I0214557

Live Fast, Die Young
The
Life and Times of Harry Greb

S. L. Compton

Windmill Writing Publications
Carbondale, Illinois

Live Fast, Die Young
The Life and Times of Harry Greb

S. L. Compton

(ISBN-13): 978-0-615-80575-7

Library of Congress Control Number: 2013938384

© 2006 by Stephen L. Compton. All Rights Reserved.

No part of this book may be reproduced, or transmitted in any form or by any means, graphic, electronic or mechanical, including photocopying, recording, taping, or by any information storage retrieval system without the written permission of Stephen L. Compton.

Manufactured in the United States of America.

Windmill Writing Publications
Carbondale, Illinois

CONTENTS

ACKNOWLEDGEMENTS

After eleven years of working on chronicling the life of Harry Greb it would only right to acknowledge the many people who helped to bring the project to conclusion. Ben, my inspiration. Mom and Dad for for all of their support while I wrote this book. J. J. Johnston whose help, input, and inspiration were truly integral in the completion of this book. J. J. is truly one of boxing's great unsung historians. Tony Fosco did an incredible service to boxing by finding and preserving footage of boxing greats, near greats, and near-do-wells. You will be missed Tony. His help in locating footage of Greb's opponents was invaluable. John Ochs, another of boxing's great unsung historians whose knowledge, interest, and materials were wonderful contributions. Pamela Bradburn for her wonderful help in editing. Mike Acri, Greg Thompson, and Paul Spadafora all of whom helped me to understand what it means to be a Pittsburgh fighter and how Harry Greb's past has influenced the modern fight scene in the Smokey City. The staff of Morris Library at Southern Illinois University, particularly Charles Flagg and David Bond, who put up with my constant nagging and almost nonstop flow of incoming newspaper microfilm to say that without their help and patience this book would not have been completed is a colossal understatement. Robert Greb, who provided much needed rare family photos and recollections that reinforced some of the ideas I had formed yet could not prove about the early life of Pius Greb and his family in the United States. Harry Greb Wohlfarth, Maria Boscia, and Sue Wohlfarth. Hank Kaplan, who provided some of the context and flavor of the times which could not be reproduced through examination of written material in anything less than a lifetime. Dr. Laurence McNamee, whose childhood recollections of James "Red" Mason were simply priceless. Rusty Rubin, whose belief in my writing ability extended far beyond my own. In truth if he hadn't been so enthusiastic about my ability this book would never have been written. Ed Cahill, who saved me a trip to St. Louis by sending me Greb's service record. Luckett Davis, boxing record compiler supreme. Luckett's almost encyclopedic knowledge of dates helped me to pinpoint important occurrences in this story that may have taken me much longer to find if ever. Clay Moyle, whose steady stream of book excerpts from his massive collection made it possible for me to avoid more library time than may have been necessary had I never met him. I wish him the best of luck on his own project's. Tim Ayres, and Rafael Tenorio, two friends who provided me with cheap, quick sources of video footage on some of Greb's opponents. Mark Ogren of Fighttoys.com, who selflessly provided me with high quality copies of photos pertaining to Greb and some of his opponents. David Bergin of Pugilistica.com, and Kevin Smith both of whom also provided quality copies of photos pertaining to Greb and his opponents. Phyllis Albacker Roseberry, who provided me with what scant information exists on Greb associates Jack and Bernard Albacker. Roy McHugh, who provided me with valuable contact information in and around the Pittsburgh area and recollections of Pittsburgh sports.

Kelly Harrington owner of Tesssaros, who never forgot me and provided me with wonderful photos of the giant square-off photo of Greb and Buck Crouse hanging in his restaurant. The staff of Northside Catholic Cemetery in Pittsburgh, Tracy Callis, Chuck Hasson, Steve Lott (one of the nicest guys I've ever dealt with in the sport of boxing), the Pittsburgh Catholic Diocese, Tim Conn, Dr. Margaret Goodman, Howard Schatz, Niek Koppen, Bob Caico, Karen Monaghan, Dan and Susan Snow, Dr. Lee B. Reichman, Dr. Bradley Smith, Lisa Carnaghi, Andrew Gray, Jen Story Fayad, Bill Heagy, Christopher DeMarco, and so many more.

PREFACE

Well, it's finally finished. In truth I never intended to write a book about Harry Greb. This project began more out of curiosity than anything else. My grandfather had boxed. He had been a great fan of Jack Dempsey's. Between his influence and the stories my father told me of Dempsey I too became a fan of the Manassa Mauler. One day in the late 1980's or early 1990's I was intrigued to pick up a boxing magazine and read an article which made mention of a 160 pound fighter who had sent the greatest boxers of his era running in the opposite direction. This man was so fearless that he even tried unsuccessfully to get a fight with the bone-crunching heavyweight champion himself to no avail. Now I was intrigued.

I had never heard of Harry Greb and could not believe that my hero would have avoided him. Over the years I read what I could on Greb whenever the odd article appeared on him in boxing magazines. These snippets seemed more of a tease than anything. Usually they seemed almost too fantastical to believe and rarely ever hinted at what really made Harry Greb tick. As the years went by there was the occasional rumor of a book in progress on Greb but nothing ever materialized. I was able to acquire a copy of the biography written about him in the 1940's but much of this seemed beyond belief as well. Tired of waiting for something authoritative to be produced I decided to spend some time at my local university's library.

Southern Illinois University has a wonderful collection of newspaper microfilm on hand and without knowing what to expect I was very quickly able to amass a rather sizeable stack of clippings detailing some of Greb's more famous bouts. The more I read the more interested I became. I began to realize that there was an excellent story here and one which deviated greatly in many ways from what had been popularly accepted about Greb's life and career. By the time my stack of research material's had reached knee high I had decided that if no one else could produce something definitive on Greb then why shouldn't I? That day, coincidently, was June 6, 2002, Harry Greb's 108th birthday.

I don't really remember how long I expected the project to take but I doubt I expected it to last more than a year, two at the most. I had made the mistake fairly early on of telling people in the boxing community that I was working on a biography of Greb. Invariably I was always asked: "When is your book coming out?" Almost always I answered: "Soon." Maybe it was wishful thinking on my part but before long people began to doubt the project would ever get finished. The problem was that I had no intention of being rushed and no intention of finishing the story until I felt I could adequately tell Greb's story. My philosophy was that if I was taking it upon myself to chronicle a man's life I owed it to that man to get the story right. In this case I felt that was extremely important given that so much has been printed about Greb, even in his own lifetime, which simply was not true.

To that end I have endeavored to present a no-frills record of Greb's life. There are no clever flashbacks or flash forwards. Rather it is a simple, straightforward, yet detailed account of Greb's background, life and career, and finally his death and legacy. I felt it was extremely important to give a clear understanding of Harry's opponents as their skill level and his dominance over them is what made him such a great fighter. In order to give an accurate picture of the fights and fighters during an era when newspaper decisions were almost universally the rule in the United State, I endeavored to utilize only first hand accounts whenever possible. In addition to this I strove to acquire as many first hand accounts as possible for each fight and event in order to give a consensus view.

Harry Greb was active in an era when films of boxing matches were popular but from which very few boxing films survive. Unfortunately to date there is no footage of any of Harry's contests known to have survived and very little on his opponents. Taking this into account I wanted to deviate from the accepted biographical norm and heavily illustrate the book in order to give readers as much of a visual reference as possible. I hope the reader will feel, as I did, that this helps them understand Greb, his style, his opponents, and his times a bit better.

This slavish devotion to illustrating the book with as many photos of the best quality as possible led to other delays. Many photos from the 1910's and 1920's do not exist anymore in any other form than newspaper photographs. Rather than reprint endless low quality copies of offset print newspaper photos, I endeavored to restore many of these photos to as close to their original condition as possible. This required a great deal of time and quite a lot of trial and error. I have no doubt that many of the photos in this book have not been seen in nearly 100 years, certainly not in the condition contained in this book.

As the project neared what I thought would be its natural conclusion I began to look for the right opportunity to publish the book with the understanding that it remain close to the vision I had when I started. In the end I decided to self-publish. This would allow me to maintain control and release the book in the form that I felt did the project and Greb justice. I believe that it is in this form which the reader will find a near complete history of Harry Greb preserved within these pages. I sincerely hope you enjoy it as much as I did working on it.

PROLOGUE

THE SMOKY CITY

Panoramic photograph of Pittsburgh as it looked at the turn of the century. View overlooking the Monongahela River.

Smokestacks belched forth plumes of black ash and fog. The cloud hung over Pittsburgh as a constant reminder of the backbreaking labor that awaited men in the steel mills. As one man remarked, "Home is just the place where I eat and sleep. I live in the mills."[1] Short of the saloons, which were plentiful, there was little else in the way of entertainment for the men of Pittsburgh. There didn't need to be. Entertainment wasn't profitable to the steel making industry. A man could expect to work an average of fourteen hours per shift.[2] It was hard work and by the time his fourteen hours were up there was little else he could think about besides sleep. A man couldn't afford to lose himself in the niceties of polite society.

Pittsburgh was more than a competitive job market, it was a place where men very often had to lay down their lives in order to feed their families. If a worker didn't give himself over completely to the mills, he was out in the street and one of the thousands of immigrants, who arrived daily, was willing and eager to take his place.

Labor unrest was nothing new to the city. In fact it had been a part of the city's history since as early as 1799.[3] However, in the 1890s Pittsburgh was exploding with new arrivals, mostly unskilled laborers, cheap labor as the steel and iron barons saw it. The only things standing in the way of cheaper labor and therefore greater profits (not to mention complete control of the company) were the organized labor unions.

The most powerful of which was the Amalgamated Association of Iron and Steel Workers of America. In 1889 the union had won a beneficial contract with the Homestead mill located seven miles east of Pittsburgh, the duration of which was set for three years. In 1892 the contract was set to expire. On the eve of this expiration Andrew Carnegie issued a notice that upon that date the mill would thereafter be Non-Union. This announcement sent shockwaves through the community and it seemed that a strike was imminent.

Talks commenced between labor and management. It was quickly apparent that not only was the Carnegie company not interested in an amicable settlement, they were fully willing to risk a strike in order to attain their goal of breaking the union. A large fence topped with barbed wire was erected around the compound, and two days before the contract between the

Mills such as this one fueled not only to the economy of Pittsburgh but also the social unrest which occasionally ended in violence.

Homestead mill and the Amalgamated Association was to expire part of the mill was shut down and 800 workers were locked out. Within days the entire Homestead mill was locked down and the workers were sent away. The strike involving thousands of workers had begun.

Andrew Carnegie and his right hand man Henry Clay Frick tried to break the strike and the unions in one move by offering the strikers individual contracts to return to work; over the course of the strike, few took this offer. Unknown to the strikers Frick sent for 300 armed Pinkertons to be employed as strikebreakers. When the Homestead workers discovered the plot passions ignited. Two barges were being towed up the Monongahela River toward Homestead, carrying the armed Pinkertons, and the Homestead strikers knew it.

When the Pinkertons attempted to dock and come ashore fighting erupted. A pitched battle ensued that lasted more than 12 hours with many people on both sides being wounded. A settlement was reached whereby the hopelessly outnumbered Pinkertons would give up and be allowed to safely leave the town. As the Pinkerton men disembarked and began to walk the gauntlet through town, the mob, swelled by more arriving workers and irate family members, once again attacked the Pinkertons. In the aftermath seven strikers and three Pinkertons lay dead, several more were wounded.[4]

Within a week Governor Robert E. Pattison called out the Pennsylvania National Guard. Carnegie and Frick wielded an enormous amount of political power leading many of the strikers to grumble that the presence of the National Guard was nothing more than a thinly veiled attempt to break the strike by protecting scab labor.

General order was restored but labor-related violence continued. Frick himself survived an assassination attempt after being shot in the neck by an anarchist supporting the cause of the workers. After the shooting Frick, true to form, continued at his desk and finished the work-

The hustle and bustle of Fifth Avenue is well documented in this photograph from 1903. Pittsburgh was showing all of the earmarks of a city on the move.

day.[5] Random labor-related violence was so pervasive that "Fort Frick", as the walled compound was now called, became almost a self-sustaining town unto itself fueled by the sweat of the scabs employed to break the strike. These acts of bloodshed had the effect of swaying the public opinion against organized labor. This, combined with the machinations of Frick and Carnegie, broke the strike and its effects would be felt throughout labor organizations for 30 years.[6]

The economic situation in the Pittsburgh area was made more difficult by the depression of 1893. This was precipitated by government spending of roughly $100 million dollars on programs which were mostly designed to enrich wealthy industrialists like Carnegie and Frick. This was compounded by an Act of Congress, which stipulated that the government would use gold to purchase silver from western states. The value of the silver as priced by the Act was substantially higher than the actual market value. This weakened the United States' gold reserves and caused inflation to spiral out of control.

This situation reached its boiling point in April of 1893 when the Secretary of the Treasury issued an announcement stating the nation's gold reserves were well below acceptable levels. As companies failed a major panic took hold over Wall Street and the value of the dollar plummeted. By year's end as many as 20 to 25 percent of workers across the country were unemployed.[7] The resulting economic depression was one of the most crushing periods in U.S. history.

The shantytowns in and around Pittsburgh began to grow at alarming rates. The winter of 1893-1894 was a terrible study in hardship punctuated by selfless individual acts of fellowship. The city spent a total of $383,678 on relief, nearly two-thirds of which was being provided by private citizens.[8] Despite the wonderful outpouring of support by the city, despair still hung over Pittsburgh's working class much like the ever-present grey haze from the mills.

In truth this was a pattern seen all across the country and one man had something to say about it. Jacob S. Coxey organized a contingent of unemployed workers to march on Washington, D.C. as a means of both protesting the rampant unemployment and lobbying for Government spending on public works which would help to employ those left jobless by the panic of 1893 and resulting Depression.

The contingent of roughly 100 men was dubbed Coxey's Army. Coxey and his men set out from Massillon, Ohio on Easter Sunday 1894 and

It wasn't known as the Smokey City for nothing. This photo taken in Pittsburgh at noon illustrated just how impenetrable the city's industrial fumes could be.

arrived at Pittsburgh on April 3. In Pittsburgh, Coxey's Army grew with support from scores of out-of-work men from the mills. But by the time Coxey's Army reached Washington its fabled march had become anti-climactic. The group never reached the advertised membership of 100,000, settling more realistically at about 500.[9] The leaders were arrested and the group was quickly dispersed. The Depression continued.

In truth, things weren't all bad in Pittsburgh. Indeed the schools, which operated at a very high standard for the day, implemented a program of handing out free textbooks to students. Some years earlier Andrew Carnegie had opened the Carnegie Free Library to the public, the first of its kind. Hospitals of all kinds were opening in the area providing a high level of health care for those who could afford it. Electric trolley cars were running downtown and new lines were being erected all the time for that new fangled invention the telephone. Somewhere in the midst of all the hustle and bustle, in the middle of the city, amid the smoke and sadness of that Depression, at a time of constant change and rapid progression, on a summer day in June a baby boy was born.

1

A CHILD OF PITTSBURGH

The Greb ancestral home of Rossdorf lies approximately 25 miles south of Frankfurt, Germany.

Pius Greb first reached the shores of the United States in June of 1881. Whether he passed into the United States through Castle Garden, which would welcome countless other immigrants prior to the completion of Ellis Island, or whether he entered the country through some other port is unknown. His exact date of arrival is lost due to the conditions surrounding his leaving home in Rossdorf, Germany. At a fair in the neighboring town of Schröck, Pius was involved in an altercation that resulted in life-threatening injuries to one Peter Kammer. Pius fled his homeland that night one step ahead of the law and eventually followed his older brother Edward who had emigrated to the United States earlier that year.[1]

Given the circumstances it is not at all surprising that he spent most of his life keeping a low profile while his only son would spend much of his life in the newspapers, on film, on stage, on the radio, and most importantly in the center of a boxing ring in front of thousands of screaming spectators.

Pius was the son of Heinrich and Maria Elizabeth Greb. He was born in 1860 in the small provincial town of Rossdorf, in the German territory of Hesse. Rossdorf was a rural community, which had been settled periodically as early as Roman times. Throughout much of the town's history it remained a quiet, sleepy village, content with remaining in the past rather than preparing for the changes which the industrial revolution would soon propel much of the world into. Pius was the fourth son of what would eventually be five sons and five daughters. He was raised Catholic and probably educated in Catholic schools.

The exact reason for Edward leaving the confines of his ancestral home are now lost. It is possible that the stock market crash of 1873 plunged his village and family into financial hardship. It is also possible that he simply grew tired of life in the sleepy village of Rossdorf and yearned for something more. What is known is that Edward and Pius were followed to the United States by their siblings Elizabeth and Richard.

This was a common pattern of migration during the late 19th and early 20th centuries called chain migration. Members of a family would begin to follow another, already established family member to the new world in the hope their chances of transition and success abroad would be improved.

Edward Greb (far left) was the first of the Greb clan to arrive in the America. He would later form a business with his brother Pius Greb. Edward is seen here with his family circa 1900.

It is likely that Edward arrived in the United States first and was followed next by Pius, then by Richard[2] and his sister Elizabeth who traveled with her future husband Peter Riehl.[3] Things begin to get murky when searching for exact dates on Pius. No ship passenger records survive with Pius' name (he may have been a stowaway or traveling under an assumed name), and to make things more confusing, the census of 1910 and 1920 have conflicting dates of arrival, neither of which is accurate.[4] Both Pius and Edward first appear in the Pittsburgh city directory of 1885 (Richard would appear in the same directory the following year).

From at least the year 1884, Pius Greb would be a citizen of Pittsburgh for the rest of his life making only periodic voyages back to his homeland of Germany. Pius was first listed in the Pittsburgh city directory as a shoemaker. In all likelihood he had arrived in the United States as an unskilled laborer eventually taking up a position as an apprentice in a shoemaker's shop owned by the Selzer family. Edward would eventually marry Philomena Selzer and it was probably through this connection that Pius found himself working as a cobbler. Edward was listed in local directories as a stone-mason, a skilled trade, and one which probably made his finding work in the exploding population of the new world much easier. This may explain the motivations of his other family members to sail for America.

It appears from the sporadic appearances of Pius in the local directory that he had a more difficult time finding stability in his new home. He probably ended up supplementing his income by working with Edward and Peter Riehl in their more successful endeavors, Riehl being a butcher and Edward working as a private contractor and stonemason.[5] In 1889 Pius declared his intention to become a naturalized citizen of the United States and in January of

Pius Greb (above) was an authoritative man and a stern taskmaster. He was the picture of Germanic stoicism and prided himself on his heritage.

1902 he was finally granted that privilege.

By 1892 Pius seems to have finally found the stability that he surely longed for upon his arrival in this chaotic city of Pittsburgh. He was now working full time with his brother Edward as an independent contractor. On April 4th 1892 Pius was able to purchase his own home located on the corner of Dauphin and Fitch in the Garfield district of Pittsburgh; he would live there for the next 53 years until his death in 1945. The house was purchased for the not-inconsiderable sum of five hundred and forty dollars. Pius had also taken a wife; he married Anna Maria Wilbert, the beautiful 28 year-old daughter of Mathias Wilbert, a Prussian tobacconist and his Bavarian wife Catherine. Pius and Anna were married on September 21st, six days after his 32nd birthday, in St. Philomena church. One month after their marriage Anna gave birth to their first child, Lillian. Despite the stigma that would certainly be attached to a union under such conditions Pius and Anna made the most of their marriage.

Nearly two years after the birth of Lillian, Anna gave birth to their second child. With midwife Mary Werle attending Anna, the Grebs welcomed a newborn baby boy into the world, on June 6, 1894.[6] Christened Edward Henry Greb, the new baby, a first-born son no less, must have surely cracked the rough, stoic exterior of his father... at least temporarily.

By 1899 the family was well established. Ida, another daughter, had been born to Pius and Anna in 1896. Pius was now working harder than ever to provide for the family. He and his brother had worked on some lucrative contracts together, the result of which can still be seen in Pittsburgh. Projects like the St. Joseph parish church in Bloomfield, which was completed in 1887, and Woolslair elementary school in Lawrenceville, completed in 1897.[7]

None of Pius' children had received any formal education as of yet but it is fair to say that the Greb family had done pretty well since its arrival in the United States. Edward had married

Philomena Selzer in November of 1884 (with Pius and Richard standing by as witnesses) and had six children; Richard had married Emma Angel, the daughter of a mill worker in June of 1888, and Elisabeth had married Peter Riehl seven months after arriving in the United States and had eight children. The Riehls were, by descendants' recollections, the more affluent side of the family. One relative remembers constantly being warned by his father to be on his best behavior when at the Riehl residence due to the fine furniture and adornments.

However, the Greb family was not immune to tragedy and hardship. At one point during the late 1890s Pius, his brother Edward, and their business partner Henry Hinnebusch, had contracted to construct a building in the city. The building was completed but the specifications were incorrect and the building collapsed. The Greb brothers blamed their partner and the partner blamed the Grebs. The business failed and the partnership was dissolved. The Greb brothers, while maintaining a close personal relationship, ended their professional relationship and thereafter took to accepting contracts on an individual basis.[8] It would result in a period of some financial difficulty for both Pius and Edward.

It seemed that the troubles had abated a bit when in 1899 Anna would give birth to Pius'

Top: Pius and his brother Edward were part of the team that completed Saint Joseph Church In Bloomfield (shown here) in 1887. Above: Woolslair Elementary School was another project which Pius and Edward Greb worked on. Construction was completed in 1897 and architectural motifs similar to those found at St. Joseph are evident in its design.

second son, Harry Pius Greb. One can imagine the joy young Edward must have felt at having a new brother. It wasn't to be. Little Harry died of meningitis that October; he was just shy of nine months old. Richard's only offspring to survive childbirth would die in 1905 at the age of five from cardiac rheumatism. More sorrow awaited Pius and Anna as their oldest child Lilly,

The industrial revolution was powered by cogs and wheels such as these shown at the Westinghouse Electric and Manufacturing Company where Harry Greb briefly worked[9]

would pass away in 1908 of endocarditis, an infection of the heart. The deaths of Pius and Anna's two children combined with the deaths of Richard's children and a child of Edward and Philomena must seem strange today but at the turn of the century it was merely a reflection of the incredibly high child mortality rate, which in some places was as high as thirty percent.

Edward Greb, the oldest of the Greb clan in Pittsburgh and the family member who seemingly began the migration from their homeland in Rossdorf, Germany to the United States, slipped into a diabetic coma and died on October 14th, 1904. He was 47 years old, just short of the average life expectancy of 48. Richard had died in the winter of 1892 at 33 years of age, and now Pius and Elizabeth were all that remained of the original four siblings who made those adventurous first steps to America.

Harry Greb's duties as a tinsmith's apprentice working for a roofing firm would have looked similar to this. The hours were long, the pay was minimal, and the work could be dangerous.

With Pius now taking contracts on a freelance basis the family was struggling to make ends meet. Pius' only son Edward would soon be expected to abandon whatever schooling he was undertaking and endeavor to find his own employment. He would be expected to work with Pius in the family business or find some other means of support. The family had by now increased in size by two, daughters Catherine and Clara, and more mouths to feed meant more debt; they would need as much income as possible. By 1909 Pius' son Edward had quit the Catholic school he was attending and took up work as an electrician's apprentice at the Westinghouse Electric and Manufacturing plant.[10] The position was the lowest work available for unskilled labor. Young Edward's employment with Westinghouse would be short-lived and uneventful. After a series of equally uneventful and unfulfilling positions he finally went to work with a roofing company as a tinsmith's apprentice, probably at Pius' urging, hoping to later utilize the boy's experience in his modest contracting business.

It was this difficult work of hauling rolled sheets of tin up ladders, often several stories in height, that Greb would later credit for the boundless energy found in his legs which one observer compared to steel springs. The work could be dangerous as well. Greb found this out on one occasion when he fell from a three story roof landing upon his head. True to the form which would later make him one of the most feared fighters in history, Greb walked away from this harrowing experience without a scratch. Such occurrences, as rare as they may have been, certainly weighed heavily on the young man's mind when considering where his future lay.

In the strict household of Pius Greb that future lay in carpentry, building, and contributing to the growth of what was now a modern industrial city. To Pius his labors were not unlike those of many other carpenters, he took pride in what he accomplished with his hands. He could see the product of his efforts and know that he was a part of the great expansion which was going on all around him. For Pius, who typified the famed German work ethic, this would take on an almost religious importance.

Indeed this powerful work ethic so prominent in the German culture was deeply rooted in religion. It had its origins in the protestant reformation and was probably tied at least in part to the Mennonite ideology of work as a form of worship. This belief in itself was similar to that of the Shakers who believed that God worked through man and thus practitioners felt a devout connection to the crafts and implements they produced. They disregarded what they saw as impracticality in their works and stripped away those characteristics that had no necessity. As a result, their work is still prized today for its ingenuity and simplistic beauty.

While Pius' own driving work ethic may have been indirectly related and influenced by such faiths they certainly weren't his only motivation. Max Weber, a sociologist/economist who published widely on the ideas of religious work ethic, would later theorize that predominantly Catholic capitalist countries prospered at a slower rate than those of their Protestant counterparts.[11] Whether such a theory was true or ultimately part of Weber's imagination is up to debate but the possibility of bettering themselves financially in what may have been perceived as a less restrictive environment was almost certainly a factor in the Greb family immigration to the new world.

In the Greb household, where German was spoken and in which strict Germanic values were adhered, to nothing as impractical as sports would ever play an occupational role in the future of any of Pius' children. Sports were nothing better than a distraction, something to read about in the newspapers or participate in at occasional church picnics. At best sports were useful for ridding young boys of too much foolishness in their system. This is where the athletic career of Harry Greb (still known as Edward) stood as he entered young adulthood. Sports would restricted to school-yard games of football, which Greb excelled at (gaining his first broken nose before ever lacing on a boxing glove), and the almost compulsory game of sandlot baseball, a sport which was sweeping the nation by storm as headlines raged with names like Connie Mack, Fred Clarke, and Pittsburgh's own Honus Wagner. Crushed no doubt by the ultra-practical world view of his father Pius, Greb would have to be satisfied with only dreams of receiving the accolades of thousands of roaring fans.

About this time another sport was beginning to gain wide appeal in the Pittsburgh area. Boxing was beginning to emerge as a major pastime in contrast to the generation previous when bouts had to be held on barges, anchored in the middle of the Monongahela or Allegheny rivers, in order to avoid the intervention of law enforcement officials. Fighters such as Albert "Buck" Crouse, Red Robinson, and Frank Klaus, in particular were headlining cards that were now being held in places such as Duquesne Gardens and Old City Hall.

Boxing was still illegal in the strictest sense of the term. Bouts were held in cooperation with local governing bodies and civic agencies, billed "officially" as exhibitions of the art of self-defense and limited to six three minute rounds or less, to be held under the Marquis of Queensberry rules. Decisions determining a winner and loser as issued by judges or officials were strictly forbidden in keeping with the atmosphere of an exhibition. Fans waiting to find out who would be determined the winner of the previous night's bout had to rely on the decision rendered by their favorite newspaper reporter. Bets were handled in this way as well: A bet would be placed on the outcome of a fight as opined by three (give or take) pre-selected

James "Red" Mason (Left) and Tom Bodkin (right) were two of Pittsburgh's most prominent and influential boxing personalities just after the turn of the century.

newspapers so, in essence, the newspaper men covering the fight replaced the judges. These decisions weren't official but they were what was relied upon to make future matches, lay bets, and weigh the abilities of fighters against one another.

Promoters couldn't accept monies outright for such exhibitions therefore athletic and/or social clubs were formed whereby persons bought "memberships" to the club promoting a certain fight. That membership allowed the purchaser the right to enter and view the boxing match without the threat of incarceration. Men like Tom Bodkin, James "Red" Mason, George Engel, and Professor Evans all ran, promoted, or made matches for such clubs and as a result they generally controlled a large portion of the boxing talent found in the vicinity of Pittsburgh.

Swelling the ranks of professional pugilists in the Pittsburgh area and adding to the talent pool was a thriving amateur boxing scene. Amateur tournaments were held, often several times a month, and governed by the Pittsburgh Athletic Association. Young athletes flocked to such competitions which promised a measure of local fame, trophies, and even the occasional chance to travel to neighboring cities to compete in inter-city tournaments.

Such tournaments were often arranged so that the best amateur fighters of Pittsburgh would fight a team of the best amateur fighters of Buffalo; the winning team would then meet the best amateurs of Cleveland and so on. Teams as far away as New York and Canada often competed in these tournaments and a fighter winning such a tournament would have placed himself in a position to demand higher purses upon turning professional due to the publicity of being an amateur champion.

The prestige of the local amateur program benefited immensely when famed boxer Joe Choynski joined the P.A.A. in early 1913 as a trainer. Choynski had fought epic battles with such men as Gentleman Jim Corbett, Bob Fitzsimmons, and Jim Jeffries, and had once knocked

The tough working-class men who populated Pittsburgh's boxing matches demanded action. As a result many Pittsburgh boxers adopted a brutal style of infighting. One of its greatest proponents, Frank Klaus, later published a treatise on the subject.

out Jack Johnson, the reigning heavyweight champion. With such a steady nurturing of talent Pittsburgh was turning out quality club-fighters and legitimate world-class talent at a terrific pace.

Pittsburgh was a rough working class town, the fighters were rough working class men, and as a result the boxing matches were usually rough brutal affairs. They were a veritable melting pot where Jews, Italians, Slavs, Germans, Poles, and just about every other race or religious denomination competed and cheered its local favorites. Action was rewarded while "stalling," or what might be perceived as not giving one's best effort, was frowned upon. This isn't to say that the fighters bred in Pittsburgh weren't clever, they simply developed a method of fighting that maximized rough give-and-take action while practicing the finer points of the manly art of self defense, a rough and tumble style of milling called infighting.

Frank Klaus was built like a tank and fought like one as well. He relied on his durability to get inside his opponent's reach and wear them down with punishing blows. Scoring impressive victory after victory he was eventually credited as being the successor to Stanley Ketchel's middleweight crown.

Infighting had probably been a part of boxing since Cain clobbered Abel but Pittsburgh fighters were likely unique in their adherence to this style. Without question the greatest proponent of infighting during this era was Frank Klaus. Klaus was arguably Pittsburgh's most popular fighter, certainly it's most renowned, and without question its most gifted.[12] He would perfect his own brand of infighting and eventually publish a book on the subject. The working class men of the city who toiled in the steel mills and factories under back breaking conditions appreciated men like Klaus for their brawn and willingness to earn their pay in the same rugged manner in which the average worker sweated for his.

Klaus had begun his career like any other local talent, fighting his way up as a preliminary boy before gaining enough fistic stature to rise to the position of a main event fighter. He gained a reputation as a durable, punishing fighter who liked nothing better than to work his way inside an opponents comfort zone and jolt away at his head and body with short powerful punches. He relied heavily on his durability and stamina and incredible physical strength.

It wasn't long before Klaus was challenging the best fighters in the world men like Harry Lewis of Philadelphia, Billy Papke, and even the middleweight champion, legendary "Michigan Assassin" Stanley Ketchel. Ketchel had made such an impression upon the psyche of the public that even today, more than a century after his tragic murder, he is remembered as one of the true icons of the sport. It's fair to say that Ketchel dominated the middleweight division and, when he was murdered by a jealous farmhand over the affections of a woman, the division was thrown into disarray.

Ketchel's death coming just months after a close fight between him and Klaus prompted Frank Klaus' ever-present manager George Engel to claim the now vacant middleweight championship in Klaus' name. Adding to the confusion found in such a situation, several other fighters made claims on the championship with varying degrees of legitimacy. Men like Billy

When power-punching middleweight champion Stanley Ketchel was murdered it left a vacuum in the division that would not be filled for three years.

Papke, who had given Ketchel some of his toughest fights, boxing master Willie Lewis and his nemesis and equally talented Harry Lewis, Hugo Kelly, Jack "Twin" Sullivan, Eddie McGoorty, Jack Dillon dubbed "The Giant Killer," and even a young French prodigy named Georges Carpentier. It seemed for a time that every pugilist who could weigh in under the limit of 158 pounds made some claim to being the champion. The public watched and waited impatiently as the mess sorted itself out to some degree of satisfaction over the course of nearly three years.

With victories over men like "Cyclone" Johnny Thompson, Leo Houck, Jack Dillon, and Georges Carpentier, Frank Klaus was rapidly gaining in both popularity and consensus opinion as the premier middleweight in the world. On March 5, 1913 Klaus was matched with former middleweight champion Billy Papke in Paris, France for what was billed as the middleweight championship of the world. Papke's cleverness and experience could not overcome

Klaus' continuous boring in and damaging smashes to the body and head. Early in the fight Papke began to foul Klaus and by the fifteenth round the referee had seen enough, ordered Papke to his corner and raised Klaus' hand in victory declaring him the new middleweight champion. The decision was greeted with approval by the spectators who judged that Klaus was on his way to a well deserved victory regardless of the disqualification. With the victory Klaus was awarded a diamond studded belt in honor of his newfound championship. Just five days after Klaus' historic victory a raw boned eighteen year old boy would compete in the first round of the Pittsburgh Athletic Association inter-city amateur boxing tournament in the 145 pound weight division. The boy's name was Edward Greb but ever after he would be called Harry.

2

UP TO SCRATCH

Exactly when Edward Henry Greb engaged in his first professional boxing match is up to some debate. James "Red" Mason, who was Greb's manager for the major portion of his career, insisted that Greb had fled the oppressive yoke of his father in the summer of 1912 and traveled with a companion to Wheeling, West Virginia where he engaged in his first professional bout against one Stoney Ritz.[1] Mason had not yet begun his association with Greb at this time and so his authority on the matter could be called into question but, if true, it is the earliest mention of Greb engaging in such a contest.

The problem with corroborating such a story is that the newspapers from Wheeling during the year of 1912 make no mention of such a bout taking place. Furthermore, when Greb later fought in Wheeling after he became a well-known fighter and indeed a champion, the local papers made no mention of him ever having fought there prior to 1919.

Stoney Ritz was indeed a young professional prizefighter fighting out of Wheeling in 1912. Given Ritz' relative skill level and development at the time in question he would have been a likely opponent for an unpolished youth just off the train looking for a professional prizefight.[2] So it is possible that the bout simply went unrecorded by the local press at the time.

Another possibility is that the bout was actually held in another location and Mason assumed that because Ritz was a Wheeling boy that was where the bout had taken place. It isn't at all unlikely that the bout took place somewhere in eastern Ohio as many Wheeling fighters were migrating west-ward in search of higher purses in places like

This rare photo of Harry Greb taken sometime in 1912 or early 1913 was published just after his upset win in the inter-city amateur tournament.

Steubenville, and Youngstown during this time.

What we do know is that by 1911 or 1912 Greb had become fascinated with the local Pittsburgh boxing scene. The boys who made up the larger part of his circle of friends had a healthy interest in the sport. Before long Greb was following them to local gyms in order to catch a glimpse of domestic heroes like Buck Crouse and Walter Monaghan while they would train. He was also sneaking off to see the local matches staged at places like Old City Hall and Duquesne Gardens. Some accounts have him occasionally acting as a towel swinger for the fighters, a job which required one to wave a towel over the fighter during the one minute rest period between rounds in order to provide oxygen and a cool breeze.[3] Harry would later say he took up the boxing to lose weight. Whatever the reason for his involvement in the sport for all intents and purposes young Edward Greb was now a boxing fanatic.

The Lawrenceville neighborhood was only a few blocks from Greb's home on Millvale Avenue and every chance he could escape the watchful eye of his father he would be off to the gyms, to the fights, or to the corner where he and his pals would hang out and discuss the upcoming bouts. There is little doubt that no small part of Greb's private time was given over to practicing the same moves he witnessed in the gyms of Lawrenceville and at the local fights. He would mimic the shifty moves of Buck Crouse or the crowd pleasing style of Red Robinson and imagine the crowds' roar of approval. Indeed, Crouse and Robinson would in time become both mentors and sparring partners for Greb. In order to fine tune his art Greb enlisted the help of James "Skipper" Manning, a jack of all trades in Pittsburgh boxing circles.[4] Whenever Greb could find the time, and sneak away from Pius' chores, he would meet with Manning and practice the finer points of the art of boxing.

By the spring of 1913 we find young Edward Henry Greb, not yet 19, preparing to enter into the local inter-city amateur boxing tournament. According to James Mason, Greb had tried to enter a similar tournament the year earlier but Pius, wanting his son playing no part in what he considered no better than a whore's game, tore up the registration papers.[5] In March of 1913 Greb would not be denied. He picked up his registration form at the offices of the A.A.U. Commissioner J. T. Taylor and on the dotted line listed "name" he signed Harry Greb, in honor of the poor little brother who never lived to see his first birthday.

This year's tournament was of particular interest due to the wide array of talent it was attracting. John Foley, considered the finest amateur heavyweight boxer and wrestler in the tri-state area, had been an early entry. Paul Milko, brother of former amateur standout Mike Milko, was another entry that local fight bugs were watching closely. Some of the other notable entries were the Webb brothers, William Miller, Art Story, and Red Cumpston, as well as future top notch professionals Ray Pryel and Johnny Fundy. The entry of the unknown Harry Greb of Garfield passed without any notice at all. Greb certainly would not be expected to stand up to such battle-tested amateurs as Story, Cumpston and Miller, all of whom had considerable experience in local amateur rings[6] and all of whom had entered the same division as Harry, the 145 pound class.

In the first round of the tournament held on March 10, 1913 Harry drew what many considered to be the toughest opponent in the weight division. William J. Miller was not only an experienced amateur boxer, having competed in local tournaments for the past several years and a member of the illustrious P. F. O'Toole Athletic Club, but he was also the defending champion in the tournament having won the 145 pound title the previous year. Miller was known as an aggressive fighter and a wicked puncher who would later be convicted of Murder for his part in the death of a drunk that he and his friends attempted to "roll."

When Miller and Greb came to scratch the audience was sure the little known Greb was in for a massacre at the hands of Miller. What the crowd saw when the gong sounded was something completely different. Miller's punching power was nullified not by Greb's skill but by his drive and will to win. When the decision was announced in Greb's favor the audience could hardly disagree yet that did little to quell their utter disbelief at such a stunning upset. The following day's sports page of the Pittsburgh Chronicle-Telegraph read "H. Greb Surprises W. J. Miller" over the recap of the previous night's tournament.[7] Harry would later intimate that this was indeed his first flirtation as an active participant in the sport.

With his win over Miller, Greb encouraged, particularly when his next opponent was announced as Art Story. Story was an experienced amateur boxer as well and like Miller he had participated in several previous local tournaments. Yet Story's success had been limited, and while not to be taken lightly, he posed less of a threat than did Miller.

When the two met on March 11 in the second round of the tournament Greb again surprised the

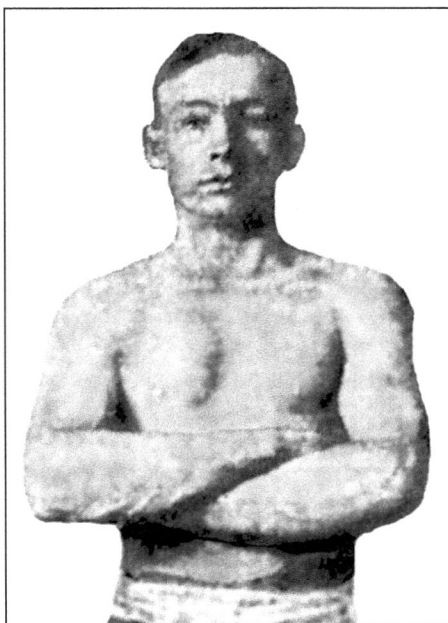

W. J. Miller (above) was considered a favorite to win the Lawrence A. C. tournament in his division until Harry Greb upset him on the opening night.

Greb defeated the more experienced Arthur Story (pictured here) in his second amateur bout.

25

audience by returning a winner via decision over his more experienced foe. The Pittsburgh Press printed only that "Greb's fighting last night was a revelation."[8] With his win over Story, Greb had earned himself a spot in the final round of the tournament to be held the following night on March 12. His opponent was Red Cumpston, a formidable fighter who like Greb's previous two opponents had much more experience.

The winners in the final round of the tournament were promised a trip to Cleveland to compete against the best boxers of that city. The only man standing in Greb's way and that rare chance at adventure was a bricklayer named Red Cumpston.

Cumpston was a sallow faced young man, with deep set eyes and curly red hair. He looked more like an undertaker than a boxer. Greb and Cumpston were both understandably determined to win the tournament and when they came together the action was furious. Round after round there was little to choose from with both fighters doing their best. At the end of the match Greb's hand was raised in victory. The Pittsburgh Press commented that Cumpston had shown great improvement and had lost by only a hairline decision, yet in Greb a new star had been uncovered.[9] With the tournament completed talk immediately switched to the Pittsburghers' chances against the Cleveland team.

When Greb defeated Red Cumpston (above) in the final bout of the amateur tournament, he won high praise from the local press and a chance to meet the best amateurs in Cleveland.

The Cleveland amateur team that would be facing Pittsburgh was a formidable one indeed. Howard Root, 105 lbs., Dick Stosh, 135 lbs., and George Koch, 145 lbs. in particular were considered heavy favorites. Again, Harry Greb would be pitted against an adversary whose experience far outweighed his own.

The Cleveland team had already defeated the best fighters that Buffalo, New York had to offer and looked forward to a victory over Pittsburgh's best. It was after the defeat of the Buffalo team that George Koch, Greb's opponent, had considered turning pro, so considerable was his talent and prestige.[10] Koch had been matched with Dan Hourigan during the tournament against Buffalo, a man considered to be one of the best amateur fighters of his weight.

When Koch defeated Hourigan he felt he had no more mountains to climb, yet decided that staying in the tournament and seeing it to the end would give him a larger bargaining chip for more lucrative purses upon turning professional. He saw little likelihood of the unknown Harry Greb upsetting his plans, and it is likely that the powers that be in the Pittsburgh Athletic Association didn't either because when the fighters left for Cleveland, Red Cumpston was along as an alternate.[11]

Regardless of the outcome of the Cleveland amateur competition, Harry Greb was scheduled to participate in his first (recorded) professional bout on April 5, the day after the tournament in Cleveland. His opponent would be Red Cumpston for six three-minute rounds. The event was the athletic carnival held by Hampton Battery B, a local National Guard unit, and Greb had the honor of headlining due to his status as amateur 145 pound champion of Pittsburgh. For all intents and purposes, Greb would end his career as an amateur at the Cleveland tournament, win, lose, or draw.

As the Pittsburgher contingent steamed out on the Pittsburgh and Lake Erie railroad that soggy afternoon of April 3 they must have been full of hope and excitement. Indeed for some of the young boxers it may have been the farthest they had ever been from home. As the team entered the Cleveland Athletic Club on the evening of the 4th they were greeted warmly by an enthusiastic crowd. There were to be seven bouts ranging from 105 pounds to Heavyweight, with the team winning the majority of bouts advancing to the next stage to face Cincinnati's best amateur boxers. All of the bouts were fiercely contested but in the end the Pittsburghers were defeated by a single bout.

The Pittsburghers carrying the flag of victory were J. J. Westwood, John Foley, and Harry Greb. The Cleveland Plain Dealer had this to say about Greb's performance:

> **Another Creditable visiting battler was Harry Greb, who showed George Koch more gloves than he ever saw at one time before. Greb out steamed George after the first round, and was so aggressive that the latter's efforts were confined largely to blocking, of which he did a good share with his face. Koch shaped up better than his opponent but, Greb's arms grapevined him persistently, and George was unable to push through the big blow.[12]**

The account, while not indicative of the heights Greb would achieve in his profession, was certainly a foreshadowing of things to come.

Upon his return Greb participated in the six round bout with Red Cumpston at Battery B's armory in the East Liberty section of Pittsburgh. Sadly none of the local papers covered the bout or gave a description of Greb's first professional fight. We do know it took place because early records of Greb list three bouts between he and Cumpston, the four round amateur bout,

The amateur team representing Pittsburgh against Cleveland. Left to right: Back Row: August Camp 158 lbs, Victor Wright (alternate), Red Cumpston 135 lbs (145 lb alternate). Front Row: Harry Greb 145 lbs, William McCullogh 125 lbs, Harry Webb 115 lbs, J.J. Westwood 105 lbs. (Not Pictured: John Foley).

a later KO which Greb scored over Cumpston and the mysterious six rounder.[13] In addition to being substantiated by early records, it is also mentioned by Red Mason in a recounting of Greb's life after Greb passed away. In retelling Greb's life story to Pittsburgh sports writer Havey Boyle Mason states "I first saw Greb in action when he fought Red Cumpston in a professional bout at Waldemier Hall in 1913...   ...Two weeks later Greb was given a second match with Cumpston and this time Greb kayoed his man."[14] Greb himself, years later, discussed his entry into the professional ranks "About two weeks later I was entered in the Pittsburgh-Cleveland amateur tournament, which took place in Cleveland. I represented Pittsburgh in the welterweight class - and I won, being the only Pittsburgher who achieved victory."

"When I got back to Pittsburgh the next day one of the local promoters told me if I'd fight Red Cumpston that night he'd give me $12. I accepted. And I knocked out Cumpston in the second round. My pals said I was good—and that I ought to quit working at the tinner's trade and

The amateur team representing Cleveland against Pittsburgh; Left to Right: Howard Root 105 lbs, Arthur Root 115 lbs, Vincent Perconi 125 lbs, Dick Stosh 135 lbs, George Koch (Grebs opponent) 145 lbs, C. J. Seegert 158 lbs, Sam Cook Heavyweight.

devote all my time to fighting. But I was a little skeptical at first. So for a long time I'd work at tinning in the day time and fight at night -whenever I could get fights."[15]

The mysterious six round bout with Cumpston and its outcome aside, we do know that by the time Greb and Cumpston were matched for a return bout, once again at East Liberty's armory, they were indeed professional prizefighters. The outcome of the rubber match between Greb and Cumpston would have a much more final ending to the series than anyone expected. Oddly enough this bout, like their first six rounder, got no press coverage (adding weight to the idea that the six rounder did indeed occur yet met with little or no publicity). We are lucky in that we have the actual account (short as it may be) of the bout from the man who refereed the fight, Yock Henninger: "Some N.G.P. boys held a smoker in East Liberty. Harry Krebbs (sic) faced Red Cumpston. It was a fast fight. Suddenly Krebbs caught Red as he was coming in. The Punch was a pickler. Cumpston hit the floor in a lump. Say, I could have counted 50 over him and then some. Cleanest kayo I have looked at and you can wager that the old boy has watched numerous in his life."[16]

It was after this final bout with Red Cumpston and its decisive victory that Greb decided to seek out a manager. Skipper Manning, who had been handling Greb previously, had neither the connections nor the acumen to bring Greb through the ranks of professional prizefighting where back room deals are as much a part of the sport as what goes on in the squared circle. After some consideration, he sought out the 44 year old James "Red" Mason, manager, promot-

James "Red" Mason, (top left) megaphone in hand, no doubt harrassing an unfortunate ballplayer opposing his beloved Pittsburgh Pirates. His professional relationship with Harry Greb began at Newell's (top right), a popular bar located on the first floor of Newell's Hotel. For years Newell's was a gathering place for Pittsburghs boxing community.

er, matchmaker, and one of the most colorful characters in Pittsburgh sporting history.

Mason had a fairly sizeable stable of fighters which featured some of Pittsburgh's best headliners. He was well known for his belief in keeping his fighters active and fighting as often as possible. It was not uncommon for a Mason fighter to engage in prizefights several times a month. It was a practice founded not out of cruelty or greed but experience, for Mason himself had been a fighter in his younger years.

Mason began fighting in 1884 in the back rooms of saloons.[17] While still actively fighting, he took up the management of boxing exhibitions staged by former John L. Sullivan opponent Dominick McCaffrey and played an active role in widening the popularity and acceptance of boxing in the Pittsburgh area. However, Mason had a rough and uncouth side which made him by turns popular and unpopular with the fickle public. He would often sit at ringside with his feet on the ring apron shouting instructions to his fighter, (something looked down upon at the time) and, if need be, obscenities at the opponent, something which got him tossed out of arenas on more than one occasion.

A baseball fanatic, Mason held various positions with the Pittsburgh Pirates from 1889 to 1900 ranging from groundskeeper to trainer.[18] Mason was a regular at the Pirates games and was famous for always carrying a megaphone in a small paper bag when he entered the stadium. With the use of the megaphone, in what can only be termed as stereotypical Red Mason behavior, he would badger and berate the opposing team (and even members of the home team if they weren't playing up to his standards).

Such behavior made him a hit with the local urchins who would attend regular games, and one elderly gentleman interviewed for this book recounted how the children would giggle with glee when Mason sounded out his famous *"LOO-KEE LOO-KEE LOO-KEE!"* directed at Cuban ballplayer Adolpho Luque.[19] Hotheaded and brash as he was fun loving and good humored, Mason could pour all of his energies into a feud (real or imagined) resulting in anything as inconsequential as sitting in front of a typewriter all night writing letters and press reports to rebuff a slight to his ego or something more serious such as an impromptu brawl. It was this dichotomy that made Mason as many enemies as he had friends, but it also made him visible and visibility was exactly what Harry Greb was seeking in the spring of 1913.

Greb was first formally introduced to Red Mason at Newell's bar.[20] He was presented by another young up-and-comer named Johnny Ray. Greb made it plain that he wished Mason to look after his career. Mason, having already seen the boy fight, asked one question: "Are you game?" to which Greb answered "Well I guess, yes. I fell off a three story house and lit on my head without being hurt."[21] A hand shake later Greb had himself a new manager. Mason freely admitted later that he had no great illusions as to Greb's promise; he was merely willing to take a chance on the youngster. In reality Mason probably expected to milk Greb's amateur success

Exposition Park, former home of the Pittsburgh Pirates, was the sight of Grebs first bout under the management of James "Red" Mason. The park hosted baseballs first World Series in 1903 but due to flooding and demands for a more modern facility it was abandoned to eventually be swallowed up by urban development. Exposition Hall can be seen in the foreground.

for what it was worth before the boy moved on to a different line of work. To this end Mason's cut of Greb's earnings was a whopping forty percent.

Mason's first order of business as Greb's pilot was to secure him a preliminary bout on a fairly high-profile card. Mike Gibbons, the St. Paul Phantom, already considered one of the great scientific boxers of the age, would be appearing in Pittsburgh to take on local welter-weight Jimmy Perry. Greb's opponent would be Ray Woods. The fight was to be six rounds or less with both fighters to weigh no more than 138 pounds.

The bout held at Exposition Park (previously home to the Pittsburgh Pirates) was not well attended due to weather concerns. In an effort to try to secure their already small percentage Gibbons' manager Eddy Reddy suggested cutting out the under card. Fortunately for Greb this suggestion was not given any consideration by promoters. In fact the entire card was nearly cancelled on account of rain until Mike Gibbons insisted on giving the meager crowd its money's worth.

Gibbons showed his complete mastery of Perry by stopping his man in the second round. On the undercard Harry Greb and Ray Woods, alias Knockout Kirkwood, would fight a sloppy six round bout which nearly all of the papers had Greb winning. It was a modest bit of exposure which is reflected by the gate receipts, which ranged in estimates from $175 to $334.[22] This is also an indication of just how little Greb would have earned for his showing. Once one factors in the expenses of the promotion and pay of all fighters on the card (eight in total), very little is left for a preliminary fighter such as Greb.

For the next month Greb probably continued his work at the roofing company and trained in his spare time while Mason tried to secure matches for him without much success. Finally, after more than a month of idleness, Greb was signed to fight on the under card of the grudge match between tough Mickey Rodgers and Red Robinson to be held on July 19, 1913; Robinson being Greb's stable mate.

As a member of Red Mason's stable, Greb had the benefit of sparring with some of the city's best boxers, Robinson included. On July 17, Greb engaged in a six round exhibition with Red Robinson at the Elks Picnic at Reels Grove to illustrate that both fighters were rounding into shape nicely for their respective bouts. The next day's edition of the Pittsburgh Press in addition

Old City Hall was witness to many of Harry Greb's early fights including his one knockout loss. In truth it was never a city hall at all but instead had served a number of purposes, most notable among those being a market house.

to previewing the main event commented "The preliminaries are going to be good ones, and some new faces are down to appear. Among them Harry Greb, a boy who looks like a comer to all who have seen him at work."[23]

Greb's opponent was to be a deaf/mute Negro named Young Blackhall but Battling Murphy was substituted the last minute. Murphy was considerably smaller than Greb and as a result Greb simply gave his man no respect. In the second round Greb badly battered Murphy, bloodying his nose, at which point the referee stepped in to stop the uneven match. Despite the obvious advantages Greb possessed over his opponent he was still being hailed as a "comer" and a welcome addition to the Pittsburgh boxing fraternity.[24]

On August 13, Greb again appeared on a card with Red Robinson, this time in Punxsutawney as part of the Western Pennsylvania Fireman's Convention. Greb's opponent was a local boy named Lloyd Crutcher. The bout lasted a minute and a half and Greb made a wonderful impression on the local population. It was commented by the Punxsutawney Spirit that "Greb is a husky lad and has developed both speed and science with his muscles. This was his eleventh fight and fourth knockout. His friends at ringside last night said he has never been bested in a fight yet."[25]

Harvey "Hooks" Evans was an experienced fighter who had already faced some of Pittsburgh's best boxers when Greb gave him a tough bout on short notice on the undercard of George Chip's KO over Frank Klaus.

Greb was next signed to fight Karl Maxwell on the under card of the bout between stable mate Al Grayber and Walter "Kid" Smith, to be held in conjunction with the Clarksburg Fair, at Clarksburg, West Virginia on September 3 at the Victoria Theater. The fair was an event which promised to draw thousands of people from the tri-state area. True to his word, Mason was keeping Greb busy and keeping his name in the newspapers, and at this stage of Greb's career little else could be expected.

Greb and his stable mates arrived in Clarksburg ready for action when it was discovered that the local Prosecuting Attorney, A. J. Findley, had declared that should such a match prove

These two photos of Harry Greb, along with the two on the facing page, were all taken at the same time. They were probably taken in mid to late 1913 as publicity photos on the event of James "Red" Mason taking Greb into his stable of fighters. They were first published in late 1913 not long after Greb's fight with Joe Chip.

as violent as one which had recently been held in Clarksburg, not only would the participants be arrested, but everyone involved would be jailed as well. As a result of such a negative response from the powers that be, the entire card was cancelled.

This did not prevent Grayber and Smith from holding an impromptu exhibition without the benefit of pay. Later that night the fighters and their friends (it is assumed that Greb was among those with Grayber) met on the streets of Clarksburg. Before long a fight between Smith and Grayber broke out that quickly turned into a free-for-all. When the dust had settled and cooler heads prevailed Smith was suffering from a cut eye and Grayber from a tin ear. Greb would have to wait for more than a month before he could expect to be paid for a fight but it

would be one that would raise his popularity in Pittsburgh far higher than any of his previous bouts.

Frank Klaus, middleweight champion, was scheduled to fight New Castle slugger George Chip on October 11 in Old City Hall.[26] Hughie Madole was scheduled to take on tough Harvey "Hooks" Evans on the under card. Despite Chip's reputation as a tough fighter and a hard puncher, Klaus wasn't taking his training seriously. He moved his quarters to Philadelphia so he could watch as much of the World Series as possible. Klaus was taking a considerable gamble by neglecting his usual regimen. He had always relied on being in the finest physical condition in order to take the punishment that he willingly accepted in order to get inside and wear his opponent down. Despite the fact that the bout was only scheduled for six rounds and was a no-decision affair, the title could still change hands if Chip were to score a knockout.

On October 8, three days before the Chip-Klaus bout, Hughie Madole engaged in a six round bout with Ray Parks. During the bout with Parks, Madole badly injured his hand and was unable to take his place opposite Hooks Evans on the undercard of the fight between Klaus and Chip. On short notice Greb agreed to take Madole's place against the smaller but more experienced Hooks Evans. It was a wonderful opportunity for Greb to show his wares against a tough young fighter in front of a championship fight audience.

As it happened that night Klaus' over-confidence got the best of him. Making the fight harder than he had, to Klaus took chance after chance by hurting Chip and then letting him off the hook, or by simply sticking out his chin and inviting Chip to hit him. Scenes like these made the fight interesting, indeed exciting, but they proved the downfall of Pittsburgh's great champion. With a lead going into the sixth and final round Klaus rushed inside and was suddenly met with a solid right uppercut and a dynamite left hook. Slowly Klaus staggered and then collapsed in a heap. Bravely struggling to his feet at the count of nine Klaus was instantly met with another thunderous left which sent him down and out for the fateful ten count. The championship had passed to a new middleweight king.

On the undercard a different kind of drama unfolded. Harry Greb and Hooks Evans fought a tremendous war to the delight of ringsiders. Fans expecting the comparatively unknown Greb to be eaten alive by the more experienced Hooks Evans were in for a surprise. Evans' greater experience showed, making Greb look amateurish at times but what stood out was Greb's resiliency and his determination to win. Round after round the two fighters clashed headlong into each other battering both head and body. Neither fighter was willing to give quarter or take it. Both fighters took the other's most punishing blows without backing up and at the end of six rounds they were both standing, bloodied but unbroken. It was the general consensus that Evans deserved the victory by a slight margin. Such a loss was hardly a setback for young Greb. His showing of grit was of such a rousing nature that he could now expect more offers from the promoters who understood all too well that the product their patrons wanted most was action.

Immediately following his action-packed fight with Hooks Evans, Greb was signed to fight Joe Chip in Youngstown, Ohio on the undercard of a match between Johnny Griffith and Tommy Bresnahan to be held on October 20, 1913. This was a huge leap in class for the young fighter from Pittsburgh. Joe Chip was in fact the brother and chief sparring partner of newly crowned middleweight champion George Chip.

Joe, like his brother, was a dangerous puncher who constantly pressed the action looking to wear his opponent down with punishing blows. He was a rugged young man sporting a mouth full of gold teeth courtesy of an errant mule kick who liked to brag about having once been blown one hundred feet by the blast of 67 sticks of dynamite while working in the mines. It was announced that Joe Chip's record included 19 fights, 15 of which had been won by knockout.[27] The bout scheduled for eight rounds at a weight of 145 pounds, promised to be an exciting chief

Mike Milko (above) as he looked during the later portion of his illustrious amateur career. Milko was a prodigious knockout artist as an amateur but failed to develop as a pro.

support to the main event and Greb would have to be in the best of shape to go the distance. As it was Greb had been training almost non-stop for several weeks and was confident of victory. However, a strange occurrence would postpone the meeting of Joe Chip and Harry Greb for over a month.

On the day of the fight it was announced that Greb would be unable to appear due to a death in the family. Indeed there is a death notice listed in the Pittsburgh Post and Pittsburgh Sun for one Catherine Greb.[28] There is one slight problem with this turn of events; there were only two Catherines in Harry's immediate family, his sister, and his grandmother on his mother's side (whose Christian name was Wilbert, not Greb), and neither of these women died on October 19, 1913 as listed. Catherine Wilbert, the least likely candidate for suspicion had died in 1908, while Catherine Greb, sister to Harry, died in 1946.[29] Further confusing matters is the fact that none of the other Pittsburgh newspapers published this death notice and no death notices of any of Greb's family members, immediate or otherwise, appear in Pittsburgh papers during this time period.

There is very little evidence at all to support the idea that Greb (or more likely James Mason) cancelled this bout due to a death in the family. In fact it is far more likely that Mason, realizing he was now in possession of a growing commodity (having already signed Greb to headline a card on October 22, two days after his scheduled bout with Chip) decided that Joe Chip posed too much risk, presented the story of a death in the family to cover his tracks and then had a phony death notice published in the paper in order to further obscure the truth.

In hindsight, if Mason did indeed prevent Greb from fighting Joe Chip, then he probably did the correct thing because the opponent who substituted for Greb, Eddie Mullaney of Akron, Ohio, utilized a clever style more suited for success against a mauling fighter, like Joe Chip, than the awkward and rushing Greb. Mullaney was knocked out in the third round.

Instead of taking his place opposite Joe Chip, Greb would next be seen in action against former amateur standout Mike Milko. Milko was a tough, rugged fighter with a wicked punch. Milko, not averse to action of any kind, found himself in the Braddock jailhouse in early June as a result of his love for fighting. He had been on his way to pick up his fiancé in order to acquire a marriage license. On the way he stopped in nearly every saloon between

Mike Milko (above) was a fierce competitor with a tremendous amateur background. In 1911 and 1912 he had 17 amateur bouts winning all of them, 13 by knockout.

Munhall and Braddock, no doubt getting up the liquid courage so many young men find necessary to take the ultimate leap into matrimony.

By the time Milko reached Steve Palschak's saloon on Seventh Street he was quite inebriated and in a fighting mood. Emulating the great John L. Sullivan, he waltzed up to the bar and declared himself the best man in the house, promptly challenging any willing patron to a fight. Without waiting for a reply he dropped the proprietor with a single blow, and went about attacking several of the patrons.

He then left the saloon in haste and continued toward his intended destination, but not before knocking down a mail carrier with one punch. At this point a police officer named Jacobs, walking his beat, attempted to apprehend Milko. Seconds later the officer was lying unconscious on the ground with Milko walking down the street toward his waiting fiancé punching every person who crossed his path. A short time later Jacobs regained consciousness and continued to pursue Milko. When Jacobs caught up, he was thrown to the ground and further beaten by Milko.

Another officer by the name of George Young came upon the scene and attempted to intervene only to meet head on with Milko's fist. Milko now realizing the odds were against him, and that he was late for his engagement (literally), began to flee his would-be captors. After a short chase and more struggle Milko was finally wrangled into a holding cell in the police station where he remained the next day, his intended wedding day.[30]

If this was how Milko behaved on the eve of his wedding, what would he be like on a night when he was expected to fight for money? Greb surely pondered this question as he prepared for the bout. Indeed there was a certain amount of animosity between the two fighters stemming at least partly from their respective amateur careers.

Milko, before turning professional, was a top notch amateur in his own right. Indeed as early as 1910 he was making a splash in the newspapers by holding his own in exhibitions with top lightweight contender Owen Moran only weeks after Moran had knocked out the "Durable Dane" Battling Nelson and drew with featherweight phenom Abe Attell.[31] Milko's performance was of such a high quality that after winning a later amateur tournament a protest was lodged against him claiming that he was a professional.[32] Milko was an amateur champion several times over and had defeated several of the same fighters that Greb defeated in the amateurs. After turning professional Milko's career seemed to be in limbo, and he no doubt harbored some ill will toward this young upstart Greb who had in such a short time made himself quite a reputation.

On the eve of the fight Milko was heard to say "If Harry Grebbs (sic) is as good as he says he is he will have the chance of his life to prove it tonight. I understand he has been doing a lot of talking about carrying the fight to me. What they call my 'haymaker' is still in working order. I haven't backed up yet in any of my bouts and I don't think he will make much of a reputation off of me." Greb for his part was extremely confident and cited his fight with Hooks Evans as proof of his ability to stand with fighters of Milko's class.[33]

The war of words finally over, the two young men squared off in the rooms of the Tariff Club on the evening of October 22, 1913. When the bell sounded the first round it was obvious this fight was going to be a tremendous struggle. Milko, knowing that Greb was considered the more clever and faster of the two, began by hammering away with short powerful body punches. However, every attempt at landing a knockout blow on Greb's jaw was a practice in futility. Greb was constantly moving in and out, up and down. The only target that presented itself to Milko was Greb's midsection, and Milko obliged. Greb for his part was beating a steady tattoo on Milko's face and torso but it was obvious that the more powerful punches were being landed by Milko. In the fourth round Milko doubled Greb over with a powerful blow to the stomach which forced Greb to hang on. In the fifth when things seemed to be slipping away from Greb he landed a beautiful right hand which sent Milko back on his heels. Instead of taking the fight out of Milko the blow simply made him more aggressive and Greb found himself in the most difficult fight of his career thus far. When the bell sounded the end of the fight, it appeared that Milko deserved the nod yet opinions were divided as to who had won. Not satisfied with such a result Milko demanded a rematch to which Greb, equally convinced of his

Joe Chip (above) would hang the only knockout on Harry Greb. A fine fighter in his own right, Chip's career was overshadowed by the accomplishments of his more talented brother, George.

claim to victory, readily agreed.

When the Youngstown newspapers found out that Harry Greb had competed in a match with Milko just days after the supposed death of his loved one they roasted him in print.

Harry Grebbs (sic) of Pittsburgh was unable to meet Joe Chip here Monday night in their scheduled eight round bout because, as announced, of a death in the family. Like the little boy who wanted to get a day off to see a ball game so was it with Grebb --it was one of his grandmothers who had died-- for last night he fought a tame six round bout in Pittsburgh with Mike Milko.[34]

Whether Red Mason or Harry saw this criticism is unknown, what is known is that Mason intended to keep Harry busy in the interim between bouts with Milko. Harry was scheduled to fight on the undercard of the re-scheduled grudge match between stable mate Al Grayber and Walter "Kid" Smith; the boys intended to bring to a conclusion the feud which began in the streets of Clarksburg.[35] It was intended to have Greb fight Kid Hackett but the match fell through and Greb was left to prepare for his rematch with Milko through simple training as opposed to fighting himself into shape, which was the method of preparation preferred by Red Mason. This was hinted at a week before the rematch with Milko when the Pittsburgh Post printed "Harry Greb, the boy that looks like a comer, is another fighter that Manager Mason intends to work from now on and if looks go for anything Greb is sure to be a champion."[36] Mason was now calling out some of the best fighters in Pittsburgh at or around 142 pounds for Greb knowing that a victory over Milko would greatly enhance Greb's reputation among local fight bugs.

The fight was to be held on the undercard of the match between Greb's stablemate and training partner Red Robinson and Harvey "Hooks" Evans. It was an intriguing match and promised to be an excellent card from top to bottom. When Greb and Milko toed the line at Old City

Hall on November 17, 1913 the stakes were high for both fighters. They both knew that a winner would be propelled into greater matches while the loser would have to work his way back up to a showcase such as this. Both fighters started out fast with Milko winging his dangerous sledgehammer like punches and Greb darting around using his better speed and agility to counter his adversary. It was an action packed fight, not at all unlike their first bout, the major difference being that Greb utilized his advantages of speed and cleverness to much greater effect. As a result, when the papers published their decisions the next day, Greb came out on top by a slight margin. It was an outstanding boost to Greb's prestige in Pittsburgh boxing circles and a boost in Mason's faith in Greb.

Within days of Greb's popular decision over Milko, Red Mason claimed for Greb the 142 pound championship of Pittsburgh and posted a fifty dollar check to be cashed by anyone willing to challenge that assertion with his fists. Mason made similar defies on behalf of other members of his stable such as Johnny Ray, Red Robinson, and Eddie Wimler.[37]

With a stable of fighters that seemed at times to be growing exponentially, Mason's attentions were understandably divided, understood that is by most with the exception of Buck Crouse. Mason and Crouse had always had a somewhat stormy relationship with Crouse leaving Mason's banner several times. Crouse was now finding it difficult to understand why Mason was wasting (in his eyes) so much time with preliminary fighters when Crouse was a headliner who could draw down good money in bouts across the country.

The ugly feud boiled over in print when it was published that Crouse had stated Mason was a tramp who didn't know he (Crouse) was alive half the time. In disgust Crouse packed his bags and left for Buffalo with Jimmy Perry in tow as his new manager. Mason got off a parting shot stating that Crouse was so good he could beat Johnny Ray any day of the week, a biting comment when one considers that Crouse was an experienced veteran fighting at 158 pounds while Ray was a preliminary fighter fighting at 115 pounds.[38]

With Crouse out of the picture for the time being, Mason now focused all of his energies on pushing his remaining fighters to the forefront of the Pittsburgh boxing scene. If successful, he could then think about taking them on tour and promoting them throughout the country at larger venues for larger purses.

The first order of business was to get Greb a spot on the undercard of the upcoming bout between Bob Moha and Tom McMahon. The bout would be held on the 29th of November at Old City Hall and Greb's opponent would be none other than Joe Chip. On the day of the fight the Pittsburgh Leader noted that Greb's bout with Chip would "...prove good, as it will give Grebbs (sic) the test needed in order to bring him around to where the public will notice him."[39]

As a warm-up to the main bout, the match between Harry Greb and Joe Chip certainly provided those in attendance their money's worth. As the two fighters met in the center of the ring at the sound of the first gong it was all slugging and no science. Joe Chip was swinging for the fences and often missed by several feet, however he was getting the better of the exchanges and managed to bloody Greb's lip. Red Mason, trying to give his fighter every advantage, began heckling Chip from ringside. As the round ended, Greb seemed to be warming up to the task and was holding his own with the brother and chief sparring partner of the Middleweight Champion.

The second round began much like the first with both boys throwing science out the window and electing to stand and trade punch for punch. Suddenly, without warning, Chip landed a massive roundhouse right swing directly on the point of Greb's chin. Harry fell in a heap near his own corner, his head striking the mat hard. Mason rushed to ringside and with his mouth full of water sprayed the unconscious form of Harry Greb in an attempt to revive him. Seeing this Joe Chip became enraged. It was the last straw after having to suffer Mason's barbs throughout the abbreviated affair. Joe rushed Mason and swung a kick in his direction. Words were exchanged and as Joe began to climb down out of the ring Mason simply held up the water bottle he had been holding and smiled, inviting Chip in. A spectator tossed Mason a heavy cane and yelled "Hit him with this Red!" With all of this excitement swirling around him Greb was struggling within his addled senses to regain his footing. Everything was a blur; for once in his life Greb found himself in the thick of the excitement and not wanting to be there.[40]

3

A YOUNG TURK

A fighter's first knockout loss can be devastating. One never knows how he will react to such an event until he has been picked up off the canvas by his seconds and revived. Some fighters are never the same; they become 'gun-shy' or simply lose their ability to take a punch altogether. Sometimes the effects of a knockout are not so overt. The effects can be subtle, merely the reflection of the fallen fighter's self-confidence. Could the fighter come back? Does the fighter have a glass jaw? Will the fighter be able to defend himself in a tight spot or will he fall to pieces the first time he gets another hard tap on the chin? These were all questions that boxing aficionados would be asking about a fighter who suffers his first KO loss. These were all questions that Greb would be forced to ask himself following his fight with Joe Chip.

Once the cobwebs had cleared from Harry's addled mind and he had come to terms with the fact that Joe Chip had knocked him silly, his naturally sunny attitude took hold and he was able to chalk it up to being an aspect of the sport he loved. He could accept it, improve from it, and move on, or he could simply quit. Greb was not a quitter. If Pius had hoped that the knockout would finally convince his only son that carpentry was the profession Harry should be focusing on, he was sorely mistaken. As headstrong as his father, Harry was now determined more than ever to prove himself to the public as a fighter.

The day after his loss to Chip, Greb immediately set about visiting all of the local newspaper offices and all of the favorite hangouts of Pittsburgh fight bugs and made it clear that not only did he come away from the bout without a scratch but that he was as eager as ever to face the stiffest competition available in the welter-

A week after his knockout loss to Joe Chip, Harry Greb came back against Battling Sherbine (above).

weight class. He added that no longer would he venture above this limit and fight middleweights weighing 156 pounds (Chip's weight the night of the fight) while he himself only weighed 142 pounds.[1]

Meanwhile James Mason had made himself very unpopular with the local Pittsburgh sports fraternity due not only to his near brawl with Joe Chip but also to his involvement in an attempt to block Dick Loadman from a lucrative fight with Kid Williams, bantamweight title claimant, in order to substitute his own fighter, Frankie Conley in Loadman's place.[2] This was the atmosphere when Greb agreed to face Battling Sherbine on December 6, 1913, just one week after his first KO loss, and Young Battling Nelson on December 12, 1913.

As Greb faced off against Sherbine on the undercard of Red Robinson's KO loss to Phil Brock it's likely that he didn't have his now somewhat reviled manager in his corner. Mason had decided that a short stint away from Pittsburgh would do his ailing reputation good. Instead Greb probably had Al Grayber in his corner as Chief Second. In fighting his first bout after a devastating knockout loss and doing so without the guidance of his manager, Greb was understandably tense in the first round. The action was sparse and Greb seemed unsure of himself. In the second round he loosened up a bit and by the third he was rapidly burying Sherbine under a mountain of boxing gloves. When the six rounds had completed Greb was an easy winner.[3]

Greb's next confidence-building fight would be in Altoona, Pennsylvania. Al Grayber would

The Mishler Theatre in Altoona, Pennsylvania was the site of Greb's bout against Bud "Young Bat" Nelson. The bout was a sort of confidence builder for Greb after his loss to Joe Chip. The Mishler Theatre still stands in much the same condition as it did when Greb fought there.

again be handling Greb's corner[4] and again Greb would be victorious. The fight was fairly even until the second round when Greb slammed home a perfect punch which sent a crimson stream flowing from Nelson's nose and mouth. That single punch changed the entire fight and suddenly Nelson lost all confidence in himself. From that point on Greb battered his opponent sending him down for a nine count twice in the third round. When Greb scored a third knock down the referee stepped in and waved the fight off, saving Nelson from further needless punishment.[5]

As 1913 drew to a close, Greb was preparing to fight for the first time an opponent with whom he would have an incredible ten bout series, Otto "Whitey" Wenzel. Wenzel was a tough, rugged fighter who had been fighting as a professional since 1910. He was well known in Pittsburgh boxing circles and faced some of the best fighters the area had to offer in the welterweight and middleweight divisions. Greb would ring in the New Year by fighting Whitey Wenzel on January 1st, 1914 on the undercard of the grudge match between Mickey Rodgers and Red Robinson at Old City Hall.

The card was replete with action from top to bottom. Rodgers earned his revenge over Robinson by scoring a decisive victory in the eyes of most present. In the semi-final Greb and Wenzel put on an action-packed bout. Both fighters sailed into each other as if they were trying to upstage the final act. For three rounds the fighters pounded each other with their best punches. After the third round Greb's harder blows seemed to tell on Wenzel and Greb took control. From that point on Greb broke Wenzel down bit by bit and when the final gong sounded no one doubted that Greb was the victor. The next day the newspapers lauded Greb's performance, one went so far as to state that "Harry Grebb fought like a bearcat against Whitey Wensel (sic) in the second

Whitey Wenzel (above) would face Greb numerous times over the years. Wenzel was a favorite of the Pittsburgh boxing fans because of his willingness to always give his best. Whatever limitations Wenzel may have possessed as a fighter he made up for them with pure moxy.

bout and won all the way."[6]

With such a sensational showing it was expected that both fighters would meet again, what wasn't expected was just how soon they would meet. Following his popular victory over Wenzel Harry was expected to face Swats Adamson on the undercard of Walter Monaghan's bout with Gus Christie of Milwaukee on January 10. Shortly before the card was to commence Whitey Wenzel was substituted for Adamson and what followed was a near repetition of their first bout. The newspaper accounts were split down the middle as to who deserved the honors in this bout. The Pittsburgh Leader presented the most comprehensive account of the fight:

> **Wenzel and Harry Greb met in the semi-final. It was the same kind of slugging as their last meeting. Both men hit hard and furious. The initial round went to Greb, as he landed the most punches. The second round went to Greb by a margin, as Greb was hitting better and harder and seemed to gauge distance better than Whitey. The slugs exchanged in the third round, if combined, would have battered down the walls of China, but Greb was the best man on giving while Whitey stood up gamely. The Northsider was game, that's all, in the fourth inning, as Greb put his full power behind every blow. But Whitey stood his ground and a couple of times came through with a wallop. It was Greb's round.**
>
> **The fifth was a repetition, only Greb did not seem able to hit as hard, as he began to show some signs of becoming tired. It was another shade for Greb. The pair became tired in the sixth and did quite a lot of wrestling and wound up with a slugging setto, as the bell rang. It was Greb's bout.[7]**

The Gazette-Times and The Press agreed with this assessment of the fight while the Post disagreed, giving Whitey the verdict and the Daily Dispatch added that "Whitey Wenzel scored a victory over Harry Greb, who a week before gave him a good lacing."[8]

The same day that the reviews came in for Greb's rematch with Wenzel an article appeared in the Pittsburgh Leader outlining the state of local Pittsburgh boxing and some of the developing prospects. In discussing welterweights the article had this to say about Greb: "Greb is a new comer and looks pretty good. He is boxing preliminaries and really has qualifications that will win him ring honors. But he has never been put to the acid test and fans cannot pass judgment on him. Greb bumped into a knockout from Joe Chip's mauler recently, but that does not seem to have slowed up Harry in the least bit."[9] The Pittsburgh Post, which judged against Greb in his rematch with Wenzel added to this the next day by stating that while Wenzel deserved the verdict "...Greb however, will bear watching for he looks like another Buck Crouse when Buck was coming."[10] High praise indeed, proving that Greb's efforts to show that the knockout loss to Joe Chip would not deter him was bringing results.

In order to gain Greb recognition outside of Pittsburgh, James Mason began to arrange a show at Steubenville, Ohio in which he would cast Greb as the headliner. The opponent selected for Greb was the dangerous Pittsburgh lightweight, Mickey Rodgers. Rodgers was a rough, brawling fighter who had been featured in some of Pittsburgh's most memorable grudge matches. Rodgers hailed from Southside, just across the Monongahela River, a neighborhood which was home to some of Pittsburgh's best fighters.

Rodgers, like Mike Milko, was almost as well known for his out-of-the-ring exploits as he was for his boxing ability. Not six months before agreeing to fight Greb Rodgers had been involved in an altercation on a streetcar during which he was thrown from the car and suffered two broken ribs, a dislocated knee, and bruising about his body.[11] Years later when Rodgers fell on hard times he turned to robbery. When brought before a judge Rodgers gave his occupation as "pugilist." The judge shot back "You're a BUM! Pugilists don't hold persons up, they knock 'em DOWN!"[12]

The match with Rodgers was one that Mason had been trying to make for the better part of a month, with Rodgers not willing to budge on

Mickey Rodgers (above) was one of Pittsburgh's most popular lightweights and a vicious brawler. He was lured out of his weight class by a large purse to fight Harry Greb only to lose a disqualification.

the weight issue. Both fighters had a healthy respect for the advantages the other brought to the bargaining table; in Rodgers' case it was his greater experience, in Greb's it was chiefly his size advantage. Mason finally agreed to 142 pounds and articles were signed whereby Greb and Rodgers were to weigh no more than 142 pounds the afternoon of the fight to be held on February 23 over a distance of ten rounds,[13] Greb's longest scheduled fight to date. The winner would then be matched in an enticing bout with Ray Parks of Pittsburgh's Northside. The Greb-Rodgers bout was highly anticipated by Pittsburgh fans and as a result a special rail car

was reserved for the sole purpose of carrying Pittsburgh fans to the scene of the battle.

Realizing that Rodgers was arguably his most difficult opponent, having defeated Hooks Evans and Red Robinson, Greb set about training immediately. After five days of feverish training on Greb's part it was announced that the fight would be postponed. Greb had injured his hand in his last fight with Whitey Wenzel without realizing the severity of the injury. The stiff training regimen which Greb had undertaken aggravated the hand and worsened it. The bout was set back to March 2.[14]

Rodgers for his part took it all in stride and kept right on training, running three miles in the deep snows that now enveloped Pittsburgh and sparring eight rounds a day. By the time of the initial date of the fight, Rodgers' weight was already down to 143 pounds and he expected to weigh 138 pounds on March 2nd. This was perfect fighting trim for Mickey and trouble for Greb.

Despite Greb's status as a newcomer, and a preliminary fighter, Rodgers was taking the bout with Greb as deadly serious. He saw Greb as a young Turk trying to make a name off of him. Rodgers knew that he was picked as an opponent because he brought name recognition to the table while being naturally a full division lighter than Greb. "The fans think that because I am meeting Harry Greb next Monday at Steubenville that I intend to enter the welterweight division, but such is not the case. I am boxing Greb and allowing him to come in above 140 pounds because I was offered a big guarantee by the promoters -and also because I think I can beat him, no matter what the weight be."[15]

As the fighters finally entered the ring on March 2, 1914 they were both trained to the minute. Each was the picture of a fighting machine with one exception; Greb's injured hand which had postponed the bout was still causing a considerable amount of pain. Before entering the ring Greb was given an injection of cocaine directly into the hand to numb the pain. It did more than numb Harry's pain; it numbed his senses as well. He complained of having what he described as something that "resembled a sleeping sickness."[16]

A large crowd was present and as the gong rang sounding the first round anticipation was at a fever pitch. Greb came out for the first round feeling as though he was in a stupor. It took a solid punch landing squarely in his face to bring him to some semblance of his senses. Even as the bell rang ending the round Greb was slow to react and stumbled back to his corner. The bout quickly degenerated from an exhibition of skill to an ugly wrestling match with both fighters mauling in the clinches. Round after round this pattern continued, much to the fans' disgust. As Greb's greater strength began to tell on his opponent Rodgers became increasingly frustrated. In the fifth round suddenly and deliberately Mickey Rodgers, ever the street brawler, sent a "well placed knee" into Greb's abdomen which doubled the boy over and promptly won him the fight on a disqualification (some reports state it was a bevy of low blows). It was an ugly fight, an ugly way to win, and capping off the unsatisfactory evening

Greb was carried from the ring in agony.[17]

With nothing in the way of boxing matches lined up for the next month, Greb spent a week or two recuperating from the hard training he had undertaken (and the foul he had received) for his bout with Rodgers. It wasn't long before he was itching to fight again and without any matches in sight he continued his training by honing his skills against his stable mates, most notably Johnny Ray, and Red Robinson who was preparing for a bout with Jack Coyne.

As Greb was recuperating, a young amateur boxer in Pittsburgh was making headlines. Fay Keiser, who had been winning several amateur competitions in the 158 pound class, was considering a

This cartoon, lampooning Al McCoy's un-looked for title winning knockout over George Chip was indicative of sentiments across the nation. He would become known as the "Cheese Champ" for what was considered his lucky victory and his unwillingness to risk losing his championship over the course of a three year reign.

move up to heavyweight in order to challenge the redoubtable John Foley, premier amateur heavyweight in western Pennsylvania, Eastern Ohio, West Virginia and western New York. It was an ambitious move and, if successful, would have catapulted Keiser to prominence in Pittsburgh boxing before ever even turning professional.[18] Just prior to the competition Keiser cancelled his entry form and agreed to turn professional by facing Harry Greb on the undercard of the bout between Gus Christie and Buck Crouse to be held April 14 at Duquesne Gardens.

On April 7 the bout between Christie and Crouse would take on an even greater importance. Both men were highly touted middleweight contenders with designs on a championship. On April 7 George Chip met Al McCoy in a no-decision bout in Brooklyn, New York. McCoy had never given any indication of being anything other than a journeyman and so when the offer was made for McCoy to fight at 158 pounds against either Joe Chip or George Chip (whichever could make the weight), George agreed despite the fact that if he lost by KO his championship would pass to McCoy.[19] Chip was a five to one favorite and it was two to one that McCoy would not last five rounds.

As the fight began everything went exactly the way fans expected; Chip pursued McCoy

Fay Keiser (pictured here, in a rare photo circa 1914 or 1915) was one of Greb's most persistent opponents. Keiser came out of the amateur ranks in 1914 to face Greb. They would have no less than nine fights over the years with the last bout being held in 1924.

with a grim determination to end matters early while McCoy literally ran from Chip's wild right hand swings. No blows were landed in the opening thirty seconds. After this point Chip opened McCoy's "defense" with a left jab that bloodied McCoy's nose, Chip then worked his way inside with two rights to the body. They clinched and Chip worked his right to the body again. The southpaw McCoy suddenly opened up with his own right to the stomach and then brought up a short left uppercut to the point of Chip's chin which sent Chip sprawling. As the crowd sat in stunned silence, it was fully eight seconds before Chip even began to stir, so devastating was the uppercut that felled him. As the referee reached the fatal ten count Chip was only just beginning to raise his shoulders from the mat. The bout had lasted 80 seconds, between 5 and 6 punches had landed and only one mattered. Just as stunned as the audience, McCoy stood in a daze not fully understanding that he was now a world champion.[20] It was a title that he would shamefully milk for over three years with near disastrous results to the division.

So it was when Gus Christie and Buck Crouse, leading contenders in the middleweight division, squared off at Duquesne Gardens on April 14, 1914, both men hoping to gain a shot at the seemingly vulnerable middleweight title. With former middleweight champion Frank Klaus seated at ringside, Buck Crouse survived a rocky third round to take the popular verdict.

On the undercard Harry Greb was taken the limit by Fay Keiser fighting for his first time as a professional. Greb carried the fight to Keiser and it was this display of aggressiveness that won him the decision in the eyes of those seated at ringside. Three papers dissented, the Chronicle-Telegraph, the Daily Dispatch and the Press, calling the bout a draw.[21]

Having turned back Keiser's hopes of making a quick reputation as a professional, Greb went back to honing his skills by working out daily with Red Robinson and Al Grayber. Robinson was preparing for yet another bout against his nemesis Mickey Rodgers, who after losing to Greb in the Steubenville debacle had decided to stay in the lightweight ranks. Greb and Keiser were signed as the chief support to the Rodgers-Robinson bout. When the time came for the two fighters to face off for their second match in a month Keiser was ready. The two fighters battled every minute of the six rounds with Greb again carrying the fight to Keiser. The Gazette-Times remarked that Greb "hit Fay Keiser seemingly 10,000 times during their six-round semi-final, but Keiser was there at the finish, beaten but willing, and he got the glad hand."[22] The Press voted for Keiser stating that "Greb grew wilder and Keiser better as the go progressed, and had the matter of decision been left to rooters, Keiser would have been handed the blue ribbon."[23]

George Lewis (above) was a talented stylist who had difficulty in acquiring opponents due to his considerable promise. In Greb he found a willing adversary.

The Dispatch, Chronicle-Telegraph, and the Sun had Greb winning the fight while the Post had the match even. In the main event Red Robinson suffered a one sided defeat at the hands of Rodgers.

Since the beginning of the year a young welterweight named George Lewis had been trying desperately to get fights in Pittsburgh. Lewis hailed from Toledo, Ohio and showed such promise early in his career that he had been selected as a sparring partner for Jack Dillon in early 1913 while Dillon was in Pittsburgh training for his bout with Buck Crouse. Dillon had been battering his sparring partners when Lewis was called for. Lewis, still barely an amateur, stepped into the ring and stunned observers with his display. He made Jack "The Giant Killer" step faster than any of his more experienced predecessors. Discussions among those who witnessed the sparring session centered around Lewis' bright future.[24] After developing his style in fights against Whitey Wenzel, Hooks Evans, and lesser lights of the local boxing scene, Lewis had become known as a talented boxer and someone to be avoided. Quick and agile with a sizzling right hand and solid defense, Lewis was avoided like the plague by area fighters from lightweight to middleweight. As a result he had to supplement his income by taking up work as a pastry chef.[25]

Noble Davis, who had taken the reigns of Lewis' career, had set about an ambitious campaign designed to acquire lucrative fights for his man. First Davis claimed for Lewis the welterweight championship of Western Pennsylvania. He then set about issuing defies in local newspapers to all of the leading boxers dangling the dubious title claim as a reward to anyone who could defeat Lewis. There was just one problem; his proclamations went unheeded for months and a fighter without an opponent is a man without a job.

One of the fighters Davis had focused upon was none other than Harry Greb. Red Mason, seeing Lewis as little more than an upstart, tired of reading Davis' claims and promptly signed Greb to dispatch the young fighter at the Southside Market House on May 25. Both fighters entered the ring confident of victory and both fighters left the ring just as confident that they had won. The match was wild, and sloppy, fought at a fast pace. Both boys were so eager to show their best that they ended up trying too hard and as a result they offered up a pleasing if somewhat ugly match. Greb was the aggressor and used his greater size to effect but Lewis was sharp and more polished. His precision punching set Greb's nose to bleed and had his face red at the conclusion of the sixth and final round. The newspapers were just as divided as the fans as to who deserved the decision. "George Lewis," stated the Post "came out on the short end in his bout with Harry Greb in the main event. Greb forced the fighting and did by far the best work at long range."[26] In stark contrast to this assessment was the Press which issued a scathing review of the fight and the fighters.[27] Unimpressed by the of lack skill exhibited by the youngsters, it grudgingly gave Lewis a slight victory. The Gazette-Times agreed with this result but added that the fight "...was a good one and well received by a handful of fans."[28] The Dispatch, while offering minimal coverage of the events, felt Greb deserved the victory. As a postscript to the bout, it was noted that while Greb, working on a guarantee received forty dollars for his nights' work, Lewis, who had been so eager for a match agreed to work on a percentage basis. The bout drew a poor crowd and as a result Lewis received nothing for the fight.[29]

After the less than decisive result of the Lewis-Greb tilt, Lewis was eager for a rematch but he would have to wait two months for his chance, for Greb was already scheduled to meet several other battlers in the near future. The first of these scheduled bouts was a third match against Whitey Wenzel on the undercard of yet another match between Mickey Rodgers and Red Robinson scheduled for just four days after Greb's bout with Lewis. The bout which preceded a popular loss by Robinson to Rodgers, got little attention outside of the verdict which most papers felt Greb deserved.[30]

Greb was next scheduled to appear in a bout with Walter Monaghan.[31] The bout would be the main event of an attractive card which would pit amateur heavyweight champion John Foley against Al Grayber, Johnny Ray against Nish Gallagher, and Kid Summers against Kid Egan. The bout would be held in Lawrenceville at Waldemier Hall. With Foley and Monaghan hailing from Lawrenceville and Greb being unofficially adopted by that section, because of his training there and his birth in neighboring Garfield, it had district fans anxiously awaiting the day when festivities would begin. An added attraction was the fact that it would be Foley's first professional bout, and taking on one of the most respected fighters in Pittsburgh.

Greb and Monaghan had been rivals for the affections of district fans since Greb started making a modest reputation for himself. Monaghan had much more experience than Greb, having faced such high caliber fighters as George Chip, Buck Crouse, and Jack Dillon. He was rugged and packed a heavy punch but one-sided losses to Dillon and Gus Christie illustrated that Monaghan was little more than a popular club fighter. Mason had refused several previous offers to box the Lawrenceville favorite due in part to Monaghan's reputation and partly because he had managed Walter at a time when a match with Greb would have been likely. Feeling the time was now right to clean up his home district, Greb signed to face Monaghan hoping to win honors as Lawrenceville's best 150 pounder.

Walter Monaghan (above) had been one of Lawrenceville's most beloved fighters. His bout with Greb was to decide Lawrencville's top middleweight.

In the intense June heat Greb trained relentlessly, eager for a decisive victory over Monaghan who had been made a betting favorite. Monaghan had been a favorite due to his greater size, experience, and the fact that Greb had been a professional for just over one year. This only served to motivate Greb. Greb didn't just want to win, he wanted a clean knockout. "I expect to beat Monahan Monday and prove that I am not afraid of him," said Greb. "Just because I did not jump at the first offer received to face Monahan is no sign that I feared him. I wanted to wait until I thought I was right; so look for me to make it a regular battle."[32] As the training period for both fighters drew to a close Greb weighed 148 lbs. while Monaghan expected to come into the ring weighing around 155 lbs.[33]

Monaghan entered the ring expecting to outsmart his younger rival, what he got was the worst beating of his life. From the first round until the final bell sounded Greb simply out-classed his larger foe. He danced in and out shooting punches from all directions circling Monaghan in a dizzy display of speed and agility. By the fourth round Greb was ready to take chances and as such he began to batter Monaghan around the ring. The Lawrenceville middleweight's face rained blood from cuts on both cheeks, his eyes were closed, his ribs looked a sickening pink color from the constant attention Greb paid them, and it would take seven stitches to patch up his bloody lips. The newspapers were unanimous in their decision as to the winner.[34]

The Pittsburgh Post was as surprised as anyone:

> **Harry Greb, the Garfield boy who has been boxing professionally but little over one year, surprised even his fondest admirers last night by handing Walter Monahan of Lawrenceville, his ward rival, one of the worst beatings that the "bearcat" ever received. Greb beat Monahan in every round; in the fourth and fifth simply hammering him to a pulp. From the fourth round on Monahan's face was cut to shreds...**
>
> **...It was by far the best scrap Greb has fought, although he appeared to be outweighed slightly.[35]**

The Press was no less complimentary of Greb's victory:

> **..."Mon" never assimilated so much punishment since he took up gloving. Greb boxed and fought rings around him, ripped open his cheeks, closed his lampteenies, and bunged up his ribs. It was an awful slaughter...**
>
> **Greb's battle was his topnotcher. He has been battling like a tenth-rater, but last night he gave flashes that would become a champion. He had his adversary bewildered. When Harry was frescoing "Mon's" mug, so much gore was being spilled that numerous weak-kneed bugs left the hall for a gasp of fresh air.[36]**

As word spread of Greb's unlooked-for victory, George Lewis again appeared on the scene calling out his former opponent. "Mason knows that I am Greb's master in the ring, and for that reason, will not make the match," said Lewis. "But he will try and make the fans believe that he has the best boy in this city. I won over Greb the only time we met and I am sure I can do it again. I am always ready to make a match with Greb at 145 pounds ringside, for a side bet of $200 and winner take all, or will split the money any way that will be satisfactory to Mason."[37]

Mason had other plans for Greb. Owing to the success of the Lawrenceville show, Mason decided to put on an encore performance at the same venue. This time Greb would be facing another Lawrenceville favorite, Irish Gorgas, and again the promotion would center on the idea that the winner would be the top middleweight in the district.

Gorgas had been fighting in the Pittsburgh area for four years under various names such as Irish Gorgas, Rooster Gorgas, and Kid Gorgas. His real name was in fact Walter Gorgas and he hailed from a part of Lawrenceville known as "Irish Town." Among other things, Gorgas was well known for his peculiar habit of training not in the early morning or midafternoon as most fighters, but well after midnight. Gorgas, like Monaghan, was little more than a rugged Pittsburgh club fighter but he was well respected in the city and figured to give Greb a more difficult time than his predecessor.

Both fighters trained in the stifling summer heat. Four days before the battle Greb weighed 152 pounds in fighting trim. The year of hard training had begun to put more muscle on his once wiry frame and he was now filling out. He expected to enter the ring at 150 pounds or about five pounds lighter than his rival.[38] Gorgas, for his part, was not overlooking his young opponent's recent victory over Monaghan and vowed revenge for the honor of Lawrenceville.

Walter "Irish" Gorgas (above) unwillingly helped to establish Greb's reputation as one of Pittsburgh's premier middleweights by suffering a six round beating.

From the outset the fight was heated. The usually smiling Greb wore a face of grave sincerity as he smashed into Gorgas round after round. Gorgas proved a much more able battler than did Monaghan, willing to assimilate punishment in hopes of landing one wild swing which would bring the fight to a premature close. With Greb easily winning the fight, at the close of the fifth round while being parted from a clinch Greb landed a light blow to the side of Gorgas' head. The unintentional punch did no damage but Gorgas cried foul in hopes of salvaging a victory that was rapidly slipping away.

As Greb sat down on his stool for the minute rest one of Gorgas' seconds, a man named Malone, crossed the ring to argue with Red Mason about the infraction. The argument became heated and Malone took a poke at Greb who immediately became enraged by the cheap shot and tore after the man with fists flying. A near riot ensued and order had to be restored by several uniformed police officers who climbed into the ring and separated the angry parties. The fight, or rather Gorgas beating continued, through the sixth and final round, and when the

New York Tribune

NEW YORK, MONDAY, JUNE 29, 1914.   PRICE ONE CENT

HEIR TO AUSTRIAN THRONE ASSASSINATED;
WIFE BY HIS SIDE ALSO SHOT TO DEATH;
EARLIER ATTEMPT ON THEIR LIVES FAILED

Coming on the heels of Frank Moran's unsuccessful bid for Jack Johnson's heavyweight championship (top) was the news that Archduke Franz Ferdinand and his wife had been assassinated (above). It was an event that signalled the beginning of the first world war.

papers rendered their unofficial decisions the next day it was to no one's surprise that Greb had taken the victory.[39]

If Pittsburgh boxing fans had overlooked the Greb-Gorgas showdown it was because events elsewhere in the world had held sway over their attention. Two days before the fight another of Pittsburgh's fighters found himself in the ultimate dream of every boxer, challenging for the heavyweight championship of the world. Frank Moran, the "Pittsburgh Dentist," was in France facing black heavyweight champion Jack Johnson. Moran had the hopes of not only Pittsburgh but much of white America riding on his chances to wipe what they considered the stain of Jack Johnson's reign as champion from the public consciousness.

Johnson had been exiled from the United States after fleeing charges that he violated the Mann act, which prohibited interstate transport of women for immoral purposes. He had wound his way through Europe before finding France to his liking. When he stepped into the ring with Moran it was more out of desperation for funds than for honor or glory. Johnson was nearly broke and it was with cold, hard cash firmly fixed in his mind that he entered the ring. He trained but little and carried a paunch that had never graced his statuesque physique in past performances.

The fight had excited the minds of boxing fans across the western world. Newspapers across the United States were prepared to read round by round telegraph reports of the fight to crowds camped outside their offices eagerly awaiting news of the event. The ringside crowd was populated by the leading heads of society and the referee was none other than young French boxing champion and idol Georges Carpentier. The fight itself was a poor one from start to finish. Johnson was either incapable of or unwilling to inflict serious punishment on his opponent. Moran for his part was game and tried his best but was no match even for an out-of-shape ring general such as Johnson.

If the Johnson-Moran fight wasn't enough to divert Pittsburgh's attentions away from the Greb-Gorgas bout then the news coming just hours after Moran's defeat was. Archduke Franz Ferdinand had been assassinated in Sarajevo. What at first seemed like the death of a rather innocuous European nobleman would tear the very fabric of European life, laying bare rifts which had existed just below the surface for years. Within a month a war erupted that would eventually spill over borders across much of the world.

With the madness in Europe still a distant murmur, Greb began to prepare for a bout with Ray Parks, a popular welterweight of Pittsburgh's Northside district fresh off a successful campaign in Wisconsin and Minnesota. In addition to the Parks bout, Red Mason had also lined up a rematch with George Lewis in Steubenville. The Parks bout would be held on July 20 giving Greb one week to prepare for his bout with Lewis on July 27. When it was announced that Greb had contracted to fight Lewis in Steubenville, for what was expected to be a higher purse than Pittsburgh clubs were currently offering, Parks backed out of the bout with Greb in hopes that the bout could be rearranged in Steubenville for more money.[40] Fay Keiser was quickly substituted for Parks and the show was saved. Keiser was certainly a much larger opponent than Greb had

John "Honey" Foley (above) had been an incredibly talented amateur heavyweight boxer and wrestler in Pittsburgh. He turned pro in 1914 facing Greb's stablemate Al Grayber. Just over a month later he would face Greb on a moments notice. Despite being heavily outweighed Greb gave Foley a boxing lesson which prompted many to call for his retirement.

George Lewis (above), the fighting pastry chef of Pittsburgh (by way of Toledo) who would prove the most tenacious of Greb's early opponents.

trained for but if size worried Greb he was in for another surprise.

Just as the preliminary card was ending the promoters went to notify Keiser that it was time for him to put in an appearance. Keiser was nowhere to be found. Someone spotted heavyweight John "Honey" Foley, former amateur champion of western Pennsylvania, in the audience and he was immediately snatched up and placed before Greb. Foley, who had been defeated only a week before by Fay Keiser, was still nursing a banged up left eye and a broken nose.[41] While he may not have been in the best of condition on account of his recent wounds, he certainly had an enormous advantage in weight; one estimate had him outweighing Greb by thirty pounds.[42] As it turned out even this was no help against his smaller opponent. Greb used his speed to stay away from Foley's powerful swings and set about puffing up his left eye and bloodying his nose. Foley made the fight interesting, mainly through his size and dogged determination, even managing to land a few blows in the fourth round, his best. Nevertheless, when the fight had concluded only two papers disagreed with the prevailing opinion that Foley had been badly outclassed, and called the fight a draw.[43]

Greb was now ready to face George Lewis, who had already given him one of his most difficult fights. The decision of their first bout was still being disputed and debated by those who witnessed it and by the fighters themselves. It was hoped that this match, being scheduled for ten rounds, would lead to a more decisive result. "I expect to score a knockout," said Lewis. "But in case such a thing does not happen, I will prove that I am the master of Greb in the ring. Do not think that I pick Greb as a soft boy, for he is not, but if he wins from me he will have the fight of his life. There is only one thing I will say about Greb. He is the only boy in this section that would agree to box me."[44] Both fighters were training at an incredible pace. Greb was sparring daily with Buck Crouse (who had made amends with Mason) and Johnny Ray, who had been preparing for an upcoming bout with Patsy Brannigan.

The promotion of the bout had been a resounding success. Fans from Pittsburgh and Wheeling arrived at the site of the battle via special trains. A large crowd was on hand to witness what Steubenville papers would call "one of the best battles ever seen here."[45] Greb tried to use his size advantage by constantly leaping in and out and mauling Lewis on the inside, but Lewis proved too clever, sweeping the last four rounds. With such a finish Lewis was able to take the decision of Steubenville's two newspapers.[46] Despite Lewis' apparent victory, reports filtered back to Pittsburgh (probably originating with Red Mason) that Greb had won the fight, broke Lewis' nose and his own hand in the process.[47] When Noble Davis, Lewis' manager, read these accounts he was furious, replying to the papers:

> That your article of the 27th, dated Steubenville, and describing the bout between George Lewis and Harry Greb does not conform with the general opinion of the sporting public of Steubenville, who witnessed this contest is evident from the fact that the article credits Greb with nine of the 10 rounds, while the popular decision was quite the reverse and gave Lewis a decided advantage over his opponent in eight of these rounds. This opinion I learned after making a personal canvas after the fight of the leading fans at the ringside.
>
> You have also been misinformed regarding Lewis' physical condition after the fight. Your article says his nose was broken, and as Lewis showed no marks as a result of this encounter I wish to positively say that this is untrue and in all fairness to the boy whom I represent, I think it is but right for me to make denial of this assertion. Greb and his manager will find both Lewis and myself perfectly willing to post a forfeit for a return engagement of these boys at 145 ringside, winner take all. I hope that you will continue to maintain your customary sportsmanlike attitude in this matter and give Lewis the credit which is justly due him.
>
> Noble H. Davis
>
> Manager of pugilist George Lewis[48]

Not to be outdone, Mason quickly fired back with his own statement:

> I have observed that the manager of George Lewis has seen fit to write you and say that the published accounts of the recent 10 round fight between his man and Harry Greb did not meet with his approval. He says that he canvassed the ringside spectators, and they all seemed to think that Lewis had won. This is indeed strange as the spectators left just as soon as the fight was over. Then, too, Mr. Davis must have been in doubt as to the outcome when he had to go among the spectators and get their opinion. I felt so good over the way the fight was going that I did not have to make a poll of the people to learn who had won. Mr. Davis again makes it appear that he and his fighter do not care for any more of Greb's game when he talks about ringside weight, as he signed for and the men have already fought twice at catch weights. Now I am willing to give Lewis another chance at Greb under the same conditions. The only reply that I will take

any notice of will be an acceptance by Mr. Davis and his fighter for a bout with Greb, say in two weeks, under the same conditions as before. We are ready to meet them at your office and sign articles if they mean business.

James Mason
Manager of Harry Greb [49]

Mason had initially hoped to schedule the bout for August 10 at Waldemier Hall in Pittsburgh. When this could not be arranged, he set about planning for an August 31 showdown at the same venue. In the meantime, Greb had to stay active and so Irish Gorgas was again called on to face Greb on the August 10 date. Greb added his own two cents when told of Davis' letter to the press. "I notice that the manager of Lewis has denied that I outboxed his man on that occasion," said Greb, "but, as a matter of fact, I held the lead practically all the way. If Lewis' manager is sincere in his statement that he desires another match, he will find me only too willing to accommodate him. I'll be ready to make a new match with him at catchweights as soon as I have disposed of Gorgas, and then the public will learn which side told the truth about the Steubenville affair." [50]

Still harboring ill feeling toward one another over the near riot in their first bout, Greb and Gorgas set about preparing for an all-out war in this, their second bout. Gorgas, ignoring the fact that he had been badly out-pointed in every round, stuck firm to his belief that he would have knocked Greb out had the fight not been interrupted. However foolish this may have sounded to witnesses of the first fight, it was a notion that helped to motivate Gorgas in his preparation for the upcoming bout.

The bout itself proved a disappointment to the large crowd who expected to see the bitter feud play out before them. Instead Greb so nearly dominated his opponent that the bout could almost be called one-sided. At the tap of the first gong Greb rushed from his corner and sent both fists whistling into Gorgas. He was on top of Gorgas all the time, giving him little chance to get set for one of his powerful punches. When Gorgas was able to get a punch started, Greb proved far too adept defensively to get caught by the wild swings. Gorgas suffered a broken nose which hindered his breathing and the pace that Greb set was far too much under such conditions. When the bout had finished, the best that could be said for Gorgas was that he held Greb even in two rounds, the other four going to Greb by a wide margin. [51]

Ten days after his fight with Gorgas Greb was probably glad to get a call asking him to take the place of his stablemate Red Robinson in a bout against Whitey Wenzel. Robinson had not fought in nearly two months, since his defeat at the hands of Mickey Rodgers. When an unexpected illness overtook him, he was forced to withdraw from the bout and Greb was substituted. For Greb it was doubtful that this was an inconvenience considering his growing appreciation of Mason's doctrine of maintaining a busy schedule. One thing is certain, the fans were much more eager to see a Greb-Wenzel bout than one featuring Robinson, who was a natural lightweight, opposing the 158 pound Wenzel.

With George Lewis seated ringside the two fighters gave the fans everything they could want and more, standing toe-to-toe slugging it out for the entire six rounds. As the final round approached Greb, sensing the fight was close, came tearing out of his corner and fought the entire three minutes at such a fast pace that the fans could scarcely believe it. The fighters made such a hit, and were so evenly matched, that the newspapers awarded a draw not wishing to take credit from either.

> ..."Whitey" Wenzel and Harry Greb fought six of the best rounds of milling ever seen in Pittsburgh, and to give it a draw would be dealing out justice to both scrappers. They were at it from bell to bell, crowding as much action into their six rounds as is usually seen in three or four bouts of that length. There must be some sort of feud existing between them; at least it appeared so last night. Wenzel led until the sixth round, when Greb rallied, and by a sensational finish, which he commenced when they came from their corners and kept up until the closing bell, piled up enough points to make the bout an even thing.[52]

With the Wenzel fight behind him and just a week to go before settling his dispute with George Lewis, Greb was in a fighting mood. He was eager to settle the argument over who had really won their first two bouts, and eager to make Lewis and his manager pay for their constant jibes. There was only one problem; Lewis would not make it to the fight. Just days before the scheduled event Lewis pulled out and was replaced by John Foley.[53]

Having taken yet another bout with Greb on short notice, after having been defeated in their first, Foley could at least boast of being in top condition for this rematch. Foley had been moonlighting in a local steel mill while in training for several upcoming fights. The rigorous mill work combined with training had left Foley in rock hard form. Lack of fitness could not be used as an excuse if he were to lose, and lose he did. Greb jumped on Foley from the opening bell and fought him to a standstill for six rounds. It made little difference that Foley was a full-fledged heavyweight. Greb pressed the action the entire fight, forcing Foley back on his heels. It was an easy, dominant win for Greb.[54]

It seems that after the Foley fight Greb became discouraged with his prospects in Pittsburgh. His father was still pressuring him to quit the sport and take up an honest trade. Greb, it seems, felt as though he were getting nowhere fast by fighting the same Pittsburgh club fighters time and again win, lose, or draw. He was certainly popular in the city but he could look to the example of fighters like Buck Crouse, Al Grayber, and Walter Monaghan who all possessed a degree of talent at one time or another in their careers yet seemed to stagnate the longer they stayed at home and as a result they ended up serving as cannon fodder for the nationally recognized boxers who passed through Pittsburgh hoping to make a few extra dollars. If Greb was to make himself known he would have to escape the confines of Pittsburgh, much as Frank Moran and Frank Klaus had, and move to one of the bigger cities, such as Philadelphia or New York where he might establish a national reputation.

So it was that Greb left Pittsburgh and traveled by train to Philadelphia with little more than dreams of "the big time" to carry him through the journey. His management with Mason was binding only by a handshake and as Mason was hardly willing to leave his stable of fighters and relocate to Philly they decided to part ways on even terms.

When Greb arrived in Philadelphia he sought out new management in the form of Billy Reynolds.[55] Reynolds' first order of business as Greb's new manager was to write to the Philadelphia Public Ledger which on Sundays printed letters from managers and aspiring fighters looking for work:

> **Sporting Editor of the Public Ledger:**
> Sir - While Philadelphia Clubs are clamoring for new faces I am making a request through your much read columns for my two protégés, Johnny Nelson and Harry Greb. The former I consider one of the best 118 - pound boxers in Pennsylvania. Greb at 154 pounds has never been beaten. Since March 10, 1913 he has fought 29 contests and won them all. All I ask is for any of the local club match-

Before finding fame with "Ripley's Believe It Or Not," Robert Ripley was a talented cartoonist whose sports centered art could be found in papers across the country. Here he spoofs the tramp lifestyle that was common among boxers during Greb's lifetime.

makers to give either of these boys a chance and the crowd is sure to get a run for its money. Greb is from Pittsburgh, but he has decided to make Philadelphia his home, as he realizes that if a boxer can make good in the Quaker City his reputation is made. Nelson at 118 and Greb at 154. Match them with anyone, champions or near champions, and see who takes the count.

Billy Reynolds

Philadelphia, September 12, 1914[56]

Reynolds' plea worked as Greb was immediately signed to face Jack Fink on the undercard of a fight between Harry "KO" Baker and Jack McCarron on September 26. Greb now found himself in the position of having to entirely reestablish his reputation. He had gone from fighting main events in Pittsburgh to being a preliminary boy again. He was not even accorded the honor of fighting in the semi-windup.

The Philadelphia Public Ledger and Philadelphia Record gave the bout to Greb while the Philadelphia Press voted the bout a draw. In all three instances the only coverage given of the fight was one sentence long. The North American was much more impressed with Greb than its contemporaries stating: "Harry Greb, the Pittsburgh middleweight made his debut before a local audience and defeated Jack Fink of Camden, in six hard rounds. It was the best fight of the night. Both lads fought at a terrific pace from gong to gong, with the Pittsburgher having the better of it by his aggressiveness."[57] Greb had truly gone from being a big fish in a small pond to being a small fish in a huge ocean.

Greb had to wait around for two months before getting another match in the competitive boxing scene of Philadelphia. With little money, little food, and few people he could rely on, Greb was finding his dreams of reaching the top in Philly a much more

Terry Martin (above) was on the downside of a once illustrious career when he fought Greb in 1914. He had challenged for the welterweight championship and faced some of the legends of boxing while still in his prime.

difficult prospect than he imagined.

When he finally received another match it was with fading former welterweight contender Terry Martin on the undercard of Young Ahearn's popular victory over Leo Houck at the National Athletic Club. Again, the newspapers differed as to the outcome. The Philadelphia Inquirer gave the bout to Greb while the Public Ledger and the Record had the bout a draw. Greb pressed the action throughout the fight using his speed and aggressiveness to offset Martin's edge in experience. During the third round the sole of one of Martin's shoes was damaged and he fought the remainder of the fight in his bare feet.[58]

A turning point in Greb's sojourn in the Quaker City came when he attended the fight between Joe Borrell and Young Erne at the Olympia Athletic Association on December 8, 1914. Owing to a high fever and an inflamed eye, Erne was not allowed to climb into the ring with Borrell. A canvas was made of available fighters and when Greb was found to be sitting in the audience he was asked if he would be willing to fight Borrell. Despite being grossly out of shape (he weighed over 170 pounds), it was the chance he had been waiting for.

Borrell was a tremendously talented fighter, truly world-class. He had faced some of the toughest men in the welterweight and middleweight divisions in the United States, France, and England. A year earlier he had nearly killed welterweight title claimant Harry Lewis as a result of a vicious beating punctuated by a knockout. Lewis would remain in a coma for days suffering from a hematoma. Lewis survived but spent the rest of his life partially paralyzed as a result of the bout with Borrell. Borrell was a good boxer and powerful puncher. His compact frame gave him incredible strength and posed a difficult proposition for any middleweight in the world, much less a hungry preliminary fighter taking the fight on a moment's notice.

This publicity photo taken of Greb during his Philadelphia sojourn in late 1914 and early 1915 shows a still maturing Greb in training togs prepared to take on the world.

Greb gave the audience his best as he fought a grim but losing battle against his more experienced opponent. Determined not to let Borrell's reputation dictate the course of the fight, Greb rushed out of his corner at the start of the opening round and began throwing punches at

Borrell as if he were back in Pittsburgh facing one of the locals. The first round found Borrell puzzled and he didn't quite know what to make of this young fighter recklessly attacking him. Borrell settled down to the task at hand in the second round and began halting Greb's rushes with thudding blows to the body. As the fight progressed Borrell's experience began to tell on Greb, the body work was beginning to slow the Pittsburgher down, and he was taking tremendous amounts of punishment. In the fourth Borrell had Greb shaken and in the fifth Borrell landed a dynamite uppercut which rattled Greb's teeth and sent him down for a count of nine with blood streaming from his mouth. As Greb beat the count the bell sounded and he wobbled back to his corner. When the sixth and final round commenced Greb came tearing out of his corner only to be met with a fusillade of punches by Borrell who was eager to end the fight. Borrell tried hard for the knockout but Greb managed to remain upright.

He had taken a frightful beating for his game effort and was given a warm applause for putting up a good showing under the circumstances. Greb was bitter and dejected over the defeat, angrily

Joseph Borrelli, better known as Joe Borrell (above) was one of Philadelphia's great middleweights. He fought many of the greatest fighters of his era across several countries.

refusing to shake Borrell's hand after the bout. Not a paper gave Greb the decision.[59]

4

A KIT OF CARPENTER'S TOOLS

Greb hobbled out of the ring with a broken nose and several damaged ribs. The beating he had received at Borrell's hands was more severe than anyone in the audience had realized. With almost no money, and nowhere to go, Greb was taken in by a young fighter from Wilmington, Delaware named Harry "KO" Baker. Baker was a blonde southpaw who, after spending time in Buffalo, had come to Philadelphia, much like Greb, in hopes of gaining wider fame. Also like Greb he was finding Philadelphia a rough place to break into. Having fought and lost to Jack McCarron, Frank Loughrey, and Borrell, he understood the trouble that Greb was experiencing. Yet, despite a hasty telegram sent to Red Mason by Greb asking to return to his management, Baker convinced Greb to try to stick it out. It was the beginning of a friendship that according to Greb's family would last for the remainder of Greb's life.[1]

Baker nursed Greb back to health over the course of a month. Once Greb healthy again Baker arranged for Greb to fight on the undercard of his New Year's Day match with Howard Truesdale. Greb would be facing Billy Donovan, a local favorite from the Kensington section of Philadelphia. Baker would lose his bout to Truesdale according to the opinions of newspapermen ringside. The bout between Greb and Billy Donovan was one in which every observer had a different opinion, although most reached the conclusion that Donovan deserved the victory.[2]

Within days of his fight with Donovan Greb received another match. This time it was a bout with Howard Truesdale, the same man who had just defeated Harry Baker. The bout would provide the opportunity for Greb to avenge his friend's loss. Greb would have a much easier time with Truesdale than did Baker.

Another publicity photo of Greb taken in Philadelphia in late 1914 at the same time as the photo displayed on page 64.

As the crowd watched that night on January 8, 1915 they witnessed the odd sight of a young fighter hopping around the ring, leaping in and out, spearing an utterly lost Howard Truesdale with long lefts while whipping rights to the body. Truesdale's large following was astonished by the ease in which Greb boxed circles around their favorite. When the last round began Greb ignored the usual practice of shaking hands and sailed into his opponent. There was nothing to it; Truesdale simply could not cope with the speed of his Pittsburgh rival.[3]

Despite his victory over Truesdale, Greb was still anxious to return to Pittsburgh. He had been in contact with Red Mason who had tentatively arranged for a lucrative homecoming bout against George Chip to be held at Duquesne Garden on January 25. With the Chip contest three weeks away, Greb was persuaded by Baker to stay in Philadelphia for the time being.

Four days after his fight with Truesdale, Greb was seated ringside for what he expected to be a fight between Tommy Coleman and St. Paul's Billy Miske. When Coleman reported for the fight with an abscess in his jaw, Greb was called upon to face Miske in Tommy Coleman's stead. Greb again agreed to take such a match on short notice, despite being at a disadvantage, hoping that it would propel him into more lucrative bouts than those he had already partaken of.

Miske was a young fighter who had come to Pennsylvania from his hometown of St. Paul, like Greb and Baker, to try to make a name for himself on the east coast. He was a middleweight with a large frame that seemed to be acquiring weight at an unusual pace and would eventually support the dimensions of a well-muscled, athletic heavyweight. He was skillful and possessed a respectable if not powerful punch. He was extremely durable and would only be knocked out one time in his career, that loss coming more than five years later in mid-1920. Miske had been born less than two months before Greb and began fighting less than three months before Greb. Despite his relative inexperience he had already faced such notables as "Kid" Ashe, Jack McCarron, and Tommy Gibbons. In addition to these professional bouts he had also fought exhibitions with future middleweight champion Mike O'Dowd, former middleweight champion Billy

Photo of Billy Miske of St. Paul (above), taken while still a young middleweight. With broad shoulders and a deep chest, Miske is already showing signs of growing out of the division.

Papke, and gigantic future heavyweight contender Fred Fulton. It is indeed safe to say that while Miske was young, he was also a dangerous man to be taken on short notice.

The two fighters fought at a torrid pace with Greb landing more often and Miske landing harder. Greb leapt from his corner in the first round and though outweighed he attacked his foe with reckless abandon, swinging left hooks to the body and head. His speed baffled Miske who was obviously unprepared for the awkward attack of the young Pittsburgh fighter. After being outpointed in the first round Miske warmed to the task in the second and began trying to time Greb for right hand counters. Occasionally these powerful rights would land but more often Greb would step inside Miske's reach and deliver hooks to the jaw. By the sixth and final round Miske, possibly feeling he was behind on points, tore after Greb from the bell and won the round by a wide margin. It was enough to earn him a draw in the eyes of most present.[4]

It was a good fight but Greb had had enough of Philadelphia. He had been mistreated, mismanaged, and mismatched. He was homesick, nearly out of money, and eager to return to Garfield and his loyal fans. Red Mason had wired Greb that Chip was out and another fighter would be taking his place. Despite this setback favorable reports of his showing with Miske arrived just in time to arouse interest in a bout featuring Greb. When Greb finally arrived back in Pittsburgh on the night of January 16, he was welcomed with open arms by fans who rather than looking down on his lukewarm invasion of the east accepted him almost as a conquering hero. It was now up to Mason to find the right opponent and the right venue to capitalize on and enhance Greb's star power; that fighter was Jack Blackburn.

"Down in Philadelphia Blackburn is a big drawing card, and I'm glad to get my chance at him," said Greb. "I know that he is cleverer than I, but I've learned a lot during my eastern experience, and think I'm about to start a cleanup campaign that will land me around the top of the heap. If I beat Blackburn it will be the biggest boost that I could have and I'm after that boost. I've got the strength to go six rounds at top pace, and I'm going to box with Johnny Ray and all the

Jack Blackburn (above) as he looked in his prime. Despite his wiry frame he was a dangerous opponent who held his own with some of the sports most legendary figures.

clever boys I can get to put me in shape to offset his cleverness."[5]

Blackburn is a character whose story is so rich that the best of Hollywood screenwriters would have scarcely been able to imagine it. He had been born in 1883 at Versailles, Kentucky. He left school at the age of 13 to work in his brother's barbershop and at age 16 began boxing. He remembered his first bout as being a preliminary fight which he fought simply for the privilege of watching the main event between Kid Robinson and Jack Barry. The first bout he actually received payment for was against one "Kid" Miller whom he knocked out for the princely sum of $2.50.[6] For the next eight years from 1901 to 1909, Blackburn moved about the country living the gypsy lifestyle that Greb himself would in time become more than familiar with. Fighting the best men from lightweight to heavyweight, Blackburn's record during this period is simply amazing. He faced such legendary men as Joe Gans, Sam Langford, Harry Lewis, and "Philadelphia" Jack O'Brien. His showing in these fights was enough to make many of the top fighters of this era steer well clear of him, a fact which was not helped by the color of his skin. He became known as a speedy fighter with a cracking left hook who knew every trick in the book.

There was another side to Blackburn though, a darker, more sinister side. Blackburn loved women and alcohol, both of which nearly destroyed his life. The frequent quarrels he had with various women often became violent; this was only made worse by the whiskey which ran through his veins as thick as blood. If Blackburn was a dangerous man while wearing boxing gloves, he was that much more dangerous while under the spell of booze. He became short tempered, uncontrollable, and unpredictable. In early January of 1909 while playing

Blackburn pictured not long after his release from a Pennsylvania penitentiary where he had been imprisoned for the murder of his friend Alonzo Polk. Note the scar running along his left cheek, given to him by his brother wielding a razor during an argument.

poker with his brother, Blackburn exploded over remarks made about the white woman he was keeping company with. A fight broke out which resulted in Blackburn being hospitalized for several cuts about the face. Later that month an argument between Blackburn's common law wife, Maude Pillion and Mattie Polk resulted in an inebriated Blackburn drawing a revolver and shooting Mrs. Polk and her husband Alonzo. The wife survived, Alonzo Polk was not so lucky. Both had been friends of Blackburn. When Blackburn sobered up he was inconsolable. Six months later, and still in the prime of his fighting career, he was found guilty of manslaughter and sentenced to fifteen years in the penitentiary.

By all accounts Blackburn was a model prisoner. He served his time by teaching boxing to warden McKenty and his sons. On January 14, 1914, after having served four and one half years of his fifteen year sentence, Blackburn was released on parole for good behavior. Upon his release Blackburn was eager to resume his boxing career. Still a legend in his own time, he was now thirty-one years old but had stayed in excellent condition in prison. His speed and timing may not have been what they once were, but he still possessed a knowledge of the sport that few fighters would ever attain. Despite such knowledge it was apparent when he re-entered the ring that he was not the same Jack Blackburn who had left the sport nearly five years before. His comeback began with mixed results. He still displayed the same cunning mastery of fistic science that enabled him to rise to the upper echelon of the sport in his prime, but he was also displaying the tell-tale sign of a fighter whose reflexes were simply not there anymore. He could see openings but could not release his punches in time to take advantage of them. As a result he was rapidly taking on the role of stepping stone while his rise to former glory seemed less likely with each new fight.[7]

"I need a couple of knockouts now to make the people realize I am as good as I was when I was taking on all comers at any weight," said Blackburn. "But I haven't underrated Greb. Down in Philadelphia they think a lot of that boy, and if I can put him away it will be a big boost for my stock in the east. I've got several matches which depend on the outcome of this fight with Greb."[8]

To Red Mason Blackburn presented the perfect opponent for Greb's return to Pittsburgh. While fights between black and white fighters were the exception to the rule in this era, Pittsburgh was fairly accepting of its African-American boxers. Fighters such as George "Kid"

SEC. ROW SEAT
D G 19
G.A.C. PRICE $1.00
Jan. 25

RESERVED SECTION
Mon., Jan. 25, 1915

Garden Athletic Club
DUQUESNE GARDEN
Monday, January 25th, 1915

Jan. 25 | GREB vs. BLACKBURN
Price $1.00
ADMIT ONE

Cotton, Young Bijou, and little Eddie Carver were all fairly popular in the Smoky City and had gained a measure of success. However, a mixed race main event was rare particularly since early 1913 when Pittsburgh's Public Safety Director John M. Morin very nearly banned mixed race bouts all together. Despite Morin's denial this was almost certainly in direct response to the charges brought against flamboyant black heavyweight champion Jack Johnson for violation of the Mann act and his subsequent marriage to a white woman. Morin's ban was short-lived at best and mixed bouts were again taking place in Pittsburgh within months.[9]

The notoriety and curiosity attached to Blackburn's name alone would ensure brisk ticket sales. Mason also played up the angle of whether the old cagey veteran could overcome the inexperienced youth, a true crossroads fight. The only thing left was to find a venue suitable enough to cash in on the venture. Mason cast his eye longingly upon Duquesne Gardens which had a seating capacity in excess of five thousand people.

In seeking out Duquesne Gardens as the venue for Greb's bout with Blackburn, it seems that Mason may have had an ulterior motive. Buck Crouse, Mason's former star, had again left the fold and was now under the management of George Engel. Engel and Crouse were trying to land a lucrative bout with George Chip who had only recently returned from a successful tour of the West Coast. If the match could be clinched between Crouse and Chip it would be the seventh bout of a particularly heated rivalry. Mason knew that Jimmy Dime, manager of George Chip, would only agree to the match if the show could be arranged at Duquesne Gardens guaranteeing a large gate and a fat percentage. Knowing this and seeing an opportunity to prevent his former protégé from making a lucrative purse, Mason quickly signed a lease with Duquesne Gardens for ten shows, later to be extended to twenty. One of the stipulations of this contract was that no other promoter could promote boxing in the Gardens until Mason's lease had been terminated. Thus Mason effec-

Pittsburgh's ornate Nixon Theatre was chosen as the site of the weigh in for the Greb-Blackburn fight, in order to add a bit of flair to the promotion.

Duquesne Gardens (above), which was generally used as an ice skating rink, featured prominently on the Pittsburgh boxing scene for years. The bleachers alone could seat well over five thousand patrons. With seating on the floor of the rink the capacity could be nearly doubled, this made it a highly sought after venue for high profile fights being held in the city.

tively secured a lucrative venue for Greb, and temporarily blocked Crouse from fighting Chip without either his approval or a portion of the proceeds.[10]

The now bitter feud between Mason and Crouse spilled over to include Greb. Crouse was jealous of the attention paid to Greb by the press and resented the fact that Greb would be benefiting from the use of Duquesne Gardens at his expense. While both men trained at the Oakland Club Crouse began making boasts and threats directed at Greb which the press was quick to pick up on and print. It was not long before the two men had to be separated lest they stage an all too real exhibition without the benefit of getting paid for their services.[11]

In keeping with the high profile atmosphere of the fight, Greb and Blackburn met at the Nixon Theatre at 5:30 on the night of the fight to weigh in for the bout. Both had posted a one-hundred dollar weight forfeit to make 158 pounds. Just before the event was to start it was arranged for pool halls and bowling alleys in Greb's home district of Garfield to close, the patrons would then spill out into the street and take part in a parade in honor of Greb which would march to the scene of the battle.

Greb had outlined his battle plan to the press long before fight night. It was his intention to stay on top of Blackburn throughout the fight. His offense would be his defense and by throwing as many punches as he could he would wear down his older opponent. Thus it was no surprise when, in the first two rounds, Greb started like a whirlwind and with little science tore after Blackburn with reckless abandon. Blackburn immediately showed the fans that he still possessed a formidable defense by blocking, catching, and slipping nearly every punch that came his way. Unfortunately for the once great fighter, defense does not win fights and before long it became clear that while he was more than capable of staying out of harm's way, his reflexes were not sufficient to counter the wild youngster in front of him who was winning rounds on aggression. Greb would lower his head, tuck his chin into his chest, and tear into Blackburn who would sidestep, parry, or clinch when Greb came near. At times the fans booed Blackburn's exhibition and questioned whether he was under wraps. Such criticisms were unfair to both Greb and Blackburn who were putting on the best fight they could given their respective age and experience.

In the third round Greb finally broke through the veteran's defense and began landing heavy punches. He was forcing Blackburn around the ring when near the end of the round Blackburn landed several hard body shots which earned Greb's respect for the moment. Blackburn returned to his corner after the round bleeding from the nose. In the fourth Blackburn followed up his brief success of the previous round and began timing Greb on the way in, landing both to the body and head. Such efforts were not enough to offset Greb's aggression but they were heartening to fans of Blackburn. Blackburn rallied in the fifth and took this round as Greb apparently took the round off, saving his strength for a fast finish. Again, at the end of the round Blackburn went on the attack and it was now apparent that he was using the age old trick employed by cagey veterans to steal rounds by a late rush.

With Garfield fans wildly cheering for their "Ickie," as Greb was known to his friends and admirers, the sixth round proved the most interesting of all. Greb came out intent on winning the round and thus he forced the action at top speed. Blackburn was forced to fight his utmost in this round and when the final gong rang many thought the round belonged to Blackburn. He may have won the battle but he lost the war; no one disagreed that Greb deserved the fight.[12]

Blackburn would continue fighting for several more years with mixed results but he would never regain the status that he once held. After retiring from active duty in 1923, Blackburn began training young fighters and within three years he had his first champion, Sammy Mandell. A year later in 1927 he trained another fighter, Bud Taylor, to the bantamweight championship. However it was not his ring record, nor his work with Mandell and Taylor that Blackburn will be remembered for. In 1937 Blackburn tutored another young fighter to a championship. That fighter's name was Joe Louis, who would forever be remembered as one of the finest heavyweights to ever grace the ring.

An interesting article appears in the Pittsburgh Gazette-Times two days after Greb's bout

Despite their friendship Greb and Harry "KO" Baker (pictured above) fought each other four times. Each bout was a vicious affair with neither fighter giving any quarter.

with Blackburn which hints at the growing tension in Greb's relationship with Pius. Apparently, Pius was losing patience with his son's chosen profession. It was one thing to be brawling in the streets, traveling to Philadelphia to get his brains knocked out by another man, or appearing in the same ring with a Negro, but enough was enough. It was high time Harry cease such foolishness and settle down to an honest profession. Family members remember that around this time Pius gave Greb an ultimatum: Quit boxing or leave home. Speaking of the dissension in the Greb household James Jerpe wrote:

> **Harry Greb has plainly told his dad that he prefers boxing gloves to a kit of carpenters' tools. "The only contracts I will make are for six rounds or better," says the Garfield mixer.**[13]

It was simple and to the point. Harry Greb was now a boxer. That was his trade, and for better or worse that is what he would put all of his energies toward. As modest as his successes had been so far, Greb now had his sights plainly set on climbing to the highest rung of the pugilistic ladder. Harry left home and took up residence in an apartment a few blocks down the street from his father's house.[14]

With the excellent publicity garnered by the Blackburn fight Mason quickly made arrangements for another bout for Greb in Duquesne Gardens. Initially it was hoped that Lancaster's tough middleweight contender Leo Houck would be the opponent but when Houck's manager, Jack McGuigan, sent word that he would not be able to work Houck's corner, making Houck unavailable, a new opponent was needed. Greb remembered his friend from Philadelphia, Harry Baker. Baker was still in Philly trying to dig up fights with mixed success. It was an opportunity for Greb to repay Baker's kindness and fill the empty slot for an opponent at the same time. Baker had been trying his best to keep busy since he and Greb had parted ways, his best showing coming against Jack Blackburn just one week before Greb faced the former great. Baker nearly knocked

Blackburn out in the first round and throughout the fight illustrated just why he was nicknamed "KO."[15] Baker's recent knockout over tough Scranton middleweight Jimmy Tighe would also make excellent publicity for a match with Greb.

Four days before his match with Baker, Greb's feud with Buck Crouse exploded. Crouse, boiling over his predicament, decided to wait for Greb outside of the Oakland gym where both fighters had been training of late. When Greb appeared the two fighters exchanged heated words and before long they were participating in an impromptu brawl. The fight lasted several minutes with Greb more than holding his own against his former friend. As the two fighters were pulled apart no one doubted that their vendetta would someday end in the squared circle.[16]

Despite their friendship, Greb and Baker both knew the stakes in winning and would be playing for keeps. One wonders if it was by accident that a misprint stating "Greb Meets Maker Tonight," appeared in the Gazette-Times the day of the fight. Before a modest

Greb (above, in 1914) returned to Pittsburgh from Philadelphia fit, more experienced, and more popular than when he left despite his limited success in the east.

house, populated mostly by Greb's Garfield fans, the two Harrys put on one of the most hellacious fights ever seen in Pittsburgh. One could scarcely believe that the two fighters had deep feelings for one another by the way they tore into each other. The left-handed Baker continually played for the stomach, ramming powerful straight lefts to Greb's midriff which caused the Garfield battler's grunts to echo through the hall.

Speed was the difference in the bout and Greb set such a fast pace through the early rounds that Baker quickly fell behind on the cards of those scoring the bout. Greb was slippery, being able to block or evade most of Baker's punches. He moved around his man at a rapid pace, burying Baker under an avalanche of boxing gloves.

The last three rounds saw the pace slow as the fighters dispensed with footwork, stood toe-

to-toe and let fly with their best punches. Baker was still sending his pile driving left into Greb's midriff but this only ignited Greb's fury as he whipped blows in from every angle. At the start of the sixth and final round Greb's fans were yelling so loudly that they could easily be heard outside of the hall. They had been whipped into a frenzy by the display of their hero and when the fight was over nearly everyone was sure that he deserved the popular decision.

The following day's newspapers let those who failed to attend know what they had missed. According to the Pittsburgh Post:

> **Harry Greb of Garfield fought like a combined human dynamo and enraged tiger against Knockout Baker of Wilmington, Del., in the main bout at Duquesne Garden last night and was an easy winner at the end. He kept after his opponent throughout the six rounds and never allowed Baker to get set. He was entitled to a clear shade in every round but the fifth, which was close. Baker probably earned an even break in this session.[17]**

The Pittsburgh Gazette-Times concurred with this assessment adding:

> **Harry Knockout Baker of Wilmington, Del., and Harry Greb of Bloomfield furnished 18 minutes of the fiercest fighting seen in this city in a long while last night at Duquesne Garden.**
>
> **Baker is a lefthander, and he hits hard, slamming to the stomach or bringing up a vicious hook. Greb fought better last night than he has ever displayed before hereabouts, and perforce he had to, for Baker would have handed him a terrible lacing. As it was Greb came out of the ring a winner by a narrow margin, acquiring the lead in the early rounds when he managed to beat the representative from the Peach State to the punch.**
>
> **The fighting these middleweights put up might be likened unto that between two gang leaders who, with their cohorts, met on the village green to settle a long - standing dispute. They threw ring science to the wind and just mauled each other.[18]**

The Pittsburgh Sun, Press, and Chronicle-Telegraph all agreed that it was an action-packed contest which belonged to Greb while the Pittsburgh Daily Dispatch had a more difficult time choosing a winner, opting instead to stay neutral but agreed that the bout was savage and satisfying from the fans standpoint.

After the fight an ice cream social was thrown in Greb's honor. Greb attended the party with his sweet heart, a girl from Washington, Pennsylvania. When word got out that Greb was seen with a pretty young woman on his arm it was reported by gossip monger Jim Jab, the article referring to her as a "Belle" of Washington, Pennsylvania. When shown the article Greb read it several times with a quizzical look. After a pause he asked a friend "What does 'belle' mean?" The friend thought about it for a moment and then shrugged his shoulders. Greb then sought out the nearest dictionary and after several minutes returned smiling, "It's all right," he said. "That guy didn't call her any names."[19]

With his two headline-grabbing wins over Baker and Blackburn behind him, Greb's Garfield fans were eager to get a glimpse of him closer to home. Mason decided it would be a good idea to cater to the loyal following and booked Greb for a match with Whitey Wenzel at the Rowe building in East Liberty, a district of Pittsburgh which makes up Garfield's eastern border. The fighters signed to make 162 pounds at 5:30pm on the night of the fight, which was billed by promoters of the Highland Athletic Club as being for the middleweight championship of Pittsburgh. On paper it was a dangerous match for Greb. It would be the fifth meeting between the two fighters. Since their last fight, six months previous, Wenzel had scored several knock-outs and won popular decisions over John Foley, Al Grayber, and Greb's former nemesis George Lewis.

Before a large crowd of passionate fans divided almost evenly in their support of the two fighters, Greb and Wenzel put on a vicious bout. With a combination of speed, aggression, and a maddeningly effective defense, Greb was able to keep Wenzel guessing throughout the fight and maintain a lead. As the fight wore on Wenzel became frustrated and resorted to trying to time Greb's rushes with uppercuts which rarely landed. In the third round Greb attacked Wenzel with such ferocity that the blonde Northside fighter nearly dove for cover. The crowd was going wild and brawls between the two excited factions were breaking out in the stands as the fight progressed.

Greb was now sending punches in nearly at will and whenever he missed one for the head he followed up with a stinging shot to the body. In the fifth round Greb fell to the floor but was up immediately and attacked that much harder. The consensus was that Greb had slipped but some argued that he was caught coming in with a short left. Seeing Greb on the canvas, even for such a brief period, may have given encouragement to Wenzel for he fought the sixth as though the entire fight depended on his winning that round. As the bell rang the two fighters clashed in the center of the ring and traded punches amid the wild shouts of the crowd. Harry Keck of the Pittsburgh Post described the finale as "...most sensational and the crowd was on its feet to the end." Greb left the ring unmarked, with even biased followers of the sport grudgingly admitting he had won the fight.

Jim Jab of the Press stated that "Greb's speed was the bright spot. 'Ickie' seemed to realize that the 40 tickets he sold to Garfield rooters demanded rapid-fire stunts. He gave them and for four frames put the Northsider off the map. Wenzel was unable to steam the tide of lefts and rights that drove his mug back and forth. Whitey got a dandy walloping in four stanzas... Give Wenzel the fifth and call the final a tossup and you will award the mess to Greb."[20]

Greb set about preparing for a March 6 match at Washington, Pennsylvania against Tommy

Mack Immediately following his victory over Wenzel. Mack was an Italian fighter from Wellsburg, West Virginia who had been making a name for himself around Washington for the past several months. Greb tore into his heavier rival and gave the Washington fans a show they could be proud of. The Washington Observer wrote:

> **Harry Greb, pride of Garfield, Pittsburgh, and rated by some ring critics of the Smoky City as the best middleweight in the state of Pennsylvania, delighted a large crowd of fistic fans at the skating rink Saturday night by his clever work in the main bout against Tommy Mack, the Wellsburg Italian. Mack never had a chance.**
>
> **Greb outdid even the most glowing of advance press notices. He worked tirelessly. Although Mack was an easy opponent for him, Greb never loafed once. He had Mack covering up all the time.**[21]

With his fame rapidly spreading through Pennsylvania, Greb was immediately signed to face Wenzel in a rematch at McKeesport in a card that James Mason was promoting at White's Opera house. When Wenzel broke his hand in training, heavyweight Jack Lavin of Cleveland stepped in and Mason quickly began to promote the bout as Cleveland's best against Pittsburgh's best.[22] In addition to this card, Mason had also stolen the rematch between Harry Greb and Knockout Baker from under the nose of Harry Edwards, matchmaker of Philadelphia's Olympia club who was eager to promote the bout. After the completion of these two bouts Greb would be pitted yet again against his rival Whitey Wenzel. With his name being broadcast almost daily in the local newspapers fighters, managers, matchmakers, and promoters were coming out of the woodwork with challenges for Greb. Even Al Grayber, Greb's friend and stablemate, was calling him out.

Greb had his way with the larger Lavin, nearly knocking him out in the fifth round, and gaining an easy popular decision despite the size difference. This victory cleared the way for Greb's anticipated rematch with his friend Harry Baker. The site chosen for the match was Duquesne Gardens to which Red Mason still held a lease. It was hoped that as an added attraction Fireman Jim Flynn, the heavyweight contender who was passing through Pittsburgh with his wife, would referee the bouts.[23]

Before a house packed full of spectators, including Harry's sweetheart who within a month would be called his fiancée by at least one paper, Greb entered the arena to a thunderous ovation from the dedicated fans of Garfield as Baker stood waiting in his corner. Greb crossed the ring and shook hands with his friend turned opponent and the audience gave another loud ovation. Jim Flynn, who had declined to referee but sat ringside, was called into the ring and introduced to the crowd by Jim Mason. With both fighters in tremendous condition, and stamping in their corners like thoroughbreds awaiting the bell, the fight began.

For the first round and a half it seemed as though Baker had learned his lessons well from

BOXING Thursday Nite, March 25
DUQUESNE GARDEN
POPULAR PRICES 50c. 75c and $1.
HARRY GREB vs. K. O. BAKER
AND THREE OTHER BOUTS.

his previous bout with Greb. He stayed calm under Greb's flailing assault and fired his power-ful left hand in an arcing uppercut to Greb's midsection. Time after time Greb's rushes were met with this tactic. Greb was controlling the fight but many felt that if Baker could continue such a strategy he had a chance to upset Greb. Midway through the second Greb caught Baker with a quick succession of lefts and rights which caused the blonde southpaw to clinch. As they clinched Greb pumped both hands to the body and Baker was clearly hurt.

By the third round the pressure that Greb was putting on Baker began to take effect. Greb danced around the ring popping in and out, up and down, all the while showering Baker with blows to the body and head. Greb had Baker groggy and worked him into a neutral corner but Baker fought back like a trapped animal, lashing out with two lefts that opened a bad cut above Greb's left eye. In the fourth Greb again had Baker in bad shape and the crowd was screaming for a knockout.

By the final round Greb had built an insurmountable lead and only a knockout for Baker could win him the fight. Baker realized this and tore from his corner; nothing could have pleased Greb more. They slammed into one another with incredible violence and it was again Greb who got the better of the exchanges. He was beating Baker to the punch with his speed which at times made his hands seem like a blur as rights and lefts bounced off of his friend's head. With the crowd in a frenzy the final bell rang and Greb was given an ovation all the way back to his dressing room.[24]

After a short rest to allow time for his eye to heal, Greb returned to training for his sixth match with Whitey Wenzel. While Greb trained for Wenzel, far from the club fights of Pittsburgh another pugilistic drama played out in the hot sun in Havana, Cuba. Reviled heavy-weight champion Jack Johnson, who had been chased out of several European countries while in exile from the United States, had found himself out of funds and in need of cash. He was coaxed into defending his championship against giant "White Hope" heavyweight Jess Willard for what looked like a relatively easy payday. Instead Johnson found himself knocked from under his crown after 26 rounds of slow attrition.

With Johnson's defeat there came a renewed interest in the heavyweight division. The cham-pionship was again on American soil and rested in the hands of a white man. Despite the mediocre quality of the new champion, it certainly seemed to white America as if things were about to change for the better in the world of boxing.

As Johnson lay dreaming in the Cuban sun, being counted out, Greb dreamed as well. His thoughts drifted to former champion George Chip. Greb had been promised a bout with Chip if he could get past Wenzel, but two days before the Wenzel bout Chip again begged off, owing to a damaged finger acquired in his rematch against Al McCoy, and the fighter selected to take his place was none other than Joe Borrell. The bout would be held the day after the Pittsburgh Pirates ushered in the National League's new season, and as such, a large crowd was expected. With blood in his eye, eager for revenge against Borrell for the beating he had received in Philadelphia, Greb entered the ring with Wenzel intent on victory.

Whitey Wenzel faced Greb in a vicious three bout series during 1915, all of which Greb won in the majority of newspaper decisions.

Wenzel was no less intent on victory. "Some of the papers gave our other fight to Harry," said Wenzel. "Well, I'll say he kept on top of me all the time, but I wasn't hurt, and I felt I gave as good as he sent. But this time I'll make sure. I never was in better condition, and I'll show the fans Thursday night. Watch for that good-night slam."[25] The loss to Greb the previous month had weighed heavily on Wenzel's mind and he was eager to redeem himself, whatever the cost. Cost indeed, for when Wenzel weighed in at $165^1/_2$ pounds, despite the articles binding the fighters to weigh no more than 162, he lost his twenty-five dollar forfeit but gained an advantage of several pounds on his rival. Wenzel became furious when told that he would lose his forfeit and declared that the scales were faulty. Greb entered the argument and both men had to be separated lest they start the festivities early.[26]

Harry entered the ring as a slight 10 to 8 betting favorite. Wenzel's showing justified such short odds. The two fighters fought as Leslie

Macpherson Jr. put it, when writing for the Post: "Two amiable wildcats fighting over a hunk of raw meat couldn't have given a better exhibition of the mauling game than did Whitey and Greb last night in their little six round setto before the Hiland (sic) Club in the East End."[27]

The battle was vicious and hard fought with Greb taking the lead from the opening round by staying at long range and sinking right hands deep into the pit of Wenzel's stomach whenever he came within range. Greb punctuated his devastating body attack with hard right hand blows to the head, one of which staggered Wenzel in the fourth, but the blonde Northsider laughed this off and continued trying to bore in. In the fifth Wenzel, sensing the fight slipping away, fought with greater urgency and caused Greb to hang on when he landed a tremendous right hand. The sixth was Wenzel's best round. He carried the fight to Greb and sliced open a large cut on his mouth with a right hand. Greb seemed to be tiring under the greater weight of

Greb tried to get revenge on Joe Borrell (above) in their rematch in 1915 but after a slow start Borrell opened up and evened the score. The newspapers disagreed as to the outcome but it could not be denied that Harry had improved upon his previous performance against Borrell.

Wenzel who had gained several more pounds between the weigh in and fight time. With Greb wobbling and looking shaky the Garfield fans screamed for Harry to hang on for the final bell but Greb surprised everyone by tearing after Wenzel and trading punches until the finish. Aside from Macpherson, who thought Wenzel won by "...a slight; -very slight- shade," the consensus was that Greb had carried the fight, his early lead being more than enough to earn him the victory.[28]

Before the ink was dry on the newspaper decisions of the Greb-Wenzel bout the ballyhoo for Greb's anticipated rematch with Joe Borrell had begun. Much was made of Borrell's fight

with Al McCoy in January in which Borrell faced the middleweight champion despite suffering a broken arm. McCoy won the fight (a fact lost in the Borrell-Greb hype) but Borrell managed to finish on his feet.[29] Harry trained for the bout so vigorously that his handlers feared he
would overtrain and come into the contest stale. He had been whipped into a frenzy by the
fight being hyped on the notion that Borrell had given Greb a terrible beating in Philadelphia[30]

The Garfield fans were out in force betting heavily on their hero despite the odds being in
Borrell's favor. As an added boost for Greb these rooters wore blue and white badges to match
the blue and white tights he was wearing for the contest in honor of the newly formed Garfield
Athletic Club. The fight began as a tame affair with Borrell content to let Greb lead despite what
Harry Keck guessed to be a fifteen pound weight advantage. The crowd quickly grew tired of
Borrell's tactics; hoping to see a repeat of the Greb-Wenzel fight of a week earlier, people began
to yell "Cut loose Joe!" In the second round, Greb opened a cut over Borrell's left eye, which
combined with the angry mob, seemed to spur Borrell into greater action. Borrell quickly
repaid the favor by opening Greb's lip which had been injured the week before against Wenzel,
an injury which threatened to choke Greb as he was continually forced to swallow his own
blood. By the fourth round Borrell had begun to take control and at the finish his infighting was
clearly tiring Greb. With the match completed, Greb was hoisted on to the shoulders of his loyal
fans and carried back to his dressing room.[31]

The newspaper reports on the fight are inconclusive at best. Every report has a different take
on how the fight played out ranging from a close win for Greb to an easy win for Borrell. It is
fairly clear that much of the difference in opinion can be attributed to whether the viewer felt
Borrell had "allowed" Greb to carry the early rounds or Greb had simply won them on his own
merit. In the first case it seems as if writers such as Richard Guy of the Gazette-Times and Jim
Jab of the Press gave Borrell slightly more credit than he deserved for his work in the early
rounds. Reviewing reports of the Pittsburgh Sun and the Pittsburgh Post, both which scored
the bout a draw, we have a closer representation of how the fight should have been judged
based on the action in the ring and not what was theorized by the observer. The Dispatch,
which had Greb winning, was probably on the other end of the spectrum, scoring against
Borrell for his perceived stalling.

Borrell took the $128 he earned from the fight and returned home. Greb rested for two weeks
while Red Mason negotiated for more fights. On May 7 Mason met with Whitey Wenzel's manager, Harry Shekels, and agreed in principle for the two men to meet for a seventh time on May
24 at Duquesne Gardens. The only hitch in signing the articles was Wenzel's reluctance to make
160 pounds at 6 o'clock on the night of the fight. Wenzel had been over the stipulated weight
of 162 pounds in their previous fight and Greb was eager to either weaken Wenzel through the
weight making process, or collect another forfeit. With Mason threatening to use another fighter against Greb instead of Wenzel a compromise was reached: The fighters would agree to post
a $50 forfeit binding them to weigh 161 pounds at 4 o'clock on the day of the fight.[32]

Wenzel entered the ring wearing white trunks and a white bathrobe with an American flag strung through his belt loops. As Greb entered the ring, his seconds walked over to Wenzel and immediately protested extra tape which was used to bind Wenzel's right hand. After a few minutes of heated discussion Wenzel returned to his dressing room for half an hour to have his hands re-taped. When he returned the fighters were called to ring center for the pre fight instructions during which neither fighter would acknowledge the other. At the start of the fight both Greb and Wenzel refused to shake hands.

The bout itself proved somewhat anti-climactic given the high expectations and legitimate bad blood between the two fighters. Wenzel had been instructed by his handlers not to take a backward step in hopes that he could prevent Greb from acquiring an early lead. Instead this played right into Greb's hands. Harry simply used his speed to stay on the outside and box Wenzel from long range. Wenzel could not cope with the greater speed and mobility of his bitter rival. Other than his lip being once again in need of stitches Greb was the easy winner. After the bout had concluded Greb walked up to Wenzel and patted him on the back to show him there were no hard feelings. Wenzel swung around, furious, with the intention of punching Greb. The two fighters ended up in a heap, wrestling in the center of the ring. Before a riot could break out police had stormed the ring and returned order.[33]

Immediately after defeating Wenzel Harry signed to face Fay Keiser in Connellsville on Decoration Day, May 31, despite having suffered an injury to his left arm during the Wenzel bout. The bout would be staged by Jack Stevens under the auspices of the West Side Athletic Club. It would be the third meeting between Greb and Keiser. Keiser had moved on from Pittsburgh and was now fighting out of Cumberland, Maryland under the guidance of Stevens after having beaten his former manager to a pulp in the middle of a Pittsburgh street. Within the last two months Keiser had fought four times in Connellsville facing Bill Fegg, Joe Chip, Tommy

Fay Keiser as he looked in 1915. He had been making rapid strides since that first professional bout against Greb the previous April. After fighting around Connellsville for a few months he would relocate to Cumberland, Maryland which he would call home for the rest of his days.

This rare photo of Greb taken around the time of his 1915 bout in Connellsville with Fay Kaiser shows his now rapidly maturing physique.

Jones, and Bull Miller. Keiser knocked Miller out in three rounds, disposed of Fegg in five rounds and won the newspaper decision over Chip and Jones. Keiser's most recent bout had been a ten round battle with Greb's stablemate Al Grayber in which the decision was disputed and argued over by both men.[34]

It was to be an ugly night for Connellsville boxing. The crowd which arrived for the bout was smaller than for shows previously staged by Stevens in the city, and of those who turned out to see Greb and Keiser square off, a vast majority had entered the premises free of charge. Adding to this unsatisfactory situation Greb broke his already injured arm in the opening round. When Keiser realized that Greb was injured he refused to take advantage of his opponent. As a result the first three rounds of the bout were tame. With the crowd growing restless and yelling "Fake!" the two fighters began to put forth their best effort. Every punch caused Greb "excruciating pain" yet he continued to fight on. Hobbled as he was, and owing to his sub par performance, Greb lost the newspaper decision according to the Connellsville Daily Courier.

Disgusted with the whole affair Stevens vowed to quit staging boxing in Connellsville, switching his focus to Cumberland where he intended to stage a rematch between Greb and Keiser on Friday June 25 at Cumberland's Miller Hall.[35]

After an extremely short period of rest to let his arm heal a bit Greb resumed training at the Oakland Club utilizing his old tutor Red Robinson as a sparring partner. Cumberland eagerly awaited the pairing of it's adopted son and Greb, for Stevens had announced his hopes that the winner would be matched with George Chip.

Greb and Keiser did not disappoint Cumberland fans. From the outset Keiser searched for that one blow which would end the fight early. He continually bounced rights and lefts off of Greb's jaw with little effect while Greb concentrated almost solely on the body. Greb's strategy was simple; he wished to crowd Keiser, pump rights and lefts to the heart and wear him down. Early in the bout Greb slashed open Keiser's mouth but Keiser continued to meet Greb punch for punch. In the fifth round Keiser slipped to the floor and Greb jumped back with his hands in the air showing he did not intend to take advantage of Keiser's position. This show of sportsmanship brought cheers from the audience. In the tenth round both fighters sensed the bout was close and both went for the knockout. The round was fought at an incredible pace and when the bell ended the bout both fighters were firing blows at the chin. The bout was adjudged a draw with an inevitable rematch eagerly anticipated.[36]

5

FASTER THAN A SPEEDING BULLET

Greb was now in great demand by promoters throughout Western Pennsylvania and the surrounding area. Mason had hoped to use this regional popularity to lure Al McCoy to Pittsburgh for a bout with Greb but McCoy's asking price was too high. Bouts with Buck Crouse, Whitey Wenzel, Al Rogers, and Jerry Cole were all under consideration as well but Greb had other ideas. He had been ringside for the match between Tommy Gavigan and Jerry Cole some months earlier in Pittsburgh. Immediately after Gavigan's four round demolition of Cole Greb wanted a match with the rangy Cleveland fighter but Mason felt Greb was not ready.

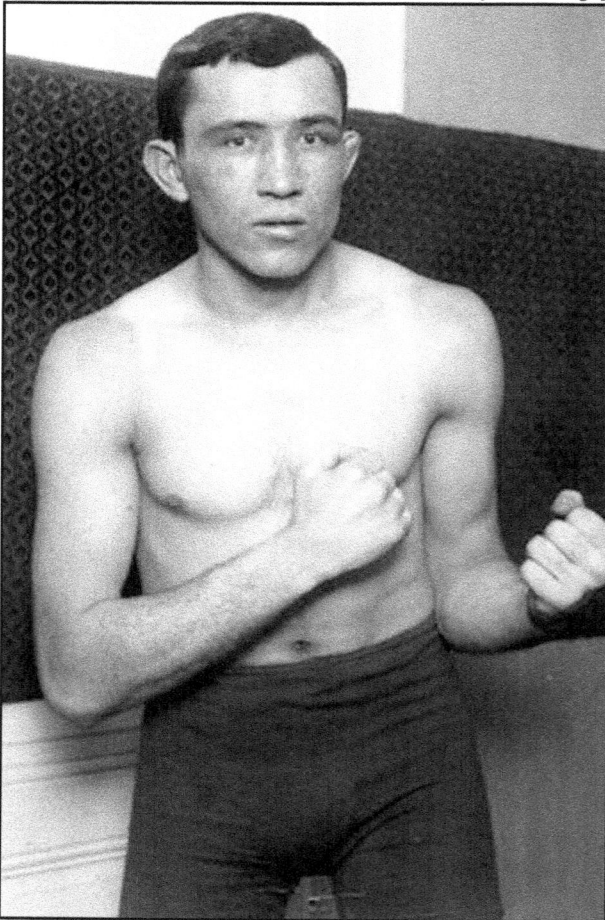

Mason now bowed to Greb's wishes and signed the fighters to face each other July 12 in Duquesne Gardens at 158 pounds. Greb set out for a hard training grind to cope with the ambidextrous Gavigan who was a talented boxer and heavy puncher. The most notable feature of this training period was the six-round exhibition he fought with stablemate Red Robinson for the Automobile Men's picnic at Keystone Park in which both fighters fought as if the match were for a

Tommy Gavigan, who would face Greb twice over the years, was a tall, rangy fighter from Cleveland. He was known as a solid boxer/puncher who held his own with the best fighters in his division.

championship.[1]

Gavigan was totally unprepared for the two-fisted assault that awaited him at the hands of Greb, despite having trained with his stablemate, featherweight champion Johnny Kilbane. After a slow first round Harry dominated Gavigan with constant aggression, pumping both hands to the body and head. In the fifth Gavigan broke through with his best punch, a resounding left hand that landed on Greb's mouth and echoed through the hall. Rather than fall, as Gavigan expected, Greb fought back more furious than ever, ignoring his blood-smeared lips which had once again been torn open. In the same session Greb shot a combination to the head and finished it off with a long haymaker to the pit of Gavigan's stomach which left the boy from Cleveland hanging on. His strength nearly gone, Gavigan fought the sixth to survive. The bout was Greb's and his boisterous fans from Garfield cheered him wildly despite two uniformed policemen being assigned to their section to keep them under control. The only consolation Tommy could take back to Cleveland was the unsatisfactory purse of $90 he received for his troubles.[2]

Nine days after his victory over Tommy Gavigan, Greb knocked out Joe Choynski's protégé George Hauser at the picnic of the Knoxville Elks held at Elwyn Grove. Choynski had high hopes for the heavyweight; needless to say his dream was never realized. Hauser had lost to the best men he had faced after having gained the fans' interest in see-saw battles with John Foley. Indeed it was John Foley who was initially scheduled to face Greb at the Elks picnic but when it was discovered that Foley was out of town Hauser took his place on one day's notice. Hauser later alleged that Greb had agreed to take it easy but reneged on his promise after the bout began. In the final minute of the final round Hauser collapsed under the weight of Greb's withering attack. The referee counted to six before picking up the heavyweight and carrying him back to his own corner with a badly damaged face and a broken rib.[3]

The Hauser fight was little more than an afterthought as much larger fights were being arranged for Greb. Only a day later he was scheduled to fight Fay Keiser in Cumberland but more important matches were being discussed behind closed doors. While George Chip had been unsuccessfully chasing his lost championship, Mason had been unsuccessfully chasing Chip. As Mason pursued the lucrative Chip match for Greb, Hugh Shannon of Buffalo was pursuing a match with Greb for his fighter Al Rogers. With neither Shannon nor Mason acquiring the bouts they wanted they did the next best thing: they fought their battles in print as opposed to the ring.

> **"Chip, so it is said, made the remark the other night after Greb
> had whipped Gavigan, that he could gain nothing by fighting the
> Pittsburgher. That may be Chip's way of looking at it, but he is
> alone in that view, and he surely would gain as much fighting
> Greb as he gained in meeting Jack McCarron two or three times,**

or meeting Walter Monohan on the Southside and getting only a draw... ...The time worn excuse of being easy won't hold in this case, as the people have paid quite a little to give Chip his start and he would be only doing the right thing by meeting Greb and showing the fight followers what he really can do against the most earnest boy turned out in this city in years."

James Mason[4]

"If Harry Greb wants to try himself against a real battler, and one who is a real favorite with the fistic fans in Pittsburgh, Al Rogers, Buffalo's middleweight championship aspirant, will give him that chance... ...Any time Mr. Mason is ready to risk his protégé's future by allowing him to fight Rogers I will be glad to make the match."

Hugh Shannon[5]

With hopes of soon acquiring better matches Greb entered the ring with Fay Keiser and fought a sloppy ten round draw. The bout featured far too much clinching for the taste of the fans. The Cumberland Times reported that despite the decision Greb appeared to have a slight advantage due to his greater ability to punch in the clinches. Pittsburgh papers printed a short report of the fight received by wire in which it was stated that Greb won a crowd pleasing fight. Given the first-hand account originating from ringside it is likely that James Mason was the author of the report published in Pittsburgh, an all too common practice in the first quarter of the century.[6]

Amid wild rumors that Greb would meet either Frank Klaus, who was contemplating a comeback, or Buck Crouse, Mason agreed to a match with Al Rogers. Rogers was a tough Italian fighter from Buffalo, New York now fighting out of Erie due, allegedly, to his employment of questionable tactics. Rogers, whose real name was Angelo Christiano, would tuck his chin in and bore into his opponents swinging both hands to the body. In the past Rogers had displayed his durability by going the distance with such men as Jack Dillon, Joe Chip, Tommy Gavigan, and Buck Crouse. His fights with Buck Crouse and Jack Dillon were particularly telling due to the fact that in both fights he had been overmatched with middleweights despite still being only a welterweight. Dillon, who won a newspaper decision over Rogers, was particularly impressed with the young Italian and Crouse had all he could handle just gaining a draw.[7]

The fighters signed to face each other on August 16 but the bout would later be set back to August 23. With an air of confidence that was rapidly becoming his hallmark, Greb entered Duquesne Gardens to the strains of a twenty-six piece band enlisted by his ever present and always outrageous Garfield rooters. The bout would be one of the most controversial events in recent memory for Pittsburgh boxing. Rogers was first to enter the ring. When the Italian began his ring walk the brass band hired by Greb's fans began to play "Nearer My God To Thee" much to the consternation of the more puritanical members of the audience. Before the fighters even entered the arena Greb's rowdy fans had been dancing and snakewalking to the music before being told rather forcefully to settle down.

The bout started fast but just before the conclusion of the first round Rogers threw a blow, the legality of which no one could agree upon, which sent Greb down clutching his groin. Greb had to be carried back to his corner for the minute's rest between rounds. When the bell rang announcing the second Greb refused to rise still claiming a foul. Referee Eddie Kennedy stated that he saw no foul prompting Roger's handlers to storm the ring demanding the fight be awarded to Rogers on a knockout. Shouts began to rise from all corners of the hall variously demanding that Rogers either be disqualified or given the fight on a knockout. Before things could escalate any further Police Superintendent Noble W. Mathews told Rogers that he could claim the fight on a foul if such was his intention but advised that Greb be allowed to continue so that the now furious patrons be given their money's worth. After a rest of five to ten minutes (depending on which source you rely upon and whether or not they supported Greb's claim of a foul) Greb arose and continued the fight.

The bout continued at it's terrific pace with both fighters giving and taking punishment. On more than one occasion after the first round Rogers hit low as he continued to work the body and Greb was inclined to complain to the referee without reply. Greb then switched his attack to the body and both fighters dished out more blows to the ribs than had been seen in Pittsburgh in many years. The bout featured ebbs and flows with both fighters taking and losing control several times. In the last round Greb punctuated the fight with a well-placed blow far below the belt giving Rogers a taste of his own medicine. After the fight Greb's rooters tried to storm the ring but were beaten back by police, prompting several brawls in the stands.

With so many unseemly elements to choose from detractors of Greb had a field day. Jim Jab was chief among them, his headlines read:

DISGUSTING EXHIBITION HURTS GAME
Sacrilege and Other Nauseating Features Mar Greb-Rogers Bout
"Ickie's" Tactics Hurt His Prestige
GREB ACTS LIKE A QUITTER.

Richard Guy was no less critical stating:

GARFIELD BOY TECHNICALLY KNOCKED OUT IN THE

Faster Than a Speeding Bullet

FIRST ROUND OF THE BOUT

Blows Come at End of Session

Rest of 10 Minutes Brings Greb Around Again and Five More

Hot Periods Are Contested

Rogers Punches the Harder

Rooting Wild, Music Indiscreet

Taking more of a diplomatic stance the Chronicle-Telegraph stated simply:

ROGERS DEFEATS GREB IN FAST GO

Buffalo Middleweight and Garfield Entry Stage Good Bout

Evening the score were those who felt Greb had been unfairly treated both during the fight and after, led by Leslie McPherson of the Post:

Greb Shades Rogers In Grueling Battle; Fouled Three Times

Followed by the Sun and the Dispatch, respectively:

Greb Beats Rogers In Hard Fought Bout

Harry Greb Bests Al Rogers In Fast Six-Round Battle[8]

With such a storm of controversy a rematch was inevitable; a rematch preceded by the obligatory war of words between the fiery Red Mason and the no less vocal Hugh Shannon.

"If Harry Greb wasn't knocked out by Al Rogers Monday night, what decision could be rendered when a referee refuses to allow claims for a foul and a fighter refuses to continue? Greb was legitimately knocked out, but he tried to prove an alibi. He was sitting in his corner fully ten minutes and was technically out when he refused to continue fighting. I consented to permit Rogers to continue the bout after giving Greb a 10-minute rest, because I am a booster for the boxing game, and I know things are not breaking any too well for the glove sport in Pittsburgh. I did not want to do it any harm by disappointing the crowd. Greb isn't in Rogers' class, and I believe he is pretty sure of it himself now. If they ever meet again the referee will be able to count a million, for Rogers certainly will give Greb all he is looking for. I am ready to rematch the boys any time. I know the big majority of the spectators aside from a few Garfield rooters, left the hall firmly convinced that Rogers won by knockout..."

Hugh Shannon [9]

"I see that Hugh Shannon, manager of Al Rogers, has written you that Rogers ought to have been given the decision the other night when his man fouled Harry Greb, and that he consented to allow his man to continue just to help the boxing game. Now it is very kind of Mr. Shannon to permit his 'champion' to continue with Greb, after Greb had sat for 10 minutes in his chair, according to Shannon. Now Mr. Shannon must have quite an imagination, or else he can be in two places at one and the same time, as after the

Angelo Christiano, otherwise known as Al Rogers, was a rugged Italian from Buffalo, New York. Barrel chested and strong as a bull, Rogers was defensively adept as well as being a tremendous pressure fighter.

show, when I went to the Garden office to settle with him for Rogers' services, he asked me what kind of a fight it had been, according to the majority of the Pittsburgh papers, and they surely were able to see the fight as well as Mr. Shannon... Now just to show how much Greb fears him, I will agree to give Rogers a return fight with Greb just as soon as he is ready to sign the articles, and will also give him the same inducements as he received before."

James "Red" Mason [10]

As Pittsburgh boxing fans continued to argue over the controversy surrounding the fight, Rogers and Greb signed for an immediate rematch to be fought on Monday, September 13 at Duquesne Gardens. Greb began training immediately, working out daily at the Pittsburgh Lyceum with Red Robinson and Johnny Ray to improve his speed. Incentive for Greb to win the Rogers bout was added when one week before the fight it was announced that George Chip had agreed to meet Greb provided he win the upcoming match. Upon hearing this news Rogers swore that he would acquire the lucrative bout with Chip by knocking Greb out. "I knocked him out in our last bout in spite of all he may say to the contrary," said Rogers, "and I'm going to do it again."[11]

Before an estimated crowd of 2,500 spectators, divided between Greb's loyal Garfield rooters (many of them now women), and a large contingent of Pittsburgh Italians come to root their countryman, Rogers and Greb set forth to settle once and for all who was the better fighter over six rounds.

Duquesne Gardens was blistering hot that night with men and women fanning themselves and removing their topcoats to gain a small measure of comfort. This irritation was compounded by the fact that Greb and Rogers failed to put on the slashing grudge match that everyone had hoped would materialize. Instead Rogers seemed overeager to land a finishing punch. His rushes were met head on by Greb and the two constantly found themselves tangled up in clinch after clinch, wrestling around the ring. Rogers complained bitterly that referee Yock Henninger, one of Pittsburgh's most respected officials, had handicapped him. This complaint was due in large part to Henninger's strict adherence to the rules disallowing any foul blows that might create such controversy as was found in the first bout. Most irritating to Rogers and his supporters was Henninger's refusal to allow the kidney punch, a dangerous blow which was rapidly being adopted as illegal across the country.[12]

With Greb being accepted as having received no worse than a draw by ringsiders he was now free to concentrate on his proposed match with George Chip tentatively scheduled for the middle of October. In the meantime Greb would be kept on the shelf resting and preparing for the most important fight of his career to date. It was during this interim period that Greb saw his name on the front page of almost every Pittsburgh newspaper for the first time.

On the afternoon of September 26 Harry and a friend named Victor Staubs were in the vicinity of the intersection of Penn Avenue and Mathilda Street when they found themselves in the middle of a commotion. A 28-year old Negro named Clarence Jackson was being reproached for "harassing" a group of white girls. Jackson challenged anyone in the crowd not approving of his behavior to a fight. Greb quickly jumped out of the crowd and before Jackson knew what was happening he was on the ground as a result of Greb's attack. The situation turned far more dangerous and potentially deadly when Jackson drew a revolver and fired. The bullet narrowly missed Greb but Victor Staubs wasn't so lucky. Greb's neighborhood friend reeled back and collapsed on the sidewalk with a bullet hole in his cheek.

In the resulting confusion Jackson made good his escape and fled north with a party of young men, headed by Greb, in hot pursuit. Jackson barricaded himself in a house on Mossfield Street, just a few blocks north of where he wounded Staubs and began firing shots from the second floor. A short while later officers Frank B. Vincent and Peter Stein entered the house and disarmed Jackson who was then identified by Greb as the man who had shot his friend. Jackson was held at the Penn Avenue Police Station pending news of Staubs' condition. Jackson was uncooperative when questioned about the incident. Staubs was taken to the West Penn Hospital where the bullet was removed from his jaw. He would eventually make a full recovery. Jackson would remain in jail until his trial on the charge of "unlawful shooting and wounding" scheduled for November.[13] Greb joked about the incident with reporters stating "I brushed those bullets away from me before they got started. I'm getting fast with my hands."[14] Pius must have been wringing his hands in disgust.

At the same time newspapers were reporting on Greb's bullet dodging exploits, the Post issued the formal announcement that Greb and Chip had finally been matched to meet on October 18 at Duquesne Gardens. The fighters had been contracted to weigh in at or under 160 pounds at four o'clock on afternoon of the fight.

Harry again set about training with Johnny Ray and Red Robinson. Ray preparing for a bout with Chip's stablemate Patsy Brannigan. Chip had been working out with Brannigan and was expected to be in Patsy's corner when he arrived in Pittsburgh for his fight with Ray. Just before the bout between Brannigan and Ray, Chip and Greb came face to face in the dressing room resulting in an ugly shouting match where Chip and Greb exchanged barbs of "You fresh kid!" and "You big stiff!" The two were quickly separated by their managers before they came to blows. The altercation merely served to further ignite the animosity between the two fighters and the public's interest in their coming clash.[15]

The labeling of Greb as a "fresh kid" was not entirely reserved to George Chip. Indeed, many questioned Mason for throwing such a promising prospect as Greb in with a former champion like Chip so soon. Chip was as rugged a fighter as existed in the division and carried a mule-kick in either hand. It was not lost on the fight fraternity that Greb had already been knocked out by Chip's younger brother Joe. In fact George had gone on record as saying he felt Greb should first prove he could beat Joe before calling out men in the class of a recently deposed champion. This was the reasoning that made Chip an easy betting favorite to not only win the fight but to stop Greb before the end of the sixth round. To Chip the bout meant little more than a warm-up for him, a stepping stone to his two goals: To regain the middleweight championship and to fight the young superstar of the Antipodes, Les Darcy, to settle the supremacy of the division.

Greb, smiling and confident as ever, increased his training regimen to twice daily knowing that a victory over Chip would give him national attention. Chip was also in hard training for the bout despite having only recently been married. The former champion owed his generally splendid conditioning to his former work as a blacksmith and miner. With this background Chip could generally expect to snap into fighting trim with a minimum amount of work. However he had no intention of losing his prestige to this young upstart and worked accordingly. He had every intention of leaving Greb looking up at the ceiling just as his brother had two years previously. Within days of the contest both men were down to the stipulated poundage and ready for action.

With more than 3,000 fans anxiously awaiting the start of festivities, Greb entered the ring. He appeared uncharacteristically nervous and it showed in the first two rounds when instead of employing his usual rushing tactics he stood off and boxed from outside trying to keep out of the range of Chip's powerful punches. Greb peppered Chip with a multitude of light punches but it was Chip who was landing the more damaging punches despite their relatively few numbers.

In the third round, with Greb's fans yelling for action, he appeared to regain his confidence and rushed Chip, refusing to let him get set for one of his powerful swings. Greb's skill at infighting was evident in this round as he landed often while evading most of Chip's blows.

Former middleweight champion George Chip (left), pictured here with younger brother and former Greb opponent Joe Chip, was still on the comeback trail when he faced Greb for the first time in October of 1915. After a period of inactivity and a recent marriage, the best Chip could muster from his younger opponent was a draw.

The Garfield fans were now wildly urging "Ickie" on, delirious at the sight of their hero taking the battle to the door-step of the former champion. Greb continued his rally in the fourth, tearing after Chip, landing three punches to one, and out-wrestling him in the clinches. Suddenly as Greb was coming in Chip timed him with two short left hooks and Greb wavered. Chip rained blows to Greb's body and head to the horror of Greb's fans and to the delight of the New Castle faction. It looked as though Greb might go down under the savage assault but he managed to hang on and survive. As the bell sounded he and the former champion were fighting on even terms.

The final two rounds witnessed Greb pecking and poking Chip with his long left and occasionally mixing in a hard blow to the head and body. Chip seemed at sea with this type of fighting and couldn't solve Greb's style. His wild rushes were deftly evaded by the fleet footed youngster and his attempts at infighting were smothered as Greb held him close until the referee could part them. After the fight had ended and the crowd began to slowly exit the arena a clamoring was heard from the ring. All eyes turned to see a near fist fight between Greb and Chip which was quickly broken up by referee Joe Donnelly before the brawl became serious.

Greb and Mason were no doubt overjoyed the next day when they read the morning papers. Four of Pittsburgh's seven newspapers had the fight a draw, feeling that Greb's high volume of punches and aggression did enough to even the score of Chip's harder punches. The Post, Leader, and Chronicle-Telegraph dissented, giving Chip a slight edge while acknowledging Greb's fine performance.[16]

This photo of Greb from 1915 was taken about the time of his fight with George Chip. Note the steely look of determination in his eyes.

The Chip fight immediately garnered attention for Greb. This attention first manifested itself when the Capital City Athletic Club of St. Paul, Minnesota, which had been preparing to pro-

mote a show with Tommy Gibbons and George Chip, decided that it would sign Greb as Gibbons' opponent instead. It was a huge opportunity for Greb. St. Paul was a hotbed of boxing talent, and was in the process of turning out some of the best fighters in the sport. Not least of these was Tommy's older brother Mike Gibbons who was rapidly becoming a legend in his own time. Mike had tutored Tommy and the younger brother was making rapid strides in the sport having already met such men as Billy Miske, Joe Borrell, and Buck Crouse who he knocked out in three rounds. Mason accepted the bout for Greb on condition that both fighters weigh no more than 158 pounds at three o'clock on the day of the fight. The bout would be held on November 16 at St. Paul's Auditorium for a scheduled distance of ten rounds.

After a short pheasant hunting trip to Rochester, Greb got down to serious training. He trained with heavyweight Frank Moran who was again riding a wave of popularity based on his win over Jim Coffey, the "Dublin Giant." In addition to Moran, Greb worked with Johnny Ray for speed; Ray was scheduled to appear on the undercard of the Gibbons fight. Mason's plans for the troupe to leave on November 7 were almost upended when it briefly looked as though Greb would be compelled to remain in Pittsburgh as the chief witness against Clarence Jackson in the Staubs shooting. However Greb was allowed to leave on the condition that he return for the trial which would be held one week after the conclusion of His bout in St. Paul.

Initially there had been some skepticism about Greb from the St. Paul sporting public. It was feared that Greb had been acquired sight unseen in order to pad Tommy's record with an easy win. To add to this confusion Greb's old opponent Walter Monahan was now living in the St. Paul area and telling everyone within ear shot that he had beaten Greb easily in their previous meeting. Billy Miske had similar stories about his match with Greb in Philadelphia earlier that year. It wasn't until Mason began sending the actual press reports of Greb's bouts to Minnesota that such fears were laid to rest.[17] Greb's first order of business upon arriving in St. Paul was to address the issue. "I certainly have come West in the hope of beating Tom," said Greb upon his arrival, "but if he whips me then he is a better boxer than we have been given to understand in the East. I am not afraid of any middleweight in the game. There are so many conflicting reports about me and my record that I am going in there Tuesday night to show these skeptics that mine is not a paper reputation. I am positive I can whip Gibbons."[18]

"I have brought him West for less than I could get right at home," said Mason. "I would have been foolish to take a long journey and a small guarantee simply to have my boy spoiled as a card in his hometown, wouldn't I? I think so well of him after his showing against George Chip to believe that he would have a good chance against Mike Gibbons, and I insisted when I made this match that if Greb beats Tommy, he is to box Mike, and the St. Paul club has promised me a chance against Tom's brother if we win next Tuesday."[19]

Greb set about training at the Gibbons brothers' gym with Harry "Fish" Warren and White Hope heavyweight Al Palzer. Palzer was immediately impressed with the young Pittsburgh fighter. "He sure can hit. He'll surprise a whole lot of fans next Tuesday,"[20] said the giant

Referee George Duffy looks on as a young Tommy Gibbons (left) prepares to hand an equally young Billy Miske a decisive boxing lesson in March of 1914 at Hudson, Wisconsin.

Palzer. Those who witnessed Greb's training made note of his speed, his aggression, and his tremendous left. The reports of these training bouts went a long way toward building some credibility with the Twin Cities fans. "The only way I can fight is to fight all the time," elaborated Greb. "You will see one real fight when Gibbons and I meet. The folks here do not give me much of a show against Tom, but they may change their minds when they see me in the ring against him. His reputation does not make any difference to me."[21]

Greb pointed to Mike O'Dowd's recent and unlooked for victory over Soldier Bartfield as an example of why he should not be counted out by the locals. "Hardly anyone conceded O'Dowd a chance to win, and yet he easily won from the leading Eastern welterweight. Out here there is an impression that Tommy Gibbons can defeat anyone of his weight, barring only his older brother. I know Tommy is a more finished boxer than I am but I don't think that will help him as much as he is relying upon. I plan to keep him busy every minute of the ten rounds. If Tommy will do his share of leading you will see a real battle. If he doesn't I figure I should win on points, because I certainly will keep after him all the time. I came west just because I thought I had a good chance to make a big advance by beating one of the Gibbons boys. I can

GREAT
Boxing Contests

Best Show Ever Held in St. Paul

TOMMY GIBBONS vs. HARRY GREB
Leading contenders for middle-weight championship.

AL PALZER vs. FARMER LODGE
Sensational heavyweight match.

JOHNNY RAY vs. TOMMY DURKIN
Philadelphia champion against Wisconsin champion.

BOBBY WARD vs. JOHNNY CASHILL
Classy featherweight match.

NEXT TUESDAY, NOV. 16
ST. PAUL AUDITORIUM

RESERVE YOUR SEATS NOW AT
Winecke & Doerr, 5th and Robert Sts.
Jack Flynn, 432 Wabasha St.
Harry Bryant, 400 Wabasha St.
Joe Mahoney, 412 Cedar St.
Ernie Jackson, 7th and Sibley Sts.
Harry Johnson, Mer. Nat'l Bank Bldg.
Pat Connolly, 928 Jackson St.
Lawrence Carr, Commerce Bldg.
Chas. Hinton, 6th and Jackson Sts.
Bob Grady, 372 Robert St.
Al. Kemmick, 618 University Ave.
Thos. O'Toole, Grove and Mississippi Sts.
Muszynski, 1199 Cortland St.
Art Banholzer, 1028 W. 7th St.
Albin Johnson, 978 Payne Ave.
Cornellissen Bros., 541 Rice St.
PRICES—$1.00, $2.00, $3.00.

get plenty of matches in Pittsburgh and I didn't have to make a long journey just to box a man I have no chance of beating."[22]

Despite his confidence Greb was a clear underdog. It was apparent that Greb was in enemy territory. The Gibbons brothers were easily the most popular and famous boxers in the Twin Cities if not the entire Midwest. Tommy had been training for three weeks with Mike and was in perfect physical condition. To add to Tommy's advantage, the elder Mike would be in his corner helping to plot strategy on the night of the fight.

A good sized crowd attended the fights and after the preliminaries, in which Johnny Ray won over Tommy Durkin, Greb and Gibbons entered the ring to hear the instructions from referee George Barton. The first round went to Gibbons who was countering Greb's aggression with short, snappy punches. Despite Greb's speed, he was having difficulty landing on his more technical opponent. The second round was worse for Greb and foreshadowed things to come. Greb was finding it near impossible to land on Gibbons who was being coached through the constant chatter of his brother Mike. Gibbons would invariably make Greb miss, sometimes wildly, and then before Greb could regain his balance he would find himself subjected to volleys of blows. Greb was already bleeding from the mouth and his face was beginning to flush from the accurate punches of Gibbons. The third round was a bit better for Greb as he got his left working, but it wasn't until the fourth that he found a margin of success against Gibbons. In this round Greb leapt in violently with a left hook to Gibbons' head which shook Gibbons and left the bridge of his nose cut and bleeding.

Gibbons came out for the fifth intent on re-establishing his dominance, but Greb met him half way and while Gibbons landed more often it was Greb who was continually forcing the fighting. In the sixth Gibbons began to pull away from Greb in the estimation of those present. He danced around the ring in the fashion of his brother, gliding about, snapping quick punches at the onrushing Greb. Greb simply could not find the target and was beginning to take a beating. By the ninth Red Mason was worried and was matching Mike Gibbons word for word in coaching the rapidly tiring Greb. Gibbons gave Greb an artistic thumping in the ninth, punctuating the round with a hard right which sent Greb back to his corner bloody and weak. As the tenth opened Mason continually shouted for Greb to survive. Greb was now exhausted, bleeding from several cuts, and fighting on instinct. Despite Mason's plea to hold on Greb continued to try for a finishing punch but his weak attempts were now easily evaded by Gibbons who tore into Greb. Greb remained on his feet at the bell but he was a sorry sight. He bled from several cuts, his cheeks were puffed, his lips were raw, and he was groggy from exhaustion and punishment.[23]

Greb and Mason returned to Pittsburgh two days later with no excuses. Tommy Gibbons had been the better fighter and that was all there was to it. Despite his clear loss, Greb had found a measure of popularity in the Twin Cities based on his gritty performance. The critics felt that he was in no way

When he fought Greb in 1915 Tommy Gibbons was still living in the shadow of his older brother Mike. He was a rapidly developing young fighter who benefitted from the teachings of arguably the world's greatest fighter.

disgraced by losing to a man who was initially favored to stop him within five rounds. Indeed the matchmaker for the Capital City Athletic Club wrote the Pittsburgh Post stating that "... Greb made such a great showing against Tom Gibbons that the fans here are clamoring to see Greb here again."[24] Because of this, Greb was offered a return engagement in St. Paul against Mike O'Dowd in late December. A fight with O'Dowd would present the opportunity for Greb to show his ability. O'Dowd was a talented young fighter riding a crest of positive publicity

Over the years the St. Paul Auditorium would host several of Greb's bouts. It was specifically designed to be used as either a theatre or public hall. Over the years it was utilized for a variety of purposes in addition to playing host to some of boxing's greatest talents.

based on his victory over Soldier Bartfield but he was much smaller than Tommy Gibbons, and his style was much different. Far from being the elusive boxer, O'Dowd liked nothing better than to be in the trenches slugging it out.

Before Greb could think about the O'Dowd fight he had a piece of unfinished business. The trial of Clarence Jackson was held on November 23 during which Harry Greb was named by Jackson as the man responsible for his incarceration. Jackson alleged that he was set upon by a mob of young men and brutally beaten. It was only when he feared for his life that he drew his pistol and fired upon the crowd, wounding Victor Staubs. Several witnesses for the commonwealth countered this testimony by stating that Jackson had been behaving "unseemly" on the street, and when reproached, offered to fight anyone on the street. It was then that Greb took up the gauntlet and knocked Jackson to the ground. According to testimony Jackson rose, drew a pistol, and fired four shots into the crowd one of which wounded Victor Staubs.[25]

The trial lasted one day after which a sealed verdict was handed down to be opened the next day. On November 24, 1915 Clarence Jackson was found guilty of felonious assault and battery by Judge John C. Haymaker. Jackson was sentenced to one year in the Allegheny County Workhouse. It was the first conviction against Jackson on a criminal record that would stretch through 1961 with violations ranging from robbery to numbers running, and narcotics to sodomy.[26]

One week after the trial of Clarence Jackson, Greb was signed to face another fighter of national prominence, his third in as many fights, on December 16. Perry "Kid" Graves was regarded by many as the logical claimant of the welterweight championship, which had been vacated by Mike "Twin" Sullivan in 1908. Much like the middleweight division after the death of Stanley Ketchel, the welterweight division had been thrown into disarray when Sullivan relinquished his title. With no clear way to decide a new champion, every fighter at or near the 145 pound weight limit began scrambling for a piece of the title. Kid Graves, with the backing of powerful Milwaukee boxing authority Tom Andrews managed to move to the forefront of title claimants by 1915.

Despite a weight advantage of at least seven pounds Greb was taking the match seriously, even going so far as to train on Sundays which he usually reserved as a day of rest. Greb had an added incentive to beat Graves due to the fact that one week before he was scheduled to enter the ring with Graves it was formally announced by the Capital City Athletic Club in St. Paul that he had been matched to face Mike O'Dowd on December 21. Graves was expected to present a difficult style, utilizing his speed and movement to offset Greb's aggression. Instead of utilizing big slow heavyweights like Al Palzer, Greb reverted to his proven method of sparring with lighter fighters such as Red Robinson and Johnny Ray. He was leav-

This photo of Greb was taken while in St. Paul to face Tommy Gibbons. He has now developed into a full fledged middleweight. The contrast in his physique between this photo and those taken the year previous is readily apparent.

ing nothing to chance with the lucrative O'Dowd match hanging in the balance.

When Graves entered the ring most in the audience felt he might be a pushover for Greb. He was much the smaller of the two and despite his reputation he had never been seen in Pittsburgh. When matched up with a young man of Greb's size the cynicism was understand-

able.

It quickly became apparent that Graves was not the out-gunned "opponent" that he initially appeared to be. He boxed with a calm, indeed a confident manner that spoke volumes of his experience. As Greb pecked and poked, sizing his man up, Graves blocked and rolled with the punches, countering when openings presented themselves. When the action got too hot he simply skittered out of danger. The first round was easily Kid Graves'.

The bell signaling the beginning of the second round had hardly finished ringing when Greb maneuvered Graves to the ropes, sent over a powerful right hand, and then shot a left to the top Graves' head. Greb went limp and fell into a clinch. As referee Joe Donnelly broke the clinch Greb muttered something but was told to keep fighting. Greb swarmed all over Graves driving him around the ring with lefts and rights. He continually tried to trap Graves on the ropes where he might land a finishing punch but his opponent was too wary.

Perry "Kid" Graves was a top welterweight of the 1910's who briefly claimed the welterweight championship. In a career spanning fifteen years he met several champions and hall of famers before finally retiring in 1921.

As the gong sounded Greb dropped his left arm to his side and walked slowly back to his corner. He was pale and his face clearly registered some pain that the audience could not understand. A doctor was called into the Greb corner to confirm what Greb already knew. His left arm had been broken early in the second round. There was no way he could continue. When it was announced that the contest was over and Greb had lost due to a broken arm the crowd began to file out in disgust. Those that lingered filled the air with shouts of "quitter!"[27] S. E. McCarty, sports editor of the Pittsburgh Leader, wrote what should probably be considered the last word and prevailing opinion of what would be Harry Greb's last stoppage defeat.

The first accident of a serious nature during a boxing bout in Pittsburgh for years occurred last night at the new Power arena fight, when Harry Greb, Garfield's pride, sustained a broken arm in his clash with Kid Graves. When the referee announced Greb had sustained a fracture of one of the bones of his left arm, the East Ender was hooted and called a quitter. Graves had been making a great showing and won the first round. The accident occurred during the first minute of the second round, but Harry plugged along to the end of the session. It was not right to accuse Greb of quitting. He has taken some hard wallopings in Pittsburgh and shown his gameness. In his battle with Tom Gibbons the Pittsburgher took a terrific lacing, but was always going in for more. Greb is game and it is wrong to accuse him of being yellow. He showed gameness by fighting out the round with a broken arm.[28]

6

BROKEN BUT UNDAUNTED

The day after his defeat at the hands of Kid Graves Greb went around to every newspaper in Pittsburgh with his arm in a splint and carrying an X-ray photo of his broken left forearm in hopes of convincing the writers that he had not quit.[1] It was a terrible way for Greb to end the year. Not only would the injury keep him out of action for the next two months, but he would also be unable to face Mike O'Dowd the following week. It was no doubt little consolation when Graves took Harry's place against O'Dowd and won.

Not wanting to be forgotten during his convalescence, and still smarting from the fans reaction to his broken arm, Greb often put in appearances to newspaper offices, gyms, and local hangouts in order to stay in the public eye. By early February his arm had healed enough to begin light training with a comeback planned for later in the month. Initially Mason had been trying to lure champion Al McCoy to Pittsburgh for a showdown with Greb but negotiations fell through when the champion continued to raise his asking price.[2] Thus Mason settled for a rematch with Walter Monaghan, who was preparing to return to Pittsburgh after more than a year spent practicing his craft around St. Paul.

Monaghan, it was said, was a greatly improved fighter having spent much time in the gyms of Twin Cities sparring with the renowned fighters there. His last appearance in Pittsburgh had been his disastrous defeat at the hands of Greb and he was eager to even the score. The bout was set to take place on February 26 at the Penn Avenue Power House.

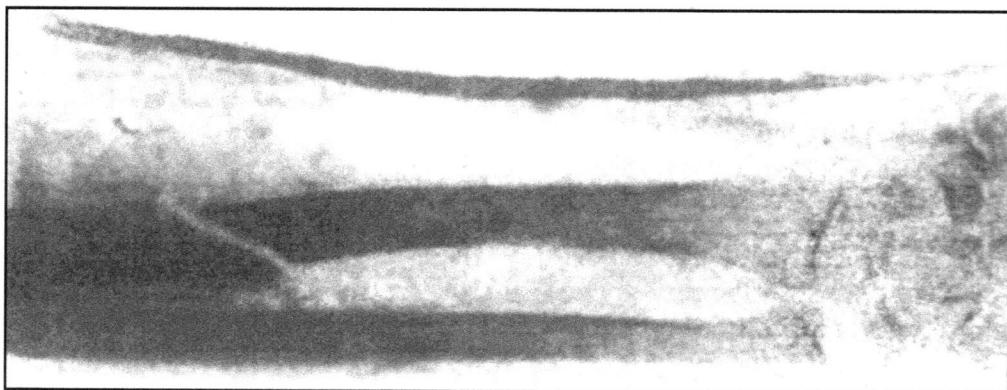

Actual X-Ray of Harry Greb's arm taken after his bout against Kid Graves. Note the fracture high on the forearm, just below the elbow.

Lawrenceville fans showed up in force that night to root the return of Monaghan, while Greb's Garfield rooters were more than prepared to cheer their hero to victory. Both boys seemed tentative in the first round. Greb particularly showed a reluctance to use his injured left. Monaghan continually tried to bore in while Greb tried to pick off these rushes from the outside using snappy lead right hands. In the second round the fight began in earnest as Greb began finding the range with his right hand. He would continually dart in to land overhand rights and then use speedy footwork to get outside before Monaghan could return fire. Several of these blows set Monaghan's nose bleeding. When Monaghan was able to get inside of Greb's right a clinch ensued followed by prolonged infighting.

The fight followed this pattern until the final two rounds when in the fifth Monaghan clipped Greb on the chin with a right hand as Greb was pulling out of clinch. Greb momentarily wobbled and looked as if he might go down but he caught himself and remained upright. He was clearly shaken and Monaghan had earned the round. In the sixth both boys, sensing the fight was close, fought at a terrific pace and when the final bell sounded it was ten seconds before referee Joe Donnelly and several cornermen could separate them.[3]

Walter Monaghan returned to Pittsburgh from the St. Paul area a much improved fighter after having trained with the Gibbons brothers. His last fight in Pittsburgh had been a severe beating at the hands of Greb. His first fight back in his hometown would also be against Greb but this time he would prove a much more worthy opponent.

Due to the competitiveness of the bout, and the natural rivalry between the Lawrenceville and Garfield fans, Mason quickly negotiated for a rematch between Monaghan and Greb to be held March 11. Unfortunately the bout was scrapped almost as soon as it had been signed when it was discovered that Greb had aggravated the injury sustained against Kid Graves. Substituting for Greb was Al Grayber, who had taken time away from boxing to manage and play on football and baseball teams. Grayber destroyed Monaghan in two rounds.

In addition to the rematch with Monaghan Greb had been signed to face Young Herman

Miller on March 18. Hoping to preserve the bout Greb insisted that his injured arm would be in condition by fight time. When the arm showed little sign of healing Greb concealed its condition from Mason and continued training. On the day before his scheduled meeting with Miller Greb met with doctors to have his arm checked. He was told that if he proceeded with the contest he ran the risk of losing the use of his left arm entirely. That was that. Greb's schedule was cleared and Al Grayber was once again chosen to fill Greb's spot.

It was the beginning of a minor feud between Greb and Grayber. Since his popularity had begun to grow Greb had resented Mason's continuing management of Grayber. He felt that one middleweight in the stable was enough to occupy Mason's time. When Grayber disposed of Monaghan in Greb's stead it served to widen the resentment. Greb felt he had been upstaged by Grayber. Grayber, despite his long inactivity, had been voicing his willingness to meet Greb in the ring for several months and it now seemed as if the two would meet in the near future.

Greb's arm was healthy enough to begin training by mid-March. His proposed opponent was to be the tough Erie, Pennsylvania Italian Kid Manuel. As Greb trained for the bout with Manuel Pittsburgh fight fans had another reason to be excited. Frank Moran, after having abandoned the madness in Europe, would be getting a second shot at the heavyweight championship on March 25. This time he would be facing Jess Willard, the gigantic conqueror of Jack Johnson. Once again newspaper offices were surrounded by large crowds awaiting round by round progress reports of the fight. A large delegation of Pittsburgh's most dedicated boxing fans had made the four hundred mile journey to watch Moran lose the newspaper decision to his much larger opponent after 10 uninspiring rounds.

With the disappointment of Moran's effort now behind them, and convinced that his title aspirations were a thing of the past, Pittsburgh fight bugs could look to the return of their favorite son to active campaigning. The Manuel bout which was held on April 1, 1916 was won by Greb in the eyes of most present; however the fight itself was upstaged by a power outage which left the hall drenched in darkness for more than two hours before the main event could start. Greb entered the ring with his injured left arm bandaged and throughout the fight showed reluctance to use it when openings presented themselves. Indeed it was his reliance on a snappy right uppercut which won him the fight and did the most damage to his Erie opponent. The fight was fairly even after four rounds until Greb set out a frantic pace in the last two rounds to seal the verdict in his favor.[4]

With his star performer on the mend, Red Mason immediately set about filling Greb's date book. Greb would first be expected to meet Grant "Kid" Clark in Johnstown on April 27. Next Mason signed Greb to face Whitey Wenzel in Charleroi on May 6. However before either of these bouts could be completed the rivalry between Greb and Al Grayber erupted again. Grayber had been signed to face Kid Manuel in a rematch of their April 15 bout which Manuel was credited with winning. The rematch was to be held two days after Greb's bout with Clark and Greb wanted the match. "I saw him first," said Greb, "I licked him once, and I can do it again." "I've a better right to him than you have," shot back Grayber. "He got fresh with me and I want to stop his clock. Now keep out of this or there'll be trouble."[5] Grayber got his wish when Mason decided that it would be best give one fight to each of his fighters and allow Greb a bit of rest rather than take two hard fights in three days.

In Johnstown Greb gave Kid Clark an unmerciful beating for six rounds before both fighters were disqualified by the referee for foul tactics. In the first round Greb unintentionally hit Clark low but allowed Clark time to recover when he

Grant "Kid" Clark (above) of Columbus, Ohio had lost to the best fighters he faced and it looked as if things would go that way for him against Harry Greb in Johnstown until he was able to draw Greb into a foul fight and they were both disqualified.

realized his error. This set the stage for the remainder of the fight whereby Clark continually complained of fouls as he assimilated more punishment. In the sixth round Clark hit Greb with three foul blows in rapid succession, Greb made no complaint but merely stepped back into the fray and paid Clark in kind. Referee Pete Buser immediately stopped the fight.[6]

Just over a week later Greb would outclass his old rival Whitey Wenzel at Charleroi's skating rink. Greb's defense was far too slick for Wenzel and his speed was the deciding factor. Wenzel was badly beaten at finish.[7] Greb's next scheduled bout was to be against Milwaukee's Gus Christie on May 13. That bout was scrapped at the last minute when Christie failed to

Kid Manuel was a strong and durable Italian fighting out of Erie, Pennsylvania, who sometimes went by the name King Manuel or Kid Emmanuel. Regardless of what name the newspapers called him he almost always gave a good account of himself.

appear[8] and Greb was left to prepare for a rematch with Kid Manuel in early June.

There was much riding on a successful outcome for Greb in his fight with Manuel. Two matches hinged on his victory, a fight with Whitey Wenzel in New Kensington on June 16 and a very lucrative and very important match with George Chip in New Castle on June 26. It was paramount that Greb make an impressive showing and he did not disappoint.

Fifty-two seconds after the start of the first round Manuel was sent sprawling to the mat from a perfectly executed right uppercut. Manuel stirred briefly at the count of five and then lay still. With Greb pacing around the fallen Italian like a wild bull, and the count nearing its conclusion, Manuel's seconds tossed water on him in hopes of reviving him at the last second. Greb flew to the ropes and made to attack the seconds. When they withdrew he returned his attention to Manuel who was now officially counted out. Greb and referee Joe Donnelly carried Manuel back to his corner.[9] Manuel remained unconscious as doctors worked trying to revive him. Greb and his seconds were prevented from leaving the arena by policemen lest charges of manslaughter became necessary. After twenty tense minutes Manuel was revived saying "It all seems like a dream to me. Where am I, anyway, and did they save the women and children first?"[10]

With Manuel so unceremoniously dispatched, the New Kensington bout with Wenzel seemed almost like an afterthought as the bout with Chip loomed. In fact Wenzel very nearly opted out of the fight when he voiced his misgivings about the fight game in general to local papers: "I told my manager three weeks ago that I was going to quit. My wife worries to death about my fighting. I'll be a full fledged moulder in a couple of months now, and I play with the orchestra three or four nights a week. I get $4 a day in the foundry and $4 or $5 a night with the orchestra, and I'd be foolish to lose my time at either job and with the family to keep on fighting."

"I'll never be a champion, no matter how hard I try. I'd always be a 'good tough boy,' a 'demon for punishment,' and fight my head off with the rest of the second and third-raters with never a chance at the big money and the laurels. I like the fight game, and the few nickels I've got in it have come in handy, but now that I can't go higher up, it's time for me to quit, so I'm through, just like I told Bill (Pickels, Wenzel's manager), only he won't believe me. I'd like to trot another heat with Greb just for old times' sake, but my wife won't let me."[11]

Apparently Mrs. Wenzel had a change of heart because within a few days Whitey relented. "Well, I hate to have them thinking I'm afraid of Icky, now that he landed a lucky punch on Manuel, so I'll fight him that 10-round fight, lick him, and then say goodbye to the ring forever. It's my wife and babies, my fiddle and my job after this, but I must lick Greb again first."[12]

The bout had a festive atmosphere being held in conjunction with New Kensington's silver jubilee celebration. Special trains ran from New Kensington to Pittsburgh to accommodate Iron City fans who made the

BOXING

New Castle Athletic Club
New Castle, Pa.

MONDAY, JUNE 26th

Geo. Chip vs. Harry Greb

Of New Castle.   Of Pittsburg
10 Rounds; 160 Pounds

Bat. Terry vs. Chas. Dunn

Of New Castle.   Of Ambridge
8 Rounds; 140 Pounds

Toughy Mur'a vs. M. Laduke

Of Ambridge.   Of Pittsburg.
6 Rounds; 115 Pounds

Admission $1.00; reserved $2.00;
stage $3.00.

First bout 8:30 sharp

Tickets on sale at Bob Hammond's Cafe, Youngstown; Hazen's Restaurant, and Sam Johnson's Cigar Stand, New Castle.

JIMMIE DIME, Promoter.

twenty mile journey to see their hometown favorites. On the sixteenth the fight was set back one day due to extremely heavy rainfall. The following day Greb punctuated Wenzel's planned retirement by easily winning the newspaper decision. Throughout the bout Wenzel was outscored in every aspect of the game from speed to skill to punching ability. When Wenzel returned to his wife and children he carried with him a badly swollen left eye and healthy respect for Greb's ability.[13] "Sure I'm through," proclaimed Wenzel. "I'm determined to quit the ring game. I just fought Greb to satisfy my friends that I wasn't afraid of him. Now the ring game is past history with me. Me for my job, my music and my family."[14]

Greb could now focus on his important match with George Chip in Chip's hometown of New Castle. The war of words had already started and it was not pretty. There was a great deal of animosity toward Greb and Red Mason generated by the New Castle and Youngstown press which had its origins in the long running feud between Patsy Brannigan (Chip's stablemate) and Johnny Ray (Greb's stablemate). The New Castle press felt that Brannigan had not received fair treatment in his most recent bout with Ray in Pittsburgh[15] and as a result they made it known that anything other than a decisive win for Greb would be met with disapproval.

> If Harry Greb doesn't fight every inch of the way here when the going is going against him, some fans are liable to haul him into court for securing money under false pretenses.[16]

And later the same paper stopped just short of accusing Greb of being a protected hometown fighter when it asked:

> Why does Harry Greb win every fight in which he participates in Pittsburgh?[17]

It didn't hurt Chip's situation any that this would be his farewell fight before his journey to Australia where he was contracted for five bouts, the first being a showdown with young Australian contender Les Darcy. The Chip-Darcy match was one of the most anticipated matches in the world with many predicting a triumph for the New Castle fighter. It had been a year and a half since George Chip had fought in his adopted hometown and he intended to give the fans a going away present in the form of a knockout. His dislike for Greb since long before their first meeting was not only undiminished but had probably grown, fed by Greb's constant jabs. "George Chip is next on my list. I'll get him, too, just like Manuel and Wenzel, but

The frightening countenance of power punching George Chip is in evidence in this photo. There was a lot on the line for Chip when he squared off with Greb for a rematch of their 1915 bout. This time he would be much more prepared and much more formidible

more like Manuel, when I meet him next week. Can I do it? Say, that's going to be a victory for me, sure, and I wouldn't surprise myself if I sunk him. You see Chip can be knocked out, as McCoy proved, with one punch. They didn't think Manuel could be stopped, but I took off my coat and I did it. I know I didn't stop Wenzel - There's a fellow who has the toughest jaw I ever walloped. He ain't human. But if I hit Chip a few times like I hit Whitey, Chip'll take a nap."[18]

To such taunts Chip merely grunted "Greb'll know a great deal more about fighting than he did before after I get through with him."[19] And illustrated his motivation later when stating, "I'm going away for a long time, and I don't want the fans -and you sporting writers -to forget about me. It's a long way to Australia, and a fellow is easily forgotten in this country unless he is right on top and kicking. So, for that reason if for nothing else, I intend to set Mr. Harry Greb down early in this fracas of ours next Monday."[20]

Even Whitey Wenzel offered his opinion of the bout based on his recent loss to Greb. "Harry Greb ought to have a very good chance of beating George Chip in New Castle Monday night, that is, if he fights as good against the ex-champion as he did against me in New Kensington. I've fought Greb several times and this last fight was the only one in which I was worried at all. He hit me harder and oftener than he had ever managed to before, and I experienced more difficulty in reaching him than ever before. And I was in pretty good shape, too. Now, if ever, Greb should outpoint Chip, and he was so nimble and hard to reach Saturday that I don't think the Madison miner will get a chance to measure him for one of those sleep-punches."[21]

Both fighters were diligent in training. Greb placed advertisements in the local papers taking on all comers in sparring and did roadwork with local marathon runner Hughey Bruce. So enthusiastic was Greb in

Harry Greb as he looked in early 1916 eager, after the layoff caused by his broken arm, to resume his career, reaffirm his popularity with local fans, and take on the best names that Red Mason could match him with.

his roadwork that he made tentative plans to run the Pittsburgh-to-Kennywood marathon two days after his bout with Chip.[22] Chip was trained to the minute, still concentrating on providing his fans with knockout. There would be no doubt as to the conditioning of the combatants.

On the eve of the battle the New Castle Herald reiterated how important this match would be in light of Chip's coming trip to Australia.

> But my, what a mournful group of fight notables there would be in this city, should Harry Greb pull an "Al McCoy" and sink Chip with one punch. All our hopes of having a champion in the city of New Castle would be smashed in the head. Snowy Baker (Darcy's promoter) wouldn't even read a letter from Jimmie Dime in such event, let alone pay good transportation for Chip to cross the Pacific and guarantee him ten thousand bucks.[23]

The George Chip that Harry Greb met that night on June 26, 1916 was a vastly different fighter than the one he had met nearly a year before. This time Chip was not feeling the effects of the long layoff and recent marriage that preceded his previous fight with Greb. Indeed the only possible distraction in Chip's life, the pending match with Les Darcy, seemed only to motivate him. Greb's speed and defense served him well but round after round Chip continued pressing forward throwing bone-crunching punches to the head body. By the mid-point of the fight Greb was in survival mode. Whenever Chip closed the gap Greb would Grab Chip's arms in a vice-like Grip seemingly following the instructions of Red Mason who sat in Greb's corner shouting: "Hold, clinch, stall or do anything, but don't get knocked out, anything to stay the ten rounds."[24]

Needless to say such a strategy did not find favor with the New Castle fans and press who already had an axe to grind with James Mason. When reports came out the next day they were not kind.

> Harry Greb, Pittsburgh's hope for middleweight honors, stayed 10 rounds with George Chip in their 10-round bout at New Castle Monday night. Greb would have succumbed long before that period, in all probability, had he stood up and fought the bearcat, and only because he is a champion at covering up and holding was he able to go the distance.[25]
>
> - Youngstown Telegram

> To go through the Chip-Greb engagement round after round would be but the story of one embrace after another. As a sticker in the clinches Greb

made the most persistent leach look like a helpless paralytic.[26]

-Youngstown Vindicator

Greb was booed and hissed several times. He was cat-called as he left the ring. However, his holding was his only salvation. Chip demonstrated he was Greb's master at everything in the fighting game.[27]

-New Castle Herald

The fight was really just a four-round affair, and they were the first four rounds at that. From then on Mr. Greb proved to be the "bear", and his clinging tactics during the last six rounds so provoked those who had put up real money that they wandered away from the building much displeased.[28]

-New Castle News

Despite such negative press Greb and his fans maintained their sunny outlook. Several hundred of these rooters had made the journey to New Castle to cheer Greb against Chip. Such a show of support from his fans meant a great deal to Greb and he took the opportunity to express his feelings on the subject in print little more than a week after his bout with Chip. "They're the kind of fellows anybody could be proud to have pulling for him. ...My friends have been criticized once or twice for their show of enthusiasm at my bouts, and I want to correct a wrong impression concerning them. They are not rough fellows. Take them singly and you won't find one of them who is not a gentleman. They let their enthusiasm carry them away when they get together, and for this reason have come to be labeled my 'gang,' but they're all fine fellows."[29]

After lasting the distance with Chip, Mason issued the announcement that he was willing to match Greb with any fighter in the country (a statement that New Castle papers scoffed at).[30] As a postscript, Chip made the long journey to Australia to face the young middleweight challenger Les Darcy. Chip did well in the early rounds, rushing Darcy around the ring and landing powerful swings to the head and body. By the sixth round Chip was clearly distressed at Darcy's ability to absorb punishment with little effect. With Chip rapidly tiring Darcy began unloading with his own heavy punches and in the ninth round a bloody and swollen Chip was battered to the canvas for the ten-count.

While Chip was still making plans for his invasion of Australia, Red Mason had decided to end the feud in his stable. On July 25 Greb was matched with rival and former friend Al Grayber for a match at the Penn Avenue Power House on August 7. Mason no doubt agonized over the decision to match two of his most promising fighters. It had become apparent to Mason that he could not continue to manage both fighters effectively. The bout would be a sort

After defeating Harry Geb in a no-decision match in June of 1916 George Chip ventured to Australia for a lucrative showdown with Les Darcy. After putting up a game battle for five rounds Chip was worn down and stopped in the ninth round. Chip is seen here being helped to his corner by his seconds and Darcy after the knockout.

of elimination and the loser would be expected to find a new manager. Greb was helped in his training by Walter Monaghan who hoped to get a match with the winner. Greb laid bare his desire for a knockout victory over his former friend, once again evoking his knockout victory over Kid Manuel. "A good stiff poke on the jaw will tumble Al Grayber just as quickly as it'll make any other man flop. I never heard that he was an iron man, and if I reach his chin as cleanly as I reached Kid Manuel's, he'll go."[31] Grayber trained in private at Esplen forsaking media interviews and even the advice of his estranged manager.

In the days leading up to the fight both men argued incessantly. They bickered about who would get the services of Red Mason. They bickered about weight (despite the fact that the bout was to be held at catch weights). Both fighters finally agreed to wager their entire percentage on the outcome, essentially making the fight a winner take all proposition.[32] For Mason's part he elected to stay neutral. He would watch the match as an impartial observer seated in press row. Grayber would be seconded by his brother Red Grayber and Joe Keally. Greb would be seconded by Walter Monaghan.

Despite stifling summer heat the Penn Avenue Power House was packed to the rafters the night of August 7 for the final chapter in the feud between Greb and Grayber. Anticipating trouble from the rabid fans of both fighters there was a large contingent of police on hand to see that the fighting didn't boil over into the stands. At the sound of the bell both fighters rushed to the center of the ring and slammed into each other with such gusto that it became readily apparent that all of the finer points of the skill of boxing would be forgotten. Grayber, using his greater size, quickly forced Greb to the ropes bending him over the top rope so violently that Greb's feet were lifted off the floor. Referee Joe Donnelly came between the fighters before Greb could be toppled out of the ring and immediately warned Grayber for his tactics.

Grayber's foul tactics continued throughout the fight and more than once it looked as if the referee would award the fight to Greb on a disqualification. Such was the case in the second round when Grayber seized hold of Greb's head with both gloves and squeezed with all of his might. The crowd let out a roar of disapproval and Grayber was sent to his corner while Greb recovered. Such tactics aside Greb was clearly the speedier fighter while Grayber seemed to realize this and pinned all of his hopes for victory on one big punch to end matters inside the distance. The third and fourth rounds saw the boxers settle down to a more scientific approach with less roughhouse tactics than previous. The fifth saw a return by Grayber to his illegal tactics and more warnings of disqualification. With the sounding of the sixth and final round Greb rushed from his corner as fresh as the first round and battered Grayber around the ring for fully one minute. This seemed to take much of the fight out of Grayber and for the next minute Greb was clearly in control. In the final minute of this final round Grayber sensed the fight slipping away and tried as best he could to catch Greb without result.

The fans and reporters were unanimous in that the fight lived up to it's grudge match billing but felt it seemed better suited for a

Al Grayber was one of Pittsburgh's most respected fighters and would eventually become one of Pittsburgh sports' elder statesmen. When he faced former friend and sparring partner Harry Greb in a 1916 grudge match a place in Red Mason's stable was on the line.

wrestling mat than a boxing ring. The newspapers that did not award the decision to Greb gave him no worse than a draw and with that Al Grayber lost the bet, his purse, and his manager.[33]

With his stable now down to one middleweight Red Mason wasted no time in filling Greb's fight card. Within a week of Greb's victory over Grayber Mason had committed Greb to fight in Cumberland, Maryland as soon as a suitable opponent could be found. Shortly thereafter Greb was signed to face Erie middleweight Jerry Cole. Cole had made himself popular in Pittsburgh over the past year by facing such men as Tommy Gavigan, Al Rogers, and Whitey Wenzel. Greb and Cole had been introduced in late March of 1915, prior to Cole's bout with Al Rogers. Sticking his hand out to greet Cole, Greb smiled, "Gee, you're too good looking to be a fighter. You're even better looking than myself."[34] From this point on both fighters periodically discussed a match with each other through the press. They would finally meet on August 28.

Cole was a powerfully built middleweight who relied on speed, ring savvy, and a flicking left jab. Realizing this Greb got down to work in the fierce August heat in hopes of shedding the extra weight he had put on to cope with the larger Al Grayber. Cole had made it well known that he intended to eschew the idea of going for a knockout, instead he would hope to build up a points lead with his rapier like left jab and take a popular decision. Greb would need to fight speed with speed and so he was up before the sun doing miles of roadwork, hiking during the day, and spent the afternoons in a steamy gym. With the fight nearing Greb was confident of his condition. "I'm in better shape now than I ever was in my life. The little extra weight

Jerry Cole was the middleweight champion of Erie, Pennsylvania when he faced Greb in the summer of 1916. Cole possessed an educated left jab and an abundance of speed. He had fought in Pittsburgh on several occasions to favorable reviews, making a match between he and Greb a natural.

I carried into the ring against Grayber is gone. I figured I'd need it in that scrap -and I did. But against Cole it would be a handicap, so I worked it off. I'm going after Cole at the crack of the bell, and I'm going to keep after him until I catch him and measure him."[35]

During the first minute of the bout Greb's training paid off. A slashing right hand broke through Cole's guard crashing into his jaw, and sending him head first to the floor with a thump. For a moment it looked as if Cole would go the same way as his townsman Kid Manuel. However he was able to get to his knees and was up at the count of nine. In this instance Greb made a rookie mistake and ruined his chances for an early knockout. He rushed Cole wildly and in his excitement missed punch after punch. When the round ended Cole was still on his feet. Despite Cole's success in beating the referee's count and finishing the round the bout was effectively over with that single right hand. From that point on Cole made little effort to stave off Greb's attack. The fight followed a similar pattern round after round as Greb leapt at Cole pouring in punch after punch only to find himself locked in an embrace, Cole's only hope of finishing the fight. In the final round Greb had Cole helpless and as the young fighter from Erie's hands dropped to his sides time and again the crowd could only believe that Greb was allowing Cole the honor of finishing the fight on his feet. At the close of the fight Cole made a feeble show of leaping over the top rope and leaving the arena, beaten though he was.[36]

One week later Harry Greb and Fay Keiser resumed their rivalry at Cumberland. Upon entering the ring Greb bowed to his admiring fans and with the tap of the gong commenced to dishing out a one-sided beating to his old rival. Keiser simply could not cope with Greb's rapidly developing speed. While leaping in and out of range Greb beat a tattoo upon Keiser's face leaving a swollen bloody mess.[37]

The Cumberland fans were so impressed with Greb's domination of Keiser that he was immediately asked back for a bout with Young Herman Miller of Baltimore. The bout, which was initially scheduled for September 26 and then subsequently moved up to September 19, nearly fell through when Greb was stricken ill with what was described only as an "infectious ailment." The promoters quickly substituted Allentown Jackie Clark in Greb's place and salvaged the card with the hope that Greb would face the winner.

As Greb convalesced Red Mason was busy making plans for his charge. Based on the strength of his wins over Jerry Cole and Kid Manuel Greb was signed to face Willie "Knockout" Brennen in Erie as soon as promoter Pete Young could secure a reasonable date. Mason had also secured George "Knockout" Brown the Chicago Greek, and Harry "KO" Baker to fill future dates with Greb in the Penn Avenue Power House. Far more exciting was the news that Red Mason had negotiated with Tom S. Andrews, Milwaukee promoter and American representative for Australian promoter Snowy Baker, to have Mason chaperone a group of fighters, including Greb, on a trip to Australia. The ultimate goal of the proposed journey would be a match between Greb and Les Darcy. The trip was scheduled to take place the following spring and stay through September, capitalizing on the cooler weather that Australia experiences during the summer months of North America.[38]

By early October Greb was ready to fight and anxious to fulfill his obligation to box at Cumberland. To this end Greb agreed to meet Allentown Jackie Clark in Lonaconing on October 16. Clark was a fast and clever middleweight who had faced many of the same opponents as Greb. A more evenly matched pair of fighters could not be hoped for. Clark, like Greb, had heard the stories of easy money in Australia, and like Greb, Clark had planned a journey Down Under in the near future. In fact the bout with Greb would be Clark's last bout before

Picturesque Lonaconing, Maryland, nestled in the Allegheny mountains, played host to a handful of Harry Greb's bouts in the 1910's. His first bout with Jackie Clark, fought at the Lonaconing Armory in October 1916, was voted by ringsiders as the greatest ever staged.

leaving for Australia. A loss might not prevent a journey by Clark to Australia but it would certainly devalue his stock among the promoters there.

On the night of the 16th the six hundred odd fans that had turned out to see Harry Greb and Jackie Clark do battle left more exhausted than the fighters. The fight, hailed by witnesses as the greatest ever staged, more than made up for Greb's cancelled bout with Herman Miller. Clark's strategy was to stand off and box Greb at long range, a strategy which quickly fell apart in the face of Greb's attack. Clark was forced to stand and fight every minute of every round. Greb constantly pressed the action, rushing into Clark with both fists pumping. Clark countered Greb's rushes with accurate punching that did little to slow Greb. Only in the seventh round did Clark gain a brief amount of respect from Greb when he landed a perfectly timed left hook which found its mark on the point of Greb's chin. Greb froze for an instant and then fought back harder than ever. After ten rounds the fight was judged a draw on the basis that Clark's greater accuracy had been equal to the aggression of Greb.[39]

Greb returned to Pittsburgh without a scratch and eager to begin training for his upcoming bout with Harry "KO" Baker the following week and another with Knockout Sweeney of New York two weeks after that. The Baker and Sweeney bouts would serve as warm-ups for his Erie bout with Willie Brennan, a bout which would change his career. Brennan hailed from Buffalo, New York, one of the great fight towns of this era, and Brennan was Buffalo's most popular fighter. A victory over Brennan might lead to a more lucrative return bout in Buffalo and more importantly much greater publicity from the larger media outlets.

Harry Baker proved easy for Greb. By the end of the contest Baker had suffered a badly cut and swollen eye and only by his great determination did he finish the fight on his feet.[40] The bout with Knockout Sweeney proved too close for comfort with an important bout against Brennan in the offing. After a sluggish first round Sweeney seemed all at sea against the raging Greb. The opening stanza was so one sided that it prompted Red Mason, ever the heckler to shout "Oy, Greb, what for you want to knock him out in one round? Then they'll say he's a bum and I ought for to be hung. Oy, Harry, don't do it!"[41]

During this opening round Sweeney seemed to sag under the weight of Greb's rushes when suddenly a fan in the stands shouted that Sweeney was a "quitter." This enraged the New York middleweight. As if waking from a slumber he fought back furiously. Between rounds Mason and Greb argued furiously in the corner. It soon became apparent to the crowd that in trying for a knockout Greb had broken his right hand, an injury which could prevent the Brennan bout and lose for Mason the appearance forfeit posted in Erie.

Sweeney took control of the fight in the second and third rounds by hammering Greb viciously to the body. Over and over his blows would land on Greb's ribs with a thud. Meanwhile Greb refused to use his injured right hand and by the end of the third round he had weakened tremendously. Mason had changed his tune after the first round shouting comically "Oy, look at his ears; get away from that stuff, Harry. Say, why didn't you take him quick like I told you? Oy, what a rough boy that Sweeney is!"[42]

Greb got an even break in the fourth using all of his guile, cleverly feinting with his near useless right and then whipping across left hooks. In the fifth Greb was desperate. He began to put his right into action, looping it instead of shooting it straight from the shoulder. By this means he was able to score and on one occasion he landed the blow with such force on Sweeney's ear that the New Yorker was turned completely around. In this round

Knockout Sweeney, the experienced New York middleweight, gave Red Mason a scare when he gave Greb all he could handle in a 6 round bout at the Penn Avenue Power House. What was supposed to be a tuneup became a dramatic struggle when Greb broke his hand in the first round.

Greb had evened the fight. The sixth was the most dramatic round as Greb rushed from his corner throwing hooks and clumsy right hands. Whenever Sweeney tried to break these rushes by clinching Greb would shove him off and continue his assault. At the bell both fighters were exhausted but it was Greb who came away the victor by a narrow, one round margin.[43]

After the Sweeney bout it was decided that the Brennan fight was far too important to cancel. Instead Greb began an intensive series of treatments with a local physician in order to mend his injured hand enough to get him through ten rounds with Brennan.[44]

Greb would need all of the help he could get in his coming bout at Erie. It wasn't a coincidence that Brennan was such a fan favorite in a fight town like Buffalo. He was an extremely strong fighter with a wicked punch. Brennan had faced the stiffest competition available in the middleweight division including such stellar names as Jimmy Clabby, Mike and Tommy Gibbons, Jack Dillon, and George Chip. Fans loved Brennan for his all-action style bolstered by his tremendous stamina. If Greb was to keep this rugged German in check he would have to be healthy.

The eyes of western Pennsylvania and western New York were on the Park Opera House in Erie the night of November 8, 1916. Fans from both Pittsburgh and Buffalo were present to cheer their favorite son. Both camps felt that it would be a rattling good bout but that their man would eventually emerge victorious. When Greb and Mason arrived in Erie that night they were no less confident. "I understand that Brennan has had some great fights in Buffalo," said Greb. "I predict that his bout tonight will be the greatest he has ever been in."[45] Speaking of Greb's chances Mason stated "He can take care of himself against any man in the world. Greb is in excellent shape and will make the best of this opportunity to get in right with Erie fans."[46]

William Brenner, AKA Willie "KO" Brennan was the favorite scion of Buffalo, New York's ample boxing community. He boasted a wealth of experience, a powerful punch, and an all-action crowd pleasing style. If Greb could show well against Brennan in Erie he would arouse interest in a lucrative showcase fight in Buffalo.

The fight began in a rather tame manner given the reputation of the two fighters for aggressive battling. As they squared off they both seemed to have a great deal of respect for one another. Suddenly Greb lashed out with his right hand.

The punch snapped straight from Greb's shoulder and crashed upon Brennan's jaw. Down went Brennan with a thud. Everyone except Greb was stunned by the suddenness of the attack and its result. Even referee Billy Bell missed his opportunity to toll a count while Brennan scrambled to his feet. As Brennan rose from the canvas his expression betrayed that he was the most surprised body in the house. Greb rushed his man in an effort to end the bout early but Brennan was able to stave this attack and fight back with vigor to hear the end of the round.

Greb continually forced Brennan around the ring with his incessant attack and continued his winning ways through the fourth round. If Harry thought Brennan was a beaten man he was sorely mistaken. In the fifth round Brennan switched his attack to Greb's body and suddenly the tide changed. Brennan started to take control with an aggressive, two fisted body attack that had Greb hanging on. In the sixth Greb showed that he was unwilling to let this opportunity slip past him. It was in this moment that Greb decided he would be something more than a Pennsylvania club fighter. He burst from his corner and fought Brennan around the ring. The fight was again in Greb's pocket and it stayed that way through the ninth round.

At the start of the tenth and final round the fighters emerged from their corners for the customary handshake. When this formality was done Greb moved in, sending rights and lefts aimed at Brennan's jaw. Greb was trying to punctuate his performance with a knockout. Brennan could do little but cover up under the assault and that is where he stayed until the final bell rang ending the fight. As the large crowd that had packed itself into the Opera House filed out they cheered and shouted Greb's name with delight.[47] Thus ended Greb's great victory over Willie "KO" Brennan a fight which signaled a turning point in his storied career.

7

BREAKOUT

With their hero defeated, Buffalo fight fans were eager to get a look at Harry Greb, and if possible to see a rematch of the Erie bout. Brennan himself was skeptical as to whether Mason would let Greb in the ring with him again. "If he does," Said Brennan "I'll gamble that Allie (Brennan's manager) will make room on the schedule for him, no matter what time he picks."[1] The Queensberry Athletic Club immediately made Greb a generous offer to appear in the city against his choice of Brennan, Buck Crouse, or Kid Wagner. Despite Brennan's thoughts to the contrary Mason wanted nothing more than for Greb to appear in Buffalo against Buffalo's favorite fighter. Two days after defeating Brennan in Erie Greb was signed for a rematch at Buffalo's Broadway Auditorium. It was the chance Mason and Greb had been waiting for, an opportunity for Greb to breakout of the Pittsburgh boxing scene and show his wares in a city that could springboard him to national prominence. Such motives were laid bare in a letter Red Mason sent to the Buffalo Courier:

Sporting Editor, Courier:

Dear Sir: - There need be no uncertainty about my quick acceptance of the proposal that I let Greb meet Knockout Brennan again in Buffalo on November 17. There are two reasons why I am eager for such a match. One is that Greb licked Brennan to the queen's taste in Erie last Wednesday and is certain as a man can be that he has Brennan's number and can repeat any time he meets him. The other reason is that I have been desirous of showing Greb before your people, for once Buffalo has seen him he will be in demand over any of the other middleweights, and after we defeat Brennan in Buffalo we will not shirk an encounter with any of them...

...We have been trying for a Buffalo crack at Brennan for a long time and I think Buffalo will be satisfied we know what we are doing in taking on your champion in his home town.

Yours truly

JAMES R. MASON

Manager of Harry Greb, Pittsburgh's best middleweight.[2]

The card was an attractive one. In addition to the Greb-Brennan headliner it would feature Tommy Burke against Kid Wagner, and three other lesser bouts. The match was squeezed into the busy schedules of Greb and Brennan each of whom already had several bouts scheduled in the near future. Brennan had fights scheduled against Jack McCarron in Dayton, Ohio November 10, and Frankie Brennan in Windsor, Ontario November 15, while Greb had a fifteen round rematch scheduled against Jackie Clark in Lonaconing, Maryland November 14.

The match with Clark was highly anticipated by fans in the Cumberland area. The previous match between Greb and Clark had aroused such interest that the upcoming fifteen round decision bout was sure to exceed the proceeds garnered by the first match. The two fighters were to weigh in at 160 pounds ringside and it was hoped that former champion Frank Klaus would referee the bout as an added attraction.[3] Both fighters were eager for a more decisive conclusion in this match and Greb especially was predicting a knockout. Fay Keiser announced he would be ringside for the bout in order to challenge the winner.

On the evening of November 14 Clark and Greb were introduced to the hundreds of fans present at Lonaconing's Armory. The weights were announced as being the contracted 160 pounds for each fighter. After preliminary instructions the fight was on. The two men met in the middle of the ring and commenced to tear into each other as if continuing where they left off in their first bout. The action in the first round was furious and few present felt the fight would see the conclusion of the fifteenth round. Greb, knowing that Clark couldn't hurt him bore in taking punishment in order to land his heavier blows. In the second round he began landing thunderous body blows which quickly began to tell on Clark. Near the end of the round Greb battered Clark across the ring and while in a neutral corner shot a terrific straight right to the solar plexus which paralyzed the Allentown fighter and sent him to his knees. Clark beat the count and before Greb could press his

Greb's rematch with Jackie Clark would take on the form of a grudge match by the time the two boxers entered the ring, with both men looking for a knock-out.

advantage the bell rang ending the round. With the bell signaling round three Greb was on Clark in an instant. Blow after blow landed on Clark's mid-section and as his opponent's guard dropped. Greb put over a right hand to the jaw which sent Clark sprawling face first to the floor, his head hanging sickeningly over the edge of the ring, and his entire body quivering in an unconscious stupor. The referee could have counted to 100, it wouldn't have mattered, the fight was over and the crowd went wild over the sensational victory.

The following day's issue of the Cumberland Times offered what was probably the only description possible of such a dramatic knockout.

> **It did not require the decision of the referee to declare the winner of the scheduled fifteen round bout last night at Lonaconing between Harry Greb of Pittsburgh, and Jackie Clarke of Allentown, and the crowd of several hundred fistic fans who attended the boxing show, was not inclined to stand around in little groups and argue for the rights and wrongs of their favorite after the fight. Harry Greb, the Pittsburgh bearcat settled once and for all times as to where honors belong when he crushed the Allentown pugilist under his powerful strength in the third round the way a cat would crush a mouse between her paws...**
>
> **...The referee kneeled at his side and tolled off the seconds directly into his ear but it is doubtful if he heard a sound. While all of this was going on Greb stood off a short distance looking down upon his victim with an air of "now who do you think is the best man."**[4]

When the referee had signaled a conclusion to the bout Greb walked over, picked Clark off the mat and carried him to his corner where it took several minutes to revive him. It was fully twenty minutes before Clark got his bearings. As Clark was being administered to, the cheering crowd stormed the ring, held Greb aloft, and carried him from the arena.

Willie Brennan did his part in preparing for the rematch as well when he came through bouts with Frankie Brennan and Jack McCarron unscathed. The stage was now set for a showdown in Buffalo and the ballyhoo had already begun. Middleweights across the Midwest were angling for a match with the winner and the promise of future lucrative matches was on the minds of both Greb and Mason. "We wouldn't have taken Brennan on again so shortly after having beaten him in Erie," said Mason "but we expect to be given consideration with Gibbons, Miske and the best of the middleweights."[5]

Brennan was far more interested in revenge than the promise of glory or financial reward. Something about the beating he had received at the hands of Greb had flipped a switch in his head; he was now almost fanatical in his drive to reverse the loss. Speaking of Brennan's bout in Ontario and the upcoming match with Greb Allie Smith said "Kayo came through alright in Windsor and will be in apple order for Greb. That's all I've got to say and Brennan doesn't want to say anything more either. You know he felt pretty sore over that Erie meeting with Greb and he is burning up with hope to reverse the tables on the Pittsburgher here Friday night."[6] Brennan added, "I never talk before a fight, but Greb is one man I want to beat. I won't alibi myself for the shade he won over me, but I'll reverse it Friday night or break a leg trying. Just keep your eye on me."[7]

With the talk completed, it was now time to fight. After Tommy Burke of St. Louis had stopped Kid Wagner in the eighth round of the final bout of a wildly entertaining undercard, Greb and Brennan were ready to decide whether or not Erie was a fluke. As the fight commenced Brennan tried to change his usually aggressive style by standing off and boxing at long range, this tactic proved fruitless as Greb would not be denied. He tore into his Buffalo rival with such fury that it set the fans in the Auditorium wild. Round after round Greb's attack grew more furious with a pace so blistering that one could hardly expect him to retain his strength. Yet, instead of weakening, Greb gained strength and speed as the fight progressed. In the first round Greb landed a right to the chin that nearly upset Brennan. By the third and fourth rounds Brennan looked to be solving Greb's awkward, aggressive style. It was merely the case of a fighter trying to keep his head above water. By round seven Greb had matters completely under control and after forcing Brennan into a corner, battered his adversary to the body and head so violently that Brennan's hometown fans now hoped only for the moral victory of finishing on his feet. From the seventh to the closing round Greb was a tornado of action, as his strength grew so did his lead. By the final bell there was no question as to the fact that Greb was the victor.

Greb was now a sensation in Buffalo.

A new middleweight sensation, a fighting tornado with all the wonderful strength, stamina, and hitting power that goes with youth and brains, was sprung on Buffalo fight fans last night in the person of Harry Greb of Pittsburgh, who outfought, outslugged, and fairly won from Knockout Brennan in the big match of a sensational bill of boxing at the Auditorium last night.[8]

Buffalo fight fans and the promoters of the Queensberry Athletic Club were so impressed by the young Pittsburgher that before he even left the arena he was signed to face Tommy Burke one week later. "Remember I said we'd beat Brennan for you," answered Mason "and then all the other champions Buffalo can produce. And if we get by Burke safely, you can't get one too hard for us."

"Jack Dillon?" asked Charley Murray, Queensberry Club matchmaker.

"Righto!" Shot back Mason. "Our boy."

"Well," answered Murray "we'll try to get Jack for the winner of the Greb-Burke bout."[9]

Burke, who had come to Buffalo from St. Louis looking for bigger purses and more public-

IN THE EARLY ROUNDS BRENNAN
FORCED GREB TO ACCEPT A LARGE
NUMBER OF SNAPPY LEFT JABS —

GREB'S MOST TELLING
BLOWS WERE — THOSE LEFT AND RIGHT
KICKS TO BRENNAN'S TUMMY —

Contemporary cartoon drawn ringside at the rematch between Harry Greb and Willie "KO" Brennan.

ity, had fallen under the management of Allie Smith. As a stablemate of Willie Brennan it was hoped that Burke would avenge his training partner and defeat Greb. "Tommy," said Smith "will give Greb what Brennan could not give him tonight, and the old Kayo is not done yet."[10] It was hoped that Burke's greater size would play a role in Greb's downfall. Burke wasn't as polished a fighter as Brennan but he had been in the ring with tough fighters such as Battling Levinsky, Jack McCarron, Frank Mantell, and Len Rowlands. He liked to boast that he never wore protective hand wraps and despite this fact had never damaged his hands. He had a powerful straight right and his over-all skills had greatly improved within the last year due to his work as a sparring partner for Packey McFarland in the latter's training camp for his bout with Mike Gibbons. It was said that McFarland helped Burke to better judge distance and take opportunities in his opponent's weaknesses.[11] While Burke could stand a lot of punishment he had two major faults which could spell trouble against a fighter of Greb's unique talents, he was a slow starter and wasn't particularly quick with his hands or feet.

With KO Brennan sparring and wrestling daily with Tommy Burke, Allie Smith was confident that his stable would regain its honor. When told that gamblers had installed Greb as a betting favorite Smith chuckled "Have they? Those birds never quit trying... The best plan to my way of thinking is to copper every bet they make. Burke may surprise 'em."[12]

Greb arrived in Buffalo on November 22 amid speculation that the winner would face jack

Dillon, champion Al McCoy, Battling Levinsky, or Jeff Smith, a fight with any of these boxers would bring a handsome prize. Greb put in light training at the First Ward Athletic Club before a large crowd of onlookers eager to get a peek at the Pittsburgh marvel. As the night of the fight arrived anticipation was at a fever pitch but suddenly terrible news arrived which threatened the entire show. Burke received word from St. Louis that his older brother, William, had been killed in an accident.[13] Burke was shattered but realized that he could be of no help to the family. He elected to stay and fight it out.

Laboring under such an emotional handicap, it is a wonder Burke finished the fight on his feet. In many ways the fight was over before it had time to begin. Within seconds of the opening of the first round Burke was backed into the ropes and forced to exchange vicious punches in an attempt to gain respect from his attacking opponent. Greb took advantage of the openings in Burke's defense and slammed a powerful left hook into Burke's jaw. Before Burke knew what had happened he was listening to the roar of the crowd from a seated position. Burke was up at the count of eight but still suffering from the stupefying effects of a punch he never saw coming. For the entire remainder of the round Greb battered Burke from one end of the ring to the next. The crowd was on its feet calling for a knockout but Burke would not go down.

It took Burke two rounds to recover and by the fourth and fifth he was again trading furiously. By the sixth Greb had things all his own way and only by being over-eager did he miss his chance for a knockout. After one minute of milling in the tenth round Greb again exploded with a left to Burke's jaw and the St. Louis battler went down. Burke, despite having suffered severe punishment, refused to stay down. Upon regaining his feet Greb pounced. Burke went down twice more and twice more he rose. This final round was now becoming a battle of wills with Greb determined to smash the fighting heart of Burke, and Burke determined to hear the final bell.

With a minute left in the round, and the clock ticking down, Greb rushed Burke to the ropes and let fly a looping right hand. It landed flush on the already wobbly fighter and Burke tumbled out of the ring and into the press row. Just as the crowd was declaring the fight over Burke pulled himself to his feet and struggled back into the ring before

Tommy Burke (Above) was a St. Louis club fighter. He came to Buffalo, like Greb, looking for wider publicity.

referee Dick Nugent could reach the count of ten. Burke may not have won the fight but he certainly won the hearts of Buffalo fans for they cheered this exhibition of uncommon bravery in the face of defeat. Down again went Burke under the blazing fists of Greb and the crowd hushed to a whisper. Slowly Burke regained his footing and when erect the crowd went wild yelling "*RING THE BELL!*" in hopes that their man would last the distance. Burke wrapped his limp arms around the onrushing Greb and held on with what little strength he had left. The bell sounded, he had won his moral victory, and the crowd gave him an ovation the likes of which few men on the losing end of a fight have ever received. [14]

Greb returned to Pittsburgh the next morning to prepare for a six round bout with George "KO" Brown the Chicago Greek. Brown's chief claim to fame was his durability and the fact that in two bouts he had gone forty rounds with Les Darcy while giving a good account of himself, no mean feat. In the first round after his dynamo rushes broke upon Brown's resilient guard Greb changed his tactics. He circled and hopped about Brown popping a left jab into the rugged battler's face. Whenever Brown was able to get close Greb followed his jab with a whipping right hand and then rushed Brown with a two-fisted attack. Before Brown could retaliate Greb would dance out of range and resume stabbing his opponent dizzy with his left. It was an easy win for Greb and one in which it was becoming readily apparent that he was beginning to meld his natural aggressiveness with blinding speed to produce a near seamless offense and defense. His style wasn't polished yet but the young Pittsburgher was definitely improving. [15]

After his easy defeat of Knockout Brown, Greb submitted to a minor operation on one of his ears which had the effect of keeping him from fighting or training for no less than two weeks. While Greb was recuperating from his surgery, and no doubt enjoying a bit of rest and relax-

JUST 8 SECONDS AFTER THE FIRST BELL GREB SPILLED BURKE WITH A VICIOUS LEFT HOOK TO JAW —

IN THE 18TH RD — GREB DUMPED BURKE INTO THE TRENCH - AND THE HARP CAME BACK FOR MORE

Burkes remarkable showing of courage in the face of physical and emotional distress was immortalised in this contemporary cartoon drawn ringside at the fight. Burke not only had to contend with the formidable Greb, but also the news that his brother had been killed days earlier in an accident.

ation, Red Mason and Buffalo promoters were negotiating to have Greb face either Bob Moha or Allie Smith's fighter and former Greb stablemate Buck Crouse. With their past history still heavy on his mind Mason nixed Crouse as an opponent in an effort to prevent Crouse from making any money with Greb. Instead, Moha was elected as Greb's next opponent, a match which was guaranteed to bring Greb more national attention than a bout with Crouse.

Initially Pittsburgh was willing to outbid Buffalo for the bout but smoky city promoters wanted the fight held on Christmas day. Greb's family pressured him to spend Christmas at home with his sisters. This, in addition to Greb's usual adherence to the doctrine of refraining from training or fighting on the Sabbath and religious holidays, convinced him to take less money in order to participate in the fight the day after Christmas in Buffalo.[16]

Moha was no easy proposition. In fact many were calling this Greb's toughest test to date. Dubbed the Milwaukee Caveman, because of his incredibly powerful build and short stature, Moha was feared by fighters all the way up to the heavyweight division. Huge slabs of muscle encased his squat frame and as far as anyone knew he had never been knocked out. For at least six years, since he gave phenom Jimmy Clabby a pasting, he had been fighting the best fighters in the country. He was known throughout the country as a tough and dangerous fighter, willing to take punishment in order to land his own damaging blows. Moha was fresh from a campaign in New York City where he had lost a newspaper decision to the streaking Billy Miske and beaten Bartley Madden as well as the huge heavyweight Joe Cox.

Mason hoped that a win over Moha would garner Greb attention in New York City and push his fighter into position for a possible showdown with Les Darcy, the Australian wunderkind whose rumored journey to the United States had sunk Mason's plans for a trip to the Antipodes. With such goals in mind Mason cancelled an upcoming bout in Scranton against Jimmy Fryer so that Greb might focus all of his attention on Moha.[17]

Greb wasn't the only one who had a lot riding on the outcome of this bout. Moha himself was looking for a championship and was scheduled to face Jack Dillon on New Year's Day. A win over Greb would only help his cause if he were to beat Dillon and demand more lucrative bouts against men such as Darcy, Levinsky, or McCoy. Another interested spectator would be Willie Brennan, still harboring an almost fanatical desire to avenge his two losses to Greb. "I won't attempt to name the winner," said Brennan "but I do know that I want Greb again and for that reason will be pulling for him. I don't want any cave man punching at me."[18]

As an example of how serious Moha was taking the bout he set up training quarters in a lumber camp in Neenah, Wisconsin. He worked daily with the lumberjacks. "I am doing the 'back to nature' stunt" wrote Bob "for I am up against a pair of tough ones in my holiday bouts. I don't know of any other boxer in the country taking on such tough birds as Harry Greb and Jack Dillon within a week's time. Therefore your Uncle Dudley is putting in his best licks."[19]

If excitement in the match hadn't already reached a fever pitch then it certainly did when news arrived that Les Darcy had arrived in New York City after a controversial exodus from his native Australia. Amid growing pressure from his countrymen to join the military and support the war effort Darcy quietly left Australia as a stowaway aboard the *Hattie Luckenbach*. After changing ships at the first port of call Darcy arrived in New York 6 weeks after his clandestine departure.

Boxing fans across the country were eager for peak at the Maitland Wonder. His pugilistic exploits in the Antipodes had set the boxing world alight and the American public had to see for themselves if the man who had defeated George Chip, Eddie McGoorty, and Jimmy Clabby was all he was cracked up to be. Promoters, managers, and matchmakers from all corners of the nation were trying to curry favor with the young Australian. Fighters from welterweight to heavyweight were lining up for a match against him while dreaming of the riches that such a money-spinning bout could bring. Greb and Moha were not immune to such allure and neither was the Queensberry Athletic Club. Charlie Murray immediately sent a dispatch to Les Darcy offering him a bout with the winner of the Greb-Moha affair and it was against this backdrop that the two fighters met on December 26, 1916.

It had been three years almost to the day since Harry Greb was knocked out by Joe Chip on one of Bob Moha's undercards and here he was stepping into the ring with the man himself. Greb was outweighed fully six and one half pounds by the Cave Man and in his dressing room this seemed to worry Greb a bit, he admitted it was a handicap.[20] Upon entering the arena the bout was delayed shortly when Greb was found to be wearing heavy bicycle tape beneath the gauze encasing his hands,[21] a practice frowned upon today but not universally forbidden in those days. After several minutes of removing the tape the bout began. Greb smiled as though

Bob Moha (above) was a veritable iron man. He was possessed of a body armored in muscle which presented a formidable sight when staring across the ring at opponents. He was an experienced and ferocious battler who could take a punch as well as give one.

he were about to take a second helping of Christmas dinner as he came out of his corner. He dazzled Moha with his speed and footwork. He cut in and out, whipping long lefts to the face ever mindful of Moha's own powerful punches. Greb had learned to gauge distance better and was now keeping Moha at the end of his reach. It was Greb who dictated the pace of the fight.

It was Greb who was laying traps for Moha and then springing into action. When Moha would invite Greb to trade Greb obliged using his quicker hands to befuddle Moha with blinding flurries of punches. To the surprise of all Greb even out-muscled Moha, shoving him back when Moha worked in close and with his opponent off balance he would leap in with a volley of punches.

Greb showed another new trick that he had not exhibited before; he continually used his left to touch and tap Moha off balance, twisting the Milwaukee fighter ever so slightly so that his punches were robbed of their full effect. When Moha succeeded at working his way inside Greb would tie his shorter opponent up in an iron grip and then dance out of danger once the referee had broken the clinch. Moha was dangerous at all times, swinging bombs that spelled "knockout" if landed. Whenever one of these swished harmlessly through the air the crowd "oohed" and ahhed" in wonder at what might happen had the blow connected.

Greb was now seeing everything that Moha was doing. When Moha was able to land Greb was ready with a snappy counter. Greb rarely got hit with the same punch twice. He was putting on a masterful display of fighting against one of the most respected men in the ring. In the eighth round Greb landed a solid overhand right that opened a cut under Moha's left eye and started it swelling. Moments later another right hand split open Moha's cauliflower ear and blood began to cascade down Bob's shoulder. By the tenth Greb was beginning to tire from the whirlwind pace he had set but the lead he had piled up was so great that only a knockout could upset his victory, a knockout which never came.[22]

"I didn't do so bad, did I?"[23] Said Greb, with a grin spreading from ear to ear. The Buffalo Courier didn't

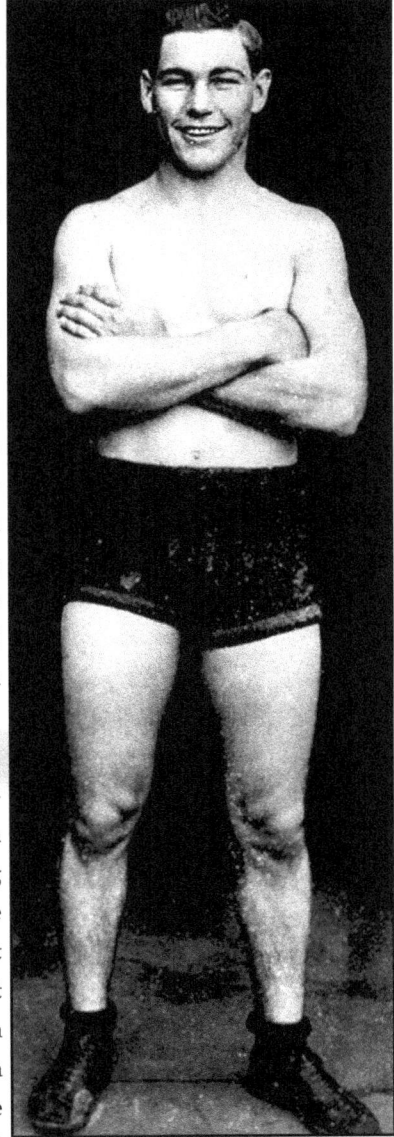

When Les Darcy (above) landed in the United States it created a sensation throughout the sport. Everyone wanted a piece of the financial bonanza that his bouts would create, Harry Greb and Bob Moha included.

seem to think so.

> Greb couldn't have planned a better style of beating Moha if he had reduced the matter to arithmetical precision. The short, powerful, terrifying figure before him was dangerous every second. Moha was about as harmless looking as a stick of dynamite. His power was shown with several punches that did not land, as much as those that did. Blows that won him his rep as a hitter were plentifully shown, but when Bob showed them Greb was somewhere else.[24]

"I knew I had to work fast with a tough hitter like Moha and granted I tired a bit on account of the pace, I won just as I had figured, and I'm satisfied. How that man can hit! No wonder he beats heavyweights. Two of his punches to my ribs made me think he had thrust his hand right through me."[25]

Moha and Greb both left Buffalo a day apart in order to train for their respective New Year's Day bouts. Moha had intended to train in Buffalo for his bout with Jack Dillon but, incensed at the unanimous newspaper decisions against him, he promptly took his business elsewhere, it no doubt added insult to injury that even his own manager admitted that Greb was the better man.[26] Greb would be facing Joe Borrell who two years earlier had given Greb such a bad beating. The match was scheduled for six rounds without a decision and Greb was eager for a more decisive showing than their rematch of 1915. "Joe Borrell's the chap that broke my nose and gave me the only disfigurement I've received in the ring," said Greb. "That's why I'm going to clean him up on Monday."[27]

Clean up he did, for Greb dominated Borrell nearly from bell to bell. Greb tore after Borrell like a wildman trying in every round after the first for the knockout. In the first round Greb seemed a bit timid. The memory of the beating he had suffered at Borrell's hands was apparently playing on his mind when that first bell rang and a tame round followed. In the second

MOHA'S BEST WORK WAS IN THE CLINCHES. ALL SHORT HOOKS TO GREB'S RIBS :-

GREB WOULD SEND HIS RIGHT CROSS TO MOHA'S CHIN- WITH PLENTY OF PUSH — BUT BOB NEVER BLINKED -

round Greb's fury exploded and he chased Borrell around the ring under a rain of boxing gloves. Borrell couldn't get set to punch and was so preoccupied with defending himself that he had little opportunity to mount his own offense. His best attempts where in the clinches when he hammered powerful blows to Greb's body. Greb quickly became wise to this and was able to block these. He rattled Borrell in the fourth and in the sixth he became so eager for a

The calm before the storm. Harry Greb and Joe Borrell square off before the January 1, 1917 bout at the Penn Avenue Power House in Pittsburgh. Greb was eager for a knock-out against Borrell as revenge for the beating he had suffered two years previous. He had to settle with a dominating newspaper decision. (Note the heavy tape used to bind Borrell's hands.)

knockout that he literally swept Borrell around the ring with wild clouts to the body and head. At the final bell Borrell was groggy but still standing. Greb was an easy winner.[28]

Celebrating Greb's victory over Borrell Red Mason issued a telegram to Tex Rickard challenging Les Darcy to a match with Greb.

> **Tex Rickard,**
>
> **World's Greatest Boxing Promoter,**
>
> **New York City.**
>
> **Harry Greb, Pittsburgh's middleweight challenges Darcy as his first opponent. Greb last week beat Bob Moha at Buffalo. Three weeks ago he easily beat Knockout Brown. He beat Miske at Philadelphia 18 months ago. Fought Chip twice; also Tom Gibbons. I will post two thousand in cash that Greb will make one fifty-eight any hour Darcy demands. Furthermore, will bet one thousand that Greb is there good and strong at the end of 10 rounds. Kindly let me know at once if there is anything doing, and I will post my cash with any New York paper named by you.**
>
> > **James Mason**
> >
> > **Manager Harry Greb**[29]

Harry would have to step in line if he wanted a crack at the Australian. Fighters were crawling out of the woodwork to face him and more pressing was the firestorm that was now arriving from Australia which accused Darcy of being a slacker and deserting his country at a time when it needed its fighting men most. Such claims where rapidly making Darcy persona-non-grata not only across the United States but across the world. While waiting for lucrative offers to pour in Darcy toured the country giving exhibitions as a means of earning an income. After one such exhibition in Philadelphia Darcy was surrounded by a crowd of young urchins. Instead of being the expected mob of admiring youths that often followed fistic heroes through the streets they had come to taunt the Australian. One bold rascal yelled "You're a cheese champion, you big slacker!"[30] The show was poorly attended and with each new day it was becoming more apparent that Darcy's stay in the United States would be a frosty one.

While waiting for the big money fights to roll in Greb needed to keep busy. He started by signing to face Eddie Coleman in Charleroi on January 13 in a ten round bout and Fay Keiser on January 29 in a 20 round bout in Lonaconing, Maryland. He would later squeeze Jules Ritchie between these two bouts for January 20 in Philadelphia. His bouts with Coleman and Ritchie turned into full blown routs with neither boxer showing much inclination to fight once they had tasted Greb's onslaught. In the first round of his bout with Coleman Greb cut out a pace that the young Ohioan couldn't cope with even at that early stage. Greb ended matters easily in the second round with a single blow to the jaw that sent Coleman down for the count.[31]

Jules Ritchie fared little better in Philadelphia. Greb pounded Ritchie about the ring send-ing punch after punch into the Lancaster boy's face. Blood streamed from Ritchie's nose and mouth after a wild right hand sent him sprawling to the canvas. In the fourth round Ritchie had lost his will to fight and could do little but clinch and run whenever Greb's flailing fists came near. At this point referee Jack McGuigan halted the bout in favor of Greb as it was apparent Ritchie wanted no more.[32]

After the match Greb and Mason quickly returned to Pittsburgh where Les Darcy's travel-ing exhibition would be appearing at a local theater. When Darcy's show arrived in Pittsburgh Greb was anxious to get in the ring with him, even if it was only for exhibition purposes. Darcy refused sticking strictly to his sparring partner Freddie Gilmore. Mason was incensed, he immediately set about a local media campaign designed to infuriate Darcy to the point of tak-ing a match with Greb. He branded Darcy as an overrated product of hype and home court advantage. Allegations which Al Lippe, manager of Jeff Smith who held a win over Darcy, was also hurling in the direction of Darcy for the same reasons as Mason.[33]

It was hoped that Greb would meet up with the Australian in Buffalo where he was sched-uled to face Willie Brennan for a third match in February. Darcy would be in Buffalo at the

This contemporary cartoon illustrates the prevailing feeling that Les Darcy's reputation carried enough weight to garner matches with the highest profile fighters in the sport but that he also intended to carefully choose his opposition. It quickly became evident that doors would be closing in Darcy's face faster than he could open them.

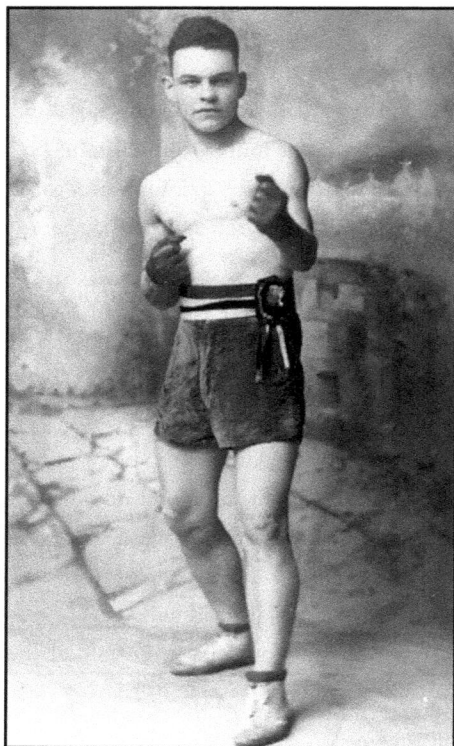

Julius Rietchey, who fought professionally as Jules Ritchie of Lancaster, Pennsylvania was literally reduced to running from his opponent when he faced Harry Greb at the National A.C. in Philadelphia on January 20, 1917.

same time and it was hoped that a fight could be worked out between the two. Darcy quickly ended any ideas of this when he arrived in Buffalo telling the local press: "Apropos of Red Mason's few remarks published in a Pittsburgh paper, I beg to say that I am the recognized champion in three classes from a country which turned out such fighters as Peter Jackson, Bob Fitzsimmons, and Young Griffo, where they do not create champions by newspaper publicity, but where ones reputation must be earned within the roped arena. That if Red Mason wishes to be convinced of my ability and will post the sum of $1,000 I will take on Greb in private for newspaper sporting editors only so that they can find out whether I am a false alarm or not. Personally I have the highest regard for Harry Greb, and would not like to spoil the boy's chances of making some real money."[34] The Buffalo Morning Express for one took a rather cold response to Darcy's bravado:

Les Darcy, the Australian, when challenged by Greb during his visit in Pittsburgh, made the great mistake of trying to treat the challenge lightly and offering to box a match in private to decide the better man, an old subterfuge to escape a dangerous opponent.[35]

Brennan had his own ideas on the matter as he was training zealously for the match with Greb, still obsessed with the idea of gaining revenge. His revenge would be doubled if he could throw a monkey wrench into the Greb's proposed bout with Darcy and this was no doubt a motivating factor in his daily workouts with Buck Crouse and the other fighters of Allie Smith's stable.

Before Greb could take on Brennan or Darcy he had to first dispose of his old rival Fay Keiser in a high stakes twenty round bout to a decision at Lonaconing, Maryland. It would be the longest bout of Greb's career to date. The match had all of the earmarks of an old time prize fight. There was a guaranteed purse of $1,000 to the winner, $500 to the loser and each fighter had posted a $1,000 dollar side bet.[36] In addition to this Red Mason was taking any bet that stated Keiser would win. Matt Hinkle, Ohio's boxing expert, had been agreed upon by both parties as the referee and when he announced the fighters to the crowd, sent them back to their corners and signaled the timekeeper to ring the bell, the fight was on.

Greb had initially planned to pace himself for the long contest but once he got wound up he couldn't or wouldn't slow down. The pace he set out was a terrific one and few in the sold out house felt he could keep it up. From the first round Keiser was taking severe punishment, particularly to the body and it was plain that he was trying to conserve his energy for a late rally when he hoped Greb would slow down. By the fifth round Keiser was bleeding severely from cuts both inside and outside of his mouth as well as a mangled nose.

By the tenth round, when Keiser had hoped to stage his rally, he was a bloody mess and weak from the body punishment he had taken. He no longer had the strength to mount a serious offense and Greb was still traveling at top speed. In the last three rounds Keiser was nearly helpless. He held on as much as possible simply trying to last the distance. His left eye was swollen, his face was smeared with gore, and his throat was parched from the blood he had been forced to swallow throughout the bout. When the gong rang ending the longest fight of Greb's career Matt Hinkle walked over and raised Greb's blood soaked glove. Keiser offered no excuses for his loss and commented that in his opinion "Greb is one of the best today wearing gloves."[37]

Greb was elated. Despite having lost nearly ten pounds over the course of the bout he was as chipper as always and celebrated the victory by downing a quart of ice cream, his favorite post-fight practice. "I went twenty rounds faster than I generally go for six or ten," Said Greb. "Keiser was dangerous until the fifteenth round, for he was strong until then. In the last few rounds he was very weak from punishment and the loss of blood and he held on grimly every time he got a chance. In the eighteenth round I said to him, don't hold on so, Fay, I'm not going to knock you out! He was cut up so

Fay Keiser had matured since that first professional bout with Greb nearly three years ago training himself into a fine club fighter. Instead of going six rounds he would travel 20 gruelling rounds with a man who was rapidly taking his place among the top men in the middleweight division.

badly and his throat was so choked that he could not answer me."[38]

With Keiser defeated Greb and his rapidly expanding following now turned their attention to Willie Brennan. Also following developments closely was Les Darcy who was still on tour in Buffalo. "I wish I could arrange it to be in Buffalo and see Greb and Brennan meet in the Broadway auditorium on February 5," said Darcy. "If anything happens to change our plans you bet I'll stick in Buffalo until after next Monday night and see them scrap. And if the Queensberry club makes a match for me later on and wants me to box their winner I'll do it."[39] When Mason heard this news he was ready to jump at the opportunity, urging Buffalo promoters to acquire Darcy's signature at any terms and Greb would be willing to face him on short notice. "That's how willing Greb is to meet Darcy."[40] Mason also issued his rebuttal of Darcy's earlier attack on him. "Harry and I had counted on being in Buffalo on Saturday. We had another reason besides desire to be on the battle ground to actuate us. Both of us wanted to see Les Darcy before he got out of Buffalo, and get something definite out of him on the subject of a battle with Greb in America. Down here Darcy issued a statement about a fight in private for nothing, but they have heard that sort of stuff before," said Mason, and added sarcastically, "one might suppose, if sincere, Darcy would have been found making a match with Jess Willard immediately afterward. But what? They say he is to meet Al McCoy, probably as poor a champion of boxing as America ever owned."[41]

Brennan had focused all of his attention on Greb. His schedule was cleared of all other bouts that he may focus solely on beating the man who had now become his great white whale. He had convinced himself that Greb had weighed too much and that going stale from a busy fight schedule had contributed more to his downfall at Greb's hands than anything Greb did in the ring. Brennan now hoped that by signing Greb to weigh in at 158 lbs. and by keeping his schedule clear until after the fight he would be in perfect trim to whip the Pittsburgh boy. In truth Brennan was rounding into remarkable form. He awoke at the crack of dawn every morning for his roadwork despite the brutal cold, and he had been boxing daily with Buck Crouse, Tommy Burke, and Kid Curley in addition to his regular hour or two of gym work. Admirers from Buffalo's east side packed the gym daily to watch Brennan train and it was felt by all that if he didn't defeat Greb he would certainly narrow the margin of defeat suffered in their previous outings.

Everything looked set for a slam bang affair when a golden opportunity arrived in the lap of Greb less than a week before the scheduled bout and threatened the entire show. James Mason received an offer from Philadelphia promoter Jack McGuigan for a match at the National Athletic Club against none other than Mike Gibbons, the St. Paul Phantom on February 10. It was an offer that Mason would have been foolish to pass up at any price. Gibbons was considered by many to be the uncrowned master of the middleweight division and Les Darcy's chief rival in the United States. A win or even a good showing against a fighter regarded as one of the greatest, if not *the* greatest fighter of any weight in the world, would increase Greb's standing immeasurably. Another factor that would certainly help Greb's publicity was the fact that Milwaukee promoters had offered an enormous sum of money to Darcy to face Mike Gibbons.[42] If Greb could defeat Gibbons, or make an impressive showing against him he would be well positioned for future lucrative bouts. Simply put it was a no-brainer. Mason accepted the match and immediately telephoned Buffalo with the manufactured excuse that Greb was having difficulty in making weight and needed more time to train.

The match wasn't a completely win/win situation for Greb and Mason. If Greb were outclassed in the bout or suffered a knockout it would show that he was still not ready to compete in the upper echelon of the sport. Furthermore, Gibbons was no fighter to be taken lightly. His schoolboy looks melted away when in the ring, and his eyes shone cold and pale. His lips formed a snarling countenance which hardly resembled the cheery little Irishman that he was out of the ring. He was known as the St. Paul Phantom for his incredible defense and ring wizardry. His footwork was so adept that admirers remarked it appeared he moved about on roller-skates. Despite his low knockout percentage he could put plenty of zip in his punches when he chose to cut loose. He spent much of his time pulling punches because of his aversion to hurting his opponents and his reliance on slick defense. Gibbons showed what he was capable of when in 1916 he fought a rematch with Jake Ahearn and destroyed him in a single round after Ahearn and his manager had infuriated Gibbons with personal taunts. Gibbons had already defeated such glowing stars as Jimmy Clabby, Jack Dillon, and Jeff Smith among many others. Adding to this already imposing resume was the fact that Gibbons had never been knocked out. No matter the outcome or the rewards that might come from it, Greb was guaranteed to have no easy time with Mike Gibbons.

With Greb lying in his sick bed, Ill with tonsillitis, Mason closed the match. Gibbons was to get 40 percent of the gate receipts which would leave little for Greb but it is doubtful that this made much difference in the decision making process.[43] Indeed, one would not be surprised if Greb's excitement was such that he began an immediate recovery upon hearing of the match. In Buffalo promoters where still in the dark as to the real reason why Mason had postponed the bout with Brennan. Brennan took it all in stride, taking the opportunity to rest and spend the day at the theater. He refused to let anything upset his focus. "Just as much more time for me to prepare in and just so much more time for Greb to worry about weight." said Brennan. "I would much rather meet Greb after he has been forced to cut down to 158, a high figure for me, by the way, than I would to try him at catch weights again and know that he was sure to be five to ten pounds heavier than I would be. I want to win this match more than any in which I have engaged in a long time and I am going to win it. I don't care how good they say Greb is nor what predictions they are making for his future. He can't make 158 pounds and beat me."[44]

One can only imagine the surprise that Queensberry Club members experienced when, on February 9, word was received that Greb would be competing against Gibbons the next day. Only the day before, frustrated by what he felt were delays attributable to Greb's inability to make 158 lbs., Brennan waived the weight limit. "Get him here and toss him in the ring with me Monday night," said Brennan. "Whether he's under, over, or just at 158, makes no difference to me."[45] It must have suddenly seemed all too clear why Mason had repeatedly delayed the match. Mason went through with this subterfuge, in all likelihood, to prevent the Queensberry A. C. from enforcing their contract with Greb and thus preventing the Gibbons fight. By the time they realized the reality of the situation it was too late. Irritated at being manipulated Charles Murray told the press "I hope Gibbons kicks seventeen kinds of stuffing out of him (Greb)..."[46] All that was left for Buffalo was to wait in anticipation for news of the Greb-Gibbons bout.

Gibbons may not have kicked seventeen kinds of stuffing out of Greb on February 10, 1917 but he certainly won the fight in the estimation of most present. Greb's still unpolished, wide open style of attack, combined with an over-eagerness to show well, played right into the cool, calculating hands of "The Phantom." Gibbons calmly met Greb's rushes with clean, precision punching. In the first round Gibbons whipped over a short left hook which positioned Greb's head perfectly for a smashing right. Greb's knees buckled but he fought on. A left jab from Greb snaked out and tore the skin from Gibbons' nose. In the second and third rounds Greb forced the fighting but could not cope with the deadly accurate counterpunches of one of the ring's greatest fighters. In the fourth Greb finally broke through Gibbons' defense and smashed a right hand to the side of Gibbons' head which left his ear badly swollen. Greb followed up this advantage with a flurry of blows that forced the St. Paul battler to rely on his famous footwork for a time. In the fifth round Gibbons again shot a right hand to Greb's jaw which sent him reeling and once again Gibbons was in control. In the sixth and final round Gibbons again landed his short, snapping right and again Greb was hurt, this time Greb clinched and held on. For the duration of the round Gibbons opened up and for the first time went on the offensive, trying hard for a knockout. At the finish Greb was still standing and the crowd cheered his effort

Willie Brennen, seen here doing roadwork for his rubber match with Greb in near zero temperatures and deep snow, was keenly focused on the match. Such harsh conditions only fortified him for the task ahead.

lustily. The only mark he carried of the engagement was a black eye which he wore like a badge of honor. Gibbons meanwhile had paid a price for his victory, his ear was badly swollen, and his eye was cut as well as his nose. The next morning the press gave all credit to Gibbons for his victory but noted that he was overly patient and that it was Greb who made the fight a crowd pleaser.[47]

Immediately after the fight, Mason and Greb rushed by taxi cab to the train station and caught the first train to Buffalo. Two days later after a short rest he was in the ring with Willie "KO" Brennan, who no doubt felt a great sense of relief when Greb finally arrived. Both men weighed exactly 161 $1/4$, and Brennan at least was trained to the minute. A large crowd was in attendance despite the extremely cold weather.

As the two fighters came out for the first round, it was apparent that Brennan was either somewhat intimidated by his opponent or he was conserving his energy, for his usually aggressive style had dulled considerably. As a result of this tactic Greb was able to take most of the first six rounds due to his high punch output, his aggressiveness, and his harder punching. Brennan opened up in the last four stanzas and to the delight of his fans began to win rounds, but his ferocious rally was met only by a smile from Greb who was confident of victory. The papers were unanimous in giving Greb the win but also agreed that Brennan had narrowed Greb's winning margin in this somewhat anti-climactic rubber match. No one could seem to agree whether Brennan had fought better than previous occasions, or if Greb had fought worse. Never-the-less the verdict was the same, "Greb shades Brennan."[48]

Greb returned to Pittsburgh after his win over Brennan for a

Mike Gibbons looked like a school boy outside of the ring, and an assassin inside. He had cold piercing eyes that belied his calculating mind. He was considered by many to be the greatest boxer of his age. When he met Greb in 1917 he gave the younger, less experienced fighter a boxing lesson.

short, unwanted rest. He harbored hopes for acquiring a fight against George Chip in one of several towns bidding for the fight, but Chip's pilot Jimmy Dime was not ready for such a match. Mason and Greb went so far as to follow Chip to Youngstown, Ohio, where he was fighting George "KO" Brown, to challenge for a match. The Pittsburgh papers were highly critical of Dime's reluctance to match his fighter with Mason's and wondered if he was ducking Greb out of fear.[49] A much more likely explanation of Dime's hesitance is that he was holding out for a rematch with Les Darcy which was rumored to take place within the near future. As a result the negotiations where fruitless and Greb was left biding his time as Mason set up other matches.

Over the course of March 1917 Greb fought three opponents: Frankie Brennan of Detroit, Tommy Gavigan of Cleveland, both in Pittsburgh, and Young Herman Miller of Baltimore, in Johnstown. Only Brennan would last the distance and he paid dearly for it, suffering a tremendous beating. Greb then signed to fight Young Ahearn in Pittsburgh at the Penn Avenue Power House. Ahearn had once had a tremendous reputation as a fighter but was now on the decline. He boasted a wonderful record, having met many of the game's best proponents regardless of weight but his downslide had started with his January 1916 match against Mike Gibbons. He had previously lost on a knockout to Gibbons in four rounds at Madison Square Garden in 1913. Thereafter he had chased Gibbons for a rematch claiming the loss was a fluke. In their zeal for a rematch, he and his manager had so berated Gibbons that the usually mild mannered Minnesotan had entered the rematch with one thought on his mind: Knockout! Before motion picture cameras and a packed audience Gibbons accomplished his goal in brutal fashion by dispatching Ahearn in the first round and leaving him in a terrible state. Ahearn would never again be the same imposing talent he had been prior to being picked up off the canvas by a frightened Mike Gibbons who feared he had killed Ahearn.

BRENNAN OFFSET GREBS SLAM BANG APPROACHES WITH A PEPPERY JAB FROM A CROUCH

GREBS BEST SHOT WAS AN OVERHAND RIGHT CROSS BRENNAN TOOK IT ON THE CHIN SEVERAL TIMES

Ahearn started out well enough against Greb. Three times Greb rushed Ahearn in the opening round and twice he was outwitted by the onetime "Dancing Master." Greb's stablemate Johnny Ray, seated at ringside commented on Ahearn "Gee, that fellow can learn me something! Here's where I pick up a few pointers."[50] At that moment Greb rushed Ahearn into a corner and as Ahearn's foot slipped outside of the ring Greb shot a blow to the stomach and then a short chopping right to the point of the chin which ended the bout barely before it started, the round being less than a minute gone. As Ahearn sat on his stool being revived by his handlers his limbs shook in nervous contractions.[51] Later as Ahearn headed to the train station he was quoted as saying, "I was hit on the jaw, that's all. Of course, it was an accident. Why, he can't box at all."[52] With that parting shot Ahearn left town to be knocked out in five rounds 21 days later by Jeff Smith.

Four days after Harry Greb knocked out Young Ahearn at Pittsburgh, President Woodrow Wilson declared war on Germany. The declaration was not unexpected but certainly left the country wondering about its future role in the conflict which for three years had cannibalized a generation of Europeans. Wilson had long resisted entry into the war, maintaining the nation's neutrality, much to the chagrin of hawkish former president Theodore Roosevelt who referred to Wilson as "a timid man physically."[53] Wilson had qualified the United States neutrality with the condition that Germany stop sinking ships without warning. When unrestricted U-boat warfare was resumed by Germany in early 1917 Wilson went before the House of Representatives and asked for a declaration of war. The day Wilson made his request before the House was the same day Harry Greb fought Ahearn. Four days later the United States was at war.

For the time being the war had little effect on Greb or his career. Initially little change was noted throughout the country in the days after the declaration. This would soon change. As days passed into

In early 1917 Greb marked time while waiting for an important match by taking on men like Tommy Gavigan, Frankie Brennan, and Young Herman Miller (above). Miller was a southpaw and the son of a well known former Baltimore fighter of the same name who had faced such legendary fighters as Joe Gans, Bobby Dobbs, and Jack Blackburn. Greb knocked Miller out in five rounds.

Jake "Young" Ahearn, one time "Dancing Master" of the prize-ring, met with a devastating defeat at the hands of Harry Greb on April 2, 1917. In less than a minute he was carried back to his corner in defeat.

weeks the entire nation seemed to rise to the task and was swept up in a patriotic fervor that grew with each new day crystallizing into a sense of duty to our cousins across the Atlantic. It would not be long before most of the nation was affected by the war. America would be in need of its fighting men, among them, Harry Greb.

Two more pedestrian bouts followed as Greb awaited something more important to come his way. The first was a 10 round bout against Al Rogers of Buffalo at Charleroi followed by a performance against Brooklyn's Zulu Kid at Pittsburgh. Greb won both bouts handily. As Greb trained daily for the two bouts, sparring with Mickey Farrell, Red Mason had sent emissaries to New York City in an effort to entice middleweight champ Al McCoy to Pittsburgh for a bout with Greb. Greb could hardly contain himself at the prospect of fighting the champion. An added attraction, if the bout could clinched, was the talk of making the bout a 10 rounder.[54] It would be the first bout scheduled for longer than six rounds in Pittsburgh in years. Despite the fact that no decision would be officially rendered Greb could still win the championship provided he scale under the 158 lb. weight limit and score a knockout; no small feat. When the match was officially announced a few days later, Greb was bursting with excitement. "You can just bet I'll try my darndest," said Greb "and you can say further that if I win the championship in this fight, I will give $500 to charity. That is a bona fide offer too."[55]

All of Pittsburgh was pulling for Greb, even former rival Whitey Wenzel came out to offer Greb his support. "I hope Greb wins..." said Wenzel "I haven't seen Harry for some time, and I'll be pulling for him when he fights McCoy. He is getting along rapidly in the game. More power to him. He works hard at his profession and he deserves his success. Give him my best wishes when you see him again."[56] Even George Chip and Jimmy Dime came sniffing around Pittsburgh in hopes of a match with the winner.[57]

Chip and Dime had by now given up on a match with Darcy who was banned from fighting in Ohio, proposed site of the Chip-Darcy bout, by Governor Cox.[58] Indeed it seemed as if every state Darcy approached answered with a ban on his hopes of boxing. The Australian was now a pariah both at home and abroad, labeled a draft dodging "slacker." In a last ditch effort to curry favor with the powers that be he enlisted in the fledgling Reserve Aviation Corps of the United States Army. This action was met with skepticism due to the fact that a condition of his signing up was that he be allowed to fight. Many critics remarked pointedly that if it was a fight he was looking for he could have simply stayed home and gone to war with his peers. With his popularity at an all-time low, it was doubtful if Darcy would box in the United States in the near future.

As the McCoy fight approached, Greb trained furiously, so much so that at times Mason had to restrict his time in the Pittsburgh Lyceum gym for fear that Greb would over-train and enter the ring stale. All the while Greb maintained his confidence. "I'm going to do it," said Greb "and when I'm champ I'll fight them all, no matter how good or how bad they are."[59] Sparring partner Jack Kelsey had worked Greb into excellent condition it was now all downhill until the battle.

McCoy, for his part, was just as confident of victory and claimed to be in top physical condition. "This young fellow Greb isn't going to be the one to make of me an ex-champion," said McCoy. "I have seen him box and believe I will win over him without trouble. I hear that George Chip has sidestepped him, but that doesn't indicate anything. Chip has tried twice to win back the title I took from him; and yet I am champion. I shall give Greb all the fight he wants in Pittsburgh and maybe they will think better of me in that city afterward."[60]

When McCoy arrived in Pittsburgh with his handpicked referee, Johnny McAvoy, he was armed with more hyperbole and willing to dispense. "If Greb beats me tonight," he said, "he will have to be a dandy. He will have to travel faster than I think it is possible for him to go, and I feel confident that I will be returned a winner."[61] The only judges would be the more than 5,000 fans and reporters from Pittsburgh's newspapers, their verdict may not have been official but it was unanimous.

On the night of April 30, 1917 fully two thousand people were turned away from Exposition Music Hall which was filled to capacity, and then some, with curiosity seekers hoping to get a glimpse of a champion in action. What they saw was a massacre. When Greb entered the ring at 9:48 PM he was given a thunderous ovation. A large group of his loyal followers from Garfield made themselves known above the clapping and Greb happily waved to them. A minute later McCoy appeared in the ring to a lukewarm reception. Among those in attendance were George Chip, Joe Chip, Jimmy Dime, and Frank Klaus.

McCoy came out for the first round with a smile on his face. The smile was not to last. Greb established that he was not some hick from the sticks in the first round when he began landing at will. McCoy did little fighting and spent most of the first two rounds covering up or on the defensive. By the third round McCoy was having a hard time maintaining his smile as blood

Harry Greb (left) and Al McCoy (right) square off for their 1917 bout in Exposition Music Hall, Pittsburgh, Pennsylvania. Between 5,000 and 7,000 fans attended the bout including several women (a rarity at the time) and 2,000 more were turned away at the doors. The gate receipts totaled more than $8,000.

poured from his nose. The Brooklynite was starting to take a beating and the crowd was booing his lack of aggressiveness. It was becoming obvious that McCoy's major strategy was simply to survive.

In the fourth Greb had McCoy reeling from his relentless attack. He battered McCoy about the ring wiping the smirk off his face for the remainder of the fight. McCoy's hope of winning a popular victory was fading rapidly. For the next several rounds he could do no better than try his best to prevent further punishment, the exception being when he very nearly fouled Greb in the fifth hitting Greb as he rose from a slip. Even in the area of stalling and trying to prevent punishment McCoy was a failure for Greb was on top of him all the time, having the champion's face smeared with crimson from a bleeding nose and a cut inside his mouth. McCoy was now unrecognizable.

In the ninth round Greb threw all caution out the window and tried hard for a knockout as the crowd cheered wildly for it's hometown hero. He knew he had the popular decision easily in hand, but the championship could only come with a knockout. As the ninth passed and the tenth began McCoy, for all of his faults, was assimilating a severe beating and still remained

Above is pictured Exposition Music Hall, located on Pittsburgh's "Point." This would be the site of Harry Greb's first championship bout. He would face Al McCoy, then middleweight champion in the first ten round bout held in the city in many years.

upright. As the bell ended the fight McCoy, knees sagging, face smeared with gore, and nose misshapen, was still on his feet. He would return home a loser but still champion. As Greb returned to his corner and began to exit the ring for his dressing room he was mobbed by the admiring crowd and disappeared out of view.[62]

The morning after the fight, those fans who were turned away, or didn't attend for whatever reason, were able to read the tale of the bout in any one of the cities many newspapers, all of which voted for Greb as the easy winner.

> Whatever claim one Al McCoy of Brooklyn possesses to the title of middleweight champion of the world must have been obtained under false pretense. Last night at Exhibition Music Hall, while 7,000 fistic fans looked on, Harry Greb of Pittsburgh did everything to the McCoy person but murder him. During ten three-minute rounds the so-called champion did little else than assimilate punishment. His left eye was closed, his nose was spread over a part of his countenance where no well-behaved proboscis has any right to be, a large cut poured forth blood and his knees were saggy and unreliable when the final clang of the tocsin indicated that the first 10-round affair in Pittsburgh for many a years had been concluded.[63]

So wrote David J. Davies of the Pittsburgh Daily Dispatch. Pittsburgh's other newspapers were no less critical of McCoy and no less complimentary of Greb's showing. The Pittsburgh

Sun expressed its opinion thus:

> Few fighters would have been able to survive the beating handed McCoy. He was badly battered in every round and gave back little punishment for that he received. He is marked from the battle, an eye being discolored. He bled at the nose and mouth, and there are welts and bruises on his body and face to show that Greb's punishment carried lots of steam.[64]

Richard Guy of the Pittsburgh Gazette-Times wrote:

> Greb looked the part of the champion, and McCoy the trial horse.
>
> There were moments when Greb had the house in an uproar. Time and again he forced McCoy to the ropes and pummeled him with rights and lefts, and the champion was released when the referee Jimmy McAvoy of New York, ordered Greb away. Then Greb kept right after the title holder and swung punches and McCoy ducked in under many; those he missed connected with him.[65]

8

BIRTH OF A CONTENDER

The McCoy bout brought Greb much prestige despite McCoy's poor reputation as a champion. Numerous offers for bouts began pouring in to James Mason's office even as Greb was preparing for several bouts he had scheduled prior to the victory over McCoy.

The first of these would be a twenty round contest against Jackie Clark to be held at Cumberland, Maryland less than a week after Greb's fight with McCoy. Clark was deadly serious about avenging his previous knockout loss at the hands of Greb and realized that a win over the recent conqueror of the middleweight champion would boost his own popularity. As a result he came into the bout in tremendous condition with a game plan much different than the one which resulted in his early defeat six months before.

Clark made a tremendous showing over the twenty round fight and the battle was declared a draw by referee Matt Hinkle. The Cumberland Evening Times felt Clark had done enough to win giving him the fight, but this decision may have been influenced by the heavily pro-Clark crowd seeing that the paper had no less than five of the twenty rounds even. The description of the fight provided by this paper makes it evident that Clark fought a highly tactical, defensive fight which would not have won him many points in the eyes of most judges.[1] Mason was furious over the decision which he felt was a robbery. He declared that Hinkle had been influenced by the partisan crowd and that Clark's defensive tactics were the only thing keeping him upright.[2] Whatever the case it was a close competitive bout which harmed neither fighter's reputation. Two months later Clark himself would go on to fight Al McCoy, winning the newspaper decision.

Jackie Clark was determined to avenge his knockout loss to Greb in the 20-round rematch at Cumberland. He would prove a much more difficult opponent than champion Al McCoy.

CHAMPIONSHIP

BOXING BOUT

=== AT ===

WEST END THEATRE

Wednesday, May 9

HARRY GREB vs. **K. O. BAKER**

Of Pittsburgh   Of Philadelphia

10 ROUNDS

JACK LIGHTNING vs. **JIMMY O'DAY**

Of Pittsburgh   Of Cleveland

(Eight Rounds)

KID YORK   VS.   BATTLING SCHULTZ

(Six Rounds)

First Bout at 9:15 Sharp.

Reserved Seats $1, $2 and $3.   General Admission 25 Cents.

The high profile matches Greb and Mason had been awaiting were now starting to materialize. Promoters in Buffalo were trying to match Greb with middleweight title claimant Jeff Smith and Mick Stambaugh of Youngstown was trying to secure Greb's services, in place of Les Darcy, against George Chip. Initially Mason agreed to terms for the Jeff Smith match in Buffalo to be held on May 8 but with critics pointing out that Greb had fought on April 30, May 5, and had a match with Harry "KO" Baker scheduled for May 9 in Uniontown it was suggested that Mason might be stretching his young protégé too thin. Mason relented and the bout with Smith was postponed.

After a short rest Greb began light training for his bout with Baker. The fight would be held in conjunction with a series of automobile races which would include participants such as the legendary race car drivers Ralph DePalma and Barney Oldfield. As an added attraction Oldfield, the most renowned race car driver of his day, was selected as the referee of Greb's bout. After the preliminaries had concluded Oldfield climbed onto the stage with his trademark cigar clinched in his teeth, shed his hat and coat, and got down to the business of overseeing Greb beat Harry Baker to a frazzle.

The only difficulty Oldfield had was in breaking some of Baker's clinches which were designed to prolong his stay in the realm of the conscious. Greb quite simply battered his old friend from the opening bell until one minute into the fifth round when Baker was counted out after being floored by a hard right to the pit of the stomach. It was a game showing by Baker who gave his best and won the hearts of the fans with his courageous exhibition but he was simply outgunned. With each successive round Baker received a more brutal beating until the third when he came out reinvigorated and tried to make a last stand. To the amazement of all present Baker and Greb stood toe to toe, trading their best punches with the sound of landed punches reverberating throughout the hall. The fourth and fifth rounds saw Baker assimilate a

tremendous amount of punishment.

At the end of the fourth round
Greb dropped Baker to the mat
with a short right and only the bell
saved the young southpaw. After
dropping Baker for a six count early
in the fifth round Greb poured
punches to the body and head
before finally scoring the fight ending knockout after a minutes fighting. It was a capacity audience that
watched the slaughter and which,
to their surprise, saw Greb carry
Baker back to his corner and kiss
him. When Baker was led to his
dressing room he had two closed
eyes, his nose and mouth bled and
his body was covered with red and purple splotches.[3]

Legendary automobile racer Barney Oldfield, seen here with his ever present cigar. Was the celebrity referee of Harry Greb's bout with Harry Baker in Uniontown. The bout was held in conjunction with a race Oldfield was participating in.

When asked a month later about the kiss Greb replied "I'm not a bit ashamed of having done it, I'd do it again under the same circumstances. Of all the 49 or 50 men I have fought, I have never felt for any of them as I feel for Baker, and here is the reason. Several years ago, when I was just dubbing around in the game, I made a trip to Philadelphia on my own book. I went flat broke there and didn't have any friends. The only fellow in the boxing fraternity there who would stake me was Baker. He took care of me and tried to get me on with him at a Philly club so I could get some money. He wasn't successful, but he tried hard.

After a short stay in the Quaker City, I came back to Pittsburgh. As soon as I could, I got myself matched up with Baker, because he wasn't getting many fights then himself. Baker came on from Philly and we fought a hard battle in Duquesne Garden. Then we had a return engagement in the Garden and later we fought in the Penn Avenue Power House arena. Every time he gave me a tough scrap and I tried my darndest to knock him out. We were great pals outside the ring and would do anything for each other, but in the ring we forgot all about friendship.

Our latest bout was the one at Uniontown last month. Again Baker gave me a hard fight. He hit me one punch to the head at the start of the third round that put me closer to a knockout than I have ever been since I started going well. I dropped him just as the bell ended the fourth round and then finished him in the fifth.

After I had put him down for the count I felt sorry for him. I picked him up and carried him to his corner and then helped bring him to. I nearly cried and I kissed him. And I am not a bit ashamed of it either.

Harry Baker is a fine scout personally. He treated me white when I didn't have a thing and any time I can do him a favor I'll be only too glad to come through."[4]

With Baker out of the way Greb was now ready to face Jeff Smith in Buffalo. Smith would prove one of Greb's most difficult opponents to date. Dubbed the "Globe-trotter" for his incredible record of fighting all over the world, by the time he retired from the ring Smith had fought in France, Australia, Britain, Canada, Mexico, and claimed to have fought in several other locales across the globe. His record was a formidable one. He had defeated such notables as Jimmy Clabby, Eddie McGoorty, Willie Lewis, and George Chip. While in Australia he fought two bouts with Les Darcy, winning one when Darcy refused to come out of his corner for the sixth round, claiming a foul which was not allowed by the referee, and losing one which ended in a controversial second round foul. While in France Smith built up an enviable record. He fought a much larger Georges Carpentier lasting the twenty round limit despite being heavily outgunned and went on to defeat Georges Bernard in a bout that the French billed as being for the middleweight championship of the world. Upon this victory Smith was awarded a jewel encrusted belt emblematic of his title.

What made Smith such a dangerous opponent was the fact that he had very few flaws as a fighter. He had a tremendous ability to absorb punishment; in fact he wouldn't be stopped in a bout until 15 years into his career. His speed and boxing skills were on par with anyone in

Buffalo's Broadway Auditorium was the site of many of Greb's fights in the Bison City, including his fight with Jeff Smith. Greb was always a favorite with the Buffalo fans for his crowd pleasing style and willingness to fight anyone.

the world. He carried a wicked punch which was capable of dropping a man cold and his stamina was unquestionable as he had traveled fifteen rounds or more no less than 12 times. The one major chink in Smith's formidable armor was the fact that he tended to rely too heavily on his defense in fights and as a result he was capable of being outpointed by a fighter who pressed the issue and took the fight to him. This was the case when he met Carpentier and quickly fell behind on points as Carpentier used his greater size to press the attack and keep Smith on the defensive.

When Greb postponed the match with Smith earlier in the month, Smith and his manager Al Lippe began a smear campaign of both Greb and Mason in the Pittsburgh and Buffalo newspapers branding Greb a "slacker" and stating that he had run out of the match with Smith. Such suggestions infuriated Mason who shot back with his own press release. "...from the way Harry is working the last few days there is certainly going to be some go, that is if Lippy Al's fighter does one-half that his windy manager has written to the papers here that he will do."[5]

As Greb trained for the Smith fight, Mason was finally able to secure a bout with George Chip. Chip's manager Jimmy Dime had been holding out for his fighter but finally signed when Mason agreed to hold the match on May 22, three days after his match with Smith. Dime reasoned that with his fighter's challenge of Greb coming so close on the heels of Greb's bout with Smith, which was expected to be a taxing affair, Chip's chances of victory would be improved. The bout would again be scheduled for 10-rounds and would again take place at Exhibition Music Hall.

When Greb and Mason arrived in Buffalo, Mason was jubilant at having two such high profile fights lined up for Greb. "We'll take two stars in four days," he said "Smith here in Buffalo and George Chip next Tuesday in Pittsburgh."[6]

As Smith and Greb weighed in for their bout at 3 o'clock on the day of the fight, it became known that Greb was four and a half pounds over the contracted weight of 160 pounds outweighing Smith by nine pounds. Lippe demanded that Greb make weight. Greb refused. Lippe then demanded that Greb at least take off two pounds, to which Greb again refused.

Jerome Jeffords, professionally known as Jeff Smith, pictured here in a rare photo from 1913 was one of the most formidable opponents Greb would ever stack up against. He could have easily been a champion in any era had he been provided the opportunity.

Finally Greb demanded that he fight at the weight he came in at or he would simply return to Pittsburgh where he had a larger purse waiting for him in the form of George Chip. When it became obvious that Greb wasn't bluffing Smith stepped in "Come on big guy, I'll take you at catch weights, and let's see how good you are."[7] It was later revealed that Smith's bravado was buttressed by an addition to his guarantee based on the weight difference.[8]

Just as the fighters entered the ring the fight was again delayed. This time because it was found that Smith was wearing heavy tape under his hand wrappings. He was immediately sent back to his dressing room by officials and ordered to remove the hard binding. It seems both fighters had a healthy respect for the others ability based on the "insurance" they were taking out on themselves.

When Smith returned to the ring the fighters argued about which corner the other would use. With this argument finally settled and the psychological warfare completed the fighters finally prepared to settle their argument as promoters intended, by beating the hell out of each other.

When the two fighters finally got down to the business of fighting Smith's Achilles heel

George Chip (right), in training for his May 22, 1917 battle with Harry Greb, pounds the heavy bag supported by Jimmy Dime (left) as Joe Chip (center left) and Tom McMahon (center right) look on. The vertical object standing in the foreground is a training tool used by Dime called a "ding-bat" which he would use as a lance from behind the heavy-bag to simulate an opponent's punches.

began to manifest itself. As Greb became more aggressive throughout the bout Smith became more defense-oriented and as a result he was falling behind on points. Everyone agreed that Smith was technically the more skilled fighter. His ability to block, sidestep, or catch punches and counter them with short snappy uppercuts and body blows was nothing short of masterful. The problem was that there was a lot more blocking than countering and all the while Greb was piling up points regardless of how wild he looked in comparison to Smith. When the final bell sounded the decision of the fans and the newspapermen was again unanimous in Greb's favor. It was agreed that Smith at times bewildered Greb with his defense but defense alone was not enough to win him the bout. Both fighters left the ring unmarked with Smith complaining bitterly about the weight difference.[9]

If Jimmy Dime had hoped Smith would take some of the wind out of Greb's sails he was sorely mistaken. Greb returned to Pittsburgh ready and willing to add George Chip to his growing list of victims. "I know Greb is coming, but he isn't 'arrived' yet," said Dime. "He is faster than Chip, I'll admit, but he don't know how to get the right 'steam' into his punches. He has to hit too often to produce results. And Chip don't. One good opening and it will be curtains for Greb."[10] Dime was putting Chip through his paces daily at their New Castle headquarters. To prepare for Greb's unusual combination of speed and strength Chip sparred with heavyweight Tom McMahon, and lightweight Babe Picato. Rounding out Chip's sparring staff

Harry Greb (left) and George Chip square off for the cameras as referee Eddie Kennedy looks on. An estimated crowd of 2,500 fans watched as Greb and Chip fought ten rounds of a grudge match that was long in the making. Note former champion Frank Klaus seated ringside at the far right of the photo.

was his brother Joe who years earlier had been the only man to pin a knockout on Greb. Dime was leaving nothing to chance and as a result Chip was in tremendous condition.

All of Pittsburgh was eager to see what was shaping up to be a genuine grudge match. Even Frank Klaus, former champion and victim of Chip, when cornered was willing to dispense with his opinion of the bout. "I think that if there is any counting being done, the referee will be pumphandling over Mr. Greb. If the bout goes ten rounds next Tuesday night, I think that Greb will be acclaimed the victor on points." Klaus added, "Harry Greb looks to me to be one of the very best middles in the country. He is a comer, sure, and he is coming strong. Fast, strong, active, and agile, he has the fighter's temperament. As soon as he learns to hit- hit hard, I mean- there will be no stopping him. He'll be champion soon enough."[11]

Both fighters appeared nervous as they entered the ring, likely eager to get the show started. Some speculated that this apparent tension was due to the fact that both fighters had weighed in under 158 pounds making them somewhat drawn and weak. Greb's seconds would be Red Mason and George Hook, his sparring partner. Chip would have Jimmy Dime and Patsy Brannigan in his corner. Frank Klaus, who occupied a ringside seat, was introduced and shook hands with Chip to a warm ovation.

As the first round opened it was relatively slow going with both fighters content to feel each other out. Greb was warned for holding and hitting. The second saw Greb commence his dancing tactics, he danced around Chip nimbly shooting in punches from all directions. Chip rushed into a clinch and shot a short left hook to Greb's jaw, Greb answered by pumping his fists deep into Chip's midsection. Greb was now carrying the fight to Chip as the former champion seemed content to lay back and wait for the opportunity to shoot one of his powerful right hands over.

The fourth round witnessed Greb tearing after Chip like a man possessed. He leaped in at his opponent, spinning him and pounding him to the body and head. More than once Chip met these rushes with well

This publicity photo of Greb taken in 1917 (along with those on the next two pages) shows Greb trim and ready for his whirlwind campaign of that year which would make him a worthy contender for the title.

planted right hands that would spin Greb around or shake him but still the Pittsburgh youngster continued his onslaught.

Chip had his best round in the fifth when he planted a powerful short right hand on Greb's mouth which shook Greb to his toes and made him fall into a clinch. As Greb's head cleared the two fighters pounded each other around the ring from one end to the other. Several times in close Chip was guilty of butting Greb, an action which left the crowd hissing.

In the sixth round Chip could be seen to tire and clinched whenever Greb came close. Referee Eddie Kennedy was kept busy breaking the fighters and finally warned Chip for butting after another such infraction had raised the ire of the crowd. After being separated the two fighters met ring center and traded powerful blows to the jaw. This only enlivened Greb as he dove into Chip pumping both fists into his adversary like pistons. Greb was warned again for holding and hitting which again caused the crowd to voice its displeasure. Just before the round ended Greb landed a hard right to the side of Chip's head which split open his cauliflower ear and sent blood streaming down the side of his head.

Coming out for round seven Chip butted again and again was warned. Greb sailed into Chip forcing him to the ropes. On the ropes Chip landed a hard right which caused Greb's knees to sag but in an instant he was back on top of Chip and using the former champ's damaged ear as a target. Chip was trying his best to protect himself but Greb was deadly accurate and at the end of the round the entire left side of Chip's face was smeared with the blood that was now flowing steadily from the damaged ear.

The eighth round was Greb's by a wide margin as Chip essayed to hold on and was most effective offensively when he was butting. At one point Greb landed a series of right hands which badly rattled Chip and

Greb was extremely conscious about his appearance and once he became a highly successful fighter he was never seen outside of his profession in anything other than tailored suits of the most current fashion. It was often remarked that in street clothes he looked more like a young business man than a pug of the prize-ring.

the crowd jumped out of their seats expecting a knockout. Chip was again wobbled in the ninth and seemed to be weakening. At one point he backed Greb into a corner and as he prepared to land his crushing right, the slippery Pittsburgher wriggled out of danger and resumed his attack.

The men shook hands for the tenth round and only a knockout could save Chip from a popular defeat. Despite this fact he either would not or could not tear into his opponent with any urgency. Both fighters were tired but it was Chip who became sloppy and continually missed. When the bell ended the fight Greb was held to be the winner by newspapermen and fans alike. The only round that could be given to the blood soaked Chip in good faith was the fifth when he had Greb hurt.[12]

The press lavished praise on Greb the following morning for adding yet another high profile name to his record of wins. Richard Guy of the Gazette-Times probably handed Greb the best compliment when he stated:

> **Greb really fought better than upon any previous occasion in this city, for he measured his punches better and hit straighter. He seemed to set himself better and there was more force in consequence.**[13]

Harry Keck of the Pittsburgh Post stated it was one of the best fights seen in Pittsburgh in years and his colleague at the same paper Florent Gibson stated that in all of the years of watching Chip box he had never seen Chip fight a greater bout despite losing.[14] David J. Davies of the Daily Dispatch commented thus:

> **Chip was outclassed as a boxer; he wasn't permitted to set himself and whenever this privilege is denied him, he doesn't share very liberally in the honors that are to be bestowed. George worked hard and doggedly, at times taking all his opponent had to hand out, in the hope that he would be able to land one of his terrible right swings.**

He failed in this very laudable undertaking, however and therein lay his undoing.[15]

With his defeat of Chip, Greb could claim his status as a legitimate contender for the middleweight championship. Within the last five months he had met such men as Mike Gibbons, Jeff Smith, George Chip, and champion Al McCoy and had never been embarrassed. With this new degree of fame, and the larger purses he was pulling in, Greb now had all the trappings of a top fighter. He was always nattily attired in the latest fashion. Children followed him around the streets of Pittsburgh and never one to disappoint his loyal fans Greb often tossed coins to them in appreciation. He spoke out publicly in favor of Liberty Loan Bonds, he had women interested in his affections, and newspapers ran stories about his exploits. His fame allowed him to branch out into other areas of sport such as supporting an amateur baseball team which boasted his name "The Harry Grebs" and acting as a newspaper correspondent at the Frank Moran-Carl Morris fight in New York City. He was easily the best known and most popular fighter in Pittsburgh if not the whole of Western Pennsylvania.

Greb's new found fame served him well on Memorial Day, just over a week after his defeat of Chip. He had been touring West View Park with several friends when the automobile he was riding in stopped and pulled over to the side of the road. Several members of his party left the car to explore the park while Greb and a friend were left alone with four women. An automobile parked adjacent to the one occupied by Greb and his companions demanded they move along. When Greb declined the passengers of the opposing car became belligerent and challenged Greb to a fight. Greb climbed out of the car in his immaculate suit, silk gloves, and tossed his cane to one of the onlookers. "Gee, it's Harry Greb!" said one of the members of the rival car. Those who had unknowingly challenged Pittsburgh's most famous fighter to a game of fisticuffs suddenly lost their nerve. "I - er - er -I -didn't mean anything," said the guilty party. "It was all a mistake."[16]

Another factor in Greb's rise to prominence, a small factor albeit a tragic one, was the death of Les Darcy. Just after Greb's victory over champion Al McCoy, Les Darcy was checked into a hospital in Memphis, Tennessee suffering from rheumatic fever brought on by an infected false tooth. Slowly but steadily his condition worsened and less than one month later he was dead. He had been in Memphis still searching for that elusive fight which

BOXING MATCH
--AT --
West End Theatre

Thursday, June 14th
Harry Grebb
of Pittsburgh, vs.
Frank Mantell
of Dayton, O.
(10 rounds)
Red Saunders
vs.
Bud Gregg
(6 rounds)
Wilbur Johnson
vs.
Jimmy O'Day
(6 rounds)
First Bout 9 p. m. sharp.
PRICES $1, $1.50, $2
Tickets on sale at Penn Bowling Alleys and West End Theater.

would make him a star in the United States. Those hypocritical sportswriters, who had hounded and castigated the young Australian as a coward in life, now mourned him in death as a hero. With Darcy's passing there was one less title claimant, one less roadblock to the championship, one less great fighter in the world.

Big money offers were now pouring in for Greb's services. So much so that Red Mason was having to turn down more offers than he could keep. Mickey Stambaugh was anxious to promote a rematch between Greb and Chip in Youngstown, offering Greb a guarantee of $2,000 with a percentage of the gate. There was already a scheduled fight with former welterweight and middleweight title claimant Frank Mantell in Uniontown and there was preliminary talk of a tour along the west coast. There was also a scheduled bout with Augie Ratner in New York City which would give Greb the chance he had longed for to show his talents in the great metropolis. There were also preliminary talks for a match between Greb and his longtime rival Buck Crouse. Greb and Mason had been reluctant to give Crouse the opportunity to make any money in a fight with Greb but the Pittsburgh fans demanded it. With the history between Crouse and Greb it was a genuine grudge match and as such it was a lucrative bout.

Greb's rematch with Chip fell through when Stambaugh lowered his offer and Mason declined to do business. The west coast tour wouldn't materialize for another seven years and the Augie Ratner bout in New York City fell apart at the last minute. These were all merely speed bumps in the eyes of Mason who was ever working on behalf of Greb to climb the ladder of fistiana. Such was the case when on June 11 he finally swallowed his pride and signed Greb for the long awaited bout with Buck Crouse to be held on June 25.

Before Greb and Crouse could put their bitter feud to an end Greb had one small detail to clear up: his bout with Frank Mantell. A small

Frank Mantell (above) was a former welterweight and middleweight title claimant at the end of a successful career when he faced Greb in 1917. He had fought and defeated several great fighters over his career but it was age more than anything else that was the deciding factor in his fight against Harry Greb.

detail indeed for half a minute before the close of the first round Mantell was lying unconscious on the floor bleeding from both nose and mouth. The old battler was simply overwhelmed by his younger opponent.[17] Mantell instantly became one of Greb's biggest supporters. Years later he remembered the fight: "I never hear of Harry Greb, but what I recall the days when he used to hang around one of the Philadelphia gymnasiums.

'The clown is what we called him then. In those days Greb looked the part. He was a well set-up kid, however, who wasn't afraid to put on the gloves with anybody. Leo Houck, Frank Klaus, myself and several others used to race to the gym in order to grab Greb first for a workout.

All Greb knew at the time was to swing his hands. He scarcely moved out of his tracks. To hit him it was simply a matter of feinting him into an opening and letting him have it.

After coming to Dayton I lost track of Greb until a McKeesport, Pa., promoter wired me an offer to box him. Remembering what a clown he used to be, and figuring I still had it on him, I took the match.

Greb's former mentor, sparring partner, friend, and eventual rival, Buck Crouse (pictured above) was a talented middleweight once considered championship material. When he met Harry Greb in 1917 it was to settle a feud that had been three years in the making.

What happened is an old story now. I got in the ring. We shook hands. The bell rang. When I opened my eyes in the dressing room I was the most surprised man in the world. How he hit me or what hand he used is still a mystery to yours truly.

Listen-- when they get so fast that you can't see 'em, I'll say they have speed, and this boy Greb is a world-beater on any old kind of track."[18]

Mantell had been on the downslide for years and the Greb fight was just another wake up call for the old fighter to hang up the gloves. It was a call he wouldn't heed. He fought on for seven more years; it was a sad but all too common end to a once talented fighter.

Crouse was likely ecstatic at getting the match with Greb. He had been banned in Pittsburgh for some time due to allegations that a cancelled fight with Battling Levinsky had been fixed in advance.[19] This, coming on the heels of rumors that Crouse had taken dives in his Australian fights with Dave Smith and Les Darcy, as well as the fixed fight he participated in at Panama against Jack Ortega, made the local authorities wary of exhibiting Crouse for public consumption. There was no evidence that any of these rumors were legitimate but when word spread of the rumored agreement between Crouse and Levinsky superintendent of Police, Noble W. Matthews, issued the order that the only men he would allow Crouse to fight in Pittsburgh were George Chip, Les Darcy, and Harry Greb. With Chip defeated by Greb and Darcy dead that left only Greb for Crouse to show against in his hometown. If nothing else he was confident of victory based on his long association with Greb "I'll whip Greb just as sure as we meet in the ring," he said. "I know his style and am certain that I can get to him. This is the opportunity that I have been waiting for to stage a real comeback; and you can say for me that there's going to be a real fight."[20]

The bout would be a scheduled ten rounder, with the fighters contracted to weigh 160 lbs. "give or take a pound" at 3pm on the day of the fight. Both fighters would be expected to post a forfeit of $300 against the agreed weight.

Driven by their long rivalry, Greb was training for the Crouse fight as if it were a championship bout. Harry Keck, of the Pittsburgh Post, upon watching Greb train wrote:

> **We had a chance to see Harry Greb work out yesterday at the Pittsburgh Lyceum. The local middleweight, who is fighting probably more than any man of his pounds in the country today and is a virtual demon for stamina, is no less a tireless worker in the gymnasium than he is in the ring.**
>
> **We have never seen a fighter who hurries through his training stunts so speedily and yet does them so thoroughly as does Greb. His program yesterday, and it is his daily routine when he has a fight on, started with about five minutes of strenuous shadow boxing. Then it was five minutes at the punching bag. Then five minutes at skipping the rope. Then five minutes at the dummy bag. Then four rounds of boxing. Then five minutes of tumbling and muscle-loosening on the mat. Then a shower and a rub and then a long plunge in the swimming pool, with lots of swimming under the surface. Then a final dive and he dressed. Never for a minute did he stop until he had finished his schedule.[21]**

Mason was also working behind the scenes on Greb's behalf adding his own bit of gamesmanship. Mason, trying to distract Crouse from the fight, found fault with the check Crouse had posted as forfeit for making weight. He questioned whether the tender was legitimate and demanded a cash forfeit in its place or risk calling off the fight. Publicly Mason gave his reasoning as feeling that Crouse could not make the stipulated weight and as such had posted a bad check in the event that he come in above the agreed poundage so that he wouldn't have to pay his end of the forfeit. "Crouse is not going to put something over on me," said Mason. "I want him to show that he is trying to make the weight. I am not going to let Harry train down to the stipulated poundage, enter the ring against a chap pounds overweight, and then collect a very doubtful scrap of paper for our pains.

If Crouse is going to try to steal a march and come in fine, fat, and strong, with a big weight advantage, I want, at least, to make it costly to him."[22]

If Mason was trying to get under Crouse' skin it apparently worked. "Mason had no business making the holler he did," shot back Buck. "He knew my check was good, and that I never tried in my life to put anything of that kind over."[23] Buck immediately put up a cash forfeit and went about his training, all the while making declarations of his victory over Greb.

Greb himself wasn't immune to playing mind games with his old enemy. He made it a point to question the legality of Buck's tactics and stated that he would request the referee watch Crouse closely in the event that Crouse use foul tactics. "I don't want to take any chances with Crouse," said Harry. "He has been guilty of foul tactics in other bouts, and I have no assurance that he won't try them on me, when he sees that he is being beaten, unless the referee cautions him in advance, and warns him that he will be disqualified for the first offense."[24]

Again Crouse felt the need to defend himself in print when such allegations became public. "Greb is going a bit too far in his intimations," he said. "He is intimating that I fouled opponents to escape a beating. Nothing could be further from the truth. It is true that I have lost one or two bouts on fouls; but they were always unintentional. I never aimed low in my life. I would not resort to such tactics, and I'll make Greb eat his words when we meet one week from tonight."[25]

Despite such distractions, Crouse' training was going well. Handling his training was Patsy Brannigan, a tremendous fighter in his own right. Brannigan was putting Crouse through his paces daily, even engaging in hot sparring sessions with him in addition to Crouse' other sparring partners Kid Smith and Al Martin. Indeed Brannigan was giving Crouse such a workout in his sparring sessions that during one such heated bout Crouse was butted by Brannigan resulting in a cut lip which caused a postponement of the big match with Greb.

Upon hearing about the postponement, Greb was disappointed. "Just my luck," he said. "I was as fit as a fiddle and intended to do my final boxing today, lay off Sunday, and be ready for the bell Monday. Now I will have to let up in my training or run the risk of going stale."[26] After his initial disappointment subsided Greb took the postponement in stride, stating that he would rather have Crouse in tip top shape so there would be no excuses. "I intend to be just right for this bout," said Harry, "and I am going to allow nothing to interfere with it. I am certain that I can beat Crouse the best day he ever saw, but I am not going to take any chances and you can gamble your last dollar that I will be fit when I enter the ring next Monday.

I ought to be in better shape than Crouse, for I have not had the hard time he has had in getting down to the stipulated poundage. I can make 160 pounds any old time I try, but Buck is having an awful time getting down even to 161, if reports are correct. He will soon have to quit posing as a middleweight and take on heavies."[27]

Greb certainly wasn't kidding when he said he was taking no chances. He resumed training six days before the bout and worked so hard during a sweltering heat wave that in less than an hour he had taken off five pounds. The speed of his workouts was increased by the addition of two lightweights, Johnny Ray and Young Goldie, to Greb's sparring staff which already included promising young middleweight Jack Kelsey. Such rabid devotion to his training regimen would need to be curbed in fear of training down too fine and thus coming into his bout with Crouse handicapped. This tendency to exercise nearly to the point of overtraining would pop up off and on throughout Greb's early rise to fame. It was a condition that would at times place Greb at a disadvantage to his opponents and no doubt worried Mason as the date of the Crouse

Harry Greb (left) and Buck Crouse square off for the cameras as referee Eddie Kennedy looks on, prior to their 1917 grudge match at Pittsburgh's Exposition Music Hall.

fight approached.

As Crouse entered the ring on the night of July 2 he seemed nervous. Behind him were his seconds Francis Murphy, Patsy Brannigan, and Jimmy Perry. Greb entered the ring before a packed house, larger than that which paid to see his fights with either Al McCoy or George Chip, and shook hands with his old enemy. After receiving instructions from the referee the gong sounded and the two men resumed their combat that began in the street outside of the Oakland Gym more than two years before.

From the start of the first round Greb's strategy was obvious. He was off-setting the longer reach of Crouse by bulling his way inside and forcing Crouse to fight at a grueling pace. The few occasions Crouse was able to get range on his punches and land effectively it merely served to whip Greb into a greater fury.

As the second round opened, Greb rushed to Crouse's corner and was on top of his man before Buck had a chance to side step the attack. Again, Greb forced his way inside and mauled Crouse around the ring. Greb was fighting at such a terrific pace that Crouse could do little but defend himself and clinch. It's fair to say that Crouse was simply being swept away by the tremendous amount of punches Greb was throwing.

By the fourth round it was plain that Crouse had no idea how to deal with Greb's attack. He simply could not cope with Greb's tactics and when he finally braced himself for another Greb onslaught he was surprised to find that instead of rushing in headlong Greb was now boxing

THE FINISH OF BUCK CROUSE

Harry Greb, the winner

Greb's best bet was his uppercut & he used it often -

In the first Greb's arms went around like a windmill -

Greb had Crouse guessing with his "mad" rushes

Greb played a tune on Buck's chin in the fift

Buck tossed the sponge at the end of the sixth -

from the outside. Still baffled by this abrupt change in tactics Crouse had little time to adjust when Greb started sending in powerful blows to the mid-section which bent Buck in half. Bleeding from the nose, and trying to protect his battered face and body, Crouse was a sorry sight at the close of the round.

The fifth and sixth rounds witnessed Crouse take a severe beating. The old contender could barely defend himself; he was little more than a magnet for the blows of the onrushing boy from Garfield. Crouse was still bleeding from the nose but much more severe was the cut lip he had sustained in training. Greb had re-opened the wound and made a target of it. Crouse's mouth was now a ghastly sight as it filled with blood and pieces of flesh which had become torn over the course of the bout.

Midway through the sixth Crouse made a feeble attempt to signal his surrender but his battered maw was in such a that he could not speak intelligibly to make his intention known. The crowd, already excited to a fever pitch by the grudge match, had come to their feet screaming for a knockout. The hall was in an uproar and Greb continued pounding his old tutor. As the round ended Crouse sat down heavily on his stool and tried to communicate with his seconds through torn and bloody lips. Seconds later a sponge was tossed into the center of the ring at Crouse's request signaling his surrender.[28]

For days the Pittsburgh papers virtually ignored the great manner in which Greb had dismantled Crouse instead choosing to flay Crouse for what was widely considered an act of great cowardice. The one-sided nature of the fight and the incredible amount of punishment Crouse suffered was disregarded in light of the end result which saw Crouse pleading with his handlers to end the fight. Greb did little to help Crouse's image when he told reporters that as early as the second round Crouse was pleading with him to take it easy and as early as the fourth round Crouse was soliciting referee Kennedy to stop the fight.[29] Crouse's reputation was forever destroyed in that fight and never again would he threaten to usurp Greb's standing as Pittsburgh's favorite fighter.

With Crouse now removed from Greb's agenda it was time to focus on fights that would garner him greater recognition nationwide. Two days after the Crouse fight Greb was in Youngstown, Ohio to challenge the winner of the Mike Gibbons-George Chip bout. Gibbons, exhibiting the same defensive wizardry that had befuddled Greb in Philadelphia, dominated Chip and Greb immediately set his sights on a Gibbons rematch. Barring a bout with Gibbons there were preliminary talks for a bout with Jack Dillon, either bout to be held in Pittsburgh's Forbes Field.

As fate would have it, Mike Gibbons could not be coaxed into a bout with Greb, as a result Jack Dillon made his way to Pittsburgh to negotiate terms for a Greb match which was finalized on July 10, 1917 and scheduled for 10 rounds on July 30. Both fighters were to weigh 163 pounds at 3pm on the day of the fight. Greb, now exercising his star power, was signed to receive 25 percent of gate the same amount as the highly regarded Dillon. The ball park would be completely dark except for the ring which would be illuminated by four 1000 watt lights. Due to the growing popularity of the sport with women a special section of the park would be roped off especially for ladies wishing to view the proceedings. It would be the first boxing match held at Forbes Field, home of the Pirates since the abandonment of Exposition Park.

Dillon was no fighter to be trifled with. True enough his best days were starting to wane but this was a fighter who, despite being able to scale 158 pounds, had been able to knockout such heavyweights as Jim Flynn and Tom Cowler, and had only recently won matches from Gunboat Smith and Al McCoy. In the year previous he had won a popular decision over Pittsburgh's own heavyweight hope Frank Moran. Dillon could punch, he was durable, and with his long experience against just about every fighter of note for nearly a decade he presented a wily adversary that many felt could put an end to Greb's incredible winning streak.

Adding somewhat to the appeal of the open air bout with Dillon was the fact that Red Mason had released a public statement claiming the middleweight championship for Greb.[30] The claim went largely ignored by everyone outside of Pittsburgh yet it still had the effect of garnering Greb some local publicity which would hopefully attract a few extra visitors to his bout with Dillon. Dillon himself was taking Greb's claim seriously (at least for promotional purposes) stating that while he had been fighting primarily light heavyweights and heavyweights, he could still make the middleweight limit. With this in mind he made it known that he intended to remove Greb from title contention when they met.

Greb was again in danger of overtraining due to his excitement over the prospect of yet another high profile bout. He had been working out almost non-stop in the oppressive July heat since the battle with Dillon was signed. Mason was justifiably worried that Greb was stretching himself too thin, particularly with the prospect of a Dayton match with George "KO" Brown on the twenty-third looming up. Greb was

Jack Dillon (above) was one of history's most formidable ringmen. He was incredibly strong for his size, extremely durable, and famous for beating men of every style ranging in weight from welterweight to heavyweight.

probably lucky when the match with Brown was postponed but Mason was still concerned that his fighter would come into the ring stale. The best Mason could do was to get Greb to take a half day canoeing trip on July 19 and hope it would be enough when he resumed his training on the twentieth with light heavyweight Charlie Schons.[31] Mason would have Greb ease off of training in this manner several more times before the Dillon fight, which appealed to Greb as he loved to swim and canoe.

Speculation was rife as to the outcome of the bout. It was conceded that Dillon had probably seen better days but he was still a formidable opponent. This anticipation was causing ticket sales to soar and a record crowd was expected. Local newspapers speculated on which fighter would be able to impose his will on the other:

> **Greb is a master at any style of fighting, long range or short, offensive or aggressive, and he usually mixes up his styles so shiftily that his foes hardly know what's coming next. But against the imperturbable Dillon, who never loses his head and is always set, can he play the dashing, slashing game he likes, and, more important still, can he keep Dillon from gaining the close-in advantage he wants and pumping away at his ribs?**[32]

Two days before the bout a near disaster struck. While sparring with George Hook Greb was struck over the right eye by Hook's elbow while slipping a punch. The eye rapidly began to swell and in an attempt to curb the swelling a leech was placed on the damaged area. After the leech was removed the wound bled for several hours despite all attempts to curb the flow of blood. Greb was taken home to rest, still possessed of a massive swelling over his eye. Despite the mishap Greb refused to postpone the bout.[33] The swelling had subsided a good deal by the day of the fight but Greb, more worried about his appearance than the effect it might have on his fight, was still concerned with the wound.

Dillon and Greb entered the ring before more than 7,000 fans eager to find out if Harry could back up his championship pretensions by beating a fighter of true championship caliber. The entire affair was given an air of class by the uniformed ushers, the announcer in full evening dress, and referee dressed completely in white. The attendance of prominent Pittsburgh socialites only enhanced the glamour of the event. In addition to Pittsburgh's upper crust, members of both the Pittsburgh Pirates and the New York Giants (who had played a game in the stadium the night before) were present in force. The crowd was the largest in the history of Pittsburgh boxing.

After the preliminaries had finished the audience was hushed in anticipation. Dillon entered the ring to a lukewarm reception by partisan crowd. Silence again fell over the arena when suddenly a great clamor could be heard, a clamor which rapidly grew into a thunderous applause. Greb was entering the arena.

Both fighters had agreed to waive the weight limit but weighed in the day before the fight simply for show. Dillon stripped to his under garments weighed $158^{1/2}$ pounds while Greb weighed 165 pounds fully dressed. Greb was resplendent in his green tights with an American flag woven through his belt loops. Dillon's white trunks shone like pearl in the intense light of the ring. Despite the pro-Greb crowd Dillon was unconcerned, even letting out a yawn before the first bell rang. Dillon had been to the big dance before, he knew what to expect, or so he thought.

In the first round Greb took command of his more experienced opponent and never let him gain control. In the second round Greb started Dillon's mouth bleeding which continued throughout the fight. At times Dillon would be forced to spit blood so as not to choke on the thick gore.

After the second round a three minute time out was needed in order to replace one of Greb's gloves which had been torn. The rest did little to help Dillon's situation as he was again forced on the defensive against the on-rushing Pittsburgher. Greb was showing utter disdain for the immense reputation of the Indiana fighter, he was now willing to box or slug and more than held his own at either.

Dillon had his best round in the fourth when he rushed out and sent a tremendous blow to

The first boxing match ever held at Pittsburgh's Forbes Field (above), home of the Pittsburgh Pirates, was Harry Greb's bout with Jack Dillon in 1917. A record crowd attended the bout which was one of the social events of the summer.

Greb's jaw. It was the same punch which had felled heavyweights yet Greb stayed upright, clinched until his head cleared, and then danced out of harm's way. Dillon tried to press his advantage but every time he seemed to hurt Greb, Harry fought back harder. Still, Dillon was doing his best work of the night and many in the audience felt the tide might be turning. It was also noted that the eye which Greb injured two days previous had begun to swell again.

Those in the crowd who felt Dillon was beginning to rally were sorely mistaken when the fifth round came about and Greb battered Dillon about the ring. Dillon tried time and again to land a crusher that would put an end to his torment but Greb was far too slippery, far too quick. This pattern continued through the sixth and in the seventh the crowd got its most exciting round of the evening. Greb went right after Dillon in this round and landed a series of punches which had Dillon hurt and wobbling. The crowd leapt to its feet and sent a roar of approval as Greb pumped lefts and rights into Dillon. They cheered wildly for a knockout but Dillon was too crafty and too rugged, the opportunity passed.

Greb swept the next two rounds and in the final stanza both fighters tried hard for a knockout with Dillon receiving far more punishment. He was in bad shape at the finish with his mouth still bleeding and his features slightly distorted. Outside of the fourth which was close Dillon had not won a round.[34]

Florent Gibson of the Pittsburgh Post summed up the fight as such:

> Only his magnificent physique, ruggedness, and indomitable bulldog courage kept him on his feet. A lesser man would have sunk under the punishment but not Dillon. Dazed, sick, staggering, and weary, he kept going...[35]
>
> ...Even at straight, old-fashioned toe-to-toe slugging Greb proved himself more than Dillon's equal. He could hit with greater rapidity and score twice while Dillon was getting his ponderous punches under way. Except that one punch at the beginning of the fourth, none of Dillon's had any appreciable effect; nor slowed Harry up. Indeed Harry fought his hardest after assimilating the occasional wallop. He was unmarked from the fight, his only sign being a slight swelling of the left eye which, injured in a training bout Saturday, started to swell about half way through the fight.
>
> Dillon bled at the mouth from the second round on, and his features, distorted in a snarl - a disgusted sort of a snarl at that, were badly battered. Dillon's facial expression differed from its usual wooden mask last night. He registered rage, disappointment, and blind, helpless fury as the fight progressed.[36]

Richard guy of the Gazette-Times added:

> Every round went to Greb by at least a fair margin. Greb was able to
> walk in, hit with either hand, and then keep Dillon from doing any dam-
> age. Greb hit as often as he desired and some of the punches had force to
> them, but, with the exception of the seventh round Dillon shook off all.
> Only at intervals did Greb make Dillon wince, then causing the Hoosier to
> spit blood.[37]

Jim Jab of the Pittsburgh Press took a much more cynical view of the fight feeling that Dillon
had come simply to earn a paycheck and little else.[38] This is unlikely considering the incredible
physical conditioning Dillon showed as well as the punishment that was forced upon him by
Greb. Jab, who when not laboring under his pen name was a certain Dr. Alfred Cratty attending the denizens of the Pittsburgh's red light district,[39] had been taking a much more disparag-
ing view of Greb's fights as of late. It was becoming an almost knee jerk reaction of his to search
for excuses as to why Greb's opponents lost while ignoring the likelihood that it was Greb who
was making his opponents look poor in comparison. As a result Cratty often found himself rendering a minority report.

Dillon's own words give more insight into the circumstances of his defeat than anything Jim
Jab could conjure up in his fertile imagination. After the fight Dillon was visited in his dressing room by Joe Donnelly, the fight's announcer. Donnelly tried to offer Dillon condolences by
stating he had tried his best. Dillon, reflecting on the fight to Donnelly, offered: "What's the use
in trying against a guy like that? What's the use in trying against a cyclone like Greb? He's too
fast for me or anybody else his weight. He didn't even give me time to spit the blood out of my
mouth. He'll lick them all. He gave me a lacing and he'll give Gibbons one if he fights Mike.
His speed and aggressiveness will take all of Mike's cleverness. He's good; no use taking any
credit away from him. He's young and good. He'll lick 'em all."[40]

Following his victory over Dillon, Red Mason decided it was time he and his charge take a
much needed vacation. They would go their separate ways with plans to return to active campaigning by Labor Day. Mason went to the quiet resort town of Conneaut Lake while Greb,
with friend Buck Glenn in tow, headed off for the bright lights of New York City with hopes of
also visiting Atlantic City.

Just days after both Mason and Greb had departed for their respective destinations, light-
heavyweight champion Battling Levinsky agreed to meet Greb at Forbes Field on Labor Day.
The bout was a scheduled ten-rounder and as Levinsky was a light heavyweight there would
be no need for Greb to worry himself with making weight. The bout would be a no-decision
contest but, as with the McCoy bout, in the eventuality that the fight be terminated in Greb's
favor via knockout or foul the championship would pass to the Pittsburgher.

Meanwhile Greb was enjoying his vacation in New York. While idle, newspapers across the Midwest were churning out stories about rumored bouts he had signed for, would be participating in, or was considering. For the most part it was all gossip. Greb had decided quite firmly that his vacation would last until his Labor Day showdown with Levinsky.

The most newsworthy piece of information that was making the rounds was Greb's claim to the middleweight championship. As details filtered out it became known that while Greb would claim the title as his own he still conceded a need to settle the matter of superiority over McCoy in a twenty round bout to a decision. To entice the "Cheese Champ" into such a match Greb posted a $1000 guarantee with a Pittsburgh newspaperman and offered to donate his entire purse to the war effort. No less an authority than Milwaukee promoter and boxing expert T. S. Andrews hailed Greb as wonderful championship material and lauded the offer adding only that the inclusion of Jeff Smith and Mike Gibbons in a sort of round robin might better decide who had a clear claim to the championship.[41]

While in New York, Greb did have a chance to attend the Battling Levinsky-Jack London bout on August 6. He came away unimpressed with his future adversary. Writing back to Pittsburgh he stated "I saw Levinsky fight down here the other night. He fought a chap named Jack London and, though he stopped London in the sixth, he doesn't scare me. In fact I had a notion to jump into the ring and fight the both of them just to show the New Yorkers down here what a real fighter looks like. I've a hunch I'll be the light-heavyweight champion on and after Labor Day."[42]

The bout would certainly prove an interesting one. Levinsky could boast advantages in weight, height, reach, and experience. He had already beaten Jack Dillon for the championship and alongside the Hoosier Bearcat, in defeat, stood Gunboat Smith, Jim Coffey, Jim Flynn, and Tom Cowler. One could never call Levinsky a great champion but he was talented, with a tricky defense and the ability to absorb punishment. He was fast on his feet and fast with his hands using a combination of clever footwork and combination punching to keep his opponents outside of his reach while counterpunching his way to victory. Never a great puncher, Levinsky's best

This photo along with that on the following page are from the same publicity shoot as the photos displayed earlier. Taken in 1917 they were designed to illustrate Greb's various ring poses, even sitting on his stool between rounds.

weapon was his rapier like jab which he used both as an offensive weapon and defensive foil.

Greb returned to Pittsburgh on August 19 and headed almost immediately to Conneaut Lake where he would limber up before serious training by swimming and canoeing. It was remembered by friends and family years later that Greb fell in love with the small resort town and would often swim the length of the lake to stay trim. One week prior to the scheduled bout with Levinsky Greb began hard training and when he returned to Pittsburgh on August 25 he was already in marvelous condition. Upon arrival he made it known that he would be training at the Pittsburgh Lyceum with his loyal sparring partners George Hook and Charlie Schons.

An article published by the Pittsburgh Post just prior to his bout with Levinsky gives a unique insight into the supreme confidence that Greb exhibited as he became more experienced:

There's one peculiarity of Harry Greb's that is his, and his alone. Harry is absolutely original in many ways, but there are few fighters who do not wax pessimistic over their condition now and then, even if it is only to alibi a possible defeat. "Aw, I feel rotten!" coming from the lips of a husky, well-trained athlete sounds rather timorous, but it is heard often.

Harry's little idiosyncrasy is to always, under all circumstances, be feeling fine. A true disciple of Douglas Fairbanks. Harry is the original cheer up guy of pugilism, even when he is mighty sick. Often he has gone into the ring when he would far rather be in bed, claiming a feeling of fitness he did not possess, and fight a furious battle to victory.

Harry claims that he is "feeling fine," and that "he was never in better shape in his whole life," with his fight with Battling Levinsky only a few days off. And this time he is not kidding himself. He really is in magnificent shape for his Labor Day battle at Forbes Field, and, although Levinsky is the biggest and perhaps the most dangerous man he has ever been matched with, he is supremely confident of the outcome.

His week at Conneaut Lake, which he spent in all sorts of outdoor sports, has put him on edge, and Monday he hopped into his final whirl of preparation, consisting mainly of boxing. Many chaps would quickly go stale if they worked at the pressure Greb works, but he is put to annex the light-heavyweight championship Monday night, and intends to be "right" when the fight starts.[43]

As with Greb's recent bouts, he had trained himself too fine, he was in danger of overtraining and was forced to take a day of rest three days before the fight. When he resumed training the next day Greb injured a ligament in his left ankle which produced a swelling so severe it was feared he would need to have it lanced. Such an injury doctors agreed was a sure sign that he had been training much too hard.[44] The bout would have to be postponed; the new date would be September 6.

Both Greb and Levinsky took the opportunity to make their way to Canton, Ohio to see Carl Morris lose on a foul to Fred Fulton.[45] Upon returning to Pittsburgh Greb resumed his workouts with but two days left before his fight with the light-heavyweight champion. Greb pushed himself to his limits in that final workout just to be sure that his leg would hold when he faced Levinsky.[46] Levinsky for his part had enlisted the help of Buck Crouse to lend a hand in his training. Crouse spent the day familiarizing Levinsky with Greb's awkward style. When both completed their training they expressed confidence in victory.[47]

With the preliminaries completed announcer Joe Donnelly entered the ring and called up a diminutive little man who was led to the ring. It was announced this man, Monte Attell, brother of former featherweight champion Abe Attell and one time claimant of the bantamweight title, was now blind and in need of an operation which would restore the sight to one eye. Attell who was always a favorite in Pittsburgh due to his fights with Patsy Brannigan was immediately showered with coins and bills from the appreciative fans. Johnny Ray, Hooks Evans, and Young Goldie weaved their way through the crowd collecting donations in their hats. When the collection had ceased it was announced that $525.25 had been raised for the benefit of Attell.

As Levinsky wound his way through the crowd and stepped into the ring he was given only a fair applause. When Greb made his appearance the stadium nearly shook to its foundations with the applause of the crowd, which while not as large as that of the Dillon fight, was still considerable. When the men stripped for action it was apparent that Greb was at a great disadvantage; he appeared to be anywhere from ten to twenty pounds lighter than the champion.

Greb came out for the first round with the intent of keeping Levinsky from getting into a rhythm with his left jab. He repeatedly rushed the defense minded Levinsky to the ropes pounding away as he got inside. This waltz continued for the next four rounds to the slight annoyance of many present as it was felt by some that Levinsky was being overly cautious in an effort to preserve his laurels. The only thing making the contest interesting up to this point had been the size differential which was preventing Greb from sweeping Levinsky totally off of his feet.

The fight finally opened up in the fifth round when Levinsky began to land with more frequency. Late in the round Levinsky landed a blow to Greb's mouth which spun Harry around and sent a spray of blood across the ring. Still, Levinsky was too hesitant to put himself in harm's way and missed any opportunity he may have had.

Greb came out for the sixth intent on retaking the initiative. He dove into the Battler furiously and drove him around the ring with a series of blows to the face. Levinsky's legs were now shaking under the bombardment and it was apparent that he was in some distress. The seventh saw Levinsky try to retake command by boxing at long range with his left and using his greater size and weight against Greb in the clinches which were frequent. Greb would not be denied however and several times broke through Levinsky's guard to score enough punches to win him the round.

Battling Levinsky (above) held the light-heavyweight championship in 1917 when he faced Harry Greb at Forbes Field. His size and defensive stance was expected to pose problems for Greb who hoped to take the championship by knockout.

The eighth was Levinsky's best round. He was warned for butting early but during one of Greb's rushes he caught the Pittsburgh fighter under the heart with a tremendous blow. Greb laughed but it was apparent to all but Levinsky that he was shaken. Levinsky, having fallen for Greb's ruse, was content to stay away and let Greb lead. The body blow had taken some of the steam out of Greb and as a result Levinsky was better able to control his rushes in this round. As the bell sounded Greb sat down heavily on his stool and allowed his seconds to work furiously over him.

In the ninth Levinsky, heartened by his work in the previous round, was more willing to

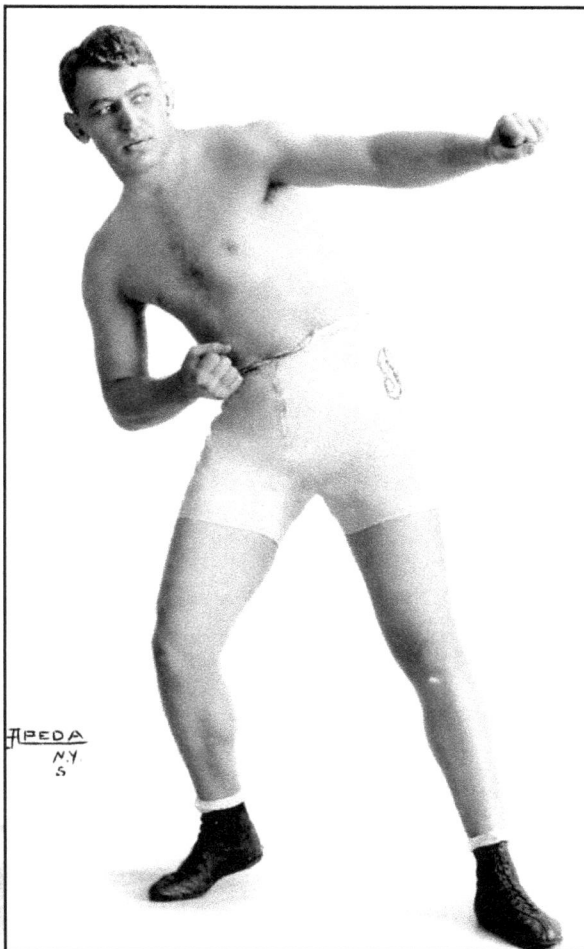

stand and trade with Greb and as a result he was met with a powerful left hook on the jaw that stopped him in his tracks. When it became apparent that Greb had recovered his strength and was more than willing to meet the Battler on his own terms Levinsky again reverted to his tactic of moving and jabbing, a policy which again brought groans from the audience.

Levinsky came out for the tenth round a tired man and eager for the final bell to sound. He was met with a raging young fighter intent on scoring a title winning knockout. Greb tore after Levinsky putting everything into his punches and swinging wildly in hopes that one of his haymakers might strike gold. It was all Levinsky could do to hold Greb off of him and suddenly a hard right landed with a thud on Levinsky's jaw and the champion dropped. Time seemed to stand still, the stadium was in pandemonium. Levinsky shook his head and was up at the count of three but clearly hurt. As the champion regained his feet Greb tore across the ring with the intent of finishing his man and bringing the title home. Before Greb could reach Levinsky the bell rang. The fight was over. Levinsky had lost the popular decision but would continue to wear his crown.[48]

In his dressing after the fight Levinsky was despondent, expressing the same frustration that plagued Jack Dillon after his defeat at Greb's hands. "Wasn't I rotten? Gee, wasn't I rotten? I couldn't get my left working. I couldn't plant my right. Gee, wasn't I rotten!"[49] Greb was ready to move on afterwards. He had one fighter on his mind and that was Mike Gibbons who as yet had not responded to any offers for a rematch with Greb. On his fight with Levinsky he commented: "Had he been my size I surely would have knocked him out. It took me a few rounds to get him down to my size and then he wasn't in the fight. He never gave me any trouble except for one body blow in the eighth round. I am sure I would have stopped him had the tenth round gone a minute longer, for he was tired and hanging on even before I knocked him down just before the bell.

I would now be light-heavyweight champion if our bout had been a 12 or 15-round affair instead of a 10-rounder."[50]

9

RUMORS OF WAR

With decisive victories over middleweight champion Al McCoy and light heavyweight champion Battling Levinsky, as well as headline catching victories such as his knockout of Buck Crouse and his wins over former champions Jack Dillon and George Chip, Harry was ready to enter the sport on the national stage. He was now ready to tackle New York City, the Mecca of boxing. If you wanted to make money, real money, in the sport of boxing you ultimately had to wind up in New York. A boxer making it big in New York could expect national headlines, bigger purses, and maybe even a championship. The downside was that New York boxing was a cutthroat world. Many fighters had traveled from the "sticks" to the Big Apple with championship dreams only to end up broken in body and spirit. If Greb were to take his career to the next level New York would be the next step.

Before taking New York by storm, Greb would have to get himself in top condition, he did so by honoring his previous fight contracts. Prior to his fight with Levinsky Greb had signed for a ten round rematch with Jeff Smith in Milwaukee to be held on September 11 in conjunction with the State Fair, and a 15 round decision match with George "KO" Brown to be held in Dayton on September 17. Greb and Smith agreed to weigh 160 lbs. at 3 o'clock in the afternoon. The bout would have a circus like atmosphere with both fighters making claims to the middleweight championship and newspapers talking of the possibility of Mike Gibbons facing the winner in a sort of unification bout.[1] To top it all off Smith had sent to Milwaukee promoters the jewel studded belt he had won in France in 1913, emblematic of his dubious claim to leadership in the middleweight division. The belt would be prominently displayed in a store-front window to help promote the bout.

Initially Smith had been made the favorite in betting odds but with a win over Levinsky under his belt odds swung in Greb's favor. The win over Levinsky had such an impact among fans of the sport that promoters across the country were now seeking him for matches. He had been offered a $300 bonus in addition to his purse by Allentown promoters to opt out of the bout with Smith and meet Jackie Clarke in that city.[2] It was while Greb was preparing to meet Jeff Smith that James Mason agreed to one of the several offers from New York Promoters. Jimmy Johnston the famous "Boy Bandit" boxing promoter had signed Greb to fight at St. Nicholas Arena against either Zulu Kid or Jack London only three days after his bout with Smith. It would be a good venue to test the waters for Greb in what was the hub of the boxing world.

Possibly feeling that Greb was getting ahead of himself with such lofty aspirations, Smith was taking nothing to chance. He spent the early part of his training in Chicago which provided him with the opportunity to train with some of the best fighters the area had to offer including Sam Langford and George "KO" Brown, who was already in preparation for his upcoming bout with Greb.[3] Smith then moved on to Milwaukee and finished his training at Morgenrath's Gym. Greb arrived late (a chronic habit of his) in Milwaukee expressing little but his confidence in beating Smith: "Far be it from me to blow my own bugle. I have made boxing my business and I go in to win. Boxing fans are perhaps acquainted with the fact that I have met and defeated some of the best middles and light heavies in America. I do not hesitate to say that I am after the 158-pound title."[4] Smith was equally confident, giving Harry all the credit he deserved yet admitting that he had his eye on a showdown with Mike Gibbons.

With White Sox owner Charlie Comiskey looking on, Harry Greb and Jeff Smith answered the opening bell for their ten round bout. In the first round Smith outboxed Greb and it looked as if his greater experience might be the deciding factor in the fight. As the second round sounded Greb, having sized his man up, began the whirlwind attack that led to victories over Dillon, and Levinsky. Smith displayed the same dazzling defense he showed in Buffalo but it was Harry who was making the fight. Greb battered Smith all around the ring barely giving him space to breathe, occasionally Smith would come back with a wicked blow to the midsection but it only made Greb fight back twice as hard. As the battle progressed it became more obvious with each successive round that Greb was simply burying Smith under a sea of gloves which Smith could only endeavor to avoid. As the fight drew to a close the crowd began to boo and hiss at Smith who was now holding on and trying to survive Greb's onslaught, which seemed to have gained momentum as the fight progressed. The Milwaukee newspapers unanimously awarded the bout to Greb and blasted Smith for his poor showing.[5]

It was by all accounts a poor fight from the fans stand-

Jeff Smith, (above) was an immensely talented fighter. He could box as well as punch. His lone Achilles Heel was his propensity to turn overly defensive. It was a weakness Greb exploited when they met to decide a suitable opponent for middleweight title claiment Mike Gibbons.

point and the blame rested entirely on the shoulders of Smith. In an attempt to make Smith atone for his poor showing the state athletic commission summoned Smith to its chambers for an explanation of the relatively minor infraction of posting his weight forfeit late. Smith refused to comply, suggesting the commission "go to hell," and promptly left town right after making it known that his check (now being held as forfeit) was worthless.[6] Smith was immediately suspended for six months in Wisconsin. Greb made many friends with his dominant performance and plans were already being made to bring him back for another engagement in the city (presumably with Mike Gibbons) as soon as his schedule allowed.

With his victory over Jeff Smith secured, Greb was now able to focus on his showcase bout in New York. He would have the honor of headlin-ing a card which included such illus-trious names as welterweight champi-

This publicity pose taken sometime in early/mid 1917 shows Greb in fighting trim and preparing to take on some of the toughest names in the light heavyweight and middleweight divisions.

on Ted "Kid" Lewis, and recently deposed welterweight champion Jack Britton. The card received minimal press and to the New York sporting public, used to frequent and spectacular events, it was just another bout, one of the many which took place on a near daily basis in the city.

The New York boxing world was a cruel and unforgiving place populated by unscrupulous managers, shifty promoters, and a multitude of pugs ranging in ability from human punching bags to virtuosos, all scraping for the last nickel like mangy dogs fighting over table scraps. Only a year earlier another young fighter had ventured east to New York in search of fame and fortune. That young fighter ended up sleeping on park benches, exploited by dishonest man-agers and eventually returned home with three fractured ribs, a broken spirit, and empty pock-ets, his name was Jack Dempsey. This was the harsh reality that Greb faced as he prepared to make his debut in "the big time" and in order to make himself known above the legion of star-

ry eyed fighters just like himself he would have to be spectacular. Unfortunately he wasn't.

What Greb and Mason had hoped would be a coming out party ended up being a no win situation. On the night of the fight Zulu Kid was prevented from proceeding with the contest by the club doctor. Jack London, a little known journeyman of modest ability was substituted as Greb's opponent. Given London's lack of ability the crowd expected a slaughter. Instead London's awkwardness and size allowed him to stay nine rounds with Greb before he was eventually sent to the canvas by a devastating overhand right. London arose on wobbly legs and after receiving further punishment the contest was halted in order to prevent further harm to the groggy fighter. The New York critics viewed the performance with disdain. London, who outweighed Greb by 14 pounds, was reasoned to be easy meat for the man hyped by Jimmy Johnston as the next Stanley Ketchel. Had Greb ended the fight in the first round the critics would have sneered that London was simply overmatched and the win proved nothing, as it was the critics smugly took the opinion that the Pittsburgher had a more difficult time with his larger opponent than his publicity had led them to believe adding a stinging parting shot that he "...does not look even like Ketchel's ghost."[7]

While in New York the most interesting publicity Harry received was for the peculiar habit of training to the strains of a live pianist. He stressed that such a practice improved his speed and timing, both of which he would need in his next bout.[8]

Greb was now off to Dayton, Ohio for his fifteen round rematch with the redoubtable George "KO" Brown. Brown, still famous for his durability, was preparing to enter the army and this would be his last bout prior to joining the war effort. He stressed his intention to make the most of it. The legendary Sam Langford had helped Brown prepare for the bout in Chicago. "Feeling fine, and am ready to fight the battle of my career and see no reason why I should not be able to beat Greb tonight so have a bet on me and rest easy."[9] This was the confidence Brown exuded as he arrived in Dayton prior to the fight. Brown's poise rewarded him little as Greb

Greb startled fans across the midwest when he forced the incredibly durable George "KO" Brown (above) to quit in the ninth round of their scheduled 15 round rematch in Dayton, Ohio.

tore into him from the opening bell, never letting Brown get set to punch. Round after round Greb forced the fight at such a pace that at times Brown became frustrated at his own ineffectiveness and resorted to using elbows and hitting on the break. Greb kept his calm in such situations, continuing to pile up points and befuddle the Greek battler with his speed. On one occasion Brown maneuvered Greb into a corner only to find that when he let fly his punches Greb was out and behind him. As Brown turned Greb shot a volley of blows to the head in such rapid succession that Brown was forced to clinch. As the eighth round came to a close Brown notified the officials that he had broken his right hand. A cursory inspection was made with no fracture being evident. James Mason stood up and announced that Greb was willing to continue whenever Brown felt comfortable despite his right to claim victory on a foul over the delay.

After a short rest Brown came out for the ninth round but quickly made it clear that he could not, or would not use his right hand to defend himself. As a result referee Lou Bauman sent Brown to his corner and raised Greb's glove in victory.[10]

Leaving Dayton with many new friends and fans, Greb now had five days to rest before taking on Battling Kopin in ten rounds at Charleroi, Pennsylvania. Kopin had been a tremendous talent in the welterweight division but had since outgrown the class and was now fighting as a middleweight. Greb made it known that he intended to continue his knockout streak against Kopin and proceeded to train accordingly. It took Greb only three rounds to dismiss his opponent as Kopin claimed a broken wrist before the start of the fourth round. Physicians examining the wounded appendage were non-committal on the validity of Kopin's claims. It was duly noted that Greb had a great advantage over his opponent at the time of the stoppage and that mismatch may not have been too strong a word.[11]

Greb continued his dizzy schedule by facing Johnny Howard at the Broadway Sporting Club in Brooklyn, New York. Greb was determined to make a better showing than his last appearance in New York. His opponent had initially been the sturdy deaf/mute "Silent" Martin. Martin bowed

Battling Kopin (above) had been a top notch welterweight who had moved up to the middleweight division when he was stopped in consecutive matches with Harry Greb.

out of the proceedings and Johnny Howard of Bayonne, New Jersey was selected as a replacement. In Howard Greb had an opponent who was both well-known and well-respected. A decisive victory over Howard would do much to warm the icy New York press to his cause. Chilly indeed was the reception Greb received upon his return to New York. Fred Hawthorne of the New York Tribune commented "Greb, upon the lone occasion when we saw him perform at the St. Nicholas Rink, a couple of weeks ago, reminded us strongly of the old farm of our boyhood days. The principle feature of that farm was the swinging gate, and Harry is like that, so it is just possible that Howard may land a swing tonight on Greb's whalebone jaw."[12] Greb's determination to show such criticisms false was evident in the first round when he sailed into Howard and sent the man sprawling to the canvas with a terrific left. Greb continually tore into his man ignoring any blows returned by Howard. In the third a right-left combination sent Howard flopping to the canvas again. As the rounds progressed Howard began to take a frightful beating. As the bell for the ninth round sounded Greb shot from his stool like a bullet from a gun and smashed Howard all over the ring finally dropping him for a count of nine. Howard arose unaware of his surroundings and unable to defend himself against the fury that Greb now unleashed upon him. Referee Johnny Haukop jumped between the fighters and escorted Greb back to his corner, raising his hand in victory. The bout signaled a slight melting of the ice between Greb and the New York press which had so harshly received him.[13]

Johnny Howard (above) of Bayonne, New Jersey was known as the "Fighting Cop." He was a well known, respected fighter when he faced Greb in 1917 in a bout that finally provided Greb with some positive coverage in New York.

After his bout with Howard, the Broadway Sporting Club tried to sign Greb to fight Gus Christie. It was a match that promoters across the country were bidding on. Tom Andrews of

Milwaukee wanted the match as well as Jack McGuigan of the National Sporting Club in Philadelphia. Mason exercised his managerial acumen by maximizing Greb's profit and popularity in bypassing the Broadway Club's offer for a chance to fight Christie in Buffalo. This may have seemed foolish in light of the plan to bring Greb greater fame in New York City but it was actually a cunning move on Mason's part. By passing up the Broadway Athletic Club's offer for a Christie bout he hoped to enter into negotiations at the club for a bout with middleweight champion Al McCoy. If Greb could continue his knockout streak in a bout with Al McCoy he would gain recognition as champion of the division. In turn Mason accepted offers from Milwaukee and Philadelphia but not for bouts with Christie. Milwaukee, he hoped, would acquire Mike Gibbons as an opponent. A win over Gibbons, still regarded by many as the best middleweight in the world, combined with the hoped for knockout of Al McCoy would cement Greb's claim on the championship. The Philadelphia bout Mason signed for would be against talented ex-welterweight Billy Kramer.[14]

The Kramer bout was the opening to Mason's planned assault on the championship. Initially it was to serve as little more than a warm-up bout yet Kramer fought the fight of his life and ended up giving Greb a difficult time. It was Greb's greater size and his furious late round rally that saved the popular decision for him.[15] He could afford no setbacks. Next Greb ventured to Buffalo, New York for the bout with Gus Christie which had sent clubs across the country clamoring for the opportunity to promote the show. Mason had selected Buffalo over more desirable locations for two reasons, the first being that Greb was immensely popular in Buffalo. The second being that two months previous Buffalo had hosted a tremendous bout between Gus Christie, and the sensational black light-heavyweight Kid Norfolk, who outweighed Christie by twelve pounds. For ten rounds the two fighters stood toe-to-toe and slugged it out. During one of the later sessions Christie landed a powerful blow which sent a spray of teeth from Norfolk's mouth that ringsiders collected as souvenirs. At the conclusion opinions varied as to who had deserved the decision. James Mason was ringside for the contest and calls went up immediately for Greb to face one of the two men. Thus the promotion was a cinch in Buffalo.

At ringside Greb weighed in at $161^{1/2}$ while Christie weighed $164^{1/2}$. Ringsiders called the first round even,

Billy Kramer (above) was a talented welterweight from Milwaukee who had grown into the middleweight division when he gave Greb a close battle in Philadelphia.

GREB: BEST BET WAS A LUNGE AT CHRISTIE'S BODY TO BE MET BY A VELVET LIKE PARRY — OF COURSE A FEW GOT BY.

Contemporary cartoon drawn at ringside during the Greb-Christie bout held in Buffalo in 1917.

the best round Christie would muster against the young dynamo from Pittsburgh. Early in the fight Greb sliced open Christie's left eye and the crimson optic became a target for Harry throughout the fight. Round after round Greb utterly dominated Christie and left no question as to who the winner would be when the final gong sounded.[16] Just prior to the match it had been agreed that Greb would finally get his long awaited rematch with middleweight Champion Al McCoy at the Broadway Sporting Club in Brooklyn. Mason's gamble had paid off, or so it would seem.

With Greb and Mason awaiting the bout with McCoy as a couple of ravenous wolves eye a lamb, a telegram was received from John Weismantle, promoter of the bout, announcing that McCoy had refused to honor his agreement to meet Greb on October 16 and that he had severed relations with his manager Jack Bulger.[17] Speculation was rife that Greb's easy victory over Gus Christie was the deciding factor in McCoy's reluctance to meet the Pittsburgh fighter and that his subsequent split with Bulger was prompted by Bulger's carelessness in matching McCoy with one of the most vicious fighters in the division.[18] Incensed at what he considered an act of cowardice, the defiant James Mason sent a press release to news outlets across the country claiming the middleweight championship for Harry Greb on the grounds that he had proven himself to be an outstanding challenger for the title and McCoy as champion had flatly refused to face him. The statement (the second such statement sent out by Mason), like numerous others issued since the death of Stanley Ketchel was not widely accepted but it was a bit of publicity that could be exploited as leverage for larger purses, and more meaningful fights.

As Greb finished out the month of October with a popular decision over Len Rowlands in Milwaukee and a referee's decision over Gus Christie in Chattanooga, Tennessee, talk of the tragedies in Europe were everywhere. Young men were registering with their local draft

James Mason claimed the middleweight championship for Harry Greb when Al McCoy (above) backed out of their scheduled ten round bout at the Broadway Sporting Club in Brooklyn, New York two days before the October 16th engagement.

offices, signing up to the colors, and shipping off to training cantonments across the country in preparation for the trenches of the western front. The boxing world was not immune to the patriotic fervor that was sweeping the nation. Mike Gibbons was prevented from accepting his showdown with Greb due to the fact that he was preparing to leave for Fort Dodge, Iowa were he would train soldiers in self-defense and eventually author a pamphlet on the use of the bayonet. Benny Leonard, lightweight champion and one of the most popular boxers of the age, was also preparing to leave for Camp Upton where he too would serve as a training instructor. While in Chicago training for his bout with Rowlands, Greb invited sailors from the Great Lakes Naval Training station to Kid Howard's gymnasium to watch him spar a heated session with Bryan Downey. During the Greb-Rowlands card, which was headlined by heavyweight contenders Fred Fulton and Bob Devere, a Canadian army officer delivered a speech from center ring calling on all able bodied British, Canadian, and American men to sign up for active service. The war that had spilled over so many borders in Europe and had seemed so far away at one time was now weighing heavily on the young care-free mind of Harry Greb. The reality that much of the world was at war was inescapable, and if Greb was in need of a reminder he need look no further than Thomas F. Enright of Pittsburgh, who became one of the first combat casualties of the American Expeditionary Forces, and whose remains would not return from that foreign land until four years later.

As the date for Greb's Chattanooga rematch with Gus Christie drew near both fighters were

Gus Christie (above) was a tough, talented middleweight/light-heavyweight who had stood up to some of the best fighters in the sport. He faced Greb three times in 1917 and lost the newspaper decision in each of their bouts.

lauded for having registered with the armed forces. It was only a matter of time now before Greb's number would be called[19] and he would be sent away to help in the war effort. It was due in large part to this fact that James Mason had Greb on such an accelerated schedule of fights. They both wanted to make as much money as possible before Greb went off to war. Nobody knew how long the war might last and what the outcome might be.

Heavyweight champion Jess Willard added to Greb's prestige when, passing through Chattanooga with his Buffalo Bill Circus, he commented "This boy Greb who fights here next week is sure to be champion of the middleweights, in my opinion. He is one of the best men in the game today. Christie is able to make it interesting for him, too, and Chattanooga folks ought to be in for a corking good fight when these two get together."[20] Christie added to this compliment with a remark taken from experience: "That boy is one fighting terror, and when they talk about him not being clever, they don't know what they are talking about. He may not be a Mike Gibbons etc. but believe me he is some bear in his own awkward style. He starts out like a whirlwind and just about the time you think he is ready to blow up he comes on stronger than ever. I have fought all of the middleweights, but never met one with so much stamina as this fellow has. He seems to be made of iron and never lets up for a moment. I hurt him, or at least I thought I did several times, but he only smiled and came back like a bull. In a long fight he will beat Gibbons and all of them, to my way of thinking."[21] This was not simply idle praise to boost the gate of the upcoming bout. Christie had indeed faced a plethora of talented fighters. His record was dotted with names like Mike and Tommy Gibbons, Kid Norfolk, Battling Levinsky, Jack Dillon, George Chip, Billy Miske, and Les Darcy. Christie had a genuine respect for Greb's ability and it showed when they finally met on October 23, 1917 at Chattanooga's Armory. In fact it might be said that Christie had too much respect for Greb as he spent most the bout holding and trying to avoid punishment. It was the opinion of ringsiders that Christie spoiled the match with such tactics and that Greb was far ahead of Christie in fistic class that he would need a better opponent to show his championship wares in the future.[22]

While Greb was preparing for the Christie rematch Red Mason was busy lining up more bouts. Negotiations had begun and stalled for a match with Kid Norfolk who had put up such a great fight against Christie in Buffalo. Buffalo promoters were eager to bring together the Negro star and the bounding Pittsburgh contender but a hitch in negotiations occurred over the weight difference. Mason was keenly aware that Norfolk could comfortably weigh 180 pounds[23] while Greb could reduce to 158 pounds if need be. Thus Mason reasoned that Norfolk should agree to weigh no more than 175 pounds at six o'clock on the night of the fight. To most this seemed a reasonable request for such an exciting match-up. Unfortunately Leo Flynn, Norfolk's manager saw matters in a much different light. Norfolk had only recently defeated Billy Miske in Boston via twelve round decision; the victory was an important one and gave

Flynn the opinion that he could dictate terms. Mason, along with most everyone else, disagreed and Norfolk was left out in the cold. It was a poor decision on Flynn's part as Norfolk's career would stagnate for the next six months while Greb's fame continued to grow.

When Leo Flynn dropped the ball on the Greb-Norfolk bout Dan McKetrick, manager of Soldier Bartfield, was quick to seize the opportunity. He immediately turned the tables on Mason and stated that if Greb would weigh 160 for a fight Bartfield would sign.[24] Mason was reluctant to agree. Bartfield was a dangerous fighter who had a reputation of making talented boxers look awful. He was little more than a blown up welterweight but he was strong, fast, durable, and awkward. His pet punch was a backhand delivered while seemingly in full retreat with his back turned on his opponent. It was odd but effective. Mason knew that allowing Greb to reduce his weight to 160 might weaken his fighter, giving Bartfield, who would have no trouble making the weight limit, the advantage. While Bartfield would essentially be fighting at his comfort level, Greb would have to keep his weight artificially low for an extended period of time, as he was already signed to meet George Chip in Cincinnati on October 29 (four days before his meeting with Bartfield) at 158 pounds. Negotiations continued for the better part of a week with McKetrick and Mason heatedly scrounging for every advantage in the articles of agreement. At one point a frustrated Mason commented on his unwillingness to budge

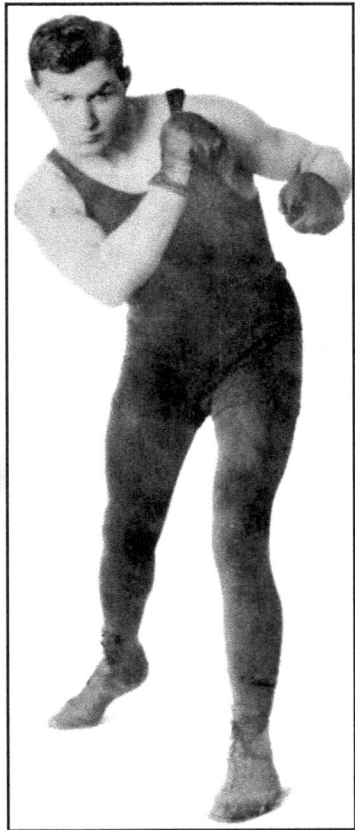

Jacob "Soldier" Bartfield (above) was one of the toughest little men to ever lace on a glove. He fought some of the best fighters in history and gave each of them a rough time

in the dialogue "Not an inch, not an ounce. That New York mob can't dictate to us. Bartfield asked for this match, not Greb. We can fight middleweights and don't have to look for men like Bartfield... ... Greb will do 160 pounds at 5 o'clock, not an ounce less, or an hour earlier or later. If the match is on, wire me; if not save the telegraph and telephone tolls by not bothering me."[25]

Finally the Queensberry Athletic Club of Buffalo was able to match the two fighters. Greb agreed to make 160 pounds at 5 o'clock on November 2, the day of the battle. Buffalo was ecstatic over the matching of what it considered two of the finest middleweights in the world. The consensus was that Bartfield posed the best chance of any prospective opponent of slowing Greb's rise to dominance in the division. Many reasoned that Greb's style of leaping in on his opponents would leave him open for one of Bartfield's sneak backhand punches.

During preparation for his bouts with Chip and Bartfield, Greb suffered a cut ear which became infected and swollen; as a result his match with Chip was postponed. At the very least this prevented Greb from having to maintain a low weight for such a long period, on the other hand it diverted Greb from his usual method training which was to fight himself into shape.[26]

Bartfield arrived in Buffalo on the day of the fight after having participated in a patriotic card for the benefit of the Red Cross and the Army Athletic Fund in New York. Buffalo was wild with excitement over the coming bout. As the first round commenced, Greb rushed out of his corner in his characteristic manner, bearing down on his opponent with a smile and the thought of overwhelming victory. Instead he met with a sudden crackling backhand left to the jaw. Greb moved in again only to be met with the same punch. The smile was now off of Greb's face and he was deadly earnest.

Round after round the two fighters battled back and forth. Whenever Bartfield smacked Greb with a solid thump Greb would retaliate with a torrent of blows. The effectiveness of Bartfield in blocking these blows amazed the crowd. A few rounds into the fight Greb changed his style and started to box effectively at long range, utilizing his superi-

Contemporary cartoon of the Greb-Bartfield bout in Buffalo. the illustration shows Bartfields famous backhand punch which he used to halt Greb's relentless attacks.

or reach. Bartfield was able to counter this style effectively but it was apparent to all that his early momentum was slowly fading. The fight grew more furious with each succeeding round as Greb's famed stamina began to tell on Bartfield. The final round was frenzied as Greb fought ferociously to turn the tide in his honor. Bartfield was visibly weakening and Greb's rushes were weighing heavily on his now shaking legs. At one point Greb attacked with such fury that Bartfield was thrown to the mat but shot up in an instant and leapt back into combat. As the final gong rang the crowd was on its feet roaring with applause. The two fighters patted each other on the back and returned to their corners. The next day's newspapers judged the fight a razor thin win for Bartfield via his early lead.[27]

Greb exploded when he read the newspaper verdicts rendered against him by the four major newspapers in Buffalo, the Morning Express, the Evening News, the Enquirer, and the Courier. When Greb read the decisions surrounded by the same reporters who had written their verdicts he was furious. "This is an outrage. Bartfield can't fight and I proved it. I beat Bartfield in every round but the third. I admit he hit me two or three hard punches in that round but in the others he never hit me as hard as Knockout Brennen used to. If ever I beat a man I beat Bartfield. Why, I could feel him sagging in my arms in the tenth round. I can't see how any man who knows the first thing about fighting or judging boxing bouts could see Bartfield in front. I don't think he was entitled to a draw. I'll bet $1,000 right now that you couldn't get him to fight me again. I have fought forty-one times in the last year and this is the first decision I have lost since Mike Gibbons. If Bartfield will fight me again, let me weigh the same. 162 ringside, I will knock him out or I'll give him my end of the purse. Get him and get him quick so I can knock his fool head off.[28]

Bartfield is stronger than most people believe, can box and hit well and is a great ring general. Maybe I tried to get him too fast the other night, but I still believe that victory ordinarily rests with the attacking party and if I meet him again I will go after him even hotter and he'll never backhand me like he did again. The Soldier was completely gone in the last round and ready to be finished. I don't believe you could ever coax him into the ring with me again. If you can shoot me a wire. If you can't any middleweight in the world will do."[29]

Bartfield had his own opinion of the matter: "Can he hit? Oi, Yoi! By golly, that boy he's got a regular sock. He hit me a right hand drive on the neck and one in the ribs that made me feel my back it's broke completely. He hit me harder than Gibbons or any man I ever met. And such a rough guy! He's a wrestler, I think. He laid on me, he shoved me, he hit me with his head, he give me the shoulder, the elbow; by golly I thought one time he wanted to roll off the platform with me. But these big guys they all get rough when they know a little man is licking 'em. And the old Soldier licked him eh..."[30]

When told of Greb's angry comments Bartfield remarked "Ah, n-o-w it begins to look like matchmaking, well, you'll have to see Danny McKetrick about that. If he says fight Jess Willard, then the Soldier will do it. I can beat Greb any time, any place, but Dan, he's the man to talk to about matches."[31]

Florent Gibson of the Pittsburgh Post speculated that Buffalo newspapers had punished Greb with a loss because prior to the fight with Bartfield he had refused to face Mike Gibbons in Buffalo in the event that he win, hoping instead to face Gibbons in Pittsburgh where negotiations for such a match were ongoing.[32] This scenario is highly unlikely. While it's true that Pittsburgh was working diligently at matching Gibbons and Greb the match was going nowhere. Gibbons was in the army, or at least preparing to report to duty, and as such promoters across the country who were bidding for his services met with frustration. Indeed Gibbons would not fight again until after the war had ended. Mason was savvy enough not to burn any of his bridges by flatly refusing a high profile fight in such a manner. Greb for his part likely would have agreed to fight anybody, anywhere, this was simply his nature.

November 14, 1917 was a day that sent shockwaves through the boxing community. On November 14, 1917 Al McCoy faced Mike O'Dowd, the Fighting Harp of St. Paul, in a bout which would be the final contest fought under New York's Frawley law, which legalized ten round no-decision boxing matches in the state. The bout, held at the Clermont Sporting Club in Brooklyn instantly revitalized the middleweight division. When the match was initially signed it seemed to many that it would be another in a long line of lackluster attempts by Al McCoy to merely survive his opponent and hang on to his cherished crown. It wasn't that O'Dowd was a bad fighter; in truth he was an excellent fighter, having only recently defeated the great English fighter Ted "Kid" Lewis. He had a nice string of victories coming into the McCoy match, and had faced men such as Billy Miske, Soldier Bartfield, and Jack Britton. O'Dowd was as tough as shoe-leather, he could punch, and he had somewhat underrated boxing skills. The problem was that O'Dowd seemed on the small side for a middleweight. He could comfortably weigh 154 pounds, and against McCoy was outweighed by ten pounds. McCoy had made a habit of being able to stay out of harm's way in no-decision matches long enough to retain his title. McCoy didn't so much beat his opponents as he outlasted them. Given the size disparity, this seemed like the likely outcome once again.

That is exactly how the fight looked in the first three rounds as McCoy did his best to clinch every time the smaller O'Dowd would bore into him with fists pumping like pistons. It seemed as if McCoy would usher out the era of the Frawley law while still maintaining his claim to the title and his unpopularity with fans everywhere who rejoiced in calling him the "Cheese Champ." In the fourth round things changed dramatically for McCoy, the fans at ringside, and the entire middleweight division. In a wild and furious exchange McCoy was sent to the canvas four times by right hands and O'Dowd was down twice (probably under the weight of his own attack more than that of McCoy's). In the sixth O'Dowd struck again with deadly accuracy. A right hand followed by a picture perfect, smashing left hook dropped McCoy in heap on the canvas. McCoy's personal referee Johnny McAvoy began to count as McCoy struggled to his feet. Once on his feet O'Dowd was on top of McCoy and rushed him furiously to the ropes

Contemporary cartoon illustrating the animosity that Greb and Chip held for one another. Chip always referred to Greb as a "fresh kid" while Greb looked upon the ex-champ as merely a stepping stone for greater things.

where McCoy was sent down again. This time McCoy took the full nine seconds to clear his head. Nine seconds wasn't long enough. As McCoy stood on unsteady legs O'Dowd backed him into a corner, shot a straight left jab which opened McCoy's defense, and then crossed a tremendous right hand which froze McCoy for an instant and then sent him toppling over on his side. As McAvoy tolled off the count, McCoy's father, tears rolling down his cheeks, tossed in the towel. The fight was over. Mike O'Dowd had won the championship by knockout and the already riotous audience went wild.[33]

With the passing of McCoy as champion Greb's focus shifted from a man reluctant to put his title at risk to O'Dowd, a lion hearted little fighter who feared no one. Things were beginning to look a lot better for Greb or anyone else who styled themselves a middleweight contender. As for the passing of the Frawley law it would now be up to the local civic governments in New York, and the states that used New York as an example, to regulate boxing as they saw fit. Whether the sport would survive was a question on every promoter's mind. While war was slowly drawing the United States and its fighter's attentions away from more leisurely pursuits, it was the war which would eventually prove boxing's savior.

Five days after O'Dowd was crowned champion, Greb entered the ring in Cincinnati's Heuck's Theatre to face his old foe and former champion George Chip. With the history between these two fighters the fans hoped to see a continuation of their previous grudge matches and it didn't help that Chip continued to refer to Greb as a "fresh kid."[34] Both fighters had posted a two hundred dollar forfeit to make the 158 lb. limit and when they stepped on the scales at three in the afternoon Greb was one pound overweight. It cost him two hundred dollars. George Chip paid for every one of those two hundred dollars with his hide. Despite a high fever, for ten rounds Greb drove Chip across the ring with a cascade of rights and lefts. In between rounds Greb would return to his corner and dunk his entire head into a bucket of ice water. Thus refreshed Greb would renew his demonic pace and continue giving Chip the beat-

1 and 2. Stills from the actual film of the fight show Mike O'Dowd landing a crushing left hook to Al McCoy's chin.

3. McCoy struggles to rise as referee McAvoy counts over him.

4. After regaining his feet, McCoy is down again. The fury of O'Dowds attack forces him to the canvas.

5. *O'Dowd backs a wobbly McCoy into a corner and lands a dynamite right hand.*

6 and 7. *McCoy drops to the canvas as if pole-axed.*

8. *As McAvoy administers yet another count, with O'Dowd pacing like a tiger, the corner of McCoy throws in the towel symbolizing the end of the fight.*

9. *Mike O'Dowd races back to his corner in jubilation. A new champion is born.*

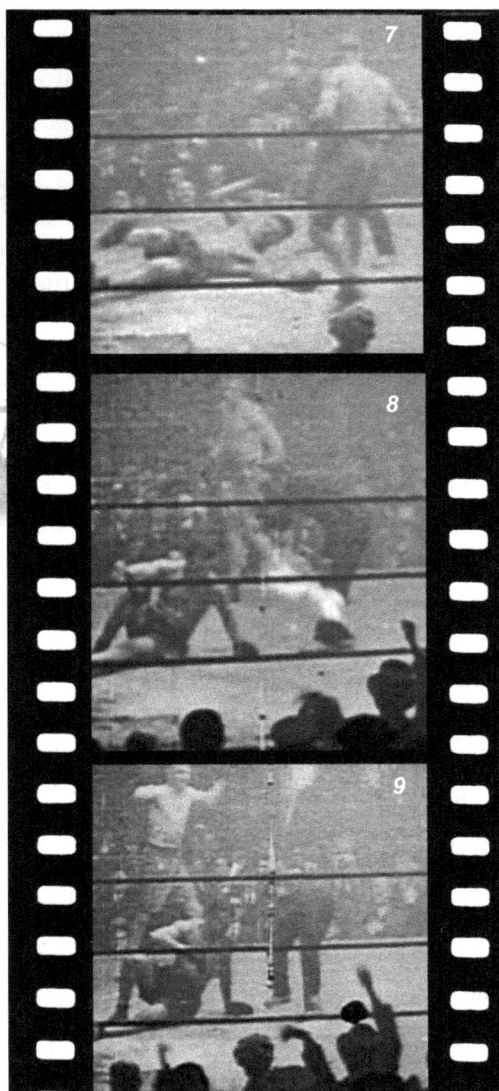

Despite his substantial girth Willie Meehan (above right) was a talented and unorthodox fighter who boasted a win over future heavyweight champion Jack Dempsey (above left) when he faced Greb in 1917. Nearly a year later he would succeed in defeating the "Manassa Mauler" once more.

ing of a lifetime. As in previous contests Greb made a hit out of his first appearance in Cincinnati. The fans went wild over his victory while newspapers ran stories about him for weeks after he left town.[35]

With a win over Chip on his record and future showdown with O'Dowd on his mind Greb headed east to Philadelphia in order to face the "Frisco Fat Boy" Willie Meehan. Meehan was something of a clown act in boxing. His rolls of fat belied an unorthodox style and solid skills that gave many of the best fighters he fought great difficulty. He had only recently arrived from the west coast after helping to slow the meteoric rise of a young heavyweight contender named Jack Dempsey. Dempsey and Meehan had squared off four times in the past six months managing to win once, hold Dempsey even twice, and lost once. Meehan had turned professional nearly ten years earlier as a scrawny 93 pounder. He quickly grew into a somewhat doughy middleweight and continued his rapid weight gain until finally topping out as a rather comic looking five foot, nine inch, 195 pound heavyweight. In the ring Meehan would use a mixture of slapstick and surprising speed to confuse his opponents. Today Meehan would be known as a spoiler, a fighter who win, lose, or draw would make his opponent look bad.

Greb easily defeated Meehan in the estimation of all present. The bout, which was a poor one to begin with, was upstaged by the exciting undercard. Meehan had a great advantage in weight over Greb weighing 187 pounds to Greb's 160, and yet Harry beat a tattoo on every part of the Californian's ample anatomy. The Philadelphia Public Ledger was quoted on the bout as

Gus Christie (left) with manager Sam Marburger (center) and stablemate Jack Dillon. Harry Greb would defeat both Dillon and Christie a total of four times in 1917.

such:

> "At times the contest bordered on a Burlesque. Meehan ducked, dodged, and slapped his opponent on the ears with his open glove. He, however, did no damage. Greb, on the contrary, decorated the fat ungainly heavyweight, leaving the latter's right eye partly closed and his nose and lips bleeding at the finish...
>
> Meehan boxed his usual slambang style, sending his swings across in wild fashion. Some landed on Greb's body. Others swished over his head. While several failed to land at all. His grotesque style and the ability of such a fat man to stand the terrific pace made a hit with the crowd. He was forgiven for his shortcomings because he boxed at top speed and gave the crowd his best."[36]

Two days after his bout with Meehan Greb was in Johnstown, Pennsylvania for a bout with George "Kid" Ashe. Ashe was a large middleweight who had faced some of the biggest names in the sport over the past five years including Kid Norfolk, Jack Dillon, Battling Levinsky, Leo Houck, Gus Christie, and others. Ashe was easy meat for Greb. He received a frightful beating at the Pittsburgh fighter's hands and had the dubious honor of staying the limit of ten rounds under speculation that Greb had been pulling his punches.[37] Three days later Greb was again on the warpath knocking out the veteran Terry Martin in three rounds, ending his career.[38]

After a brief return to his hometown Greb left for Cincinnati to face Gus Christie for a third time. Christie had only recently recovered from a rather novel surgery. He had willingly gone

George "Kid" Ashe was a respected jour-neyman who had fought several of the sports top fighters. He provided cannon fod-der for Greb's attack when they met late in 1917.

under the knife in order to shave the bones of his brow ridge down to prevent cutting and swelling during fights. If Greb could convinc-ingly defeat the "new and improved" Gus Christie for a third time he was expected to return to Pittsburgh and treat his hometown fans to a Christmas day boxing show featur-ing his old nemesis Whitey Wenzel.

With the memory of Greb's sensational vic-tory over George Chip still on their minds, Cincinnati fight fans packed Heuck's Theater for a sellout crowd anticipating another sensa-tional performance. Greb delivered, battering Christie about the ring. Harry won every round of the fight and kept his opponent so busy blocking punches that he had few opportunities to mount his own offense. The next day Cincinnati sports enthusiasts were bustling with excitement over Harry's dis-play. The Cincinnati Enquirer's glowing report underscored Greb's rapid rise to appar-ent dominance over the light heavyweight and middleweight divisions:

"Never in the history of the local prize ring has a boxer given more sat-isfaction than Harry Greb, the Pittsbu-rgh bearcat, who made his second appear-ance last night at the Queen City Athletic Club shown in a 12 round bout.... If there is any part of Christie's anatomy that Greb did not hit last night it was below the belt, as Harry never missed the mark any time he aimed a blow...

From the first round on it was plainly evident that it was Greb's night, although Christie put up a good fight and did his very best. But Christie or no other man has any business in the ring with this wild man from Pittsburgh, as he is in a class by himself, and at present writing can whip any man in the game with the possible exception of big Jess Willard, and it is no cinch that Willard could beat him if Greb keeps up his current pace."[39]

With such a glowing endorsement being dispatched to news outlets across the country Greb returned to Pittsburgh where he would show his wares for the first time since defeating Battling Levinsky. It was not by accident that Greb had not appeared in his hometown for so long. During the buildup to his bout with Levinsky he had been angered by the news that Pittsburgh promoters had offered Benny Leonard $7,500 to face Phil Bloom. Greb felt that in light of such a guarantee he was being short changed by promoters at home who were taking his new fame for granted.[40] So it was by design that Greb had begun his semi-exile from Pittsburgh to fight in other locales which promised higher purses.

Despite the passage of only a few short months Greb had fought fifteen times in ten different cities against some of the best fighters in the world. He had scored five knockouts, won 9 decisions officially or otherwise, and lost only one verdict in the eyes of newspapermen (if not himself). It seemed like an eternity since he had the opportunity to exhibit his skill for his loyal fans in Pittsburgh. It was suitable that his opponent would be Whitey Wenzel whom he had first faced one week shy of four years ago when barely just starting his career.

The long lasting ring feud between Whitey Wenzel (above) and Harry Greb, came to an abrupt end on Christmas day 1917 when Greb easily outclassed his old rival.

After taking a hiatus from ring work for a period Wenzel had returned and was working his way back to form. He was improving to such a degree that of his three previous opponents, one had been sent to the morgue and another to the hospital. Jimmy Wilson had died as result of injuries suffered in his November 28 bout with Wenzel when he was knocked down, his head striking the edge of the ring. Three days later Wenzel's next opponent, former Greb sparring partner Charles Schons, was in a Pittsburgh hospital as a result of a fractured collar bone suffered at the hands of Wenzel. Wenzel was tough and experienced not to mention that he had a firm grasp of Greb's style and tactics garnered in his nine previous bouts with Greb.

Greb for his part wasn't taking any chances. His grueling fight schedule had left his hands in poor shape and he was forced to limit his boxing preparation as a result. "A fellow's got to have a perfect pair of hands to make an impression on Wenzel. He's one of the toughest birds I've ever met and I know from experience that I have to put all I've got into a punch to faze

him. You can't do that if there's anything wrong with your hands so I'm not taking any unnec-essary risks."[41] Wenzel had his own ideas about the fight. "I am hitting harder than ever now and I don't think Greb can wallop me hard enough to hurt me. Therefore I am going to wade in and try to stop him. Watch me, I fought Greb nine or ten times before I retired nearly two years ago and I always gave him a good fight. I won't fail to repeat on this occasion, for I know just how much a win over Greb will mean for me."[42] With that the two fighters prepared to give each other a lavish Christmas dinner: a knuckle sandwich.

Unfortunately for Wenzel Greb's development, in the interim between their previous bout and this, had been such that Whitey was nowhere near his class in this, their final meeting. Greb easily dominated the fight from start to finish. In the fifth round Greb sliced open Wenzel's eye and blood streamed down his face for the remainder of the fight. Hinting at the hand problems Greb had alluded to prior to the fight, he allowed Wenzel to finish the full ten rounds on his feet in what most felt was an obvious display of mercy.[43]

After the fight Greb gave Wenzel credit for being a game opponent. "Don't you let anyone tell you that Whitey can't still hold his own. He can hit just as hard as any time I have fought him, and we have met nine or ten times. He still has that wicked uppercut and against a slow-er man might do a lot of damage. I had to watch myself at several stages during the bout. He's

Scenes like this were becoming commonplace in late 1917. Young men piled onto trains waiting to take them to training camps across the nation in preperation for war. They were treated as celebrities in the newspapers and people flocked to see them off.

far from through- that fellow Whitey."[44] Conspicuously working Greb's corner, swinging a towel, had been a man in the uniform of the United States Army. The man was an old friend, Bill Gemmell, who had since joined the army and was preparing to sail for France and the trenches of Europe which by now had destroyed so many young lives. Scenes such as this were becoming all too common in Pittsburgh and around the country. Young men were flocking to the service of Uncle Sam. Men in uniform could be seen in towns across America sharpening their skills for the bloody fighting which now engulfed Europe. Gemmell had worked many of Greb's early fights and had arrived back in Pittsburgh to spend the holidays with his family and friends. He would be returning to camp in Texas on January 2nd and his presence only served to remind Greb that the nation was mobilizing for war and an uncertain future.

10

HELL'S HARP

As the nation celebrated the beginning of a new year, Greb took a short break from his gypsy lifestyle to relax with friends and family and prepare for one more bout in the Pittsburgh area before again going on tour. Newspapers were touting Greb as the most active fighter of the previous year, having participated in 37 professional bouts and earning a respectable $28,753. Including newspaper decisions he had lost two bouts, drew one, won thirty-four, and stopped thirteen of his opponents.[1] It was a record to be proud of but with war rapidly thinning the ranks of professional fighters Greb and Mason knew that their days were limited. Greb would soon be called to action. With this in mind they began making plans for an aggressive campaign in which they would earn as much money as possible before Greb would be called to the colors. The ultimate goal would be a fight with Mike O'Dowd, the "Fighting Harp" of St. Paul, who now held the middleweight championship and who was preparing to enter the army at Fort Dodge.

Greb's first start in 1918 would be against heavyweight Terry Keller of Dayton, Ohio. Keller had faced such prominent men as Jack Dempsey, Bill Brennan, Tom McMahon and Fred Fulton. However Keller was little more than a sparring partner level journeyman who served as an "opponent" for many of the fighters he fought. Despite this fact the size difference between Greb and Keller was looked for to make for an interesting fight. What transpired was a slaughter.

To the strains of a musical ensemble seated at ringside Greb waded into Keller with reckless abandon. Punch after punch slammed into Keller's sorry anatomy and at several times had him weak and groggy. So over-eager was Greb for the knockout that during a clinch in the ninth round he took a wild swing, missed Keller, and dropped referee Scotty McLarren who was attempting to separate the two

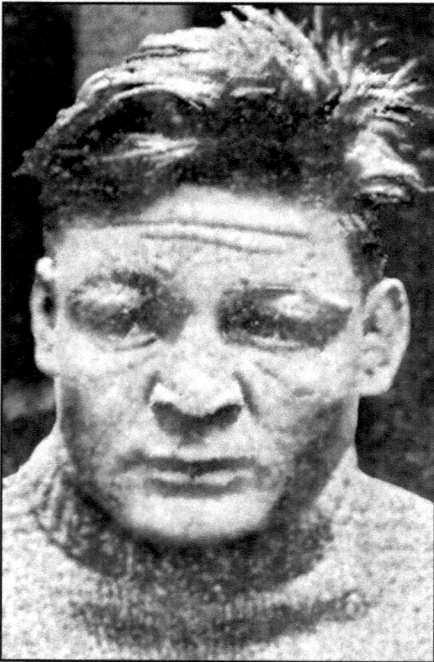

This rare photo of Terry Keller (above) illustrates what he called his "cauliflower eyes."

men. McLarren was up immediately, unharmed, and the one-sided beating resumed.[2]

Even while Greb was preparing for his battle with Keller his thoughts were occupied with another upcoming bout, his rematch with Battling Kopin, who two months earlier in his bout with Greb had retired with a broken arm. Kopin had been complaining long and loud that he would have won if not for the injury. These boasts irritated Greb to no end and he set out to prove once and for all that it was Kopin's chin and not his arm which which was composed of more than a little fine china. "Kopin will not bother me, I am going after him from the start this time and if I don't make short work of him, I'm a fish."[3] Kopin, for his part, was training at the League Island navy yard in Philadelphia, having recently joined the navy in hopes of getting a crack at the Kaiser.

When Kopin and Greb squared off in Charleroi's Rink during a snowstorm on January 14th two things were apparent: Greb was trained to the minute and Kopin wasn't. Both men started quickly with right hands, Kopin bringing a chopping right to the side of Greb's face and Greb answering with thudding right uppercuts. Near the end of the first round both fighters were falling into a clinch when Greb sent an uppercut deep into Kopin's midsection. The Jamestown battler collapsed on the mat, was summarily counted out, and dragged back to his corner by his seconds. Greb had proven his point.[4]

Now Greb and Mason made the five day trek by train down to New Orleans, Louisiana for a twenty round bout with Augie Ratner of New York. Ratner had been a tremendous amateur talent, winning several championships, and was expected by most authorities to have a splendid professional career. As an amateur he had been both a New York State champion and Amateur Athletic Union champion.

As Greb and Mason wound their way south Mason lit up telegraph offices in every whistle-stop arranging matches for Greb in Latrobe, Lonaconing, Bridgeport, and negotiating with St. Paul promoters for a bout with Mike

Former amateur star Augie Ratner (above) took a gamble in more ways than one in his fight with Greb. He came out on the loser's end in more ways than one as well.

O'Dowd. St. Paul promoters had balked at Mason's demand of $2,500 and twenty-five percent of the gate receipts insisting that Mason take one or the other. Mason held out knowing that it would be O'Dowd's last chance at a payday before leaving for an indefinite tour of duty. Mason was playing a dangerous game with Greb's championship dreams but the gamble paid off. Two days into their journey south Mason made the announcement that he had secured the O'Dowd match for $2,500 and a privilege of twenty-five percent of the gate receipts. Mason accomplished another coup during the negotiations in addition to getting his purse demands. He had made such an issue over Greb's "inability" to make the middleweight limit that promoters stipulated Greb *must* weigh 158 lbs. or less, making the match a championship contest if Greb were able to knockout O'Dowd or win via disqualification. In an age when fighters were regularly forcing opponents to sign contracts stating they would weigh *over* the championship limit, in order to protect their title claim, it was a triumph of Mason's wily intellect getting O'Dowd to agree to such a match with such a highly regarded opponent.[5]

When Greb arrived in "The Big Easy" he immediately set about training, surrounded by throngs of curious onlookers. Ratner had been in New Orleans for some time already, having two weeks prior knocked out Sailor Hildebrand in one round. So eager was Ratner's manager Scotty Montieth to rush his young star into the limelight that he took a major gamble with Ratner's purse agreeing to pay Greb's guarantee and the cost of the promotion out of Ratner's percentage of the gate receipts before taking any money for themselves. If the match sold poorly it could leave Ratner with empty pockets. It was a great display of confidence on Montieth's part yet risky none the less.[6] When Montieth saw the relatively small turnout (due in part to a last minute change of venue) he quickly bet two hundred dollars on Ratner to stay the 20 round limit in hopes that they would recoup at least some of their losses. With Ratner's bet serving as a backdrop to the story of the fight, the men set about their task.

From start to finish Greb outclassed Ratner. He was simply too big, too strong, and too experienced for the young New Yorker. Often times he would batter Ratner's defenses down by sheer strength and muscle him around the ring as if the former amateur star were a rag doll. It was a case of man against boy. Greb was so much stronger that in the third round he sent

---

TONIGHT!   8:30 P. M.   **TONIGHT!**

DAUPHINE THEATER
(STEAM HEATED)

HARRY GREB vs. AUGIE RATNER
20———ROUNDS———20

PRICES: $1.00 $2.00 $3.00

Above Prices Include War Tax.

Tickets on Sale at Tortorich's Cafe, 118 Baronne Street

Ratner sprawling against the ropes and down to the canvas for a short count with one right hand to the shoulder. As the fight wore on Greb seemed to gain speed and strength while Ratner resorted to holding and defensive tactics in order to gain the moral victory (and the $200 bet) of staying the limit with Greb. In the seventeenth round Greb landed a succession of blistering rights and lefts to his opponent's jaw leaving Ratner reeling about. The chance was there for a knockout but Greb allowed Ratner too much time to clear his head and the opportunity passed. When the final bell rang referee Remy Dorr raised Greb's hand in victory.[7]

Greb, upon a brief return to Pittsburgh after the fight, stated that "He (Ratner) was in good shape and he gave me a good fight. However, had I been on the scene training for a few days before the fight I would have stopped him. I didn't get into New Orleans until last Sunday morning, after having spent five days on the road, making the trip by easy stages. It took me 10 rounds to get warmed up to my work and it was not until after that stage that I piled up my winning margin."[8] Greb also let it be known that he would appear in the upcoming boxing benefit for the Camp Lee tobacco fund in early February and that he was always willing to fight free of charge for any show benefiting the war effort, provided it didn't clash with previously scheduled bouts.

With his victory over Ratner secured, Greb sent a one sentence telegram to the Bridgeport Telegram. It stated simply:

"Will be in Bridgeport Friday afternoon some time.

Harry Greb."[9]

Zulu Kid was unimpressed with Greb's recent progress in the sport, particularly his win over Ratner in New Orleans. "Augie Ratner is by no means the best middleweight in the world. As a matter of fact I slipped him the walloping of his young life not so long ago in New York. Greb's victory over that boy means nothing in this fight. If it really concerns the bout any then it will show that I will be on the advantage. I fought Greb before as you well know, and I must say one thing and that is that Harry is one of the toughest men I've met in a very long while. I expect a tough fight to-night and am fully prepared for one. But, I do expect to win and win before the 12th round rolls on."[10]

The card, scheduled to begin at 8:30 pm was pushed up one hour to 7:30 due to a curfew issued by the National Fuel Administrator, Harry A. Garfield, forcing all managers of theatres, clubs, cabarets, and restaurants nationwide to close by 10:30 pm. The measure was designed to conserve fuel and energy for the war. Greb lay to rest the boasting of Zulu Kid with a terrific one sided battering of the Brooklyn Italian.

Greb, that sensational and crack light heavyweight of the Steel City all but knocked out the Zulu Kid and The Telegram decision goes to him by a magin-

ALL STAR

Boxing Exhibition

Tuesday, January 29th

CASINO, State St., Bridgeport

STAR BOUT—15 ROUNDS

160 POUNDS AT 3 O'CLOCK

HARRY GREB of Pittsburgh, Pa.,

VS.

ZULU KID of New York

SECOND STAR BOUT—10 ROUNDS

135 POUNDS AT 3 O'CLOCK

LOUIS BOGASH of Bridgeport.

VS.

AL THOMAS of New York

THIRD STAR BOUT

JOHNNY MARTIN of New Haven

VS.

YOUNG EDDY of Greenwich

Every Boxer must weigh in at 3 o'clock on the day of contest at the Alpine Hotel.

Manager and Matchmaker	Referee
BILLY HOGAN	**TERRY LEE**
Announcer	Timer
FRANK BRAITHWAITE	**M. F. O'CONNOR**

Doors Open at 6:30 P. M. Sharp   Bouts at 7:30 P. M. Sharp

TICKETS $1.10 AND $2.25

RESERVED SEATS GUARANTEED OR MONEY REFUNDED AT BOX OFFICE.

This Show Will Be In Every Way Up to Standard Established by the Management.

that is as wide as the Atlantic Ocean.[11]

These were the words of Bridgeport Telegram sports writer Roger Ferri. Greb showed Bridgeport fans every facet of his now enormous ability. He danced around the ring taking potshots at the Kid from outside and then with a sudden leap he would be on the Italian in the blink of an eye hammering tremendous power punches to the head and body. When Zulu Kid got set to retaliate Greb would be gone, leaving the Kid to flail at the ozone. Greb's foot work was so fast, and his leaping attacks so swift that he was compared in speed to a bantamweight, and in skill to Johnny Dundee, one of the great little fighters of all time. In the fourteenth round Zulu Kid made a haphazard rush at Greb only to be met with a tremendous right hand swing that staggered him and sent blood flowing from a deep cut over the his right eye. Blood now poured down over the side of Zulu's already beet red face and just as the fight looked to be heading into a decisive conclusion the clock tolled 10:30 and the bout was promptly stopped in compliance with the curfew order. Greb left the ring to thunderous applause.[12]

The day after the fight the sports editorial was glowing in its praise of Greb:

Talking about that fight- That boy Greb can sure move his 170 pounds about

the ring. He's as fast as a featherweight on his feet and can hit from any old angle at all and most of the blows go where they're sent, too. He fights with a combination of the styles of Johnny Dundee and Johnny Kilbane, especially when the latter pulls that "round the mulberry bush" stuff.[13]

Greb left Bridgeport immediately in order to face Jack Hubbard, so-called heavyweight champion of the U. S. Navy, of Newark. Hubbard, like Terry Keller, was a fighter who had lost to the best fighters he had faced, usually by knockout. Combine that with the fact that Hubbard was utterly lacking in the skills necessary to be a top fighter and you have the makings of one of Greb's more pedestrian fights.

Greb had originally been scheduled to face Zulu Kid in Lonaconing but when he achieved such a decisive victory in Bridgeport Maryland promoters dropped the Italian in favor of someone who would not be so readily identifiable with defeat at Greb's hands. En route to Lonaconing Greb sent word to his loyal fans in Cincinnati that "I haven't got time enough to train for all my fights. I need the money and want to get all I can before I go into the army next month. For O'Dowd I will be in the best of shape. Too bad he will not fight me 20 rounds for a decision, but I will not let that worry me. I want to say right here that I am going in at the sound of the gong to put him out, and anyone who takes a chance on me can rest assured that they will get a run for their money...

...The promoters tell me that it is a hard matter to secure opponents for me. I am sorry that such is the case. I will fight any man in the world and do not ask a fortune for my services. I would at least like an opportunity to make one more fight in your city before I enlist. I want to be a soldier. I have not asked exemption and stand ready to answer the call. I never asked a man to do

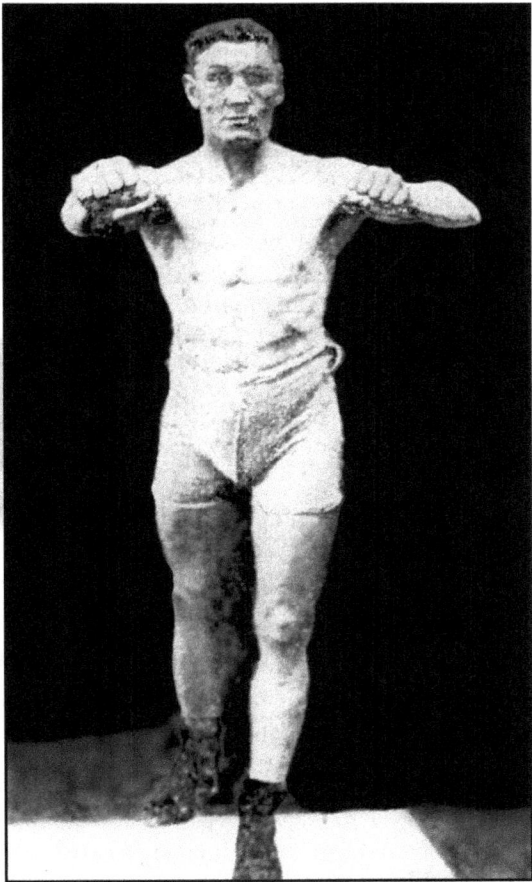

Billed as the "heavyweight champion of the United States Navy", Newark, New Jersey's Jack Hubbard met several talented fighters before being secured to fight Harry Greb in Maryland in early 1918. Unfortunately for him his fights often ended with him being counted out by the referee.

Frank Klaus (above) had not fought since his second knockout loss to George Chip. He had been entertaining the idea of a comeback for years until he fought Harry Greb in an exhibition bout in early 1918. Greb battered Klaus for three rounds with Klaus only occasionally showing signs of his once formidable skill.

me a favor in my life, and do not want to start in on Uncle Sam now that he needs all us young fellows to help him swat the Kaiser. I only hope that I can make good for my country."[14]

With this Greb entered the ring against heavyweight Jack Hubbard who for two rounds traded blows with Greb punch for punch. In the third round Greb landed a dynamite right hand that sent Hubbard down, striking his head hard on the canvas. Realizing that Hubbard had probably suffered more from striking his head on the hard floor than from the actual knockdown punch, Greb offered to let him continue despite being counted out. Hubbard gave the idea a thought and then decided he had received enough punishment for one day. It was Greb's fifth professional bout in one month.[15]

When Harry returned to Pittsburgh he found the whole town buzzing about his upcoming exhibition bout with Frank Klaus. Klaus hadn't fought since his second loss to George Chip more than four years earlier. Initially Klaus was to referee the exhibition bouts but then decided that he would rather fight saying "No I won't referee for the show; I'll fight. Why shouldn't I? I'm in the best of shape and feel as good as I did when I was champion. Is Greb on the card? Have you got anyone to box him? If not, let me go on with him. And, listen, don't put any cushions on my hands for the fight. Give me regulation five-ounce gloves, so I can sting him when I hit him. We're good friends and all that, but I just want to see how it is nobody seems to hurt

Greb. I'll bet I could make him go some when I was champion, and I know I can do it now. I'm serious, what do you say?"[16]

Upon acceptance of his offer, Klaus returned to his home district of Braddock and set about a rigorous training program in order to prepare himself for the bout. At J. S. Goldstein's gym in Braddock he put on a public workout which reminded onlookers his former speed and conditioning. It appeared as if a real fight was in the making.

Meanwhile, Greb had his own problems. As he continued to train diligently for his busy schedule it became apparent that his bout with Gus Christie in Latrobe, scheduled for February 8 was falling apart at the seams bit by bit. Several delays had hurt the promotion and while things seemed to be set for the show to go on, it was still on shaky ground. Adding to Greb's pressure was the fact that Tommy Gibbons and his manager Eddie Kane had set up camp in Pittsburgh and decided to use Greb's newfound fame as a means of garnering cheap publicity. Gibbons and Kane had arrived for a series of fights to be held in Pittsburgh and, knowing that Greb's schedule was as full as any fighter in the country, began calling him out. Kane even went so far as to offer a $1000 dollar side bet to the winner; money easily brandished about when there is little hope of the match being made. Despite Kane's transparent attempts at an inexpensive public relations campaign it no doubt irritated Greb to have these outsiders come to his hometown and make outlandish claims on his name.[17]

As Greb entered the ring at the Penn Avenue Powerhouse to face former middleweight champion Frank Klaus in three two minute rounds it must have been with a heavy heart for he had just that day found out that his match with Gus Christie in Latrobe had been called off when Christie, no doubt still smarting from the three recent beatings at the hands of Greb, called in sick. Just before the start of the bout the crowd became aware that Tommy Gibbons was in the hall and began to applaud. A constant banter between the fans of Gibbons and those loyal to Greb began with the start of the bout. "You ain't afraid of Gibbons, are you Harry?" yelled a Gibbons supporter, a fan of Harry's shot back "Put Gibbons in the ring with Harry!" In the first round Greb drew blood from the old-timers nose. At the end of the round Red Mason shouted "You can put Gibbons in here for the other two rounds if you want." Greb, growing tired of the scene and wishing to remain impartial, shot back "Shut up, Red!" At that moment referee Joe Donnelly called Gibbons to the ring and introduced him to the crowd, an act which met with a resounding cheer from the disappointingly half capacity crowd. The second round saw Greb, smarting from the day's circumstances, tear into Klaus raining blows down upon him. Klaus showed flashes of his past form leaving the fans wondering what a match between the two fighters in their respective primes would look like yet, despite the short rounds, Klaus became winded easily and couldn't sustain his once famous stamina long enough to see if he could hurt Greb any more than any of Greb's recent opponents. In the third round Greb, sensing that Klaus had little left in the tank, slowed the pace of the fight and coasted the final round.[18]

With the Christie match now cancelled Greb could concentrate on his upcoming title bout with Mike O'Dowd in St. Paul. Within the last week Mason had signed Greb for a match with Bob Moha in Cincinnati on February 18 ten rounds to a decision and a rematch with Jack Dillon in Toledo in the early part of March. The Moha bout would serve Mason's favorite practice of having Greb fight himself into shape, being one week before the O'Dowd match.

On February 15, 1918 Greb left his beloved Pittsburgh for St. Paul via Cincinnati where he first had to dispatch of Moha. Before leaving Greb gave reporters his assessment of the fight in a manner that is enlightening to both Greb's approach to the sport and his insight into the outcome of his upcoming championship match:

"I feel it in my bones that I am going to knock out O'Dowd. I have dreamed several times since the match was made that the championship will be mine and I honestly feel all the confidence in the world in my ability to stop O'Dowd.

Sadly Mike O'Dowd (above) is a little remembered champion. Yet, in his day he was a great fighter who feared no one and fought the best men in his division. He was a breath of fresh air in a division that had stagnated under the reign of Al McCoy.

I will either knockout O'Dowd or be out pointed in the attempt. If I don't knock him out, don't be surprised to if you get word from St. Paul that O'Dowd out pointed me.

Now I don't think O'Dowd could ever outpoint me if I went into the ring just to get the better of him. I have seen him fight and know his style and it ought to be easy for me to hop about and plaster him from all angles. But, in this bout, it will be up to me to try to knock him out as I cannot win the title on points. He is a rugged customer and can take a lot of punishment, but I think I know how to go after him to knock that crown off his head.

Mike is one of those fellows who fight all the time, much along my order. However, unlike my jumping style, he comes into his man on a direct line. I am glad of this, for I think I have the right sort of tactics to beat him."

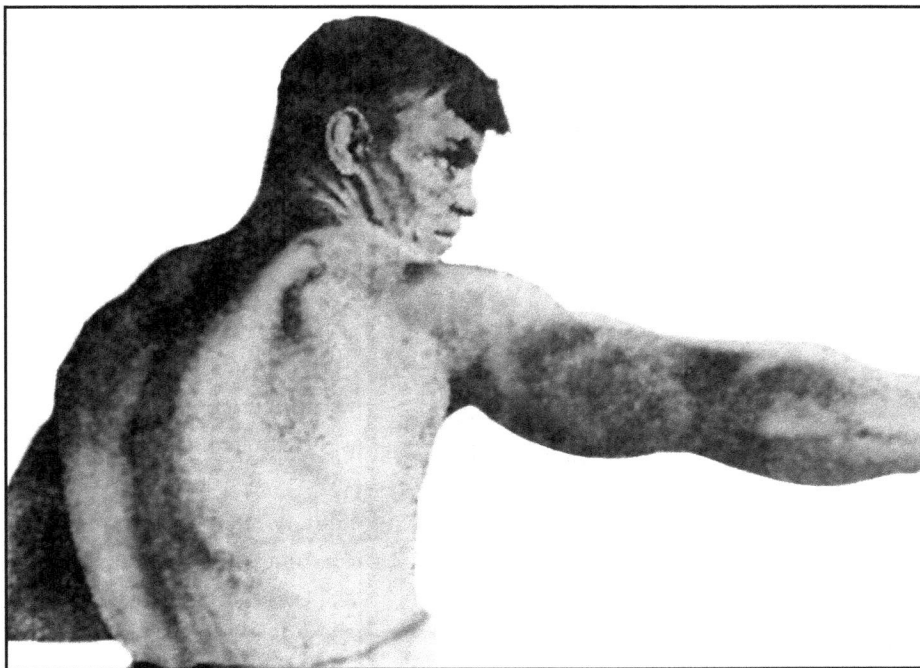

Its easy to see from this photo why Bob Moha was called the "Milwaukee Caveman." In February of 1918 Greb warmed up for his championship bout with Mike O'Dowd by giving Moha a frightful, bloody beating in front of awed Cincinnati admirers.

I am not going to show him a lot of speed in our bout, but I am going to set for all my punches, and every time he comes in I am going to wallop him on the chin just as hard as I can. If he doesn't go down under the bombardment it will be no fault of mine."[19]

Red Mason added his own parting shot to the surprise of all. He called Eddie Kane's bluff and accepted terms to meet Tommy Gibbons. It was a sly move by Mason and one which met with immediate praise and a predictable result. Kane promptly priced Gibbons out of the fight and decided to turn his publicity machine on Mike O'Dowd. Kane and Gibbons cooked up the idea that O'Dowd's claim to the championship was tenuous and that since Tom's brother Mike was almost universally accepted as the master of all middleweights, and was now away with the military, Tommy should graciously accept the reigns of champion as a sort of steward of the division and his family's honor. The idea was ludicrous and was taken seriously by no one. It was seen for what it was, an attempt by Kane to cash in on the public's interest in the upcoming O'Dowd-Greb match.[20]

If O'Dowd was taking the claims of Tommy Gibbons lightly he certainly was not taking Greb's challenge lightly. He had trained diligently for what he knew was his toughest challenge. Despite heavy snowstorms O'Dowd continued his outdoor roadwork, trudging miles in snow that was often up to his knees. He would return to the Wabasha gym in the afternoon and

Going to War

Last Public Appearance Before Joining the "Colors"

MIKE O'DOWD

of St. Paul.
Champion Middleweight of the World.
vs.

HARRY GREB

of Pittsburgh, Pa. Contender of Title.
10 Rounds.

St.Paul Auditorium, Monday Eve., Feb.25

PRELIMINARIES.

DEL HANLON of St. Paul vs.
GUS BLOOMBERG of Minneapolis.
10 Rounds.

JOE BOWMAN vs. BILLY EMKE.
6 Rounds.

FRANK ROSE vs. JOE BOWERS.
6 Rounds.

PRICES $1.00, $2.00, $3.00, $4.00, $5.00.
FIRST BOUT 8:15 SHARP.

box several rounds with the clever welterweight Jock Malone and light heavyweight Billy Empke. Fans who watched him spar were surprised to see O'Dowd working not on his rushing, boring-in tactics, but on his movement and more refined boxing skills.[21]

O'Dowd, now one of the great forgotten champions, was a tremendous fighter. He had come into the sport idolizing Mike Gibbons and even when they had long since retired after having fought three slashing bouts, O'Dowd credited Gibbons as the best. O'Dowd had been born in 1895. His education took him through elementary school until more pressing matters, such as putting food on the table, intervened. He worked as a telephone line repairman for a time and reportedly played semi-pro football. Like Greb, once O'Dowd took up boxing, or "fightin'" as he called it, he never looked back. Fighting was in O'Dowd's blood and it was never more apparent than when he was in the ring tearing in on his opponent. Little more than a beefed up welterweight, O'Dowd could hit with tremendous force and was as strong as a bull. As Greb stated, he generally fought his man coming in looking to land punches to the head and body. He would bob and weave presenting a difficult target but despite the aggressive style he was also a talented boxer with deceptively fast hands. After five years in the ring O'Dowd's face bore the signs of his trade. He had lumps of scar tissue over both eyes which gave him a forlorn look. His ears where heavily cauliflowered, his lips had a battered, swollen look to them and his nose had obviously been broken several times. Despite the evidence that many gloves had fallen on this face O'Dowd had never been knocked out.

Before Greb could face this Harp from Hell he first had to get by Moha and get by him he did. Greb battered Moha unmercifully and dominated the fight in a fashion that left no question as to who referee Lou Bauman would pick as the winner.[22] When Bauman announced Greb the winner over the blood-soaked Moha the house let out a roar of approval. Greb's only reminder of the event was a swollen left eye. The next day the Cincinnati Enquirer was glowing in its praise:

> Greb never fought better in his life. He jumped out at the tap of the gong and after hitting his stride never let up only for the short rest between rounds. He was here, there, and everywhere and his antics not only amused the crowd, but so badly fooled Moha that half the time he had to look about to find where his man had gone...

> ...There may be better battlers in this world than Greb, but Cincinnati has never gazed upon his equal. Old-timers who sat around the ringside last night remarked that they would give any price had Greb been alive in the palmy days of Kid McCoy...

> ...Greb, as usual, hit his man with every kind of punch imaginable. Blows landed all over Moha's body, from the top of his head to the middle of his spine. The remarkable endurance of the Pittsburgh boy caused spectators to gasp for breath. He is a wonder among wonders and has the world beaten for stamina.[23]

RIGHT UPPERCUT. MARCH!

MIKE O'DOWD IS TO HAVE CHARGE OF A SQUAD ENROUTE TO CAMP.

Contemporary cartoon illustrating O'Dowds expected induction into the army. O'Dowd was expected to ship with a small squad under his command to Camp Dodge within days of the conclusion of his bout with Greb.

After beating Moha, Greb and Mason quickly boarded a late train to Chicago and on to St. Paul. They had intended to approach St. Paul at a more leisurely pace but dispatches from the Twin Cities threatened a confiscation of Greb's forfeit if he arrived on the scene late.[24] Thus Mason and Greb hurried their way to the battleground. They arrived on January 20, five days before fight time and Greb immediately set about training across the river in Minneapolis.

Greb's first day of training proved something of a false start. He intended to do some light roadwork and finish off the day in the gym. Unaccustomed to the harsh Minnesota winter, Greb cut his roadwork short and spent the rest of the afternoon thawing out. In addition to the rigors of the weather, Greb was five pounds over the 158 pound limit. He was already in fighting trim and reducing five pounds in five days would be no easy feat. To add to these worries he was in enemy territory (nothing new to him) and O'Dowd had clearly won the hearts and minds of Twin Cities inhabitants. Indeed for some time St. Paul had been vilified in other parts of the country for it's treatment of out-of-town fighters, at least since Kid Williams lost a fight to "Kewpie" Ertle on a disputed foul in what many felt was an attempt to rob Williams of his bantamweight championship.

In order for Greb to gain support among the locals he would have to show well in training. Minneapolis fans got their first opportunity to see Greb in present condition when he held public workouts at Jimmy Potts' Gymnasium on February 21. Immediately opinions began to change from rabid support of O'Dowd to a fear that Greb might prove "too much" for their favorite. Over in St. Paul fans were holding to their loyalties and heavily favored O'Dowd stating he never looked better. A day later Greb held open workouts in St. Paul, at Gates gymnasium, for the first time and after giving his sparring partner, Jack Reed, a terrific beating O'Dowd's fans felt their hopes melting away.

Greb was looking tremendous but he was still overweight. If he could not make the limit of 158 lbs. he would not only lose his weight forfeit but also any hope of triumphantly returning to Pittsburgh as the middleweight champion of the world. On February 23 Greb tapered off his gym work and took a long run through the snow covered streets of St. Paul in an attempt to drop those remaining pounds, nothing worked. In a frantic attempt to lose the remaining weight Greb spent the evening before the bout in a Turkish bathhouse sweating down to the prescribed limit.[25]

On the day of the fight sports were offering no better than even money on the outcome of the fight. O'Dowd had been a prohibitive favorite early in the betting but two days before the fight his lead had been shaved down to place him a 7 to 5 favorite and finally on fight night it was even money. The bout had been heavily promoted on the idea that both Greb and O'Dowd would soon be drafted and thus this could be the last time to see either of them before the end of the war. As a result the bout was expected to draw anywhere from $12,000 to $20,000 making it a highly successful promotion.

The night before the fight both fighters were brimming with confidence as they spoke to reporters. "I have beaten better men than O'Dowd has ever met, so why shouldn't I whip him?" said Greb. "This fight is important to me only because it gives me a whack at the title. I never felt surer of winning, but you can never be sure of a knockout. It all depends on the way O'Dowd fights. If he stands up and fights he will be stopped. If he runs, he may last."[26] To this O'Dowd answered "I have never been in better condition and I feel confident of beating Greb. I have seen him fight twice and know his style. If he whips me I shall have no alibi. He'll get plenty of chances to stop me if he can, because he won't find me running away from him."[27]

With the ballyhoo finished, the weigh in proceeded the next day at 3 P.M. as planned and the results were shocking. O'Dowd stepped on the scales and settled the beam at 156 lbs. exactly as expected. When Greb stepped up, the room waited in anticipation knowing of Greb's inability to lose his excess weight. As the beam slowly settled the examiner announced "155 and three-quarters!" It wasn't a good sign. Greb had been so anxious to make the middleweight limit that he had taken off far too much weight. It would remain to be seen how it would affect his performance.

At fight time Mike O'Dowd entered the ring looking every bit a champion in his green velvet robe embroidered with golden harps.[28] After shaking hands and receiving instructions the fight began in front of a smaller than expected crowd. As Greb came out of his corner it was apparent that the long hours spent in the steam of the Turkish bath reducing weight had weakened him. From the outset Greb acted on his pre-fight promise of going straight for a knockout and completely disregarded any idea of winning a newspaper decision. He tore in after O'Dowd winging wild left hooks to the body and head. O'Dowd met these rushes with a tight defense and short counterpunches. The round was generally ruled even. In the second round the action resumed where

Mike O'Dowd is the very picture of a boxer with sad eyes, cauliflower ears, a broken nose, and scarred lips. His face encapsulates the rugged life that fighters sustain for glory and riches.

it left off yet, to everyone's surprise, instead of being met head on by the usually mauling O'Dowd, Greb was met with a stiff left jab. The greater surprise was that despite Greb's strength and ruggedness he simply could not get past O'Dowd's jab.

As the second and third round progressed it became apparent that O'Dowd's strategy was radically different than anyone had expected. He was backpedaling away from Greb's rushes and instead of trying to slug with Greb as promised he was working almost exclusively with his jab and clinching when Greb worked his way inside. Greb for his part was growing increasingly wild as he looked for the knockout, often missing widely and looking decidedly amateurish. The fight opened up again in the fifth round when Greb, after having been outpointed or held even in the previous rounds, broke through O'Dowd's defense and forced the Irishman to slug away. Slug away he did and in Greb's weakened state he was getting the worse of the exchanges.

The fight again changed in the sixth with Greb now becoming more effective. His rushes, wild as they were, were now tiring O'Dowd and his swings were either connecting or falling just short of the mark. Greb now went back to his old tactics of bouncing in and out making himself a more difficult target and leaping in when on the attack. In the seventh Greb landed a hard right to O'Dowd's jaw which wobbled the hometown favorite. Greb followed the advantage up by smashing O'Dowd to the ropes and blasting away with both hands. A terrific exchange ensued and while Greb got the better of it he came away with a split lip. O'Dowd took a brutal eighth round in which both fighters began to show signs of weakening. In the ninth O'Dowd was clearly fading fast and Greb, hoping to speed up the process, began by pumping lefts and rights into O'Dowd's stomach. Near the end of the round Greb shot a quick left and right to O'Dowd's chin and the Harp staggered. Greb immediately leapt on his man and was battering him about the ring when the bell sounded.

The fighters arose slowly for the tenth and final round, shook hands, and resumed the engagement. Both fighters tried to give their best in the tenth but after a short burst of brutal infighting the round degenerated into a sloppy affair punctuated by mauling and clinching. As the gong sounded ending the fight it was apparent that both fighters were spent. Greb came away with a split lip and O'Dowd a swollen eye and the championship.[29]

The next day newspapers were split as to who won the contest. The majority voted for O'Dowd but by what margin and in what rounds he had won this victory was as much in dispute as to how large a role Greb's incredible weight drain played in the fight.

The St. Paul Dispatch ruled in O'Dowd's favor without going into any details of the actual fight, commenting only that while Greb did most of the leading, O'Dowd was more effective. Fred Coburn of the Minneapolis Tribune disagreed with this assessment stating that it was in fact Greb's aggressiveness which earned him the fight. The St. Paul Pioneer Press gave the verdict to O'Dowd. The Minneapolis Journal agreed stating that O'Dowd won a clear but "not wide" margin. Ed L. Shave of the St. Paul Daily News announced in his headline that the bout was a draw but admitted "Strictly scoring the bout on points Greb would be entitled to a shade, but a draw verdict harms neither."[30] It is interesting to note that Shave made the prediction that if Greb weighed in over the middleweight limit he would beat O'Dowd, weighing in under the limit would seemingly weaken Greb and thus give O'Dowd the advantage. Shave made mention of Greb's all night sojourn to the Turkish bath in his attempt to make weight and gave the Pittsburgh battler credit for never breaking his attack and trying his best at all times. It was little consolation that George Barton, dean of Twin Cities sports writers voted for Greb in his column published by the Minneapolis Daily News.

Barton's resume as an authority on all matters fistic was extensive to say the least. He had been a professional fighter of some repute during the turn of the century having handed a defeat to former champion "Terrible" Terry McGovern. While fighting in the ring Barton supplemented his income by working as a sports editor of the Minneapolis Daily News when he had graduated from high school. After retiring from boxing Barton trained fighters, counting among his pupils no less than Mike Gibbons, considered by some to be the greatest fighter of the age. Barton was also one of the most respected referees in the Twin Cities area. In 1952 Barton would be awarded the James J. Walker Award for Long and Meritorious Service to the sport of boxing. From 1952 to 1953 he was the head of the National Boxing Association. Barton was a leading member of the Minnesota State Athletic Commission from 1942 until 1969. The day after he resigned his position with the Commission he died. During his lifetime he refereed over 12,000 boxing matches performing his duties in a manner that prompted Nat Fleischer to name Barton one of boxing's top three all-time great referees. No less an authority picked Greb as the winner over O'Dowd on February 25, 1918.

"Having neglected to use grasshoppers for sparring partners," said Barton "Mike O'Dowd was unable to fathom Harry Greb's jumping-jack antics, consequently the "Fighting Harp" was outpointed by his Pittsburgh rival in their 10-round bout at St. Paul Auditorium last night." Giving Greb five rounds, two to O'Dowd and counting three even Barton added "While Greb won there was nothing so very decisive about his victory, for the championship did not change hands, nor was either fighter badly punished."

"The Pittsburgh Mauler undoubtedly weakened himself doing such a low figure (155 3/4 lbs.) all of which made his work last night all the more remarkable."[31]

Within days O'Dowd would be on his way to a military training camp and there was nothing for Greb but to board the train out of St. Paul without a championship and prepare anew for the rigorous schedule that Red Mason had planned. America was now fully engaged in the war effort and it was anyone's guess as to when or if Greb would ever get another shot at the title. In the meantime his major concern was making as much money as possible in order to secure his financial future once he was called on to serve his country.

11

OVER THERE

With Mike O'Dowd behind him and military service almost certainly ahead of him, Greb and Mason set about an ambitious schedule designed to create a nest egg. The schedule called for Greb to fight at least once a week over a period of at least two months in places such as Bridgeport, Connecticut, Cleveland, Ohio, and Buffalo, New York. It would be a taxing tour and one which would leave little time for much more than counting their money.

The first opponent on this campaign was Jack Dillon who agreed to fight Greb in Toledo, Ohio. Dillon was eager for the chance to get revenge against Greb for their previous meeting. He was also hoping that a win over Greb would propel him into bigger matches against heavyweight contenders Jack Dempsey and Fred Fulton. "Dillon is after more than Greb," said Fred Harter, Dillon's business manager. "He wants to get a crack at Billy Miske and Jack Dempsey... By beating Greb we intend to go after all the big fellows, with a Fulton match our objective."[1] Feeling that he would have a greater chance of catching the elusive Greb with a knockout punch in a longer fight than their ten round Pittsburgh engagement, Dillon requested a fifteen round bout but settled for a fight of a twelve rounds. With negotiations completed the bout was set for March 4, 1918 in Toledo's Coliseum to be fought at catch weights.

Dillon had struggled to regain his old form since his last meeting with Greb more than six months earlier. He had faced such men as Mike Gibbons, Billy Miske, and George Chip in the interim but had come out on the losing end in those matches. It was hoped by Toledo fans that the Dillon of old would appear before them and prove a worthy foe for the Pittsburgh fighter. Dillon himself upon arriving expressed some concern about Greb's speed stating: "If I can catch the race horse (Greb) tonight I'll know what I'll do."

"At present I am rather uncertain. Somehow the impression seems to prevail that Jack Dillon is a dead one. Well I'll try to show them something different. Greb is a high class boy and don't you forget that fact. But he is in motion all of the time and he is the hardest kid to box I ever saw. You never know what he is going to do next."

"I wanted to box Greb 15 rounds because I knew I could catch him in that time and beat him, but Red Mason is too foxy and 12 was his limit. I think I can get Greb in 12 rounds tonight."[2]

JACK DILLON vs. HARRY GREB TWELVE ROUNDS **COLISEUM** MONDAY EVE. MAR. 4 **TWO OTHER GOOD BOUTS**

Twelve rounds, or fifteen rounds, it would not have made any difference. Dillon spent the balance of the fight soaking up punishment from Greb without being able to return. Greb was simply too fast, too aggressive, and too slippery for Dillon to mount any kind of offense and thus the nearly three thousand fans that paid to see the fight were treated to the sad spectacle of a once great fighter suffering a terrible beating. The Toledo News-Bee estimated that Dillon landed only four punches over the course of the 12 round fight and none where of any consequence. Dillon fell back on an age old trick used by fighters whose legs can't support them under heavy punishment, he fought with his back to the ropes allowing the ring to support his weight as Greb used the "Hoosier Bearcat" as a human punching bag.[3] The Toledo Blade's account of the fight probably gives the most even account both in illustrating the decline of Dillon and the rising star of Greb:

Whoever thought to see the day a Toledo audience would jeer Jack Dillon; or see him helpless before the onslaught of an opponent, waving his hands impotently, to ward off an attack from any two-fisted human?

Yet, this was the spectacle presented the largest crowd that ever assembled in Toledo to see a boxing match. From the first gong to the last Dillon was powerless.

To attempt to keep track of the punches Greb rained upon the sturdy Hoosier would have been futile. The blows were pulled from everywhere. They came overhand, sidearm, roundhouse, straight across, shot up from below, or were pumped in from an angle until Dillon was literally swamped.[4]

The Blade even went on to suggest that Greb had held back from knocking out Dillon.

As press reports began to filter out around the country of Dillon's showing at the hands of Greb the embarrassed Toledo Boxing Commission felt the need to take action. They quickly decided that Dillon had appeared out of shape and thus cheat-

Jack Dillon

INDIANAPOLIS, IND

Greb effectively ended the status Jack Dillon (above) once held as a top fighter when the two met in Toledo, Ohio. Greb dominated so thoroughly that many called for Dillon to be banned from Toledo rings as unfit.

ed the public of a genuine performance. This explanation, after press reports at Dillon's train-ing exhibitions (and ringside) stated the Hoosier to be in fantastic physical condition, seemed unjustified never mind that it totally disregarded the likely scenario that Greb was much bet-ter than he had been given credit for. The Commission fined the Toledo Athletic Association $50 for its handling of the fight and put the matter behind it.

James Mason leapt to Dillon's defense stating: "I am sorry to see a great fighter like Jack Dillon 'roasted' in this way. Because when Toledoans know Greb better they will appreciate that he handles most opponents the same as he did Dillon."[5] Dillon defended himself by pub-lishing an article in the Toledo Times one week after the fight stating:

> **Harry Greb, the Pittsburgh boxer will be the next middleweight cham-pion of the world if he can get down to 158 pounds. He has the speed of a lightweight, and the aggressiveness of a McGovern, and best of all, he always is in splendid condition.**
>
> **Greb's only weakness is his inability to hit hard. But fast and clever box-ers are fast supplanting the sluggers of a few years ago in the mid-dleweight division. If Greb can retain his present form, and I see no rea-son why he can't, he is only a boy, he will step to the front.**
>
> **He has the advantage of boxing only short contests and has the endurance to go at top speed all the time. Heavy hitters and stronger men have no chance with him in short bouts.[6]**

Dillon for his part would fight on for another five years without ever again reaching the upper echelon of the sport. His bout in Toledo with Greb would be their last meeting in the ring and if their first meeting signaled the end of Dillon's status as a top contender the Toledo bout sim-ply put an exclamation point on that fact.

Leaving Toledo behind them Greb and Mason headed east to Cleveland to face New York's Mike McTigue. McTigue had been born in County Clare, Ireland in 1892 and had come to the United States sixteen years later. He had taken up boxing in 1909 but had yet to make an impression on fans of the sport. He was a solid practitioner with good defensive skills and a respectable punch but he tended to rely too heavily on defense and was often chided for fight-ing not to win but simply to hear the final bell. While not actively campaigning McTigue had been enlisted as a boxing instructor at the New York Athletic Club, a position which kept him fit and prepared to make the stipulated weight of 162 pounds for the Greb fight.

When 3 o'clock chimed in the offices of the City Athletic Club Greb was not present for the weigh in. McTigue who weighed in at $158^1/_4$ disregarded Greb's absence and refused to accept Greb's weight forfeit. "I'll fight him if he weighs a ton" was the Irishman's brave reply. Rumor quickly spread that Greb had refused to weigh in because he was far in excess of the contracted weight. Red Mason stated that the match was contracted at catch weights and thus there was no call for the fighters to weigh in. This explanation seems more like splitting hairs than a genuine justification for Greb's absence, especially considering one of Greb's seconds had appeared at the weigh in to make sure McTigue made the weight. In all likelihood the truth lies somewhere in-between.[7]

In front of a smaller than expected crowd Greb squared off before Mike McTigue, advertised as the middleweight champion of Ireland. Before the first round had completed it was obvious that the matchmakers had made a terrible mistake in acquiring McTigue's services. After Greb's initial onslaught McTigue proceeded to hold, cover up, lay on the ropes, and take whatever measures he deemed necessary to finish the ten rounds on his feet. Round after round the crowd registered its disgust with a torrent of boos, hisses, and jeers. By the eighth round the small crowd had started to shuffle out of the arena being well satisfied that McTigue was not willing or able to bring out the best in Greb. Those who remained in the hall were not shy about voicing their disgust. Once when McTigue let loose a feeble jab a spectator shouted "You've got him going, Mike! Tear into him again!" As the final round began to close, McTigue was hanging onto Greb for dear life with the fans shouting invectives at him. Another self-styled comic yelled "Don't roast Mike. Just wait until he gets started!" The final bell rang seconds later. McTigue escaped the fight with minimal injury, suffering only a cut above his left eye.[8]

It was a dismal contest. Fans from Toledo who had traveled to Cleveland to see Greb came back convinced that his showing against Dillon was not an aberration. "If we had such a show

More controversy followed Greb in Cleveland when he faced New York Irishman Mike McTigue (above). Greb irritated local officials by refusing to weigh in and the friction was further compounded when McTigue failed to put up a competetive bout.

here they'd run the promoter out of town," said one fan. Another added: "You talk about the way Greb handled Dillon. He did worse things to McTigue, who is a young fellow with a splendid record. In New York he is well thought of. He is boxing instructor at the New York A. C. and one of the cleverest boxers imaginable. He has beaten most of the middleweights in the east, but he was a plaything for Greb.

At times Greb rained punches upon him so fast that McTigue turned his back and covered his head with his gloves. He tried to box, but Greb would not let him and finally he spent his time trying to hold Greb's arms. The referee was kept busy prying them apart in every round."[9] The real fight had only just begun.

Dissatisfied with Greb's refusal to weigh in, the fight card, and the fact that many felt Greb had allowed McTigue to stay the distance, the Cleveland boxing commission had decided to lay blame squarely at Greb's feet. They confiscated his forfeit money despite the fact that McTigue had refused to accept it, and even now were threatening to enforce a statewide ban on him.[10] This could mean the loss of a large amount of the money Mason and Greb had hoped to acquire before entering the war, considering Greb now had plans to fight in several Ohio towns as part of his pre-war tour. The one-hundred dollar forfeit was no small matter either. The fact that the commission was using Greb as a scapegoat became apparent when Greb was asked to appear in a patriotic benefit in Cleveland in the near future, gratis, in exchange for the return of his forfeit. It appeared that Greb was being blackmailed into helping the somewhat battered Cleveland boxing scene.[11]

Greb and Mason left Cleveland with matters still unresolved. In fact it would be several months before the whole episode would be entirely cleared up to the satisfaction of all parties involved. Next on the Greb agenda was a fight with Willie Langford in Buffalo on March 18. Talk still lingered about the failed negotiations to match Greb and Kid Norfolk in Buffalo months earlier. Greb's detractors felt he had drawn the infamous color line, refusing to face a Negro fighter. In order to put these rumors to rest and show that he was willing to face anyone, white or black, Greb signed to fight Langford, a black middleweight.

Willie Langford was a rugged fighter despite being on the small side for a middleweight. He carried a powerful right hand and was always in tremendous condition. Langford had a wealth of experience having fought from New Orleans, Louisiana to Canada. He had faced heavyweights such as John Lester Johnson, fought for the "colored" middleweight championship, and faced such note worthies as Young Ahearn, Mike Glover, Jack "Twin" Sullivan, and Ted "Kid" Lewis. Despite these attributes Langford never seemed to be able to bring his talents together and as a result he spent his career as the "opponent."

Playing up to his opponents ideas that Greb had drawn the color line, Mason demanded a higher than usual guarantee in order to face a black fighter. Langford certainly was not a very threatening opponent and Greb had never drawn the color line in the past either publicly or privately yet he or rather Mason was not averse to using it as a means of acquiring the quick funds which had been the goal of their current tour.

The pre-fight press was thankfully tactful in it's ballyhoo of the fight. There was little race baiting in comparison to other fights of the era, the most commonly discussed subjects being the intentions of both fighters to end the match before the conclusion of the sixth and final round as well as the hope that this match would lead to one between Greb and Norfolk. When told of Greb's intentions to end matters quickly Langford responded "Don't talk about him stopping me. Just figure out that I may be the man to do the stopping."[12] To such comments Mason replied: "Well, if Langford's a whirlwind they may break even but he better be a whirlwind for I am going to let loose a boxing tornado against him."[13]

A Tornado is just what Langford met that night before more than 2,000 spectators, many of them uniformed service men. From the opening bell Greb attacked with a fury that nearly swept Langford off his feet. Throwing punch after punch he battered down Langford's defense and sent him reeling around the ring. One could be sure that Willie Langford had never seen the singular style of Harry Greb in any of his previous opponents as his face was frozen in a mask of shock throughout the contest. At one point Greb missed a wild swing and nearly went through the ropes. With head and shoulders dangling through the ropes and over the edge of the ring Greb let loose a punch "...from way out in the audience and bashed Willie alongside the head," much to the crowds delight. Langford never had a chance to test his potent right hand as Greb battered him all through the six rounds, keeping the Langford entirely on the defensive. Despite Greb's assault Langford never once took a count and while he was bleeding and dizzy at the final bell he could boast the moral victory of

Willie Langford was a rugged middleweight with a lot of experience when he faced Greb in Buffalo over six rounds. Both fighters vowed for a knockout but the best Greb could accomplish was a one-sided beating which left Langford bloody and reeling.

Tornado Harry Sweeps Langford
Across Ring at High Speed

GREB SLAMMED, DOVE, JUMPED,
MISSED AND HIT LANGFORD
TO THE BEST HE
KNEW - SOME
KNOWLEDGE

having finished on his feet.[14]

After the fight Greb gave Langford praise as a hard puncher and a better man than he expected, adding that he would beat a lot of white boys if given the opportunity. Sitting ringside was Willie "KO" Brennen, on furlough from Camp Upton. Still not satisfied with Greb's superiority over him he began to lobby for a fourth bout with the Pittsburgh star. "Brennen was the first man I boxed in Buffalo," said Greb, "and much of my subsequent rise to the position I have today, at the door of the middleweight championship, dates from that first Buffalo bout. Brennen at his best makes the average man I meet look like a joke, but I'm ready for him."[15]

After spending a day visiting friends in Buffalo, Greb set out again to continue his tour. He had now been tentatively scheduled to face Packey McFarland in the four round exhibition for charity in Cleveland in order to get his weight forfeit back from the McTigue debacle on April 4, Gus Christie in Latrobe, Pennsylvania on April 5, George Chip in Denver in "early April," Steamboat Bill Scott on April 8 in Muncie, Indiana, Tommy Robson in Boston on April 10, Jack McCarron in Toledo on April 12, George Chip, again, at Bridgeport, Connecticut on April 15, Silent Martin in Akron, Ohio on April 18, and an as yet unnamed opponent in Atlanta on April 24.[16] If all went off without a hitch Greb would box nine men in twenty days traveling several thousand miles by rail. The Toledo Blade estimated that in four nights alone between his scheduled bout with Bill Scott and his bout with Jack McCarron he would travel over 1,300 miles and fight thirty-four rounds.[17] It was a dizzying schedule and one which was much discussed in the newspapers.

Cracks began to form in the plan not long after Greb's defeat of Langford. He was already showing signs of stress after having campaigned at an average of nearly one fight a week since the beginning of December. Without warning the Patriotic exhibition in Cleveland was cancelled indefinitely leaving Greb's one hundred dollar weight forfeit still hanging over his head. The next hitch came when Greb was forced to postpone his bout with Robson because it was scheduled too close to the bout with McCarron in Toledo; Robson would have to wait until later in the month. This allowed Greb time to concentrate on his fights with Bill Scott and Jack McCarron. One week before his match with Bill Scott a substitution was made and in Scott's

BOXING Campbell's Auditorium
Mon., Apr. 8, 8:30 p.m.
HARRY GREB vs. FRANK MANTELL
Pittsburg, Pa.   Providence, R. I.
——TEN THREE-MINUTE ROUNDS——
See the Greatest Boxing Contest Ever Staged in Muncie.
——HIGH CLASS PRELIMINARIES——
Tickets on sale at Kirby House Cigar Stand and Littlefield and
Stout Pool Room.
ADMISSION $1.00————————————————RINGSIDE $2.00

An original advertisement for Greb's ill-fated pre-war tour. The bout with Mantell was cancelled when Greb refused to fight the third substitute for original opponent Steamboat Bill Scott.

stead was placed heavyweight Jack Reed of New York. Three days before the bout Reed was replaced with Frank Mantell. On the same day Greb was receiving yet another opponent for his Muncie bout he received word that his Latrobe bout with Gus Christie had been cancelled by the local District Attorney with no reason given for the action. Things were not looking good for Greb's final push before entering the service of his country.[18]

The strain of Greb's yo-yo dieting, his troubles in Toledo and Cleveland, his now crumbling tour, and the fact that his final physical examination for the draft had recently been completed (meaning time was running short to re-organize the tour), was causing the usually happy-go-lucky fighter to suffer seriously from nervous tension. As a result of this stress he developed a large boil on his forehead. As if a boil on such a vulnerable spot for a boxer wasn't bad enough another bit of bad fortune cropped up. Mantell reported to the fight in Muncie with a bad back but offered to substitute heavyweight Terry Keller in his place. Feeling feverish and irritated by the now third substitution Greb refused to go on with the show.[19]

While in Muncie Greb, hoping to stave off the effects of the boil on his forehead, had the offending carbuncle lanced. He rapidly developed an infection from the procedure and while in route to Toledo was forced to stay over in Cincinnati. While in Cincinnati Greb's face began to swell grotesquely. His right eye which was directly under the boil had swollen shut and the entire right side of his face was puffed like a balloon. As the infection grew worse Mason wired that they would not be able to honor the Toledo fight with Jack McCarron. Greb was raced back home to Pittsburgh and immediately hospitalized. Initially it was hoped that Greb would be released from the hospital within days and resume his schedule, beginning with the now postponed McCarron fight in Toledo, but it quickly became apparent that this would not be possible when Greb's condition became severe. It was thought that blood poisoning had set in and Pneumonia was threatened. Greb was quickly quarantined in Mercy Hospital, suffering a high fever and delirium, family and friends were strictly forbidden from seeing the ailing fighter.[20]

With Greb expecting to be drafted within the next month, and his recovery expected to last at least two weeks, it was apparent that his plans of a lucrative tour were now over. It would be the end of April before Greb was strong enough to begin making plans both for the service and for his career. By this time he had been considering joining the United States Naval Reserves. Johnny Ray, Greb's friend, stablemate, and sparring partner, had been a member of the Reserves for a year now and no doubt this influenced Greb's thinking. He likely took note of Ray's participation in patriotic boxing exhibitions and his work recruiting and training young sailors and decided that it would be a more glamorous position than spending the hot summer in a crowded army cantonment. Greb was in Philadelphia to witness Ray's performance in the boxing carnivals held for the benefit of the third Liberty Loan drive. Harry and Ray traveled to New York together where Ray was scheduled to take part in another boxing benefit on the final night of the Liberty Loan drive. During the journey Greb agreed to participate in the benefit as well. When the two fighters arrived in New York they parted company as Greb traveled on to Atlantic City to begin training for the upcoming event which would be held on May 4.

The ring was pitched on the quarterdeck of the training ship U.S.S. Recruit, a full scale mockup of a naval battleship constructed in Union Square Park. A sixty-eight piece band was present to provide music for the spectators and the show was packed from top to bottom with boxers turned naval personnel. Adding to the glamour of the event was famed announcer Joe Humphries, and referee Mike Leonard, former "Beau Brummel" of the boxing ring who participated in boxing's first filmed bout back in 1894. Greb was scheduled to face former middleweight champion Al McCoy in the event. Harry trained for this bout as if it were more than an exhibition. It was vital that he get himself into top condition because he was already scheduled to face Soldier Bartfield on May 10 in Pittsburgh. It was still not clear if Greb's illness had any lingering effects. With this in mind, Mason watched Greb closely as he worked himself into

Connecticut's Greatest Boxing Show

Biggest Held in Years

UNDER AUSPICES OF THE

UNION BOATING CLUB

AT CASINO

STATE STREET

Monday Evening, April 15

—o—

15 ROUNDS

George Chip, the Boy Who Knocks them Out, vs. Harry Greb, The Boy Wonder.

—o—

10 ROUNDS

Frankie Conifrey, of New York, vs. Louis Bogash of Bridgeport.

—o—

10 ROUNDS

Young Brown, of Bridgeport, vs. Charlie Bergen, of New Haven.

—o—

Matchmaker & Mgr., Billy Hogan.

Referee, Joe Terry Lee.

Announcer, Frank Braithwaite.

Timer, Michael F. O'Connor.

Tickets are on sale at all the leading cafes and hotels. They will be on sale at the Casino from 9 a. m. on day of show. Information bureau, Hotel Alpine, Phone Barnum 6619. Also Atlantic Hotel.

Admission, $1.10—Reserved Seats, $2.25—Ringside Seats, $3.25-$5.50.

condition.

Before an estimated gathering of forty-thousand onlookers Greb faced not one but three opponents for charity. Greb faced heavyweights Jim Coffey and Joe Bonds, the fighters apparently taking turns facing one another, switching off each round. After being adjudged the winner, Greb then took on Al McCoy for four rounds and was again deemed the winner. In each fight Greb gave no quarter and asked none in return.[21]

When Greb failed to return to Pittsburgh on May 6 to resume training for Bartfield the local press was flabbergasted. They could not understand how a man just recently out of his sick bed could take an opponent like Bartfield so lightly by neglecting his training. Rumors quickly circulated that Greb had remained in the east to enlist in the Navy. These rumors were confirmed when it was officially announced that on May 7, 1918 Greb had joined the United States Naval Reserves.[22] In addition to Johnny Ray, Commander Newton Mansfield, formerly of Pittsburgh, had persuaded Greb that the Naval Reserves were the place for him. Mansfield had been in contact with Washington in an effort to get Johnny Ray reassigned from his post in Philadelphia to New York where he could train troops and travel around the country boxing in exhibitions and bouts, which would serve as a platform for recruitment. When Greb was approached with the same offer he jumped at the chance.[23] Greb later explained the arrangement by saying, "You see, I am one of the Navy's recruiting stars. The officers use me and my little troupe as often as possible for the purpose of stimulating naval recruiting. Every time I appear in the ring they expect great things of me because I am the champion of that branch of the service. Every time I score a knockout it is a great stimulant for the recruits, who immediately want to be where I am. Get the idea?"[24] This would allow Greb to fulfill his patriotic duty while continuing his boxing career in good conscience. He was scheduled to report to active duty on June 5, which would allow him time to fulfill his obligations to face Bartfield in Pittsburgh, as well as face Al McCoy in Cincinnati on May 13, Clay Turner in Bridgeport on May 15, and even squeeze in

Greb is seen here on the left taking the fight to Joe Bonds, one of three opponents he faced in the patriotic boxing exhibition aboard the U.S.S. Recruit constructed in Manhattan's Union Square Park, for the Third Liberty Loan Drive.

With his health recovered Greb made the transition from civilian to service life when, following the advice of Johnny Ray and Commander Newton Mansfield, he joined the United States Naval Reserves at Pelham Bay Naval Training Center in New York City.

another bout with Bartfield in Toledo on May 29. Greb was now ready to make up for lost time.

Bartfield and Greb weighed in for their rematch at the Pittsburgh Natatorium with both fighters weighing in under the stipulated limit (160 give or take a pound), only to have the bout postponed to May 20 due to inclement weather. There was nothing left but for Greb to head to Cincinnati for his rematch with Al McCoy. Greb battered McCoy so thoroughly that by the fifth round spectators began to slowly file out of the theatre. The bout barely served as a workout for the Pittsburgher.[25] Greb, with Red Mason in tow, then hopped a train and after a brief stay in Pittsburgh the party made the trip to New York City where they then completed the journey to Bridgeport, Connecticut via automobile. In Bridgeport Greb would be facing "Chief" Clay Turner, who had won popularity in the city a month earlier with an upset disqualification win over George Chip.

After several stirring speeches promoting the war effort by local military boosters, Turner fell to defeat before Greb's relentless attack much like Al McCoy two days earlier. Sporting a height, weight, and reach advantage Turner was able to make the contest interesting by occasionally rocking Greb with hard right uppercuts one of which cut Greb's right eye. When

Turner was able to land such telling blows Greb fought back harder. He would force Turner across the ring with lightning quick blows all the while utilizing his incredible speed to dodge, duck, and slip blows. In the fifteenth and final round Greb battered Turner throughout the three minutes with little return. Turner left the ring bleeding from the nose and mouth and sporting a badly mangled right ear.[26]

With victories over both Al McCoy and Clay Turner added to his record Greb was now ready to return to Pittsburgh for his postponed match with Soldier Bartfield. There was little question that Greb had fully recovered from his illness and was now ready to face Bartfield, just as there was little question that in order to avenge his earlier defeat at the hands of Bartfield he would have to be at or near his best. The Soldier was relieved to hear that Greb had returned to Pittsburgh with no ill effects from his recent bouts, he wanted no more delays. Bartfield had been in Pittsburgh training for more than ten days and he was focused on beating Greb and getting back on the road. With Greb back in Pittsburgh, everyone from Bartfield to promoter Jim Routley to the fan on the street was assured that the highly anticipated match would come off without a hitch.

A small shower on the afternoon of the fight threatened to postpone the bout yet again but it passed before the preliminaries started. Forbes Field was not packed to capacity, as expect-ed, by the time the preliminaries ended. The rain storm seemed to frighten off the less hardy adherents to the sport. Nonetheless as Bartfield waited in the middle of the ring for Greb to appear a thunderous cheer went up. Slowly Greb emerged from under the stands followed by Red Mason and Johnny Ray. He was clad in bright green tights with an American flag on his right leg. The fighters were announced by Joe Donnelly who also presented Greb with a pres-ent from his hometown admirers. After the final instructions both men returned to their cor-ners.

From the outset Greb took command of the fight. He was intent on not letting Bartfield get out in front as he had in Buffalo the previous winter. Greb used his nine pound weight advan-tage to great effect, meeting Bartfield's rushes and turning them back. Each round Greb was able to stem Bartfield's attack by landing first, harder, and more often. In the third Bartfield, sensing that he was slipping behind, tried to mount an effective attack. Greb seemed surprised by Bartfield's ferocity but quickly warmed to the task. He dug his toes into the canvas and slugged hard with Bartfield. Before long Bartfield was giving ground or trying to clinch to evade Greb's rally. The crowd roared with delight as Greb fought his way out of the clinches and forced Bartfield to retreat with a vicious assault. Several times Bartfield tried to catch Greb coming in with his pet backhand punch but Greb was able to evade this dangerous weapon. As Bartfield grew desperate he was repeatedly warned and hissed by the audience for using his elbows and throwing low blows. Despite such tactics Greb made no complaint and continued his attack.

After the fifth round Greb began to slow a bit allowing Bartfield the opportunity to get back into the fight. They fought at an even pace during the sixth round with Greb coming back to take the seventh but it was in the eighth that Bartfield was able to win his first clear round of the fight. He was able to get in close and bang hard shots to Greb's body which offset the harder punching of Pittsburgh's favorite. In the ninth Bartfield repeatedly stung Greb with hard uppercuts and body shots. It was apparent to all that Greb was fading fast. Neither man heard the bell sounding the end of the round and continued to throw punches. They were quickly separated and dragged back to their corners. The tenth and final round was the most sensational of the fight. After several clumsy clinches opening the round a fight broke out when Bartfield twice deliberately head-butted Greb. Greb furiously drove Bartfield around the ring forcing Bartfield to stand his ground or be literally fought off his feet. As the bell sounded he and Greb were standing toe to toe trading vicious punches with Greb getting the better of it.[27]

Although adjudged the winner by the press and fans alike Greb had nothing but praise for Bartfield. He admitted that Bartfield had given him one of his stiffest fights and that he remained a tricky proposition. It was a proposition that Greb would have to take on yet again in Toledo on May 29. The bout had been rumored prior to their match in Pittsburgh causing a minor controversy owing to the fact that two such fights so close together might give the impression that the fighters were taking part in staged bouts to minimize the risk of injury while continuing to fight often and earn more money. Red Mason temporarily put such concerns to rest by swearing that Greb had no such match planned with Bartfield in Toledo. On May 21, the day after Greb and Bartfield met at Forbes Field, Mason sent word to Ed McDaniel, matchmaker of the Toledo Athletic Association confirming that his signed contract and weight forfeit were in the mail binding Greb to face Bartfield at Swayne Field.[28]

Before Greb could face Bartfield in Toledo he was first scheduled to face heavyweight contender Gunboat Smith at New York in Madison Square Garden as part of a patriotic boxing carnival to benefit the Red Cross. For this contest Greb agreed to fight without pay or expenses. The card would be a gala event, studded with stars from top to bottom. An estimated $30,000 gate was expected from a packed house. In Gunboat Smith Greb would be meeting one of the most experienced battlers in the ring. Though past his prime Smith was a dynamite puncher who had gained notoriety early in his career by knocking former heavyweight champion Jack Johnson clear out of the ring during a training session. Among his victims he could count Frank Moran, Sam Langford, Battling Levinsky, and heavyweight champion Jess Willard. Despite this impressive resume Smith had struggled the last few years with the best competition he had faced. Despite remaining a drawing card he was on the downside of a once promising career.

A capacity crowd filled Madison Square Garden on May 24, 1918 raising $52, 225 for the Red Cross. Prior to the start of the boxing matches bands played, songs were sung, and patriotic speeches were made. The Garden glistened with colorful flags and Red Cross posters draped everywhere. Beautiful young society women dressed in the uniform of Red Cross nurses passed up and down the aisles soliciting donations for the cause. The box seats were filled with

ANOTHER BLOW FOR THE KAISER

the greatest names of New York society. Greb and Gunboat Smith met following an exciting bout between Battling Levinsky and Jim Coffey.

Initially Smith seemed amused by someone of Greb's size forcing the fight. His amusement quickly changed to desperation when he realized that Greb was so fast it was hard to land clean on him. Greb continually darted in and peppered the old Gunner with short snappy punches before quickly dancing out of range of Smith's vicious right hand swings. The crowd cheered both fighters lustily when referee Kid McPartland sent them to their corners after the conclusion of the final round. The crowd was so enthusiastic that after 1 A.M. when the show was dragging on an announcement was made that bouts would be shortened to four rounds. This threw the crowd into an uproar and six round bouts were continued well into the early morning hours.[29]

Busy as ever Greb was back in Pittsburgh the next day to attend the marriage of his sister Ida to John Elmer Edwards. Yet another day later Greb was at the Bessemer building in downtown Pittsburgh soliciting funds for the Red Cross.[30] It was not until 11 p.m. on May 27 that Greb boarded a train

229

Soldier Bartfield faced Greb three times in 1918 and continued to prove that he was one of the most difficult opponents in the ring with his curious combination of punching power, durability, and awkwardness.

for Toledo with James Mason in tow. Greb arrived in Toledo the next day and set about putting the finishing touches on his training for the rubber match with Soldier Bartfield. Bartfield had been in Toledo for four days and couldn't be happier with the distance of the fight, believing that a longer fight would provide him with more of an opportunity to stop Greb. "Greb can't hurt me if he hits me all night," said the Brooklynite. "I know he shows everybody a lot of gloves, but he's not a punisher, and I'll eat everything he shoves my way. I can clout him as often as he wallops me, and I'll sting him a lot harder. I had him almost out in the sixth round at Pittsburgh, but he was able to stall his way thru the period and was all right when the gong rang for the seventh. You'll find him tired and weary after the tenth on Wednesday, and you'll see me full of zip and ginger fizz. I may not stop this Pittsburgh bird, but if I don't I'll be greatly surprised."[31]

Of course Harry had his own ideas when he entered the ring at Swayne Field. He immediately saw that Bartfield was serious about trying for a knockout. Bartfield set himself and waited for Greb to walk into one of his dangerous backhand swings. Greb was by now well acquainted with Bartfield's pet punch, he would rush in and force Bartfield off balance, peppering him with quick stinging punches. When Bartfield would shift his weight to whip that backhand into Greb's mush Harry would already be on the other side of the ring with a smile on his face. Bartfield was further hampered by the insistence of referee Ollie Pecord that he fight cleanly without using his elbows or head. Prior to incurring the wrath of Eddie Kennedy in Pittsburgh for foul tactics Bartfield had beaten Jack McCarron in Toledo largely on the use of illegal tactics. Pecord had no stomach for this behavior and in the sixth round when Bartfield was rapidly growing frustrated with his inability to break through Greb's defense he was warned for using his elbows. Seeing Bartfield's frustration, Greb stepped in with a right hand, and backed out before Bartfield could retaliate, adding insult to injury as he laughed at his foe.

Bartfield finally connected with Greb in the tenth round as Greb was moving away. Off balance, Greb dropped to the mat with a smile on his face and immediately rose, still wearing the

BALL PARK | **SOLDIER BARTFIELD** vs. **HARRY GREB** | for greatest bout ever staged in Ohio the night before, and spend Decoration Day in Toledo.
Wednesday Eve., May 29 | FIFTEEN ROUNDS——TWO OTHER STAR BOUTS

boyish grin that had bedeviled Bartfield all night. All three of Toledo's major papers agreed the knockdown was more the result of Greb's balance than any injury. After rising, Greb continued his attack and by the fifteenth he had Bartfield a beaten man. When the final bell rang there was no doubt as to the winner. To show that he could do more than absorb punishment Bartfield turned a somersault in mid-ring. Not to be outdone Red Mason walked to the center of the ring and turned one of his own. The next day the fight was hailed as the greatest ever seen in Toledo.[32] Unfortunately the bout was a financial flop but this didn't prevent the enthused Toledo promoters from planning a show in the near future between Greb and Jack McCarron.

After a short stay in Pittsburgh, Greb and Johnny Ray left for New York where they would be stationed aboard the land battleship U.S.S. Recruit. While still in training Greb agreed to appear in a boxing carnival to be held in Madison Square Garden to raise funds for the entertainment of soldiers wounded in the war. The show nearly didn't go on due to a police order devised to prevent the staging of the boxing exhibitions. Managers Jimmy Johnston and Billy Roche were taken to the station house and only released when an eleventh hour injunction was granted to the committee in charge of the carnival by Supreme Court Justice Charles Guy barring the police from preventing the event. In the second bout of the evening Greb easily out pointed Zulu Kid before a crowd of 7,500. As a squad of shipmates from the Recruit watched from Greb's corner he cut the Zulu Kid's face to shreds over the course of six rounds leaving

The Battleship U.S.S. Recruit was a scale replica of a United States warship constructed at Union Square, Manhattan. It served as a recruiting station, and training center for the United States Navy during World War I. Harry Greb reported for active duty on June 30, 1918 and spent the majority of his service attached to it.

FRANKIE
BURNS
AND
JACK SHARKEY.

HARRY GREB OF THE
U.S. NAVY AND 'THE ZULU KID'

THERE WERE ALL SORTS OF
FIGHTERS THERE.

LONG RANGE STUFF
BY FRED FULTON.

him a badly battered and bleeding fighter at the conclusion of the contest.[33]

After helping to raise an estimated $15,000 for the benefit of wounded service men Greb was given leave by his commanding officer W. T. Conn to face Gus Christie in Bridgeport on June 24. The day before the bout Sam Marburger, manager for Christie, sent word that Christie had injured his shoulder in training and would have to postpone the bout. Promoter Billy Hogan would hear nothing of the sort. Instead he enlisted the aid of Brooklyn middleweight Frank Carbone to substitute for Christie. Before the bouts began Chief Yeowoman of the United States Navy Mrs. George Alexander Wheelock gave a stirring patriotic speech calling on all citizens to aid in the "salvation of mankind."

"Look at Harry Greb over there," preached Wheelock. "He is an example of the kind of boys that are in the navy." To punctuate Mrs. Wheelock's pride Greb gave Carbone a stiff, one-sided beating. The Bridgeport Post estimated that Greb hit Carbone forty times for every one he received. The Bridgeport Telegram was no less emphatic when it stated that the honors had gone to Greb "by 48 and one-third miles."[34]

Greb's leave was further extended by his superiors so that he might travel to Rock Island, Illinois for a July 4, bout with Bob Moha and Cleveland, Ohio for an exhibition bout which would serve to honor Greb's previous obligation to the Cleveland commission, designed to gain back his purse from the McTigue fight. When Greb arrived in Rock Island he was described by the Rock Island Argus' staff writer L. C. Johnson as "just a big, good natured, unspoiled boy, every inch a gentleman."[35] After being introduced by Chief Yeoman A. E. Benson and used as the centerpiece of an impassioned plea for new recruits Greb defeated Moha in an action packed bout.[36]

The day after defeating Moha Greb, now being billed as the middleweight champion of the navy, was in Cleveland preparing for his exhibition bout. It was another gala event. The elite of Cleveland's society were present in box seats sprinkled among the crowd of 8,000. Several bands played patriotic songs as Chief Yeowoman Wheelock gave one of her now famous speeches. Women dressed as Red Cross nurses moved throughout the audience soliciting donations, which would eventually reach $1,864.35, swelling the total profits to over $14,000; and then there was boxing.

The card featured such stars as lightweight contender Rocky Kansas, featherweight champion Johnny Kilbane, welterweight champion Ted 'Kid' Lewis, and featherweight contender Johnny Dundee among others. Motion picture cameras commissioned by the Cleveland Plain Dealer were on hand to film the events after which the movies would be shown in local theatres in order to raise more money for the fund. One of the fights

FEROCIOUS RING MAULER

which made the film was Greb's exhibition against Danish heavyweight Oscar Anderson in which Greb danced rings around his larger opponent while punching him dizzy.[37] Greb had initially been scheduled to face Packey McFarland who failed to appear. When no other middleweight would agree to face Greb he pointed to the big Dane saying "I'll box him rather than have the crowd disappointed." Greb faced his man in the center of the ring, "If I get hurt it will be my fault," he said. "If you get hurt it will be yours, we must box on the level,"[38] and they did.

After a short stop in Pittsburgh Greb was again back in training for yet another all-star boxing carnival. This time he would appear in Philadelphia opposite Soldier Bartfield on a card featuring Lew Tendler and Frankie Callahan in separate bouts at Shibe Park. The card, while not officially a benefit had many of the features of one. The United States Marine Band played patriotic songs as the crowd accompanied them, yeowomen and sailors moved through the audience taking donations for the athletic fund of the Naval Reserves, and Naval Reserve forces acted as ushers. The show was a success as 10,000 satisfied customers waited anxiously for their hometown hero Lew Tendler to take on lightweight contender Irish Patsy Cline.

There was excitement galore when Greb fought Bartfield. In the first round Greb went down

SEE THE

Fight Movies

of C. A. C. Patriotic Boxing Show NOW at

THE MALL

Barney Adair vs. Charley White, Harry Greb vs. Oscar Anderson, Rocky Kansas vs. Cal Delaney, Johnny Kilbane vs. Larry Hanson, Ted Lewis vs. Jack Twin Sullivan, Matt Brock vs. Johnny Dundee, Johnny Griffiths vs. Vincent Jorkoni, and others.

to his knees for a short count from a blow to the mid-section but rose quickly and re-entered the fray. During the third round Greb rushed Bartfield into a corner with such force that the middle rope was snapped and the fight was delayed until it could be replaced. Another feature of the bouts was the use of a whistle to sound out a warning when ten seconds remained in the round. During the course of the action the ten second whistle sounded and Greb, thinking the round had ended, raised his hands to signify a cessation of activity Bartfield took advantage of Greb's momentary lack of defense and began to whale away at his mid-section. Luckily no damage was done. During the fight Red Mason sat ringside with his feet on the apron shouting encouragement to Greb and was only silenced when he was threatened with removal from the field.[39] The bout itself was a hard one and hard to judge, newspaper's disagreeing as to the winner.[40]

Even as Greb was preparing to take on Bartfield Red Mason was negotiating a bout for Greb which would prove one of the most important service bouts of the war. The bout would be a scheduled ten round contest between Greb and Eddie McGoorty at Fort Sheridan, outside of Chicago, for what was being billed as the middleweight championship of the armed forces. Both fighters agreed to weigh no more than 165 pounds. Despite the fact that decisions were forbidden in Illinois the fight would be fought to a referee's decision, being that the bout was under the jurisdiction of the United States Army. The men would split forty-five percent of the gross receipts and the rest would go to the athletic fund of the camp. Special trains would run from Chicago to the camp allowing boxing starved Chicago patrons the opportunity to see high class professional boxing.

McGoorty was a veteran of the ring, despite still being in the prime of life at 29 years old. He had been something of a boxing prodigy, having had his earliest mention in the National Police Gazette in 1900 at the age of 10.[41] He fought regularly in amateur competitions and impromptu matches around his native Oshkosh, Wisconsin before winning the state amateur lightweight championship in 1904. The next year McGoorty turned pro and quickly made a name for himself locally as a clever, hard hitting fighter with a jaw-rattling left hook. By 1912 McGoorty had built up such an impressive resume that he began to claim the middleweight title which had been secured quite handily by Frank Klaus. After a pair of inconclusive no-decision bouts in which Klaus maintained his grip on the championship McGoorty headed down to Australia to cash in on the burgeoning boxing market there. While in Australia McGoorty, still claiming the middleweight championship, lost two important contests to Les Darcy and slowly slid into a black hole of gambling and alcoholism.

After years of relative inactivity McGoorty began a comeback early in 1918 which saw him reel off respectable wins against such men as Phil Harrison, George Chip, and Frankie Brennan. His recent fights combined with his military training at Camp Grant had helped him attain some of his past form and he was again talking about a run at the middleweight or light-heavyweight championship. McGoorty viewed Greb as an important stepping stone toward that goal and to this end he acquired the help of a trio of well-respected veterans. He would have in his corner former middleweight champion Tommy Ryan, former featherweight title claimant Eddie Santry, and welterweight contender Fred Dyer all of whom expressed the utmost confidence in McGoorty's conditioning and ability to defeat Greb. "I never saw him fight," said Eddie, "but they tell me

Eddie McGoorty, known as the Oshkosh Terror had been a contender for nearly a decade when he faced Harry Greb in mid 1918. He was an intelligent, fun loving fighter with a devastating left hook.

he tears in from the jump and never lets up. Looks as if that sort of fighter ought to give me a chance early in the game to plant one on the chin. And one is all I want."[42]

The fact that the bout was being billed as for the championship of Uncle Sam's armed forces meant that newspapers across the nation would focus their attention on Ft. Sheridan for the afternoon contest. To show their faith in McGoorty the men of Camp Grant raised $5,000 to back McGoorty in his coming bout.[43] Greb's fellow seamen purchased a wrist watch and promised it to Greb on the event that he defeat McGoorty. His officers aboard the recruit added to the war-chest by stating that if Greb could defeat McGoorty he would be given occasional furlough to continue his career.[44] It had all of the makings of an attention grabbing bout with the only competition for headline space being a poorly promoted eight round no-decision contest between heavyweight contenders Jack Dempsey and Fred Fulton, which had already been run out of several venues and seemed always on the verge of collapse.

Army versus Navy, one of the greatest rivalries in sports, helped to draw four thousand people to the bout which was moved into the cavalry drill hall for fear of rain. Ed W. Smith sportswriter for the Chicago Evening American and one of the most respected referees in the nation was on hand to officiate. Corporal Eddie McGoorty and Seaman Harry Greb met in the center of the ring at Ft. Sheridan staring intently at one another as referee Smith looked on. Flash bulbs popped signifying that the next day's Chicago Tribune would feature a large photo of the scene preceding the battle. Focusing intently on the ring were officers and enlisted men, naval personnel from Great Lakes Naval Training Center, and civilians who had made the 30 mile trek by special train or by one of the several small automobile caravans which set out earlier in the

Harry Greb has a look of steely determination on his face as he squares off with Eddie McGoorty prior to their July 27, 1918 match at Fort Sheridan, Illinois billed as being for the middleweight championship of the armed forces of the United States. Celebrated referee and boxing writer Ed Smith looks on.

day. The undercard featured several matches between soldiers of the fort and during the festivities it was announced from ringside that Jack Dempsey had knocked out Fred Fulton in less than 30 seconds of the first round.

From the tap of the first gong Greb was on top of his man. McGoorty was forced to use every trick in his vast arsenal to maintain an even pace with the rampaging sailor. It was in this round that McGoorty landed his best punch, his legendary left hook square on Greb's chin. Greb took the punch and continued to rip into McGoorty working both fists furiously to the head and body. Those at ringside whispered that at the pace he had set Greb would run out of steam before the fifth round. In the third round Greb battered McGoorty around the ring swelling his left eye and leaving him tottering when the bell ended the session. When the eighth had come and it was apparent that Greb was still as fresh as the first and McGoorty was puffing hard to get a bit of oxygen to his lungs it was nearly a foregone conclusion as to which branch of the military the palm of victory would go.

McGoorty fought valiantly those last three rounds. He was pushed and pulled by the strength of Greb as though he was a limp dishtowel, his punches, though sharp and accurate, failed to halt the Smoke City man, who landed three for every one he took and showed a coolness and ring intellect that won the respect of all present. The crowd burst into wild applause when Ed Smith walked over to Greb after the finish of the fight and raised his hand in victory. It was a sensational triumph for both Greb and the Navy.[45]

The next day Greb's terrific victory was overshadowed by reports of the Dempsey-Fulton contest. What had initially seemed a fiasco was now being promoted as the emergence of a major star in boxing. Despite suffering from weak ticket sales (the show was a financial failure), a poor undercard (which was halted prematurely), a riot in the stands squelched by threats of calling the card off, and the unsatisfactorily abbreviated conclusion to the main event which rendered films of the fight useless, it had succeeded in bumping all other major sports stories including the Greb-McGoorty fight. The papers focused on the emphatic way in which Dempsey had dispatched heavyweight champion Jess Willard's top contender in 23 seconds without allowing Fulton to land a single blow. Overnight Jack Dempsey had been turned into a knockout sensation ready for the greatest prize in sports: The heavyweight championship. However, Dempsey was not alone in his ambition and he quickly became a target for every fighter eager to make a name for himself or get a straight shot at Jess Willard. Suddenly a victory over Dempsey could provide the opportunities that couldn't be acquired in years of fighting through the tank towns of North America. Greb joined the multitude of fighters eager for a shot at Dempsey and a ticket to the big time.

Greb returned to New York covered in glory and ready for his next bout, a contest in Philadelphia against light-heavyweight champion Battling Levinsky. The bout, which was originally scheduled for July 30, would be postponed twice before being rescheduled for August 6 at Shibe Park. When Greb arrived in Philadelphia he was wearing a medal indicative of his victory over McGoorty and eager to announce his willingness to face Dempsey. "If I do not win from Levinsky at Shibe Park tonight they can pass me up and take Levinsky, but I do want a chance at Dempsey and I think I am entitled to it."[46]

Greb trimmed Levinsky with relative ease[47] and then stopped by the offices of the Philadelphia Press with Red Mason in tow to reiterate his eagerness to face Jack Dempsey. He then made the short trek to Jersey City to again add Chief Clay Turner to his list of victims. Turner had been a sparring partner and second for Dempsey for the abbreviated match with Fred Fulton leaving him in excellent condition for his bout with Greb. Not even training with the top heavyweight contender was enough to prepare Turner for Greb who piled up points with a vicious body attack and smothered Turner in the clinches.[48]

Greb was now thrust into a period of inactivity in which matches with Eddie McGoorty, Jack Dempsey, Tommy Gibbons, Soldier Bartfield, and Clay Turner failed to materialize. The proposed Dempsey match was especially disappointing when it was learned that Philadelphia promoters, who had initially been interested in Greb, had decided instead to sign Battling Levinsky to the match. Greb's inability to get matches was made worse when naval authorities denied Greb permission to fight Jack McCarron in Philadelphia when he failed to give proper notification to his superiors of the proposed contest.[49] Greb quickly made sure to gain the proper permission from his commanding officer for a series of planned bouts the first of which was to be held in Pittsburgh on September 21. Little did he know it would be his last professional boxing match of the year.

The opponent selected to face Greb was Billy Miske, the same young man who Greb had

Fred Fulton and Jack Dempsey shake hands prior to their 23 second encounter which upstaged Greb's victory over Eddie McGoorty for the army-navy championship. Clay Turner can be seen just over Dempsey's left shoulder.

come out of the crowd to face nearly four years earlier in Philadelphia when both were relative novices. Since that time Miske had grown into a heavyweight, weighing a lean 185 pounds, and had reeled off victories over such men as Jack Dillon, Battling Levinsky, Gunboat Smith, and Carl Morris who outweighed Miske by a whopping fifty pounds. In addition to this he had been able to hold both Jack Dempsey and Fred Fulton to draws in recent matches.

While training for the match

Greb continued his duties aboard the U.S.S. Recruit where he was able to exercise and stay in condition by giving public sparring exhibitions. He arrived in Pittsburgh from New York early on September 20 amid speculation by even his most ardent fans that he had finally chosen an opponent who could take his measure and give him a sound beating in doing so. Prior to leaving New York Greb had requested he be placed in active service. The war was rapidly winding down and he was

Billy Miske, The Human Stumbling Block, Makes Things Tough For Other Heavies

MISKE IS A STUMBLING BLOCK FOR THESE AMBITIOUS HEAVIES.

BILLY MISKE

eager to see action before it was over. He left for Pittsburgh after being told to expect his sailing orders when he returned.[50]

"Gee," said Greb. "You're bigger than you used to be,"[51] said Greb when confronted by Miske, who was fully fifteen pounds heavier than Greb when they stood ring center with their managers to hear Eddie Kennedy's instructions. Greb quickly complained that Miske was wearing excessive bandaging on his hands. Already at considerable disadvantages in height, weight, and reach, Harry wasn't about to let Miske enter the fray with bandages that would make his hands like cinder blocks. After removing the offending bandage Miske returned to his corner, prepared for combat. Greb immediately attacked using the unorthodox style which he had by now perfected. He bounced in, hopping up and down, jumping from side to side, slinging punches anywhere that Miske left an opening, and bounding out of reach before Miske could counter. He seemed unable to fathom Greb's strange style, and had difficulty timing Greb's rushes. As a result Miske was made to seem slow and confused. After five rounds Greb had a fairly sizable lead through his incredible speed and ability to keep Miske from getting on track.

By the sixth round Miske was beginning to have some success. He punished Greb's body in close and then ripped powerful right hands to the chin. Over the second half of the fight Miske and Greb exchanged rounds first one then the other taking control. In the ninth round Miske backed Greb into a corner and crossed a ramrod right hand which re-opened a cut above Greb's right eye. The cut, which had been opened in sparring ten days earlier by Johnny Ray, imme-

Billy Miske had come a long way, both physically and professionally, since he last faced Greb in 1915. Now campaigning as a light-heavyweight and heavyweight, he was eagerly seeking a championship. He had made a name for himself as a stumbling block for many of the highly rated contenders.

diately began cascading blood down the side of Greb's face. Miske seized the opportunity and punished him to the body and head, paying careful attention to Greb's already damaged eye.

Greb gamely tried to fight back under the handicap but he was ineffective and badly beaten at the close of the round. Greb came out fresh from the minutes rest and immediately went after Miske to make up for the last round. Miske met Greb head on and immediately began blasting away at his face and midsection with powerful right hand swings. One of these straight rights caused Greb's knees to sag and it looked for an instant as if he might go down but he remained upright and even managed to launch his own attack to Miske's stomach. Greb was too weak to sustain his assault and his judgment of distance was off due to the renewed blood flow seeping into his eye. It looked again as if Greb might go down under another barrage from Miske but the St. Paul fighter was arm weary and his punches lacked the force to hurt Greb. As the bell rang ending the bout Miske and Greb collapsed into each other's arms, embraced, and exchanged compliments. Referee Kennedy left the ring covered in blood muttering "It was a tough finish."[52]

Florent Gibson and Harry Keck, both writing for the Pittsburgh Post, agreed that Greb had won the bout by virtue of his early lead. "Had not Miske been subjected to a Greb barrage all through the fight which," wrote Gibson, "producing no startling results, gradually wore him down, he might have been able to stop Harry in the last two rounds. Conversely, had Harry's eye not been cut open, it is possible that he might have made Miske crumble as suddenly as the Kaiser's lines in the west, in the last two rounds." He added that "Those who render their verdicts according to the last round or two are going to discredit Greb and do Miske small justice."[53] However it was to this argument that James J. Long of the Pittsburgh Sun, Richard Guy of the Gazette-Times, and George L. McCoy Jr. of the Pittsburgh Leader subscribed. All had Greb leading through most of the bout but agreed that Miske had more than evened up the contest in the final two rounds to which the Pittsburgh Post editorialized "Merely in search of information, we'd like to have a number of Pittsburgh fight critics explain

Harry Greb was intensely proud of his service in the navy. He took every opportunity to show off his uniform, often wearing it into the ring before bouts. His superiors capitalized on his success in the boxing ring by using him as a tool to stimulate recruitment and war fund donations. In addition to this and his other wartime duties he donated his time to various war charities.

how they figure, according to their own dope, that Greb had the first eight rounds and Miske the last two, and still Miske outpointed Greb."[54] One week later allied forces would make a decisive break in the Hindenburg Line which would hasten the end of the war.

Irritated by those who felt he had lost the fight in those closing rounds Harry began lobbying for a rematch with Miske as soon as promoters could match the two. It was hoped that the two would face off again in October not long after Greb's scheduled bout with Clay Turner in Boston on October 1. Neither of these bouts would take place until the following year. All places of public entertainment were now closed in Boston to protect against a deadly sickness which was spreading through the city, indeed it was spreading through much of the world, killing at an alarming rate. What first seemed like an innocuous cold quickly turned into a killer the likes of which the world has never seen. The disease festered and incubated in the training camps, trenches, and ports of the war. It was then spread throughout cities and towns via rail lines and steam ships. It was quickly dubbed the Spanish Flu due to the high mortality rate of those infected with the sickness in Spain. By the time it had burned itself out in 1919 it had

Harry Greb (left) can be seen here being backed into the ropes by Billy Miske in the ninth round of their September 21, 1918 bout at Forbes Field in Pittsburgh. Greb was comfortably ahead before receiving a bad cut which allowed Miske to mount a furious assault in the final two rounds.

killed anywhere from twenty to forty million people, more than the sixteen million military and non-military deaths which resulted from the war. Greb couldn't even report back to his station as many of his shipmates were now quarantined. As a result he returned to Pittsburgh with orders to be prepared to sail when he could safely return to his ship.[55]

When Greb finally left for New York a large crowd of admirers gathered at the East Liberty station to wish him a fond farewell. To show their fondness of him they presented Greb with a wrist watch before the train slowly chugged its way east. Red Mason was, for once, happy to see Greb go. Greb had recently purchased an expensive new car and drove it every chance he got. Mason would comment that he drove in the same manner he fought. "Yes, sir;" exclaimed Mason. "Just like that. Misses things narrower than anybody I ever see. Added 10 years onto my life to ride with him. Don't exactly bust any speed laws, or anything like that, you know, but -well, all I gotta say is, EXCUSE ME from riding with him in the future."[56] Harry would accompany Johnny Ray to New York where they would be stationed aboard the armed transport ship U.S.S. Sierra. Greb would be working on the gun crew hauling the 108 pound shells used in the main gun, a task, he commented, that was excellent for keeping in fighting trim.[57]

Not long after receiving his new assignment Greb was notified by his commanding officer that upon reaching France he would be transferred to London where he would participate in the British Empire and American Services Boxing Tournament. The tournament, held under the patronage of King George was set to take place on December 11 and 12 in London's Royal Albert Hall. It would be a joyous celebration of allied strength made sweeter by the fact that on the eleventh hour of the eleventh day of the eleventh month of 1918 the armistice that was signed when Germany was forced to accept the futility of its struggle went into effect officially ending the bloodiest conflict in human history. The tournament would feature contestants from all military branches of South Africa, New Zealand, Canada, England, Australia, and the United States. Some of the stars of the ring that would appear were Jimmy Wilde, Mike O'Dowd, Eddie McGoorty, Augie Ratner, Johnny Basham, and Bombardier Billy Wells.

Tragic news reached Greb while he was away. On the afternoon of November 25 Jimmy Mason, Red Mason's five year old son, was playing with his little sister when he decided to look for Christmas gifts hidden in the house. He lit a candle and began his search. During the course of his adventure his clothes caught fire. The frightened little boy ran about the house trying to put out the flames as quietly as possible lest his parents find the mischief he had been up to. It was three year old Dorothy who alerted her parents and said "James is burning up!" Red quickly put out the flames using a blanket and rushed his badly injured son to Homeopathic Hospital where he was given only an even chance of survival.

From his hospital bed Jimmy raised his little head and looked at his weeping father

OVER THERE

"Don't cry, papa." All night Red and his wife Carrie kept a vigil as the boy occasionally asked his father to tell him stories of Indians, soldiers, and wild animals. He asked "Daddy are there two Kaisers? Will the soldiers get one and Harry Greb (who he idolized) and Johnny Ray get the other one on the ocean?" Both parents sat helpless as the little boy slipped from this life.[58] Mason later shuffled aimlessly into the office of Ralph S. Davis, sports editor of the Press, his eyes red and swollen and his clothing disheveled, "My little boy is dead," he said, "burned to death. His mother had bought him some things for Christmas and had hidden them. He was hunting them and his nightgown caught fire -and he's dead -and he was a fine little fellow." Upon which he burst into tears. The next day Anna Greb, Harry's mother paid her respects on behalf of Harry who was by now on his way to Europe.[59]

Harry Greb arrived in London on November 30. He immediately had trouble getting used to the cold, damp climate and complained bitterly of the food. "Fish was the chief dish and we got it three times a day," he said. "How could anybody fight on that diet?"[60] Such handicaps caused Willie Meehan to remark upon his return "I have been half frozen ever since I left here on November 20, and I never expected to get warm again!"[61] Five members of the team came down with flu and injuries prevented several other members from training or competing. Old time lightweight champion Jack McAuliffe was present to help familiarize the Americans with the rules of the tournament which would be a modified version of the Imperial Services Boxing Association code which governed military boxing and strongly resembled the English amateur

boxing rules. Even the British understood this to be a severe handicap to the experienced boxers of the United States. Many of the boxers complained bitterly of the abbreviated training time and lack of adequate training facilities.

According to an account by team member Ritchie Mitchell Greb had a terrible time in London.

> "Greb arrived in London several days before I did, which was a week before the tournament," said Mitchell. "Previously to that Harry had engaged in a street mixup with three Limies -that's the American name for Englishmen -and he flattened them. Harry had a difficult time squaring himself with a policeman who came along and it looked for a while as though he might spend his London visit in jail.
>
> "Happy at being released by the bobby, Greb started to cross the street. Looking at his left he was struck by an automobile coming from the other direction. He was knocked unconscious -Harry had forgotten that the current of traffic in London is just opposite to that in America, keeping to the left side of the street instead of the right.
>
> "Greb was removed to a hospital and received three stitches in his head. His legs and body were also badly bruised. But that was only the beginning of his ill luck. On account of his legs he could not do road work so he decided to box -he was still about six pounds heavy and the bout was to take place within a few days.
>
> "Picking out a big fellow who could not have hit him with a yard stick, Greb mauled the daylights out of the Englishman for three rounds, until--
>
> "Greb turned to go to his corner after the third round, and his sparring mate not hearing the bell let go a haymaker, which split Harry's lip. Two stitches sewed it up. And still the worse was yet to come. He couldn't do roadwork -his legs were sore; he couldn't box, his lip was damaged. Yet what worried him most was the possibility that he might not be permitted to take part in the tournament because of being overweight.
>
> "As a last resort he hied himself to the Turkish Baths. While in the hot room he slipped and fell, and four more stitches were put in his head.
>
> "It seems to me the United States navy was entitled to the tournament on Harry's gameness alone"[62]

The grand old Royal Albert Hall was a sight to behold on the eleventh day of December 1918. Flags of many nations draped the ring posts, pillars, and ropes. The packed audience was like a sea of military uniforms. It was even announced that King George would add to the splendor by gracing the event with his presence on the day of the finals. As Greb sat in the dressing room

SOUTH AFRICAN TEAM.

Back Row :—L. Cpl. E. C. Baker, Pte. G. Horrocks, Cpl. Maurs, Cpl. Green.
Front Row :—Sgt. Coles, D.C.M., M.M., Pte. Klepper, 2nd. Lieut. Meierterkamp (captain), Pte. A. Davis, Pte. C. A. Thomson.

ROYAL NAVY.

Front Row :—Ldg. Smn. Smith, A. B. Hall, A. B. Davies, Stkr. Harvey, Chief Instr. O'Neil, Lt.-Com. Burnett (captain), Ldg. Smn. Hayes, Cook's Mate Stephens, A. B. Pattern, Pte. Jagger.
Back Row :—Sgt. King, Ldg. Smn. Powell, Sgt. Ponsford, P.O. Gummer, Ldg. Smn. Key, Pte. Parker, Sgnlmn. Wilkinson, Sgt. Braddock, A. B. Hole.

Top: The South African team which competed in the Inter-Allied boxing tournament, Lance Corporal E. C. Baker (top inset), Greb's first opponent in the competition, saw little of the tournament, being knocked out within a few seconds of the first round. Sergeant William Ring (above inset) of the Royal Navy Team (above) faired better by defeating Greb in three rounds on a decision that Greb angrily disputed.

preparing for his bout the commanding officer came in and announced that Ritchie Mitchell had just been robbed in his bout against Jack Miller of the British Army. Greb was told that he would do well to score a knockout otherwise he faced the prospect of losing another hometown decision.

Greb was to face Lance Corporal E. C. Baker of the South African team. At the bell the fight-ers were ordered by the referee to shake hands and step back before initiating combat. As the two fighters stepped forward and clasped hands Greb leapt back and immediately jumped in with a left hook that rocked Baker to his heels. Before Baker knew what was happening Greb was on top of him raining blows. A right hand to the jaw followed by a left hook to the body dropped Baker unconscious. The bout was over before it had begun and Greb's victory had horrified the prudish British officials and fans alike. He was booed and hissed for what they called the "pretense" of a handshake. The first day of the tournament ended with the British Army leading with twenty-one points. The Americans returned to their lodgings still smarting from what they considered a bad decision against Ritchie Mitchell and an unusual scoring sys-tem which awarded points that at times seemed to them to be arbitrary.

The next day word was received that King George would not attend due to a cold he had caught while in France and that his son Prince Edward would appear in his stead. The first bout of the day would be Harry Greb's match against Sergeant W. Ring of the Royal Marine Artillery. Greb was warned immediately by the referee to give a more earnest handshake and step well back before initiating combat, which he did. He then proceeded to attack Ring, as the London Daily Telegraph wrote, "...in a way that suggested a human windmill."[63] Ring was the immediate favorite of the crowd due to the fact that Greb had by now been cast as a villain for his rough fighting of the day before. It seemed that at every step Greb was pestered by the ref-eree and could never get started. He ripped and tore at Ring only to be warned for low blows. He was again warned for fighting in the clinches. Finally he simply rushed in throwing punch after punch as Ring was content to pop left jabs into Greb's face. Every British account of the fight differs, some saying Greb suffered great punishment, others saying Ring won through his cleverness and ability to block Greb's blows. It is surely one of the mysteries of a tournament which seemed to have its share of controversy that one of the most accomplished boxers in the world had been defeated by a complete unknown. Indeed, it was Ring's hand that was raised at the end of the three rounds to the great joy of the Englishmen present. It was a bitter pill for the competitive Greb to swallow.[64]

> "We finally got through three rounds and at the end Ring got the deci-sion," complained Greb. "I was confident I had won, but later was told the decision went against me on these counts:
>
> "First, because I was warned so often; second because I was wild, miss-ing many punches, and thirdly, because my opponent had managed to show great cleverness in eluding me.
>
> "According to that system maybe I did lose. I started a hundred punch-es to Ring's one. He was on the defensive most of the time, covering and

blocking and devoting his energies to making me miss, for all of which he was piling up points. On the other hand, every time I landed a punch, that meant a point for me, but if I happened to miss the next punch that wiped out the point I had just earned. Every time I was warned for an infraction of the rules, with which I was not familiar, I lost another point. Oh, it's a great system. I wonder how many points I owe myself!"[65]

Harry (left) launches an attack against Seargent William Ring of the Royal Marines. Ring won a baffling decision over his American opponent which left Greb with a bitter taste in his mouth and looking forward to returning to the United States.

The British had their own complaints. When Memphis Pal Moore was returned the winner over British hero Jimmy Wilde, the legendary "Mighty Atom," a near riot ensued as the crowd erupted in catcalls which continued for several minutes. It was the upset of the tournament and would be talked about for months. Only with the intervention of another legend, former champion Jem Driscoll, did the crowd quiet down and the tournament resumed. "When Pal Moore rightfully won from Jimmy Wilde, the English favorite, the spectators raised the roof with their booing," continued Greb. "Which they kept up until Jem Driscoll, coach of the English team, stepped into the ring and, like the true sportsman he is, announced that he was satisfied with the verdict."[66]

In the end the British Army came away victorious with a total of fifty points. The United States Army was a distant second with thirty-nine points, while Greb's Navy team came in fourth place with thirty-two points, just behind the Royal Navy and Royal Air Force who tied for third place with thirty-two and a half points. In the aftermath Prince Albert presented the winning team with the trophy emblematic of victory. To each member of the winning team a small replica of the trophy was presented. Each member of the running-up team received a small enamel medallion. Gold medals were presented to the winners of each weight division and silver to the runner-up. Every participant received a souvenir certificate marking the occasion. The next day a luncheon was held for all participants of the competition at the Savoy Hotel in which endless speeches were made extolling the virtues of the allied forces and the tournament. Photographs were made of the luncheon "with a view to having a permanent record of the greatest assembly of boxing men that had ever been brought together in the history of the art."[67]

On December 14 Greb and many of his teammates boarded the Cedric, a military hospital ship, for home. They passed time on the voyage by giving exhibitions to the great joy of the wounded soldiers returning home from a very different kind of battleground. When they finally arrived in New York ten days later they were treated to a hero's welcome. Newspapermen flocked to get the inside story of the tournament and the Americans were eager to please. Pal Moore was the hero of the hour due to his unlooked for victory over Wilde. There were grumblings over the defeats of Greb, Joe Lynch, and Mitchell as well as the point system and rules governing the bouts but these were quickly forgotten as the fighters looked forward to getting on with their careers and a future without war. Greb summed up his journey in his typical manner, quick and to the point: "I wouldn't trade the lower end of Fifth Avenue in Pittsburgh for all of London."[68]

The future looked bright for Greb. He was now home and the war was over. He expected to be mustered out of the service before long and could resume his career. Most importantly he had a wedding to plan.

SAVE THE HONEYMOON FOR LATER

Little is known today of the young woman who would become Mrs. Harry Greb. During their marriage and after her death Greb went to great lengths to insulate his family from the media attention that surrounded an athlete of his stature. What is known is mostly conjecture and hearsay from sources that can be considered less than reliable. Some accounts place her as a chorus girl in the Academy Theater's regular burlesque show, a story which is hard to confirm given that generally it was only headliners who were named in the advertisements of such shows. Descendants of Greb tell

> *The honour of your presence is requested*
> *at the marriage of*
> **Miss Mildred Kathleen Reilly**
> *to*
> **Mr. Harry Edward Greb**
> *on Thursday morning, January the thirtieth*
> *nineteen hundred and nineteen*
> *at nine o'clock*
> *Epiphany Church*
> *Pittsburgh, Pennsylvania*

the story that she was a beauty queen before she married Greb. Still other accounts have her as a childhood sweetheart of Greb, the least likely scenario.

What is known about Mildred Reilly is that she was born in Wilmerding, Pennsylvania to Thomas and Irene Reilly. Thomas had been an Irish immigrant who had since passed away leaving Irene to support Mildred, and her two other children, as best she could. One contemporary newspaper report at the time of the wedding had the courtship between Mildred and Harry taking place over the course of the previous year. He certainly could not have chosen a better wife. She was an attractive young girl of 18 with plump rosy cheeks, beautiful doe-like eyes, and an attractive figure. If she wasn't a chorus girl or beauty contestant, it is easy to see how such rumors persisted. The wedding itself was set for January 30 but first Greb was eager to get back into the ring.

His first bout after returning from London was scheduled for New Year's Day in the Southside Market House against heavyweight Jack Heinen of Great Lakes Naval Training center. The fight suffered an eleventh hour cancellation. The official reason given was that Heinen had failed to secure leave from his commanding officer to face Greb in Pittsburgh. However rumors persisted that the real reason the bout had been called off was because ticket sales had lagged due to the fact that Heinen was completely unknown in Pittsburgh.[1] Instead of facing

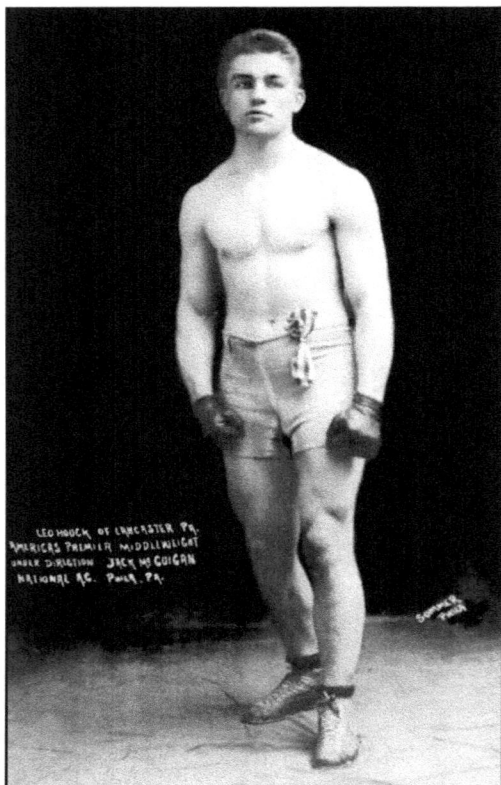

Leo Houck (or Hauck) began fighting in 1902 at the age of 14. His career spanned nearly a quarter of a century and during that time faced an absolutely stellar array of fistic talent. He was incredibly popular with fans in his hometown of Lancaster, Pennsylvania.

Heinen Greb would now look forward to four matches that Mason had arranged for him, all to take place prior to his wedding ceremony. He would be expected to meet Leo Houck in Boston on January 14, Young Fisher in Syracuse on January 20, Knockout Sampson in Pittsburgh on January 23, and Soldier Bartfield in Columbus, Ohio on January 27.

In his first performance in Boston Greb had little difficulty outpointing Leo Houck but the match was poorly received by the press. Houck, Like Eddie McGoorty, had been fighting since early childhood. By 1910 he was holding his own with the best men in the middleweight division. A year later he was claiming the middleweight championship by virtue of his 20 round victory over Harry Lewis in Paris. In 1912 he lost his tenuous claim when he was stopped, for the first of only two times in his career, by Jack Dillon. Houck was a natural athlete who, in addition to boxing, excelled at football, baseball, and basketball. He was continually buoyed throughout his career by the support of his hometown fans in Lancaster, Pennsylvania who loved him for his defensive genius and willingness to stand inside with his opponent and fight. He was a heavy puncher but not of the knockout variety, staying close to his opponent blocking and countering with short thudding blows. In Boston Houck, unnerved by Greb's wild attack, spent nearly the entire fight in a defensive shell leaving the fans and press greatly displeased. Houck had fought several important bouts in Boston, his quality was known to the fans. Since Harry was a stranger in Boston he was made the scapegoat for the unsatisfactory fight. They felt that he should have been able to do more with an opponent who was so obviously unwilling to engage. Despite the lack of enthusiasm Greb was asked back by the promoters for another opportunity to show his wares.[2]

Less than a week later Greb was in Syracuse to meet the local favorite Young Fisher. Fisher was a short compact middleweight who had met several good fighters in his career yet he had never been able to overcome his status as a local clubfighter. He was a rough fighter to the point of being dirty and his overly physical style of combat had earned him the nickname

"Caveman" by his peers. Despite his limitations Fisher was eager to face Greb. "I'm full of confidence and never felt better in my life," he said. "It is the first time I ever have really trained as I should, because I know Greb is the toughest man I ever met. I'll do my best to knock him out, as I always do."[3]

Greb labored under several slight handicaps in his bout with Fisher. First, the rust that was evident in his bout with Houck still plagued him. He was overweight and had difficulty losing the excess poundage. As a result he spent the evening before the bout in a Turkish bath hoping to melt away the extra flesh. In addition to his weight concerns Greb was anxious that he would not be marked up about the face with his wedding so near.

After a delay of thirty minutes while both sides argued over the heavy tape Greb used to bind his hands the fight began. Greb had to use all of his guile to preserve his features for Fisher was eager to win at all costs. From the first

Charles Fazio, professionally known as Young Fisher, was a rough and willing middleweight from the Northside of Syracuse, New York. Despite never being more than a tough club fighter he faced some of the best competition available.

round on Fisher fought an exceedingly foul fight. It was quickly apparent that despite his poor judgment of distance Greb was the much better fighter. To even matters Fisher began to use his elbows, raking them across Greb's face.

Growing increasingly angry at Fisher's tactics in the second round Greb shot over a hard right hand that sent Fisher to the canvas. Things got uglier in the seventh round when Fisher began to head-butt while continuing the liberal use of his elbows. Greb continued to pummel Fisher until the end of the round when in a clinch Fisher deliberately stomped on Greb's foot. At the bell Greb limped back to his corner.

Fisher tried to follow up on his ill-gotten advantage in the eighth round by again slashing Greb with his elbow. Greb fought like a wild man and forced Fisher to retreat from a vicious onslaught. The beating continued through the ninth and in the tenth roun Fisher resorted to biting Greb on the left forearm which sent Greb into a rage. Both fighters began to wrestle and

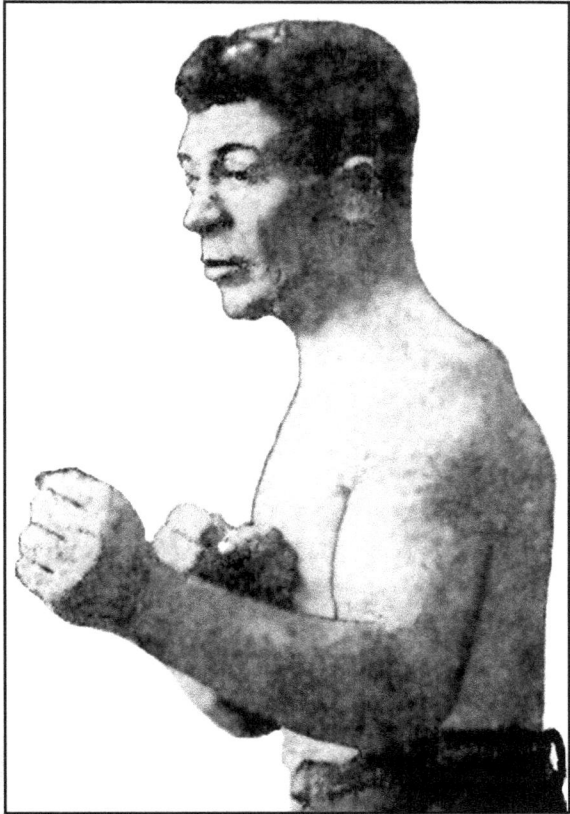

wound up writhing on the floor. The action was barely able to resume before the final bell ended the fight.

Harry was adjudged the easy winner despite the sloppy performance.[4] After the bout Greb, who was usually respectful of his opponents outside of the ring, couldn't resist taking a jab at his enemy when he stated that Fisher was the worst fighter he had ever faced in all his years in the ring.[5]

After leaving Syracuse, Greb returned to Pittsburgh where he easily defeated Paul Sampson, pitching the boxing equivalent of a no-hitter.[6] Two days later he was at City Hall filling out a marriage license. In Columbus Greb used his speed and size to stay on top of Soldier Bartfield. As usual Bartfield proved a cagey opponent but Greb who was now entering his prime was simply too big and too fast for the smaller man. It was the fifth and final time these two warriors would meet in the ring.[7]

Greb quickly returned to Pittsburgh to prepare for his wedding. For a young man such as Greb, who lived life at a pace comparable to that in which he fought, the two days he had to prepare for one of the most important events of his life was an eternity. Mildred and Harry were to be wed at 9am at the Epiphany Church, located right in the heart of downtown

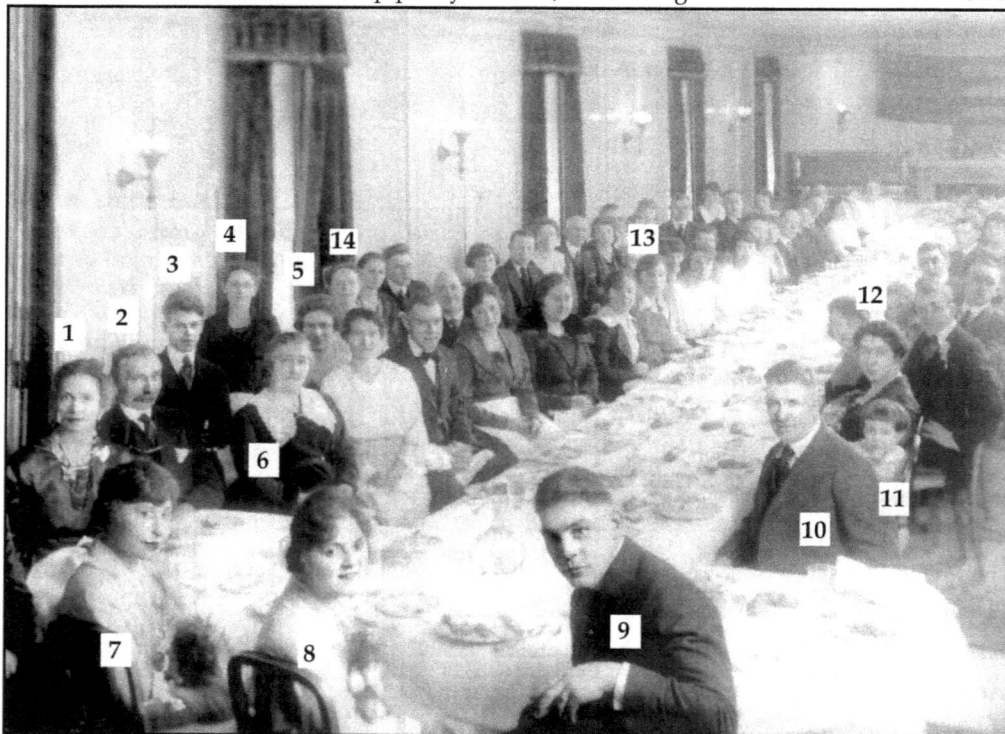

Mildred and Harry host a lavish wedding reception breakfast at the Fort Pitt Hotel. The principles are: 1. Anna Greb, 2. Pius Greb, 3. J. Elmer Edwards, 4. Elizabeth Riehl, 5. Ida Edwards, 6. Irene Reilly, 7. Catherine Greb, 8. Mildred Greb, 9. Harry Greb, 10. James "Red" Mason, 11. Dorothy Mason, 12. Caroline M. Mason, 13. Clara Greb, 14. Charlotte Edwards.

Pittsburgh. Greb, true to form, arrived late. He did however have a good excuse as he had been out early in the morning doing roadwork for his upcoming bout with Tommy Robson.

The service began at nine-thirty with Father O'Connell performing the ceremony as Harry tugged nervously at his dress suit. Greb's best man was Leo "Poof" Kelly, a childhood friend who remained close to Greb throughout his life. Harry's sister Catherine served as bridesmaid to Mildred. The church was packed with people who had been invited by the young couple via an open invitation. After the ceremony Greb and his new bride treated one hundred select guests to a lavish breakfast at the Fort Pitt Hotel during which Red Mason announced that the ceremony had taken place on the occasion of his eighth wedding anniversary.[8]

Harry and Mildred make a fashionable couple as newlyweds in early 1919. Mildred often accompanied Greb to his fights and made a hit with fans who weren't accustomed to seeing women ringside.

The honeymoon would have to wait. That afternoon Greb and his new wife were accompanied by Red and Carrie Mason and their daughter Dorothy on a train bound for Cleveland where Greb would face Tommy Robson the next day. The bout was contracted for catch weights so when Cleveland authorities found Greb and his party dining and demanded Greb weigh in before the fight Mason was livid. There was no point in weighing in he argued as there was no stipulated weight limit. Greb and Mason accompanied the officials back to the back room to further debate the matter. There Mason and Jimmy Johnston, manager of Robson, argued. Johnston threatened to pull Robson out of the fight if Greb didn't weigh in. To bring the dispute to a close Greb stepped on the scales with a steak dinner in his stomach and dressed in full winter clothing. He weighed 178 pounds which led those present to estimate his weight at being about 168 without the dinner or clothing.[9]

Robson showed himself to be a tough, game fighter. Despite Greb's advantage in weight Robson continually attacked. His chief weapon was a wicked right hand punch which he tried to land on Greb time and again without success. The crowd cheered his willingness to accept the punishment that the human buzz saw from Pittsburgh was meting out in order to get that one deciding punch in. The entire house was so taken with the smaller man's courage that as the final bell rang out even Greb threw his arms around Robson's neck and kissed him on both cheeks. "You gave me a great tussle kid," said Greb.[10]

Robson was no less complimentary of Greb. "He did not hurt me," said Robson, "but never before did anyone hit me so often and get away without any damage to speak of. Now the question is: 'How does he do it?' How can any man of his weight dance and leap and keep on top of you the way he does without becoming exhausted? And he can go 20 rounds the same way. He is the biggest freak in the ring, and I know the only way I will ever be able to beat him is to land a haymaker and with him sprawling all over me I don't see how I can do it even then. I think Jack Dempsey is the only man who can put him away for the count."[11] A theory Greb was increasingly anxious to test.

After the Robson bout Greb and his new bride returned to Pittsburgh and a new home. Greb had purchased a new house in the East End of Pittsburgh and had it completely furnished so that it would be ready when the couple returned to begin their new life together. Four days later Pittsburgh watched its rising star win via technical knockout in the third round over Len Rowlands when Rowlands refused to answer the bell for the fourth round claiming he was hit low. The bout was easy money for Greb and the press knew it. They were merciless in their criticism of Rowlands as well as the current state of boxing whereby promoters such as Red Mason who held interest in boxing clubs could pick and choose "soft touches" for their fighters.[12]

Greb divided a week in Pittsburgh between his new bride and fine tuning his conditioning. He was expected in Syracuse on the tenth of February to face one of his toughest challenges yet. His opponent would be rising heavyweight contender "KO" Bill Brennan. At six feet one inches tall and weighing around two hundred pounds. Brennan was arguably the most intimidating combination of speed, size, and punching power that Greb had yet faced. Brennan began fight-

"KO" Bill Brennan was a powerfully built, athletic fighter who had been ranked right at the top of the heavyweight division for several years when he first met Harry professionally in 1919.

ing around 1913 he began fighting and racked up an impressive string of knockouts which led to his nickname. By 1916 he was considered a top heavyweight and in 1918 he met another rising star in Jack Dempsey. Fate was unkind to Brennan, who, according to legend, broke his ankle in the second round of that fight but gamely fought on before being stopped in the sixth, the first stoppage loss of his career. The ankle and World War 1 led to a period of inactivity for Brennan and he was now on the comeback trail.

Greb was now in excellent fighting trim. The Syracuse sports marveled at his conditioning. At the opening of the first round Greb took the initiative and never let up. Early in the fight Brennan, while still being outpointed, was able to stay competitive with his smaller, faster rival. This had all changed by the middle of the fight. Brennan, who by now had missed scores of powerful rights and lefts, was second guessing himself. Whenever he lined Greb up for a fight ending punch and let it fly he hit nothing but air. Greb was making the fight look easy. When the final bell sounded Greb was the only possible victor.[13] According to the Syracuse Journal "Brennan tried hard, but whenever he seemed to have one of his blows aimed at Greb, it would go wild. Although Brennan was in splendid condition, he was unable to touch the scrappy middleweight from Pennsylvania, who was on his toes from the first bell to the final."[14] The Syracuse Post-Standard added that even though Greb was "outweighed by several pounds, many inches shorter, the battler from the Pennsylvania city gave an exhibition of speed, footwork, and fighting ring generalship that seemed to dazzle and bewilder Brennan and cause him to look like a selling plater in a futurity scheduled to be run by thorobreds only."[15]

"Lots of persons," said Greb, "thought I was going too high to tackle a heavy fellow like Bill Brennan, but I handled him alright last night and never a mark to show for it."[16]

Eager to preserve the public's high opinion of Brennan, Leo P. Flynn, manager of Brennan's affairs, under the guise of the Syracuse Herald, sent false reports of the fight over the newswire claiming Greb had been badly beaten and marked up over the course of the fight.[17] Despite the fact that the actual Syracuse Herald had given Greb every round of the fight, some of the local Pittsburgh newspapers picked up the story and printed it. This made Greb furious. "I'll show him," Harry exclaimed. "Get this fellow for me again. Bring him to Pittsburgh. I want to show him up here, where my friends can see me do it."[18] As a result Mason made tentative arrangements for a Brennan rematch to be held in Duquesne Gardens the following month.

Prior to the Brennan fight in Syracuse Greb and Mason stopped off in Buffalo to sign a bout with Battling Levinsky February 17. On the return trip from Syracuse Greb made the rounds of Buffalo newspaper offices to give the writers copy and help promote the fight. "I'll be in great shape for Mr. Levinsky," said Greb. "I've got an account to settle with that young man. We boxed once in Pittsburgh. That's my home town. You know he wanted to make a good showing. All the gang was there. In the first round Levinsky clips me over the eye. Bing! I got a slit. Couldn't do my best after that. But he didn't sneak the decision. Not over me. I should say not. Even with a slit eyebrow I boxed him silly. All the papers said I won. That's good enough to

Mister Harry Greb."

"I'll trim Levinsky right this time. Wait and see. I never made a bad showing here did? I should say not. And I won't this time."[19] Later on the same trip Greb expressed his eagerness to break into the heavyweight division and gain a fight with the winner of the proposed championship bout between Jess Willard and Jack Dempsey. "Me for the heavyweight class," he said. "I've cleaned up the middleweights and my victory over Wild Bill Brennan shows I can go through this light-heavyweight (sic) class just as easily. Look at that Jack Dempsey. Getting $27,500 for a chance at the heavyweight title. Say, boy, that's going to be my dish someday, just watch me."

"Just about a couple more months and I'll be recognized as one of the real heavyweight contenders. The Levinsky match will put me a long ways toward that goal and I can beat him just as sure as the Marines can wallop all the Germans in the world. I'll give him all I got Monday night and then me for some of these so-called heavies. They'll be heavy when they hit the floor, I'm thinking."

"Fight Dempsey, why not? I hope he wins. I'd like to meet him in a year for the title. I'd just as soon meet either him or Willard they both will look alike to me when I'm ready to let Red Mason go ahead with the match."[20]

Dempsey himself was by now well aware of Greb's intentions. He was reminded of the fact during a short stay in Pittsburgh when asked what he thought of his smaller rival. "I never saw Harry in action, but I have heard an awful lot about him. They say he is as good in the tenth round as he is in the first. A fellow has to be good to win a reputation like that. Among the fighters I have also heard that Greb is a good, clean boy. I am sorry I am not going to have a chance to meet him here."[21]

Greb was not the only one who had Dempsey on his mind. Levinsky had left his work in the naval shipyards with little training to face Dempsey on November 6 of the previous year. The fight was no contest. Levinsky was poorly conditioned and Dempsey obliterated him in three rounds. Levinsky had fought twice since his devastating loss to Dempsey, once against Leo

When light-heavyweight champion Battling Levinsky faced Greb in early 1919 he was looking for a rematch against Jack Dempsey who had knocked him out the previous winter. Levinsky would face Greb four times in 1919.

Houck, and most recently, a 12 round points victory over Jim Coffey, the Dublin Giant. Levinsky had now worked himself into the same terrific conditioning that made him the light heavyweight champion. His ultimate goal was a revenge match against Dempsey or a match with the winner of the Dempsey-Willard bout.

Both fighters were in perfect condition when they received referee Dick Nugent's instructions. Mildred watched from the balcony as they returned to their corners. The bell rang and Greb quickly moved to the center of the ring. Boxing from a crouch he made it difficult for the ten pounds heavier Levinsky to land his vaunted jab. Greb would spring from his crouch firing left hooks to the body only to follow up with a looping right hand to the jaw. Despite losing the first two rounds Levinsky was still showing his old time form and defensive ability. He made Greb miss often and occasionally landed with sharp counters. By the fourth round Greb's frantic pace had begun to tell on Levinsky who no longer wore a look of confidence. The combination of Greb's vicious attack and completely unpredictable style had Levinsky totally confused.

This light heavyweight champion, with over ten years of experience and well over two hundred fights to his name against the best fighters in three divisions, was up against a Greb that he simply could not cope with. He tried to rally in the seventh, much to the delight of his fans, and in the eighth he managed to re-open a small cut over Greb's eye sustained in training. From this point on Greb put on so much pressure that Levinsky nearly crumbled. Greb buckled Levinsky's legs with a long left hook forcing the quivering Levinsky to hold. During the ninth and tenth Greb battered the rapidly fading fighter who could only cover and hold to avoid further punishment. The fighters embraced as the final bell rang to the eager applause of the crowd of 5,000.[22]

When speaking of the fight the next day the Buffalo Courier gave one of the great descriptions of Greb's unique and unorthodox style.

> Starting at the first tap of the bell, Greb never stopped charging at the foxy and clever Levinsky. Never a moment did he let up, springing, leaping, swinging, and jabbing from all angles. Wild as a hawk, apparently, yet his punches went home to the mark and the very fury and relentlessness of his attack wore Levinsky down until, in the last two rounds, when Levinsky perceptibly tired, Greb was all over him, shooting rights and lefts from everywhere...
>
> ...Levinsky showed all of his wonderful defensive skill, or he would have been well beaten, but he couldn't figure Greb and keep him figured. The minute Levinsky solved one attack Greb started another style. Twice Bat measured Greb perfectly and as he leaped in, jabbed with the left and whipped the right to the same mark, but Greb only smiled, crouched, leaped and tried from another angle. His style bewildered even the spectators. He would start to hook, then change the

One of the most colorful fighters of the teens and twenties was Chuck Wiggins (above). Wiggins was a hard fighting, hard living Hoosier. Often at odds with the law, he would eventually die under questionable circumstances while in police custody in 1942.

punch and hit straight. Wild swings apparently hewed for the body were suddenly lifted to the head and smacked Levinsky smartly about the ears...[23]

Greb now had eleven days to prepare in Pittsburgh for his next series of bouts. He would face Chuck Wiggins in back to back bouts in Toledo and Detroit on February 28 and March 3, then Leo Houck in his hometown of Lancaster, Pennsylvania three days later on March 6.

Wiggins was a young man born to fight. Fast on his feet with a great talent for slipping and countering punches. He was tough and rugged and always willing to stand in and slug with anyone. When he wasn't getting paid to fight by promoters he trained for the ring by cleaning out bars in drunken brawls. The Indianapolis police department had a small squad dedicated to "pacifying" him when he was on one of his drunken tears. Chuck Wiggins was a handful.

Greb's popularity was now such that his name was guaranteeing large crowds in both Toledo and Detroit. Even casual fans of the sport were eager to see this young man who was willing to fight tirelessly against all comers. Wiggins, who was already well respected in Toledo, arrived on ground early to begin training for the biggest contest of his career. He worked out daily with former Greb opponent George Lewis. The sparring sessions between these two were such that one fan remarked, "That was worth $3 of any man's money. I never saw two such fast boys before."[24]

During the preparations for the card Promoter Ad Q. Thatcher made the six hour journey to Chicago in hopes of meeting with Tex Rickard to secure Toledo's bid for the upcoming Willard-Dempsey heavyweight championship bout. Coming on the heels of a Greb-Wiggins bout (which was already expected to be the largest gate in the history of Toledo boxing) a bout for the heavyweight championship would be a huge boost for Toledo. Thatcher missed Rickard but met with sportswriter Ed Smith who reserved a seat at the press table for the Greb-Wiggins fight which already had reservations for twice as many press credentials as the usual Toledo boxing match.[25]

As fast as Chuck Wiggins may have been Greb made him look as though he were standing still. Using every trick in his vast repertoire Greb kept his less experienced foe guessing throughout the twelve rounds and was returned the easy winner by fans and press alike.[26] Toledo fight patrons who expected Wiggins to give Greb a better fight in that city than had Jack Dillon and Soldier Bartfield were not only mistaken but greatly surprised by the ease in which Greb demonstrated his mastery. Dick Meade of the Toledo News-Bee was shocked and disappointed at the one sidedness of the interesting stylistic pairing:

> All the vaunted speed of Wiggins, his uncanny left hand, his punishing right, and his blocking ability melted away into thin air once Greb got underway.
>
> Chuck was a mechanical toy that Harry did with as he pleased. The Pittsburgh boy didn't try to put Wiggins away or give him any nasty punishment, but he made a sucker out of Chuck and showed him to such an extent that Billy Rooks, who had the pair slated for Detroit Monday night, is looking for somebody to face the Pittsburger.
>
> Wiggins didn't have a thing. He tried to jab with his supposedly wonderful left, but Greb's jaw was never there. Harry's speed was wonderful. He was quick as a thought, as a flash or anger, and always was about five seconds ahead of his opponent.
>
> Greb was so darned swift in the ring that he would wait until Wiggins' fast jab was within six inches of his jaw, and then slip his head to the side as the punch flashed by.
>
> Wiggins always waited for Greb to come in, which is suicide without an argument. Harry would cock, prime, and aim his blows and then crack the bullseye.
>
> When he wanted to, Harry would tie Chuck into knots with head feintings. And when he combined head action with hand passing and feet stepping, Wiggins didn't know whether it was raining or snowing, night or day, here or there, in and out, up or down, this or that, beer or skittles, doughnuts or coffee, or whiskey or soda.
>
> Greb would feint Wiggins into hysterics, spasms, or whatever it is that makes one unimportant, futile, or not at all necessary.[27]

Billy Rooks, promoter of the proposed Greb-Wiggins bout in Detroit was not ready to write Wiggins off. "Wiggins was scared to death, not of the man in the ring but of Greb's reputation, and he was expecting something every minute, that Greb did not have," said Rooks. "I am confident that fight tonight will be a thriller, because I know in my own mind that Wiggins can do better than he did at Toledo. He knows what Greb has now, knows that he isn't a superman, and will be more confident."[28]

Rooks' confidence was not well placed as Wiggins was again completely outclassed by Greb. Harry treated the fight as little more than a workout, continually staying ahead on points but never trying overly hard for the knockout. Indeed Wiggins was so outclassed that his corner contemplated throwing in the towel. "I would have thrown in the towel," said cornerman Jimmy Byrne, "but Greb asked Wiggins to quit. Chuck told him that he could kill him, or bite him, but he would not quit, and that Greb couldn't knock him out."

"Chuck had several ribs cracked, he has a badly damaged left ear, and a battered right one, and his mouth is all cut up. Wiggins was badly hurt in this fight, but he refused to be put out...

"...Wiggins couldn't do a thing with Greb. We planned to have him step in and break up Harry's rushing attack, but he's too powerful and would sweep Chuck back."[29]

Detroit fans were so disappointed with the uneven match that early on they began to hiss and boo. By the fifth round they were slowly filing out knowing that the bout held no surprises in store before the eighth and final round.[30]

Leo Houck fared no better three days later. Despite being in the best shape that local fans could remember Houck was nothing more than a workout for Greb. The Lancaster fight fans, who worshipped the ground Houck walked on, were forced to admit that if Greb stood in Houck's way for a chance at the championship he could hang up the gloves now. The Lancaster sportswriters who were reluctant to give Greb credit for beating Houck in Boston were now forced to admit Houck lost every round to Greb and had no answer for Harry's speed, strength, and aggressiveness.[31]

Greb and Mason hurried back to the train station in order to make the late train to Pittsburgh where Greb would have nearly two weeks to prepare for his St. Patrick's Day rematch with Bill Brennan. Leo P. Flynn was confident of his fighters chances against Greb even going so far as to offer $2,500 of his own money to bet against Greb.[32] Jack Dempsey who had been in Pittsburgh giving sparring exhibitions gave his opinion of the fight. "If Harry Greb thinks he is going up against an easy proposition in Bill Brennan he is much mistaken," said Dempsey. "He gave me

Lancaster's Fulton Opera House served as the venue for Greb's bout against hometown hero Leo Houck. The building was first erected in 1852 on the foundation of Lancaster's colonial jail. In addition to Greb it played host to Horace Greeley, Mark Twain, and George M. Cohan among other luminaries at different times during its operation.

one of the hardest fights I ever had, and I have no doubt that he will give the Pittsburgh fans their money's worth when he opposes Greb."[33]

Confidence expressed in a man opposing Greb was again misplaced. Brennan was easily outpointed. After dominating the fight with his speed Greb opened up in the final round and battered his much larger opponent. At the finish Brennan was a sorry sight with a badly mangled eye and swollen lumps all over his face.[34]

Now avenged of the false news report sent out by Leo Flynn, Greb had another score to settle. A fighter named Eddie Trembley had been making the rounds on the east coast claiming to have knocked Greb out while in England for then Inter-Allied tournament. In fact Trembley had been stretching the truth more than a bit. He had been the fighter who Greb was sparring with in England while suffering cuts from the automobile accident. When Greb discontinued the sparring session so as not to aggravate his wounds, Trembley claimed a victory. When Trembley returned to the United States he and his manager R. H. Kain were well aware that few people would know the truth about that sparring session and filled the newspapers with stories of how Trembley had knocked out Greb.

The two fighters were matched for a bout at Johnstown, Pennsylvania by Jack Lewis. While Greb prepared for his bout with Trembley tragedy again struck Red Mason. On March 19, Carrie, Red's wife, passed away after a short bout with pneumonia. Carrie had never fully recovered from the shock of little Jimmy's death. Her own death Left the 47 year old Mason as the sole support of his little three year old daughter Dorothy. He would never remarry.[35]

As offers were coming in rapidly from all over the country Greb was left for a few days to handle his own affairs. He quickly agreed to another appearance in Buffalo against George "One Round" Davis who had challenged him to a match prior to his recent bout against Levinsky. Mason had already matched Greb for a third bout with Billy Miske to be held at the end of the month and a bout between Greb and Tommy Madden was in the offing for Butler, Pennsylvania.

Before Greb could get Trembley into the ring word was received that Trembley had promptly left his manager and would not be appearing in Johnstown. With just a day before the scheduled fight, word was sent out for a replacement. Greb had agreed to face anyone the club could acquire sight unseen. On short notice Harry "Happy" Howard of New York accepted. Howard was a veritable beanpole of a fighter, standing between six feet two inches and six feet six inches tall yet weighing between 155 and 160 pounds. Unfortunately for the fans in Johnstown Howard's height was his only distinguishing quality and he was badly beaten at the end of the ten rounds.[36]

When the rubber match between Greb and Miske was finally signed both camps were surprised. The Greb camp felt that Miske was lucky to get the popular verdict after the previous bout. Harry himself was eager to get Miske back to Pittsburgh and prove to his fans that he was the heavyweight's master. Miske's followers felt Greb was not only lucky to escape a KO but was foolish to sign against the man some considered Jack Dempsey's only rival for heavyweight honors. Miske had broken his hand in a bout with Tom Cowler in January, an injury which rendered him inactive for two and a half months. Three days prior to his bout with Greb Miske came back to knock out Cowler in the fourth round. There was much at stake for both fighters as they were both eager for a shot at a big money fight with the winner of the Willard-Dempsey bout. The loser would have much ground to make up in order to attain such a fight.

A record crowd was present to see the Greb-Miske fight on March 31. Masses of fans stormed the entrances, poured through windows, and simply overwhelmed the auxiliary police force called in to keep the peace. Just before the start of the fight Miske was handed a telegram which he read in his corner. It said: "Baby arrived at 6:30; Everything going well. Father" Miske was now the father of his second child, Douglas.

Billy Miske and Harry Greb met for the third and final time during the spring of 1919. The bout was followed by controversy surrounding Miske's performance. Tragically Miske would not live to see his thirtieth birthday. He died New Year's Day 1924 of a kidney ailment.

The bout itself was marred by the atrocious officiating of referee Jack Dillon. Despite being a betting favorite Miske showed a reluctance to use his previously damaged right hand. As a result he was more inclined to get inside and bang away at Greb's body which made for a softer target than the head. It was this same strategy that won Miske a knockout over Cowler.

From the outside Greb was able to use his speed of hand and foot to outwork Miske and beat him to the punch. In the third round Miske rushed Greb and pummeled his body. Suddenly a minute before the close of the round Greb turned away from the action and limped to his corner claiming a low blow. Referee Jack Dillon saw the blow but refused to award the bout to Greb on a foul and despite Greb's reluctance to continue Dillon refused to award the bout to Miske on a TKO. Inexplicably Dillon allowed the round to end without resuming the action. Neither fighter nor their corners, or even the crowd made a protest but it served to underscore the usually competent Dillon's shoddy performance.

Save the Honeymoon for Later

The bout resumed in the fourth round and beginning with the fifth Greb was in control. It was a good fight with ebbs and flows. Miske showed a marked superiority at infighting due in large part to his size and strength advantages yet he was kept at bay by Greb's darting left hand and lightning quick one-two's. In the final round Miske brought blood from Greb's mouth prompting Greb to attack with a furious rally. The crowd, which paid between ten and twelve thousand dollars, went home pleased yet a select few were perplexed. They could not understand why Miske didn't uncork his powerful right in the same manner he had the previous fall. This was a small, yet vocal group.[37]

To counter the criticism of his performance referee Jack Dillon tried to pass the blame on to Billy Miske claiming the St. Paul Heavyweight had not given his best. On the morning following the fight Dillon turned in a report to Sheriff William S. Haddock stating that while Greb had given his very best, Miske had, in his opinion, pulled his punches. Dillon then released the report to the press. This sent an outrage through the community. The public was angry at the possibility that either the fight may not have been on the level or that Jack Dillon was trying to displace blame for his inability to control the action.[38]

A special detective employed by Public Safety Director Pritchard during the fight to make sure the show was professionally handled found nothing amiss. Jim Routley, matchmaker for the fight, laid the blame squarely with Jack Dillon who was the sole arbitrator. Dillon had been instructed, stated Routley, to call the fight off if he had even the slightest notion that the fighters were not putting forth their best effort.[39] When Jack Reddy, manager for Miske, received word that Miske was not only being accused of throwing the fight but was now temporarily barred from fighting in Pittsburgh by Sheriff Haddock, he was incensed.

Reddy issued his own statement tossing any responsibility for the outcome of the bout squarely in the lap of Dillon. "Dillon, the referee, has more nerve than the Kaiser," he fumed. "He knows nothing about boxing or he would have done one or the other when Greb quit in the third round; count him out or give him the bout on a foul."[40] With the majority of the public of the opinion that the fight was fought legitimately and no proof of deception on the part

Brooklyn's Tommy Madden met some of the best fighters in the middleweight and light-heavyweight divisions during his long career. Among them was Harry Greb whom he faced in Butler, Pennsylvania in 1919. Between 1917 and 1926 he faced five men who were, at one time or another, world champions.

of either fighter, the controversy quickly died out. Boxing, which had been briefly halted in Pittsburgh, resumed again and within a few months Billy Miske would again be allowed to fight in the city.

Greb did not remain idle long. He took three days of rest before resuming his training. On the first day back on the training grind he knocked out Tommy Madden of New York in the second round at Butler, Pennsylvania. After a first round spent feeling Madden out Greb came out for the second and put his over-matched opponent away with a four punch combination.[41]

Greb was next scheduled to face Tommy Robson in Syracuse five days later. However, during an appearance by Jack Dempsey at the Syracuse Arena two days before the scheduled fight it was announced that Robson had injured two ribs and would be unable to appear. The only available opponent was Young Fisher who had made such a sorry showing against Greb earlier that winter. The audience was asked if Fisher would make an acceptable substitute to which the audience readily gave their blessing.[42]

Greb, no doubt remembering the foul fight he encountered the last time they met, punished Fisher severely. In the fourth round he knocked Fisher down with a hailstorm of blows. He slowly rose only to be knocked down a second time. This time he was saved by the bell. By the fifth it was apparent that Fisher was ready to be taken out but Greb held back. He chose instead to torture his opponent, as if he were child plucking the wings from a captured fly. The Syracuse fans could only congratulate the grit and courage of their hometown boy for staying the full ten rounds. It was estimated by both the Syracuse Journal and Syracuse Post-Standard that Fisher failed to land a dozen clean blows over the course of the fight.[43]

Greb and Mason left Syracuse early the next morning, taking a train to Buffalo where Greb

George Jaus, better known as George "One Round" Davis stood over six feet tall and weighed between 185 and 195 pounds of solid muscle. He packed a powerful right hand punch but often left himself open to counters when trying to land it. Interestingly, over the course of his career he faced middleweight champion Harry Greb, light-heavyweight champion Battling Levinsky, and heavyweight champion Jess Willard.

would face heavyweight George "One Round" Davis. Davis had been a popular fighter in Buffalo before the war. He packed a paralyzing right hand punch which garnered him several first round knockouts early in his career and his nickname. He would later explain that the nickname became something of a curse in that he constantly felt pressure to live up to it. Attacking from the tap of the gong in the hope of getting a knockout he often left himself open to coun-

WHILE DAVIS WAS TRYING TO GET HIS POWERFULL RIGHT HAND FREE OF WHAT WAS HOLDING IT-- GREB JUST SHOVELED GLOVES ALL OVER THE ONE-ROUNDER

ters and as a result had more than a few knockout losses on his record. He was now in the midst of a comeback after having spent several years on the Pennsylvania mounted police force. The first bout in Davis' comeback was a one round knockout over late sub Jack Jones on the undercard of the Greb-Levinsky fight two months previous. Davis entered the ring before Greb and Levinsky had a chance to square off and announced to the audience that he wished to challenge the winner. And so it was that Davis received his shot at Harry Greb.

"I'm not kidding myself that I'm a speed marvel," said Davis, "or that I have a chance to win from Greb in a boxing match. But one thing I do know, and that is that I can hit ten times as hard as Greb and that he can't go through ten rounds without being hit. I'll be punching from the minute I get in there and if I can get one home it will spell finish for Greb. I know I can take his best wallops and he cannot take mine. I'll keep shooting and the first shot that I land him will bring him down. Of that I'm sure, and that's the only chance I've got."[44]

With his hopes for victory pinned on a knockout punch Davis' went to work against Greb and quickly realized just how hard it was to hang a decisive blow on the whirling dervish from Pittsburgh. Greb was so fast that before Davis could start his powerful right hand Harry was either inside smothering it, or nimbly dancing out of range. Davis appeared painfully slow compared to his younger, smaller rival. Once Greb got warmed up he was on top of Davis' all the time, refusing to let Davis mount any kind of offensive. Davis could do little more than attempt to block the multitude of punches Greb was throwing in his direction. In the fourth Greb managed to close Davis' right eye. In the sixth Davis began to bleed from the mouth and most shocking of all, Greb was actually out-muscling Davis' in the clinches.[45]

After the fight Davis seemed happy just to have won a couple of rounds on the scorecards of some of his more generous fans. "I took a high shot when I consented to fight Greb," said the bruised and swollen battler. "People may think I'm crazy, but I'd fight him twice a week for six weeks if I could get the chance. I'd almost consent to fight him for nothing, for I think it would do me a lot of good. If I got all the chances I wanted at Greb I'd bet all I ever hope to see that someday I would beat him, and then could beat him every day in the week. Greb is the fastest and perhaps the strongest one of the heavyweights. I say heavyweights advisedly, for if he didn't weigh 180 Tuesday night he never weighed a pound. I think I did well with him."

"I admit his speed bewildered me at times, for I make no claim for speed, but I'll try and get it, and meantime there are a lot bigger and maybe slower fighters than Greb to whom I can turn my attention. I've started and I'll see it through. That's all I have to say."[46]

Immediately after the fight Greb and Mason met with Frank Oppenheimer matchmaker of the Fairmont Athletic Club in Erie, Pennsylvania, in order to sign a contract to face Leo Houck in that city on April 25. On that date, for the third time in four months, Greb easily defeated Leo Houck, winning every round. After the bout there was slight criticism that Greb had refrained from knocking out the durable Lancastrian in order to preserve his hands for his upcoming bout with Battling Levinsky in Canton three days later. The criticism may have been justified but it may just as easily be attributed to a turf war that was playing out in the press between Oppenheimer and Charley Finneran of the Olympic Athletic Club over promotional dominance in Erie, resulting in parties loyal to Finneran criticising Oppenheimer's show.[47]

Three days and four hundred miles later, Greb was in action again at Canton. In a terrific exhibition of skill and stamina Greb outpointed Battling Levinsky over 12 rounds. The bout was a no-decision match and as such Levinsky's light-heavyweight crown could only be lifted in the event that Greb might score a knockout. Failing to do so, he had to be satisfied with a clear cut popular decision. Fighting out of a crouch Greb would slip inside Levinsky's defense and quickly spring up throwing volleys of blows before nimbly dancing out of range. Several times during the bout Greb landed terrific blows to Levinsky's nose which sent a spray of blood.

Throughout the bout Red Mason could be heard at ringside engaged in a war of words with Levinsky's manager "Dumb" Dan Morgan. "What are you doing Harry," called Morgan to the leaping, bounding Greb, "-playing circus? Why don't you tie a string to yourself. Get down to earth me boy, down to earth. Never mind Bat, if he doesn't come down soon we'll try for a pilot's license, or else get a shotgun."

Mason quipped back: "Oh, I say Morgan, that circus of ours is all right; we're using Levinsky for the center pole. Watch him straighten up."[48] The two managers kept this banter up for the duration of the fight. Of the twelve rounds Levinsky was only given two or three depending on which source one quotes.[49]

Greb returned to Pittsburgh, staying for a week before he and Red Mason hopped a train for Boston where he was expected to face Clay Turner. It would be an opportunity for Greb to make a more favorable impression upon the Boston boxing fraternity than his previous appearance in that city when he faced Leo Houck. It will be remembered that upon that occasion the press had been critical of Greb due to the spoiling tactics of Houck. Turner was well acquainted with Greb's unorthodox style from their two previous engagements and had prepared accordingly. He focused on Greb's body, which proved an easier target than his ever moving head. Turner tried to engage Greb at close range but Greb quickly saw what his opponent was about and maintained his distance.

In the first round Turner was dropped by a vicious left hook and by round's end he was bleeding from the mouth. After the third round Turner's eyes were beginning to close rapidly and by the fifth round he was completely out of the fight. Using fast footwork to stay outside of Turner's punching range Greb would dart in and out, hammering lefts and rights to Turner's body. By the end of the fight Turner was nearly helpless, flailing blindly at the swift moving shadow in front of him, and robbed of his stamina by the vicious body attack of Greb.[50] After the bout Turner was taken to the local hospital. Greb waited to make sure that Turner's condition was not serious. Upon learning that Turner had suffered four broken ribs, in addition to the various cuts and bruises already evident at ringside, Greb and Mason hopped a train bound for Pittsburgh where he would face Willie Meehan in two days.

Greb's whirlwind schedule was beginning to take a physical toll. He arrived in Pittsburgh suffering not only a black eye from his bout in Boston but also boils. This same affliction which plagued Greb the previous year during his active campaigning could threaten his schedule for the immediate future. Such a setback would prove costly as Greb's popularity was now such that his schedule was being booked months in advance. In Meehan he would be facing a hungry fighter, a hunger which didn't just feed the rolls of fat that boiled over his waistline. Like Greb, Meehan was eager to gain a lucrative match with the winner of the Dempsey-Willard contest. Now that Dempsey had secured his title shot Meehan was more famous than ever based on his success against Dempsey the previous year.

Meehan showed to greater advantage than most

Eugene Walcott, otherwise known as Willie Meehan, the "Fat Boy" of the prize ring, remained a thorn in the side of contenders when he faced Greb in a 1919 rematch. He hoped that a victory over Greb, combined with his two wins over Jack Dempsey, would vault him to a match with the winner of the Jess Willard-Jack Dempsey bout.

GREB HAD A
CIRCUS · DIVING·
SWINGING AND
CLOUTING - ALSO
MISSING BART
MADDEN

of Greb's recent opponents. Harry found it difficult to hurt Meehan due primarily to Meehan's $32^{1/2}$ pound weight advantage. In the fourth Greb managed to open a cut over Meehan's right eye. Both fighters showed little regard for the punching power of the other and as such the fight had plenty of action. The following day Greb was returned the winner by Pittsburgh's sporting press due to his greater activity and greater speed.[51]

Tex Rickard had now secured Toledo as the site for the heavyweight showdown between Jess Willard and Jack Dempsey and tickets were in great demand. Red Mason was handling the sale of tickets in Pittsburgh for Rickard and had a tentative agreement for Greb to box in Toledo on the eve of the fight against either Bill Brennan or K.O. Brown. This match was eventually postponed and then cancelled altogether at the request of Rickard who probably felt it would hurt the gate of his big attraction.[52] Nevertheless Greb would have plenty on his plate to keep him busy. In just over two weeks after his fight with Meehan he had already added victories over heavyweight Bartley Madden in Buffalo, and Tommy Robson in Syracuse to his record.

After the Robson bout it was announced that Greb had been offered a position as sparring partner for heavyweight champion Jess Willard as he prepared for his upcoming Toledo bout with Jack Dempsey. Greb refused. His schedule was now booked up well into July with bouts that would prove far more lucrative than the sparring sessions that Willard now offered.[53]

"Greb is a busy boxer, and he can make more money in real fights than he can by helping Willard train," said Red Mason. "Moreover there is a chance that someday, if Harry gets heavier, he may get a crack at Dempsey himself."

"Greb will be one of the busiest boxers in the country the next two weeks. His next bout is with Joe Borrell at Philadelphia, in the National league ball park. June 16, two nights later he meets Happy Howard at Erie, and the following night he meets Bartley Madden at Canton. On June 20 he clashes with Jeff Smith at Martin's Ferry, and on June 23 comes his battle at Forbes Field with Mike Gibbons."

"Greb hasn't time to help condition Willard. He is kept busy fighting his own battles."[54]

Most important of the above mentioned bouts was the rematch with Mike Gibbons in Pittsburgh on June 23. Greb had been chomping at the bit to get Gibbons back in the ring with him for over two years and he finally had his opportunity. He would enjoy this. He had a score to settle with Gibbons and the fact that Gibbons held out for an enormous guarantee and the right to dictate terms before signing didn't improve Greb's disposition toward him.

Prior to his bout with Greb, Gibbons cancelled all of his future fight dates with the exception of a tune-up against George Chip in Terre Haute. Greb for his part maintained his busy schedule. He would continue to adhere to the Red Mason philosophy, believing that to rest is to rust. He traveled to Philadelphia on June 16 where he destroyed his old tormenter Joe Borrell. In the second round Greb hit Borrell so hard with a single punch that Borrell turned a somersault before stopping to take a nine count. In the fourth round Borrell went down again, this time from a body-punch. Two minutes and five seconds into the fifth round the referee was forced to halt the one sided contest. Borrell had been backed into a corner and with his hands at his sides, unable to mount any discernable defense, took blow after blow. After his hand was raised by referee Lew Grimson Greb leaped over the ring ropes, jogged into the stands and kissed his beautiful wife to the cheers of the audience. He was cheered all the way back to his dressing room.[55]

Greb continued his "training regimen" by outpointing lanky Brooklynite Happy Howard in Erie and knocking out inept trial-horse Yankee Gilbert, all within four days of defeating Borrell. Gilbert had been a late replacement for Jeff Smith who was originally slated to face Greb across the river at Martin's Ferry, Ohio. The venue of the bout was switched due to local opposition from several veterans' organizations who felt that boxing

BOXING

At the COOLEST SPOT IN ERIE
Fairmont A. C., 14th and State
WEDNESDAY NIGHT

Harry Greb vs. Happy Howard
World's Middleweight Champion   Of Brooklyn.
TEN ROUNDS

Jerry Cole, 160, vs. Jimmy Gray, 160
Of Erie   Tipton Slasher of Syracuse
EIGHT ROUNDS

Young Rogers, vs. Young Scholl
Better Known as Masked Marvel.   Of Buffalo
SIX ROUNDS

One Other Bout To Be Arranged
PRICES—$1.50, $2.50, $3.50 and $5.00. Seats now selling at the Lawrence Hotel, Two K's, Hook's, Hall's and George Stephaney's.

Heavyweight Yankee Gilbert was a woefully inept fighter who often disgusted fans and officials alike with his almost complete lack of knowledge of the art of self-defense. He faced Greb in 1919 resulting in similarly unflattering reviews.

was not appropriate family entertainment. Greb entered the ring first at which time the lights went out. When the lights came back on it wasn't Jeff Smith standing in the ring but a little known heavyweight named Yankee Gilbert. Red Mason addressed the audience notifying them that Jeff Smith's manager had sent word his fighter would not be able to appear. It was obvious from the start that Gilbert was completely outclassed by Greb. He was down at the end of the first and by the second the audience had already begun filing out. Greb was disgusted with such a poor substitute and repeatedly called for the referee to stop the contest. Finally, in the fourth round the referee mercifully halted the travesty, sending Gilbert to his corner after having been knocked through the ropes. Needless to say Wheeling was not overly enthused about seeing Gilbert in the future.[56]

When Greb returned to Pittsburgh he found that Mike Gibbons had been a busy boy. Press reports had filtered into Pittsburgh daily. Gibbons had been training diligently with a bevy of sparring partners. Stories originating the Gibbons camp were printed daily telling of how Gibbons would refuse to shake hands with Greb, how he would knock out Greb, and how it was Greb all along who had prevented the match from taking place earlier. This last statement irritated Greb to no end.

"I never sidestepped Gibbons in my life," stated the defiant Greb. "I have been trying to get him to agree to reasonable terms for a bout for years. I'll make him eat his words when I get him in the ring Monday evening."[57]

Gibbons entered the ring first, checked the ropes, and the floorboards. Greb entered next and while the fighters were having their gloves put on Greb's ever present Garfield rooters serenaded him from the grandstand. A near capacity crowd waited with bated breath as Greb and Gibbons posed for photographs at 10:17 p.m. After receiving the final instructions by referee Ed W. Smith the two rivals returned to their corner to await the bell.

The game plan of both fighters was apparent from the outset. Gibbons would attempt to minimize the exchanges while trying to make Greb miss and counter with short accurate punches. Greb for his part intended to bury Mike under an avalanche of blows to prevent Gibbons from mounting any discernable offense. So it was that whoever would be able to fight *his* fight would ultimately be adjudged the victor. In the first round Greb attacked relentlessly, wildly even. Leaving himself open he hoped to draw leads from Gibbons who despite his 31 years still possessed one of the most impenetrable defenses in the sport. Gibbons was much too smart for such a tactic. While Greb pecked and poked attempting to find a chink in Gibbons armor Gibbons maintained his composure and blocked or slipped many of Greb's punches, throwing in the occasional counter. There wasn't much to choose from the men after the first. Gibbons had been more accurate but Greb was far busier, the general consensus was an even round.

The second round was similar to the first with the exception that Greb was now utilizing his reach advantage by holding Gibbons off with his left and raking him with right hands. Gibbons returned to his corner after the round spitting blood. The third showed Gibbons in all of his defensive glory. He made Greb miss time and again. In return Greb made Gibbons miss several blows on the inside and then countered with a hard right, the hardest punch of the fight so far.

In the fourth round Gibbons came out of his corner rubbing his nose with the thumb of his glove, his trademark known the world over. He seemed to be finding his rhythm. He was still having a hard time mounting any offense due to Greb's high rate of activity but he was now preventing Greb from scoring effectively while letting fly with eye-catching counter punches. Greb came back after the fourth to reclaim lost ground. He broke through Gibbon's defense and the two traded furiously as Greb forced Gibbons

Harry Greb and Mike Gibbons square off for the cameras as referee Ed Smith looks on. Their long awaited rematch held at Forbes Field, Pittsburgh, was a grudge match of sorts, eagerly anticipated as a showdown between two of the worlds best middleweights.

into retreat. Greb pursued Gibbons to the ropes, battering him into a corner. It was the best round of the fight and the pace was telling on Gibbons.

Gibbons came out, much like Greb in the previous round, intent on re-establishing himself. As he attacked Greb he left himself open and in an instant Greb was on his man, showering Gibbons with blows and again forcing him to the ropes. Gibbons did his best to block and counter but Greb's pace was blistering and he could not overcome the younger man's momentum. Both fighters returned to their respective corners at the end of the round showing signs of battle; Greb suffering a cut under his right eye, Gibbons bleeding from a cut nose.

The seventh was a slow round, both fighters having exerted themselves greatly in the previous two rounds. The slow pace benefited Gibbons who made Greb miss time and again while keeping him at a safe distance with his rapier-like left. Gibbons came out confident in the eighth. In a clinch he tapped Greb on top of the head and smiled, which only made Greb fight harder. Greb increased the pace of his attack incrementally over the final three rounds to the point that in the tenth he was all over Gibbons, barely giving the St. Paul legend room to breath.

Near the end of the round Greb slipped to his knees and Gibbons took full advantage of Greb's liability by hitting Greb as he rose. Greb didn't complain and it wasn't enough to swing the margin of victory in his favor.[58]

The next day the majority of Pittsburgh's newspapers judged Greb the winner. The loudest dissenting opinion was that of the Pittsburgh Press' Jim Jab who always found it difficult to give Greb credit for anything he did in the ring. Richard Guy of the Leader, who was occasionally at odds with Greb, remarked that "Greb looked better in action last night than at any time I have ever seen him. His general physical condition seemed splendid and he fought with the spirit and speed of a champion. Indeed, he performed like one with the exception of his punching, which was light. At times he boxed all around Gibbons, just like a champion would a second-rater."[59]

The show was a success on many levels; setting records for attendance and gate receipts. However, the high price needed to secure Gibbon's services meant that what should have been a financial bonanza for the Keystone club was only a slight profit. The fight illustrated that it would be difficult for local boxing clubs to sign important bouts without operating at a near-loss. Pittsburgh promoters would have to think long and hard before agreeing to terms like those Mike Gibbons demanded.[60]

Another interesting side note, which hints at the stress Harry's busy career placed on his now pregnant young wife, was noted by the Post. Just before Greb left his dressing room for the bout a phone rang in the Post's sports department. It was Mildred Greb looking for her husband. The attendant who answered the phone notified her that he was fighting Mike Gibbon's that night.

"Well, I just know it's a scheme for him to stay out late tonight. Licking that fellow oughtn't keep him away from home at this hour."[61]

For the next four days Greb nursed an injured ankle which he suffered in the fall he took in the last round of his bout with Gibbons. He then proceeded to travel west to Tulsa, Oklahoma to once again face Bill Brennan on July 4. The bout would provide western fans unable to make the long journey to Toledo to see the Willard-Dempsey contest the opportunity to witness a high class boxing card in their own backyard. The card was arranged by John "The Barber" Reisler. The same John Reisler who, for the past year or so, had been trying to hamper the career of Jack Dempsey.

Reisler had previously managed Dempsey when the young heavyweight had come from the west to New York in hopes of making a name for himself. More eager to make a quick buck with the young fighter from Utah than to nurture his talent he made plans to quickly overmatch Dempsey against a top heavyweight and reap the profits. When Dempsey refused several of the matches Reisler offered a fight was arranged between Dempsey and a black journeyman named John Lester Johnson at the Harlem Sporting Club. It was a rough fight and according to legend Dempsey suffered three broken ribs.

Rather than stay in the east and continue fighting for Reisler, a dejected Dempsey headed west and faded for a time into relative obscurity. It wasn't until he was brought under the management of Jack "Doc" Kearns that he found a manager wily enough and energetic enough to bring Dempsey along to the point where he would one day challenge for the championship. However, as soon as Dempsey started making a name for himself as a possible challenger for Jess Willard Reisler appeared claiming that he and not Kearns was Dempsey's rightful manager. He continually hounded Dempsey with court orders and lawsuits either to prevent Dempsey from fighting or to get a cut of the purse. He was never successful but he would remain a thorn in Dempsey's side throughout much of the latter's career.[62]

On the way to Tulsa Greb and Mason stayed in St. Louis for two days to train and make contacts for possible future fights in the city. While there Greb worked out at Harry Cook's gymnasium where he took on all comers. Brennan was already in training in Tulsa having just left St. Louis where he faced Billy Miske in a disappointing eight rounder. He sparred daily with Roughhouse Ware and Lee Anderson.

On July 2, Greb arrived in Tulsa eager and excited. Jack Kearns had just announced that Newark, New Jersey was offering $35,000 for a fight between Greb and Jack Dempsey provided Dempsey defeat Willard. "Frankly I don't think Greb would have a chance with Jack," said Kearns. "But, if he wants to mix it with him and some promoter is game enough to gamble on the venture, he can have the fight."[63] In order to get such a match Greb would need to remove Brennan from his path and continue his winning ways. He first needed to find suitable sparring partners. Unable to locate any from the crop of local fighters a request was sent to Brennan and Leo P. Flynn that Greb be allowed to work with Anderson and Ware. Initially Brennan was unwilling to allow his opponent to benefit from his sparring partners but finally relented.

"Well," said Brennan, "if you think you can get any value out of them after I'm through with them, I guess it's all right. Go ahead."[64]

At the Brady hotel, where both fighters set up training camps, Greb battered Ware relentlessly and then took on Lee Anderson for three fast rounds. Anderson, who would eventually boast wins over Gunboat Smith, Kid Norfolk, Sam Langford, and Tiger Flowers showed his burgeoning talent and gave Greb the much needed sparring he was looking for. Tulsa fight critics were amazed at Greb's speed and stamina. Those that left the Brady hotel that afternoon came away with the impression that if Greb were still standing at the end of fifteen rounds with Brennan he would be well ahead on points.[65]

The Brennan fight would be held at the Tulsa Convention Hall. John Reisler had spared no expense in preparing the card. He had workmen secure dozens of large electrical fans throughout the hall and made arrangements for all windows and skylights to be opened, allowing a free circulation of air to hold back the July heat. Arrangements had also been made for a wire direct to ringside from Toledo so that returns of the heavyweight championship could be announced to the crowd between rounds.

A deafening roar was sent up from the crowd watching the semi-final between Earl Puryear and Bobbie Hughes when it was announced during the eleventh round that Jack Dempsey had knocked out Jess Willard to win the heavyweight championship. What the crowd could not have known was how brutal Dempsey's demolition of the giant Willard actually was.

The Treaty of Versailles had only been signed the previous week, officially ending World War 1, yet what Dempsey did to Willard that hot July afternoon looked much like the start of World War 2 when Germany steam-rolled the hapless Poland. After the first knockdown the giant Kansan, who outweighed his smaller opponent by nearly sixty pounds, was helpless. He floundered around the ring as Dempsey battered him to the canvas again and again. After the seventh knockdown referee Ollie Pecord apparently tolled the fateful ten with Willard reclining in a neutral corner. The jubilant Dempsey rushed into the audience to celebrate when suddenly Jack Kearns frantically called him to return to the ring. The fight wasn't over; the bell ending the first round which could not be heard over the uproar of the crowd had saved Willard. For two more rounds they battled on as Willard somehow succeeded stayed upright. Finally between the third and fourth rounds Willard threw in the towel and a legend was born.

Bill Brennan and Harry Greb met for the third of their four fights on July 4, 1919 at Tulsa, Oklahoma. Brennan remained a top drawing card for the next four years before finally retiring in late 1923 to open a nightclub. Six months later on June 15, 1924, he was shot and killed by two thugs under mysterious circumstances.

Maybe Brennan was motivated by his former opponents' victory over Willard. Maybe he was simply more prepared for Greb's speed and unorthodox style after having faced him twice before. Whatever the case, Brennan provided more opposition than in any of their previous engagements; actually managing to win a few of the fifteen rounds. Despite his adjustments it wasn't enough. Greb was far too fast and used his elusive footwork to avoid any toe-to-toe exchanges that might benefit the much larger Brennan. When Greb's punches were not enough to stave off the heavyweight he brought his elbows and thumbs into play. As the fight progressed Brennan began to tire from the fast pace

Greb set.

In the ninth round Brennan's left glove split open exposing his thumb. As time was called so the glove could be replaced Red Mason bellowed "That's an old stall when a fellow is getting beat!" For one of the few times in his life Mason was left silent and red-faced when in the thirteenth round time had to be called to replace Harry's glove. In the fourteenth and fifteenth rounds Greb abandoned his dancing style and went right after Brennan. He stood inside with Brennan, dug his toes into the mat, and bounced powerful lefts and rights off of Brennan's head. Brennan returned to his corner after the fourteenth with a bloody right eye, looking haggard and worn. In the fifteenth Brennan tried one last desperate rally to turn the decision in his favor but it was for naught. Greb indulged Brennan's attack and the round ended evenly. Referee Ed Cochrane raised Greb's hand in victory to the applause of the crowd but it was unnecessary. Nobody in the audience doubted that Greb had defeated his opponent.[66]

Ten days later Greb was in Philadelphia to face Battling Levinsky on an all-star card promoted by Phil Glassman at Shibe Park. Greb was now such a drawing card that he could demand and receive more money than the light-heavyweight champion. The bout was aggressively promoted on the idea that both fighters were looking for a shot at Jack Dempsey's heavyweight championship.

According to the Philadelphia Press Greb seemed "...like the most plausible one to make a serious bid for the title."

"Against a man of Willard's bulk Greb would have been hopelessly out of the running. But, although Dempsey beat Willard, he brings the title back into the class of men who are within the scope of the average heavyweight and that means there will be more on the carpet with a chance and more action."

"Greb is a wonderful fighter. Hardly a full-fledged heavy yet, he will be before long as he has the frame, the bones, muscles, and sinews of a big, powerful fighter. He is fast, a terrific puncher, and clever. Added to that he is all that Dempsey is and he seems to be the approaching meteor in the pugilistic firmament."[67]

Greb easily defeated a reluctant Levinsky. The battler seemed intent on making Greb

BUT YER NOT GOIN' TU LICK ME, BAT

NOW YOU SEE THE REASON WHY I MUST LICK YOU, HARRY

GREB

LEVINSKY

TWO SOULS WITH BUT A SINGLE THOUGHT

HARRY GREB AND "BATTLING" LEVINSKY WHO MEET IN THE SEMI-CLASSIC

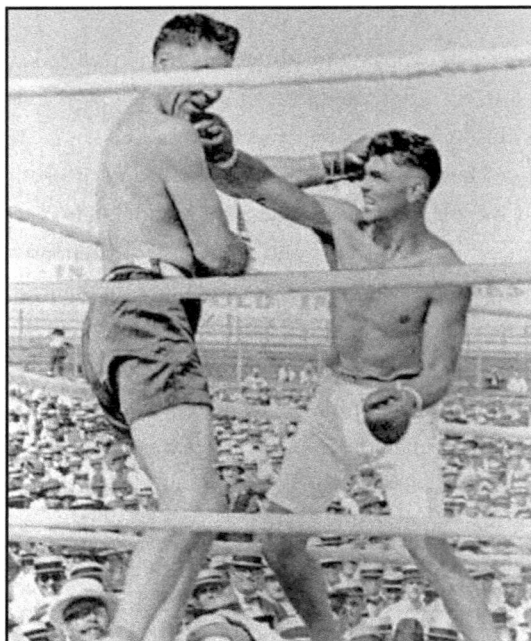

Jack Dempsey launches yet another furious assault on a reeling Jess Willard in the first round of their historic heavyweight championship match. Willard would be battered to the canvas seven times in losing his title.

look bad and finishing on his feet more than actually fighting. He continually clinched and covered up, refusing to fight back as Greb probed for openings. Finally at the urging of the impatient crowd Levinsky began to open up a bit more over the last two rounds providing Greb with opportunities to score. It was a poor fight and after the six rounds had concluded Greb's standing with the public in Philadelphia was somewhat diminished.[68]

The one fighter in this country who seemed to have a chance with Dempsey was Harry Greb, the Smoky City fighter, but after Monday night's showing Greb also seems to be down somewhere near the bottom of the ladder.

Of course it must be admitted that no fighter would have had much chance of beating Levinsky the way he fought in the Shibe Park arena. We hand it to Greb for having a lot of speed and endurance, and suggest that if the fight game palls he might enter marathon running for he traveled at least six miles chasing Levinsky.

-Philadelphia Press[69]

Two days later Greb put Levinsky's non-performance behind him by easily getting the better of George "KO" Brown in Wheeling, West Virginia. Brown, though game, and willing to fight at all times, barely won a round. At the finish of the ten round contest Brown sported a badly swollen right eye and his torso was blotched with red welts from the terrific hammering Greb had subjected him to.[70]

In just over a week's time Greb would partake in a contest that while not historically significant was extremely important to him and his honor. It was a contest that he had long been eager for. On July 24 he would face Joe Chip, the only man to ever knock him out, in Youngstown, Ohio. In the six year interim since their last fight Chip had been a busy young man. He had maintained his status as a respectable yet unspectacular fighter until the outbreak of the war when he promptly joined the army and temporarily ended his professional career. In the army he fought exhibition bouts and helped train soldiers in self-defense.

After the war he began his comeback and even managed to knock out former middleweight champion Al McCoy. Most recently he had been employed by Jess Willard during the latter's training for the Dempsey match. Chip was in camp to provide Willard with a speedy sparring partner. The heavyweight champion got more than he bargained for. Chip gave Willard some of his most difficult sparring sessions rocking the champion several times with left hooks and taking the fight to his employer.[71] Chip managed to make Willard look bad enough that a few days before the fight he was told he would not be sparring with champion for the duration of his stay in camp. The experience had left Chip in fine condition and confident of his chances against a man he had already knocked out once.

The match meant a lot to Greb as he eagerly stalked a meeting with Jack Dempsey. If he were to get close to a meeting with the power-punching heavyweight champion questions would arise about his ability to take a punch based on his loss to Chip. With Connecticut promoter Joe Mulvihil offering a $50,000 dollar purse,[72] and Jimmy Shevlin of Cincinnati bidding,[73] in addition to the offer from New Jersey already in Doc Kearns hands, for a championship match

Joe Chip is seen here on the attack against Jess Willard at the heavyweight champion's training camp for his defense against Jack Dempsey. Chip provided Willard with some of his most intense sparring sessions and was eventually removed from actively sparring with the champion for making Willard look bad.

between Greb and Dempsey, it would be important for Greb to erase any doubts about his durability. Joe Chip would have to be defeated in a manner that left no question about what happened at Old City Hall back in 1913.

Youngstown had been brought to a fever pitch over the coming bout. The Chip brothers were local favorites living less than twenty miles away. So brisk was the sale of tickets that promoter "Mick" Stambaugh actually attempted to slow down sales as he met with difficulty arranging more seating at the Idora Park baseball field where the bout was to be staged.[74] Fans from eastern Ohio and western Pennsylvania all wanted to know if Chip could pull a repeat of his previous victory or had Greb progressed too far out of his class. Even Jimmy Dime, manager of Chip, admitted that Chip would have to score a knockout to win,[75] for Greb, who Dime felt was the best bet to beat Dempsey,[76] was a hard man to outpoint once he got those piston-like arms moving. Brother George's only prediction on the fight was that "Greb is a tough old bird, fast, and always going."[77]

An added worry for the Chip clan was Greb's weight. Joe was a somewhat small middleweight, weighing well under 158 pounds while Greb could comfortably fight in the 160's. Well aware that Red Mason was a man who could and would take any advantage possible, those close to Chip worried that Mason might forfeit the $200 dollars he had placed to bind Greb to the stipulated poundage of 161 on the day of the fight, allowing Harry to come in at an advantageous weight.

At three o'clock on the day of the fight at the Tod House Hotel's Turkish baths Greb weighed in exactly at 161 pounds as contracted. Joe Chip stepped on the scales in his street clothes and weighed 162. Both fighters had made weight now they simply had to relax until fight time.

People from all walks of life rubbed elbows at the fight. The ringside seats were completely sold out and beyond those it was standing room only. The fight broke the previous attendance record for a boxing match held at Youngstown established when Mike Gibbons and George Chip met there on July 4, 1917. There was also the added attraction that it was the first boxing match held at night in Youngstown. At 10:25 pm the fighters received their final instructions in ring center from Referee M. J. McHale and returned to their corners to await the bell.

Many had questioned whether the memory of his knockout at the hands of Chip would affect Greb's performance. If Greb was haunted that night by memories of their previous engagement it wasn't showing. The usual confident smile graced Harry's lips as he entered the ring and remained throughout the twelve rounds. From the outset Greb forced the fight, refusing to let Chip set his feet to deliver one of his powerful punches. Each round was a repetition of the first with Greb becoming increasingly dominant. He worked circles around Chip. When Chip succeeded in planting his feet Greb was either on the other side of the ring, far out of danger or behind Chip, grabbing him in a vice-like grip. He would leap in, flailing with both fists, forcing Chip off balance or back him to the ropes to unleash a torrent of blows.

According to referee McHale writing as sports editor of the Youngstown Telegram:

> Harry Greb of Pittsburgh who seems destined to be the next legitimate opponent of Jack Dempsey for the world's heavyweight championship, made his debut before a Youngstown audience last night and the general verdict was; "THAT BOY GREB IS SURE THERE."
>
> Greb outpointed, outboxed, outslugged, and "out-everythinged else" Joe Chip of New Castle, in every one of the scheduled twelve rounds. Only that Chip was such a glutton in absorbing punishment he never would have survived the early rounds.[78]

The other local papers agreed that Greb had won the contest handily but criticized his lack of punching power as a handicap if he ever met with Dempsey.[79]

"He made capital of the knockout he scored over me," explained Greb "so when I got him in the ring again I gave him a good beating. I could have knocked him out -he wanted me to - but I let him stay just for meanness."[80]

13

BABY AND ALL

Having exorcised the ghost of Joe Chip, Greb could move forward with what would prove the most active year of his career. According to Red Mason Pittsburgh was now bidding on a Greb-Dempsey championship stating that they were willing to top any offer previously submitted for such a match.[1] Greb was always willing to face Mike O'Dowd or Battling Levinsky for their championships but neither seemed eager to give him a decision match. O'Dowd had already far out-priced himself for a match with Greb in Pittsburgh.[2] Levinsky for his part was only willing to put his title on the line for an equally outrageous price. The only men he would face in decision bouts were either overmatched or weighed more than the light-heavyweight limit thereby precluding them from claiming the title in the event that they defeat the champion. The bottom line was that neither Levinsky nor O'Dowd were willing to fight Greb to a decision match with the championship on the line for anything less than an unreasonable sum of money.

So it was that Greb set his sights squarely on Jack Dempsey. Why not? They had fought many common opponents; Terry Keller, Willie Meehan, Bill Brennan, Battling Levinsky, and Billy Miske all former Dempsey opponents and all defeated by Greb at various times. Maybe Greb didn't carry a heavyweight punch but he didn't rely on a single punch to win his fights in the first place. He used speed and elusiveness to frustrate and outpoint opponents a tactic which would stand him in better stead than trying to go toe-to-toe with the murderous punching champion. Dempsey was a heavyweight but at just over six feet tall and weighing 187 pounds he wasn't any larger than Billy Miske or Bill Brennan, both hard punching heavyweights who Greb had shown he could com-

Terry Keller (right) seen here serving as sparring partner to Jack Dempsey as Dempsey prepares for his title winning bout with Jess Willard. Just over one month later Keller was given a bad beating by Greb in Dayton, Ohio.

pete with on more than even terms. To Greb it was more than logical that he be considered a rival for Dempsey, now he needed to keep winning and keep convincing others of that fact.

The road to this goal must have seemed like an endless blur of railroad tracks vanishing on a far distant horizon. In just over six months Greb had traveled well over seven thousand miles to face 21 men in 17 different cities and towns over the course of 31 fights. Amazingly he won every bout either on points or in the majority of newspapers judging each fight. To a boxer of any era a championship means more exposure, greater fame, greater demand for your services, and all of these things added up to the bottom line, the reason why fighters punish their body through training and combat: more money. If Greb wanted to be paid like a champion he would either have to win a title or fight so often that it would leave little time for a personal life. And so his life became one train ride after another, one hotel after another, one fight after another.

As Greb hurtled toward this goal he first encountered Terry Keller before Dayton, Ohio's Miami Athletic Club. Keller was now fresh off a stint as a sparring partner helping to prepare Jack Dempsey for his historic victory over Jess Willard. Despite this experience Keller was years removed from any important victory and his once great promise had fizzled.

A large crowd was present to witness Terry Keller, with Jimmy Dime in his corner, absorb a terrific beating. The bout was little more than a repeat of their match the previous year. Bets were made at ringside on whether Keller had succeeded landing more than 10 blows over the course of the 15 round fight. Greb rarely missed a punch, the vast majority of which painted Keller's face with bruises and crimson splashes of blood.[3]

Less than two weeks later Greb was squaring off once again opposite Bill Brennan. Pittsburgh promoters hoped to match the winner with Jack Dempsey. With both Brennan and Greb being talked of as prospective opponents for Dempsey it was imperative that Harry defeat Brennan as easily as he had in their previous meetings in order to maintain his stature as a threat to the champion. Outweighed by 26 pounds Greb once again easily outscored Brennan leaving him with a badly cut eye and a bloody nose in the process. The audience was smaller than hoped for due to a street car strike and poor weather those that did attend were unanimous in the opinion that a more challenging opponent would be needed to test Greb's mettle in the future.[4]

Red Mason was now booking Greb for engagements at a dizzying pace in locales ranging from St. Louis to Philadelphia. On Labor Day Harry would face Jeff Smith in Youngstown, Ohio in a card promoted by the Youngstown Football and Athletic Club, two days later he was expected to meet Battling Levinsky in Wheeling, West Virginia promoted by the Wheeling Athletic Association. Both bouts where highly anticipated and both were being touted by promoters as breaking all attendance records in the Ohio Valley.

Jeff Smith was still being promoted as middleweight title claimant and logical contender for the throne based on his long years of meritorious service in boxing rings around the world. The

Despite being outweighed by 26 pounds Harry Greb (light trunks) is seen carrying the fight to the much larger Bill Brennan. Greb easily defeated the man that many were considering the top contender for heavyweight champion Jack Dempsey's crown. Brennan would here-after refuse to face Greb, electing to protect his standing as a contender.

bout had all of the hallmarks of one participated in by Jeff Smith. There was the jewel encrusted belt carried over from France by Smith on display in a local store window, the bombastic promotion of Smith's ability by manager Al Lippe, and endless mentioning of Smith's bouts against foreign legends Les Darcy and Georges Carpentier. Also noted was Smith's service to his country during the war training troops in self-defense at Fort Dix.

The bout would be held in Idora Park in order to accommodate a large crowd and scheduled for the evening to avoid conflicts with other popular Labor Day sporting events. With Champion Mike O'Dowd seemingly unwilling to face either fighter for anything less than a king's ransom it was one of the most sought after marquee events of the season and as such Matchmaker Mick Stambaugh was forced to beat offers from Philadelphia, Denver, Kansas City, Pittsburgh, Buffalo, Milwaukee, and Minneapolis in order to sign the fighters.[5] The two combatants agreed to split seventy percent of the gross receipts. They would weigh 161 pounds at 3 o'clock on the afternoon of the fight. To which Smith boasted that if Greb made weight Smith would stop him inside of the scheduled twelve rounds.[6]

Smith was taking his boast seriously. In their two previous meetings Greb had handily defeated Smith; it was now up to Smith to gain some measure of revenge. As a result Smith was honing his skills by training with some of the best fighters the east coast had to offer including Battling Levinsky, Soldier Bartfield, KO Loughlin, George Ashe, and Eddie Moy.[7] He had turned down several offers for matches during the interim so that he might focus all of his attention on Greb.

A slow drizzling rain fell for twelve hours preceding the match culminating in what looked like a downpour before the skies finally cleared allowing the undercard to begin at 8:15 pm. Demand for tickets had been so high that extra

Jeff Smith displays his treasured belt emblematic of his tenuous hold on the "middleweight championship." The belt, reputed to be worth $2,500, was studded in gold donated by French Humorist Bernard and Ivory which was donated and carved by noted sculpture Paul Moreau Vauthier.

bleachers had to be erected to satisfy the expected crowd of between six and eight-thousand. However, with the day now chilly, damp, and overcast, the crowd was a much smaller than expected 5,000. The crowd was eager for action, after a satisfying if somewhat unspectacular

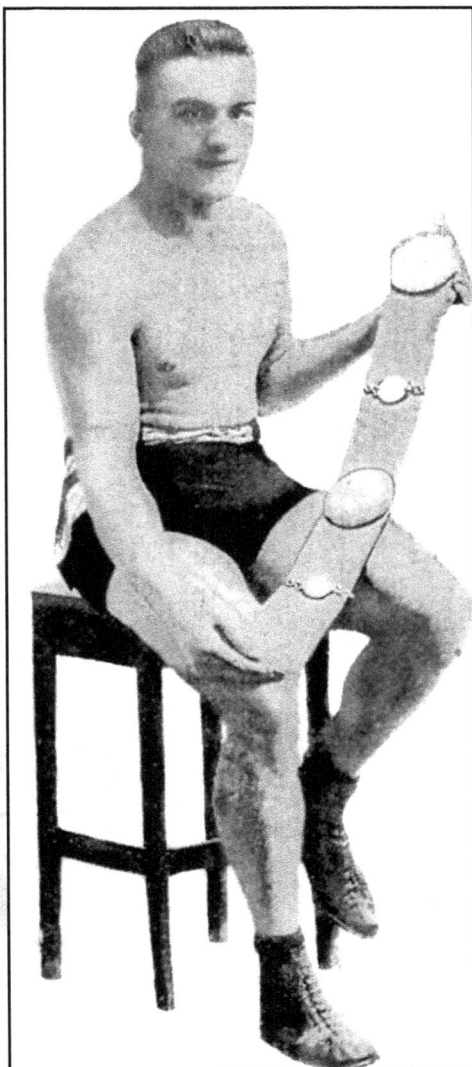

Battling Levinsky (right) stands with lightweight champions Benny Leonard (center), and Battling Nelson (left) while partaking in the festivities sorrounding the heavyweight championship fight between Jack Dempsey and Jess Willard in July 1919

undercard, when announcer Tom Bannon introduced the fighters.

From the outset Greb used his speed to leap in with rapid fire combinations and slip out of range before Smith could counter. When Smith's eye was split open by a Greb punch in the second round it was apparent that Smith would be in for a long night. Whenever Smith managed to work his way in close Greb would grab his arms tightly and hold until the referee was able to pry them apart upon which time Greb would resume his long range tactics. This strategy drew the ire of the crowd and of the referee who repeatedly warned Greb. In the eighth round the action was halted and Greb was told that if he continued to clinch he would be disqualified. From this point on there were no complaints from the crowd or the referee of Greb's tactics yet Smith was still unable to overcome Greb's speed and aggression.

Smith's only measure of success came in the tenth round when he snapped Greb's head back violently with two wicked punches. This momentum was short lived though as Greb leapt upon Smith and pumped both gloves to the head and body forcing Smith to the ropes in a defensive shell. In this same round Smith's glove split causing a halt to the match until a replacement could be located at which time Harry gleefully proceeded to continue his domination of one of the most gifted fighters in the world. When the match had completed Frank Ward of the Youngstown Vindicator estimated that Smith landed only nine clean punches on Greb.[8]

Two days later Greb was in Wheeling, West Virginia to face Battling Levinsky. The bout had been scheduled for the Wheeling Park Casino but with demand just as it had been for the Smith bout the venue was changed to the State Fair Grounds to accommodate a crowd of between eight and eleven thousand. The ring was pitched directly in front of the grandstands with an extra set of bleachers borrowed from the local high school. The promotion was boosted by the fact that Levinsky was still light heavyweight champion and while no decision would be officially rendered the championship could change hands in the event of a knockout or disqualification.

With his eye on this end Mason wrote to the Wheeling Register that Greb "...is ready for the best in the light heavy division. He will work from the first gong with but one intention, and that will be to put Levinsky away and cop the light heavyweight title."[9]

Levinsky was equally confident of victory: "I think I will successfully defend my title here tomorrow night, as I am in the best of condition. I know that Greb is a good boy and one of the greatest in the ring, but I will climb out of the ring after our ten round bout the winner."[10]

Levinsky arrived in Wheeling on September 1 and immediately set about training at the American gym. The day before the fight about three-hundred people packed themselves into the gym to watch the light heavyweight champ go through his paces and were greatly impressed with his conditioning.

The bout itself was a lackluster one. Levinsky, as had become his custom, particularly when facing Greb, assumed a decidedly defensive stance. He rarely elected to exchange with his smaller opponent, instead seeking refuge from the multitude of punches that Greb was throwing his way. This overt lack of aggression drew boos from the crowd and left many wondering just how fit Levinsky was, despite his showing in training. In the sixth round Levinsky fell through the ropes and the resulting clamor was so loud that the fighters failed to hear the bell ending the round and fought until their seconds could tear them apart. This happened again at the end of the tenth and final round when both fighters failed to hear the bell and fought for fully one minute after the round before the referee and seconds were able to part them.

The bout was a disappointing one aesthetically and financially. The undercard outshone the main event due in large part to Levinsky's strategy of survival. Financially the bout was a bust because of the crowd of an estimated seven to ten-thousand fans present only about half paid. How several thousand non-paying customers were able to crash the gate was never adequately explained.[11]

Two weeks later Greb was in St. Louis to face Silent Martin, the deaf mute middleweight of Brooklyn, New York. Martin was a formidable club fighter, always in excellent shape, and possessed of a wicked punch, which in his most recent bout had rendered Young Fisher unconscious in the second round with a

Deaf/Mute Thomas "Silent" Martin overcame his disability to become a capable and sought after fighter off the teens and twenties. During his career he would face eight world champions across three divisions.

The St. Louis Coliseum was erected in 1908 and played host to the 1910 Democratic National Convention, Veiled Profit Balls, and various sporting events such as Harry Greb's 1919 showdown with Silent Martin. It was the only time Greb would appear in that city professionally, possibly due the disappointing turnout. The Coliseum could seat 10,000 but only two thousand fans showed up.

broken jaw. Martin was guided in his career by equally deaf mute manager Fred W. Meinken who used sign language to communicate with his fighter between rounds.

The match was signed by Tommy Sullivan of the Future City Athletic Club for eight rounds at the St. Louis Coliseum. Martin arrived in the city the day before the fight and fine-tuned his skills at Harry Cook's gymnasium. Greb arrived on the day of the fight and took up light training at Sammy Dixon's gym.

The attendance of two thousand was smaller than hoped for. Those fans that did show up were treated to a performance that they would not soon forget. Entering the ring suffering from the same boils which had plagued him on his strenuous campaign the previous year, Greb dominated Silent Martin with a combination of elusive footwork and pinpoint punching accuracy. For three rounds Greb focused on landing powerful right hands which were obviously designed to wear Martin down. However in the third round Greb broke the little finger of his right hand and rarely used it for the rest of the fight. Despite this handicap Greb was so dominant that members of the audience began to file out early, feeling that each round was simply a repetition of the previous round. At one point between rounds as Martin's seconds feverishly doused him with water a spectator nearby raised his umbrella to shield himself from the splash drawing laughs from the throng.

The next day's newspapers judged the fight an easy, one sided win for Greb. Martin was given high marks for bravery but one paper judged that he landed only three solid punches over the course of the eight round bout.[12]

John E. Wray of the St. Louis Post-Dispatch was thoroughly overwhelmed by Greb's agility and style:

> Greb threw off his bathrobe and stood up in the ring a splendidly muscled young man, whose biceps appeared large enough to guarantee knockouts at any time...
>
> But it was not his build that won him notice. The moment the bell rang there began an exhibition the like of which has never been seen here on the part of a heavyweight. Greb immediately began leaping and prancing about like a dancing faun, darting in and out, leading and landing constantly, springing up and down, launching himself forward like a cat, then retreating with a backward spring almost before his blow had solidly reached its mark.
>
> He threw his 168 pounds around the ring with an agility never before equaled by a heavyweight. The ring creaked and groaned, and literally shook with the violence of his activity.[13]

Sailor Ed Petroskey had been a tough contender during the early part of the 1910's. He acquired his nickname by serving several terms in the United States Navy. He was trying to mount a comeback in 1919 when he ran into Harry Greb in Philadelphia.

Greb spent the next month focusing on his beloved baseball while his injured hand healed and spending time with the now very pregnant Mildred. Baseball fans, less fanatical than Greb, across the nation waited eagerly for the 1919 World Series. With the war now over and the nation ready for a lighter form of distraction the powers that be in baseball decided on a best of nine world series. It would become one of the most controversial sporting events in history. Once the World Series had ended with an upset win by the Cincinnati Reds and the pain in Greb's hand had subsided, he appeared in Philadelphia to box a six rounder against Sailor Petroskey.

Sailor Ed Petroskey had fought the biggest and best names that boxing had to offer in the

first half of the teens but he was now a throwback to a time that was rapidly disappearing in the sport. Bald and flabby Petroskey was a shadow of the muscular blonde warrior that had held his own with the stars of the middleweight division half a decade ago. In fighting Greb Petroskey was hoping to jump back into the mix after a layoff of over a year. Agreeing to face Greb as a means to this end would prove a mistake.

Petroskey was strong and willing but little else. In the first he was able to catch Greb with a powerful right hand that rocked Greb who grabbed and held as both fighters tumbled to the mat. Upon rising Greb exposed Petroskey's rust using his extraordinary speed and footwork to hit Petroskey nearly at will. Greb was on the move continually and occasionally grabbed the ring rope with his left gaining leverage for the right uppercut. As the fight progressed Petroskey became frustrated with his inability to land on Greb and began a verbal tirade which only prompted Greb to further shower Petroskey with blows from all angles.

Dorothy Mildred Greb was born to Harry and Mildred on October 16, 1919. She was adored by her father who, despite being on the road almost constantly, doted on his little girl.

In the fifth round Petroskey began to bleed from the nose and mouth and by the end of the bout the audience had begun to laugh as Petroskey missed Greb with wild swings. Once again it was estimated that he had failed to land more than half a dozen blows during the half dozen rounds. After the bout it was announced that Greb had broken his left hand and would be unable to face Tommy Robson the following week in Jersey City.[14]

Greb again returned to Pittsburgh to nurse his injured hands and take care of Mildred in her final week of pregnancy. Three days after his fight with Petroskey Harry was blessed with the birth of his first child. On October 16, 1919 Dorothy Mildred Greb was born. Harry Greb was now the father of a beautiful, plump little girl. With his schedule now clear for the time being and needing to nurse two broken hands, Greb had a little more than a month in order to get acquainted with the newest member of his family.

As Harry rested Red Mason continued to pursue a lucrative schedule of matches for Greb. Mason had hoped to match Greb with the now aging Frank Moran in an all-Pittsburgh bout however two poorly received showings by Moran in Pittsburgh and Cumberland served to kill any demand for the match and Mason was left to ponder other opponents.[15] In addition to working out Greb's itinerary Mason was also acquiring more talent for his stable (which now included Johnny Kirk, Irish Chick Rodgers, Patsy Scanlon, Reed Brown, Buster Brown, Johnny Welsh, Gus Camp, and Val Grunan). As if his plate was not already full enough, Mason was the planning the possible purchase of a gym, which he hoped to maintain with Greb as Partner. If there was one man who could run the tireless Harry Greb ragged it was the tireless James "Red" Mason.

By early November Greb's hands had healed enough that he was able to begin training. Not wanting to take any chances with Greb's damaged hands Mason refused all offers until November 17. On that date Greb battered George "KO" Brown so completely that the Greek left the ring bleeding profusely from multiple cuts and wearing a badly swollen face. Greb's hands had held up well under the constant battering Brown's face subjected them to leaving Greb in fine condition for his upcoming bouts with Larry Williams and Zulu Kid three days apart.[16]

The day before Greb was to step into the ring with Williams Red Mason received a long distance telephone call from Buffalo. Promoter Charles J. Murray was in desperate need of a replacement on short notice. In five days he had a card which originally featured Willie Meehan facing Canadian Heavyweight Champion Soldier Jones. Meehan had already been on ground for the match when he received word that his wife was terminally ill and immediately turned around and headed back to San Francisco. Murray was in need of a replacement and Mason was more than willing to allow Greb to face the Canadian slugger on short notice.

In defeat Williams provided Greb with one of his more competitive bouts of the season. Using his obvious height and

Larry Williams was a serviceable if unspectacular light-heavyweight hailing from Bridgeport, Connecticut. He had hovered on the periphery of the upper echelon of the middleweight and light-heavyweight divisions for several years prior to meeting Harry Greb for the first time in late 1919.

weight advantages (he outweighed Greb by 16 pounds) Williams was able to punch with Greb and as a result the bout fell into a pattern of action packed exchanges in which Greb usually came out ahead based on his higher work-rate. It was a pleasing card and the large crowd which filled the South Side Market House was a testament to Greb's continued popularity among his hometown fans.[17]

Several of those fans no doubt made the trip to Beaver Falls three days later, on Thanksgiving Day, to watch Greb severely batter Brooklyn's Zulu Kid. Greb was back in the gym the day after his bout with Williams continuing to sharpen the skills which prompted the Beaver Falls Evening Tribune to remark:

"Greb displayed the finest exhibition of the manly art ever seen in the valley and the surrounding towns were well represented at the bout. He exhibited a quality of boxing, with a variety of blows that completely mystified his opponent who saw little but a mirage before his eyes and had the crowd with him from the start."[18]

Harry and Red left Beaver Falls immediately for Pittsburgh in order to spend Thanksgiving with their families then caught a 9 o'clock train to arrive late that night in Buffalo for his match with Soldier Jones. There was a great deal of natural interest in Buffalo regarding a Greb-Jones match. Greb had always been popular in Buffalo but now Jones was making a name for himself in the Bison City. He had faced three opponents before Buffalo crowds in recent months, having lost a disqualification to the geriatric Jack "Twin" Sullivan, and winning emphatic first round knockouts over Stanley Meyers and George "One Round" Davis. The Davis victory was cause for much scrutiny by boxing fans who were quick to note that Jones did to Davis what Greb couldn't accomplish in ten rounds.

John Horace Beaudin, professionally known as Soldier Jones, came from Gaspe, Quebec and was already Canadian Heavyweight Champion when he first faced Harry Greb in 1919. The Soldier, who gained his nickname by serving during the Great War, packed a knockout punch but he was wild, which often resulted in losing disqualifications or leaving himself open to counters which found his weak chin and left him stretched out cold.

Furthermore at five feet ten and one half inches tall, weighing 180 pounds, and possessing terrific hitting power Jones would present Greb with a formidable physical challenge.

In addition to those qualifications Jones possessed in the ring, he was also a light-hearted gregarious young man of twenty-two who was quick to laugh and enjoyed bantering with the fans that showed up at the gym to watch him train.

"They tell me Greb is a flying, galloping speed boy and that I'll be lucky to hit him with a whip, but all I want is a chance to hit him once. The punch that brought One Round Davis down will bring him down, too. He may make me look silly for a while, but I'll guarantee to get him a couple of times in ten rounds."[19] Later Jones added, "If Brennan (KO Bill Brennan) couldn't drop me, I'm sure Greb isn't going to."[20]

For all of his physical advantages and bravado Jones was clearly overmatched when presented with the speed and cat-like reflexes of his Pittsburgh rival. Jones was reduced to flailing away with his powerful right as if trying to catch smoke. In the third round Jones finally landed one and sent Greb reeling several feet. It was the worst mistake Jones could have made. In the fourth round Greb slowed his footwork and began to stand flat-footed trading punches with his rapidly tiring rival.

Near the end of the fourth Greb landed a punishing blow flush on Jones' face which left his lips and nose bloody. As the Soldier sagged Greb pounced on him like a blood-thirsty animal. Several punches dropped Jones but he was saved by the bell. Greb continued his fury in the fifth and after being knocked down four times Jones was saved from further punishment by Referee Joe Suttner.[21]

In the dressing room after the fight Greb gave Jones due credit for his punching power. "No," he said, "you bet I wasn't fooling in the third round."[22] Later, before returning to Pittsburgh to spend a few days with his family before setting out to face Clay Turner in Syracuse, Greb remarked: "Say, Jones should go to Pittsburgh and box Frank Moran. What he would do to him would be plenty."[23]

On December 1, the day before Harry was to face Clay Turner in Syracuse word was received that Turner had injured his knee while doing roadwork and would be unable to attend the fight. Bartley Madden was substituted in Turner's place much to Greb's disappointment. However there was one consolation to accepting Madden as a substitute: Madden had been touted as a possible opponent for Jack Dempsey in the near future and as such Red Mason, being the astute manager that he was, was able to see the upside that if Greb were able to eliminate one of Dempsey's possible opponents he would be that much closer to challenging for the championship himself.

Greb was further disappointed when he was told at the last minute that Bartley had not arrived in Syracuse. Greb, it was announced, would be expected to face the Negro welterweight Panama Joe Gans. With the crowd waiting in anticipation Red Mason climbed over the top rope followed by Harry Greb, who was still wearing his street clothes and announced that

Cyril Quinton, otherwise known as Panama Joe Gans, was one of the best fighters of his era but circumstances beyond his control prevented him from ever challenging for a world title, namely the color of his skin. He and Harry came close to facing one another in December 1919 but once again the color of his skin prevented the match.

Harry had drawn the color line and would not face Gans.

Angered by the prospect of not getting to see their main event, the crowd began to hiss and boo. Greb, who was visibly irritated at the situation and pained by being called a "yellow coward," stepped forward to explain that he had promised his new wife that he would not fight a Negro. At one point in his address Greb made reference to "niggers" which drew the wrath of the crowd and, understandably, Panama Gans. Greb apologized to Gans for his remarks and then tried to diffuse the situation by offering to box any white man the club could find on short notice. Young heavyweight Frank Rice was suggested by some members of the audience but he failed to appear when the shout went up. After thirty minutes of waiting in the vain hope that a fight would materialize the crowd slowly shuffled out after being promised that they would be able to honor their tickets at the next show the club put on.[24]

Many, looking at the situation out of context, have seized upon the incident as an example of racial prejudice on the part of Greb and Mason. Others have tried to use the event to show that Greb feared Gans. Neither argument seems very likely. Gans while admittedly being a talented fighter had hardly proven himself to be a great threat to a man who had faced numerous world champions and top contenders of all sizes without a hint of regret. Indeed the most impressive name on Gans' resume was Jeff Smith, who Harry had already defeated several times. Newspaper accounts of the Gans-Smith bout are inconclusive as to the winner. It would not be out of the realm of possibility to suggest that Greb knew next to nothing about the young welterweight from Barbados.

When one examines the situation within the context of 1919 America it becomes readily apparent that Greb and Mason's actions were quite reasonable. 1919 had been a year of tremendous racial tension in the United States. Throughout the summer and fall nearly 30 cities had experienced devastating riots with hundreds of casualties. Lynching was now at an eleven year high. Many of those who did not sanction such violence found it prudent to avoid "race mix-ing." Tensions ran high after what would eventually be dubbed the "Red Summer of 1919" and in such an atmosphere Greb's actions, even his promise to Mildred, were easily understand-able.

Greb and Mason made their way back to Pittsburgh and the incident was quickly forgotten. On the way back they stopped off in Buffalo where Greb was anxious to reiterate to the wait-ing reporters that he was ready and willing to face any heavyweight who stood between he and Jack Dempsey.[25] With that objective foremost in his mind Greb stood across the ring from Clay Turner on December 10 in Buffalo intent on exacting revenge for the embarrassment he expe-rienced in Syracuse.

Outweighed by seven pounds, Greb used his size to his advantage by fighting at a terrific pace. Turner succeeded in matching Greb for the first two or three rounds before that pace began to tell. Turner was able to land his left, particularly to the body, but Greb was able to shrug off such blows and come back with his own unending stream of punches from all direc-tions. He re-injured his left hand in the fourth but this didn't deter him from trying at every opportunity to go for the knock out. When the final bell rang Turner was sporting a cut eye, cut mouth, and bloody nose. He was a sorry sight and one which for years to come would typify Greb's opponents.[26]

"I would rather fight ten Battling Levinskys or ten Kid Norfolks than one Harry Greb," said a bewildered Clay Turner afterwards.

"There's a dash and snap about Greb that discourages a fighter. I hit him half a dozen solid right-hand punches under the heart in the second round and he came at me harder than ever. In the third I measured him and as he started to duck I let go with the left. It was as fair a left hook as ever landed. It hit him right on the chin. He half wheeled, then smiled and, instead of slowing up, leaped in with both hands pumping punches. I took all the fight out of Kid Norfolk with the same kind of body smashes I gave Greb, but Harry never let on he felt 'em. I know they hurt, for his body reddened under the attack, but he never let up or stayed away. He's too young, too powerful, too full of pep and stamina. He probably could fight twenty rounds and tire the best man in the game. I haven't the slightest fear of Levinsky, Gibbons, Bill Brennan or the others, but Greb is one man I'll take my hat off to. He's the best heavyweight, or light-heavyweight, in the game, the next best man to Jack Dempsey."[27]

Fans and media present at the bout echoed Turner's opinion adding that Greb would sure-ly prove a more difficult test for the heavyweight champion than France's Georges Carpentier who was now being considered the front-runner for a shot at Dempsey's title.

Two days later Harry traveled to Endicott, New York to headline a bout put on by Bill Fischer and the Endicott/Johnson City Athletic Association. His opponent was Mike McTigue who since his sorry showing against Greb the previous year had continued meandering aim-lessly through the fistic landscape facing journeymen and contenders with mixed results.

Despite being able to count on a sizeable contention of Irishmen showing up to his fights he remained somewhat unpopular due to his cautious style.

McTigue was able to give a better account of himself in Endicott but it was Greb's aggression that won him nearly every round. With both fighters weighing 162 pounds Greb was able to continually back McTigue up and force him into a defensive shell while piling up points.[28] He was compared by the local press to such fistic luminaries as Johnny Dundee, Benny Leonard, and Jack Dempsey. Gordon Williams of the Binghamton Press queried how Greb could do it? How could he continue to fight at such a terrific pace for the duration of a bout and seem to get stronger as the rounds progressed?[29] It was a mystery that press and fans alike would ponder for years to come.

Next up for Greb would be a fight before Pittsburgh fans against Billy Kramer who had given him a tough six round bout two years earlier in Philadelphia. Kramer was now nearing the end of his career. With the help of his manager Willus Britt he had continued to get fights with top opposition such as Mike Gibbons, Jeff Smith, and champion Mike O'Dowd but he had lost by knockout to those three and was losing more than he was winning overall.

Possibly remembering the tough fight Kramer had given him in Philadelphia Greb tortured Kramer. Smiling, laughing, and demonstrating his complete fistic mastery over Kramer in every aspect of the sport Greb toyed with his opponent as the crowd of the Southside Market House grew restless. In the seventh round referee Loudon Campbell stepped in and sent Kramer to his corner signaling an end to the one-sided bout. The audience leapt to its feet showering Campbell with a cascade of cat-calls. The bout may have been one sided they reasoned but Kramer had not been on the verge of a knockout. Campbell gave into the audience's wishes and allowed the burlesque to continue. For three more rounds Greb battered a game and determined Kramer who despite being bloodied and bruised managed to stay upright until the final bell.[30]

One week later on December 22 Greb was in Philadelphia to again fight Clay Turner. He was preceded by a letter printed in the Philadelphia Public Ledger written by Willus Britt stating that the recent Greb-Kramer bout was the greatest seen in a Pittsburgh ring in many a long age and that Kramer had given a great account of himself despite Greb using dirty tactics and sporting a twenty pound weight advantage.[31] Such was the state of boxing during the early 20th century when managers sent out a plethora of false reports through the newspapers in order to maintain the status of their fighters. It would be up to Greb to debunk such a story through his showing against Turner who was conceded one of the best in the light-heavyweight division.

The crowd which gathered at Philadelphia's Olympia to watch two of the best light-heavyweights in the world witnessed a virtual repeat of Greb's victory over Turner in Buffalo twelve days earlier with the exception that it was considerably more one-sided in Greb's favor. When Turner landed his powerful blows to Greb's body Harry simply laughed and launched into a tornado-like attack. After the bout Greb and Mason repeated their call for a bout with Jack Dempsey.[32] When told that many thought Greb would be too small for the champ Mason answered "That's all bosh, though, for Harry has fought heavies time after time. He defeated Bill Brennan four times; Battling Levinsky five times, and Billy Miske three times. This would indicate he can handle himself with the heavies, doesn't it?"

"I want to fight Dempsey." said Harry. "Don't look surprised. I weigh less than 170 pounds, while the champion scales around 190 or 195. That doesn't bother me. I've fought other big fellows- truly not the caliber of the champion- but big, tough fellows, and I always managed to hold my own with them. Bill Brennan is almost as big as Jack and I beat Bill. Battling Levinsky and Clay Turner are big fellows I boxed and they never hurt me." When told that none of these men hit as hard as the champion Greb retorted "That's true, but I have faced many hard hitters and none of them made an impression on me."

Greb closed by expressing his interest in facing French idol Georges Carpentier. Both Greb and Mason conceded that it was unlikely that the Frenchman would face anyone and risk losing a lucrative payday before squaring off with Dempsey "But if Carpentier decides to meet one or two first class men before tackling Jack," said Mason, "I'll take the first boat to France and send Harry against him and he will beat Carpentier."[33]

Greb had a reasonable expectation of being able to fight for a championship in either of the middleweight, light-heavyweight, or heavyweight classes. He was now in his physical prime; his previous 12 months of campaigning had proven that. He had fought an amazing 45 bouts in 1919 despite having gotten married, had his first child, and suffered a forced six-week hiatus due to broken hands within that period. More amazing was the fact that he had not lost a single consensus or official decision despite facing some of the most respected fighters in the history of the sport. Greb was considered by many, not the least of which was Billy Rocap, sports editor of the *Philadelphia Public Ledger*, as the light-heavyweight champion via his domination of that weight class and its champion. Most fans considered Greb a sure bet to win the middleweight championship and conceded that he was a leading contender of the heavyweights with a strong possibility of upsetting Jack Dempsey for the title.

As 1919 drew to a close a world of possibilities lay at Greb's fingertips.

14

MIKE'S BROTHER

Harry returned to Pittsburgh anxious to spend his daughter's first Christmas at home. He had declined numerous lucrative offers for bouts and expressed his interest in getting a nice a Christmas tree for Dorothy instead. When questions arose about Harry's inactivity it was announced that he had been confined to bed with an attack of Ptomaine poisoning.[1] Bouts with Augie Ratner and Captain Bob Roper were cancelled. This puzzled many fans. Greb was initially expected to recover quickly but when several weeks had passed and Greb still had not resumed his busy schedule it was revealed that he had broken his arm in the fourth round of his Philadelphia bout with Clay Turner.[2] Greb and Mason had kept the injury secret so as not to hamper his ability to schedule fights when they chose to resume march to a championship. Mason would often book seven or eight bouts in advance for Greb and it was feared that if promoters got word that Greb was prone to injuries they would not book him in fights so close to one another.

As Harry convalesced the United States entered a new era, an era which is now counted as one of the most colorful and storied in this nation's history. On January 16 the Volstead Act went into effect with the Eighteenth Amendment to the Constitution mandating the prohibition of "intoxicating beverages." Radical changes to the political and social landscape took place virtually overnight. Criminal organizations rapidly bonded together to form vast nationwide networks fueled by the proceeds of illegal alcoholic beverages. These criminal organizations made headlines but far more important was the fact that overnight every American citizen who sneaked a taste of booze, a vast percentage of society, was labeled a criminal. As oppressive as this might sound it actually had the opposite effect. Americans, who have always been fascinated with criminal society, had suddenly felt liberated by the fact that they were breaking the law every time they took a drink of alcohol and suddenly the twenties began to roar. Underground nightclubs sprang up like wildfire where the utterance of a password or knowing the right person could gain admittance to dancing, music, and all manner of spirits from bathtub gin to imported champagne.

Some of those who felt the effects of prohibition were the immigrant masses many of whom like the Greb family were Catholic and typically used wine during religious service. Many of these, like Pius Greb, took to making their own wine for such purposes. Occasionally Greb tasted his father's homemade wine but at this point prohibition had little effect on Greb's life. He was far too focused on his career and winning a championship to waste his time looking through the bottom of a bottle. Besides, to Harry there was nothing more intoxicating than being behind the wheel of a speeding motorcar, his greatest vice.

It had been hoped that Greb's first opponent after his arm healed would be Soldier Bartfield in Philadelphia. However Bartfield promptly left the country for Poland where he hoped to find his mother from whom he had little contact since the start of the Great War. With that bout cancelled Greb would have to wait until early February to face Bartley Madden at Kalamazoo, Michigan. A week before the fight Madden sent word that he would be unable to show for the bout due to illness. Zulu Kid was quickly substituted in his place and the card was saved.

As Greb prepared to meet Zulu Kid Pittsburgh was buzzing with the rumor that Harry had signed contracts to meet Jack Dempsey in Buffalo on May 30 over a distance of ten rounds.[3] Greb was scheduled to receive $15,000 to Dempsey's $50,000. It was said that Dempsey had not yet signed the articles of agreement but had promised to do so as soon as he was sure there was no chance of meeting Georges Carpentier within the next six months[4] in what would surely be the largest bout in boxing history.

The bout with Zulu Kid seemed to be going the way of their previous engagements with Greb controlling the action fairly easily when in the fourth round he suddenly landed a hard right that re-injured his still healing arm. For the next four rounds he fought with his right hand hanging limp by his side occasionally feinting and punching exclusively with his left. The crowd, thinking Greb was not trying his best, grew increasingly weary of the display and began to shower the ring with hisses and catcalls. Secretary McAuley of the local boxing commission halted the bout in the eighth round and demanded an explanation. Greb revealed that his arm had been re-injured and insisted that under the circumstances he was doing his best. He begged that he be allowed to continue. "I've never been stopped in the ring yet," he argued, "and I don't want to start now. I want to go on."[5] The bout was allowed to continue and despite the handicap Greb was able to do more damage to Zulu Kid in the final two rounds than in the previous eight. The local newspapers felt that Greb had done enough to earn the victory thru his speed and footwork and noted that a local physician entered the ring to examine Greb and made the announcement that "The arm had been broken. Any person examining it can discover a bone out of place about three inches below the elbow."[6]

The announcement that Greb had broken his arm sent panic through the Pittsburgh fight community. Greb had been signed to face Captain Bob Roper in six days at Exposition Hall and such an injury would surely cause a cancellation. Wanting to preserve the match, Red Mason quickly sent telegrams out to all of the Pittsburgh newspapers stating that the story of the broken arm was untrue.[7] Upon returning home Mason in his usual mercurial style stated that "it is all a lie and a gross injustice. Greb's arm which was broken December 22, last, is now in pretty good shape and will not interfere in his taking part in his bout with Captain Bob Roper at the Expo. True the arm is not as strong as normally, and punching a hard head like the one on Zulu's shoulders didn't do it any good. But, there is absolutely no truth in the report that it is broken. However, the dampening effect of the rumor locally, has caused us to ask for a postponement of the Roper fight until the night of February 21, one week later than the scheduled date. With the false rumors spread broadcast, and the effect it would have on the crowd at the Roper fight, we want two weeks here among the fans who anticipate going to the Roper fight to prove that Greb's arm is in good shape and that he will be able to use it to best advantage against Roper."[8]

Greb began training for Roper a week before the fight after giving his injured arm maximum time to heal. So intent was he on making a good showing that he even trained straight through Sunday, a day he usually reserved for rest and family pursuits. Roper, although fairly new to the limelight, was being primed for a run at Jack Dempsey's crown. According to biographies published about Roper during his career he had enlisted in the Army at 18 and served in the Philippines and China. He learned to box in the Philippines while fighting the Moros under general Black Jack Pershing, winning the island championship. Upon returning to the United

States in 1916 he won the army championship. At the outbreak of the war Roper was commissioned as a Captain in the army and served as an instructor of machine gunnery and light artillery at Fort Oglethorpe, Ga. Captain Bob was discharged in December of 1918 and immediately turned professional.[9]

Standing just under six feet tall and weighing around 190 pounds roper had all of the physical tools required to excel in the heavyweight division. His courage was exhibited by his willingness to travel anywhere and face anyone. In pursuit of his quest for the heavyweight championship Roper traveled down to Mexico and found himself under the tutelage of exiled former heavyweight champion Jack Johnson. Johnson had announced that he would groom Roper for a run at the championship. After returning to the United States Roper notched his biggest win to date by defeating Frank Moran.

Trained to the minute and with heavy tape binding his hands Roper outweighed Harry by fifteen and a half pounds. The packed audience

William E. Hammond, professionally known as Captain Bob Roper, was a tough and respected journeyman fighter who had been groomed for a shot at the heavyweight championship by none other than former champion Jack Johnson.

with many in attendance being forced to stand wondered if Greb had bitten off more than he could chew. After two rounds of trying to match Greb's furious pace the crowd began to see that Roper would not be the man to defeat their hero. In an effort to preserve his recently injured hands and arm Greb worked his way in close and pounded Roper's body furiously. In order to stave off punishment Roper continuously tried to hold Greb tight but Greb was able to shake off his larger foe and continue his rapid fire assault.

Only in the fifth did Roper threaten. He lashed out with a right hand that landed squarely on Greb's jaw sending Harry back on his heels across the ring. Roper followed up his momentary advantage with a furious assault but Greb was able to slip and block most of the blows before quickly regaining his composure and resuming his beating of the former army captain. The one sided nature of the fight left many onlookers shouting to Roper to steer clear of Dempsey for the foreseeable future.[10]

Just before his fight with Bob Roper, Greb was approached by Mike Burke working for Akron promoter Art Kauth for a proposed bout on March 9. Hoping to get exposure in a new town Greb readily signed the contract. "Fill in any man's name you can secure who is a topnotcher,"[11] Greb said. The promoters immediately signed Clay Turner and despite the fact that Greb had already beaten Turner five times ticket sales were brisk. When tickets were placed on sale at the Hamilton cigar store there were over three hundred orders. "It's the biggest first day's advance sale I've ever had," stated proprietor Frank Niel.[12]

Having already demonstrated that he seemingly had Turner's number Greb motivated himself with the goal of stopping Turner within the twelve round limit. He set about training with stablemate Johnny "Zip" Kirk who was working out for a bout with Johnny Ray, who by now had left Red Mason's stable. The Kirk-Ray fight was an ugly grudge match in the making and Greb was all too happy to help Kirk prepare for his former sparring partner.

Ray and Kirk were scheduled to face off the day before Turner and Greb met and as Kirk weighed in for the fight that afternoon he was attacked by Johnny Ray

Clay Turner (above) faced Harry Greb an amazing seven times over the course of two years. The last time coming in June of 1920.

and his partisans. The assault, which left Kirk bleeding from the neck, would foreshadow events to come. Before a packed and excited crowd Kirk started the fight by battering Ray around the ring. This continued for two rounds when as the bell sounded ending the second round Kirk tapped Ray on the shoulder in a gesture of familiarity. Ray quickly lashed out and suddenly several of his supporters rushed into the ring and beat Kirk to the floor, kicking him in the groin repeatedly. The riot was quickly put down by local police and the proceedings where immediately halted with several of those directly involved in the assault being arrested.[13]

It was an ugly incident that threatened to destroy boxing in Pittsburgh. Greb himself was implicated by some reports as having knocked out Young Lightning, a former boxer and Ray partisan during the fracas.[14] As police court magistrate J. J. Sweeney set about sorting things out Greb and Mason were on a train bound for Akron where Greb once again battered Turner into a bloody pulp. Turner gamely took everything Greb threw his way without flinching, always hoping to land his own powerful swings but, in the words of Addie Adams, writer for the Akron Evening Times: "Greb gave one of the finest exhibitions of fighting ever seen in Akron. A flash of speed, he was all over the ring, in and out, ducking, side stepping, and hitting the rugged Indian with everything he had."[15]

While at ringside for the fight Red Mason received a long distance phone call from Buffalo asking for Irish Chick Rodgers to appear there against Chip Davis. Upon returning to ringside Mason told reporters that the call had been Buffalo trying to match Greb with Jack Dempsey. A few days later Mason traveled to Buffalo to second Rogers against Davis and upon returning to Pittsburgh it was announced that Mason had made the trip to Buffalo to sign the articles of agreement for the Dempsey bout.[16] It was alleged by certain newspapermen in Buffalo and Pittsburgh that these stories had been entirely concocted by Red Mason in order to publicize his fighter at expense of Dempsey.[17] It certainly wasn't out of the scope of possibility given Mason's history. If the wily Mason could not get a fight with Dempsey he would at least attach the heavyweight champion's name to Greb's in a way that kept the press and public interested.

It had been expected that Greb would face Larry Williams in a rematch in Pittsburgh the week following his fight with Clay Turner but as the controversy of the Kirk-Ray bout continued to cast a shadow over the sport a postponement was necessary. James Routley, matchmaker for the Keystone club had felt the promotion might be hurt when enemies of Red Mason had stated publicly that he was a silent partner in the Keystone club, receiving special privileges which might give the impression of bias in favor of Mason or his fighters by the club and its officials. In light of such allegations Routley decided that it would be best to wait until after the official inquiry into the riot had concluded before staging a fight featuring Greb.[18]

While waiting for the air to clear in Pittsburgh Greb and Mason traveled to Dayton, Ohio to face Tommy Robson. Robson came to Dayton confident of his chances of upsetting Greb.

Robson had always been able to give a wonderful showing against Greb but was handicapped by his lack of size. With two bouts against Greb under his belt Robson knew exactly what to expect from his larger rival. He continually pressed forward trying to get Greb to stand still and slug but Greb was too smart for this. Knowing where his advantage lay Greb kept the fight at long range utilizing his size to pepper Tommy with bursts of punches from all directions. In the ninth Tommy caught Greb with his money-punch, a right hand loaded with TNT that landed right on the jaw and sent Greb flailing against the ropes. Robson tried to follow up his advantage but Greb was once again too big and too strong and at the end of the twelve rounds referee Lou Bauman raised Harry's hand in victory.[19]

"Greb is the most puzzling boxer in the world," said Robson. "He is not clever. But he is so uncannily tireless and such a perfect perpetual motion machine that it is impossible to get away from him. His arms never cease going- jabbing, hooking, swinging- every minute of the whole round. He'll start a right swing and you'll duck it to let it go over, when wang! you'll get a crack on the eye from a left uppercut, started about the same time he swings his right. He's wearing rather than a dangerous puncher, and, believe me, he'll give Dempsey a mighty interesting fight despite the fact that he's shy about 15 pounds in weight. He would have Dempsey tied in knots taking punishment. Dempsey might get him, but I think Greb would give a better fight than a lot of the men they are taking as contenders."[20]

After several days of testimony during the inquiry into the fight between Johnny Ray and Johnny Kirk and its aftermath, where it was revealed that referee Loudon Campbell was almost totally incompetent, Mason and the Keystone club came away virtually unscathed. Johnny Ray would not fight for nearly a year. Kirk would only have two more fights over the course of the next month before being sent to prison for four years for robbery, he would never box again. With the investigation over and the major players more or less exonerated boxing could continue in Pittsburgh and with it Greb's bout against Larry Williams.

There was much riding on Greb's upcoming bout

Tommy Robson of Malden, Massachusetts, was a smallish middleweight who made up for his lack of size with excellent conditioning and a powerful punch. Despite sporting victories over four champions he was too inconsistent to be a real threat to the title. However, he always gave a good account of himself and gave the fans their money's worth.

with Williams for both he and Pittsburgh. For the city itself it was extremely important that the bout be a clean and satisfying exhibition of boxing without controversy. There was the very real possibility that were anything untoward to transpire during the competition the entire sport might be clamped down for good. That was even if the local fans hadn't been so disgusted by the Kirk-Ray riot as to avoid the sport altogether. Adding to the pressure was the fact that it would be Greb's final bout in the city for several months and he wanted to leave a lasting impression on his fans.

Those wondering whether the Kirk-Ray affair had hurt the sport in Pittsburgh got their answer when only a little more than half of the seats were filled to see Greb's farewell fight. Seated ringside among the interested onlookers were five members of what would be termed the Municipal Athletic Committee which would hereafter oversee the sport in Pittsburgh. They were treated to a prototypical Greb performance. He improved upon his previous showing against Williams by minimizing exchanges and using his speed to outpunch Williams and keep the tall blonde on the defensive.[21]

After the fight Greb angrily rebutted allegations that a fight with Dempsey and himself was a figment of Mason's imagination. "You can just put that down as some more 'knocking' on the part of certain persons who begrudge me the success I have won in the boxing game," said Greb. "If anybody doubts that negotiations are on for a bout between Dempsey and myself let them write the promoters of the Queensberry Club in Buffalo, who have any amount of correspondence with Jack Kearns, Jack Dempsey, and Jim Corbett with regard to the bout. It would not profit me anything to claim that I had a match pending with Dempsey if I had not; I would be simply making myself ridiculous in the eyes of everybody."[22]

Dempsey had his own battles to wage, outside of the ring. In late January he was the victim of a scathing exposé by the San Francisco Chronicle which had been digging into his war record. Dempsey's former wife Maxine had published a letter stating she had unimpeachable proof that Dempsey and Kearns had conspired to dodge the draft, effectively keeping the champion out of the war and on the streets making money. Before long the federal government took interest in the allegations and on February 24 a grand jury handed down an indictment of Dempsey on the charge of conspiracy to avoid the draft. The melodrama would play out in the courts and the newspapers until mid-June when Dempsey was acquitted but his reputation had suffered.

Harry, with Mason in tow, left almost immediately after the Williams fight for Denver where Greb was scheduled to face George "KO" Brown on March 25 with the winner of that bout scheduled to face "Captain" Bob Roper on April 5. From there Mason and Greb would head to San Francisco and Los Angeles in search of warmer climates and more lucrative bouts. They spent two days and two nights on a train bound for the mile high city and, with barely enough time to shake off the trail dust, Greb entered the Stockyard Stadium and furnished western fans with a one-sided drubbing of the Greek battler. Having faced Brown four times in the past three and a half years he knew just what to expect from the old brawler and left him with a badly lacerated face. More impressive was the fact that Greb showed no signs of suffering under the mile high altitude despite having just arrived the day before.[23]

Immediately after the match Jack Kanner signed Greb to face "Captain" Bob Roper. Harry had made such a hit with local fans that a great crowd was expected. Kanner hoped to match the winner of the bout with Tommy Gibbons in late May. When asked about his thoughts on a match with Gibbons, the young man who had given Harry a hiding back in 1915, Greb replied "I beat Mike Gibbons in Pittsburgh last summer which shows I must have improved some since battling Tommy four years ago."[24]

George "KO" Brown was winding down his long career when he faced Harry Greb for the fifth time in 1920 at Denver, Colorado. Brown would fight only a handful of times after this final encounter with Greb.

Mason had still hoped to continue on to the west coast but Harry was beginning to get homesick. Mason tried to keep Greb occupied by taking him to see some of the splendor of the Rocky Mountains but to no avail. Desperately missing his family Harry wired for Mildred and Dorothy to come to Denver with him and continue on to the coast.[25]

It is not recorded whether Mildred and the six month old Dorothy actually made the trip to Denver. If they did they would have seen Harry give a near repetition of his previous bout with Roper where, save for a single round, Greb dominated his larger opponent.[26] Abe Pollack of the Rocky Mountain News wrote that Greb was "...one of the classiest men who has shown in Denver in years and appears to be a worthy opponent of any man of his weight in the world. He is like a moving target in the ring and it is difficult for any opponent to land a hard punch. His footwork was like a dancing master. He always keeps going and it is a miracle how he can stand the pace he sets."[27] Rick Ricketson of the Denver Post was no less impressed with Greb's speed, elusiveness, and stamina comparing his footwork to Irene Castle, a famous dancer of the 1910's and 20's.[28]

During the bout with Roper Harry injured his arm yet again and was forced to cancel his planned tour of the coast. He and Red boarded a train the next day and began the two day journey back to Pittsburgh where they hid Greb's injury by stating that he had contracted a bad cold.[29]

Captain Bob Roper (left), and his manager Sig Hart are seen here arriving in Denver, Colorado on the morning of March 29, 1920 for his twelve round match with Harry Greb at the Stockyard Stadium.

Within days of returning to Pittsburgh the local boxing community was buzzing with the news that French idol Georges Carpentier would be coming to the city to give an exhibition. As a cash cow Carpentier's influence could not be denied. He had been a fixture on the international boxing scene for close to a decade. The Frenchman had been considered something of a child prodigy. By eighteen he had already faced some of the stiffest competition in the world and with the onset of the Great War he had enlisted and served with distinction, being discharged a war hero. Over the course of the previous year Carpentier had re-acclimated himself by facing a steady stream of second and third raters to win the European heavyweight championship and was now being talked of as a possible opponent of Jack Dempsey. His movie star good looks, and war record meant he was instant box-office. This tour was designed to give the American public an opportunity to view the much talked of fighter for themselves and help promote the idea of matching the Frenchman for the heavyweight championship.

Greb's mouth must have watered at the prospect of getting to size up Carpentier. In addition to providing a sizable purse the Frenchman would also be an almost sure springboard to a match for the heavyweight championship if the so-called Orchid Man could be cornered into a bout.

As Harry's arm healed it was announced that he was matched by James Routley of Pittsburgh's Keystone club for two very important bouts. On May 12 he would face Tommy Gibbons at Forbes Field, and on May 29 he would be face Mike O'Dowd at the same venue. The O'Dowd bout would be a no-decision affair but with the weight set at 158 pounds Greb would have a chance to win the middleweight championship by a knockout or foul. The weight agreement also gave Greb the opportunity to prove that he was still a legitimate middleweight despite the persistent belief that he had now grown out of the division. It was something of a coup for Routley to get O'Dowd to sign for the match as the champion made it clear he considered Greb his most difficult opponent calling him "the roughest in the world."[30] Routley was forced to offer the highest guarantee ever offered a fighter in Pittsburgh for the champion's services.[31]

Before Greb could get a taste of the championship he had to get by Tommy Gibbons. Harry had quite a lot of animosity toward Gibbons as a result of Gibbons' manager Eddie Kane's continued, erroneous claims that Harry had been ducking a match with Tommy for years. For years Pittsburgh promoters had frequently tried to sign Tommy to a bout with Greb only to be met with exorbitant demands from Kane. Denver promoters met with the same difficulty in matching the two fighters when Kane sent them a simple telegram in response to their efforts:

Five thousand guarantee with privilege of 35 per cent. Three tickets and one thousand for training expenses. Rush answer.

EDDIE KANE, Manager of Tommy Gibbons.[32]

These were extremely high handed demands for the times and venue prompting the Denver Post to print the headline TOM GIBBONS ISN'T OVERLY ANXIOUS TO MEET EITHER GREB OR ROPER.[33] Similar headlines had been printed in the past when trying to arrange a match between Greb and Gibbons. Given the fact that Gibbons met Roper less than a week after he lost to Greb in Denver it can be safely assumed that if Gibbons was going to be looking across the ring at Harry Greb he (or Eddie Kane) wanted to be well compensated.

Since beating Greb in 1915 Tommy had labored in the shadow of his older, more talented, and more famous brother Mike. While Mike was being considered the uncrowned king of the middleweights Tommy had been quietly building a resume as a top middleweight and light heavyweight yet never seemed able to escape the promotional tag of being

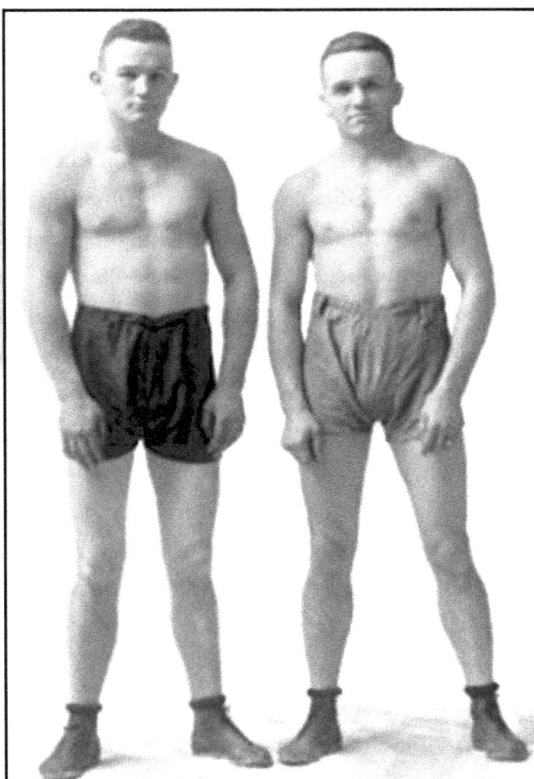

Tommy Gibbons (left), seen here with brother Mike, was slowly and quietly making a name for himself in the boxing world but crawling out of his brothers shadow would prove a difficult task.

"Mike's brother." Being the younger sibling of the great St. Paul Phantom helped sell tickets but it had to be hard being known more for his brother's accomplishments than his own which were considerable. He had fought over thirty times since meeting Greb in 1915 against mostly top opposition and managed to go undefeated. He was a classy boxer in the St. Paul style who used a modified form of his brothers famous footwork and despite having only scored two knockouts in that four year period he was a stiff puncher, particularly to the body. It's fair to say that despite his inability to immerge from his brother's shadow Tommy was a difficult proposition for any fighter in the world.

Reports were issued that Greb began training for Tommy Gibbons on April 26 and spurned all offers for his services prior to the Gibbons bout, showing that he was taking Tommy seriously and not as just another opponent.[34] However, Greb and Mason were keeping secret the fact that Greb's arm still had not adequately healed, hampering his ability to train properly. Reports were issued almost daily attesting to the intensity of Greb's workouts when in fact he was able to do little more than roadwork.[35] Greb seemed unfazed by his lack of a well-rounded training regimen. He was confident that he could beat Gibbons handily.

On May 3 Greb took some relief from the training "grind" to see Georges Carpentier exhibit his skills at Duquesne Gardens before a much smaller than expected crowd. Carpentier climbed into the ring and asked to see Frank Klaus, his onetime conqueror. "Hallo there, Klaus," said Carpentier as the former middleweight champion clambered up the aisle. While Carpentier was adjusting his gloves before the festivities began Harry Greb climbed into the ring and was introduced to Carpentier. Greb took the opportunity to announce that he was challenging the Frenchman to great applause. Harry eased into his seat and watched with rapt intensity, studying his possible future opponent. When Carpentier had finished showing his skills against his sparring partner Jules Lenares Greb remarked: "He's good. Yes, good. But I'd like to fight him."[36] The general consensus of opinion was that Carpentier was no match for Dempsey and Greb could hardly contain himself at the thought of facing the much hyped European champion. "Oh, boys what a fight we'd make! And I can lick him too."[37]

Three days later as Greb still dreamed of meeting Carpentier there was a major upset in the boxing world that shook Harry from his dream. Mike O'Dowd had traveled to Boston to face a local club fighter named Johnny Wilson. Little in Wilson's professional past suggested that O'Dowd would have anything more than a walkover.

Originally from Harlem, Wilson had turned professional around 1911 but failed to distinguish himself from the multitude of journeymen and club fighters that populated the east coast. He won some and he lost some against varying degrees of opposition while continuing to work at times as a tinsmith, sheet metal worker, and Western Union Courier. Despite the influence of his manager, underworld figure Vincent Morello, Wilson's career stagnated until he moved to the Boston area where he found himself under the management of popular former professional baseball player Marty Killilea. Wilson racked up a string of modest victories and found himself as an opponent for O'Dowd.

The only difficulty that O'Dowd's manager could foresee for his fighter would be Wilson's southpaw stance. Mullins had prepared to protect O'Dowd's title by forcing Wilson to accept Hector McInnis, a friend of Mullin's, as referee. It seemed that everything had been arranged for a successful O'Dowd defense and an easy purse. What Mullins and O'Dowd weren't banking on was the fact that Wilson was trained to the minute and sported one of boxing's best body attacks. In addition to this Wilson was a full sized middleweight with great upper body strength. In the second round Wilson whipped over a left hand that dropped O'Dowd. As the fight progressed Wilson was able to control the bout with his body punching.

When McInnis raised Wilson's hand in victory O'Dowd was furious. He rushed from his stool and shouted: "The least I should have got was a draw!"[38] Mullins quickly sent telegrams stating that Mike was robbed and that Wilson had fought an exceedingly foul fight. "I was up against it in Boston," stated O'Dowd. "Will I ever fight Wilson again? Well, you can bet your bonnet if I do it won't be in Boston. The referee always was supposed to be a friend of mine. But he found a better friend. That is the way I size it up."[39]

No one was more stunned by the upset than Greb. "Just to think," he said, "that I have been trailing O'Dowd all this time for a match only to have him lose the championship as soon as articles on closed."[40]

The O'Dowd match was now in jeopardy if for nothing else than the fact that the huge guarantee which had been promised to O'Dowd was now far out of line for a fighter who no longer wore the championship. There had been talk of trying to acquire the services of the new champion in O'Dowd's stead. But it seemed highly unlikely that the Wilson would consent to risk his recently won laurels against his top contender in his very next fight. Adding to the confusion was the fact that Wilson was virtually unknown. "The last time I was in Boston someone suggested a match between Wilson and me," said Greb commenting on the new champion. "'Wilson?' he said. 'Nothing doing. He'd be only a setup for Greb and the fans wouldn't turn out for it."

"Southpaws are easy for me," added Harry. "If

Johnny Wilson (right), born John Francis Panica, with his manager Martin Killilea. Wilson defeated Mike O'Dowd for the middleweight championship of the world on May 6, 1920.

the Keystone Club is thinking of canceling on O'Dowd I wish it would offer Wilson O'Dowd's guarantee and get him for me May 29."[41]

The day after Wilson defeated O'Dowd Red Mason wired Boston that he Greb would be willing to meet Wilson "...at any weight the latter selects and post any amount that Greb can lick him."[42]

With O'Dowd out of the picture at least temporarily Greb had to refocus for his upcoming bout with Tommy Gibbons. Explaining why he felt he needed to defeat Gibbons: "In all my fights," he said, "only five men ever have been able to score victories over me-- that is, victories that were generally conceded. They were Joe Chip, George Chip, Mike Gibbons, Tommy Gibbons, and Joe Borrell.

"Borrell licked me in Philadelphia when I was a novice and went on with him as a substitute opponent. He broke my nose and licked me considerable. In return, I've whipped him several times, and the last time I met him I knocked him out in his home town.

"Joe Chip scored the only knockout that ever has been recorded against me. That came in one of my first professional bouts, away back in 1913. I avenged it when I gave him a drubbing in 12 rounds in Youngstown last summer.

"George Chip gave me a whipping in 10 rounds in New Castle when I was just starting out as a main-bouter, but I have walloped him plenty a number of times, beating him so badly the last few times that he would never box me again.

"I took on Mike Gibbons on short notice in Philadelphia several years ago and while a lot of persons thought I won, most of the newspaper decisions went against me. I wiped out that mark at Forbes Field last June. That cleans me up, with the exception of Tommy Gibbons, and I'm going to wipe the slate when I get him in the ring Wednesday night.

"When I met Tommy Gibbons the first time, I was green. It was my first main bout of any importance out of town and I fought Tommy right in his home town, St. Paul. I got along fine for six rounds, but in the last four he gave me a healthy beating. It would be foolish for me to say he didn't beat me, for he did. And he marked me up a lot doing it. I knew I was whipped after that fight.

"There are a few other bouts in which the decisions have not gone entirely in favor of me, but I do not regard them in the light of defeats. A boxer generally knows when he is licked and when he isn't, and the five instances I have enumerated are the only ones in which I am willing to concede that I did not win. Reports of my bout with Mike O'Dowd in St. Paul did not favor me but the Minneapolis papers gave me the decision and I know in my heart that I won. Reports from Buffalo when I fought Soldier Bartfield there went against me, but I know I won that bout, too, and I have demonstrated several times since that I am Bartfield's master. When I fought Billy Miske at Forbes Field I consider I won, for I was leading the first eight rounds and was in trouble in the last two merely because of a cut over one of my eyes. Had I lost that bout, I would not be ashamed or afraid to admit it.

"Looking back over my career I feel satisfied that I will be all even with myself if I polish off Tommy Gibbons Wednesday night. Am I going to win? Just watch me. I have had a long lay-off and rest and feel better than ever before. I am in good shape and Tommy had better be right if he wants to make any kind of showing."[43]

If Greb was unable to train as he needed to Gibbons was diligent in his training, even stopping off for a day in Chicago on the way to Pittsburgh so as not to miss a day of training. "Gibbons is banking as much on a knockout as he is on winning on points," said his manager Eddie Kane. "He is punching harder than ever, and if he catches Greb coming in with one of those hard, straight right handers it will be all over in a hurry."[44]

On Wednesday May 12 at 3pm both fighters stepped on the scale with Gibbons weighing exactly 165 pounds, the stipulated weight, and Greb weighing slightly less. However by five o'clock threatening weather had moved into the area and after a conference between all interested parties it was agreed that the fight would be postponed to Saturday.

It was questioned as to whether the fighters would be forced to make weight again on the new date. Eddie Kane was adamant that his fighter had fulfilled his contractual obligation to make weight and that no further weigh in would be honored. With Gibbons coming down in weight to face Greb and possibly gaining a slight edge by not having to make weight on the afternoon of the fight Mason was quick to insist that the fighters weigh in again or lose their forfeit of $500. "The articles call for the men to weigh in at 165 pounds at 3pm on the day of the contest," said Mason. "Tomorrow is the day of the contest and the boxers will have to weigh in again, just as if there had never been a postponement. Gibbons is not going to get away with anything like that. He will weigh in again at 3 o'clock tomorrow afternoon, or on whatever day the bout is held, and if he doesn't scale under he will forfeit his weight deposit of $500."[45] It was finally agreed that there would be no second weigh in, much to Mason's consternation.

By the time the preliminaries started at 8:41 the stands were already half full. By the time Greb entered the ring at 10:18 12,000 fans cheered him wildly. A few minutes later Gibbons arrived to great applause as well. The two fighters greeted each other and checked their bandages. Their ringside weights were announced as 166 for Gibbons and 165 for Greb.

The first round opened slowly with Greb rather tentative until the middle of the round when he opened up with a volley of lefts and rights. Gibbons kept his composure and weathered the storm to maintain an even round with Greb. Many observers noted that Greb was not as fast or sharp as he had been in previous bouts. The second seemed to be going much the same when during an exchange Gibbons landed a powerful right hand under the heart that took the steam out of Greb. By the third it was plain to see that things were going to be rocky for the hometown hero. His left eye was swelling badly and he seemed slower than usual.

During this round Kid Coffey, a former boxer working in Gibbons corner, began heckling Greb. One of Greb's corner men went to the Gibbons corner and a fight ensued at ringside causing Greb's man to be ejected.

Greb was having difficulty finding his range and those punches that were on target were blocked and countered by Tommy who was now fighting in a form every bit as marvelous as that of his legendary brother. Pittsburgh fans were stunned to see Greb back up and fight on the defensive with Gibbons not only pursuing him along the ropes but out-speeding him as well. It was as if Greb was being forced, round by round, into the role that so many of his opponents had assumed when facing him, that of complete and utter helplessness.

Greb fared only slightly better in the fifth and sixth, though Tommy was now talking to him disdainfully, admonishing him to fight. Harry was rapidly weakening under the precision punching of the St. Paul boxer and whenever he tried to come back with his own attack it had little or no stopping power to the point that Gibbons no longer feared retaliation. Greb was a pitiful sight as the ninth rolled around. His left eye had been completely closed for several rounds, his face was puffed, and his body was red from the constant battering of Gibbons. Greb was forced to resort to clinching tactics in order to survive as his own fans jeered him and called for Gibbons to knock him out.

The final round witnessed Greb hanging on as the referee tried time and again to break the fighters. Gibbon's mercilessly pounded Greb's ribs, sinking his gloves deep into Harry's midsection. Greb tried desperately to fight back but was unable to mount anything resembling an effective attack. Just before the bell ended the fight Harry lashed out with one last desperate punch which found it's mark bloodying Gibbons' mouth but it was much too little and much too late. The fight was over and Greb had been handed what was possibly the most one-sided beating of his career.[46]

The fighters congratulated each other through bloody lips but it was Gibbons who was in receipt of the crowd's adulation. Nearly every fan of the sport in Pittsburgh, be they casual or fanatic, felt Greb would win and win easily. In losing, and losing as ingloriously as he did, Greb broke their hearts and they turned on him for it. He stood in his corner nearly alone but for a few of his handlers and closest friends as Gibbons soaked up the applause of the crowd. In his dressing room after the fight a smiling Gibbons said "I could have knocked Greb out in any of the late rounds, but I wanted to show him up before his own people."[47]

The next day Harry was about town to prove that some reports of the fight exaggerated the punishment he had received. He was bruised, swollen, and sporting a black eye but he was not missing any teeth, as had been reported.[48] The defeat was so comprehensive that Greb was forced to admit that it had been a bad beating he had received. Rather than be cowed by the loss Greb was eager to prove that it was an aberration. He was so anxious to wipe out the defeat that he was willing to face Gibbons within two weeks despite Gibbons plans to travel to Europe seeking bigger purses. He was ready to cancel his fight with Mike O'Dowd at the end of the month in order to face Gibbons on that date. "Yes, Gibbons beat me. But there is more to it than most persons are aware of," complained Greb. "In the first place the referee, who was brought in from out-of-town, didn't give me any the best of it. Three particular times he permitted

After his shocking victory over Harry Greb in May 1920, Tommy Gibbons, seen here flanked by Jim Moore and his manager Eddie Kane aboard the Royal George, headed to England to seek more lucrative bouts. When it became apparent that the Europeans wanted none of Tommy's game, they visited family in Ireland and returned home to face Harry in a rematch.

Gibbons to do things contrary to the rules agreed upon previous to the fight. 'Break clean and step back' were the orders. But in the second round Gibbons swung hard coming out of a clinch and caught me flush on the jaw. Not an inch did he step back. Again in the fourth a low blow dented the cup I was wearing. The referee couldn't help but see the blow, but did not even caution Tom. In the seventh Gibbons butted me with his shoulder and bruised my right eye. Each of these blows hurt, every one of them was foul, but the referee, who was brought here without our sanction, said or did nothing. I am willing to call off the bout with O'Dowd on the 29th if Gibbons will delay his trip long enough to meet me again. Or I will give him the date I have with Johnny Wilson on June 12. Gibbons is the best man I have ever met and I want another opportunity of showing the local fans that I am his master."[49]

Richard Guy would later allege that Harry had been up all night partying before the fight.[50] Greb gave another account of his defeat to Harry Keck: "I under-rated Gibbons a lot," he said, "and thought I would have no trouble with him. Perhaps I should have had a few bouts under my belt before meeting him, to put me right after my long layoff. I felt the lack of work when I tried to get started. All I ask is that Gibbons postpone his trip to Europe, if he is still thinking of going through with it, and consent to fight me here again on May 29."[51]

All of the excuses aside, and there were many from Greb and his supporters, Gibbons was simply the better man and performed brilliantly in what may very well have been the greatest performance of his career. In trying to discredit Gibbons' victory Greb drew the ire of a large swath of Pittsburgh's boxing fans.

As Gibbons left Pittsburgh for the east where he would board a steamer for England he scoffed at Greb's challenge. "Greb knows that is impossible," he said. "Our transportation is all purchased, and all plans made to sail this week. However, we will not be away forever. In fact, we'll be back soon, and then, if Harry wants another beating, I'll give it to him at any time and place that suits him."[52]

On May 17, while in Canton to see the match between Mike O'Dowd and welterweight champion Jack Britton, Jim Routley was able to finalize articles for the proposed rematch between O'Dowd and Greb. However twelve days was very little time to promote the bout and attract a crowd sizeable enough for the Keystone Club to break even, much less pay the fighters their guarantees. In addition to this difficulty Greb was demanding that the weight agreement for 158 pounds be waved now that O'Dowd was no longer champion. O'Dowd had already agreed to take a cut in his purse for losing the championship and he was not willing to allow Greb to come in at an advantageous weight. When the Keystone club could not negotiate a settlement and failed to begin advertising the bout a week prior to the agreed upon date Red Mason declared that he considered the bout off and left Pittsburgh with Greb in tow for Conneaut Lake where Greb would continue training for upcoming bouts.

Many in Pittsburgh, who had already had their confidence in Greb shaken by his defeat at the hands of Gibbons, felt that Greb was running out on a difficult challenge. Routley had tried in earnest to make the match but it seems that the promotion ran out of time prompting Greb and Mason to forgo the headache and move on to bouts that were already guaranteed. Harry

Convention Hall in Rochester, New York was originally constructed in 1868 as a Naval Armory. It often played host to social events and before long it was turned over completely to be used as a convention hall. Harry Greb appeared there in June 1920 as he worked himself back into condition with a one sided drubbing of Frank Carbone. The structure still stands, having been heavily renovated in the 1980's, and now houses Rochester's prestigious Geva Theatre.

was roundly criticized for this action in the wake of his loss to Gibbons.

One such bout was scheduled for June 2 in Philadelphia. Promoter Jack Hanlon had initially hoped to match Greb with a young up and coming light heavyweight named Gene Tunney. When Tunney learned he would be expected to face Harry Greb he declined, leaving Hanlon to sign Clay Turner instead.[53]

After dropping Turner in the first round, Greb easily dominated him, putting an exclamation point on their series of bouts.[54] It would be the last time they would meet professionally. They had faced each other seven times with Greb always coming out ahead. Turner would continue to fight for a little over two more years before retiring after a second round knockout at the hands of Jeff Smith.

Mason continued to line up fights for Greb with the ultimate goal of working him into top physical condition for a planned return with Tommy Gibbons as soon as the latter returned from Europe.

Mason had hoped to sign Bill Brennan for yet another go with Greb but the big man was now one of the names mentioned most prominently as an opponent for Dempsey and he wasn't about to ruin his chances of a title shot by losing another one sided decision to his much smaller antagonist.

Frank Carbone was a tough, if unspectacular, journeyman of the 1910's and 20's. His record was a veritable who's who of top flight competition and despite coming up short against most of them he would eventually sport knockout victories over future champions Johnny Wilson and Mike McTigue as well as a decision over hall of famer Young Stribling.

On June 21 Harry and Red Mason returned to Conneaut Lake with Val Grunen, Irish Chick Rodgers, and Dee Kelly where he would get down to the task of hard conditioning. In little over a week Greb would travel to Rochester, New York to face Frank Carbone who he had beaten so easily two years ago. Mason committed Greb for a match one week after the Carbone bout against Chuck Wiggins in Cincinnati. "My big aim," said Greb, "is to get several fights away from Pittsburgh for the next month to prepare me for a return bout with Tom Gibbons, which I believe will be arranged for Forbes Field the latter part of July. My manager tells me that Kane and Gibbons have wired the Keystone Club asking for terms and I'm pretty sure the match will be arranged. Meanwhile I will meet Carbone, Wiggins, and anybody else in out-of-town bouts.

I figure the matches just ahead will put me on edge for the Gibbons fight -an edge I lacked when I stacked up against the St. Paul battler in the recent fight at Forbes Field."[55]

Greb's training stunts in the small resort town of Conneaut Lake drew crowds of vacationing spectators. His every thought was strained on his obsession with getting even against Tommy Gibbons. "I am willing to sacrifice some share of the gate receipts to Gibbons," said Greb, "if the St. Paul man will agree to meet me again, as I will not rest well until I've taken his measure, which I feel confident of doing."[56] The matches that Mason had lined up for Greb were little more than an afterthought to the fighter. It was obvious that he was viewing them more as sparring exhibitions in preparation for Gibbons.

On their way to Rochester Mason and Greb stopped off at Buffalo where they picked up a match in early July from Charles Murray of the Queensberry Club. Carbone came into the bout coming off a good performance against former champion George Chip and boasting of the fact that he had once knocked out the new middleweight champion Johnny Wilson. Greb outweighed Carbone by seven pounds and seemed to be his old self throughout the fight. He danced lightly in and out, peppering Carbone with blows from all directions. He smiled throughout the contest and laughed at Carbone's wild attempts to land a punch. In the first round Carbone split his right glove and was fitted with a lighter one. Fighting against an ordinary fighter this may have been an advantage for Carbone, whose best punch was his right, but Greb was much too fast to allow the Italian to land with any regularity or force.

Bob Moha's long career was winding down when he faced Harry Greb three times in 1920. For ten years he had been facing some of the toughest opponents in the world and even now was hoping for a shot at Jack Dempsey's championship.

At one point in the bout Carbone landed several low blows but Greb refused to claim the bout on a foul, electing instead to continue his dominance of the Brooklynite. Between the ninth and tenth rounds one of Carbone's seconds spilled smelling salts in his eye causing Frank to leap off his stool with a yell. It took over three minutes to clear his eye out before the fight could resume. The rest, if it can be called that, did not benefit Carbone, especially with Red Mason protesting the halt. When all was said and done it was yet another easy victory for Harry who was rapidly rounding into his old form.[57]

The day after Greb defeated Carbone Red Mason replied to a wire from Mike McKinney in Canton, Ohio stating that Greb would be available on July 5 to face Bob Moha in twelve rounds at catch weights. As Greb prepared for Moha Mason entered into negotiations with Eddie Kane for a return bout with Tommy Gibbons. Gibbons and Kane had recently returned to the United States from England where Tommy was unsuccessful in acquiring the lucrative matches against European soft touches that he had desired. In Canton, Mike McKinney had high hopes of matching the winner of Greb-Moha with Gibbons for Labor Day. So it was with added urgency that the Keystone Club began lobbying to put the show on for July 31 at Forbes Field.

McKinney turned up the heat on Pittsburgh by offering to match Greb with Jack Dempsey for Labor Day adding that he hoped to beat out Buffalo's Charlie Murray for the match.[58] It was to no avail; Mason was firm in his commitment to staging the bout in Pittsburgh in front of the same fans who had witnessed Greb's Waterloo. It was imperative that Mason rehabilitate Greb's image in his hometown. Kane and Gibbons could not have been happier in accepting what they considered an easy big money match for Tommy. "Why not?" said Kane, "boxing is Gibbons' business, and I can't conceive of any bout being easier for him than another with Greb."[59] Later he remarked "I was a bit surprised when Greb demanded a return match, for Tom has twice beaten him. When these lads meet again, Tom will knock him out."[60]

Any hope that Mike McKinney had of bringing Greb together with Gibbons or Dempsey in Canton was completely lost when only two-thousand fans turned out to watch Greb completely outclass Moha. It was for the best that so small a crowd filed into the Canton Auditorium because what they witnessed was a fairly lackluster fight with Moha content to hold and survive until the final two rounds when, feeling that Greb was slowing up a bit, he started trying to land punches in earnest with little success.[61]

After the bout with Moha, Greb and Mason motored to Akron, Ohio to watch Bob Roper outpoint Bob Martin and then returned to Pittsburgh where

Tom Sharkey (left), old-time contender of the heavyweight wars from 20 years earlier poses with Harry Greb at the Fort Erie Races. This photo was taken on the afternoon of July 8, 1920, the day Greb faced Larry Williams in Buffalo.

they spent the next day playing handball to keep Harry sharp for his match the next day in Buffalo against Larry Williams. The match would be held at the Ferry street baseball park in conjunction with the Fort Erie horse races. A great crowd of sporting men was expected despite the poor weather.

The day of the fight Harry attended the Fort Erie races where he met one time heavyweight terror Tom Sharkey. Greb must have taken a measure of confidence in his aspirations for a heavyweight title from Sharkey, who once gave former heavyweight champion Jim Jeffries all he could handle for 25 rounds, for when they came face to face Sharkey and Greb were nearly the same size, and Jeffries, it should be remembered, was a larger man than Dempsey.

That night Sharkey was ringside to witness Greb easily defeat Larry Williams[62] prompting the writer for the Buffalo Express to write: "...many of the spectators are today more willing than before to admit that, if Greb's challenge to Jack Dempsey is ever accepted, the champion may have a much livelier time subduing the light heavy than he had demolishing the Goliath Willard to annex the title."[63]

Within days after returning from Buffalo it was officially announced by the Keystone Club that Harry Greb would meet Tommy Gibbons in a return match at Forbes Field on July 31. The official weight would be set at 163 pounds at 10am.

Gibbons announced that after defeating Greb he would seek a match against Dempsey for the champion. "If the coming battle is to name the one that will meet Dempsey," commented Mason, "it will, I am sure, be my man, Harry Greb."[64]

It was the intention of Greb and Mason to leave no stone unturned in his training. Another defeat to Gibbons would be devastating both professionally and psychologically. No excuse would be able to erase the fact that Gibbons was his master were he to suffer another loss at the hands of Mike's brother.

"I am going to put my automobile in the garage for the next week and devote myself to real work,"[65] said Greb. In fact Greb traded his auto in for a train as three days later he and Mason headed east in search of the best sparring partners available. "I will have no alibis to offer if I am beaten again," said Greb two days before departing, "I feel fine now, and I have mapped out a busy program for the coming week. There will be no foolishness on my part, my friends can bank on that."[66] Many in Pittsburgh felt that it was a folly for Greb to train in New York where many fighters had been lured by the siren song of the primrose rose path only to be lost among the many broken down stumble-bums known as has-beens, second-raters, and ham-eggers.

Mason had other ideas. He had a plan that if successful would put Greb in fantastic shape and deposit him at the head of the line of contenders for Dempsey's championship. They were going after the man himself: Jack Dempsey.

Since being acquitted on the slacker charge Dempsey had traveled to New York City where he set up training camp at the Van Kelton Stadium at eighth avenue and Fifty-Seventh Street.

There he set about the task of getting in shape for a proposed bout with Bill Brennan. His manager Doc Kearns advertised Dempsey's training in newspapers and charged fifty-five cents for admittance, drawing large crowds daily. Big Bill Tate had been Dempsey's chief sparring partner in these training sessions but the champion was eager for good men to help him round into shape and so he was glad to have the addition of Greb in his camp when the Pittsburgh middleweight arrived on July 27 and announced his readiness to assist the champion.

It was a gamble on the part of Red Mason to allow his protégé to face the man they had been chasing in a training exhibition in front of several hundred spectators. If Greb was made to look bad it would forever sink any talk of a match with the champion. There was also the very real threat that Greb could suffer an injury forcing the postponement or cancellation of his bout with Gibbons which would only add fuel to the fire that was the belief that Harry wanted no part of another beating at the hands of Gibbons. After all, Dempsey was well known for being as ferocious in sparring sessions as he was in actual matches. Only days before Greb and Mason left for New York Dempsey had been working out in light sparring with bantamweight Midget Smith and knocked the little man completely senseless. Years later Dempsey would take on cub reporter Paul Gallico in a sparring session which resulted in Gallico being knocked out in less than a round. Bill Peet of the Pittsburgh Dispatch even theorized that Dempsey could only gain confidence from sparring sessions with Greb, a confidence that would allow him to quickly dispatch Harry in the event of a proposed fight between the two.[67]

Mason had no intention of any of these possibilities happening. He knew his fighter and knew that it was a winning situation. Harry would be able to show several hundred fans and reporters that he could compete with the heavyweight champion on even terms without fear and in the process would get the best sparring he could possibly ask for to prepare him for Tommy Gibbons.

Greb boxed four hard rounds with Dempsey on July 27 before a large crowd. Dempsey was glad to have Greb in his camp and stated that he wished he could have helped Greb prepare for his bout with Gibbons in May. The next day after word had filtered out that Greb was working with Dempsey the Stadium was stormed with fans eager to see the two great fighters in action. There was such a demand for seats that admission was raised from fifty-five cents to one dollar. Doc Kearns was so impressed with Greb's performance that he made arrangements with Red Mason to have Harry brought to Michigan where it was announced that Dempsey would defend his title against Billy Miske on Labor Day prior to facing Bill Brennan. Promoter Tex Rickard, acting as time-keeper during the sparring sessions, was equally impressed by Greb's ability to extend the champion and announced that he would do his best to secure Johnny Wilson for a championship match with Greb in October. Dempsey himself told onlookers that Greb was the first man to give him a real workout.[68]

The following day Harry was again facing Dempsey in a sparring session. This time the doors had to be closed long before the fighters took to the ring because the stadium had been filled to capacity by fans eager to see the two future legends in action. No less of an attraction was motion picture idol Douglas Fairbanks who was acting as referee. The audience was surprised to see the smaller man tearing into Dempsey with no regard for the champion's power and no fear. In the second round their heads collided and Dempsey was forced to retire from the session with a large swelling over his left eye. Rather than disappoint the audience Dempsey boxed a playful exhibition with Fairbanks to the crowd's amusement and was unable to spar the following day owing to the swelling.[69]

The training bouts were a huge success for Mason. Greb had benefited greatly from sparring with the champion and the publicity was exactly what Mason had hoped for. George Underwood, writing for the New York Evening Telegram, was already stating that Dempsey would likely be matched with Greb in the near future.[70]

Harry returned to Pittsburgh brimming with confidence. He now knew that he could stand in the ring with the heavyweight champion and need not fear the man the press had dubbed the "giant-killer." If he had nothing to fear from Dempsey then surely the prospect of Gibbons would hold no dread for him.

The morning of the fight Mason was informed that Eddie Kane had refused to allow his fighter to weigh in. Mason was furious, it was now the second time that Kane had refused to allow his fighter to make weight for Greb. Mason marched Harry over to the Americus Club where Kane and Gibbons were preparing for the match and in the presence of all he had Greb climb onto the scales where he tipped the beam at 160 $\frac{1}{2}$ pounds. Kane maintained his insistence that Gibbons would not weigh in. There had only been a verbal contract for the fight and as such there was no legally binding agreement for Gibbons to weigh under the agreed upon 163 pounds. Kane and Gibbons were not above going back on their word to gain an advantage over Greb. For a moment it looked as if Mason would pull the plug on the entire match until Sheriff Haddock was called on to barter a compromise whereby Gibbons would be allowed to fight without weighing in and in exchange Greb would be paid half of Gibbons' weight forfeit amounting to $250 dollars.[71]

Half way through the preliminaries ominous grey clouds began to move into the area but the rain held off. Gibbons entered the ring at 4:25 as a 10 to 8 favorite with but one writer in Pittsburgh giving Greb a chance to win. Greb entered a few minutes later and for a moment the bad blood between the two parties spilled over into an argument over which corners the fighters would occupy. Referee Jack Dillon flipped a coin and Greb won the call. Mason taunted Kane and Gibbons "Don't get sore," and "I've got you beat at the start."[72] Gibbons just smiled as if to reiterate his boast that he spoke with his fists.

Many commented that Gibbons looked the larger man. Greb sized his man up before leaping in and beginning his aggressive attack. The first round went to Greb who drew blood from Tommy's upper lip. It looked as if the fight might take a line similar to their previous bout with Gibbons taking over in the second. He repeatedly landed hard, precision blows to the body and head, countering Greb's rushes with impeccable timing and picking off his punches before they reached the mark.

Greb began to pick up speed after round three and each round thereafter he increased the pace. By round four Tommy was beginning to look puzzled, this was clearly a different Greb than the one he had faced in May. In the fifth Greb rocked Gibbons with three straight power punches, two rights to the head and a left to the body that seemed to momentarily take something out of Tommy. Several more body punches hurt the St. Paul battler. Tommy returned to his corner bleeding from the nose.

As Gibbons stalked Greb hoping to corner him and land a crushing knockout blow, Greb danced around the ring with his back to the ropes, leaping in to attack, throwing a multitude of blows, missing some but landing many. When Gibbons got close enough to land something Greb would clinch, breaking up Tommy's rhythm, and wait for the referee to break them before resuming long range tactics. At times Greb was so fast and elusive that he seemed to be everywhere and nowhere. On more than one occasion he actually popped up behind Gibbons.

During the fifth a light rain had begun which by the start of the seventh had turned into a downpour. Many of the estimated 10,000 in attendance began to run for the grandstands where there was shelter from the rain and lightning, which was now crackling around the stadium. Several of the ringside reporters ducked for cover under the ring to be shouted returns of the fight from those who stayed to brave the weather. Greb seemed to draw strength from the rain. He ripped into Gibbons relentlessly with blows to the body and head. Gibbons caught Greb coming in with a right cross to the chin which landed with a flash of lightening and a clap of thunder. Greb dropped to a knee but he bounced up without a count and as Gibbons tried to follow up his advantage Greb met him full tilt and attacked with such fury that Gibbons was forced to give ground. Gibbons returned to his corner with a cut over his right eye.

The ring was now filled with water and the two fighters splashed about as they waged combat. Gibbons seemed to be growing frustrated with Greb's increasing pace and ability to improve upon their previous encounter resulting in his use of foul tactics. Greb remained unfazed and with each round seemed to be widening his margin of victory. He fought the last two rounds wearing a confident grin and continually disregarded the force of Gibbons' weakening blows to wade in and punish his rival. As the ninth round dawned the storm clouds were so dark that the fighters were barely visible from the grandstands. The rain continued to fall thick and heavy, and lightening crackled across the river valley.

In the final round Greb cut loose from the bell and put on such a display of pure aggression, fury, and non-stop punching that Gibbons was bewildered and unable to answer. The crowd was on its feet rabidly cheering the hometown boy. Screams for a knockout could be heard over the dull roar of the rainstorm. Those who didn't cheer stood awed by Greb's ability to fight at a pace far greater than the start of the fight against such a taxing opponent in the final round.[73]

When the final bell rang Greb's fans rushed the ring in jubilation, their hero had reversed

his previous setback in a brilliant performance. Red Mason turned a handstand in the center of the ring to celebrate as Eddie Kane and Tommy Gibbons stood by. "Harry came back just as I knew he would,"[74] shouted Mason. Kane was indignant and refused to concede defeat.

The bout had been a tremendous success for Pittsburgh, shattering the previous attendance record set by Greb's bout with Mike Gibbons. It also drew a record for gross receipts, set during the same fight,[75] by roughly two thousand dollars, and of course the hometown hero

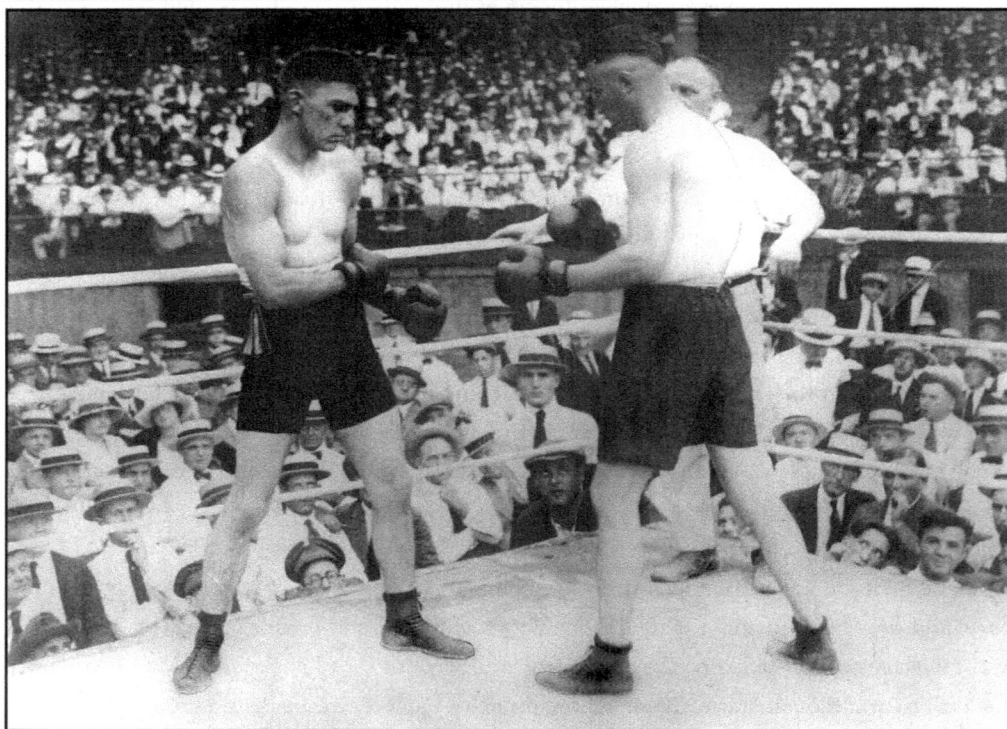

Top, left to right, James "Red" Mason, Harry Greb, Referee Jack Dillon, Tommy Gibbons, and Eddie Kane receive final instructions. Above, Harry Greb and Tommy Gibbons square off just before the start of their third dramatic bout.

had redeemed himself. As far as the newspapers were concerned the majority voted for Greb. Six of the seven local papers wrote about the fight, of those six four returned Greb the winner, one, the Gazette-Times ruled the bout a draw (although oddly a tally of the rounds had Greb winning by a margin of 3 to 2 with 5 even), and as was to be expected the crotchety, conspiracy expounding Jim Jab writing for the Pittsburgh Press ruled in favor of Gibbons despite giving Greb great praise for his performance and admitting that many would disagree with him. It comes as no surprise that the only newspaper report of the fight which ended up in Tommy's scrapbook was that written by Jim Jab.[76]

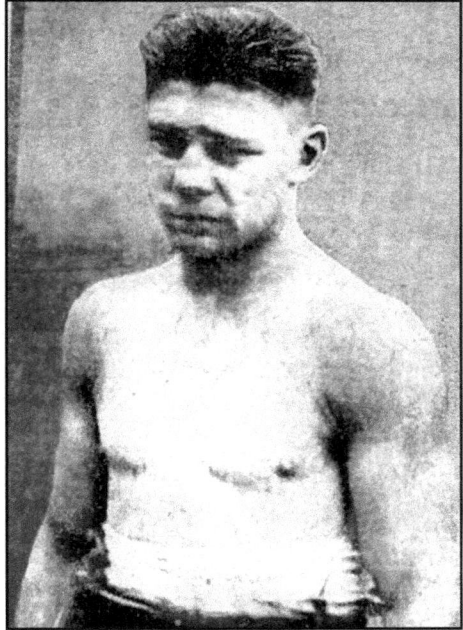

Top: Greb looks focused on the task ahead just prior to the opening bell. Above: Tommy Gibbons (left) and Harry Greb are seen here in the first round of their third fight, feeling one another out. Greb is seen darting in and out as Gibbons stands more erect trying to find the range with his jab to bring over a crushing right hand.

Above: Referee Jack Dillon looks on as Greb (center) leaps in with a flying attack on Tommy Gibbons in the second round. Below: Greb (left) is seen tying up Gibbons in an attempt to break his rhythm in the third. Inset: Gibbons (right) steps inside a long hook and plants a solid jab on Greb's jaw backing him into the ropes in the third.

Above: Tommy Gibbons (center) tries to ward off a terrific body attack by Harry Greb in this action photo from an unspecified round of their July 31, 1920 bout at Forbes Field, Pittsburgh. Below: Tommy Gibbons (left) winces as Harry Greb launches his trademark windmill attack in the sixth round of their third fight. A light rain had already begun to fall and by the next round it had begun to rain so hard that photographs would be virtually impossible.

15

CHASING THE CHAMPIONS

Harry spent the day following his dramatic victory over Gibbons celebrating with friends and family and racing along Pittsburgh's roads in his automobile. Two days later he took Mildred and Dorothy to Atlantic City. They made the trek via his beloved auto and toured Harrisburg, Baltimore, Washington, and Philadelphia on the way.

As the family enjoyed their vacation Mason was busy behind the scenes booking an ambitious schedule for Greb. Harry had already agreed to face Chuck Wiggins at Kalamazoo on August 20 in order to show the fans that his fight with Zulu Kid earlier in the year was not indicative of his ability. Mason was also able to squeeze a bout with Bob Moha into Greb's busy schedule for August 14 in Cedar Point, Ohio. Promoter Mike McKinney was still very eager to stage a bout between Greb and Gibbons in Canton but Eddie Kane had refused to allow his fighter to face Greb again. Greb had also readily agreed to travel to Michigan in later in the summer to help Jack Dempsey prepare for his defense against Billy Miske.[1] Dempsey and Kearns had been so impressed with the intensity Greb brought to their training sessions that they demanded Promoter Floyd Fitzsimmons make room for Greb to appear on the undercard of the Miske fight in a semi-final bout.

Boxing was now poised to reach a level of popularity unparalleled in it's history. As thousands of young soldiers had returned home they brought with them a love of the sport acquired in training cantonments across the nation. Boxing's stars had contributed greatly to the war effort, adding to the sport's patriotic luster. With the passing of the Walker Law in New York, being held up as an example of how the sport could be cleanly governed and brought into the mainstream combined with the damage done to baseball's reputation in the fallout over the Black Sox scandal, boxing appeared on the verge of becoming America's national pastime. Harry and Mason were eager to take advantage of this surge in popularity.

Mason set about calling out Battling Levinsky in the hope that he could arrange a fifteen round light heavyweight championship fight for Greb. He was willing to bet Levinsky $500 to $1000 that Greb would stop Levinsky inside of fifteen rounds.[2] Floyd Fitzsimmons tried to arrange for Greb to meet Levinsky on the undercard of the Dempsey-Miske bout but Levinsky's manager Dan Morgan declined. Morgan was already in talks with Francois Descamps, manager of Georges Carpentier, to arrange a championship bout between the two and there was no way Morgan was going to risk his chance at a monster purse against Carpentier by losing Levinsky's championship to Greb for $3000. Fitzsimmons contacted several other fighters to fill the date but was finding it difficult to acquire an opponent for Harry.

Greb had little trouble outpointing Moha in a bout colored by the two fighters' taunts of one another.[3] Less than a week later Greb was in Kalamazoo to face Chuck Wiggins. Wiggins had greatly improved since their last meeting a year and half previous. In the interim Wiggins had traveled to Australia, defeating the heavyweight champion of that country. Wiggins had been steadily increasing his level of opposition and his ability to beat men much larger than himself was rapidly gaining him a reputation as a fighter much in the mold of Harry Greb himself. He had developed himself into a rugged, shifty fighter, who boasted a nasty mean streak and considerable knowledge of the ring. It was expected that Wiggins would give Harry all he could handle. Many of his recent bouts had been waged in Kalamazoo and he was quite popular there among the fans. If ever an opponent was made to show Kalamazoo what Greb was truly made of it was Wiggins.

"I am certain to win against Wiggins," said Harry, "I know his style and will stop him. Just say for me that I am all right this time. Both arms are as good as new and I have trained to step ten rounds at top step, without a seconds let up."[4]

"This is just the fight I have been waiting for," said Wiggins in response. "I never would have consented to meet Greb here, if not certain of defeating him. He has shaded me twice, but that was in my early career and he will meet an entirely different man in the Kalamazoo ring. Greb is fast and aggressive, but I have got some speed myself and can rush through ten rounds with any of them."[5]

Kalamazoo fans got every penny's worth of fighting action when Greb and Wiggins faced

off. Wiggins outweighed Greb by two pounds at 167 and was in perfect condition. For all his speed and ring savvy though Wiggins was unable to contend with Greb. He was once again far too fast, far too slippery for the Hoosier. According to Howard P. Hall: "Greb owed Kalamazoo a good fight to make up for the unfortunate meeting here with Zulu Kid last February. He paid the bill last night with compound interest. Kalamazoo had never seen Greb when he was right and his showing against Wiggins was a revelation. He landed easily three to four clean blows to one for Wiggins. We all know how fast Wiggins is."[6]

As the fight progressed Wiggins became frustrated with his inability to catch Greb cleanly and resorted to foul tactics. On several occasions he butted Greb or elbowed him. The crowd quickly turned against the man who had been a favorite there and booed Wiggins. Greb was unfazed by these tactics and continued to educate Wiggins on the finer points of the noble art of self-defense. Despite the stifling heat Harry finished the show by fighting the tenth round as fresh as he had the first. Wiggins left the ring with a cut nose and swollen left eye.[7]

Floyd Fitzsimmons and Jack Kearns had been present at the Wiggins bout and both agreed that another Wiggins-Greb bout would be a great attraction. Still having trouble securing a quality opponent to meet Greb on the under-card of Dempsey's defense against Miske, Fitzsimmons was quick to sign Wiggins. Kearns tried to get Greb to come to Benton Harbor and start working with the champion immediately but Greb demurred, wanting to spend a few days at home before joining Dempsey's camp.

Wiggins had been scheduled to face Milwaukee's Ted Jamieson in Grand Rapids on August 27 but the cut on his nose received in his bout with Greb became infected. Both of Wiggins' eyes swelled shut and he was forced to cancel the bout with Jamieson the day before.[8] Matchmaker Morrisey of the East Grand Rapids Athletic Club placed a long distance call to Red Mason and on short notice Greb accepted the bout with Jamieson for the largest guarantee ever offered a fighter in Grand Rapids history.[9] The bout was rescheduled for August 28 to allow Greb time to travel from Pittsburgh. It was a great opportunity and a stroke of luck for Jamieson. "If I beat Greb I will amount to something," he said. "I couldn't add much to my reputation by walloping Wiggins, but Greb is just about the class of his

Theodore Jamieson was the son of Scottish immigrant parents. He had been a national A.A.U champion and runner up to the A.E.F. championship. His first professional fight was against his much more experienced hometown rival Bob Moha and he continued to face tough opposition throughout his career.

division at present and if I beat him I'll have the honor myself. And if I lose it will be no disgrace."[10]

The bout meant a lot to both fighters as Milwaukee promoter Tom S. Andrews announced that he would pay a large guarantee for the winner to fight before his club.[11] It was a purse that Jamieson was determined to get and he showed it as soon as he got within striking distance during the first round. As he and Greb felt one another out for an opening Jamieson shot over a powerful left that dropped Harry to the canvas with a thud. Before a count could be started Greb regained his senses and was up by the count of four. Jamieson, sensing his opportunity, tried to capitalize on the surprise he had sprung and tore after Greb like a man possessed. Harry calmly picked off the inbound blows and spent the round warding off Jamieson's assault.

Greb spent the early part of the second round warding off a Jamieson assault and then went right back to his old style of tearing in with a multitude of punches. Despite smothering his opponent and having most of

Harry works out on the pulleys in this rare photo circa 1920. Greb was always proud to train in his United States Navy training togs.

the fight his own way Grand Rapids newspapers were split on the verdict.[12] The Grand Rapids Herald voted the bout a draw while the Grand Rapids News felt Greb had done more than enough to earn the decision. According to the Herald: "From start to finish it was one of the greatest fights ever fought in a Grand Rapids ring or in any other ring anywhere in the world. If the Dempsey-Miske fight at Benton Harbor on Labor day is as good, those who pay $30 for ringside seats and $3 for war tax will be getting their money's worth. Time after time the two men stood toe to toe and weaving around the ring flailed away with both hands until they literally fought themselves apart."[13]

The News reported that "the Pittsburgher, after his head had rid itself of the myriad of stars and comets, came back and punched the Milwaukee gamester full of holes, earning the decision. Jamieson didn't know that there were so many boxing gloves manufactured."[14]

Two days later Greb arrived at Dempsey's training camp ready to help the champion put

the finishing touches on his conditioning. It no doubt bothered Greb that Dempsey was making the first defense of his championship against a man Greb himself had beaten. The championship match itself was little more than a payday for the champion, a formality. Many openly scoffed at Miske as a legitimate threat to the champion. It was no secret that Miske had been ailing for some time now, suffering from a mysterious malady that had sent him to the hospital the previous year.[15] Indeed Miske had fought only once in over a year and that being a pointless second round knockout over Jack Moran. In later years Dempsey would admit that the match had been arranged in haste in order help Miske financially.[16] Whether he knew it or not Miske was in fact dying of a kidney ailment and needed as much money as possible to set his family up before he passed away.

Dempsey took the training seriously and once again showed his unwillingness to take it easy on even the most inexperienced sparring partners when a young soldier named Riley arrived in his camp begging to train with the champion. Dempsey knocked the young man out in the second round; afterwards Riley was allowed to stay in camp but he no longer sparred with Dempsey.

Harry had been shadowboxing nearby and surveyed the scene as Riley was lead from the ring in a stupor, his keen, analytical mind had been working, studying the champion. Greb knew that if he was to maintain his place as one of Dempsey's top contenders there was no way he could allow Dempsey to manhandle him as the champion had done with Riley. Indeed if Greb wanted to continue hurling challenges at Dempsey he would need to show to great effect against the champion when it came time for the two to spar together.[17]

That time came the following day. Brimming with confidence, Greb leapt at the champion with the call of time. The fans and newspapermen who had flocked to ringside to see the champion condition himself sat in awe as Greb took the fight to his larger antagonist and made Dempsey look slow and amateurish in comparison. Initially the champion had planned to spar only two rounds with Harry but was so frustrated with his showing that he begged another round. Dempsey was unable to capitalize on the extra round and Harry continued to make the champion miss and counter with his own wicked punches that had the crowd roaring.[18]

Word spread fast that Dempsey and Greb had put up a sensational sparring exhibition full of surprises. P. T. Knox, writing for the Pittsburgh Gazette-Times described the exhibition like this:

"The bout with Greb was a real one, it was the best workout Dempsey has had. The Pittsburgher was in prime shape, and although he only weighs 165 pounds, he gave the champion a real honest-to-goodness battle. Greb was all over him and kept forcing him around the ring throughout the session. Dempsey could do little with the speedy light heavyweight, while Greb seemed to be able to hit Dempsey almost at will. Time and again Greb made the champion miss with his famous right and left hooks to the head and countered with heavy swings to the head and hooks to the body.

Greb was a veritable whirlwind. Twenty-five pounds lighter than the champion, and about four inches shorter, Harry made the champion step very lively. He had to jump off the floor to hit Dempsey in the head when the latter was standing up straight, but managed to do it and landed without leaving himself open to Jack's snappy hooks and short swings."[19]

The following day, September 2, more than two thousand people made the trek to Dempsey's training camp in hopes of witnessing another terrific sparring session between the champion and the middleweight upstart. As Dempsey's trainer Teddy Hayes called "time" Greb rushed the champion with an attack so furious that Dempsey was taken completely by surprise. It wasn't until Greb landed a powerful left hook to the body that shook Dempsey out of his surprise and forced the champion to stand and fight. The two fighters then put on a tremendous display of boxing that drove the audience wild.

The training bout continued at a furious pace in the second. The two fighters had complete-

Harry Greb (center) poses with heavyweight champion Jack Dempsey (left) in this photo which was probably taken at Dempsey's training camp for championship fight against Billy Miske. It was Greb's greatest desire to face Dempsey in the ring and he spent much of his time lobbying for the opportunity to meet him in a bout.

ly forgotten themselves and thrown all pretense of a training bout out the window. Jack Kearns and Red Mason, from the fighters' corners, begged the fighters to calm down. Their worst fear nearly came true when midway through the second round the two fighters collided heads and Dempsey came away spitting blood. After the second round had ended Teddy Hayes admonished the crowd to refrain from cheering the fighters on to greater levels of ferocity. If Dempsey were injured and the fight called off it would mean a lot of money lost for everyone involved. After a third round replete with action the audience cheered for fully ten minutes at the remarkable display by both fighters.[20]

The following day, the final day of training, another crowd of over two thousand fans arrived to see another brutal session. They were disappointed. Greb and Dempsey squared off for three tame rounds with only occasional bursts of excitement. After Dempsey's tongue had been cut the previous day the two fighters had been instructed to take it easy.[21]

Miske, for his part, was kept busy denying that he was ill. He insisted that his hospital stay had been the result of having his tonsils removed and what he called a slight curvature of the spine. His sparring was hampered by injuries and a lack of quality sparring partners. With the ballyhoo in full swing most in the press were unwilling to admit that Miske was no longer a quality challenger despite at least one writer noting that his skin color was a "sickly pallor" when he entered the ring to face Dempsey.[22]

Harry and Red Mason intended to bet as much money as they could on the champion but they had to be sure of their investment so Mason sent Harry to Miske's camp on September 4 to get a feel for the challenger. Harry arrived at the camp before training had gotten underway and ran into Billy. They spoke briefly before Greb left with the impression that he was unwelcome. After returning to camp Greb sparred a few rounds with Soldier Riley for the enjoyment of the fans that showed up.[23]

Two days later on September 6 fifteen thousand boxing enthusiasts arrived to watch the heavyweight championship of the world. After a lackluster bout between the legendary Sam Langford and Dempsey's chief sparring partner Big Bill Tate Greb met Chuck Wiggins in the six round semi-final. Before the bout Eddie McGoorty, still searching for one last big payday, challenged the winner. It was a furious bout with Wiggins showing great speed and skill and even employing some of Greb's famous tactics learned in their previous meetings. Greb, as was his custom, came on after three rounds and began to punish Wiggins, cutting him above the eye and leaving him with a bloody mouth at the close of the contest. Most of the observers felt that Greb deserved the decision but a few dissenters argued that a draw would have been fair.[24] The referee, E. W Dickerson, sports editor for the Grand Rapids Herald, unofficially declared Greb the winner in his column the following day. Dickerson called it the fastest six rounds ever fought.[25]

Greb hopped out of the ring, quickly changed, and followed Dempsey into the ring to act as a second. After the usual announcements and introductions were made, Dempsey proceeded to go after Miske with the single minded purpose of finishing the fight quickly and mercifully. Gone was the ferocious scowl which had become a trademark of the champion. In its place was a sober, calculating look which betrayed the rather poorly kept secret that this bout was less about a championship and much more about charity. Dempsey quickly and easily ended matters in the third round. Before Miske had regained his feet following the final knockdown many of the spectators had begun to file out of the arena muttering "set-up," "it was framed," and other such exclamations of dissatisfaction.[26]

It was the almost unanimous opinion of ringsiders that the Greb-Wiggins bout had stolen the show. It certainly garnered the largest applause. Many of the sportswriters and spectators publicly stated

Facing page: E. W. Dickerson, referee for the undercard bouts of the Dempsey-Miske fight, is photographed here just before the start of the preliminary. Top: Harry Greb (right) is on the attack against Chuck Wiggins in this rare photo from their semi-final match to Jack Dempsey's championship defense against Billy Miske. Above: Jack Dempsey looks on as a forlorn Billy Miske tries to beat Referee Jimmy Daugherty's count after suffering a knockdown. Miske would go down in defeat midway through the third round.

Ted Jamieson
M LWAUKEE, WISC.

A match with Georges Carpentier had been proposed for the winner of the rematch between Greb and Ted Jamieson (above) but more important to Harry was to prove to the public that he could take Jamieson's measure.

that Greb or even Bill Tate would have posed a much greater threat to the champion than Miske, who appeared a shadow of his former self. "Dempsey couldn't do anything with me in the gym, and he was trying." said Greb the week after the fight. "We used eight ounce gloves and not the big pillows a lot of people seem to think. I just kept him busy moving around and scored at will. They took movies of Jack working out every day, but they never took any of my bouts with him, because he didn't show to any particular advantage when I speeded up and used the old footwork and threw a barrage of gloves. However, I don't think Jack would want to box with me in a regular fight just now. We got to be pretty good chums when we were together, and unless business demands, there is no reason why we should quit enjoying our friendship to go through a bout. Nevertheless, I am confident from my showings with Jack that he can't do anything with me."[27]

Red Mason returned to Pittsburgh with Harry ecstatic with the results of their trip. Greb had received wonderful press due to his showing against Dempsey in the training ring which led Mason to surmise that Dempsey and Greb would meet for the championship within the year. Mason had also succeeded in signing Greb for a rematch with Ted Jamieson in Jamieson's hometown of Milwaukee on September 22. It would be an opportunity for Greb to avenge the knockdown he suffered against Jamieson the previous month. There was also the added incentive that Georges Carpentier had instructed his American liaison, Jack Curley, to enquire about arranging a match with the winner of Greb-Jamieson in Milwaukee in November.[28]

With so much to look forward to Greb was a veritable wave of destruction against Jamieson. He punched holes in the Milwaukee Scot from long range but fearing disqualification he refused to fight in close which drew the ire of the audience. When assured by the referee that the rules of the state allowed infighting Greb went to work on Jamieson and gave him the beating of his young life. In the third the two fighters leapt at one another and the resulting collision of heads left Jamieson with a badly cut forehead that stained his chest a bright crimson. During the fourth round Jamieson sustained a broken right thumb (some accounts state the injury occurred as early as the second round). At the end of the fifth round Jamieson begged referee Houlehen to stop the fight. Jamieson agreed to continue but his showing was so pitiable that Houlehen was forced to stop the bout at the end of the sixth, awarding the fight to Harry on a sixth round technical knockout. Jamieson had failed to win a single round. Later that night X-rays confirmed that Jamieson had indeed suffered a fractured thumb.[29]

After the fight promoter Frank Mulkern presented Harry with a contract to meet Jack Dempsey over 10 rounds for $17,500 on October 26. Greb eagerly agreed when Mulkern added that his friend Dempsey had made him "a halfway promise" for the bout. "I know I can beat Dempsey in 10 rounds," stated Greb. Of course I will be spotting the champion in the neighborhood of 20 pounds, but others have done the same thing and got away with it and I feel I can turn the trick."[30]

If Dempsey could not be secured both Frank Mulkern and rival promoter Tom Andrews hoped to bring Georges Carpentier to Milwaukee to meet Greb. However, the potential bonanza was on extremely shaky ground. Doc Kearns was not interested in matching Dempsey so tough. Kearns had instead been pursuing a fight with Gunboat Smith in Boston for months without success. Carpentier had been in talks for a match with Battling Levinsky on the east coast with the ultimate prize being the light-heavyweight championship. The bout was finalized while Milwaukee promoters were still planning Greb's bout. If everything went to plan Carpentier would defeat Levinsky in sensational fashion to win the light-heavyweight championship setting up a mega-showdown for the heavyweight championship with Jack Dempsey the following summer. In order for this much anticipated match to take place Dempsey would need to continue his winning ways and as such Kearns saw fit to try to match him with men well below Greb's caliber.

Unable to get anyone to sanction a bout between Dempsey and Gunboat Smith who was now several years past his prime, Kearns turned his sights to Bill Brennan who Dempsey had already defeated once and whom Greb had beaten four times. Again, Boston refused to sanction the fight and for a time it seemed as if Milwaukee and Greb were back in the running. Mulkern's plans began to unravel when the state commission issued a statement declaring that they would find it difficult to sanction a bout between Dempsey and Greb due to the weight disparity.[31] When the Milwaukee Sentinel and Milwaukee Journal both jumped on the band wagon, calling for Mulkern to abandon his plans to match Dempsey with Greb, the fight fell apart.[32]

Trying to keep his fighter busy Mason signed Greb for a bout with Chuck Wiggins at South Bend, Indiana. Upon hearing that Gunboat Smith needed a top shelf opponent to prove his worth for a Dempsey fight, promoter Eugene Kessler made the appropriate long distance calls seizing the opportunity to increase the prestige of his event by promoting it as an elimination bout between Greb and Smith. In short, Wiggins was out and Smith was in. It was a natural match for both fighters. For Smith, Greb presented a world class opponent who, once beaten, would propel Smith to a shot at the title. For Greb it was another opportunity to remove a possible contender for the heavyweight championship from his path.

Smith had made a name for himself on the West Coast, bursting out of the training camps of former champions Jack Johnson and Stanley Ketchel to become a serious threat for the heavyweight championship. He was a tall, raw-boned fighter who combined solid skills, a sharp left jab, and a powerful right hand to climb to the top of the list of challengers for Jack Johnson's crown. That had been years ago though and by the time Jack Johnson had lost the title to Jess Willard down in Havana Gunboat Smith's best days were behind him. Smith had continued to face the best competition he could find, acting as something of a gate keeper in the division but by October of 1920 he was losing more than he was winning and seemed to be hanging on for one last big payday.

Floyd Fitzsimmons who promoted the Dempsey-Miske bout in Benton Harbor traveled to South Bend to make arrangements for the winner to face Dempsey.[33] Owing to such a great opportunity Red Mason asked for a postponement of one week from October 14 to October 21 in order to have more time to train. Extra seating had been arranged and a special section was being set up for Notre Dame students. Handling the sale of tickets to Notre Dame students was none other than legendary Notre Dame footballer George "The Gipper" Gipp,[34] who would die tragically two months later.

Despite the fact that Smith was in the waning years of his career he initially received more press in the South Bend newspapers and reigned a favorite in the betting odds due in large part to his former standing. One article even went so far as to refer to Greb as a trial horse for Gunboat Smith.[35]

As Greb and Smith prepared for their elimination bout another match was taking place in a Jersey City ballpark which would ultimately decide an opponent for Dempsey. Georges Carpentier met Battling Levinsky on October 12 in order to show his wares to a curious American public. In a one-sided bout Carpentier stopped Levinsky in the

Greb (above and facing page) as he appeared in training in 1919 or 1920.

fourth round, winning the light-heavyweight championship and placing him one step closer to a lucrative shot at the heavyweight title the following year. Immediately following the Frenchman's victory many fans and reporters intimated that the fix had been in.[36] It certainly seemed plausible. Levinsky had been easily brushed aside after showing up woefully out of shape with a paunch and double chin as if he had neglected to train for his biggest bout in years. Furthermore, the bout was a no-decision bout meaning that in order to retain his title Levinsky would merely have to survive to the final bell, a tactic the usually durable and defense savvy champion had been more than willing to employ in recent years to retain his title.

It had been obvious that Jack Curley, Carpentier's American representative, Tex Rickard, Jack Dempsey and Jack Kearns had been eager to match the Frenchman with the champion in a bout that would generate hundreds of thousands of dollars, if not millions. The problem was that despite Carpentier being an extremely bankable fighter he had done little of late to earn him a shot at Dempsey and lacked credibility with most Americans. That's where Levinsky came in. If Carpentier could not only win in an emphatic fashion against Levinsky but also annex a championship in the process he would gain instant credibility and jump ahead of several fighters to the top of the list of potential heavyweight title challengers.

An investigation was ordered into the fight after the local commissioner stated publicly that he felt Levinsky had not tried to win the bout but nothing came of it and it was quickly forgotten. Such things are generally impossible to prove and so it was that Carpentier was now considered the front runner for a shot at the heavyweight championship.

With Carpentier's victory over Levinsky fresh on the public's mind Mulkern and Andrews continued to lobby for a match between the Frenchman and Greb. Andrews had been able to secure Greb's signature to face Carpentier and while on the East Coast to see the Carpentier-Levinsky bout hoped to sign Carpentier. Frank Mulkern had been in contact with Carpentier as well but was surprised to hear from the Frenchman's representatives that they felt Greb would not be competitive with Carpentier and thus refused to fight him. This met with a highly critical response from Milwaukee press. "Carpentier's refusal to box Harry Greb here on grounds that Greb could

not furnish enough opposition to make the match interesting is ridiculous and disgusting. 'Get the money and take no chances,' seems to be the motto of glittering Georges...

...We have a sneaking hunch that the Pittsburgh wild man would spoil whatever chance Mons. Carpentier has of getting for a goal by Jack Dempsey. Greb, despite his Paul Swan steps and apparent awkward style is a great boxer, and Carpentier would have to step his best to beat him over a route of any distance."[37]

Greb and Mason arrived in South Bend via the New York Central Railroad on October 19. Gunboat Smith who had been training in Chicago with Captain Bob Roper arrived the following day and both fighters put the finishing touches on their workouts at the local Y.M.C.A.

Greb entered the ring first. As he marched up the aisle he told fans close by "I'm going to get him alright."[38] Gunboat Smith followed, entering the ring as the betting favorite. Harry weighed 165 pounds and the old Gunner was ten pounds heavier.

The bell signaled both fighters to the center of the ring. The two hopefuls spent a few moments feeling each other out for an opening. Harry pressed forward, while Gunboat seemed unwilling to engage. As Greb moved in Smith let fly a crisp right hand that Greb was able to get away from. Greb leapt forward on the attack, forcing Smith to the ropes with a vicious body attack that left the Gunner doubled over and gasping for air. Suddenly Greb swung a long left hook that caught Smith squarely on the right eye with such force that the eyeball was forced backwards out of its socket. The punch clearly hurt Smith who was now reeling around the ring in agony with Greb in hot pursuit, showering Gunboat with blows. Smith tried to find sanctuary in a clinch but was quickly parted by the referee. A final chopping right hand sent Gunboat to the canvas. Smith rolled around in agony as Referee Ed Smith of Chicago tolled the fatal count. The time was two minutes of the first round.[39]

When the stunned audience finally realized that the fight was over they began to shout and complain that the fix was in. This quickly changed when it was realized that Smith was in serious distress and a doctor was called from the crowd to attend the stricken fighter. The right side of Gunboat Smith's face was an ugly swollen mass and the left side was beginning to swell as well. The doctor ordered that Smith be taken immediately to a clinic and feared that he may lose the eye completely. In later years Smith would claim it had been a thumb which did the damage but shortly after the fight he remarked "Greb hit me harder last night than either Carpentier or Dempsey hit me when I fought them. That poke in the eye was one of the hardest I ever got, and it stopped me on the spot."[40]

After the fight with Gunboat Smith Red Mason and Floyd Fitzsimmons met at the Oliver hotel to discuss terms for championship match against Jack Dempsey at Benton Harbor. Nothing was set in stone but both Mason and Fitzsimmons remained hopeful that they could acquire the champion's services for a match with Greb. Tom Andrews and Frank Mulkern maintained hope that one of them could match Carpentier and Greb in Milwaukee. Greb was eager for the match but it seemed unlikely the Frenchman would risk losing the Dempsey bonanza as a result of a possible loss. So the only thing left for the team of Greb and Mason was to bide their time, book fights, and keep winning.

After leaving South Bend Harry and Red paid a short visit to Cleveland and then returned home to Pittsburgh. Shortly after arriving in Pittsburgh Greb suffered a painfully swollen ingrown toenail which caused the postponement of his planned fight with local heavyweight Mickey Shannon. Shannon had been born Raymond J. McMillan in 1897 near Frostburg, Maryland and became a standout baseball and football player while attending Staunton, West Virginia military academy. It was during this time that he began his first tentative forays into the world of boxing by facing far more experienced fighters in Fay Keiser and Al Grayber. After losing both of those fights by knockout he concentrated on football and baseball and by the time the United States was ready to enter the Great War Shannon left the

Despite weighing little more than a light-heavyweight Gunboat Smith had for years been a top contender for the heavyweight championship, and even claimed the White Hope Heavyweight Championship. Smith sported a powerful punch but was on the downside of his career when he faced Greb in 1920.

academy to enlist. Shannon enlisted in the army and was stationed at Camp Gordon where he met Mike Gibbons, the camp boxing instructor.

After the war Shannon moved to Pittsburgh to work at Carnegie Steel. At night Shannon appeared in local boxing bouts to supplement his income. Charles Kolb, a local boxing personality who had relocated to New Jersey, took notice of Shannon's promise and brought the young fighter to New Jersey to concentrate on boxing full time. On July 21, 1920 Shannon knocked out Ed Williams on the undercard of the bout between Captain Bob Roper and Charlie Weinert. When Weinert was unable to continue due to a foul Shannon, who had been watching from the audience, volunteered to take Weinert's place and defeated Roper. The two victories in one night caused something of a sensation and Shannon's career seemed to be on the fast track.

Greb and Shannon finally met on October 28 and Shannon, weighing 191 pounds, immediately set about using his twenty-seven pound weight advantage by wading into Harry and

Mickey Shannon was a short, powerfully built heavyweight. He was an excellent all-around athlete who was making rapid strides in boxing when he suffered a setback at the hands of Greb and died tragically after a match later that year.

forcing the fighting. Greb, instead of dancing and leaping around the ring, oddly elected to stand toe-to-toe with the heavyweight which allowed Shannon to have great success in the first and second rounds. In the third Shannon continued to back Greb up but instead of the much smaller man wilting under the pressure it was Shannon who seemed to be tiring as Harry continued to stand his ground and trade punch for punch. By the close of the third round Shannon had slowed perceptibly. Harry took over in the fourth and from this point on did not take a backward step. In the seventh he suckered Shannon in by feigning weakness and then suddenly lashed out with a powerful right hand that landed high on the head and sliced open Shannon's eyebrow. In the ninth a short left hook dropped all of Shannon's 191 pounds to the canvas for an eight count. The final round saw an exhausted and bleeding Shannon being battered from pillar to post and glad for the final bell.[41] Florent Gibson, writing for the Post, pointed out that Greb seemed unusually willing to trade punches and extended the theory that Greb was out to hurt Shannon;[42] it was later discovered that Greb and Red Mason had wagered that Greb would stop Shannon inside of ten rounds.[43] Gibson later noted that in his opinion the fight should have been stopped as early as the sixth round to save the young prospect unnecessary punishment.[44]

Despite winning handily the fight had been taxing enough that Harry was compelled to postpone a match the following day against Bartley Madden in Kalamazoo, Michigan. The Michigan commission took offense to Red Mason's handling of the affair and demanded Greb's appearance on the 10th of November. "You will have to box Bartley Madden of New York in Kalamazoo November 10, according to your contract, post $300 forfeit at once, have expenses of postponed fight deducted from your contract price or be barred from boxing in all states that control boxing through commissions. You must be in Kalamazoo by Monday November 8. Wire answer to us today, also to Kalamazoo Athletic Association," stated the telegram from the Michigan commission.[45]

"I am not in the habit of saying much before a bout takes place," said Harry on the eve of the fight. "I prefer to do my talking afterwards. I am going to show Bartley Madden tonight that I did not "run out" on the former match as he seems to think. I know he is a top-notcher but I figure it will be all the more to my credit to dispose of him for that very reason. No one needs to worry about me. I'll be right there at the finish and be perfectly able to take care of myself all the way through the bout."[46]

Before a capacity crowd, which included Mildred Greb, Harry punched holes in Bartley Madden. Harry weighed 167^1/$_2$ to Madden's 185 but the difference in weight mattered little. It was a vintage Greb performance with Harry all over his man and only the legendary toughness of Madden and his dangerous right hand making the fight interesting.[47]

The next day Red Mason, Mildred, Bill Sweeney, and Harry began the journey south to New Orleans for a November 15 fight against New Orleans' top middleweight Happy Littleton. When the Greb retinue arrived in New Orleans they immediately set about arranging for quality sparring to prepare Greb for Littleton, who had been making a great name for himself since losing a twenty round decision to Martin Burke the previous year. Mason immediately introduced his young fighter to a heavyweight he would be working with. It was Jack London the fighter Greb had faced in his first bout in New York City three years earlier. London had grown into a heavyweight and had recently relocated to New Orleans in search of fights. In his first sparring session with Harry he was knocked out inside of one round and thereafter refused to spar with his former adversary.[48]

For nearly fifteen years Bartley Madden served as a gatekeeper in the light-heavyweight and heavyweight divisions. Sporting an iron chin and a powerful right hand Madden was a stiff proposition for all but the best.

When he wasn't training Harry and Mildred spent time seeing the sights of the Big Easy. Mildred had been eager to see the French Quarter and was no doubt enjoying this time with Harry. She had been busy rearing the couple's daughter and now that Dorothy was a year old she was able to stay with Harry's family while Mildred got away with Harry for what was a much needed vacation from the everyday rigors of a lonely housewife.[49]

The fight with Littleton was cancelled due to threatening weather though Harry and Red Mason agreed to return at a later date if the match could be rescheduled.

Greb and company quickly boarded a train and headed 1,000 miles north for Milwaukee where Harry was signed to face Bob Moha on November 22. With Georges Carpentier back in France and Jack Dempsey likely to face Bill Brennan at Madison Square Garden in December, Frank Mulkern had exercised his contract with Greb to face the best opponent that could be acquired. Whether Moha fit that description at this point in his career is debatable but it was at least hoped that he would present Harry with a formidable challenge.

A few days before the fight Eddie Kane, manager of Tommy Gibbons, arrived in Milwaukee to issue a challenge for the winner to face his fighter. "I truly believe either Gibbons or Greb has the necessary ability to whip Dempsey," said Kane. "Either one of the boys is faster than Jack and it is my opinion they can outpoint him any time they meet."[50]

Mildred watched from ringside as Harry used his speed of hand and foot to dominate Moha, winning nearly every round and cutting Moha's lip severely in the process. Weighing an unusually high 170^3/$_4$ (a pound heavier than the stocky Moha) one wonders if Greb was taking a working holiday with his young wife. As Greb smiled and danced throughout the contest, amusing himself and putting on a show for the audience, Moha became increasingly frustrated and bewildered. At times he became so befuddled that he simply froze, staring at his opponent and absorbing punishment.[51]

The next day Bob's brother, acting as manager, met Harry and Red. "Fine cut you gave Bob when you bumped him with your head," said Vincent.

"Bumped heads, eh??" replied Greb. "You mean I hit him with the gloved hand, not once, but many times."

"Well, I have $2,000 here to say you can't do it in a 20 round bout at 160 pounds; yes, 162 pounds. I will get a club to stage it," said Vincent.

Growing angry, Harry replied "Look, I have been easy with Bob, but here, (turning to Mason), let me have $1,000 to call this bird."

Both men handed their stake to T. S. Andrews who looked on as the two men argued. "Now the weight must be 160 at 3," said Vincent.

"Say," said Harry, "before we go any further we will make the bet $5,000 and meet in a private room to a finish, or any way you want it. The weight will be what you suggested -162 pounds -and that goes any time."

Vincent Moha withdrew his roll of bills and placed it back in his pocket. "Yes," said Greb, "and any time you have $5,000 to spare just put it up and I will be ready for Bob and all the light heavyweights or middleweights around. Money talks and my money is ready."[52]

Harry and Bob Moha never again faced one another across the ring as adversaries. Apparently Vincent thought better of matching his brother against a man he had never beaten in six fights for $5,000 a side.

Harry and his entourage returned to Pittsburgh the next day. Within days of returning Greb had agreed to appear in an exhibition bout against Jack Burke to celebrate the reopening of the

Pittsburgh Lyceum where Harry routinely trained. Harry even agreed to act as boxing instructor for the newly remodeled establishment. It was just one example of Greb giving back to his community which included sponsoring a local semi-professional football team: Harry Greb's Fort Pitt Eleven, and donating thousands to local Catholic churches.

As Harry prepared for his next bout against Jeff Smith at Motor Square Garden in Pittsburgh he was reminded of the danger inherent in his profession. His recent opponent Mickey Shannon languished in a coma at a Jersey City hospital, the result of a bout against Al Roberts of Staten Island. Mickey was winning the fight going away after four rounds. He had dropped Roberts in the fourth with the bell saving the New Yorker from a possible knockout. Roberts roared back in the fifth and quickly dropped Mickey for a nine count. From that point on Roberts battered Shannon. Early in the sixth Roberts again dropped Shannon after a particularly vicious assault. In falling Shannon struck the base of his skull. After the referee had tolled the fateful ten count ringside doctors rushed to the stricken fighter's aid. One of Shannon's seconds, Al Thomas, was helping manager Charlie Kolb to administer to Shannon. He asked several times, "How do you feel, Mickey." Suddenly Shannon's eyes opened and he answered, "All right, Al." He then slipped into a coma and never regained consciousness. Ray MacMillan, professionally known as Mickey Shannon, died the following day of a brain hemorrhage.[53]

The same day that Shannon passed away Jeff Smith was forced to back out of his bout with Harry and promoters quickly substituted Jack Duffy as his opponent. Despite coming highly recommended by the likes of Tex Rickard, Sam Langford, and Jack Dempsey Duffy was a poor opponent for a fighter of Greb's caliber. More of a sparring partner than an actual contender, Duffy was a poorly skilled fighter whose chief weapon was a respectable right hand. He had bounced around the Midwest fighting mainly out of Chicago (which is probably where Langford became associated with him) before finally ending up in New York where a couple of impressive knockout wins over lesser competition garnered him the small bit of attention that led to his bout with Harry Greb. The Motor Square Boxing Club realized that Duffy was a less attractive opponent than the ultra-talented Jeff Smith and offered refunds to any patron not wishing to have their ticket honored. Greb's fans were so anxious to see him in a local ring again that not a single refund was requested, as it turned out they probably should have. Harry continually battered Duffy, who offered absolutely nothing in the way of competition. It was said that Duffy was likely the worst opponent Harry had ever faced in a local ring. Duffy was dropped twice in the fifth, the last knockdown seemed a sure finisher but the bell ending the round saved Duffy who never-the-less refused to come out for the sixth round. Greb could have finished his man at any stage of the fight but merely chose to toy with him, battering his features mercilessly so that by the fourth round Duffy was a swollen bloody mess. Duffy landed only one blow during the fifteen minutes of fighting and went several months believing he was suffering one or two broken ribs from the fight.[54]

Three days after Greb battered and toyed with Jack Duffy, Jack Dempsey defended his heavyweight championship against another of Harry's victims, Bill Brennan. It was expected to be a relatively easy fight for Dempsey. The champion after all was a man killer who demolished his opponents and Brennan was a journeyman often lost in the vast stable of fighters managed by Leo P. Flynn, who had lost four of four fights to a middleweight (Greb) and had in fact already been defeated by the champion in 1918.

Yet Brennan had learned quite a bit from his disastrous first fight with the champion. He trained with some of the best sparring partners available and promised to give the champion the fight of his life.

Dempsey and his manager Doc Kearns had hoped for a short, decisive knockout to maintain the myth of the champion's invincibility. He had to know he was in for a much longer night and tougher fight when in the second round he was rocked with right hand counters from the challenger. Brennan was mapping out the strategy that would eventually be used to take the title from Dempsey: Keep him on the end of a sharp jab and blister him with left hooks, and right hands when he tried to bull his way past the jab. When Dempsey was able to work his way in close to land his damaging short punches Brennan would tie him up until the referee separated the men.

The fight was a close and unexpectedly competitive one when in the tenth round Brennan landed a powerful right to the side of the champion's ear splitting open the scar tissue and spilling blood down the champion's neck and over his shoulder. In the eleventh Brennan cut Dempsey's mouth and by the end of the round had the blood smeared across the champion's face. Despite inflicting such injuries on Dempsey Brennan was fading fast and in the twelfth he succumbed to the champion's vicious body attack.[55]

It had been a close shave for Dempsey, whose reputation had suffered slightly from what was one of the more difficult fights of his career. Brennan was more popular than ever and eager to meet the champion again, feeling he could further improve upon his performance. The day before the fight John McGarvey and John Bell, representing the Motor Square Boxing Club, personally offered Jack Kearns $50,000 with a privilege of 50 percent of the gate for Dempsey to face Greb but

Rudolph Prevratsky, who fought professionally as Jack Duffy was a fairly obscure Chicago middleweight who happened into a fight with Greb when Jeff Smith was injured, forcing a postponement.

after such a taxing defense the champion was in no mood to negotiate and could think of little but getting his ear looked at by a specialist and heading home.[56]

Rather than wait for an opportunity to face the champion, as Brennan did, Greb continued his hectic schedule. On the twenty-first he would face Captain Bob Roper in Boston and on Christmas day he would face Jeff Smith at Motor Square Garden in Pittsburgh.

Roper was riding a wave of popularity due to a highly publicized points victory over Bob Martin, former A.E.F heavyweight champion, who was being groomed for a shot at Dempsey. Roper's skills had improved under the tutelage of Jack Blackburn and he was making news by touting his new found belief in the power of psychological warfare. He would employ these tactics throughout his career by entering the ring with a shaven head, or a snake around his neck, or a skull and crossbones sewn onto his trunks, in hopes of unnerving his opponent. It was in Boston that Roper had defeated Bob Martin and the Faneuil Club which was promoting the Greb-Roper bout hoped to match the winner with either Dempsey or Bill Brennan.

The pairing of Greb and Roper had been so highly anticipated in Boston that local police were forced to halt the sale of tickets and by the time the doors opened more than two thousand eager fans were turned away. It was a packed house, estimated to be the largest indoor crowd in the history of Boston boxing, which featured many of the lights of Boston society. Before the bell for the first round had ceased to sound Harry was in Captain Bob's face with a volley of blows and never let up.

The advice of Blackburn, a former Greb victim himself, did little to help Roper who round

Bill Brennan (right) spears Jack Dempsey with a long left. Despite having been beaten easily by Greb four times Brennan gave Dempsey arguably the most difficult fight of his seven year reign by punishing the champion on the outside with jabs and straight rights while checking the champion's infighting with precision uppercuts and strategic clinching.

In 1920 Captain Bob Roper (right) sought the guidance of past master and former Greb victim Jack Blackburn (left) whose long career was now winding down and giving way to a career as a trainer, culminating in the rise of Joe Louis.

after round was snowed under by a veritable blizzard of boxing gloves. "Take the fight to him and back him up," implored Blackburn. "Keep him on the run, it's the only chance you have of beating this bird." Eddie Long, Roper's manager sat in stunned silence, unable to believe that his fighter was a mere plaything in Greb's hands. Greb's corner stood in stark contrast. Red Mason paid little attention to the fight, talking and joking with ringsiders, supremely confident that Harry would easily defeat his larger opponent.

Harry started so fast that even his most ardent fans questioned whether he would be able to maintain the pace but he actually fought the tenth round faster than the first, with each successive round a repetition of the one before. In short, Greb won in dominant, one-sided fashion. Boston sportswriters agreed that Roper had failed to land more than a dozen blows on his rival in the thirty minutes of fighting.[57]

After the fight Greb and Mason left for Pittsburgh on barely speaking terms. Greb and Mason usually accepted a guarantee with a privilege of the gate but on this occasion Red Mason accepted a flat guarantee. Eddie Long, on behalf of Bob Roper, accepted a percentage of the gate and when the receipts were counted from this record breaking attendance it was found that both Roper and the promoters made more than Harry, who was furious at Mason for taking such a foolish gamble.[58]

The bout with Jeff Smith was heavily promoted on the hopes that Smith would stand and fight Greb instead of crawling into his defensive shell as he had done in their previous bouts much to the consternation of those who wanted to see a real fight. As it turned out, Smith once again showed marvelous defensive ability but only flashes of his true fistic brilliance. Round after round Greb piled up points often inviting Smith to trade blows or leaving himself open in hopes that Smith would initiate an offense but the Bayonne battler steadfastly refused and was at times booed.

After the fight Smith remarked to William Peet, sports editor for the Pittsburgh Dispatch: "I

GREB LANDS AT WILL IN HIS BOUT WITH CAPT ROPER

His Punches, Delivered From All Angles, Puzzle the Chicago Heavy—Crowd of 8000 See Battle Here

would rather battle Jack Dempsey than Harry Greb. He violates all the rules of the ring and gets away with it. In the tenth round I saw a chance to shoot in a right uppercut and put all my weight behind the blow. It landed flush on Greb's chin, but did not bother him for a minute. He came back at me like a ton of bricks and I was forced to cover up to protect myself."[59] Cover up he did and when the fight was over it was up to Smith and his manager to come up with an excuse for yet another sorry showing against Greb.[60]

With the Smith fight behind him and the year at an end Harry could concentrate on where his career lay. He was frustrated that despite being one of the biggest draws in the sport and well known across the country he was no closer to his dream of winning a championship. He was no closer to the big money fights he craved. Despite defeating several of the best fighters in the world across three weight divisions he felt his career was stagnating and it was time to make a change. Harry decided that he would celebrate the birth of 1921 with a change in management.

16

A PARTING OF THE WAYS

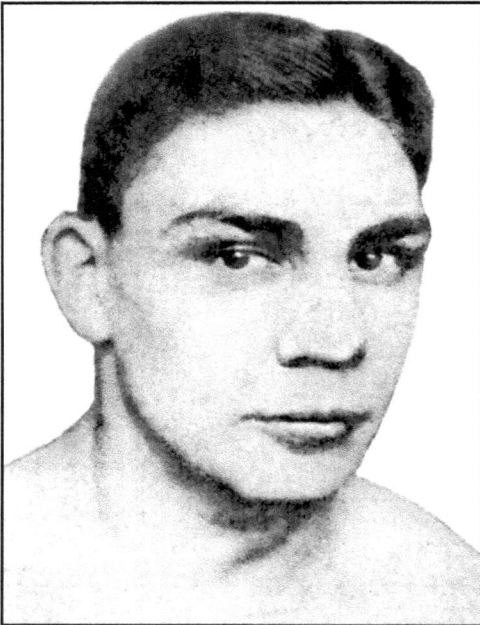

Harry as he appeared in early 1921, probably taken in Boston in January or February.

The news had spread through Pittsburgh's boxing community like wildfire. Harry Greb had, for all intents and purposes, fired Red Mason as his manager. There had been grumblings from Harry for some time now but few expected such a change. It seems that the change was precipitated by Mason's inability to get Greb a shot at the title, any title. The last straw was Mason's handling of the purse for the Roper bout.

"Yes, it is true we have quit," said Harry. "The constant wrangling and quibbling got on my nerves and as Mason seemed to have no particular interest in me other than the money which I brought him, I thought it best to bet someone else. I have been fighting now for eight years and have never gotten into the big money class, although I have beaten the best fighters in the world with the exception of Dempsey. I am 26 years of age and have but a few years more to go, and if I don't benefit now I never will. In those eight years I have made but little money compared to the other fighters, and I mean to make use of the few years remaining to get enough so that when second raters begin to beat me I'll have enough to retire and go into business,"

"When Mason first took me eight years ago he had a contract with me calling for 40 per cent. This continued until a couple of years ago when it was reduced to one-third. During this time I averaged 30 fights a year, and in most of them got less money than the man I defeated. I was all right as long as I could fight, but when injury or illness forced me to layoff for a while Mason never came around. In the match with Gibbons which was to be held in New York soon, Mason said we were to get $4,500 which did not seem enough for me, as the fight here would be worth more than that and only be 10 rounds, without a decision. Other fighters are getting big money under the 15-round decision bouts in the East, and I feel that I am able to stand up before any of them. Mason did not want to make these matches, apparently, and I wanted to go there and cut in."[1]

Red always had a rocky relationship with his fighters but most agreed that there was no one in Pittsburgh who could keep them as active as Mason. Activity to a fighter in the teens and twenties meant money and Mason was a genius when it came to getting his fighters work. The problem was that Mason seemed to have a fairly limited grasp when it came to taking a fighter to the next level. He had brought fighters to the brink of superstardom in the past only to watch them burn out before realizing their potential. In Harry he had a fighter who had been a contender for more than 3 years but for whom a truly big money bout or a title shot always seemed just out of grasp, despite the fact that Harry was recognized as a leading contender in three of boxing's eight accepted weight divisions. The question now would be who could help Harry break into boxing's big time, and the answer was right under the noses of Pittsburgh's fight fraternity.

Greb's new manager George Engel (left) piloted Frank Klaus to a middleweight championship. He is seen here with Frankie Madole (center) and Klaus in Paris sometime in 1912.

When it was announced that George Engel would be replacing Mason the match seemed a no-brainer. Engel, like Mason, was a Pittsburgh native who had boxed back in the rough and tumble days when matches were held in the back rooms of saloons or on barges in the Monongahela River to avoid police intervention. In fact Harry had been associated with Engel during his ill-fated trip to Philadelphia in the winter of 1914/1915. Engel had worked Harry's corner during his fight with Borrell in which Harry had been so badly abused. With his ever present cigar, Engel was the quintessential old time fight manager who had already piloted one of Pittsburgh's natives, Frank Klaus, to a middleweight championship and in so doing had developed contacts from coast to coast and even in Europe. If Greb wanted to break into the big time in New York, Engel knew who to talk to. If Greb wanted to spend a winter in

California fighting four-rounders for easy money, Engel had the contacts. If Harry wanted to go to Paris and negotiate a fight with Carpentier, Engel could take him.

When informed of Greb's decision Mason feigned relief. He argued that Greb had been a prima donna, demanding all of Mason's time, and jealous of any time Mason devoted to other fighters in his stable. It was a transparent attempt to conceal his anger at having been ousted and replaced by a longtime rival. Mason's true feelings were shown when he began a series of scathing attacks on Harry in print.

Harry seemed optimistic about his future with Engel and ready to start a fresh campaign. In two letters dated January 2nd and 6th, 1921 reprinted here without corrections Harry explained his position:

Dear Friend George,

Just a few lines to let know I have received your two telegrams and was glad to hear from you. The papers here give me a big write up the day I split from Red.

Well George how is every thing going I have been takeing a rest but will start in training today.

Duke Kelly while passing through called me up on the phone and told me they had me booked to box Leo Houck in Dallas Tex on January 14. I suppose Mason did not say anything about me leaving him and the club don't know any difernt. Anyway I am going to send you the address of the promoter and you can get in touch with him Mason told them one thousand and tickets would be o.k. but it is up to you now I really think he would be a good (illegible) is not enough money. But whatever you do will be o.k. the promoter address in Dallas Tex is Larry Meinert 1612 Main St. Dallas Texas

I will close for the time being

With Best Wishes

Your Friend

Harry Greb [2]

My Dear Pal George,

Your letter received today and was very glad to hear from you.

George I sure am glad I made the change I did in making you manager. Now since it is done I am really very happy and would not take twenty thousand dollars cash to go back to him.

He has his hamer out knocking already but everybody knows Red Mason.

Well George I have been training for the last four days and now I am in pretty good

Pittsburgh,Pa.,   December,30th, 1920,
Harry Greb of Pittsburgh Pa, now employs George Engel of
New York City as his business manager under the
following terms,

            FIRST. the said Greb is to devote all of
his ability as a boxer or otherwise to the carrying out of
this contract and is to assume no emplyment of any kind,
that shall not be considered as undertaken under and
controlled by this agreement,

            SECOND. This agreement shall continue in
force for a term of Two Years from date, unless sooner
dissolved by mutual consent,

            THIRD. The said Engel shall have all the
rights and all the powers and perform all the duties that
are usually had by a boxing manager,

            FOURTH.The said Greb shall receive SEVENTY
(70) percent of the net profits of this agreement and the
said Engel shall receive THIRTY.(30) percent thereof,

            FIFTH. From the Gross receipts of this
engagement shall be deducted the training expenses of said
sum, and any expence incurred by the said Engel in carrying
out this agreement, and the balance shall constitute the
net profits above referred to,

            SIXTH.In all matters of business policy
to be pursued hereunder the said Engel shall have the
controlling voice,

            The intention of this agreement is
that said Greb shall devote all his personal time and
efforts to the carrying out of the same, and the said Engel
shall act as his business manager, and in the construction
of this agreement where itsterms are in dispute or do not
cover the custom that usually prevails in such agreements
shall govern,

            Signed in duplicate,

GEORGE ENGEL

HAS TAKEN OVER THE MANAGEMENT OF

HARRY GREB

The Light Heavyweight
Champion of the World

HARRY GREB

GREB IS ONE CHAMPION WHO
BELIEVES IN WORKING AND IS
ALWAYS IN SHAPE AND FIT TO
FIGHT HE WILL FIGHT ANYBODY
FROM 165 POUNDS TO HEAVY-
WEIGHTS. ANY CLUB THAT WILL
GIVE GREB A REASONABLE
GUARANTEE TO CONVINCE US
THAT THE CLUB ITSELF HAS
SOME PATRONAGE. WE WILL BE
ONLY TOO GLAD TO GIVE THEIR
OFFER IMMEDIATE ATTENTION

WRITE, WIRE OR PHONE GEORGE ENGEL

PHONE WESTCHESTER 1528   2518 MACLAY AVE., BRONX, N. Y. CITY

Duplicate of the contract (left) entered into between Greb and Engel. The union was met with much enthusiasm as Engel had previously guided Frank Klaus to a middleweight championship and had excellent connections in the important East Coast market. Immediately after signing Greb Engel had promotional announcements (above) printed.

shape and from now on with about four days notice will be able to take on any fight you arrange.

If I were you I would get in touch with Tortorich in New Orleans as Mason had me matched with Happy Littleton for 15 rounds to a decision and he was to receive twenty five hundred with the privelidge of twenty five per cent of the hous with all expences, but I am sure you can get more than that.

I was talking to John McGarvey matchmaker of the Motor Club here and I give him your address he is going to get in touch with you for a bout with Tommy Gibbons he said he would give 33⅓ per cent of the hous but I think you can get a guarantee of five thousand with the privelidge that would be ten rounds no decision and I am sure I can beat him but try to get him to make one sixty three at three oclock the last time we were to do that weight but he lost his forfeit and I weighed in at one sixty one and he weighed 168 but still I beat him easy. I think it would be a good match for me here.

Well George how about the flat we are anxious to go to New York City and you and

I can work together better see what you can do for me to go there the first of next month.

That certainly was a nice write up Walter St. Denis had about you. Am enclosing a clipping out of the days paper what Mason said try to send a story in the papers here that I am a big booster for Pitts and that I will travel all over the world to box but it will always be Harry Greb of Pittsburgh and that will show that red headed bastard up.

Will come to an end hoping to get a long letter like this from you soon.

> Regards From
> Mrs Greb and Myself to you
> And your family,
> Harry Greb

The bills you got out are fine we will have som pictures taken later. Get my clipping books from Boston, Hugh McGregor has them.[3]

Five days later Harry was back in the ring, this time working in the corner of his sparring partner, Jack Burke, for the latter's bout with Young Bob Fitzsimmons. Burke lost the bout by trying to employ the same unusual style that had made Greb famous. Red Mason in attendance used the opportunity to criticize Greb for spoiling Burke's once promising ability.[4] For the past two weeks Mason had been trying to gain a measure of revenge against Harry by sending press reports to various local papers stating that Harry wanted no part of Tom Gibbons and that he would forsake Pittsburgh for New York in order to turn local sentiment against him. Harry was eager to refute such slanders to the point that he had it announced at ringside for the Fitzsimmons-Burke fight that he was "Harry Greb of Pittsburgh, who says he will always make Pittsburgh his home."[5]

As Mason waged his own private war against Greb, George Engel was busy lining up fights for his new charge. He had already been in contact with Johnny Wilson about a middleweight title shot. Wilson's demands were ridiculous ($10,000, forty percent of the gate, his own referee, Greb had to weigh 158 pounds and if he weighed over 158 Wilson would not accept a forfeit and would refuse to fight.)[6] prompting Engel to continue to line up busy work for Greb. First on their agenda would be an old acquaintance of Greb's from his early days.

Johnny Celmars had been born just three months after Harry in Pittsburgh in the neighboring Lawrenceville district. He turned professional a few months after Greb and like Greb quickly distinguished himself as an exciting young club-fighter. In late 1915 Celmars moved to Toledo, Ohio where for three years he faced some of the best local talent before joining the army during the war. After being discharged in early 1919 he resumed his career and headed west. When he was signed to face Harry in Dallas on January 20, 1921 he had been fighting mostly in California. Celmars had never really developed much beyond club-fighter status but he was a willing brawler who made up for his lack of skill with blood and guts determination. Harry remembered Celmars for his long string of early knockouts and one particularly rough training session.

An article in January 19, 1921 The Dallas Morning News provided great insight into Greb's feelings on the upcoming bout:

> "Celmars? I know him. He's a tough baby."
>
> This was the comment of Harry Greb of Pittsburgh on his arrival in Dallas yesterday afternoon on Johnny Celmars of Toledo, the opponent selected to face the Smokey City craftsman in a ten round go tomorrow night at the coliseum as the headline feature of the soldiers and sailors athletic club.
>
> Greb dropped off an afternoon train, chinned a few moments with the promoters, declared that he was ready to make weight, 162 at 3 o'clock and then milled through a lively workout at the Young Street Station. Greb has an old score to settle with Johnny Celmars. Johnny is the boy who is responsible for the fact that Greb wears gold teeth in the front of his mouth in place of the molars that nature bestowed upon him.
>
> "Johnny will have to come across with a dentist's bill for what he did to me six years ago," Greb said laughingly Tuesday night and that started fireworks.
>
> "Celmars and I lived in Pittsburgh together years ago and we used to work out together in the local gyms," He said. "This happened about six years ago, Johnny hooked a wild one into my jaw and knocked out two teeth and loosened another," He said "and the old boy is still loose." He said with a smile.
>
> The story dispels the general prevailing notion that he and Celmars are strangers. The two were hometown boys together and worked out together numerous times according to Greb's own statement.
>
> Greb was lavish in his praise of Dallas "You've got a real city here," He said. "I was sort of expecting a small town and when I got out of the station I thought I had got off at the wrong place." Asked concerning rumors that he was to box Dempsey Greb expressed himself somewhat reservedly "Well I'll tell you," He said, "and you can figure out the dope yourself. My former manager had promised to pay Dempsey $75,000 for a bout in Pittsburgh and we thought everything was settled by the signing when he backed out. He did the same stunt in another case when we guaranteed him $65,000 to fight me in Milwaukee. He refused to fight me. That ought to tell the story," He said "I'm willing to meet Dempsey at any time," He went on, "and don't bar him or any other man."
>
> Greb had a word of praise to say for Celmars and recalled the year when Celmars

had 15 straight knockouts in as many weeks. "He carries a stiff punch," He said "and if he can hit as hard as he could when I knew him years ago I don't care to have him catch me on the jaw."[7]

Speaking to the Dallas Times-Herald Harry made clear his thoughts on a bout with Dempsey:

"I stand ready to meet World Champion Jack Dempsey right now, anywhere in the world.

Three eastern clubs, Tex Rickard's, the Milwaukee Sporting Club, and St. Paul's A.C., have my signature to sets of articles to face Dempsey, but so far he has failed to live up to his verbal promise to give me a crack at his title...

Afraid of Dempsey? From the manner in which Jack is sidestepping me, it looks like the shoe is on the other foot. Dempsey's a fine fellow, but we're talking of his ring abilities. I have seen him in action in many of his bouts, have worked with him in his training, and I know that I can beat him...

Any good man who can keep away from Dempsey, who is able to occasionally get in and 'register' will get Jack's goat and after that the remainder should be easy.

To all aspiring challengers for Jack's crown, I would give this advice.

Side step him, make him miss-- and this is easy, in my opinion, carry the battle to say six rounds, and then you have him..."[8]

After speaking to the press Harry had a reunion of sorts with another fighter from his past. Tommy Burke, who had been defeated by Greb five years previous in Buffalo, had been fighting around the Dallas/Fort Worth area for the past several months. Burke now found himself staring once again across the ring at Pittsburgh's cyclonic contender and once again he found himself deposited on the canvas after a hard right hand during a five round sparring session.[9]

Greb was true to his word in his promise to punish Celmars. He constantly befuddled Celmars with dazzling speed and many times Celmars would spin around thinking Greb was behind him so fast was Greb's attack and ability to move around Celmars and out of harm's way. In the third round he opened a bad cut over Celmars left eye which bled throughout the contest. By the end of the fight Celmars had two badly swollen and bruised eyes which forced him to pay a visit to the emergency room. Both the Dallas Times Herald and Dallas Morning News estimated that Celmars hit Greb less than six times in the thirty minutes of fighting.[10]

After a brief return to Pittsburgh Harry headed with Mildred to New York where the couple would meet George Engel and travel from there to Boston to face Pal Reed. Reed was an aggressive southpaw who according to the press of the day had never been knocked down and had only lost once in his career and that being a close decision to current middleweight champion Johnny Wilson. A day or two before the match Reed suffered a cut lip in training and it was briefly feared that the bout would be postponed. When Greb faced Reed in the ring, seeing his damaged lip and the seventeen pound weight advantage that he held over Reed he decided to take it easy and simply outbox his smaller, injured, outclassed foe. Despite the fact that Harry let up on Reed many observers felt it was one of Greb's most brilliant performances and gave him much credit for his sportsmanship in refusing to attack Reed's injured lip.[11]

After the Reed fight Harry was forced to take a month off while George Engel recovered from a bout of the grippe. Meanwhile offers were pouring in for Greb's services. Promoters in New York and the Midwest were vying for a match between Tommy Gibbons and Harry but several details needed to be worked out before the two camps could come together. In the meantime Harry was scheduled to appear in Boston again on February 25 to face Jeff Smith once again. During the promotion much was made of an offer to have Smith face Georges Carpentier in Monte Carlo for $35,000 but two days before meeting Greb Smith received a telegram from Paris notifying him that Carpentier would not meet him for fear that it may jeopardize his upcoming bout with Jack Dempsey.[12] With Harry's recent showings in Boston against Bob Roper and Pal Reed still fresh in the minds of boxing fans ticket sales were brisk.

Harry arrived accompanied by a friend who would work his corner in place of George Engel who was still confined to bed. Greb was installed as the favorite but Smith was confident of victory despite having lost to Harry in all of their previous encounters. The crowd, which was estimated to be the largest indoor crowd to witness a boxing match in Boston's history, was treated to an excellent contest. Early on it seemed as though Smith might be able to get an edge on Harry by timing his rushes and landing heavily to the body or shooting hard uppercuts in close but as the fight wore on Harry's tireless attack and greater aggressiveness began to wear Smith down and while the fight was competitive Greb was awarded the decision unanimously by both judges and the referee.[13] Only Doc Almy, writing for the Boston Post felt Smith deserved the victory but was so criticized for his opinion that he was later forced to explain his position.[14]

After the fight Harry headed to New York to the visit his ailing manager. He walked in and dumped three thousand dollars in cash on his bed and said "Here's our dough!" He then sat in a chair by Engel's bed, keeping him company for hours and telling him not to worry about the business.[15]

While in Boston Harry was handed a challenge from a young Canadian heavyweight named Jack Renault. Renault implied that Greb was afraid to face him[16] and added that he was willing to face Harry in his Pittsburgh. Harry immediately agreed to put the young upstart in his place and Jim Routley of the Birmingham Club set about arranging the match for March 16 at Expo Hall .

Renault had turned professional in 1918 after spending a couple of years in the amateur ranks while working as a mounted policeman. In three years of fighting he had only suffered two defeats, one being a disqualification loss in his second professional bout. Late in 1919

Harry and Mildred are seen here in a photograph taken the day of his bout with Pal Reed in Boston.

Renault moved from Canada to New Bedford, Massachusetts where he began to gain more exposure. Standing six-foot-one and weighing nearly 190 pounds Renault was being billed as the light-heavyweight and heavyweight champion of Canada when Routley signed him to face Harry.

Harry entered the ring weighing 165 pounds, giving up twenty-two pounds and five inches in height but these disadvantages didn't deter him from bringing the fight to Renault. From the first round it was evident that Renault, who was a natural counterpuncher, was uncomfortable with Greb's aggression and speed. He showed himself to be big, strong, fast, and fairly skilled but none of these attributes helped to cope with Greb, who won the fight by a wide margin despite Renault's good showing.[17]

George Engel, still weak from his recent illness, left for New York immediately after the bout to continue his recovery. One wonders if Engel was present the following evening when Johnny Wilson successfully defended his middleweight championship against Mike O'Dowd. O'Dowd complained bitterly to the referee that Wilson was hitting low, head-butting, and had used an oil in his hair which blinded O'Dowd when rubbed in his face. When the split decision in favor of Wilson was announced O'Dowd wept openly.[18]

Harry Greb (third from right), is pictured here with his semi-pro football team the Golden Tornados of Garfield. In 1920 they had an impressive season winning six, drawing three, and losing one to Beaver Falls. Their greatest win that season was a 7-0 victory over neighborhood rivals the Bloomfield Tigers.

Harry was eager to get a crack at Wilson's championship but while Engel negotiated for the match he needed to stay busy and next on his agenda was the long postponed bout with Happy Littleton in New Orleans, scheduled for April 1st. Bartley Madden, who had been in town for a fight, offered to work with Littleton to prepare him for Greb since he had faced Harry twice before.[19] Fans were impressed with how well Littleton showed in sparring and were eager to get a glimpse of Greb, who had been delayed in Pittsburgh taking care of Mildred. Mildred had been increasingly suffering from illness over the past several months and was once again feeling the effects.

When Harry finally arrived two days before the bout he dazzled onlookers by offering his head to sparring partners and challenged them to hit him. By clever ducking and weaving he was able to avoid all the blows aimed in his direction.[20] He remained, as usual, supremely confident, treating the bout as little more than an after-thought, or a sparring session. When Littleton sent word to Harry that the fight would be on April Fool's Day and that Harry might be the one to get fooled Greb simply smiled, and yawned.[21]

When Greb and Engel arrived at the Auditorium they were greeted by another record breaking crowd. Nearly nine thousand people had paid just under $16,000 for admission. A jazz band was on hand to entertain patrons as they ambled to their seats. With the clang of the opening bell it was apparent that Littleton, despite all of his promise, hard training, and popularity, was in over his head. He fought gamely but Harry was too smart, too experienced, and far too fast. After the second round Littleton was lost amid a shower of blows and was scarcely able to find Greb to land one of his own. He was rendered so ineffective that one fan stood up to insult him and after the round Littleton made a half-hearted attempt to get to the man. He probably wished it was the heckler he was fighting and not Harry because with each successive round his face began to assimilate bruises and cuts from the constant torrent of blows. In the eighth round Harry began to let up but, game to the core, Littleton slurred through bloody lips, "come on, don't show me no mercy." Harry obliged and the one sided beating continued.

In the final round Happy was reeling and looked as if he may finally go down but he was saved by the bell. His handlers grabbed him and walked him to a neutral corner where he buried his face in his gloves as his knees shook with weakness. One eye was closed, and his lips were puffed but he could hang his head high knowing that he had gone fifteen rounds with one of the greatest fighters of the age.[22] "I believe I could have had four hands, and all of them brand new, and not beat him," said Littleton, "He is a great fighter and there's no one can take it from him."[23]

Harry and Engel returned to Pittsburgh via train on April 4th and spent just enough time in town to watch the fight between Whitey Wenzel and George Chip before they boarded a train

This photo was taken moments before Harry Greb's 15 round decision victory over Happy Littleton, April 1, 1921, in New Orleans. Left to right: Willie Sehrt (Littleton's manager), Happy Littleton, Referee Al Wambsgans, Harry Greb, and George Engel.

for Canada where Harry would face Jack Renault in Montreal and Soldier Jones in Toronto.

On April 6th, a mere five days after facing Happy Littleton, and nearly 2000 miles away, Harry fought Canadian heavyweight Jack Renault for the second time in less than a month. This time Renault and Greb weighed in at ringside before the fight with Renault sporting a fifteen pound weight advantage at 182 pounds. His greater height, weight, and reach proved to be of little refuge from Greb, who out-boxed Renault from the outside, out punched him from the inside, and even out-muscled the larger man whenever Renault attempted to tie him up.

In the second round Harry landed a blow that dropped the former Mountie and from which he never fully recovered. In the fifth Renault rushed Harry to the ropes and landed a hard right that shook him but the blow only served to anger Greb and he battled back so hard that he once again dropped Renault. When the bell rang ending the round Renault staggered drunkenly back to his corner. From then on it was all Greb and he was adjudged an easy victor.[24]

Greb and Engel stayed in Montreal until the day before his bout with Soldier Jones. Weighing six and a half pounds more than Greb, Jones was another heavier opponent sporting height and reach advantages who found Harry an unmanageable tyro in the ring. Greb started out slow, wary of Jones powerful right hand but in the second the contest broke wide open. Jones landed a powerful right to the body that sent Harry to the canvas. He sprang up quickly laughing sheepishly and continued out-boxing his rival. Jones said something angered Greb early in the third round and Harry, intent on punishing the Canadian, rained blows down on Jones, knocking him to the canvas four times before the close of the round. In the fourth Harry sent Jones to the canvas twice more before finally ending the contest with a third knockdown in that round. When the referee finished the count Harry picked Jones up and carried him back to his corner.[25]

As Harry and Mason mapped out a busy schedule Mildred traveled to Saranac Lake New York, considered one of the leading institutions for treating Tuberculosis. Her health had been rapidly failing and she had by now been diagnosed with Tuberculosis. By now she was rapidly losing weight, and experienced bouts of prolonged weakness, her skin was pale and feverish. Her nerves were often frayed, with Harry's long absences from home only compounding the stress.

The treatment of Tuberculosis at Saranac centered around the philosophy that strict bed rest and prolonged exposure to the cool dry mountain air would benefit those inflicted with the disease. To this purpose, rather than being a centralized institution, Saranac Lake was populated by small dwellings dubbed "cure cottages." These dwellings featured multiple open air porches upon which the patients would sit or lay in the open air for long hours with little to do but hope for an improvement or wait to die. It was a tedious, and often times depressing, way of life.[26] Mildred was treated at #67 Park Avenue,[27] a cure cottage which stands today as the Walker Cottage and is now on the National Registry of Historic Places.

Two days after the Renault fight Harry arrived in Pittsburgh and immediately approached

Above: Two photos of Mildred Greb, likely taken at the New Brighton summer home that doubled as Harry's training quarters in 1921

organizers of the all-star boxing card to benefit the destitute women and children of Ireland hoping the promotion could find room for him. The committee was eager to have him participate knowing that he was the greatest drawing card in Pittsburgh but they nettled Greb when they insisted he face a fighter such as Tommy Gibbons, Kid Norfolk, or Fred Fulton. Harry argued that he could draw down a huge sum of money facing opponents of that caliber in the east, particularly Tommy Gibbons who Tex Rickard was offering to match with Greb in Madison Square Garden for a princely sum. He certainly wasn't going to face a top contender for the $750 he was being offered.[28] When the committee demanded that Greb face a top contender or he wouldn't be on the card at all Greb walked away from the promotion and left Pittsburgh for Saranac Lake where Mildred was recuperating from her illness.[29] When the committee was approached by a contingent of Harry's fans asking them to reconsider they relented and Harry was matched with Bartley Madden in the final bout of the evening.[30]

In mid-April Johnny Ray and Johnny Dundee took part in a historic bout in Pittsburgh. It was the first boxing match ever broadcast live by radio which would revolutionize the sport. The fight was broadcast by KDKA in Pittsburgh using Florent Gibson as announcer. The broadcast was a novelty that ushered in a new era and it was decided that the benefit for the Irish would be broadcast live via radio for fans as far away as Maine and Mississippi.

Headlining a card which saw Fred Fulton knock out Jack Temple in the first round, and Johnny Ray outbox Charlie Dunn, Greb easily out-boxed Bartley Madden. He started out fast enough for the first two rounds but in the third round he opened a cut over one of Madden's eyes and from that point on he let up refusing to punish Madden too much, knowing that neither of them were being paid enough to kill each other. In the eighth and ninth rounds as the crowd grew restless Harry opened up a bit but slowed down again in the tenth and final round. Despite his lackadaisical performance Greb was easily considered the winner.[31] In six short months Madden would go on to administer a severe beating to Fred Fulton only to see Fulton receive a gift draw decision.

While Harry spent much of his free time training and attending to Mildred at Saranac Lake, George Engel had been busy behind the scenes arranging bouts for Harry. He had succeeded in signing Harry for a lucrative three fight deal with the Birmingham club against Johnny Wilson, Frank Moran, and Kid Norfolk at Forbes Field. As the details of this match were worked out Harry agreed to face Jimmy Darcy in Boston on Friday the 13th of May, followed by Jeff Smith in New Orleans on May 20th, and Chuck Wiggins at South Bend on May 28. With Johnny Wilson showing no inclination to face Greb it had been hoped that the match between he and Frank Moran could be arranged for the near future in a showdown of two of Pittsburgh's most celebrated fighters.

Jimmy Darcy was a bull strong, heavily muscled middleweight who was now being managed by Jack Dempsey's manager Doc Kearns. Kearns had high hopes of matching his newly acquired fighter with Johnny Wilson for the middleweight championship. He turned pro in 1915 fighting out of Portland, Oregon and eventually made his way south to California. In six years of fighting Darcy had met some of the most talented fighters in the game. He won some and lost some but always fought to the highest standard.

Darcy tried his hardest, he stood and traded with Greb, but Harry's speed, skill, and aggression were too much to overcome. In the second round he cut Darcy's mouth. In the fifth he opened a bad cut over his left eye and knocked him down for a five count. Most observers felt, like with many of Harry's previous encounters, that he could have knocked Darcy out but was content to carry him. It proved another easy decision victory for Greb and afterwards he and George Engel left for New York where they would take a connecting train south for his bout with Jeff Smith in New Orleans.[32]

Harry had signed for a fifteen round bout with Smith but Al Lippe, Smith's manager held out hopes that he could double cross Greb and have the distance changed to 20 rounds, believing that Smith's greater experience at that distance would give him an advantage. Mason and Greb argued that they had been contracted to fifteen rounds at a certain amount of money and if the distance was extended by five rounds the purse should also be increased. "That's the bunk they're handing out about Smith licking me in twenty rounds," Greb said angrily. "I'll fight him all night in a locked room, if I get paid for it, and the same thing goes for twenty rounds. My business is no different than the occupation of any other man. I get paid according to my contract. Insofar as me being afraid to go twenty rounds, that's silly. I'm younger than Smith and am sure that I can stand twenty rounds in this heat just as well as he can."[33] With promoters unwilling to increase Greb's purse the bout was kept at fifteen rounds.

Valeri Trambitas, otherwise known as Jimmy Darcy, was a strong and rugged middleweight from the West Coast. By the time he first faced Harry Greb in 1921 he had relocated to the East Coast where he joined Jack Dempsey's stable under Doc Kearns and hoped to win a title.

The bout was fought along similar lines to their previous five encounters with Smith fighting out of a defensive shell and looking for opportunities to counter Greb's attacks. When Greb closed the distance on Smith the New Jersey battler would invariably clasp Harry in a vice like grip. Despite all of Al Lippe's pre-fight bluster about knocking Greb out and wanting a longer fight Smith was being hissed by the audience and cries of "fake" where sent up. Smith, however, was very clever and quite successful at landing hard body punches in close. He was doing enough subtle work to catch the eye of experienced onlookers and when referee Wambsgans called the bout a draw at the end of 15 rounds the crowd was satisfied even if most felt Greb deserved a slight lead. Harry and his manager were furious and shouted "never again!" as they left the ring.[34]

The New Orleans Times-Picayune argued that while the fight was close Smith had done enough clean, clever, and classically styled boxing to win the fight. The New Orleans States felt it was Smith who was lucky to have escaped with a draw and the New Orleans Item stated that the draw was just but added that most felt Greb had deserved the victory.

Harry and George left New Orleans the next day for South Bend, Indiana where Harry would face Chuck Wiggins for the fifth time. Wiggins was determined to beat Greb and left no stone unturned in training. He worked out at White River, burning through sparring partners at an impressive rate. He knew the task ahead of him was a difficult one and trained accordingly. "Bet your money on me," he said. "I will show Greb more gloves than he ever dreamed of. That affair at Benton Harbor will not compare with this one when it comes to speed. Greb is a hard man to fight. You've got to figure him all out. He is so different from any other boxer and it takes experience with his style to master it."[35]

Harry and George arrived in South Bend on May 23 still fuming over the decision rendered in New Orleans against Jeff Smith. "Smith wouldn't box," he complained. "I hit him a hundred times in the early rounds and he continually clinched and held on. So I decided to fight him at his own game and resorted to infighting."[36] After a short rest he began his training by doing light roadwork. The following day Engel left Harry to his training and returned to Pittsburgh where he hoped to finalize arrangements for Harry to face Frank Moran.

The newly formed South Bend Athletic Club had hoped to draw a large sporting crowd by holding the bout on Memorial Day (called Decoration Day in 1921) in conjunction with the Indianapolis 500 races and a large track meet being held at Notre Dame. To add to the festive atmosphere it was hoped that Georges Carpentier, who had only recently arrived in the United States for his challenge of Jack Dempsey on July 2, would referee the match or at the very least attend. Carpentier had traveled to the United States with French race car driver Albert Guyot, who would be participating in the Indianapolis 500, and planned to travel with his friend to witness the races. An invitation was sent to Carpentier suggesting he stop in South Bend for the Greb-Wiggins bout but Carpentier's Indiana trip was quickly prohibited by Tex Rickard who didn't want anything unforeseen to happen to Carpentier that might jeopardize the promotion of the Dempsey fight.[37] With Carpentier out as a possibility the selection of the referee became much more difficult with the fighters unable to agree on a suitable arbiter. Finally Floyd Fitzsimmons was agreed on and the promotion could proceed.

As Dempsey and Carpentier trained for their bout speculation was rife as to whether Harry would join his training camp. Greb had made such an impression the two times he had visited Dempsey's training camp that many were eager to see he and the champ spar once again. Outwardly Kearns expressed a willingness to have Greb assist the champ, when pressed on the subject, and Greb was open to the possibility as well. "I am willing to assist Dempsey train to beat Carpentier,"

Harry fought Jeff Smith (above) twice in 1921. Greb won the first bout in Boston but three months later was awarded a bitterly disputed draw in New Orleans.

asserted Greb, "for I want to see the crown stay in America. I know Jack can easily whip the Frenchman if he is in condition and I will do anything to help him attain the best condition. After my bout here I will go to Atlantic City and spar with the champion."[38]

The day before the match with Wiggins Harry polished off his training with fifteen fast minutes of handball, four rounds of sparring, and twenty minutes of rope skipping and shadowboxing. When he finished he was as fresh as the moment he started and looked more than ready to do it all over again. He was in tremendous condition and he would need it. The South Bend News-Times was the only paper in South Bend to publish a Sunday edition and thus they were the only local paper to provide coverage of the bout:

In May and June of 1921 Greb faced Chuck Wiggins for the fifth and sixth times in his career. The South Bend News-Times called the first bout a draw. The Terre Haute Star awarded the second bout to Greb.

A lightning finish by Chuck Wiggins, Indianapolis light heavyweight battler, in the final round of their ten-round classic at Springbrook Park Saturday afternoon, brought the crowd of 1,500 to its feet yelling for a knockout and earned him a draw with Harry Greb of Pittsburg, his principal opponent for the light heavyweight crown.

The final round was the climax to one of the most hard fought, slam-bang, evenly matched battles ever staged anywhere and certainly for action its like has never been seen in South Bend. From the sound of the gong in the first round to the end of the tenth, the onlookers were kept on their toes, hardly daring to turn their heads to light a cigarette for fear a K.O. would be slipped over and they would "muff it." Instead of getting slower and slower as most fights do, it got faster and faster.

Going into the tenth round, Greb looked like a sure winner. The "rubber ball" from Pittsburg had been dealing out terribly telling blows to Wiggins' body from the third round on and had been pecking away at a nasty cut under the Hoosier boy's right eye which he had opened in the fourth frame.

He began his rushing, give-and-take style of milling in the very first round and neither wasted any time trying to feel the other out. Greb's tactics seemed to suit Chuck all right so he adopted a similar method himself. They stood toe to toe through the first four rounds, while fans wondered how long they could keep it up without one of them dropping. And if anyone had dropped in the early frames it would have been Wiggins for Harry clearly outpointed and outslugged him in addition to excelling in the infighting. Then too Greb's peculiar shifting attack and defense made it hard for the Hoosier to fathom where the next blow would come from.

The fifth round was a classic to watch. Wiggins stung Greb with his first real telling blow and it served to arouse the "dynamo's" ire. He cornered his blonde opponent and rained a perfect fusillade of blows at close quarters upon him. Wiggins returning each nearly blow for blow. Their gloves were working like pistons nearly the entire round, and old time fight fans characterized it as the fastest frame they had ever witnessed.

In the sixth Greb got Chuck in the corner again and it looked bad for the Hoosier as Harry was slipping in some socks that would have stopped most battlers. But Wiggins' remarkable forte for assimilating punishment served him in good stead and he managed to weather the storm. Again in the following round Greb looked as though he was about due to slip over the knockout. He got Wiggins coming in with a terrific left hook to the jaw and followed with a right and left to the midriff, but Chuck countered with two light taps and then clinched, managing again to survive the onslaught.

The eighth round was even with Wiggins showing remarkable stamina, in that his legs had as much spring as at the beginning and he still had plenty of courage to force the fighting. The ninth was a repetition of the sixth and seventh and was easily Greb's round as he drove home three of the stiffest jolts administered throughout the fight without return.

The final round goes to Chuck Wiggins who displayed his remarkable staying powers and courage then if ever. Greb came in fast when the gong sounded and ran straight into a hard left jab flush to the jaw which turned the Pittsburg star halfway around. It slowed Harry up for fully a minute during which time Chuck tried to retrieve the ground lost earlier in the fight. Greb came back strong during the last two minutes and he and Wiggins sure gave the bugs a thrill as they slammed each other all over the ring until the final bell sounded ending a wonderful scrap between two great battlers, neither of whom knows the meaning of the word "quit." Referee Fitzsimmons can testify to the truth of that.[39]

Harry and George headed to New York where they hoped to catch a glimpse of Georges Carpentier whose training camp was now in full swing. When they arrived they were greeted with a strange sight. Georges' camp was being conducted completely in secret. The audience allowed to watch his training was kept to a minimum, an odd strategy in a day when a fighter could greatly increase his income by charging admission to his training sessions. The press theorized that it was to keep secret the fact that Carpentier was not only overrated but had also been grossly overmatched against Dempsey. For his part Greb was not impressed by the Frenchman, who had surrounded himself with a sparring staff that, with the exception of the now ancient Joe Jeannette, was depressingly laughable. When asked who Greb was picking to win the July 2 bout he replied: "Dempsey is my choice for every cent I've got."[40] Greb offered to spar with Carpentier whose manager Francois Descamps smiled and declined.[41] Upon returning to Pittsburgh Greb was less diplomatic in his opinion of Carpentier "I watched Georges work out and I think he's a false alarm."[42]

When Dempsey was told of Greb's prediction the champion replied: "Harry ought to be a good judge of the way things will go in Jersey City. Greb is a classy Pittsburgher. If he says I'll win I guess he knows what he is talking about."[43] For the most part Greb was fairly open about his strong belief that Dempsey would demolish Carpentier in less than six rounds but on occasion he would enthusiastically argue with observers that the Frenchman would win. It was a ruse, slyly calculated to increase the betting on Carpentier and thereby increase any winnings Greb would receive when Dempsey won.

On June 24 Harry was back in Indiana to once again face Chuck Wiggins. This time the match would be held at Terre Haute under the auspices of the Terre Haute Athletic Club at the I.I.I. league athletic field. Wiggins was out for blood, feeling that Greb was overlooking him. "If Greb thinks he can box me and then jump right in and work with Dempsey he is badly mistaken," said Chuck. "I'll fix him up so he won't want to see a boxing glove for weeks. It looks to me as if he merely is trying to cheapen me and he can't get away with it. I'm in shape for the match and I'll shoot at him everything I have. And if he wants to get rough, well, watch me."[44] Greb denied looking past Wiggins. "I'll be in Dempsey's camp Wiggins or no Wiggins," said Greb. "But he isn't to be lightly held. Chuck can hold his own with any of the big boys, but, of course I believe I can whip him at any stage of the road."[45] The bout itself was, once again, closely contested with Harry being adjudged the ultimate victor. The Terre Haute Star gave three rounds to Greb, two rounds to Wiggins, and had five rounds even.[46]

As it turned out Harry would only be a part of Dempsey's training camp as a visitor. When Jack Kearns read the newspaper reports that Harry was on his way to help the champion train he promptly announced that Dempsey would not be needing any more sparring partners.[47] Further frustrating Harry were the erroneous reports emanating out of Boston that within days he would be facing Johnny Wilson. Greb had no knowledge of such a match and within a few days another bizarre report surfaced from Boston stating that the match was called off due to Greb's inability to make weight. It seemed that someone in Johnny Wilson's hometown wanted the public to think Harry could not be seen as a serious contender for the middleweight championship.

As the world waited with baited breath for what was sure to be the largest sporting attraction in history, Engel was hard at work finalizing details for Harry's all-Pittsburgh bout against heavyweight warhorse Frank Moran. The deal was finally agreed upon a couple of days after Harry's bout with Wiggins. The fight would be staged before the Birmingham Boxing Club at Forbes Field on July 18. Both Moran and Greb hoped the match would propel them to a title shot against the winner of the Dempsey-Carpentier match.

Before he was to face Greb Moran was scheduled to face Bob Martin in New York on the eve of the Dempsey-Carpentier bout. Martin, an ex-soldier, was extremely popular, having won the A.E.F. heavyweight title. He was being groomed for a shot at the heavyweight title by his wily manager Jimmy "Bow-tie" Bronson and many in the fight community were already speaking of him as a logical contender to the crown. If Moran could defeat Martin in New York on the eve of the championship contest and then return to Pittsburgh and defeat Greb it would be a major coup resulting in a well-spring of support for his championship aspirations.

Harry refused to take Moran lightly despite his long years of service. He intended to take a short trip to New York and New Jersey with Mildred where they would join George Engel in visiting Dempsey's training camp and then enjoy the big fight from ringside. After July 4th Harry would head to Brighton, where he owned a summer home, and set up training camp.

One of the first publicity photos of Harry taken after signing George Engel as his manager.

At Dempsey's camp Greb, looking sharp in a blue suit and silk shirt, watched intently as the champion worked, analyzing every move and studying the champion's armor for weak points. "Look at those shoulders," he whispered in awe.[48] Despite being impressed with Dempsey's physical appearance Harry felt Dempsey's condition and training left much to be desired. "I've just laid a $500 bet that Carpentier will not come up for the sixth round and I still think I'm going to win, but Dempsey doesn't look any too good. He missed too many punches there against O'Hare and Williams and his legs kind of sagged as he moved around. I thought he'd look better. When I worked out with him at Benton Harbor prior to his fight with Miske he was much faster on his feet and he hit more accurately. I think he's going to win, but I wish he was in better condition than he showed just now."[49]

Left to right: Harry Keck, unknown, Havey Boyle, Greb, unknown, and George Engel pose for a photo together on the occasion of visiting Jack Dempsey's training camp in late June 1921. The champion was busy at work preparing for his anticipated showdown with Georges Carpentier.

Harry and George spent three days visiting the Dempsey camp while they stayed at the lovely New Belmont Hotel right on the boardwalk in Atlantic City. On their second day at Dempsey's camp George and Harry brought their wives and introduced them to the champion before getting down to business. Engel and Kearns discussed a possible match between Dempsey and Harry to be held on Labor Day. Afterwards Engel immediately notified the Pittsburgh Dispatch that Kearns had promised Greb first crack at the champion if he defeated Carpentier.[50] While Engel and Kearns talked business Dempsey asked Harry if he would be interested in seconding him against Carpentier. Greb declined stating he intended to challenge the winner. "Down in my heart I feel that I can outpoint Jack in a 10 or 12-round fight," said Harry, "and down in his heart he feels the same way."[51]

Early on July 2nd what would be the largest audience to ever witness a sporting event began to file into the arena. It was a hot day punctuated by periods of drizzling rain. The undercard featuring seven bouts was slow and uninteresting but the crowd was buzzing with anticipation of the main event. The semi-final bout featuring Billy Miske and Jack Renault was put off so that the main event could start on schedule and avoid the rain which seemed eminent. Just before 3 o'clock a roar of excitement went up as the first strains of the French national anthem, played by a brass band on hand to entertain, pierced the arena. Then suddenly Carpentier, the war hero who held the hopes of his nation on his shoulders emerged followed by his constant companion and manager Francois Descamps. Moments later Dempsey himself came into view wearing his lucky red sweater, looking grim and serious.

When both fighters came into view it suddenly became apparent to ringsiders why

Carpentier had spent most of his training camp preparing in secret, far from prying eyes. True he looked every bit an athlete but his slender, pale frame seemed more suited to dancing than to absorbing the powerful punches that Dempsey was sure to deliver. In truth, the bout was a mismatch both on paper and in the ring. By and large Carpentier, throughout his career, had either lost to the best fighters he had faced (Klaus, Papke, Dixie Kid, etc.) or his major wins had been accompanied with some controversy (Gunboat Smith had in many eyes in been unfairly disqualified and Battling Levinsky had, according to some, thrown his fight with Carpentier). Simply put it was a bout that was too lucrative not to be made and too ludicrous to be competitive. Dempsey, who was a fast, durable, and skilled two fisted slugger had far too many tools for the relatively one dimensional Carpentier, who from his earliest days to his retirement fought out of a modified crouch from which he would leap in from long range, trying to land his admittedly dynamite right hand. If an opponent could take this punch, or avoid it consistently he could render Carpentier as ineffective as a child.

From the first round Dempsey's plan was apparent, as was the fact that he was easily Carpentier's master. He would rush in close under Carpentier's exaggerated jabs and right hands and deliver punishing body punches and illegal rabbit punches to the back of the head in hopes of slowly grinding the Frenchman down to a point where he could land his knockout punch which he had dubbed "Iron Mike." In the second round, after sparring for a bit, Carpentier finally found a home for his powerful long right hand. Dempsey wobbled and Carpentier followed it up with two more punches that sent Dempsey to the ropes on unsteady legs but his head quickly cleared and he was again fighting Carpentier on even terms. The third was a repetition of the first with Dempsey forcing Carpentier to fight hard. The end came abruptly in the fourth. Dempsey rushed out of his corner seemingly intent on finishing his overmatched opponent and after a short left-right combination Carpentier collapsed in a heap and looked to be finished but at the count of nine he sprang to his feet and rushed Dempsey only to be put down for the count with a hard right to the body.[52]

As the audience ambled out of the arena Miske and Renault fought an uninspired bout. "It ended just as I thought it would," Harry said to Bill Peet of the Dispatch after the bout. "Although I will say that Carp had Dempsey in a bad way during the second round. I am not bragging, but you can bet Jack will never sock me with "Iron Mike" if we ever meet and I sincerely hope we do very soon."[53]

Harry had extended his stay in the east so that he and George could enter into negotiations with Tex Rickard for a bout with either Jack Dempsey or Georges Carpentier, who had expressed an interest in fighting another American in October. Rickard held talks with Engel and agreed to consider Greb as an opponent for Georges. Also in the running for a match with either Dempsey or Carpentier was Tom Gibbons, who had put on weight since his last bout with Greb and was now in the midst of an eleven bout knockout streak that included the durable spoiler Willie Meehan. In order to consolidate his claim Greb offered to fight Gibbons

Frank Moran broke into professional boxing in Pittsburgh before moving east to gain wider attention. He had already challenged for the championship twice by 1921 when he he prepared for a much anticipated all-Pittsburgh showdown with Harry Greb which he hoped would propel him to another shot at the title against Jack Dempsey.

for the privilege of facing Carpentier.[54]

Eager to make an impressive showing against Moran Harry opened training camp at his summer home in Brighton Heights. He invited the local press to come out and watch him train in order to add some excitement to the promotion but almost immediately his training hit a snag. On July 12, in New York, Frank Moran fought Bob Martin, the bout having been postponed to that date so that it wouldn't have to compete with Dempsey-Carpentier bout. In the seventh round Martin landed a combination that dropped the red headed veteran flat on his back where he remained while the referee counted him out. Within days it was announced that the Greb-Moran bout was off.

With the Moran bout off the logical replacement would have seemed to have been Bob Martin but Martin's manager Jimmy Bronson refused to let Bob face Greb, admitting that Martin was not ready for such a test yet.[55] With Moran now deemed unsuitable, and Johnny Wilson still avoiding a fight with Greb, the only other option was the to fulfill his contract with the Birmingham club and face Kid Norfolk. The bout with Norfolk had been talked of for years. Since the match had first been suggested back in the summer of 1917 in Buffalo Norfolk had continued to be a presence in the heavyweight division notching important wins over Billy Miske, Clay Turner, Larry Williams, and Bill Tate for the Negro heavyweight championship on the undercard of Dempsey's defense against Bill Brennan. He had also suffered a few losses along the road which, combined with the color of his skin allowed promoters and matchmakers to avoid giving him a title shot. He suffered a second round knockout at the hands of an old, overweight Sam Langford, two decisive points defeats at the hands of Clay Turner, and most recently a punishing knockout loss at the hands of Lee Anderson in which he lost his championship and the sight in his left eye.

After his bout with Anderson Norfolk took some time to recover and adjust to seeing the world through one eye. His manager Leo P. Flynn offered his services as a sparring partner for

Dempsey during the latter's training for Carpentier. Flynn offered Norfolk's services under one condition: that Dempsey agree to give Norfolk a title shot. Jack Kearns refused and Norfolk never got his chance to show the world what he could have done with the champion either in a match or sparring.[56] When Norfolk was offered a chance at Greb, one of the most respected contenders in three divisions, he jumped at it. His only stipulation was that he needed more time to get into shape than the July 18 date allowed so the Birmingham club re-scheduled the bout for August 29 to be held at Forbes Field. For Harry it was another opportunity to remove one of Dempsey's contenders and maintain his status as a top contender for Dempsey's crown.

As Harry continued his training Engel was involved in the laborious task of trying to negotiate a championship match with Johnny Wilson. Dick Curley, working for promoter Harry Hyams had matched Harry and Wilson for a bout in East Chicago, Indiana to be held in August.[57] Those plans were completely upset when on July 27 Wilson came close to losing his title at the hands of Bryan Downey in Cleveland. In the seventh round Wilson was dropped hard by a short right hand. His handpicked referee Jimmy Gardner began to count "one, two, three, four, five, six, seven, eight, nine, nine, nine, ten!" Downey walked back to his corner convinced that he was the new middleweight champion only to turn and see Gardner inexplicably wave the fight on. Downey showered Wilson with blows dropping him for a count of six and then another knockdown upon which Gardner counted "one, two, three, five!" At this moment Wilson's manager, Killelea, leapt into the ring and attempted to assist Wilson to his feet, in clear violation of the rules of boxing. Downey's manager, Jimmy Dunn, tackled Killelea to prevent his interference. Remarkably Gardner then disqualified Downey for "hitting Wilson while he was down."[58] The Ohio boxing commission disagreed and named Downey middleweight champion. Wilson was still almost universally acknowledged as the champion but his reign was now wearing thin on fans who were tired of his handpicked opponents and officials. Finally it became apparent that Wilson had no intention of facing Harry when it was announced that he would fight Bryan Downey in a rematch promoted by Tex Rickard at Boyle's Thirty Acres, the same arena where Dempsey faced Carpentier.

Harry took a short break to have his tonsils removed then returned to hard training. With such a full plate it now seems amazing the Greb would take on more responsibilities but that is exactly what he did when he accepted a position as boxing instructor for the Pittsburgh police force. As part of his inauguration into this new position Greb would participate in the Victory Field Day sports card promoted by the Pittsburgh Police Pension Fund. He would appear in a four round exhibition bout against former opponent Johnny Howard, himself a police officer of Bayonne, New Jersey. The exhibition was scheduled for two days before Harry's bout with Kid Norfolk.

On August 15 Harry was in Jersey City to appear in an exhibition bout against Mike Burke for the benefit of disabled soldiers. When he returned to his training camp at New Brighton he wired for the services of Burke and Larry Williams who had impressed eastern sportswriters

Top: Harry Greb's summer home in New Brighton, PA. which doubled as his training camp. Above: Harry and Larry Williams sparring in preperation for Harry's bout with Frank Moran. Having fought Williams three times and witnessed Williams give Dempsey a hard workout in training for Carpentier convinced Greb of his quality as a sparring partner

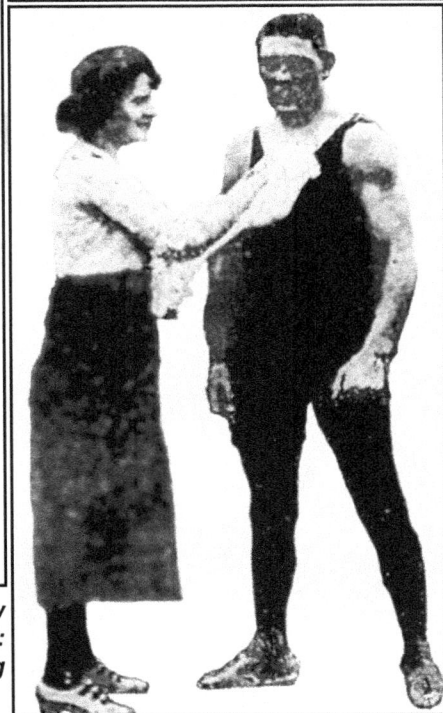

Above and top right: Scenes from Harry's New Brighton training camp for the Moran bout. Right: Mildred toweling Greb off after a hard training bout.

with his ability while helping to train Dempsey for Carpentier. Norfolk, like Greb, was leaving no stone unturned in his own training. Back in New York he was working out daily at Grupp's gymnasium with Bartley Madden, Harry Wills, Bill Brennan, Bill Tate, and Panama Joe Gans.

One week before the fight a rumor had spread through the Pittsburgh fight community like wildfire that Greb and Norfolk had reached an agreement whereby neither would give his best effort.[59] The rumor was entirely false and found to be so after a brief investigation.[60] The origin of the slander most likely rests with Red Mason who for months now had been unleashing his vitriol against Harry through his contacts in the press. With such a smear campaign in full swing against him Harry was glad for the investigation. "This gives me a chance to uncover the persons who are unfriendly toward me," he said. "I could gain nothing by 'framing' a bout with Norfolk and would be foolish to attempt to do so. Murder will out sooner or later, and if I were to be guilty of any underhanded tactics in my dealings with the Pittsburgh followers of boxing, I would not dare to show my face here to deny the charges. Just say for me that I, too, am glad to avail myself of the public showdown which you have suggested."

"I expect Norfolk to give me a hard fight. Of course, I expect to beat him. I wouldn't be much of a fighter if I was in the habit of anticipating defeat."[61]

Harry had been burning through sparring partners at an alarming rate. In addition to Mike Burke and Larry Williams he was battering members of the police athletic team to the point where some surely wondered if they would be able to compete in the upcoming festivities. On the 27th he faced off against Johnny Howard in a four round exhibition that he easily dominated, even giving the crowd a laugh by clowning around with referee Dillon.[62]

Two days later Harry found himself staring across the ring at a fighter now regarded by some as one of the greatest boxers to never win a championship. With nearly 6,000 fans in the stands and an estimated 40,000 more listening to the fight via radio the bell rang opening what

Greb (right) launches one of his characteristic flying attacks at Bayonne's Johnny Howard during the third annual Victory field day as Referee Jack Dillon looks on. Harry trained the police boxers and donated his services for the event free of charge.

would be a legendary contest. Giving away 17^1/$_2$ pounds Harry seemed tentative at first, not sure what to make of Norfolk, who was fast, possessed a sharp, accurate jab, and could hit hard with both hands. Norfolk opened by nullifying Greb's speed with his jab and working his way in close. Early in the fight Greb clinched and held repeatedly, tugging, pulling, and pushing Norfolk around the ring in an effort to tire the larger man. It was a tactic adopted out of necessity as Norfolk had an uncanny ability to catch his punches and counter effectively.

Things looked bad for Harry when in the third round Norfolk tore after him pumping punches in from all directions before a hard right backhand punch to the jaw sent Harry down in a sitting position. But just when it looked darkest Harry sprang up without a count and jumped on Norfolk with a furious rally. Norfolk checked Harry's rush with a hard left hook to the body and resumed command just as the bell rang ending the round.

Norfolk went on the attack again in the fourth looking to put Greb down for good but Harry was too heady for this and continued to pull Norfolk in close where the two fighters would pound away at the body. Up to the fifth round it would not have been a stretch to call the fight one-sided in favor of Norfolk but in the fifth Norfolk began to slow perceptibly and it was noticed that he was breathing hard while Harry seemed relatively fresh. As the sixth opened the two fighters met in the center of the ring and traded blows furiously. Suddenly the crowd jumped to its feet with a shout as Norfolk was forced to break ground, being chased to the ropes by Harry who was raining blows upon his foe. Norfolk emerged from the melee bleeding from the left eye. The cut suffered against Lee Anderson had been reopened and Norfolk looked worried for the first time in the fight.

Greb's rally had excited the audience and a dull roar was growing as the fighters came out for the seventh. Greb, sensing the tide was turning, leapt to the attack, tossing punches at Norfolk with reckless abandon. Time and again the larger fighter was forced to break ground. Midway through the round Greb backed Norfolk to the ropes and landed a combination that sent Norfolk's head spinning but he refused to go down. With the fight now seemingly in hand Greb started to play to the crowd by getting behind Norfolk and attacking from this indefensible position which brought forth laughter from the audience.

In the eighth round, shaken and confused by this total reversal, Norfolk continually looked to his corner for advice. Harry was now pressing the fight and, whether in close or from a distance, was outfighting and outpunching Norfolk. The ninth was very much like the eighth and when the fighters met in the center of the ring to shake hands for the tenth and final round Norfolk smiled a sheepish smile of gold teeth. Harry had been holding back for a big finish in the ninth and once again he continually chased Norfolk to the ropes, battering him relentlessly. Norfolk was now bleeding from the mouth and both eyes were cut while Harry was relatively unmarked save for a puffed left eye. The final bell found Greb once again battering Norfolk around the ring.[63]

The newspapers were split straight down the middle as to the winner. The Sun, Gazette-

This publicity photo of Harry was taken in New York two weeks before his ten round bout with Kid Norfolk.

Times, and Press felt Norfolk won, agreeing that Norfolk dominated the first six and Greb dominated the last four. The Post, Dispatch, and Leader all felt Greb won handily by scores of 6-4, 6-3-1, and 9-1 respectively. The Chronicle-Telegraph did not have a reporter present and instead used a thinly rewritten version of Harry Keck's account found in the Gazette-Times. Of the reporters who voted for Norfolk all gave Greb credit for a superb effort against a fighter who outweighed him by so much. Jim Jab, Greb's constant antagonist felt it was a hard thing to pick a winner. Bill Peet of the Dispatch called it the closest fight he had witnessed in years. Regis Welsh stated that both fighters had categorically erased any notion that the fight had been fixed, while Richard Guy of the Leader, who posted the ludicrously one-sided score of 9 rounds for Greb and 1 for Norfolk, stated that there was no shame for Norfolk in losing such a tremendous fight.[64]

The following day referee Yock Henninger announced publicly that had he been allowed to render an official decision he would have awarded the fight to Greb by a close margin of victory. "Greb won the fight." said Henninger, "Not by the great margin that some would have you believe. But the advantage was sufficient in my mind to have given him, had it been required, the decision without question. Greb showed plenty of stuff even when Norfolk was going good early in the fight and from the sixth round on had the black boy so tired that two or three rounds more would have put the decision beyond argument."[65]   The announcement by Henninger riled those who felt Norfolk held the advantage. It was argued that such a public proclamation by the referee was tantamount to rendering an official decision thereby unethical if not illegal.[66] It was a feeble argument given that it was common place during the era for newspapermen to referee fights and then print their decision in following day's column.

After the fight Norfolk spent a few days convalescing in Pittsburgh before announcing that he would call off all fights he had previously scheduled for several months due to injuries he had sustained against Greb.[67] What was not announced and would not be known for several years was the injury which Harry had suffered. When Harry Greb stepped down out of the ring that evening he left behind him the vision in his right eye. At some point in the fight a punch from Kid Norfolk had sufficiently damaged the eye. To what extent the eye was rendered sightless is now up to debate. What makes it difficult to determine is the fact that Harry was absolutely terrified if it was discovered that he was now fighting with one eye he would be forced to abandon the sport he loved and so he kept the injury secret from all but a few close friends and relatives.[68]

Amazingly, despite such a serious injury, Harry was in the ring again one week later against Chuck Wiggins at Ashland, Kentucky's Clyffeside Park. The weather threatened to cancel the show briefly which hurt the gate but the storm clouds and rain cleared in time for the two fighters to continue their grudge series. Over the first half of the fight Wiggins was showered with boos and catcalls for repeated low blows but Harry continued on about his business nonplussed. Wiggins abuse of the rules earned him warnings from the referee several times only to have Harry's nod of approval symbolizing the fact that he was more than capable of taking care of Wiggins on his own. In the seventh round after one particularly low blow Harry took matters into his own hands and floored Wiggins with a low blow of his own. Wiggins sat on the canvas complaining of the low blow but found no sympathy with the audience or the referee

Kid Norfolk in a photo circa 1916 or 1917. Around Norfolk's waist is the belt emblematic of his winning the championship of the Panama Canal Zone.

who continued counting over him. From this point on the fight was a no holds barred brawl with Greb slowly grinding Wiggins down to win the newspaper verdict.[69]

On the same day that Harry faced Wiggins, Johnny Wilson defended his middleweight championship against Bryan Downey in the fight that had prevented Harry from getting his title shot. It was an abysmal bout in which Wilson fought an entirely defensive fight. He could only lose his championship by a knockout or disqualification and so he kept as much distance between himself and Downey as possible and rarely took chances that would leave him exposed for a blow. Downey seemed wholly incapable of forcing Wilson to fight and as a result after a tedious twelve rounds the press deemed the audience of 30,000 the loser.[70] Tex Rickard was livid and conspired with the New Jersey Boxing Commission to withhold Wilson's purse

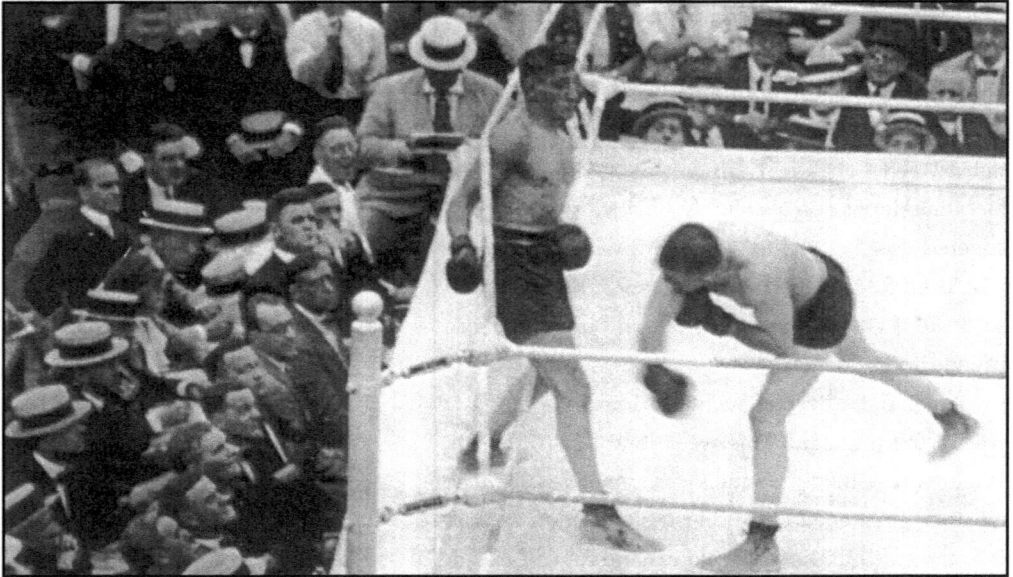

Bryan Downey (right) is seen on the attack against middleweight champion Johnny Wilson during their bout at Boyle's Thirty Acres. The fight was a rematch of their contro-versial fight in Cleveland. Wilson's performance was so poor Tex Rickard refused to pay him for his services unless he faced Harry Greb for the championship.

which amounted to an estimated $35,000. "This time he thought only of the money," said Rickard, "which was guaranteed. I think a man like Wilson ought to be thrown out of the ring for life. He is a disgrace to boxing, and the match was a disgrace to myself."[71] From this point on Rickard made it his personal mission to see Wilson defeated and relieved of his champi-onship. For this purpose Rickard selected Harry Greb.

As Rickard plotted of ways to remove Johnny Wilson from the pugilistic landscape, George Engel continued his aggressive marketing of Greb on the East coast by sending Harry in against Joe Cox at the Palace of Joy Sporting Club at Coney Island, New York on Tuesday September 20. It would be the first time Harry would fight under the Walker law which had legalized box-ing in New York and allowed decision matches. Cox was a heavyweight of the "White Hope" era who stood between six feet, two inches and six feet, five inches. He fought between 200 and 220 pounds and over a ten year career he had faced many of the top contenders of the heavy-weight division including Gunboat Smith, Bill Brennan, Luther McCarthy, Arthur Pelkey, and even sported a technical knockout over Jess Willard. Cox was a terrific athlete but as a boxer he was lukewarm at best. He'd been knocked out seven times and despite his advantage in size wasn't expected to defeat Harry.

Spotting Cox 35 pounds Harry easily evaded most of the wonderfully conditioned heavy-weight's blows and landed his own punches nearly at will. Twice Cox landed with all of his weight behind his punch and sent Harry flying across the ring only to have the smaller man leap back in his face like a maddened hornet. Short of these two punches Cox could not find any success against his speedy foe and by the tenth round those at ringside were impressed that the heavyweight had managed to stay the distance.[72]

Harry's showing against a man so much larger was enough to impress New Yorkers and convince them that Harry was ready to fight a championship. George Underwood of the New York Evening Telegraph speculated that Greb would knock out Johnny Wilson and be a good match for anyone in the middleweight and light-heavyweight divisions.[73] One thing was certain: New York finally wanted to see more of Harry.

To that end George Engel entered serious negotiations with Tex Rickard for the long awaited fourth bout between his charge and Tommy Gibbons. Engel quickly accepted terms for Harry to meet Gibbons at Madison Square Garden in a fifteen round decision bout. With Harry's signature sewn up all that was left was for Rickard to track down Gibbons' manager Eddie Kane and secure his agreement. Gibbons and Kane where now traveling throughout the west adding knockout after knockout to Gibbons' record in hopes of creating interest in a match with Dempsey or Carpentier and this busy schedule was making it difficult for Rickard to reach them. When word finally reached the pair in Buffalo that Greb had agreed to face Gibbons in an attractive bout in the metropolis Kane replied "Oh, no, he couldn't think of matching with Greb while there was prospect of a meeting with Georges Carpentier."[74] In other words Gibbons wasn't going to risk a possible title shot by losing to Greb.

While Harry waited for Rickard to finalize the fight, plans were made for him to once again face Jimmy Darcy in Buffalo where Greb had always been a fan favorite. Harry hadn't fought in Buffalo since facing Larry Williams there the year before and his fans were eager to see him in action. Jack Kearns had

JOE COX

Top: Greb arrives in New York for his bout With Joe Cox at the Palace of Joy in 1921. Bottom: Joe Cox was a big heavyweight from Missouri who ten years earlier had defeated future heavyweight champion Jess Willard. He outweighed Harry by 35 pounds when they met in 1921.

The second Madison Square Garden located at 26th and Madison Avenue was completed in 1890 and thru Tex Rickard's promotional acumen became a powerhouse in Boxing. When a fighter fought at the Garden he knew he had finally arrived.

bet $500 on his fighter to defeat Greb, a bet Kearns would lose. The only surprise came in the fourth round when Harry leapt in with both feet off the ground and ran right into a left hook that deposited him on the canvas. More surprised than hurt Harry sprung up immediately and "...cut loose like a wild man backing Darcy to the ropes with a smothering two-handed attack that was wonderful to behold. The punches came so fast Darcy halted only when he hit the ropes and grasped Greb with both hands in an enduring hug." For his temerity Darcy suffered a cut on his nose and one over his left eye. From that point on Harry had things well under control and when his arm was raised at the end of the fight the largest crowd of the season agreed as did all four of Buffalo's newspapers.[75]

While Harry was preparing for his match with Darcy Tex Rickard contacted George Engel with an offer to headline at Madison Square Garden on November 4. Having no success cornering Gibbons Rickard had acquired the services of New Jersey heavyweight Charlie Weinert. It may not have been the lucrative offer Engel was waiting for but he couldn't afford to pass it up. It would be Harry's first time headlining a card at Madison Square Garden, the Mecca of boxing.

Weinert was one of the most skilled boxers of the era but his love for the nightlife and distaste for training made him a maddeningly inconsistent fighter. Throughout his career he would rack up an impressive string of wins only to lose before fulfilling the promise his ability showed. Then he would start all over again building impressive wins only to lose once more. At the present time he had rededicated himself to the sport and was coming off a knockout over Georges Carpentier's chief sparring partner, Paul Journee, which had garnered quite a lot of favorable press. To prepare for his fight with Greb Weinert, for the first time in his career, went away to a training camp. In the Orange Mountains he worked out daily hoping that a victory over Greb would win him the lucrative match with Bill Brennan that had been promised the winner by Tex Rickard. The winner of the eventual bout with Brennan would face Dempsey for the heavyweight championship of the world. With this plum in sight Weinert worked as he never had before. No less intent on winning Harry trained daily at the Pittsburgh Lyceum eager to make a big hit in the Big Apple.

Both fighters finished hard training on November 2. "Greb is in the best condition of his career," said George Engel, "and he is very anxious to beat Weinert for it means a bout with Bill Brennan and then possibly a setto with Dempsey. Greb is in earnest about fighting Dempsey. Everybody was scared to tackle Kid Norfolk, but Harry got him in Pittsburgh and gave him a beating."[76]

Though Harry was an 8 to 5, and in some places 2 to 1, betting favorite there were those who felt Weinert, conditioned and on top of his game, could defeat Greb, particularly if he was able to make it out of the early rounds. Understanding this Engle and Harry devised a strategy whereby Greb would crowd Weinert early, preventing him from utilizing his reach and skills to get out in front with an early points lead. Weinert was viewed as something of a front runner and it was felt that if he fell behind early he would be easily dominated.

It was a wonderful night of boxing for the fans. The audience of 9,000 was nearly as excited about the semi-final, which brought together Fay Keiser and Young Bob Fitzsimmons, as they were about the main event. The interest revolved around whether or not Young Bob had inherited his father's legendary punch. He had not. But, he didn't need it to defeat Fay Keiser in an interesting bout which warmed the crowd up for the main event.

After silver tongued Joe Humphries announced the fighters, giving their weights as $178\frac{1}{2}$ for Weinert to $163\frac{3}{4}$ for Greb, the two fighters returned to their corners and the fight began. Harry started the fight exactly as planned, rushing in close and pumping lefts and rights to Weinert's

Charlie Weinert was born in Budapest, Hungary and immigrated to the United States where he began boxing at an early age. Standing six feet two inches tall Weinert used his natural athleticism to become a classy stylist. Ultimately his inconsistency in the ring prevented him from reaching his full potential.

head and body. Weinert backpedaled and did his best to fend off Greb's attack. Near the end of the round Greb countered an uppercut with a long right sending the Jersey man reeling. Harry immediately pounced on his wounded foe firing both hands so rapidly that at times it looked as if they were landing simultaneously. Weinert quickly collapsed in a heap for a count, the duration of which varied according to the sources of between four and nine seconds. Weinert rose on unsteady legs and Harry's Achilles heel reared its ugly head. Over-eager to land the knockout blow he became wild and missed his chance when the bell rang saving Weinert from the embarrassment of a first round knockout loss.

Weinert's corner brought him around with smelling salts and sent him out for the second round, but he found little respite as Greb continued his onslaught. In the third round Harry split Weinert's lip with a left hook. Harry absolutely brutalized Weinert in the sixth, seventh, and eighth. After these sessions Weinert returned to his corner wobbly, confused, and with blood dripping over his chin. In the eleventh, fourteenth, and fifteenth rounds Weinert tried to mount a feeble comeback but this newfound aggression only made Harry fight harder and forced Weinert to accept more punishment. Weinert's only relief came with the clang of the final bell which found Weinert's eyes nearly closed, his lips oozing blood, and bleeding from a cut under his left eye. The decision was unanimous in favor of Harry who had now taken New York by storm. The nearly $10,000 he received was the largest single purse he had yet received in his eight and a half year career.[77]

17

THE ST. PAUL ASSASSIN

Harry was not about to rest on his laurels. One week after his fight with Weinert he would face Billy Shade in Pittsburgh at Motor Square Garden. Leo P. Flynn, who was already balking at letting Bill Brennan face Harry a fifth time, had agreed to let Shade face Greb. Flynn had recently acquired Shade as part of a package deal along with two other Shade brothers, George and Dave. Shade had made his early career fighting four rounders in California under the management of Frank Tabor. He posted a respectable record but had failed to develop past the club level until deciding to try his craft in Australia. In less than a year between 1920 and 1921 Billy Shade fought ten bouts, winning nine and losing only one via disqualification. While in Down Under Shade was reputed to have won the welterweight, middleweight, light heavyweight, and heavyweight championships of Australia.[1] Upon his return to the United States his contract was purchased by Flynn and he was given two fights in New York, one against Homer Smith, and a showcase bout at Madison Square Garden against Fay Keiser both of which he won.

There was a great deal of speculation that if the bout was competitive the two fighters would be rematched at Madison Square Garden through Flynn's connection with the institution. The fight itself was greatly anticipated, being Harry's first bout in the city since facing Norfolk, and as such KDKA would again be ringside to broadcast the fight blow by blow.

Shade was able to make a good showing in losing nearly every one of the ten rounds. Some in the audi-

Billy Shade (left) is shown here with his manager Frank Tabor not long before Billy left for Australia, where his accomplishments made him a much sought after commodity upon returning to the United States.

ence, not the least of which was Regis Welsh, reporting for the Post, felt that Harry had carried Shade so as not to beat him too badly and ruin his chance at the lucrative rematch in the Garden.[2]

Two days later Harry's appearance in an exhibition bout for the Knights of Columbus set tongues wagging. Working Harry's corner was none other than Red Mason. Mason and Harry had been increasingly more friendly to one another in the past few weeks and with Harry's contract with Engel due to expire soon there was talk that Harry and Mason might renew their professional association. However, later in November Harry explained his position when he re-signed with Engel. "Engel has done me a lot of good," said Harry. "He has gotten me bigger money than ever before in my life, and made it possible for me to gain the inside circle in New York's biggest rings."[3]

On November 25 Greb was in Newark to give fans that had missed his demolition of Weinert a chance to see him in person. His opponent would be six foot two inch, one hundred ninety three pound Kalamazoo heavyweight Homer Smith. The enormous physical advantages sport-ed by Smith (he outweighed Harry by twenty-seven pounds) were of no help. In the very first round Greb lifted all of Smith's 193 pounds off the canvas with a right uppercut and then pro-ceeded to shatter his nose with a left hook. Despite the small crowd Harry refused to coast and tried his best to knock Smith out. As early as the third round Smith tried to quit in his corner but his seconds urged him to continue. Smith gamely fought on for two more rounds but dur-ing the five rounds he had failed to land more than half a dozen weak blows and after the fifth referee Erhardt was notified that Smith could not continue owing to a broken rib.[4]

Tex Rickard was now actively trying to match Harry with Johnny Wilson for December 16 at Madison Square Garden. After his two disastrous fights with Bryan Downey Wilson had found it nearly impossible to acquire meaningful bouts or make the kind of money that a champion could expect. He desperately needed the $35,000 that Rickard still held for his poor performance at Boyles Thirty Acres. Yet, Rickard made it known that the only way Wilson would see that money

Homer Smith was a heavyweight from Van Buren county, Michigan. During his long career he faced six world champi-ons and the best contenders of the heavyweight division.

would be to face Harry Greb.[5]

As Engel awaited word from Rickard he sent Harry in against his old adversary Fay Keiser in Philadelphia. It had been nearly five years since Harry had decisively defeated Keiser in that bloody twenty round affair at Lonaconing. Since last they met professionally Keiser had served with distinction during the war. He attained the rank of sergeant and in France after the war lost a close decision to Bob Martin for the A.E.F. heavyweight championship. In September Keiser had finally gotten a rematch with Martin and gave the highly publicized heavyweight a beating. The victory earned Keiser a break at the big time in New York where he faced Billy Shade and Young Bob Fitzsimmons, losing both fights but giving a decent account of himself. Harry easily defeated Keiser over eight rounds closing his left eye, bloodying his nose, and puffing his lips in the process.[6]

On December 10, four days after Harry defeated Keiser, Martin Killilea met with Tex Rickard in a final attempt to acquire Wilson's purse for the Downey fight. Rickard told Killelea that the only way Wilson would see his money would be if he signed to face Greb. Killilea tried to get Rickard to accept Mike Gibbons (who had recently lost to Tommy Robson and was clearly past his best) as an opponent. Rickard refused and Killilea left.[7] The two met again a few days later and again Killilea tried to get Rickard to release the funds without facing Greb and again Rickard refused whereupon Killilea signed a contract stipulating that Wilson would fight anyone of Rickard's choosing at Madison Square Garden in February.[8]

When Engel received word that Wilson had agreed to terms for a title bout with Harry he immediately made an appointment with Rickard to sign for Greb. On December 21 Engel signed the contract stipulating that both fighters would post $10,000 to bind their appearance. The weight would be 160 pounds at 2 pm on the afternoon of the fight. The official date

On December 21, 1921 Harry Greb was signed to face Johnny Wilson for the middleweight championship. Wilson however signed the above contract and then promptly tore it up when he was paid monies owed to him by Tex Rickard.

of the fight would be established before January 5 and would probably be February 10 or 16. Rickard would release no details about the compensation each fighter would receive.

Two days after he was signed to face Wilson Harry traveled to Syracuse, New York to face light heavyweight Whitey Allen. Allen was a transplanted Swede who had been boxing on and off for nearly ten years with only modest success. Allen, weighing 175 pounds, sported a twelve pound weight advantage and five inches in height. But, like many of Greb's previous opponents, Allen only suffered more for these advantages. For six rounds Harry battered Allen relentlessly. Finally at the end of the sixth round, with Allen doubled over the ropes in his corner unable to fight owing to a horribly swollen and bloody face, referee Hamill was forced to declare Greb the winner.[9]

Within days of his defeat of Whitey Allen ugly rumors began to be reported by the press that Johnny Wilson had no intention of fighting Greb.[10] The stories, attributed to close associates of Wilson, stated that Wilson only agreed to fight Harry in order to receive his money from the Downey fight. Wilson and Killilea were gambling on the argument that the Greb contract was signed under duress and as such should be void.

Herbert Allard had immigrated to the United States from Sweden in 1910 at the age of 18. He fought professionally as Whitey Allen out of the Bronx, New York.

As the story began to unfold in the press Harry headed to Cincinnati, where he remained wildly popular, to once again face Chuck Wiggins. After ten rounds Harry was judged the winner by every newspaper in the city.[11] Harry had finished the fight without a mark and as fresh after the tenth as when he entered the ring despite being outweighed 11^{1}/$_{2}$ pounds. Exasperated by his untiring opponent a bloody and bruised Wiggins commented "He's one tough baby, I would rather fight almost any of the big fellows than Harry, yet promoters keep sending for us."[12]

As George Engel and Harry were boarding the train to leave Cincinnati they were handed a telegram confirming the rumors in the press. Wilson had officially refused to face Greb. "It's an outrage," exclaimed Engel. "I have posted $10,000 to bind the match with Wilson, and Greb had agreed to make 160 pounds at 2 o'clock. The match was to have taken place on January 6 at Madison Square Garden and I called off a half dozen good fights to get Greb in shape for the Wilson bout. I will take the matter up with Promoter Rickard as soon as I reach my home in

New York."[13]

If Wilson and Killilea had hoped that the public would side with them they were sorely mistaken. There is some merit to the argument that Rickard had no right to withhold Wilson's pay. Yet, the way in which Wilson and Killilea went about getting the money, backing out on a contract to fight what most observers agreed was the man most deserving of the opportunity, rather than take the matter to the courts, only compounded Wilson's problems. Sympathy swung heavily in favor of Harry who had been forced by Killilea to come up with a $10,000 appearance forfeit, no easy task, and who had been forced to turn down several lucrative offers for fights in order to block out time to prepare for the title bout.

Two days after Killilea and Wilson backed out of the bout Wilson was banned by the New York State Athletic Commission.[14] Very quickly thereafter every state which had its own commission followed suit (Ohio and New Jersey had already banned Wilson for the two Downey fights). The public viewed Wilson as a coward, unwilling to face the best, and only interested in preserving his crown for financial gain. If Wilson intended to cash in on the championship without ever risking it the powers that be were fully prepared to step in.

On January 16 the National Boxing Association, which was holding its annual convention in New Orleans, ruled that Johnny Wilson would be barred from participating in boxing matches in the United States for a Period of one year.[15] Another development witnessed at the convention was a new rule the NBA was toying with which would strip a champion of his title if he didn't defend it against a worthy opponent within a reasonable amount of time. Between Wilson's reluctance to face his most threatening opponents and the various governing bodies' bans against him it appeared more and more likely that Wilson would be the first boxing champion to be forcibly stripped of his title outside of the ring.

The following day Wilson and Killilea appeared before the New York State Athletic Commission to plead their case. Their pleas, however, fell on deaf ears. The commission refused to lift its indefinite suspension and took no time at all to consider Wilson's case, giving the impression that their minds were firmly set. Killilea left the meeting visibly upset.[16]

As Harry's title hopes faded and

And They Call Him Champion!

Johnny Wilson's professional nightmare continued to be played out in the press it became apparent Greb would need to get active again. The earliest Engel could arrange a bout for Greb was late January. The Olympic Athletic Club in Grand Rapids had offered Harry a date and Engel readily agreed, offering to let the club pick the best man they could obtain. Initially they settled on Bob Roper but when he was injured while winning a bout against Paul Sampson a week before Kansas heavyweight Hugh Walker was substituted.[17]

Upon hearing that Roper was injured Harry and Engel cancelled plans until they were notified that a substitution had been made. The delay caused Harry and George to arrive in Grand Rapids later than expected. They were promptly notified by Thomas Bigger, chairman of the state athletic board of control that the rule stating that fighters must be on hand four days before a fight must be observed resulting in the bout being set back to February 1.[18] Harry readily agreed to the postponement and even received permission to return home for a couple of days to be at the side of Mildred who was once again dangerously ill.[19] However, when he received word that her condition had improved he chose to remain in Grand Rapids and continue training for Walker only to return to Pittsburgh the following day with new word that Mildred was still seriously ill.[20]

In discussing Greb's upcoming bout in Grand Rapids E. W. Dickerson, sportswriter for the Grand Rapids Herald and a fan of Harry's, remarked that despite being soft spoken, kind and considerate outside of the ring Harry was merciless inside. Dickerson felt that no man in the world could defeat Greb in 10 rounds including Jack Dempsey. Dickerson was squarely in the camp of those who felt Harry was Jack's logical and most deserving white contender.[21]

While Harry nursed Mildred George Engel returned to New York where he hoped to negotiate with Tex Rickard for a lucrative bout in the city. Rickard had been hoping to match Georges Carpentier with Tommy Gibbons. In the previous year Gibbons had knocked out 20 of the 22 men he faced making him a sought after attraction. Carpentier, for his part, showed little or no inclination to return to face the stars of the United States when he could make a fortune fighting lesser lights like George Cook. As it became apparent that Carpentier was not going return for some time Rickard did the next best thing. If the middleweight champion would not face his top contender, a man being hailed as a threat to Dempsey and Carpentier would not face Gibbons Rickard would match the two avoided fighters in a bonanza that would decide who had the right to face Dempsey. Thus, on January 30 Harry received a telegram from Engel announcing that he was close to having Harry matched to meet Tommy Gibbons in mid-March.[22]

Harry returned to Michigan just long enough to give Hugh Walker a one-sided beating. Walker used his 26 pound weight advantage to absorb punishment and keep coming forward but at times Harry landed a dozen or more punches without return. Round after round Harry would batter his larger foe until his face swelled and bled from cuts and yet round after round Walker's corner would patch him up and send him out to plod forward, always looking for the one punch that would end things. It never came.[23] "I landed a hard punch every once in a while," said Walker after the fight. "When I tried to follow it up Greb was not there, but was either behind me or in another part of the ring. I have fought most of the best men in the heavyweight division and thought I knew something about speed. Greb showed me that I did not know the true meaning of the word as applied to boxing. I trained for this fight as I never trained for one before and entered the ring under the impression I could corner him, but I was unable to do so and he beat me. He beat me and that is all there is to it. The best I had was not good enough."[24] Harry left the ring without a mark to make the journey back to Pittsburgh.

On February 8 Tex Rickard formally announced that Gibbons-Greb IV was set for Madison Square Garden on March 13. The match was instantly popular with press and fans alike. Harry had several obligations to fulfill before heading to New York to prepare for Gibbons. He was scheduled to meet Jeff Smith in Cincinnati on February 20 after which he would appear in Toledo against Bartley Madden on the 24th (he would cancel this bout shortly before facing Smith) and then return to Pittsburgh to appear in two exhibition bouts on the 25th and 26th against George Hook after which he would be off to Boston to face Billy Miske on the 28th.

Taking on Smith, especially in light of the close call in New Orleans the previous May, was certainly a daring move with the lucrative Gibbons bout less than a month away and a possible title shot equally close. Apparently one close call in New Orleans, which Harry insisted he won, wasn't enough to offset the memory of five relatively easy victories over Smith.

With Harry getting copy daily in all of the major cities due to the Wilson affair and the upcoming match with Gibbons he was able to negotiate for the largest sum he had ever received in Cincinnati. Indeed he was now receiving larger purses in general than at any time in his nine year career and he knew that if he kept winning they would only get bigger. Smith had a lot on the line as well as he hoped to sail for France at the end of the month to obtain a rematch with Carpentier.

Greb trained for his match with

A good drawing pair

'GREB SMITH

IT LOOKS AS IF THE SOLDIERS' SHOW WOULD CATCH A FULL HOUSE.

C'MON AN' FIGHT!

YELLOW!

EXCUSE ME, BOYS!

GREB SMITH WILSON

HIS NIBS, JOHNNY WILSON, HAS DUCKED BOTH OF THESE BATTLERS. THEY PLAY TOO ROUGHLY FOR JOHNNY

THERE'LL BE PLENTY OF NEW SPRING HATS ON DISPLAY, JUDGING BY THE ADVANCE RESERVATIONS.

AFTER HIS BOUT WITH GREB, SMITH WILL SAIL FOR EUROPE TO PICK ANOTHER QUARREL WITH CARPENTIER.

Smith at the Pittsburgh Lyceum, partaking in his usual routine of handball, shadowboxing, bag punching and sparring with George Hook and Wild Bill Reed. Upon arriving in Cincinnati he trained at the Yokum Club, taking on anyone willing to spar with him. Fans who watched Harry train were impressed with his condition as well as that of his opponent, who was putting in his training at the Fenwick Club.

The bout was very nearly disastrous for Harry. By the second round Greb's lips were cut and bleeding from Smith's accurate counters. In the fourth, while coming out of a clinch, Smith opened a cut below Harry's right eye. Despite Smith's accurate and damaging punches Greb was scoring often and his aggression was keeping him ahead on points. Smith's willingness to lay back and wait for Greb to attack irritated the fans who felt he could outpoint or even knockout Greb if he just opened up and went on the attack. It was to no avail and despite Harry leaving the ring with a badly swollen and bleeding face he was regarded the winner by two of the three Cincinnati papers to cover the fight, the other voting the bout a draw.[25]

In an article written for Ring Magazine three years later Harry would call the Cincinnati fight with Smith his hardest fight. "I just outsmarted Jeff. He knew he had me going and all that, but he wouldn't take a chance."[26] By his own admission Harry returned to his hotel and spent the next day there having hot applications applied to the eye fearing further aggravation to the injury sustained in the Norfolk fight.[27] Soon after the fight with Greb Smith received word that Carpentier had cancelled their fight, opting instead to face England's Ted "Kid" Lewis.

After treating the offending eye, Harry returned to Pittsburgh where he continued training for the Gibbons and bout. On the 26th he faced his sparring partner George Hook in an exhibition bout before the Duquesne Council Knights of Columbus. Harry was the feature attraction of the evening's entertainment, which featured vaudeville and several boxing bouts. Harry tore into Hook for three rounds and his performance prompted wild applause from the audience.[28] The following afternoon Hook and Greb did it again, this time for four rounds as part of the Pittsburgh Lyceum's annual smoker. Once again Harry was afforded a rousing ovation and those present remarked that he was in wonderful condition for his upcoming bout at Madison Square Garden.[29]

The same day of the second consecutive exhibition against Hook Harry cancelled his bout in Boston with Miske. The Gibbons bout was shaping up to be the most important bout of the season, perhaps the year, and Harry wanted nothing to jeopardize it. Rickard was already in preliminary talks to match the winner with either Carpentier or Dempsey at Boyles Thirty Acres. Doc Kearns seemed agreeable to the idea adding only that the winner would have to show great form otherwise Dempsey would probably face Harry Wills instead.[30] Francois Descamps wanted the winner to face Gene Tunney who had recently defeated Battling Levinsky in an uninteresting fight for the "Light Heavyweight Championship of America." The winner of that bout, Descamps regally declared, would have the right to face his champion.[31] Dempsey himself, who would be appearing in New York with the "Get Together" stage company, had arranged for his performance to go on earlier so he could leave and be ringside for the fight in order to size up the two contenders for his crown.[32] "You may tell the public," said the champion upon arriving, "that I am more than tired of appearing as a footlight favorite. I intend to see the Greb-Gibbons bout at the Garden on March 13 and will probably battle the winner."[33]

Given his remarkable knockout record of the past year, which had prompted some in the press to dub him the St. Paul Assassin, and the ten extra pounds he had put on since last he faced Greb, Gibbons was made an 8 to 5 favorite. Gibbons had always wanted to be able to face Harry in a longer bout and without having to struggle to make weight. It was felt by the odds-makers that these factors gave Gibbons the edge over Greb. Lightweight champion Benny Leonard was picking Gibbons to defeat Greb despite his close relationship with George Engel, as was welterweight champion Jack Britton, much of the New York press, and even a majority of Pittsburgh sportswriters. Frank Coultry, general manager of Madison Square Garden was quoted as saying that after receiving orders for tickets from London, Paris, Toronto, Mexico City, and other exotic locales he was convinced he could sell out the arena without opening the box office.[34]

The only real competition the bout had to be the biggest and most important heavyweight matches of the year was from the upcoming bout between Harry Wills and Kid Norfolk scheduled to take place eleven days before the Gibbons-Greb bout. This bout was also being billed as an elimination bout with the winner in line to face Dempsey. Jack Kearns played both sides against the middle by stating that, like the Gibbons-Greb bout, the winner of the Wills-Norfolk bout would have to win spectacularly to be considered a challenger.[35] Win, lose, or draw much of the press was already writing off Harry Greb as well as the winner of the Wills-Norfolk bout. Regardless of who won either bout, and what the power brokers decided was the right course for the heavyweight champion, within one month two challengers with exceptionally strong claims would emerge to demand the right face Dempsey for the heavyweight championship of the world.

On March 2 Harry arrived in New York where he intended to divide his training between Billy Grupp's gymnasium and Philadelphia Jack O'Brien's gym located on the roof of Madison Square Garden. He first stopped at the Garden where he was greeted by mob of admirers. After a brief visit with Jack O'Brien Harry spoke with reporters and expressed his thoughts on the upcoming bout. "When I finish with Gibbons on the evening of March 13," he said, "the boys will be convinced that Harry Greb will be the proper fellow to take a whack at Jack Dempsey's title."

"Am in pretty good shape and only need a few days to get good enough to hand Mr. Gibbons a startling surprise."

"A good fellow and a corking good fighter is Gibbons, but that won't stop me from treating him to a lacing. Can't understand why the fans in this city figure Gibbons should rule the favorite. That, however, cuts no figure when it comes to real fighting. Will start in Saturday and do some work. Then look out for the Pittsburgh Bearcat."[36]

Midway through the promotion Tex Rickard resigned his post as head of the Garden in order to focus on a myriad of legal troubles which had been dogging him for months and now seemed to threaten his very freedom. These issues could easily fill a book of their own but in short they ranged from minor distracting financial problems to very serious criminal allegations.[37] With Rickard no longer actively promoting for the time being Frank Flournoy took over the handling of the match which was now being promoted as a charity benefit for the Milk Fund of the Mayor's Committee of Women, which provided milk to children in need.

The night that Harry arrived in New

Top: Harry Greb arrives at Madison Square Garden on March 2, 1922 amidst a crowd of onlookers. Harry's first order of business was to meet with Philadelphia Jack O'Brien, who operated a gym on the roof of the Garden, and make arrangements to begin training. That meeting is depicted above as George Engel and Harry are welcomed by the former light-heavyweight champion.

York Harry Wills and Kid Norfolk staged their own elimination match to a nearly sold out Garden. Norfolk, outweighed by 35 pounds, succumbed to a Wills right uppercut in the early seconds of the second round proving conclusively that among the heavyweights Jack Dempsey need look no further than Harry Wills for a bonafide challenger.[38] However, Wills had been a top contender for Dempsey since Jack had won the championship and seemed no closer to a title fight even now than he had been during the three previous years. If Dempsey continued to refuse to meet a black fighter for the championship, the winner of the Gibbons-Greb bout would be in an excellent position to declare himself chief among Dempsey's white rivals. As such more than nine hundred press credentials were requested from all over the country for the Greb-Gibbons bout.[39]

The next day as Harry arrived to train at Philadelphia Jack O'Brien's he was again greeted by a large crowd who came to watch him go through his paces. Harry shadow boxed and played handball with Bill Bradley before heading to the steam room. Afterwards he posed for photographers. Harry got a taste of what it was like to be a champion as he was photographed more that afternoon than at any other time in his life thus far.

For the next ten days Harry worked like a Trojan every day, sparring with Bill Bradley, Andy Miller, Al Roberts, and Pat McCarthy. None of these men proved any match for Greb, despite being ordered by Engel not to hold back, but Greb was glad to tirelessly punch them around the ring as he built up the incredible stamina he had become famous for and which he would need to avoid Gibbons' deadly punch for 15 rounds. Gibbons was training at the Commonwealth Sporting Club in Harlem,

having arrived from Chicago where he worked at the Arcade. In Harlem he sparred daily with Greb victim Whitey Allen and welterweight Jim Montgomery.

Despite Harry's impressive training stints the odds were lengthening in favor of Gibbons. In fact the odds were now more in favor of Gibbons in Harry's own hometown of Pittsburgh. With much of the promotion focused on the idea that the winner would face Dempsey it seemed almost lost on a large section of the press that Gibbons could lose. A strange double standard began to emerge whereby Gibbons would earn a shot at Dempsey by beating Greb, a middleweight, yet Greb, who had already defeated several of the noted heavyweights, was being increasingly written off against the champion even if he were to defeat a heavyweight of Gibbon's caliber. Fred Keats, writing for the New York Sun, was one example of a writer who had totally written Harry off. In discussing major matches for the future he listed Gibbons facing Carpentier, Dempsey, and Gene Tunney. No mention was made of Harry as a possible opponent for these men.[40] It understandably annoyed Harry. Grantland Rice argued that even in the event of a Greb victory the Pittsburgher would be too small.[41] Dempsey himself had inadvertently refuted this argument when discussing the Wills-Norfolk bout claiming that any man weighing 170 pounds was a match for anyone in the world.[42]

Walking into the Garden on the night of the fight one would have been greeted with the sight of a sellout crowd packed literally elbow to elbow and nervous with the anticipation of

Preceding page and top: Harry posing for cameramen while training for Tommy Gibbons. Above: Harry Greb exhibits his impressive biceps to George Engel and curious cameramen. Facing page top: Harry spars with Boston's Pat McCarthy in preparation for Gibbons. Facing page below: Harry strengthens his stomach muscles in anticipation of Gibbons bodyblows.

seeing the two celebrated gladiators. Thousands were turned away at the door. The crowd was populated by the elite of New York society, the Astors, Vanderbilts, Roosevelts, Longsworths and more sat side by side with the lowly denizens of the fight crowd. By five o'clock police lines had formed for several blocks to control the massive crowds that had arrived early for the fight. By seven o'clock the Garden doors were closed and the show was already being hailed as a major success. The box office had brought in more than twice as much as the Wills-Norfolk fight proving at the very least that the winner could argue they were more bankable than any of Dempsey's current leading contenders.

After the preliminaries had completed Gibbons trotted into the ring and tested the ropes by bouncing off of them. Harry followed wearing a beautiful vanilla colored robe and emerald green trunks. He crossed the ring and shook hands with Tommy. He must have taken heart from the nearly 300 familiar faces of Pittsburgh residents that had made the trip to New York to see the fight. Gene Tunney was introduced as ready to defend his American Light Heavyweight championship against the

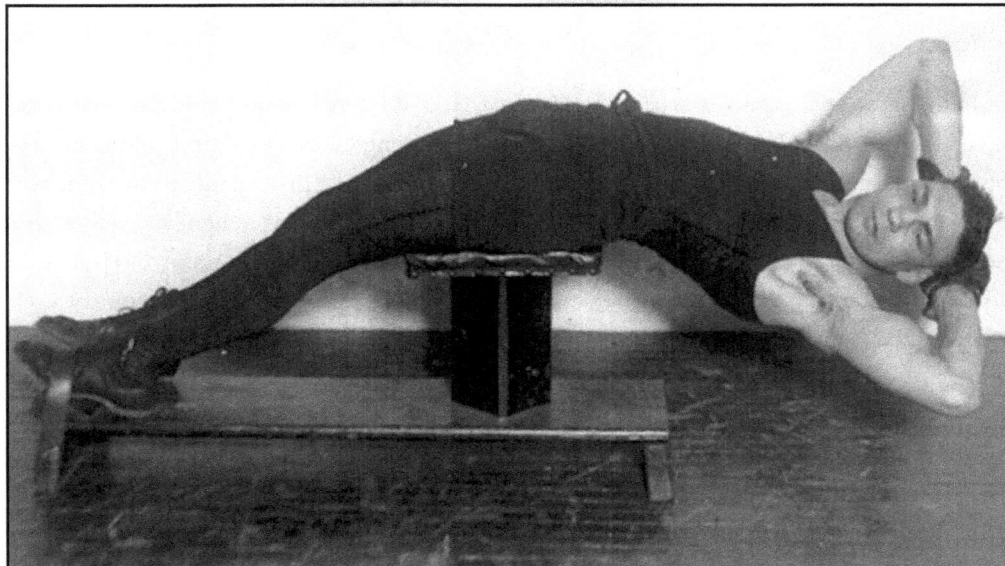

GREB JUMPS AND LEAPS ABOUT AND IS AS FAST AS OILED LIGHTNING —

HARRY GREB

THERE'S MUSIC IN TH' AIR I HEAR IT EVRYWHERE 'TIS LITTLE BIR DIES SING ING — AND I HEAR SLEIGH BELLS RING ING !!!

SOCK!

TOMMY GIBBONS

GIBBONS IS SLOWER OF FOOT BUT HAS A WALLOP THAT WOULD MAKE A MULE JEALOUS

CAN GREB'S SUPERIOR SPEED BEAT GIBBONS HEART-BREAKING POKE ????
WE SHALL SEE, BOYS, WE SHALL SEE

—THIS IS WHAT THESE LADS HAVE ON THEIR MINDS — AND INCIDENTALLY, WE WILL SAY THAT HE WHO COPS FROM J. HARRISON DEMPSEY WILL NEED BOTH SPEED AND A LULL-A-BYE MIT — —HOW 'BOUT IT ?

OODLES OF COIN

winner, followed by Johnny Dundee. Gibbons and Greb posed for what seemed like a wall of photographers after which they received Kid McPartland's final instructions.

When the bell rang sounding the first round Gibbons had hardly turned around to face Harry before he was met with a furious attack that brought cheers from the audience. The fight was being fought at a furious pace with Harry continually rushing in, gripping Gibbons tight with one arm, and strafing him with the free hand. At the end of the first round both fighters returned to their corners bleeding from the mouth. Greb's corner, which was comprised of Engel, Billy Gibson, Willie Lewis, and Tom Dolan, must have been elated after the opening round.

In the second the moment of truth for Harry arrived. If Harry had outboxed Gibbons in the first as most believed then it was surmised that before long Gibbons would land his terrible punch and send Greb to the floor. After setting Harry up for the first minute or so of the second Gibbons timed him coming in and let go with his money punch, a left hook to the liver that nearly folded Greb in half. Very quickly he followed it with another and as Greb danced around trying to avoid punishment yet another left found his mid-section. For a moment Greb looked to be in distress and the wise ones nodded approvingly that it would only be a matter of time.

Harry knew he could not let Gibbons take the lead and with this in mind he came out for the third intent on continuing where he left off in the first. He danced around Gibbons whipping in lefts and rights and making his flat-footed opponent look slow in comparison. More than once Gibbons bounced sickening right hands off of Greb's head but Harry would not be denied. For every punch Gibbons started Harry was landing two or three and very often getting there first.

It was the same old Harry in fourth when near the beginning of the round Gibbons threw a combination only to find his ducking, swirling opponent had somehow popped up behind him. Harry was continually in and out throwing punches from all angles and wriggling out of danger whenever Tommy seemed set for a punch. Near the end of the round Harry again managed to appear behind Gibbons landing a volley of blows and making the St. Paul battler look silly.

Jack Dempsey arrived ringside between the fourth and fifth rounds and witnessed Gibbons try to take a page from Harry's book at the start of the round. As the bell rang he rushed from his corner and launched an attack before Harry had managed to emerge for the round but his

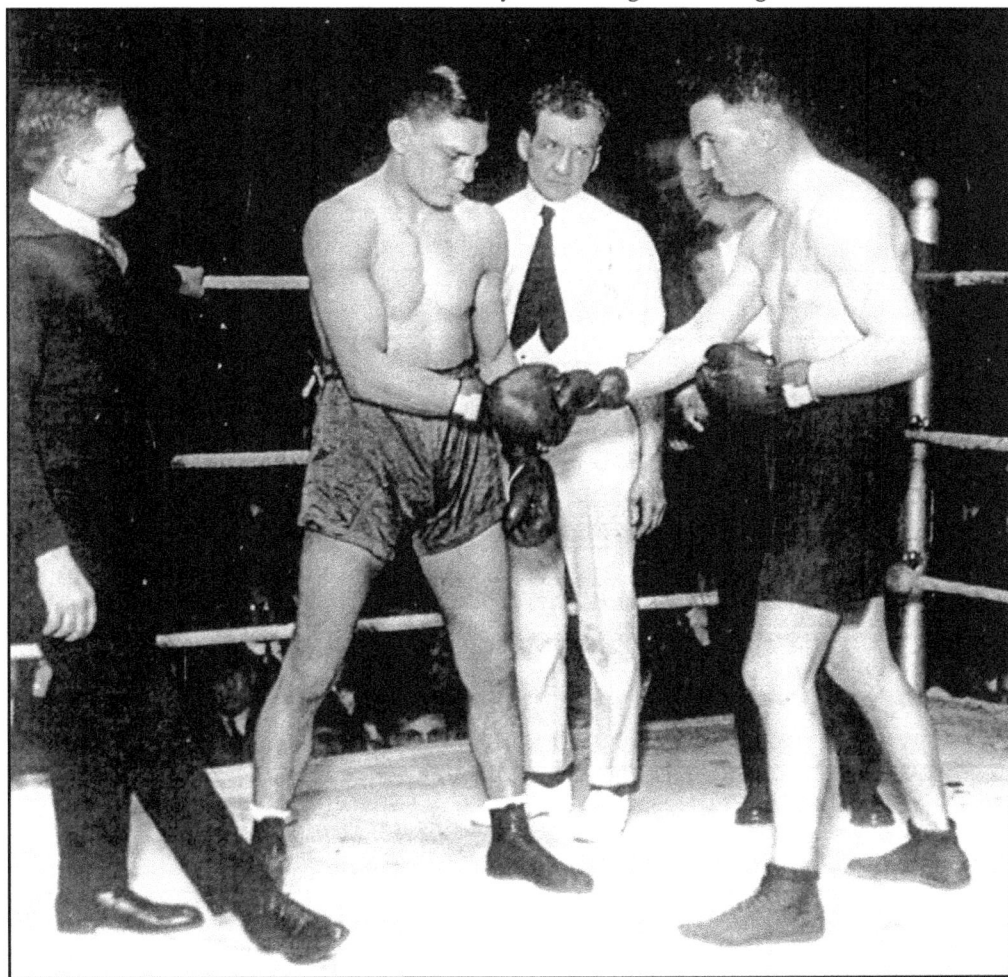

George Engel, referee Kid McPartland, and announcer Joe Humphries look on as Harry shakes hands with Tommy Gibbons prior to their fourth, final, and most important showdown on March 13, 1922.

Top: Greb (center) and Gibbons (left) pictured in a clinch during the first round. Above: Greb (center) misses a right hand in the second round. Facing page top: Harry Greb (left) throws a right hand at Gibbons' jaw as Gibbons prepares to whip over his powerful left hook to the liver in the fourth round. Facing page bottom: referee Kid McPartland(left) keeps a close eye on the action as Greb (left) and Gibbons fight in close during the tenth round. Note the position of Greb's right held close to the body and under the chin to protect against gibbons' deadly left.

temerity was met with a right and left to the jaw as Greb nimbly danced away. It was obvious now that Gibbons was trying to mount an assault that would sweep away Greb's lead and in so doing he managed to land a terrific left hook that snapped Greb's head back but only angered Harry, who rushed in with both arms flailing. Once again Tommy landed several hard left hooks to the body and was now seemingly leading Harry into traps much like he had done six years earlier.

In the sixth the two fighters fought evenly with Gibbons landing the harder punches as Harry forced the fighting. The seventh was much the same with Gibbons taking the lead but portents of things to come were seen near the end of the round when Harry stood toe to toe in his own corner and slugged with Gibbons.

The eighth was Harry's biggest round of the fight. After the two briefly fumbled around for an opening Harry opened up and began landing punches almost at will. He made Gibbons miss and then countered beautifully until the last thirty seconds when Greb amazingly increased his already torrid pace and smothered Gibbons with a blur of punches that at times seemed to leave Tommy dazed and confused.

Greb continued the ninth much as he had in the eighth as Gibbons tried to clinch in order to break Harry's rhythm. Gibbons seemed discouraged and aware that the fight was slipping away from him. He began to load up on his punches trying to land one shot that would change or even end the fight. Twice he landed hard right hands to Harry's mouth splitting his lip but Greb was confident and merely shrugged such blows off. At the close of the round Gibbons mouth hung open gasping for breath.

Gibbons was able to mount something of a comeback in the tenth by countering Greb with clean, crisp punches and had his best round since the second in the eleventh when he again seemed to hurt Harry with body shots but he could not put Greb away, something which many in the audience where now whispering he would have to do to win the fight.

In the twelfth round something happened that must have been very discouraging to Gibbons. After having probably taken the tenth and eleventh rounds Gibbons set Harry up and landed a perfect left hook that once again twisted Greb's head around yet had no real effect. From that point on Harry took over and never looked back. He kept the weakening Gibbons constantly turning, moving, chasing while he poured in punches. The audience could not understand how this middleweight was able to take such punishment from one of the best heavyweights in the world and come back to take nearly all of the championship rounds with a display of stamina rarely if ever equaled.

In the fifteenth Gibbons tried madly to corner and finish Harry but on the rare occasions when he was able to pin Greb he was met with a discouraging assault through which Harry would fight himself free. At this point even Gibbons' most ardent fans could be heard to say that it was Harry's fight beyond question. The two fighters were trading blows in Harry's corner when the final bell rang just as Greb punctuated the fight by bouncing a right hand off of

Gibbons' head.

After a short delay in tabulating the scorecards of the judges Joe Humphries moved to the center of the ring and shouted: "The winner -Greb! Greb, the winner!" As the audience broke into wild adulation George Engel and Willie Lewis lifted Greb high into the air where he waved excitedly at the crowd. Gibbons dejectedly crossed the ring with a sheepish smile and congratulated Harry. The decision had been unanimous.[43]

Harry had been outweighed by seven and one half pounds, he was smaller in almost every measurement, didn't possess a powerful punch, and at fight time the odds against him lengthened to 2 to 1 and yet he had overcome all of this to defeat a man who had already beaten him twice in impressive fashion. It was a remarkable accomplishment that, combined with the financial success of the show, meant that Harry Greb had arrived in boxing's big time.

Reporters interviewed Jack Dempsey ringside for his opinion of the fight. He stated that Greb in his opinion easily deserved the decision for forcing the fight, which was in his estimation the best and fastest fight he had ever seen. He stated that Greb would be a difficult opponent for any heavyweight in the world and that he would be willing to fight him.[44] Doc Kearns, who seemed livid that Gibbons had lost, was non-committal but told Richard Guy of the Pittsburgh Leader that he would let Dempsey fight Greb as soon as he was made an offer from a reputable club.[45] In the audience Gene Tunney smiled, he had hoped Greb would win as he would later admit he feared having to defend his championship against Gibbons.[46]

After the fight Harry sat in his dressing room basking in the glow of such a momentous victory. The room was packed with more than fifty people all trying to have a word with Greb. Four policemen stood guard at the door preventing at least a hundred more from bursting into the already tight quarters. It was announced that Harry would begin a theatrical engagement the following week which would tour several states and Canada. He was now at the height of his fame and adding to the elation he was now feeling was the fact that he would be carrying home the largest check he had ever received, $17,000 (not including the considerable sums that

ANOTHER FLAT TIRE

OLYMPIC THEATRE

TODAY—"BEHOLD MY WIFE", featuring Mabel Julienne Scott, Milton Sills, Winter Hall, Elliott Dexter and other notable stars. The development of a crude Indian maiden, married for spite by the dissolute son of an aristocratic British family, into a beautiful, cultured woman, forms the theme of "Behold My Wife". The scenes are laid for the most part in the rugged Canadian Northwest, and the story is declared to be as strong as the scenery. George Melford produced the pictures for Paramount release.

Extra attraction—Harry Greb and Tom Gibbons fight pictures in two reels. A chance to see the man who will be Dempsey's next opponent.

WEDNESDAY and THURSDAY—"SHAME", featuring John Gilbert. One of the most heartgripping stories ever screened. Starting in the Orient and ending in the great Northwest of Can-

he and Engel had wagered), $4,500 more than Tommy Gibbons had received.

Harry and George stayed in New York a week to finalize the details of the theatrical tour. Tom Bodkin, former Pittsburgh boxing personality who was now acting as a booking agent for theatres on Broadway, had approached Engel and Greb and arranged all the details. The tour would be a multi-week engagement over the Columbia circuit with Hurtig & Seamon's Theatrical Enterprises. Harry's first performance would be March 20 at the Gayety Theatre in Pittsburgh. It would afford Harry the chance to return to his hometown in triumph.

The tour date would afford Harry the chance to appear before a wider audience, make some relatively quick, easy money, and build interest in the Dempsey fight. Dempsey had announced that he would travel to Europe which made a Greb fight impossible until summer at the very earliest. Matters were not helped by the fact that the New York press was still completely writing off Harry as an opponent for the champion. Tentative plans were made for Harry to face Gene Tunney for the American Light Heavyweight championship in May once the tour was completed but this match seemed unlikely to further Greb's reputation as he was heavily favored to easily defeat Tunney.

While still in New York Harry was asked to write a series of newspaper articles about the Gibbons fight and his plans for the future.

"...I had decided on that program weeks in advance of the bout. That is the only way to beat Gibbons. Don't let him get set, and beat him to the punch by stepping inside as he telegraphs his intentions with his right.

My constantly changing style of attack had Gibbons bewildered as I figured it would. Some will say that Gibbons had an off night.

I don't believe that is fair to me. I think that my style, which Gibbons was unable to solve, was entirely responsible for my opponent's poor showing.

...In baseball they consider the pitcher who has a change of pace a wise guy, a tough fellow to beat.

I have carried that baseball idea into the fight game. I believe in mixing them up, using a change of pace.

A flat-footed boxer like Gibbons is helpless against that style. That is why I beat him so decisively.[47]

...When I was matched to fight Gibbons the public viewed the bout in much the same manner as it did the Willard-Dempsey go.

Gibbons, with an advantage of ten pounds in weight and four inches in height, was regarded as far too husky for me to have a chance with him.

I feel that I demonstrated the folly of size being a fighter's most important asset.

There are a few other things a fighter must have besides size, among them being aggressiveness, footwork, cleverness and courage.[48]

...In my bout with Tommy Gibbons I entered the ring with two definite ideas, one was to throw as many gloves as I could in the general direction of Gibbons, the other was to keep out of the way of his right hand.

Gibbons is a hard puncher. I will concede that he hits harder than I do. However, he must be set to be effective. On the other hand I never set when starting a punch, often I am going away when it lands.

That, of course, is the real reason why Gibbons has greater punching power. If I adopted flat-footed tactics I probably could put twice as much steam back of my blows.

However, such a system would immediately rob me of one of my best assets, nimble pair of legs.

If good footwork can neutralize punching power by keeping a fighter off his balance then I am for good footwork.[49]

...Prior to my bout with Gibbons a lot of fight experts said that I didn't relish body punching.

A number of them who doped Gibbons to win by a knockout claimed that Gibbons would wear me down by stomach punching when in close and weaken me for a right-cross to the jaw that would end the bout.

Other critics said that Gibbons would outgame me. That was a big laugh with me. Regardless of what kind of a fighter I am, I know that I have courage.

As a matter of fact I know that I am gamer than Gibbons. In other words,

I feel that I outgamed Gibbons in our last bout.

To bear out such a statement one needs only to read the account of the fight. I conceded height and weight to Gibbons, yet throughout the bout I carried the fight to him.

Gibbons was never aggressive. He seldom led. If I had not been aggressive there wouldn't have been much of a fight.

This talk that Gibbons would outgame me is still a sore spot with me. I have never yet showed a bit of yellow, which is more than can be said for a great many of the fighters I have met.

Other critics said that Greb can't take it, which is a saying in fight circles that applies to fighters who can't stand grueling punishment.

Gibbons has been credited with having a knockout punch. I took the best that his right hand could deliver and shook it off.

In addition the much talked about infighting in which Gibbons was supposed to excel also failed to pan out. I feel that I inflicted most of the damage that was done at close quarters.

I think that my Gibbons bout should silence for all time the opinion of some of the critics that I couldn't take it.[50]

...What about a go with Jack Dempsey?

That is a question a lot of fight fans and experts have fired at me since my victory over Gibbons.

The way some of them put the question to me, I know they expect me to answer that I have no desire to meet the champion.

If the public is enough interested to attend, and some reliable promoter will handle the match, a Dempsey bout is perfectly suitable to me.

As a matter of fact, a bout with Dempsey is the ambition of my life.

That is why I jumped at the chance to take on Gibbons. Some of my friends didn't approve of such a match. They figured Gibbons punching power was too great.

...Realizing that Gibbons was generally regarded as the logical contender I wanted to eliminate him and thereby win the position he occupied in the fight game.

I feel that my victory has entitled me to such consideration. I regard myself as the logical contender for the title, despite my size.

What is more, I have better than an even chance to win the title.

I have no thought that I could knock Dempsey out. That wouldn't be my plan of battle. I would fight him much the same as I did Gibbons. Gibbons has a punch, but it was of no use to him.

I am honest when I say that I feel that I can outbox Dempsey in a bout of twelve to fifteen rounds.

There would always be the chance of a knockout by Dempsey of course. That would be the best bet. There was always that chance in my bout with Gibbons.

I am honest when I say I think I can outbox Dempsey. Of one thing I am positive, I would make a far better fight than did Carpentier.[51]

...Some fighters are unfortunate as to their weight.

Packey McFarland was such a fighter. His best weight was about 137. It was practically impossible for him to make the lightweight limit, which in his day was set at 133.

If he carried more than 137 pounds it was of no advantage to him, since at that weight he was at his best.

I regard myself in much the same light as Packey McFarland. It is a bit tough for me to make the middleweight limit. I am at my best at about 163.

In the light heavyweight class I am forced to give away from ten to twenty pounds.

And, of course, if I decide to take on any of the real heavyweights I may be forced to give away as much as forty or fifty pounds.

If Johnny Wilson didn't run out of his match with me after getting the $30,000 which was being held up because of his bad fight with Bryan Downey I would be wearing the middleweight title today.

I can make 158 pounds as I had agreed to do for Downey. It requires some effort, but I can make it and be strong. I don't want to appear boastful, but Wilson, with his left-hand style, is made to order for me.

If Gibbons had beaten me Wilson might have agreed to take a chance. I don't believe Johnny would now take a chance with his title with me unless someone dopes him.

Now that I have beaten Gibbons some of the critics say that I should take on Gene Tunney. In a way that is rather funny to me.

When Tunney was mentioned as a possibility for Tommy Gibbons, Tunney's manager said that his fighter wasn't ready for such game, that in a year or he would meet Gibbons.

Well, I have defeated Gibbons, who was regarded as too tough for Tunney by his manager, so why should I have to meet Tunney?

Fighting, however, is a business with me, and I will meet any fighter in the country if some real promoter offers a worthwhile purse.

Yes sir, I regard myself as an unfortunate fighter. I don't think I am chesty when I say I am a better fighter than either Wilson or Tunney, yet both of them carry around titles."[52]

18

THE FIGHTING MARINE

As the train eased into Pittsburgh's Union Station a massive throng had formed, eager to catch a glimpse of the man who had defeated Jack Dempsey's chief rival. As Harry emerged from the train shortly before 10 a.m. a great shout arose from the crowd which surged forward to meet him. With Harry and Engel were Mildred, looking somewhat healthier than she had in months, his sisters Clara and Ida as well as his mother, brother-in-law and his close friends the Albacker brothers Jack and Happy (Bernard). His two sisters and mother had boarded the train at East Liberty to avoid the mayhem which had been brewing downtown.

Harry and his entourage were quickly shuffled into automobiles and paraded downtown before crowds that lined the streets holding signs singing the praises of their native son and advertising his appearance at the Gayety which would start that afternoon. Adding to the festive atmosphere was Danny Nirella's brass band, which headed the procession. On several

Harry Greb and George Engel are mobbed at Union Station by friends, family, and curiosity seekers upon their arrival by train to Pittsburgh after his much publicized victory over Tommy Gibbons. From left to right: J. Elmer Edwards, Ida Edwards, Anna Greb (behind Ida), Mildred Greb, Harry Greb, Happy Albacker, George Engel.

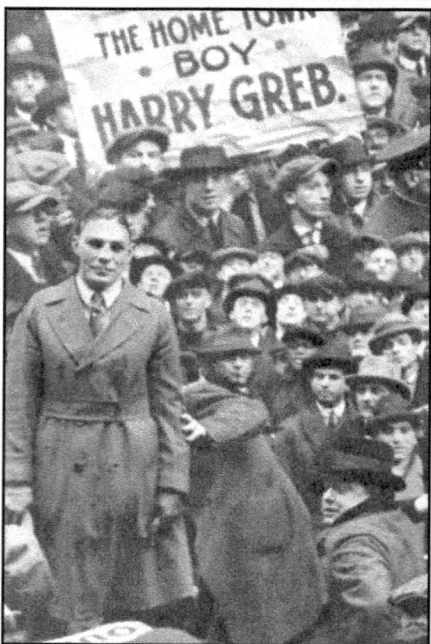

Top, above, and facing page top: Harry is greeted in Pittsburgh by a massive crowd of well-wishers. Photos were taken in front of City-County building facing northeast. In the background is the courthouse. Facing page bottom: Harry and George Engel are welcomed at the City-County building by city officials.

occasions Harry tried to stand and address the crowd but the clamor was too great for him to be heard and he finally gave up with a smile and a wave.

The parade crossed over Liberty Avenue to Fifth Avenue and then onto Grant before finally arriving at the City-County building where Harry would be welcomed in the council chambers by president Daniel Winters and other dignitaries. The presentation, which was supposed to be relatively private, nearly turned into pandemonium when the eager fans refused to wait outside. Hundreds stormed the building, knocking over furniture. A large window was shattered and a glass water bottle was overturned, smashing it and sending water cascading across the floor. Once the riotous crowd had settled down several of the councilmen officially welcomed Harry back from the fight and spoke on his behalf. Harry then told the councilmen how he had defeated Gibbons and answered questions from the audience.[1]

After leaving the City-Council building Harry was driven to a local hotel where a luncheon was given in his honor. Continuing the fast paced day Harry then arrived at the Gayety where he put on his first per-

formance. He seemed a little nervous but warmed up quickly. The show consisted of Harry and George Engel being introduced by Tom Bodkin after which Harry reiterated his love of Pittsburgh and his happiness at being back home. He would then tell the audience the story of his unlooked for victory over Gibbons, and his eagerness to face Dempsey and bring the heavyweight championship back home. After the spoken portion of the show was completed Harry would shadowbox for a round, skip rope for a round, and then spar for three rounds with Young Frank Gotch. Despite his nervousness the packed audience left satisfied.[2]

After the performance Harry was whisked away to a local radio station where he addressed radio listeners. Later in the evening Harry returned to the theatre for his second performance before finally having a chance to relax.

The whirlwind schedule kept up all week. The following night Harry purchased tickets for five hundred of the city's newsboys. They gathered in the evening and, headed by Harry, marched several blocks to the theatre where twenty of the boys were selected by lottery and given a new suit of clothes by Harry. The following night the Hotel Henry held "Harry Greb Night" where a party was given in Greb's honor. Upon arriving Harry was given a raucous

Top: Harry Greb addresses radio listeners upon his triumphant return to Pittsburgh after defeating Tommy Gibbons. Above: The silver loving cup awarded to Harry by citizens of Garfield in honor of his victory over Gibbons.

standing ovation. Shouts of "speech! speech!" went up to which Harry offered: "I'm not much of a talker. My only hope is that I can someday bring the heavyweight championship to Pittsburgh."[3]

During his final performance in Pittsburgh the audience was packed with admirers from the Garfield district. Afterwards he was presented a silver loving cup filled with red roses and topped by the flag of the United States. After completing the evening engagement Harry was honored by the Pittsburgh Press Club.

Before leaving for his next engagement in Toronto on Sunday March 26 Harry was honored by the Pittsburgh Lyceum where he had trained faithfully for years. Boxing exhibitions were put on for his benefit and a band headed by Greb's friend Happy Albacker provided musical entertainment. Harry himself was adamant about exhibiting his skills for the members and went four rounds with Jack Barry. At eleven o'clock that night a train bound for Toronto chugged out of Pittsburgh with Harry aboard. He had been afforded the greatest reception of any boxer in the history of the city. Not since the Pirates won the World Series in 1909 had anyone been feted like Harry had over the previous week.

George Engel had taken a separate train for New York where he would go to negotiate terms for a future bout with Jack Dempsey in Philadelphia for eight rounds.[4] It was expected that if Harry could show well over that distance he would be given a title shot. While planning his upcoming trip to Europe Dempsey commented on this development: "I will probably come back and fight Harry Greb on Labor Day. I picked Greb to beat Gibbons. Greb is big enough for me. He will weigh as much as Fitzsimmons did. He is a busy swinging fighter, coming in all the time and slipping the other fel-

AN ARTIST'S IMPRESSION OF GREB—BOXER-ACTOR

HARRY GREB NOW AN ACTOR MAN

Greb's·Manager·
Geo. Engle·is·on·
deck·with·his·
.see-gar.

Wallops·his·sparring·
partner·Frank Gotch·
around·the·stage·
for·three·rounds

Lwek Looper·

Ducking·scenery·
will·keep·Harry·
in·trim

As·
light·on·
his·feet·
as·the·
chorus·girls

low's punches. They are talking of matching us and I guess it will go through."[5]

With Dempsey unavailable to fight for the time being Harry's next opponent was selected to be Gene Tunney for the light-heavyweight championship of America. The title was a synthetic one, having been created by promoters eager to fill the gap created when Georges Carpentier took the world title back to France. The American light heavyweight championship itself had never existed prior to Gene Tunney's lackluster victory over faded former champ Battling Levinsky and indeed it would cease to exist after Tunney had moved up to the heavyweight division.

Tunney was given little chance to retain his championship against Greb. He had throughout his career been plagued by brittle hands, an overly defensive style of fighting, an aloof personality, and worst of all extremely protective matchmaking which had helped to preserve his undefeated record. In truth, despite having been a professional fighter since 1915, Tunney had only faced a handful of men who could have been classed as contenders and some of them had already been past their best at the time they met Tunney.

In Toronto Harry performed before sellout crowds sparring with Pittsburgh heavyweight Red Flaherty. He also visited military hospitals and performed before convalescent soldiers.[6] The following week the troupe performed the same show in Montreal where Harry was beginning to the feel the effects of the busy schedule and again a week later in Buffalo where he lamented being considered a challenger for three titles and yet unable to corner any of the champions into facing him. After leaving Buffalo a homesick Harry returned to Pittsburgh for one day before heading to New York City to fulfill his engagement there and finalize details for his fight with Tunney.

While Harry had been performing in Buffalo, Tunney had taken advantage of the talk of a proposed Greb fight to exhibit his wares in Pittsburgh. His opponent was Jack Burke, a mediocre Pittsburgh heavyweight, and sometime protégé of Greb's. Tunney won the fight by knockout in the ninth round but was jeered throughout the contest for his overly cautious style. Calls of "You'd better stay away from Greb!" could be heard throughout the hall several times.[7]

With Tunney's manager Frank "Doc" Bagley seemingly holding negotiations up Frank Flournoy called both Bagley and Engel to Madison Square Garden in order to finalize the fight. Initially it seemed as if the match would fall through due to Bagley's exorbitant demands. First Bagley refused to risk Tunney's title in a fight to a decision. Instead he wanted the fight held in New Jersey where Greb could only win via knockout or disqualification.[8] After this objection was overcome there was still the matter of how the purse should be divided. Greb was by far the more popular and recognizable fighter of the two but Tunney held a title. If Greb wanted to win that title he would have to pay for the privilege.[9]

The talks broke down without an agreement and after several days with neither Engel or Bagley willing to budge, and the fight slipping away, Greb gave in, making it known that he was willing to face Tunney "for little more than the privilege of getting a shot at the young Irishman."[10] As a result Tunney would get a whopping thirty-eight percent of the gate leaving only fourteen percent for Greb. The fight was signed to be held on May 26 (later changed to May 23) at Madison Square Garden for a scheduled distance of fifteen rounds to a decision for the American light-heavyweight championship.

In the minds of most observers the signing of the contract meant that Greb was virtually guaranteed a championship, such was the belief that his victory over Tunney was a forgone conclusion. Tunney had turned professional in 1915 but had failed to garner much attention initially. It was not until after he had won the light heavyweight championship of American Expeditionary Forces that he received any national press at all. This much publicized tournament meant that Tunney could count on returning to the United States with some interest attached to his boxing career. Yet, Tunney failed to capitalize on the country's enthusiasm for war heroes and spent the next two years facing sub-par competition and garnering little attention or respect from the press due largely to his personality and cautious style. This was most prevalent when Tunney was given the opportunity to showcase his talent on the undercard of the Jack Dempsey-Georges Carpentier fight. Instead of making the most of such a plumb assignment Tunney and Soldier Jones fought a terrible fight and by the time Tunney had knocked Jones out in the seventh round few in the massive audience cared.

Six months later despite fighting opposition of little note Tunney was given the opportunity to fight the severely faded Battling Levinsky for the "light heavyweight championship of America." Again Tunney won, and again the fight was a disappointing affair.[11] To Greb, and indeed many other fighters, Tunney's victory must have seemed a hollow one. It had been nearly five years since Harry had first defeated Levinsky in Pittsburgh in 1917, narrowly missing knocking the Battler out and thus capturing the world title.

Harry certainly felt he had little to fear from Tunney. Yet, despite all of the evidence to support Greb's confidence, there were things that hinted at Tunney being a special fighter. He was young and strong to be sure but he also had a single minded focus on his chosen profession. This professional attitude meant that Tunney came into the ring against every opponent trained to the minute, never taking any opponent for granted. While many criticized Tunney's cautious approach it was an approach borne not out of fear but out of calculation. Tunney studied his opponents, picked apart their weaknesses, slowly broke them down bit by bit, and won as he pleased. These attributes combined in Tunney to see him through his seven years of professional fighting undefeated. This is what Harry would have to contend with when he went up against Tunney May 23 and also why Harry opened as the narrow favorite at 6 to 5 odds.[12]

As part of his preparation for Tunney Harry would face a New York club fighter named Al Roberts at Boston over ten rounds. Roberts, who billed himself as the light-heavyweight champion of Staten Island, was expected to give Harry a good warm-up for Tunney. In fact Roberts had been defeated by Tunney two years earlier and was eager to defeat Greb and take his place against Tunney for a revenge match.

On May 8 Harry was ringside at Motor Square Garden to see his sparring partner Patsy Scanlon lose to Bricky Ryan. When Harry was introduced before the fight he received a rousing reception. Four days later he was in Boston to face Roberts. Despite Harry wading in seemingly wide open Roberts was unable to land effectively. Three times Roberts hit the canvas and three times he arose to survive the first round. Greb continued his savage attack in the second, cutting Roberts' eye. In the third Roberts sustained a split lip and in the fourth he was floored twice more. Roberts

Alfred Heidler was the son of German immigrant parents. He supplemented his income from working on the railroads by boxing as Al Roberts. He billed himself as the heavyweight champion of Staten Island and managed to fashion a fairly impressive record despite never devoting himself to the sport full time.

continued to weaken under Harry's pressure in the fifth. In the sixth a picture perfect right hand sent Roberts down hard. Roberts got to his feet at the count of nine but a half punch - half push sent him down for the seventh and final time.[13]

Harry's victory over Roberts did not come without criticism. Over the past several months Harry had made a not so subtle change to his style. It was a change born out of necessity. Since sustaining the injury to his eye Harry's depth perception had been compromised. In order to better judge his distance Harry would often loop one hand behind an opponent's neck and pump punches to the head and body. Strictly speaking it was an illegal tactic and one for which Harry was becoming increasingly criticized. Both W. C. Spargo of the Boston Traveler and Jack Conway of the Boston America went so far as to say that Harry should have been disqualified against Roberts for just this tactic.[14] One wonders how, if at all, their opinion would have changed had they known that for all intents and purposes Harry had faced the seven pounds heavier Roberts blind in one eye.

On May 16 Harry arrived in New York to once again train at Philadelphia Jack O'Brien's gym for his upcoming bout with Gene Tunney. Despite heavy rains fans turned out in droves to watch Harry train. What they witnessed were feats of stamina nothing short of breathtaking. Harry sparred with Red Flaherty, Jack Barry, and Bill Thomas, who in their first session went after Harry with guns blazing looking for a knockout. Unflustered, Harry let Thomas expend his energy and then spent two rounds battering his exhausted sparring partner around the ring to wild applause.[15] Harry supplemented his sparring by adding Billy Walker and Billy Walthour to his staff and despite often traveling fifteen rounds or more in a day he still put out the call for more sparring partners.

Greb and Engel were so confident of victory over Tunney that they made clear their true goal was Dempsey. "...Within three or four months you're going to see Greb in the ring with Dempsey," Engel was quoted. "Greb has one idea fixed in his head. It's that he can whip Dempsey over any route from fifteen rounds up, or a shorter route if Jack insists on it. He has helped Dempsey train several times and he knows every move Dempsey makes. Dempsey never has been able to hold Greb off and he couldn't do it in a fight. 'The way to whip Dempsey,' Greb says, 'is to keep him on his heels. Don't let him set for a punch. Stay on top of him and never stop hitting, and he can't do a thing.' If Greb gets on with Dempsey the world is going to see the busiest fifteen rounds, if it goes that far, ever pulled off in a ring."[16]

Harry himself expressed his own thoughts on the matter after one workout: "I am not underrating Tunney," Greb said. "They say he is in wonderful shape and is punching hard. I'm glad of that, for I want everyone to say I licked a real fighter next Tuesday night. The wise ones thought Tommy Gibbons would have a pink tea with me and I fooled them and proved beyond a shadow of a doubt that I was his master. I don't like to boast, but as far as I am concerned the winning of the light heavyweight crown is a mere formality. I am just as confident of beating Tunney as I was of whipping Gibbons. I am going after Carpentier next and if he is not to be had, well then I will set sail for Champion Jack Dempsey."[17]

Eager to prove himself to his numerous doubters Tunney was training diligently at Harry McCormack's farm at Red Bank, New Jersey. Tunney sparred daily with Young Hickey, Larry Williams, and Willie Ryan, trying to alter his normally defensive style to that of a more aggressive stance. Tunney was rapidly rounding into supreme condition and wowed the small crowds that came to watch his training with his powerful left hook to the head and body. It was on this left hook that Tunney and Doc Bagley were pinning all of their hopes. They made it known throughout the training camp that Tunney would be looking to knockout Greb and wouldn't be satisfied with the same lackluster victories that Tunney had settled for in the past. "You never saw Gene let out, but you will see him do it tomorrow," said Bagley on the eve of the contest. "We have brought him along gradually, letting him win under wraps for the most part. He could have stopped some of the men he has met in a punch or two, but a man never learns very much that way. Gene has been in there to get experience against all comers, and now that he has it, watch him step. He will stop Greb before the limit, and I think he will do it with a left hook."[18]

The day before the big fight the Pennsylvania Hotel began to fill with arrivals from Pittsburgh, all anxious to see their man win the championship. There was a crowd from Pittsburgh of several hundred strong at ringside in Madison Square Garden the night of the twenty-third but despite this impressive number the total of nearly 10,000 paid attendees did not quite live up to expectations and can probably be blamed on the fact that most considered Greb a sure winner. The betting odds on the fight had now settled between 3 to 1 and 7 to 5 in favor of a Greb victory. Despite this few backers could be found for Tunney and betting was light.[19]

That afternoon Harry weighed in at 162½, or twelve pounds less than Tunney. Prior to the fight George Engel paid a visit to Tunney's dressing room to inspect Tunney's hand wraps and found that Tunney had bound his hands with the heavy tape that gave a distinct

Gene Tunney was a wonderfully conditioned athlete with a cold, calculating mind, evidenced in his pensive stare emanating from this photo taken in the early 1920s.

The calm before the storm: Greb and Tunney pose for the cameramen prior to their historic match. Former fighter Kid McPartland, acting as referee, looks on as famous announcer Joe Humphries peers over Tunney's shoulder.

advantage to the wearer. While this practice was not uncommon in previous decades, if agreed upon by the participants, it was rapidly falling out of favor. Tunney was forced to unwind his bandages and rebind his hands under Engel's watchful eye.[20] As Tunney entered the ring he was given a rousing ovation by his partisan hometown crowd. In reply Harry's small by comparison, yet no less boisterous, rooting section did their best to raise the roof when Harry hopped through the ropes.

The fight itself started out poorly for Tunney and went from bad to worse. Harry came out for the first round intent on making an impression on his less experienced foe. After a few minutes of sparring Harry leapt in and shattered Tunney's nose with the first landed punch of the fight. Greb then proceeded to tear into Tunney, blasting away at head and body, and bulling the ex-marine into the ropes and corners where he would continue to belabor the champion.

Tunney fought back furiously in the second and third rounds in an attempt to stem Harry's relentless attack yet every time it looked as if Tunney had landed a solid punch Greb would come back fighting harder and more furiously than ever before. Such tenacity seemed to befuddle and confuse the champion. By the end of the fourth round Tunney, Greb, and referee Kid McPartland were covered in the blood that had continued to flow from Tunney's misshapen nose in sickening rivulets.

Things got worse for Tunney in the sixth round. Early in the round a cut which Tunney had sustained in training was reopened by what was variously described as a punch or an accidental clash of heads. In the following round the fight began to get ugly with Harry being booed by the pro-Tunney crowd for the liberal use of his head and elbows, while Tunney had begun to let his body punches stray below the belt and rabbit punched in the clinches.

By this point Harry was in complete command of the fight but Tunney was making him work all the time through sheer dogged determination like a wounded lion fighting to his last breath.

If Tunney had hoped that the pace would eventually tire Greb he was sorely disappointed when in the eighth round it appeared to many that Greb actually seemed to be gaining speed. He danced around Tunney, popping punches from all directions before opening another bad cut, this time over Tunney's right eye. Between rounds Doc Bagley, one of the all-time great cut men, worked feverishly over Tunney to halt the flow of blood, only to see his work undone and the cuts reopened each succeeding round.

Greb took the ninth and tenth rounds through his speed and aggression. By now Tunney sensed that he was desperately behind on points. In the twelfth he fought back valiantly in an attempt to salvage the fight by scoring a knockout. The rally was

Top and above: Two scenes of Tunney and Greb fighting in close during their first fight. The bottom photo is of sixth round action.

short lived though and by the fourteenth round Tunney was an exhausted, gruesome, and pitiful mess. He no longer had the stamina for any sustained attack and could only hope now for the moral victory of lasting to the final bell.[21] He succeeded but it was a hollow victory at best and his reward was that his features had been battered beyond recognition. Jack Lawrence of

Top: Greb is seen on the attack against Tunney during the sixth round as referee Kid McPartland looks on. Above: In a clinch during the sixth round Tunney is seen bending Greb backwards and nearly forcing both out of the ring near Tunney's own corner.

the New York Tribune describe Tunney as a "weird and gruesome spectacle" by virtue of the "ragged gashes" over each eye, his battered nose, and his puffed and bleeding lips.[22] The damage was not restricted to Tunney's face. His torso was swollen and turned a sickening pink, having been punched raw by the Pittsburgh dynamo. As the two fighters awaited the decision Tunney paced nervously in his corner while Greb was confident. Joe Humphries stepped to the center of the ring to announce in his legendary voice what had already been obvious to the majority of those present. Greb had won the light-heavyweight championship of America.

Tunney met Greb, who was being carried around the ring by his handlers, to congratulate him. Greb clasped both sides of Tunney's face and kissed him on the forehead. Tunney was dejected but offered no excuses for his loss. Harry then energetically leapt over the top rope and trotted back to his dressing room without a mark on his face or a hair out of place.

In the other corner it was a completely different story. Halfway back to his dressing room

Tunney collapsed and was carried to a table where, after regaining consciousness, his boxing trunks had to be cut off, so extensive was the swelling around his midsection.[23] Tunney lay on the table, unable to move, in a state of pain and utter exhaustion. When he was able to move he was taken to the hospital to have his wounds treated and then returned to his Red Bank, New Jersey training camp where he would convalesce for over a week.

If Tunney was unwilling, initially, to make excuses for his loss he quickly changed his tune. Three days after his defeat he issued a statement through his manager which had no doubt been bolstered by a small minority of New York newspapermen who issued oddly slanted stories about the outcome of the fight. One writer even went so far as to state that he would have given Tunney no worse than a draw despite Tunney admitting for the rest of his life that he lost in

As the fight progressed Tunney became increasingly desperate in his attempts to finish on his feet, often forcing referee McPartland to pry them apart in order to keep the action flowing.

horrible, one-sided fashion. Tunney would echo these stories by stating that headbutts had been the result of his broken nose and various cuts and that the resulting blood flow had been the reason he lost his championship. This all came in spite of the fact that the majority of written accounts state that the damage to Tunney's nose came from a punch and the cut over his left eye came from an accidental clash of heads.[24] Bagley added that in six months Tunney would be ready for another crack at Greb.

To be sure Greb's frantic style of fighting against Tunney at times skirted the rules of the sport but the idea that a man who had fought over two hundred bouts without a disqualification (if one excludes the double disqualification against Grant "Kid" Clark) got the better of the officials' verdict in Tunney's hometown before a partisan Tunney crowd while facing a defending champion is simply ludicrous. Indeed, Greb's most egregious foul was his repeated holding and hitting. It was this foul which would be most prominently mentioned for the rest of his career and was necessitated by his lack of depth perception which was a result of his injured eye.

Engel responded to Tunney's allegations in early June stating "Tunney says Harry used unfair tactics, such as indiscriminate use of his head in the clinches and hitting low, but he knows deep down in his heart that he was licked fair and square. This is the first time I've ever heard a squawk from one of Harry's opponents, and he has fought several hundred men. Everybody knows Greb is one of a few of the cleanest boxers in the pastime. He doesn't have to resort to mean tricks to win. He's got so much class over the many middle, light-heavy, and heavyweights that I have all I can do to induce some of them to step in the ring with him.

We'll give Tunney another chance but he'll have to stop alibiing, that is, quit saying he was

Facing page: As the final bell rang Tunney and Greb embraced and congratulated each other. Above: As George Engel looks on Joe Humphries announces that Harry Greb has just won the American light-heavyweight championship. Moments after this photo Greb was hoisted onto his handlers' shoulders and carried around the ring.

fouled out of his title. Do you know that in the thirteenth round Greb begged me to let him go out and knock Gene out, but I told him to take it easy, because he was so far ahead and he didn't have to score a k.o. to insure victory.

As soon as Tunney comes out and says he was whipped fair and square, we'll sign up for another fight. Until then he'll have to box some suckers and wait until we are good and ready to box him again."[25]

On June 15 Tunney finally left his quarters at Red Bank to post a certified check for $2,500 to bind a return bout with Greb in six months. He had spent most of the previous three weeks recuperating, recovering from one of the most brutal beatings ever sustained in a boxing match.

Harry only lingered in New York long enough to wrap up some business before quietly returning to Pittsburgh. The next night he was introduced from the ring prior to the Johnny Ray-Charlie White contest and received a raucous applause. Over the next couple of weeks Harry basked in the glow that is often afforded conquering heroes, relaxed, and even found time to act as a guest referee at several local amateur boxing matches and charity events.

The Tunney fight seemed sure to propel Harry to his greatest desire, a fight for the heavyweight championship against Jack Dempsey. Yet, Dempsey had returned from his European vacation with an entirely changed attitude toward a fight with Greb. Upon arriving in Los Angeles Dempsey expressed his hopes for a return match with Georges Carpentier stating that Greb was a "mighty good man" but "out of the question as a heavyweight possibility simply because he's too light."[26]

For his part Tex Rickard was far more interested in seeing Greb face Carpentier for the world light heavyweight title. Immediately after his victory over Tunney Rickard cabled Carpentier

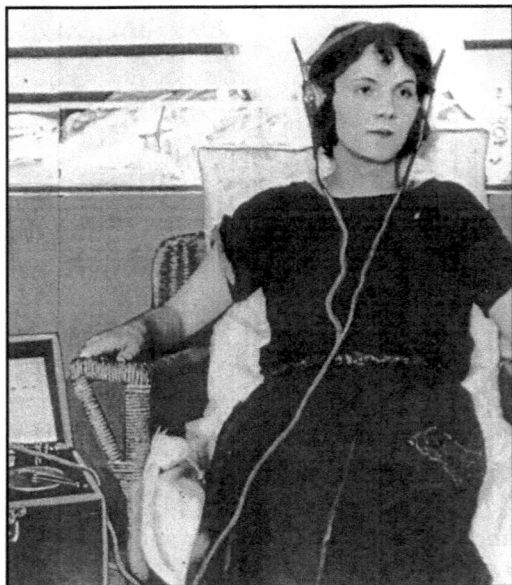

With Mildred's illness now progressing to the point where she could no longer travel without great difficulty she was confined to listening to Harry's bouts via radio. She is shown above listening to the Greb-Tunney bout on a reciever specially installed for her by Westinghouse technicians. She would also be listening to Harry's upcoming bout with Tommy Loughran which would be the first boxing match broadcast from Philadelphia.

an offer of $150,000 to face Greb for the championship.[27] When presented with this prospect Greb remarked "I'll fight Carpentier, any time, any place."[28] But Harry would soon find that Carpentier was no more eager to face him than Dempsey had been.

Before receiving word back from Carpentier Rickard began laying plans for another one of his legendary promotions featuring Greb and the Frenchman at Boyles Thirty Acres. Yet Carpentier quickly and inexplicably began throwing up roadblocks to the match. First he demanded that French promoters be given the first opportunity to bid the match in hopes that he might defend his title at home before his loyal and partisan fans.[29] This in itself was an odd request given the fact that no French promoter could come close to competing with Rickard's massive offer. Engel responded that he and Greb would go where the money was but since the money was very obviously in America, having already turned down two $10,000 offers to box in London, they would stay put until such time as a better offer materialized. Engel added that Carpentier had always been treated fairly in the States, had won his title there, and should have no complaints about defending it there.

"I don't think the Frenchman cares to have anything to do with Harry, for he has been warned about Greb's stuff," said Engel. "He'd rather stay over there and pick up some soft dough. I know plenty about Carpentier's style of milling for I had Frank Klaus when he whipped him some years ago and my orders to Harry, if they are carried out, will find George stretched out on the floor taking the 10 count."[30]

With the press clamoring for a Greb-Carpentier match Rickard was forced to wait a maddening two weeks with no official reply to his offer. Rickard sent a second cable to Carpentier and four days later, on June 10, Rickard finally received word from Carpentier's manager stating that Carpentier would instead face Marcel Nilles and Joe Beckett before any possible match with Greb.[31] Suddenly Engel's words seemed prophetic as Carpentier was being roundly criticized for his choice of opposition. In reality Carpentier had not been formally obligated to face Nilles and Beckett and indeed would not fight either man until the following summer.

"I believe there is no doubt that Carpentier is afraid to risk his title against Greb," declared Engel. "He was made a wonderful offer by Rickard, but his wily manager cabled he could not afford to accept it because Georges has two fights scheduled with as many bums in Europe. Fine state of affairs. Imagine a man with some brains turning down $150,000! Enough money to save the whole of Russia. Apparently Carpentier has been given the well-known lowdown on Greb's prowess, for I can't see how he could possibly pass up that amount of money except for the fact that he knows he is in for a licking if he consents to swap punches with my boy."[32]

Even as Rickard tried to coax the light-heavyweight champion into the ring with Greb other forces were working hard to force Johnny Wilson into finally defending his championship against Greb. The New York State Athletic Commission announced that Johnny Wilson must honor his previous contract to face Greb or risk having his title declared vacant in the state of New York.[33] In such an eventuality many states would follow suit. Wilson scoffed at such declarations but within a week, in an effort to buy them time, Wilson's manager Martin Killelea issued a statement to the press in which he proclaimed Wilson ready and willing to sit down with Rickard and sign contracts to defend his title against Greb.[34]

However as the June 20th deadline set by the commission approached Rickard tried in vain to contact Killelea without success. With Wilson's repeated and overt refusal to enter into negotiations in good faith for a fight with Greb given as the cause, the commission declared Wilson's title vacant and open for competition.[35] It was a historic, and potentially damaging, precedent that had never been seen in the ring since the inception of the Marquis of Queensbury rules. As the only two contenders with an official challenge on record backed by a forfeit it was hoped by the commission that Greb and Brooklyn's Dave Rosenberg would soon begin negotiations for a championship match.

While New York promoters and commissioners were trying to drag champions in two divisions kicking and screaming into a fight with Greb he was preparing for his next match. Intent on making good on a promise to have his first fight as American champion in Pittsburgh he had agreed to face Hugh Walker on June 26 at Forbes Field in a bout promoted by the fledgling Pittsburgh Boxing Club which had been formed by Greb's close friend Eddie Deasy.

"Walker," said Greb, "Is an early starter and if a fellow isn't careful Hughey piles up quite a lead at the start."[36] Harry found out just how right he was in the first round he walked into a punch that sent him reeling across the ring. He spent the remainder of the round on the defensive. From the second round on the fight belonged to Greb by increasingly wider margins. When the fight was over Walker was a bloody mess, much like he had been after facing Greb in February.[37]

The day after Greb's victory over Walker John J. Bell, the head of the Motor Square Garden club, announced that he had secured Greb's agreement to face Jack Dempsey in a no-decision match in Pittsburgh to be held at a specially built arena on Labor Day. Bell had received financial backing to offer Dempsey a purse of $100,000 and planned to leave within a day for New

Kansas City's Hugh Walker fought Harry Greb twice in 1922. He had been fighting professionally for seven years with mixed success as he boxed to supplement the income he earned from selling ice cream.

York where he hoped to secure the heavyweight champion's signature.[38]

"A clash between Greb and Dempsey in Pittsburgh would prove highly successful. I am sure," said Engel. "Pittsburgh is Harry's hometown and the folks there are wild about him. I am sure he could give Dempsey enough action in a ten-round bout. Greb himself is confident he can outpoint the champion over this distance, and there are plenty of Greb admirers who have confidence in Greb's active, untiring style."[39]

On July 5th the Pittsburgh Boxing Club announced that it too was eager to acquire Dempsey's services to face Greb and would match the Motor Square Garden Club's offer of $100,000 and fifty percent of the gate. Kearns announced from Chicago that he had received the offers from Pittsburgh but was making it increasingly clear that he preferred facing either Bill Brennan or Jess Willard to Greb or Harry Wills.[40] John Bell was adamant that he would need two months to prepare and promote a labor day show and would need confirmation from Kearns soon in order to begin working. To this end Bell issued a statement that if he did not receive word from Kearns by July 9 there would be little point in proceeding.

It became clear that Kearns was unwilling to risk Dempsey's crown against threatening opposition when he published a list of who he considered to be Dempsey's top challengers: 1. Jess Willard, 2. Bill Brennan, 3. Harry Greb, 4. Georges Carpentier, and 5. Harry Wills.[41] In addition to this Kearns made the odd choice of bypassing Pittsburgh, which was on his way from Chicago to New York, and then announced to the press that he could not understand why he had not heard from Bell.[42] As Kearns continued playing games in the press it became apparent that he had no intention of pitting Dempsey against Greb. When a frustrated Bell had finally come to this realization he stated: "It is too late now to think of arranging the bout for Labor Day. Had Kearns accepted my offer when I made it, almost two weeks ago, I could have gone through with the show Labor Day. As it is now, my contractor says the time is too short to permit of building of the arena and having everything in order."[43] Bell added that he hoped to salvage the match for a later date but, with Kearns seemingly playing everyone against each other, there seemed little hope of this.

While he waited for larger, more lucrative bouts Greb prepared for his next match. He was scheduled to face young Tommy Loughran in Philadelphia on July 10 (a rematch against Whitey Allen for Bellaire, Ohio having been cancelled due to foul weather). At 19 years old and still relatively inexperienced Loughran was already being hailed by his fellow Philadelphians as a future great by virtue of recent victories over such experienced campaigners as Bryan Downey, Fay Keiser, Jimmy Darcy, Mike McTigue, Frank Carbone, and Jackie Clark.[44] While not classed as a hard puncher, Loughran was fearless, perfectly conditioned, and a very clever boxer. Coming into the ring with a level of confidence that bordered on arrogance it was expected that Loughran would present Greb with an interesting challenge.

Tommy entered the ring at 163^1/$_2$ pounds to Greb's 167 and it was quickly apparent that he would be the crowd's favorite. The audience gave Loughran a thunderous applause while a band from his St. Monica's Catholic Club entertained the fans. For the first two rounds Loughran thrilled his fans by holding his own with his more experienced foe but class began to tell in the third. In the fourth Harry landed a left-right combination square on Loughran's nose which started a steady stream of blood that went unchecked throughout the fight. In the fifth round Loughran opened a cut over Greb's eye that only spurred Greb on to greater action. In the eighth and final round Loughran brought his fans to their feet with a wonderful rally but Harry was too strong and fought his younger rival off, battering him around the ring. After the final bell the two fighters smiled at each other acknowledging the other's ability.[45]

"Loughran is a good, sturdy fighter," said a smiling Greb after the fight, "and he has a bright future. I think in time, with careful handling, he will be one of the leading fighters in the country."

"He needs to develop a punch for what he showed didn't bother me much. He is a bit green at the game right now but should develop. He is inclined to rough it but that will be lost when he gets real ring experience."

Tommy Loughran (left) was a nineteen year old middleweight from Philadelphia when he first met Harry Greb. Despite his youth and relative inexperience he had already established himself as a favorite in his hometown by running up a string of wins against well known fighters. The men are pictured here prior to their July 1922 match.

"I've had a long strenuous campaign and feel pretty well tired out. I plan to take a vacation and perhaps will start up again in a month or six weeks. When I do, it will be with idea of getting a match with Georges Carpentier. The Frenchman is the only logical opponent I can see at the present time. I will be glad to meet him for the world's light heavyweight crown anywheres, but prefer to fight in this country, although I am willing to fight in Europe."

"It doesn't look like I will meet Jack Dempsey as things have about fallen through regarding the match."[46]

Greb stuck to his promise of taking a vacation. In fact he had been scheduled to appear on the Sports Alliance Show in Long Island in a four rounder two days later yet the cut suffered against Loughran was severe enough to prevent him from appearing. It would be two and half months before he would appear in the ring again.

While waiting for promoters to secure a Dempsey-Greb match Harry traveled to Saranac Lake to look over available cure cottages for rent. Mildred's condition had continued to deteriorate and Harry's long absences only complicated matters. He found that every time he returned to her she had grown weaker and lost more weight. Harry even discussed retiring from the ring in the hope that it might help her condition but was determined to make one last big payday against either Carpentier or Dempsey in order to leave the sport financially comfortable. Plans were made to sell their home in Pittsburgh and relocate to Bloomingdale, New York. Bloomingdale was situated just six miles from the health spa located at Saranac Lake where Mildred would benefit from more aggressive treatment. While there Greb looked over prospective training quarters as well.

By the end of July Mildred was being treated at a local sanitarium and her condition was listed as serious. Harry had closed on a small cottage owned by S. W. Barnard at Bloomingdale and by late August he and Dorothy moved in. They were accompanied by Mildred's mother who would look after Mildred and Dorothy while Harry was away earning the family's living. The couple enjoyed long stretches together during July, August, Sept, and October and, despite Mildred's condition, they were happy, finally having some time to be a family together as Greb slowed his schedule to be with Mildred.

While in Saranac Harry still could not pry himself away from the sport he loved so dearly. He engaged in an exhibition bout to raise money for Elizabeth Skeels, who had been widowed four years earlier when her husband had been killed by a falling tree and was now denied compensation. Harry faced his old foe Jimmy Darcy who had come to Saranac with Jack Dempsey and stayed to vacation and train for his upcoming bout with Young Fisher. Keeping time and acting as master of ceremonies for the match was none other than legendary baseball player Christy Mathewson who was himself staying at Saranac for treatment.

To keep busy, while Mildred was placed on a program of strict bed rest, Harry hunted and fished. To stay in shape he trained at the local Boys Club sparring with Jimmy Darcy and Leo Caghil, who occasionally accompanied the Greb family on their retreats.

As Harry tried to relax and enjoy his time off from the sport the business of boxing continued in his stead. Pittsburgh promoters continued to try to piece together a match with Dempsey and failing that a hometown rematch with Gene Tunney. Meanwhile Greb and Engel were inexplicably suspended from fighting in New York by the State Athletic Commission. The reasoning that the commission gave for its action was that Greb had failed to make a match with Dave Rosenberg for the Middleweight Championship, shorn from Johnny Wilson less than one month earlier. Engle had tried to attend the meeting which resulted in the suspension but arrived late and was not allowed to address the Commission. He told reporters present that he and Greb had been busy fulfilling prior engagements which prevented them from obligating themselves to a fight with Rosenberg.[47]

Baseball legend Christy Mathewson (left) shakes hands with Greb. This photo was likely taken during the summer of 1922 while Greb and Mathewson worked together on an exhibition card at Saranac Lake.

Wilson himself was now feeling the economic pinch that the Commission's ruling was having on him. He had fought Al DeMaris earlier in the month in Rutland, Vermont before a crowd of less than five hundred fans and was paid less than $700 for his trouble. He continued to lobby for the opportunity to have his suspension removed. The boxing world was divided in its assessment of the situation. Many were tired of Wilson and his unwillingness to face worthy contenders under anything but highly favorable terms and yet the New York Commission, and particularly Commissioner William Muldoon, seemed to be handing out increasingly dictatorial rulings which many surmised were an attempt at consolidating boxing's power base squarely in New York. To many in the press this was never more apparent than when the Commission appointed New Jersey's Phil Krug to face Rosenberg in Madison Square Garden for the championship. One would have been hard pressed to find a place in the top ten middleweights in the country, had such a ranking existed at this time, for either Krug or Rosenberg, yet both boxers were from the New York vicinity and would be expected to defend the championship locally on a regular basis to the benefit of promoters and the tax collectors.

The match itself held few surprises when it finally came off. Rosenberg defeated Krug as was expected yet failed to impress as a championship caliber fighter. The only real interest in the fight was whether Krug would last the distance, which he managed to do through an

Dave Rosenberg (right) of Brooklyn squares off against Phil Krug of Harrison, New Jersey in a match designed by the New York State Athletic Commission as being for the middleweight championship they had relieved Johnny WIlson of. The Commission had made a half hearted attempt at securing Greb to face Rosenberg for the title but his busy schedule prevented his participation, Krug was then secured to face Rosenberg.

inspiring exhibition of grit and determination. Yet, despite the efforts of both fighters, few regarded Rosenberg as a true champion and few today remember him as such.[48]

As Harry prepared to re-enter the ring news crossed the Atlantic that would surely have been of interest to him. Georges Carpentier had lost his championship under sensational circumstances. Rather than face any of his top challengers Carpentier chose instead to play it safe by facing a little known Senegalese export named Battling Siki. Despite being heavyweight champion of France, Siki was little more than a crude brawler, better known for his erratic behavior and unwillingness to train than his modest wins over European club fighters.

It was expected to be an easy knockout win for Carpentier. The stage was set for a triumphant homecoming at the grand opening of the new Buffalo Velodrome before the largest audience ever turned out for a boxing match in France. Adding to the luster of the event, and the purse of the fighters, motion pictures would be taken and widely distributed throughout Europe. To make sure that everything went according to script, and that the hero won, it had been arranged between Carpentier's handlers and Siki's that Siki would take his beating for a few rounds, just long enough to make the films interesting, before collapsing completely and convincingly at the champion's feet.

The problem developed early in the fight when Siki, perturbed at Carpentier's unwillingness to pull his punches, began throwing leather with wild and reckless abandon that had Carpentier stunned and dazed. The film of the fight shows Carpentier's manager Descamps making his way around the ring to Siki's corner to angrily plead that their agreement be honored. It was to no avail. In the sixth round Carpentier was sent kicking to the canvas and, while trying to claim a foul, was seemingly counted out. In a last ditch effort to save the hero's title the referee attempted to disqualify Siki for tripping but this obvious attempt at favoritism sent the massive audience into an uproar and the decision was reversed in favor of Siki by ringside officials.[49]

To the French it was an outrage and unbelievable that the beloved idol could have lost to such an inferior opponent and a black one at that. Within days plans were being hatched to take away Siki's championship and somehow give it back to Carpentier. In the face of such tactics Siki did the only thing he could to counter his critics: he went public. He told the entire story of how he had been approached to fix the fight. Bringing to light the dirty little secret of Carpentier's protected status did little to ingratiate Siki to the officials in power or the public and before long Siki found himself further ostracized by the European sporting community. As this drama played out offers for huge sums of money poured for Siki to face Harry Wills, Jack Dempsey, and Harry Greb. To this Harry remarked "Any time, anywhere, for any reasonable amount of money. I have had three offers already to meet Siki and to all of them I have replied that I am ready to talk business as soon as he signs a contract."[50] It looked for a time like the near decade long log jam in the light-heavyweight class may finally be clearing.

With all of these changes taking place Harry re-entered the ring on September 26 in Toronto against White Hope heavyweight Al Benedict. Benedict began his career in 1910 knocking out two men in a tournament publicized to find a successor to Jim Jeffries. Billy Madden, promoter of the show, took notice of the young Italian giant and decided to manage him to the title. Unfortunately Benedict's dreams soon met with the reality of his glass jaw. What ensued for Benedict was an up and down career with far more downs than ups. His record remains largely incomplete but he was stopped no less than 23 times by a wide range of opponents. In facing Benedict Harry was stepping in for Bill Brennan who had taken ill and was forced to back out of the engagement.

Those who thought the massive size disparity might bode well for Benedict can be forgiven. Yet, after Harry landed half a dozen hard punches in the first round to gain Benedict's respect the fight was completely under Greb's control. In the second Harry overwhelmed Benedict dropping him three times before the referee waved the fight off. Greb arrived in Grand Rapids the following day sporting only a slight swelling over one eye as a reminder of Benedict's five inch height advantage and thirty-seven pound weight advantage.[51]

Three days later Harry was to meet Captain Bob Roper in Grand Rapids. Roper was being given a chance to make good on his failure to meet Greb in February, having drawn a suspension for his failure to appear. Roper arrived in town early to prepare for the fight and signal his intention of going

Albert De Benedictis of Salerno, Italy, otherwise known as Al Benedict, was a heavyweight of the White Hope era. Despite his impressive physique (he stood 6' 1" tall and weighed 200 lbs.) he never developed into a leading contender.

through with the match. Sparring with his younger brother Tom, he immediately made a hit with fans who remembered him from his match with Bob Martin the year previous.

Excitement was high when Greb arrived. His fans in Grand Rapids were eager to see him perform after hearing of his major victories on the East Coast. "I know it will make some people laugh but I am positive I can defeat Dempsey in a 12 or 15 round decision bout," he said to eager listeners. "Of course I wouldn't expect to knock Dempsey out. My biggest thought would be to keep from getting knocked out."

"That is all I would have to do in order to win a decision bout with Dempsey, who is no harder to hit than anybody else, and who, I feel sure, would have as much trouble reaching me as the others have had. I haven't the slightest fear of Dempsey, regardless of the fact that all the experts say he is much too big for me. When a fighter enters the ring there is always the danger that he may be knocked out. That is the only thing I would have to guard against."

"Dempsey is strong and can hit. If he reached me on the button it would be curtains. However, I feel that in a limited bout I would be able to stay away from him, in the meantime I would be doing so much execution that the judges would have to award me the decision."[52]

During sparring for the Roper match Greb was accidentally butted by Irl Croshaw, resulting in a swollen eye. When he faced Roper he fought a very conservative fight in an attempt to protect the eye as well as his delicate hands. Promoters in New York were trying to arrange a match between Greb and Bob Martin which would be worth $15,000 to Harry. A cut eye or broken hand would place such a windfall in jeopardy. As a result of Greb's strategy, and Roper's inability to maintain the aggression he had shown in the first two rounds, the bout was not an aesthetic success. Greb won handily but the bout was slow and only occasionally did Harry rally his fans. By the end of the fight, with a Greb victory a forgone conclusion, the boos began to fall and even Roper seemed resigned to an eventual loss.[53]

When Greb and Engel made their way to New York in order to face Martin they found that the New York State Athletic Commission refused to allow Greb to face Martin as the match had been arranged while Greb was under suspension.[54] Greb immediately applied to have his suspension lifted only to be notified that he must first submit to face Wilson at catch weights or for the light heavyweight championship of America. The commission was set to reinstate Greb when he signed the articles to face Wilson under such terms and deposited $2,500 as evidence of his intent.[55]

When Wilson and his manager Martin Killelea failed to respond to the commissions call his indefinite suspension was made definite and permanent. Any boxer who was found to oppose Wilson in a match or exhibition anywhere outside of the commission's jurisdiction would suffer an immediate suspension as well.[56] With the middleweight championship situation as muddled as it had been in years there was only one thing for Harry to do: stay busy.

To that end Greb fought his old opponent and sparring partner Larry Williams at Providence, Rhode Island on October 25. Williams was now in the twilight of his career and spent the majority of his time in the ring as a trial horse and sparring partner for boxing's elite. Williams hadn't won a fight in years and was in fact coming off a stoppage loss to Floyd Johnson the previous month. It figured to be an easy victory for Greb and that is exactly what it was. Despite boasting a seventeen pound weight advantage Williams could do nothing with Greb. From the outset Greb began punching holes in Williams' defense seemingly looking for a knockout. He punctuated the first round by landing a left hook with such force that it violently snapped Williams head around.

Harry spent the next two rounds punishing Williams, softening him up for the inevitable. Early in the fourth round Greb got home with a left hook, right hand, left hook, and a straight right along the ropes that buckled Williams knees momentarily before he collapsed to the canvas. Williams rose at the count of nine on wobbly legs and was met

Prior to meeting Greb in October of 1922 Larry Williams (right) helped to prepare Gene Tunney (left) for his disasterous and unsuccessful defense against Greb.

with a torrent of punches from all angles which battered him from corner to corner. A final right hand sent Williams toppling to the mat just as his corner man Willie Lewis tossed in the towel to signify his surrender. Williams was led to his corner bewildered, bleeding, and battered, his career would be over before the year was out. Williams eventually made his way to Hollywood and acted in bit parts in movies before succumbing to the effects of pugilistic dementia.[57]

Next up for Greb would be Bob Roper in Buffalo on November 10. This match had initially been scheduled for October 23 but had to be postponed when Roper aggravated a hand injury. There was no love lost between the two fighters and Roper in particular was eager for a victory over Greb. Harry took the bout in stride, as would be expected with four previous victories over Roper under his belt, training at home. In a letter to the promoter Greb spoke of his intention to bring along two of the street urchins who idolized him:

Dear Charley,

I want you to pick me out two good seats, right up close and hold

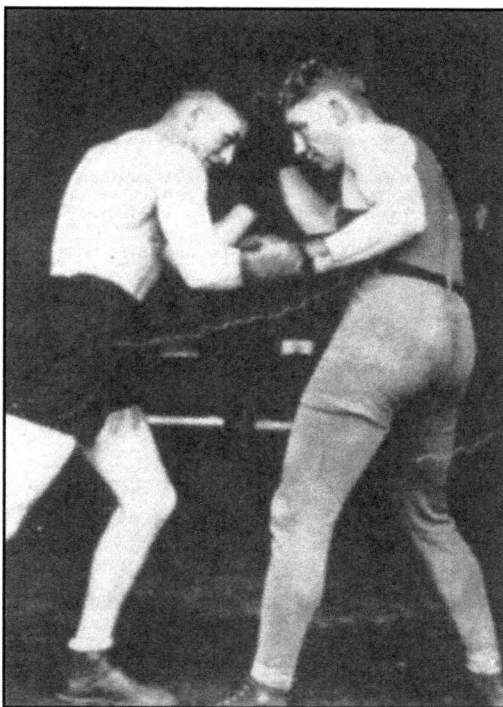

them for me. I don't care if I have to pay for these. But be sure to get me good ones. I have two mascots. Tim and Jim I call them. They are newsboys here in Pittsburgh. They've been my boosters since I broke into the big league. They're orphans, but fine boys. They're going to have a holiday at my expense. I'm bringing both to Buffalo and I want them to have the best in the house. Wait until you hear these two leather-lunged rooters root. They can out yell any two men I ever heard. I'll be over to Buffalo about the ninth. I'm working at my own gym here in Pittsburgh and will be in tiptop shape. Quite a bunch coming from Pittsburgh. I hope Roper doesn't crack any more flivvers before the tenth.

With Best Wishes to all, I am, sincerely yours,

Harry Greb

Pittsburgh, Oct. 30th, 1922 [58]

Adding to the hype of the fight was the possibility that the winner would be matched with Floyd Johnson who had recently made a splash in the division by knocking out Bob Martin in New York City. The bout would have proven a lucrative one but when Engel discovered that Bill Brennan was being floated as an opponent for Johnson instead he was livid. "Why, I will let Greb fight Johnson and Brennan seven and one-half rounds on the same evening in the same ring," said Engel, "and I will contribute $1,000 to any charity named if either one will consent to meet Harry. Together with that I will guarantee that Greb will beat the stuffing out of both." [59]

As fans listened at home to the proceedings on the WGR radio station Greb and Roper entered the ring to begin the headlining bout of a card that had drawn a record attendance to the Broadway Auditorium. It was the first boxing match broadcast live via radio from Buffalo. Always a practitioner of psychological warfare Roper entered the ring with his pet cobra Maggie wound around his neck. When referee Dick Nugent called the fighters to the center of the ring to shake hands and deliver instructions Greb spied the serpent and laughed, telling Roper to keep it at a distance.

Despite outweighing Greb by twelve pounds at 180 lbs. Roper was unable to cope with Greb's speed, andsurprisingly his strength. From the outset Harry set a tremendous pace whereby he would spring around Roper with his hands at his sides before leaping in viciously with a volley of punches. Before long Roper was gun-shy and attempted to clinch and wrestle Greb around the ring. Greb proved the stronger of the two and at times would manhandle Roper into the ropes and beat a tattoo of blows to the head and body. Despite being a fairly one sided fight it was at times viciously contested with referee Nugent having difficulty prying the fighters apart or keeping them from fighting after the bell when rounds ended. The fighters often resorted to foul tactics, illustrating their mutual dislike for one another. At the end of the fight both of Ropers eyes had been cut, his nose was bleeding, and his lips were puffed and glued together with gore. He was a sorry sight and according to three of the four Buffalo dailies he couldn't even claim a round of the fight for his troubles.[60]

Within a week after the Roper bout in Buffalo rumors began to spread that all was not well between Greb and Engel. Harry began being quoted in the press as saying that he would not renew his contract with Engel and even intimated that he may return to Red Mason. Greb noted that he felt Engel had not kept him busy enough, not garnered him the large purses he was entitled to after such attention getting wins as the Gibbons and Tunney bouts, and even intimated that Engel had been taking more money than he was entitled to.[61]

These are strange accusations in light of the fact that Engel had taken Harry from a well-respected but stagnating fighter to worldwide prominence and the forefront of three divisions through his efforts to gain a match with Johnny Wilson, Georges Carpentier, Battling Siki, and Jack Dempsey. It is true that he had not kept Greb as busy as Mason had but Engel's policy seems to have been one of quality over quantity and his connections on the East Coast cannot be underestimated in Greb's rise. Engel himself, years later, hinted at a situation that, if Greb knew about, would have certainly hastened his departure from Engel. Engel stated that one evening at a fight at Madison Square Garden he was approached by Harry McCormack the close friend of Gene Tunney's at whose Red Bank summer home Tunney trained for Greb. McCormack intimated that Tunney was interested in leaving his manager Doc Bagley and asked if Engel would be interested in handling the ex-marine. Engel stated that he could not handle Tunney while handling Tunney's current rival. Instead Engel offered to have his close friend Billy Gibson, manager of Benny Leonard, handle Tunney and later he (Engel) and Tunney may reach some agreement.[62] We

Harry Greb looks none too eager to get close to the snake wrapped around Captain Bob Roper's neck. Greb and Roper met for the second time in 1922 on November 10 in Buffalo, New York. Once the snake was removed and the bell rang beginning the fight it was a different story.

have seen in the past in regards to his relationships with Buck Crouse and Al Grayber that Greb could be extremely jealous of fighters in his stable. Had Greb gotten wind that his manager was working behind the scenes to the benefit of his rival and recent victim there is no doubt that his natural jealousy and distrust would have gotten the better of him.

Engel attempted to downplay the gossip, which was now being printed across the country, before finally placing a telephone call to Greb in order to get to the bottom of the matter. Confronted, Greb admitted that what had been quoted in the papers, attributed to him, was accurate. Engel lost his temper and after a heated argument Greb notified Engel on the spot that for all intents and purposes he was fired. As a manager from the old school where fighters were not employers but chattel to be controlled by their managers this enraged Engel.[63] On November 20 he had to admit that things between he and Greb had grown strained at best and that a split was likely.[64]

Greb had been under a great deal of stress due in large part to Mildred's condition which was worse than ever and had him greatly concerned. In early December an attempt was made to take her to Arizona where the dry climate might improve her condition. She and Greb were accompanied by a private physician. When the couple arrived in Pittsburgh they were notified that to attempt the completion of the journey would likely kill Mildred. The trip was abandoned with Mildred forced to stay in Pittsburgh and wait for the inevitable.[65]

In addition to this he had apparently suffered a relatively minor cut over one or both eyes during his recent bout with Roper, during a head cold the eyes both became infected and began to swell almost totally shut, once again he was reminded of the possibility of total blindness.[66] If his personal life seemed in turmoil his professional life soon seemed to spiral out of control as things with Engel rapidly turned ugly. What had been a personal, private argument was now being played out in the newspapers. Frustrated with the situation Greb went to the papers with stories of unfavorable contract conditions (Harry went so far as to refer to himself as a slave under Engel),[67] he intimated that Willie Lewis had done all of the training work for Engel and that when Engel was working Harry's corner for the Gibbons bout he was under the influence of alcohol.[68]

Engel had his own way of paying Harry back for the remarks. Noting that he still had a few weeks left on his contract Engel began in short order furiously booking Greb for half a dozen bouts. It seemed unlikely that Greb would be able to fulfill these engagements given the condition of his eyes, his inability to train properly, and Mildred's health. If he failed to fulfill his obligations he would likely face sanctions from those local governing bodies and any associated governing bodies, if he was somehow able to fulfill his obligations Engel could expect to be paid his managerial fee. It was a win/win situation for the calculating, cigar chomping ex-fighter.

Not to be undone by the machinations of Engel, Greb took his case to the New York State Athletic Commission. The Commission promptly sided with Greb, suspending Engel until it could further investigate Greb's claims that Engel had improperly withheld portions of his purse from the Roper fight, and invalidated all but one of the fights Engel had obligated Greb to. That lone fight that the commission wished to see held was the rematch with Gene Tunney, and the only fight Engel booked that the Commission and New York in general would profit from, which would be held approximately two hours prior to the expiration of Engel's contract with Greb.[69]

The sleazy undertones of the situation in which Greb would be compelled to face Tunney were not lost on Westbrook Pegler who had already heard ugly rumors of an attempt to rob Greb of any chance of victory were he to face Tunney. Making his views on the subject plainly known he stated: "If Greb takes on Tunney with his own manager on the hostile side he will be in danger of more than Tunney's attack. For there is work afoot to have the referee restrict the leaping, mountain-goat style of Harry which is at once his attack and defense."[70] The Pittsburgh Post agreed with Pegler's stance that Greb would be justified in avoiding the Tunney rematch under such conditions and added that "...should there be any move on the part of the referee to cut Greb down to a flat-footed fighter, Tunney, with superior reach and weight would make a "sucker" out of him. But, should such a move be made, it will be the first time that the style of a champion, or any fighter, has been determined by a commission or referee."[71]

Within days it was readily apparent that given his physical condition and that of his ailing wife Greb would not realistically be able to defend his championship on December 29 as planned. Mildred's health was now rapidly deteriorating. She had lost an enormous amount of weight and her ability to breath was now frighteningly restricted. The once beaming and plump cheeked young woman was now a thin shadow of her former self. The light that once danced in her eyes had faded as had the smile that typified early photographs of her. She was now too weak and too ill to make the planned trip to Arizona. Harry would have to stay close to home throughout the winter in order to be by her side.

As Harry's infected eyes continued to bother him into December he sought treatment in a local Pittsburgh hospital. While there one of the doctors attending him discovered his secret and quickly spread the rumor that a muscle in one of his eyes had been detached and could not be corrected.[72] Greb declined to comment on the stories and spent the next two weeks convalescing and attending to Mildred.

By the end of December Harry was ready to begin training again. He planned to take on a few fights in order to fight himself back into shape and first on the list was Bob Roper on New Year's Day. The Pittsburgh fight fraternity wasn't overly enthused about the selection of Roper as Greb's opponent. They were well aware of the fact that Harry had faced the former army captain a number of times since Roper first appeared against Greb in Pittsburgh back in 1920 and had been returned the winner every time with relative ease. However Greb was granted special consideration given his recent condition and the stress he was laboring under at home.

The match was formally finalized less than a week before it was scheduled to take place, giving Greb little time to train. He set about working himself back into shape immediately at the Pittsburgh Lyceum, sparring hard rounds with Leo Caghil and amateur heavyweight Red Seifert. Greb illustrated just how seriously he was taking Roper when interviewed at camp. "When you wear a crown," he said, "every fight is an important one. You never know when someone might land a 'lucky one' and blooie goes your hard earned championship. No sir, Roper is not going to catch me out of condition. I will train just as hard for Roper as I would if I were called upon to meet Gibbons, Tunney, or the rest of my challengers,"[73]

A large New Year's Day crowd filled Motor Square Garden, eager to see Harry in action for the first time in six months. Those who didn't attend the event in person were able to listen to the fight broadcast blow-by-blow provided by the Pittsburgh Post and Westinghouse on KDKA. The first six rounds of the contest were slow with Roper not eager to take the same kind of punishment he had in past bouts against Greb. At 188 pounds Roper sported a twenty-four pound weight advantage over Greb and former featherweight Yock Henninger had a difficult time controlling the action, seemingly getting the worst of it in many cases.

By the seventh Roper was completely frustrated by his inability to have any success with Greb. Roper had two options: sit back and take another beating, or take the fight to the alley. He did the latter. Roper rushed at Harry but instead of throwing punches he forced all of his 188 pounds upon him, bending him backwards over the top rope until it appeared to some that his back might break. As had become his habit when an opponent opened up, Greb stepped on the gas and proceeded to cut Ropers mouth and left eye. Whenever Roper could get close enough to grapple the smaller buzz saw he would rake the laces of his gloves across Harry's still healing eyes.

The fighters failed to hear the bell ending the ninth round and continued to battle. Someone yelled to Harry that the round had ended and he dropped his hands, ready to return to his corner when Roper landed a light punch to Harry's head. Enraged, Harry leapt to the attack and it was a short while before the two fighters could be separated. Greb came out for the final round still angry over the previous rounds ending and attacked viciously. Roper tried to meet this attack head on but was swept away by its fury. The bell rang to end the fight and still Roper attacked, landing a right after the bell and once again the fighters refused to be parted, hammering away at each other. Pittsburgh referee Jack Dillon, now acting as Greb's chief second jumped into the ring and tackled Roper. In a heartbeat the ring filled with spectators and special police before a full blown riot could erupt. Roper had to be escorted out of the arena by a cordon of police. Even as the disgruntled fans shuffled out of the arena many of them couldn't help but comment that Harry, despite winning easily, seemed to have lost something. He would need more work to get it back, if indeed he was ever able to regain the peak of his old dynamic form.[74]

19

TROUBLED TIMES

Immediately following the unsportsmanlike ending of the Greb-Roper bout both fighters were suspended by the Pittsburgh Boxing Commission until they appeared before that body to explain themselves. With no manager to settle his affairs Harry met with Chairman Sixsmith in private and explained his side of the events. A few days later during a special session of the Commission Greb was reinstated clearing the way for a planned rematch with Tommy Loughran to held on January 15 at Motor Square Garden.

Harry had been in New York while the Commission met. He would spend a week in the East training, scouting possible managers, and attending the upcoming bout between Floyd Johnson and Bill Brennan. Harry intended to bet heavily on Johnson and hoped to challenge the winner. Harry also intended to sign himself for several bouts that would serve the purpose of working himself back into championship form. Ultimately he was able to sign himself for fights against Billy Shade on January 22, Pal Reed on January 30, and two or three others in the following weeks.[1]

Upon his return to Pittsburgh Greb appeared in an exhibition bout against Jack Munro with none other than Red Mason working his corner. Harry was so pleased with Mason's performance that he arranged for Mason to work his corner during his bout with Loughran the following night.[2]

Red Mason and Harry Greb shake hands to seal their deal whereby Mason would renew his position as Greb's manager.

Entering the ring in green tights with Mason in his corner Greb seemed to be rounding himself back into form. He was still not at his peak but he was now good enough that he easily defeated Loughran. Greb mixed up his game by working around Loughran from the outside and then rushing in, where Loughran was at a significant disadvantage at infighting. At times the fight was rough with Loughran repeatedly using his elbows and Greb landing head butts.

Throughout the bout Harry was his usual supremely confident self, smiling, talking to Loughran, and playing up to the audience. By the eighth round Greb was so dominant that the crowd began yelling for a knockout as Greb battered Loughran around the ring.[3]

Within days of his victory over Loughran the story broke from Paris that a match between Greb and light heavyweight champion Battling Siki was close to being finalized.[4] Greb had already agreed to the terms but he expressed the hope that the bout would be staged in the United States by Tex Rickard adding that if there was no alternative he would travel to France for the bout.[5]

When Harry returned to New York to begin training for his bout with Billy Shade he was incensed to find that Rickard was negotiating a heavyweight championship bout between Jack Dempsey and Tommy Gibbons. He made it clear to several newspaper outlets that he felt he was Dempsey's most deserving challenger and even expressed a willingness to once again defeat Tommy Gibbons in order to erase any doubt that it should be he and not Gibbons who received the lucrative title shot.[6] His pleas largely fell on deaf ears and he was forced to continue fighting and winning in hopes of forcing a match with heavyweight champion.

Greb met Billy Shade at Jersey City on January 22. He was either unwilling or unable to fight at his best and, despite winning in fairly one sided manner, the fans once again noted a marked decline in Greb's ability compared to the last time they had seen him. In the seventh round Shade walked into a left that deposited him squarely on the canvas. He was up immediately only to return to being out-gamed by his rival. At the conclusion of the bout Greb was far ahead on points (it was estimated Shade landed no more than a dozen blows) but the audience booed the fighters just the same for Shade's lack of a competitive showing and Greb's apparent unwillingness to finish his man on the several occasions he had Shade hurt.[7]

Greb was also booed on occasion throughout the bout for holding and hitting which, combined with his early inaccuracy, hinted at his damaged eye and the resulting lack of depth perception. The foul of holding and hitting would be an increasing complaint against Greb from his opponents as the years went by.

Once again Red Mason had worked Greb's corner for the bout. All along Mason had denied that he and Greb had reached an agreement for Mason to manage Greb. After Mason had traveled to Jersey City to work Greb's corner, leaving his two fighters Cuddy DeMarco and Patsy Young to fend for themselves while fighting the same night as Greb, it came as no surprise when Greb and Mason made the announcement that they had officially reconciled.[8] In hiring Mason, as had been the case with Engel, Greb announced that his intended purpose was to ultimately gain a match with heavyweight champion Jack Dempsey.[9]

The following day Greb was in New York to defend himself against Engel's insistence that he defend his title against Tunney. Much was revealed at this meeting of the Athletic Commission. Greb was notified that he would indeed have to defend his title against Tunney in New York City and that Engel, not Mason, would receive the manager's portion of Greb's purse.[10] Only days earlier Tunney had purchased his contract from the very capable and respected Doc Bagley and aligned himself with Billy Gibson (with Engel possibly acting as the intermediary brokering the deal). This created the almost unbelievable possibility whereby Greb was being forced to defend his championship against Tunney, in Tunney's hometown, and with Engel working Tunney's corner (as he often did for Gibson's fighters) while being paid out of Greb's purse. It was Greb's intention to stave off this possibility for as long as possible in hopes that he would be able to prevent Engel of his money. Using his wife's increasing illness and his relative lack of conditioning as an excuse Greb was able to get Chairman Muldoon to postpone the defense for a later date.[11]

At the same meeting Greb signed to defend his championship against Tommy Loughran on January 30, the same night he was scheduled to face Pal Reed. The Loughran bout, scheduled to be held in Madison Square Garden, would be much more lucrative than the Reed match prompting Greb to offer Newark promoters $800 to call off the match. The best the Newark promoters could offer was to postpone the match until February 5 and ask for $1,500 from Harry for expenses in postponing the fight.[12]

Harry returned to New York to train for Tommy Loughran after a brief visit home to see Mildred. The day before the fight the New York Evening Telegram printed a small article detailing a rumor of Greb's ailing eyesight.[13] Between his increasingly obvious lack of depth perception and the rumor now out about his poor vision it seemed that Greb's closely guarded secret was now on the verge of becoming one of the sport's worst kept. Tommy Gibbons

Harry Greb and Tommy Loughran face off in the ring prior to their January 30, 1923 American Light Heavyweight Championship held at Madison Square Garden.

Top: Loughran (left) misses with an overhand right over the top of Greb's head as Greb lands his own right. Above: Greb (left) holds Loughran's head with his left hand while hammering away to the head and body with his right. Over the years this would be Greb's most common foul, the stories of his dirty fighting have largely been blown out of proportion based on this one tactic which was probably necessitated by his decreased vision.

noted the decline as well in commenting on the proposed Greb-Loughran title bout. "Greb was at his very best when he fought me last year, but I think he's slipping and opportunity may be knocking at Loughran's door. He's got a chance of a lifetime and he should make the most of it."[14]

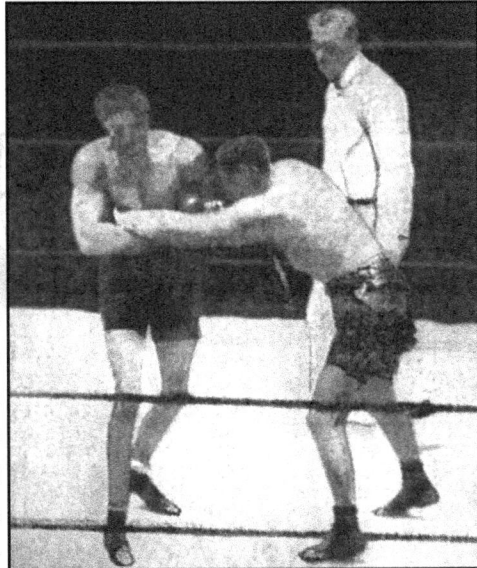

Top left: Loughran (left) and Greb exchange jabs. Top right and right: Loughran (left, in both photos) holds Greb's left arm and punches with the right. Greb can be seen working his head onto Loughran's chest to smother Loughran's effectiveness. Loughran was criticized for exaggerating Greb's use of his head in order to score points with the judges.

Both fighters weighed in at 166 pounds and entered the ring supremely confident. As in his previous bout Greb was wildly inaccurate in the early going against Loughran. Through the first few rounds the only success Greb could find was when he was able to work his way in close and flail away with both arms. As the rounds wore on Greb found that he could practice his favorite tactic of holding Loughran's head with his left and pounding away with his right. When all else failed Greb used his head and elbows liberally. These tactics combined with his early ineffectiveness conspired to turn the fans against him. As the bout progressed Greb's aggressiveness, regardless of how sloppy, forced Loughran into a defensive shell and he rapidly fell behind on points. By the later rounds Loughran had seemingly become timid and disheartened.

In the tenth Greb landed a hard body shot which doubled Loughran over and sent him against the ropes. He immediately tried to claim a foul but the referee was having none of it

Greb (right) backs Loughran into a corner, measuring with his left for the overhand right.

and Loughran continued to fight. In the fourteenth Loughran landed a similar blow on Greb which doubled the champion over but Greb gamely fought on. He gave no quarter and asked none in return.

Loughran rallied in these final two rounds. It was enough to win the crowds acclaim but not enough to win the fight. Loughran had waited too long to launch his counter attack and Greb had simply piled up too many points. The audience, displeased with Greb's tactics and the overall unsatisfactory nature of the fight, booed the champion as he left the ring and cheered Loughran.[15]

The papers were all in agreement that the fight had not been up to the standard of a championship. All agreed that Greb had deserved the victory on points but some felt that he should have been disqualified. Others noted that Loughran had held on far too much, and that he had played to the crowd, making Greb's infractions seem worse than they were. "Had Tommy kept clean early we would have had a nice fight," stated Greb a few days later. "But when he tried to get rough I showed him a few tricks and then he began complaining."[16] It was noted that Loughran had been warned for his tactics by the referee but what was indisputable was that sentiment in New York had drastically shifted against Greb.

The day after the fight Greb met with Tex Rickard and notified him that he was prepared to defend against Tunney. The match was made for February 23, the only date available for Madison Square Garden. Greb would now have another three weeks to fight himself into condition.

Sitting ringside at the Loughran fight was Pal Reed who would be hard at work with his stablemate, welterweight champion Mickey Walker, preparing for his bout with Greb the following week and what he considered the chance of a lifetime. Reed hoped to take advantage of Greb's seemingly diminished form. Decisions were not allowed by law in New Jersey but Reed could win the championship by stopping Greb within the distance. Reed was beaming with confidence due to his showing against Loughran earlier in the month. Loughran had come into the fight a prohibitive favorite only to find great difficulty solving Reed's southpaw style. In the fourth round Reed dropped Loughran for a nine count and seemingly took the fight out of the young Philadelphian. Reports differed as to who won the match but given Greb's lackluster showing against Loughran Reed must have thought his chances looked pretty good.

Despite outweighing Reed nine and a half pounds, Greb showed his versatility and a great respect for Reed's powerful left by continually boxing off of Reed's right side in order to increase the distance his left had to travel and limit its effectiveness. He even confused Reed by occasionally switching to southpaw himself. Despite fighting at an already fast clip Greb seemed to increase his speed and strength as the rounds went on. At the conclusion of the fight Harry wrapped his arm around Reed and walked him to his corner congratulating him on his game effort. He had completely outclassed his blonde foe.[17]

Eleven days later Greb was in Syracuse to face Young Fisher for the third time. It would be his final tune-up before facing Tunney for the title. Greb easily won every round of the bout. The monotony of Greb's domination was interrupted in the later rounds when at one point Fisher rushed Greb into the ropes so violently that one of the corner posts broke bringing the ring ropes down. A five minute break was needed for repairs before Greb could resume playing a tattoo on Fishers face and body. After the final bell a dazed and bloody Fisher worked his way over to congratulate Greb who replied "You're a game kid." Red Mason then sprayed Fisher with water from his mouth in his trademark fashion bringing a close to the evening.[18]

Pal Reed was a hard punching southpaw who faced 6 world champions during his career. He fought Harry Greb 3 times from 1921 to 1924. While fighting he attended classes at Harvard University and even coached their boxing team for a time. After retiring from the sport he coached boxing at the University of New Hampshire.

In the weeks leading up to the second fight with Tunney talk of a predetermined victory intensified and there was a great deal of evidence to suggest that such talk was more than just rumor and innuendo.

Much had changed since the last meeting of Greb and Tunney, particularly in the previous two months. Tunney was now employing Billy Gibson as his manager. Gibson

was considered to be one of the most connected and most powerful managers in the sport of boxing, particularly on the East Coast. In addition to Gibson's clout, Tunney's friend and supporter Al Smith had recently been elected governor of New York. Smith took office on January 1 and within a month had begun making plans to place another good friend of Tunney's, William McCormack, brother of Harry McCormack, at whose Red Bank, New Jersey home Tunney regularly lived and trained, in a position on the New York State Licensing Committee. The Licensing Committee would not be formally established until mid April but it's makeup, and intended purpose of restricting William Muldoon's power, had been a topic of much debate. Muldoon had been at odds with Senator Jimmy Walker, a Smith ally, for some time. Walker, Smith, and McCormack were all Democrats (like Tunney) and all belonged to the powerful and infamous Tammany Hall political machine. Walker and McCormack would both be touched by scandal and allegations of corruption within a few short years.

Both Gibson and Tunney were close friends with powerful New York bookmaker Tim Mara. Mara would go on to found the New York Giants, due in no small part to the help of Gibson. Both Mara and McCormack had bet on Tunney in the first Greb fight and lost a substantial amount of money and were eager to lend support to Tunney in order to help him regain his championship.[20] In a 1930 article detailing the behind the scenes deals that helped Tunney gain recognition later as a challenger for Jack Dempsey it was noted that "letters from Billy Gibson, Tunney's manager, also spoke of 'straightening out angles'; of getting people, many of them well known in Manhattan and national politics, 'lined up' or 'in our corner' and of 'working on others'" using Mara as an intermediary.[19]

Gibson was never shy about associating with, and soliciting help from, underworld figures. Early in his career when Gibson needed help acquiring a boxing license he turned to Arnold Rothstein, a veritable Moriarity of modern crime who has been implicated in everything from fixing the 1919 World Series to laying the foundations of the modern Mafia. Since that time Gibson had made sure to stay on friendly terms with Rothstein, who even owned a percentage of Gibson's highest profile fighter, lightweight champion Benny Leonard. In 1926, on the eve of Tunney's Heavyweight Championship bout with Jack Dempsey, Gibson and Tunney signed over a 20% interest in Tunney's future earnings to Philadelphia racketeer Max "Boo Boo" Hoff for the remarkable sum of one dollar and "other good and valuable considerations." When one reads further down the contract to reveal that it would only go into effect in the event that Tunney win the championship it becomes obvious that those "good and valuable considerations" were Hoff's "assurances" that Tunney would win.[21]

By the time Tunney eventually got his shot at Dempsey he had signed over 75% of his future earnings to Hoff, Tim Mara, and Gibson in exchange for their influence peddling. When Tunney failed to honor the contract with Hoff, the racketeer sued. Mara would also sue Tunney for payment for services rendered when Tunney turned his back on Mara after winning the championship.[22] Tunney eventually settled out of court with Mara while Hoff's lawsuit was ultimately unsuccessful but the dirt that had been dredged up about Tunney's back room dealings, much of which was actually admitted to by Tunney, is instructive.

In addition to the powerful figures aligned behind Tunney, both legitimate and underworld, Tunney would freely admit in later years that he regularly paid sportswriters that they may print favorable copy about him in the hopes of furthering his career.[23] A cursory look at a few of New York's papers leading up to the rematch with Greb gives an indication that Tunney's dollars may have been hard at work.

The selection of the referee for Greb's rematch with Tunney was also a point of contention. The commission refused to release the name of the referee which sent conspiracy theorists buzzing. The two leading candidates being spoken of by the press were Kid McPartland and Patsy Haley. McPartland was being heavily criticized by the pro-Tunney press because of his handling of the first Greb-Tunney bout. Yet, surprisingly Greb had apparently asked specifically that the usually strict Haley be allowed to referee the contest rather than McPartland.[24] This may have been in part because of McPartland's recent controversial disqualification of Tommy Gibbons in a bout with Billy Miske in which Gibbons was well ahead on points. Conversely Haley had recently refereed the Carl Tremaine-Irish Johnny Curtin bout in which Curtin quit, claiming he was fouled, the foul was not allowed by Haley and Tremaine was ruled the winner. Greb may have felt that in light of these recent performances Haley was the safer bet. Despite this recent ruling Haley had shown in the past and would continue to show for years to come that he was not afraid to disqualify fighters for even marginal infractions.[25] If Greb did indeed lobby for Haley over McPartland it was a decision he would come to regret.

As Tunney sparred with Wolf Larsen and Larry Williams he was being drilled by Billy Gibson on the use of dirty tactics, despite all of the hyperbole denigrating Greb's alleged foul fighting and the Tunney camp's hope for a referee who would be especially mindful of Greb.[26]

A few days before the fight Gibson stepped up his rhetoric lobbying the commission to protect Tunney against Greb's alleged illegal tactics. He wrote a letter to the commission asking that the judges and the referee be instructed to pay close attention to Greb and deduct points for any infraction. Gibson made particular note of Greb's holding and hitting.[27]

Two days before the bout Greb visited William Muldoon pleading his case and even stating that both he and his wife had been receiving threatening letters from pro-Tunney interests. Muldoon replied "You have won all your fights, and I have never heard of you being disqualified for foul tactics, no matter if the bout was in Maine or Texas. It is quite apparent that the referees do not regard you as a foul fighter, even if some of your opponents make the charge. The referee who will officiate at the bout will judge the bout on what is done in the ring and not by threats or accusations made by Tunney or his partisans."[28]

The threatening letters and rumors of a fix had so worried Mildred that she appealed to Chairman Muldoon from her sick bed to protect Harry and ensure that his title would not be taken via skullduggery. Muldoon personally wired Mrs. Greb to notify her that Greb would be treated fairly by New York officials.[29] It was enough to satisfy the Greb family for the moment but while Muldoon remained a vocal figurehead his position was tenuous and it was spoken of freely in the press that his powers were in the process of being curbed by Walker, and Smith. It remained to be seen what effect Gibson and Tunney's influential friends would have on the match.

For months Pittsburgh newspapers had been alluding to a plot to rob Greb of his crown. As Pittsburgh fans filtered into New York in anticipation of the match they wrote home with troubling stories:

Corroborating in every phase the various rumors out of New York that there is a well laid plan on foot to rob Harry Greb of his title when he meets Gene Tunney Friday night in Madison Square Garden, a well known local fight follower who arrived in New York yesterday stated by long distance telephone last night that the condition is without parallel in sport history. "I've seen many placed where fights were fixed and where fighters were robbed, but if what I heard today in inside boxing circles can be true, Greb hasn't a chance in the world to beat Tunney," is the gist of what was said last night by telephone. And the beautiful part of it is that, according to the ruling New York boxing commission, should Greb be disqualified, he will not be entitled to any part of the purse, such a ruling having been affected by the commission several weeks ago.

According to the informant, who says that had Tunney received the kind of treatment in Pittsburgh when he knocked out Jack Burke here that Greb has been getting since his return from Syracuse, there would have been a howl around the world, which forever would have placed this city on the boxing blacklist.

The thing has become so apparent, according to this report, that local fight fans already on the scene, who have friends in the metropolis, have been warned "not to wager a nickel," as it seems to be a foregone conclusion that Greb's style, the kind which they agreed when he beat Gibbons was the greatest in the ring, will be barred in every detail and the first violation of the referee's rulings will result in Greb being thrown out of the ring, disqualified and deprived of his title, to say nothing of confiscating his end of the purse.

The best proof that a referee friendly to Tunney will likely be the final selection was forecasted yesterday when at the regular meeting of the commission, no referee was selected, this being left until the day of the fight.

Prominent fight managers, those inside in the tricks of the New York game, said that never before in their careers had they seen things so well laid to accomplish a purpose. The native New Yorkers are daily being stirred up by inflammatory articles in the newspapers regarding Greb's style and his tactics since winning the title and with a capacity throng expected, men well known in the game are advising Pittsburgh friends that to bet on the result without a foul clause, would be the height of folly.

Tunney is keeping away from the crowd in the downtown section, not being permitted out of his training camp in Red Bank, N. J., while Greb, according to this informant, yesterday afternoon during his training at the Garden gym was booed and hissed and hooted at every phase of training he attempted to undertake. While the officials of the Garden have said nothing concerning the outcome of the affair, which is common talk, according to this long distance informer, that they are permitting matters to take their course, without interruption. It was rumored yesterday that two judges, who have worked in previous fights, who had been scheduled for the affair, have been called off, the selection of these, as well as the referee, being withheld until the last minute.

This Pittsburgher, who, contrary to general belief, is not connected in any way with the local fight game or fighters, stated that conditions are such that should Greb be disqualified and lose his title on a foul it will be the worst thing in the boxing game in years. Hangers-on around Madison Square Garden, accosting out-of-towners at the box office in the Garden when they go to purchase tickets, openly boast that "things are set," and "Gibson is boss," etc., according to this informant, and the fact that they have been warned not to bet on Greb's chances without a "foul clause" bears out the fact that the style which Greb used once has gone into the discards for this particular fight.

Despite all the talk, the informant states that he watched Greb try to go through his work today, and that after a 15-minute workout Harry forsook the gym for the road. Later in the Hotel Theresa, where Greb is quartered, Greb told his party that "regardless of everything they're trying to do, I'll beat Tunney and beat him so badly that should he get the decision everyone in the hall will know that I have been robbed."[30]

The confusion over whether the fight would be fought and judged on its merits was reflected in the betting. Greb opened as a solid 8 to 5 favorite to retain his crown. The odds quickly shifted further in Greb's favor at 2 to 1. However, as talk of a "sure thing" for Tunney began to build momentum a flood of Tunney money swung a 2 to1 margin for Greb to 6 to 5 or better in favor of Tunney.

The day before the fight Harry rested and went downtown to greet Argentine heavyweight Luis Firpo on his arrival to the United States for his upcoming match with Bill Brennan. Firpo planned to be ringside the following evening to watch the Greb-Tunney match.

The threats against Greb had been so numerous that the night of the fight a special police detachment was issued to escort him to and from the ring. Harry entered the ring weighing 165^{1}/$_{2}$ pounds, eight and a half pounds less than Tunney. When asked about his condition Greb remarked "Bully. They thought they could unnerve me by making public statements to the effect that I am the foulest fighter in the ring, but their scheme did not work. Other than upsetting Mrs. Greb, who feared that the threats of Tunney's followers might be carried out, I have paid no attention to their cries. I know my ability, know that I am not a foul fighter, and feel confident the crown will continue to rest upon my head for a little while longer after tonight's fight is over."[31]

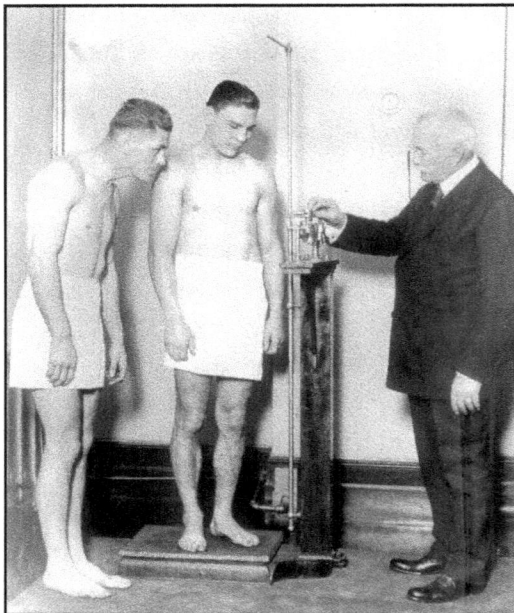

Shortly before the fight it was announced, as expected, that Pasty Haley had been given the assignment to referee. The judges for the contest would be Charles E. Miles and Charles Meighan. Red Mason and Tom Dolan would be Greb's corner men. George Engel was not in Tunney's corner as had been expected. Engel had probably feared losing all or a portion of the percentage he nefari-

*Top: **William Muldoon (right) weighs Harry Greb as Gene Tunney watches intently.** Above: Greb and Tunney square off in the Madison Square Garden gym for photographers prior to their February 1923 rematch.*

ously guaranteed himself by signing the match after Greb had lodged a protest against his presence in Tunney's corner with the commission.

Greb entered the ring first to a chorus of boos and mingled cheers. Tunney followed to a cheer the likes of which nearly raised the roof off the Garden. The capacity crowd was clearly in favor of the hometown boy and when the fighters were announced they once again showered Greb with derision and Tunney with applause.

After the announcements, which included the introductions from ringside of both Floyd Johnson and Luis Firpo, Haley called the fighters and their seconds to ring center in order to deliver final instructions. Billy Gibson immediately began to instruct Haley on Greb's various tactics, to each of which Haley issued a warning to Greb. A comical scene then ensued with Greb questioning the use of each tactic and illustrating their use on Tunney. The crowd stood by for ten minutes marveling as Greb jerked Tunney's head to and fro while the ex-marine stood by passively taking it all in to the amusement of the audience.

Finally an exasperated Greb asked Haley pointedly if he would even be allowed to fight with both hands, implying that he was being forced to fight with one hand behind his back by the obviously partisan referee.

By the time the bell rang sounding the first round odds had once again shifted in Greb's favor at a margin of 8 to 5, as late arrivals from Pittsburgh had brought a flood of money swinging the odds. Such was the rumor of a fix in Tunney's favor that the vast majority of these late bets had a no foul stipulation whereby a disqualification of Greb would render all bets off.

Greb paced in his corner awaiting the bell. He seemed like a ball of pent up energy that could not wait to get at his rival. When the bell finally sounded an irritated Greb leapt from his corner and went straight at Tunney. He darted in and out with such speed of foot that Tunney seemed confused. In order to slow Greb down Tunney clinched continuously, using his size and strength to tire Greb. This incessant clinching led to several unsatisfactory exchanges at close quarters. Time and again they would be separated whereupon Greb would leap in with scoring punches before the inevitable clinch.

During one of these clinches Greb leaned over Tunney's shoulder to trade barbs with a ringside heckler. As early as the first round Tunney seemed intent on playing for Greb's body, hoping to sap the champion's strength. Greb seemed cautious of his style and tactics, afraid to get too aggressive or too wild for fear of being disqualified. Billy Gibson's propaganda was having an effect.

Greb came out for the second round once again on the aggressive and once again met with a clinch by Tunney. Tunney then wrestled Greb to floor. Greb rose quickly and attacked Tunney, rocking him with a series of blows to the head. Tunney fought back valiantly and landed a couple of body blows that caused Greb to clinch. Despite letting Tunney fight and wrestle in the clinches Patsy Haley stepped in immediately to break Greb's clinch. Greb then leapt in, landing his own body blows in answer to Tunney's attack. The round ended with both fighters in a clinch. Haley followed Greb back to his corner and warned him to keep his punches up.

The third began with a clinch and once again observer's noted that Greb seemed unusually cautious. The round illustrated the necessity for Greb's reserved tactics. At one point he was booed by the partisan crowd for landing two legal blows against Tunney and at another point he was warned for clinching by the referee despite Tunney initiating the vast majority of clinches. Tunney landed some hellacious body shots in this round but when he returned to his corner at the end of the round he was suffering a cut left eye which seemed to be troubling him.

The fourth was another ugly round with much clinching. Tunney began rabbit punching in the clinches but finally Haley stepped in and warned him. Tunney was able to land the cleaner, harder punches in this round.

In the fifth round Tunney landed a hard punch to Greb's mouth that, combined with his success in the previous round, seemed to wake Greb's natural instincts. Finally Greb started to dance around in his well known, incomprehensible style with his hands waving around to distract and disorient his opponent. Tunney continued to have success to the body but Greb's fans must have breathed a sigh of relief in this round as the old Greb seemed to be slowly coming to life. In the sixth Tunney seemed to slow down slightly while Greb increased his pace. He worked in close to his larger opponent and whipped a hard right hand to the jaw. Tunney tried to reply but Greb made him miss, pumping both arms to Tunney's body. Tunney's only reply was to repeatedly clinch whenever he could wrap his arms around Greb.

In the seventh round Greb pulled ahead further. He increased his pace once again, while once again Tunney seemed to slow perceptibly. The former Marine's right eye was cut by a left hook in this round and he seemed confused by Greb's ability to rapidly change tactics and style.

Greb came out for the eighth smiling as if knowing what the round held in store for his adversary. He quickly went to work on Tunney landing several right hands to the jaw that Tunney was unable to counter. The audience, seeing Greb's surge and the success it was having, increased its hostility towards the champion. It had no effect on Harry who continued forcing Tunney around the ring with stiff punches and tying up his larger foe whenever it seemed like Tunney would attempt a counter-attack.

Between the eighth and ninth rounds Tunney and Billy Gibson called Patsy Haley over to complain of Greb's tactics. Greb came out for the round landing a dynamite right hand that sent Tunney reeling across the ring. Greb pounced on his man and as he worked both fists to the head and body in close he was warned by Haley for holding. Despite Haley's interference Greb continued to belabor Tunney. Tunney tried to regain some of the momentum by backing Greb into a corner and firing away but Greb simply laughed and fought his way out.

Tunney came out determined to make up lost ground in the tenth. He threw a hard body shot and tried to follow up but was once again swept back by Greb's assault. This continued, varied, and relentless attack seemed to confuse Tunney and he seemed unable to take the initiative against Greb and keep it. Both fighters were warned for rough fighting. While fighting along the ropes Tunney stuck his head outside of the ring while Greb attacked. The pro-Tunney audience booed and Haley warned Greb. After the round ended Red Mason dumped the entire contents of the ice bucket over Greb to cool his hard charging stallion.

The fight was rapidly getting out of Haley's control. At one point in the eleventh Tunney lowered his head and came into a clinch without a punch in an attempt to butt. Greb held out both hands waiting for the referee to break the fighters and no warning was forthcoming for Tunney's infraction. Tunney continually tried to use his greater size to maul, and wrestle Greb with only a token warning from Haley. As the fight slipped away from Tunney he became more desperate and Greb, fighting back in kind, was warned for his actions. At this point Tunney seemed to be running out of gas while Greb seemed stronger than ever.

In the twelfth it looked momentarily as if Haley's admonitions might end the contest early when after a couple of clinches he grabbed Harry's arm and yelled twice "Don't do that!" Greb simply went back to work carrying the fight to Tunney only to be interrupted once again with another warning from the increasingly dictatorial referee. At this point Haley and Greb entered into a heated argument and for a moment it looked as if the argument would become physical. Once again Harry returned to his work and when the round ended he was followed to his corner by Haley who was now verbally berating Greb.

In the thirteenth round Greb continued his assault but seemed much more cautious in the clinches. Despite this Tunney continued to play up to the referee's sympathies by constantly complaining, choosing even to complain to Haley after being hit by a clean left hand. All the while Tunney continued his rough work inside before he was finally warned at the end of the round for wrestling Greb into the ropes.

Tunney had been losing the first minute and a half of the fourteenth round when he brought the crowd to its feet by stunning Greb with a right hand smash to the chin. Tunney's fans, who had been disappointed all night with Tunney's lack of aggression, finally got what they had been calling for. Tunney, smelling victory, attacked. Greb clinched while his head cleared and then blocked or dodge all of Tunney's follow up blows. As the round drew to a close Greb's head had cleared and the two fighters were engaged in fierce infighting.

The fighters shook hands for the fifteenth and final round and then went to infighting, where they remained for most of the round. Tunney's fans were once again surprised by their favorite's lack of aggression, particularly in light of the previous round's success. The round was even with Tunney landing heavily to the body and Greb landing several eye-catching uppercuts and continuing to use Tunney's damaged right eye as a target.[32]

And here the words of Regis Welsh seem to sum up the conclusion of the evening:

Like the tread of a murderer to the gallows, Joe Humphries walked from one judge to the other, looked over the ballots, the box of which had been stuffed from

Facing page top: Harry Greb leaps in and crashes a long right hand to Tunney's jaw.
Facing page center: Despite Harry's increasing reputation as a dirty fighter the tactic he was most often criticized for was holding and hitting, likely necessitated by his lack of depth perception due to his impaired vision and perfectly illustrated by this photo.
Facing page bottom: Harry Greb (facing the camera) weaves in as Tunney backs away during the third round. Top left: Harry (closest to the camera) ducks under a Tunney right in the seventh round. Top right and bottom left: The two fighters wrestle, notice how Tunney rests his chin on Greb's head to give the appearance of being butted by Greb. Tunney was harshly criticized for this tactic, designed to draw sympathy from the referee. Bottom right: Tunney (facing the camera) holds Greb's arms on the inside during the eleventh round.

Referee Patsy Haley keeps a close eye on the action as Greb (right) and Tunney flail away furiously at one another during a mixup in the second round. Haley was heavily criticized for his perceived bias against Greb.

the time the match was made, and New York had a new champion to its home-brew list, as clean a fighter, as gentlemanly a lad as ever lived, but one who will suffer forever as the victim of a well-laid plot and a championship of which he is no more deserving than a prohibitionist is of becoming owner of the Schlitz brewery.[33]

Greb stood in his corner, with a half stunned bemused grin as Humphries announced "The winner, and our new light heavyweight champion, Gene Tunney!" After all, hadn't he been warned for the previous four months that he could not win against Tunney in New York? With swollen knots all over his face and cuts around both eyes Tunney slowly walked over to shake hands with Greb. The overwhelmingly pro-Tunney audience paused momentarily, seemingly surprised by the decision then let out a raucous cheer but those who felt Greb had won or deserved no worse than a draw made their voices heard as well and a great debate raged throughout the arena as to the merits of the verdict.

Greb and his handlers slowly and quietly made their way to the dressing room, as they endured the shouts and taunts of Tunney's supporters. Interviewed in his dressing room Greb stated "I was deliberately jobbed. I was warned several days ago that it was all fixed so that I would get the works and the title would be handed back to Tunney. I have never been disqualified in my life and yet I was warned by the referee before and picked on all through. I forced the going all the way and won the majority of the rounds- but Tunney gets the decision. It is a pretty cheaply won honor."[34] To another reporter he remarked: "That was a pippin, that was a pippin. If ever I beat a man, if ever I tamed a man, I tamed Tunney. I was told, my manager was told, they were out with guns. They surely were. But this thing does not break my nerve. If Tunney will give me the same chance I gave him, that's all I want. I'll fight him any place, any time, for any purse. I can lick him seven days a week. This is a fine thing.

"I never was hurt. He never stopped me for a second, but he whined and whimpered to the referee for help, and he got it. Haley was on me half a dozen times, until I lost my temper and argued with him. I'd like to battle him fifteen more rounds right now."[35]

Tunney had his own version of events: "Greb's blows did not hurt me at any time and I think I proved my ability to stop his style of attack. Greb's holding handicapped me some, but he didn't gain much by his tactics. I was forced to complain to referee Haley frequently, but his warnings seemed to have little effect."[36]

Referee Haley was cornered by a mob of curious sportswriters and though under an official gag order he felt the need to defend his decision which was rapidly coming under scrutiny. "I am not permitted to talk to newspaper men but since you pin me down I might as well say that Greb was guilty of fouling in various ways from the second round on. I warned him, and would have tossed him out of the ring several times had it not been for the fact that Tunney seemed strong and I did not want to disappoint the spectators. How Greb has got by so long without being disqualified is a puzzle to me."[37]

The boxing fraternity was still in an uproar the following day when the opinions of ringsiders were published and the returns came back overwhelmingly in favor of a Greb victory. Of those newspapers present the New York Morning Telegraph (both Sam Taub and James P. Sinnot), New York Evening Mail (both Warren Brown and Ed Hughes), New York Herald (Charles Mathison), New York Evening Journal, Newark Evening News, Newark Star-Eagle, Brooklyn Daily Eagle, Brooklyn Standard-Union, New York Tribune (Grantland Rice), Philadelphia Public Ledger, Pittsburgh Post, Pittsburgh Gazette-Times, Pittsburgh Press, Boxing Blade, and Staten Island Advance all felt that Greb should have won the decision.

Only the New York Sun, New York Evening Telegram, New York Times, New York American, New York Globe, New York Post, New York Call, and New York Morning World voted for Tunney. The Sun had a caveat with their decision stating that Greb scored more points but that they deducted points from Greb which allowed Tunney to pull ahead.

The New York Evening World, The New York Tribune (Jack Lawrence), New York Herald (Walter Trumball), and New York Daily News called the bout a draw.

In addition to the newspapermen such experts as William Muldoon, Frank Flournoy, Dumb Dan Morgan, and Tom O'Rourke were vocal in their opinion that Greb won. Bantamweight champion Joe Lynch told a gathering of reporters "Yes, they want me to risk my title in there, too, but after what I saw tonight, me for overseas until I get another crack at big money, and then I'll come back and let them do it to me just like they did to Greb."[38] Nat Fleischer who had recently founded Ring Magazine chose to sit on the fence.

The few critics who sided with the decision were at times half-hearted and at times almost comically one sided:

> Although Tunney deserved the decision, he won more because Greb put up a poor fight than because of anything remarkable that he accomplished. The local man was not at his best. His hitting was not as effective as usual and he was not as aggressive as he should have been. If Greb had put up one of his good fights he would have won. If Tunney had put up one of his best fights he might have scored a knockout.
>
> -Fred Keats, New York Sun[39]

> On actual points, Tunney won by an unquestionable margin, taking eleven of the fifteen rounds. One of the rounds was even and three went to Greb. Harry would have taken a couple more stanzas were it not for the points which, as rendered imperative by the rules, had to be deducted for infractions of the rules...
>
> ...As far as butting was concerned, Tunney was almost as much at fault as Greb, for Gene repeatedly ducked in such a manner that Greb could not help sticking the top of his head into Tunney's face. Tunney also leaned forward when Greb used his jumping attack and the collision of heads and chins were inevitable...
>
> ...At times it looked as if Gene deliberately was drawing butts to win by a disqualification of Greb. And at times it looked as if Referee Patsy Haley, earnest and conscientious in his endeavor to prevent infraction of the rules, went a bit too far and hectored and annoyed Greb unnecessarily...
>
> -George Underwood, New York Evening Telegram[40]

> Tunney carried off nine of the fifteen rounds. The Greenwich Village boxer won the first five and with his furious assault in the closing rounds carried off the twelfth, thirteenth, fourteenth, and fifteenth. In the fourteenth session Tunney almost floored his rival with a terrific right to the jaw. Greb recovered quickly, however, and resumed his peculiar style of battling, plunging, and tearing in wildly, his arms swinging incessantly but without any sense of direction
>
> -James Dawson, New York Times[41]

> It is safe to say on last night's showing that he can always whip Greb, who has slipped back many pegs without question. It was bitter milling from the start. Tunney was far more active than usual, and when Greb came out with a rush Tunney met him half way.
>
> -Bert Igoe, New York World[42]

The Decision was a just one. the majority of Tunney's rooters, and he was the overwhelming favorite, were apprehensive until Joe Humphries dispelled their fears with his announcement, but there should not have been any doubt as to the result. Tunney won cleanly.

-Dan Lyons, New York Globe [43]

The critics of the decision were numerous and vocal:

Harry Greb sure got the tar end of the stick in his set-to with Gene Tunney in the Garden Friday night. Patsy Haley, who refereed the scrap, complained after the fight about the ex-American light-heavyweight champion's tactics. How about the low lefts that Tunney shot over at least a dozen times during the fifteen rounds? Also, how about the new champion roughing Greb to the ropes time and again?

However, what's the use talking? Greb, in the opinion of all the fair minded fans who witnessed the scrap, received the worst decision ever handed down under the Walker law.

-Sam Taub, New York Morning Telegraph [44]

I would not go so far as to say that I think the decision in the Gene Tunney-Harry Greb light-heavyweight championship bout at Madison Square Garden warrants an official investigation. I do say that I believe that Harry Greb had the better of the fight by a wide margin and should not have been deprived of his title...

...Let us assume, therefore, that the decision expressed the honest belief of those who rendered it. They must pardon me, however, for saying that, despite its admitted honesty of purpose, it is a sad commentary upon their competence as judges of matters fistic.

-James P. Sinnot New York Morning Telegraph [45]

The decision calls for a sweeping investigation by the Boxing Commission- the sooner the better for all parties concerned.

-Ed Hughes, New York Evening Mail [46]

Aside from the fourteenth round I fail to see how the officials could pick Tunney over Greb. The affair was fiercely fought and both men were doing a lot of clinching and holding. If there was any rough work Tunney was as guilty as Greb...

...Billy Gibson, manager of Tunney, generally is considered the biggest factor in the return of the American light heavyweight boxing crown to Gene.

-Bert Dodge, Newark Star-Eagle[47]

The decision was what the boys call a "gun." The verdict was probably the most unsatisfactory one rendered in New York since the Walker law judging from the general outburst of protest following the announcement that Tunney was the new champion.

Greb gave Tunney as bad a beating as he handed Gene when he took the light heavyweight championship from him in their previous encounter. There didn't seem to be the least bit of doubt as to Greb's superiority after the ninth round of the match last night, and though rumors floated thick and fast that it was "in" for Tunney to win if the contest was at all close, not even those that thought they had the inside track figured that there was a possibility of Greb getting the worst of it, he made such a decisive job of the fight the majority of the fans seemed to think.

-Newark Evening News[48]

The worst Harry Greb deserved in blowing his title of light heavyweight champion of America to Gene Tunney, in the Madison Square Garden ring, on the evening of February 23, was a draw. They fought 15 rough rounds before a capacity assemblage. I figured the Pittsburger deserved the verdict but apparently the judges and referee docked Harry plenty for some unintentional foul stuff he pulled and they agreed on Gene as the winner.

-Clarence S. Gillespie, Boxing Blade[49]

We have with us today a new light heavyweight champion -Gene Tunney of Greenwich Village. This by the grace of the judges Charles Meegan, and C. E. Miles, who decided that he had defeated Harry Greb of Pittsburgh after 15 rounds of mauling and clawing that was dignified by the term of boxing at Madison Square Garden last night. That decision would have made Daniel blink his eyes with surprise and would have caused Solomon to call out his guards. It will go down in ring history with the decision that Wyatt Earp gave in San Francisco when he awarded a fight to Tom Sharkey over Bob Fitzsimmons.

No one was more surprised over the decision than was Tunney. I was sitting in his corner when Joe Humphreys, the announcer, after looking at the written decisions of the judges said: "A new light heavyweight champion -Gene Tunney." In that manner Humphreys announced the winner. A look of complete surprise passed over Tunney's face. For about 15 seconds it did not dawn upon him that he was the champion. Then his lips broke into a smile.

-W. C. Vreeland, Brooklyn Daily Eagle[50]

In plain words, last night's match was either a "job," as Harry Greb bitterly insists, or the defeated champion was guilty of his usual foul tactics. Otherwise, and this is the expression of a sincere admirer of the Greenwich Village lad, Tunney did not prove that he is the better man of the two in his fight last night.

-Ed Van Every, New York Evening World[51]

Greb did most of the fighting, most of the hitting, and most of the holding. He used his head repeatedly, but even considering the number of points he lost in this way, he still deserved the decision. At the very worst he might have got a draw.

-Grantland Rice, New York Tribune[52]

It was drawing it very fine to wrest the championship title from a man when the battle seemed to be so close at the end.

-Harry Newman, New York Daily News[53]

Tunney took two rounds, the third and the fourteenth, yet even those who had made the verdict possible by their early malice, public and private, were amazed at the audacity of the decision.

Veteran ringsiders, watching every action, stood up and howled in loud derision. But the die was cast, Greb had been robbed and the nefarious work of those here who do things had borne fruit.

- Regis Welsh, Pittsburgh Post[54]

Unless we miss our guess the decision in this bout will become famous in boxing history. It will be echoed and re-echoed many times and it may shake the very foundation of the game in this state, not that Tunney did not put up a good fight and do himself justice, but giving him full credit for all that he achieved the victory is a hollow one for him. Officially he is the winner, but to all other intents and purposes Greb came out of the scrap with a lion's share of honors. The worst Greb should have been given was a draw and even that would have been a howling injustice, as we see it.

-Harry Keck, Pittsburgh Gazette-Times[55]

Two days after the fight the New York Tribune and New York Herald revealed that decision had not been a unanimous one. The two judges had split in their decision, Charles Miles voting for Greb, with Haley's deciding the championship.[56] Despite chairman Muldoon stating that he felt the decision against Greb was "unjustifiable" he would stand behind the ruling of the officials appointed to their task. Muldoon considered the matter closed and refused to entertain allegations of fight fixing.[57] The Pittsburgh Post hinted that Muldoon's reluctance to act was due in no small part to his position as the odd man out in Governor Al Smith's soon-to-be reorganized boxing commission.[58]

On February 26 Greb and Mason visited the offices of the New York state boxing commission and issued a formal challenge to Gene Tunney which was accepted by the chairman who also refused to accept Greb's $2,500 forfeit binding the match in light of the unsatisfactory nature of the decision. While there Greb collected his purse for the Tunney bout which after a $4,555.36 deduction for George Engel's share and $781 for tickets advanced to Greb he was left with $13,568.17. In addition to this it was announced that Greb had accepted a handsome offer of $50,000 to face Jack Bloomfield in London in May. Fate had other plans though and more immediate concerns would prevent Harry from making the trip.

Harry and Mason left by train for Pittsburgh late that night and as they made their way home another story regarding Greb broke in the newspapers which caused a minor sensation. In discussing the controversial decision of the Tunney-Greb match in his column "Chilly Sauce" Charles Doyle writing for the Pittsburgh Gazette-Times alluded to the "propaganda" against Greb which appeared in some of the New York papers. He then went on to quote a story Greb told him in relation to the first bout with Tunney as a means of illustrating how business was done in New York: "I got quite a nice sum for that fight," said Harry, "but I left plenty of the coin right in New York. Shortly after the bout I was informed it would be proper for me to give $3,000 to the newspapermen of New York, the money to be used in booming a bout with Jack Dempsey. I wanted to fight Jack, but I could not see where I should give up my own money for such a project. I fought the proposition for a while, but finally gave up the money under protest."[59]

The story caused much grumbling among the New York sportswriters and they quickly seized upon it. For his part Greb denied having ever made such a claim and there are good arguments both for and against the legitimacy of whether Greb actually said what was quoted and the allegations attributed to Greb. Whether Greb made the statement or not Doyle had exposed a now accepted fact: In New York you had to pay to play.

The charge was laid before Chairman Muldoon who refused to acknowledge it as anything more than gossip. For a time the New York World, which had been squarely in Tunney's camp, refused to let the matter die and swore to launch its own investigation into the claims but the matter was quickly dropped.

Upon returning home Greb found Mildred's condition had deteriorated. He immediately postponed the trip to Hot Springs that Red Mason had previously arranged; where they planned to enjoy spring training with the Pirates and relax. Mildred was not expected to live long and Harry wanted to be close at hand.

Greb took a brief recess from his bedside duties to be honored at a special smoker staged by the Pittsburgh Lyceum. There Greb boxed a three round exhibition with Tom Higgins before a packed and enthusiastic house. Afterwards he was honored with a loving cup inscribed with the words "The Pittsburgh Lyceum's appreciation of the Greb-Tunney bout February 23, 1923, in Madison Square Garden. He lost the decision but won the fight. Here expressed and presented Sunday March 11, 1923."[60]

The following week the Knights of Columbus planned a similar smoker yet Harry was forced to cancel his appearance. Mildred had steadily grown worse just over the last week and finally on March 18 at only twenty-two years of age her suffering ended and she passed from this world leaving behind a devastated husband and a three year old daughter.

Mildred's funeral was held three days later at Harry's Jackson Street home and mass was observed at Sacred Heart Church. Harry's world must have seemed like it was spinning out of control as he watched his wife's casket sink into the earth. In less than a month he had lost his title, and his wife. He had been rendered a single father at the age of 28 and continued to be hounded by hostile press-men. Reminded of his own mortality, Harry had a will made out the same day as Mildred's funeral.

According to his friends Greb was inconsolable. True to form Red Mason knew of only one cure for any ailment: Activity. He promptly set about negotiating matches for Harry and quickly signed him to face Jeff Smith in Atlanta in July. Using this as pretext for getting Harry as far from Pittsburgh as possible he whisked him away to the resort town of Hot Springs, Arkansas to tour the spas, enjoy the fresh air, and train with Harry's beloved Pirates.

While it may seem somewhat cold hearted that Mason was attempting to smother Greb's worries with work the strategy could not have come at a more fortuitous time. Events where now in motion that hinted at a possible break in the logjam in both the middleweight and light-heavyweight divisions.

The day before Mildred's death light heavyweight champion Battling Siki had inexplicably traveled to Dublin, Ireland to face Irish ex-patriot Mike McTigue for the crown on St. Patrick's Day of all days. How Siki expected to defeat an Irishman in Dublin during the Uprising, on St. Patrick's Day

This loving cup was presented to Greb by his friends at the Pittsburgh Lyceum during a smoker staged in his honor. The inscription reads: "The Pittsburgh Lyceum's appreciation of the Greb-Tunney bout February 23, 1923, in Madison Square Garden. He lost the decision but won the fight. Here expressed and presented Sunday March 11, 1923."

is anyone's guess but when Siki was declared the loser after chasing the ever timid McTigue for 20 rounds he seemed to be the only one who had not been given the script.

McTigue was now a champion, New York was his home, and Greb had already defeated him with relative ease on two occasions. Quick to seize the opportunity, Tex Rickard was now aggressively trying to sign McTigue to face either Tunney or Greb for the championship.

In the middleweight division it was announced that Johnny Wilson's contract had been purchased for $50,000 by Frank Marlowe. Marlowe, whose real name was Gandolfo Curto, was a sportsman, gambler, and underworld figure who would eventually reach the highest echelons organized crime, before being gunned down in 1929. With Marlowe's muscle now backing him Wilson suddenly got brave. He began aggressively lobbying to be reinstated in New York and when notified that he would be expected to defend his championship against Greb he agreed, thinking that Greb could no longer make the middleweight limit or would at least be weakened in doing so.

The long expected shake up in the State Athletic Commission finally took place in mid April. Governor Al Smith moved on the Commission and curbed much of Chairman Muldoon's power by relocating it within the newly appointed Licensing Committee, primarily in the hands of Smith crony, and Tunney's friend, William McCormack.[61] With this change it was expected that fighters who had been made persona non grata under the increasingly dictatorial edicts of Muldoon, such as Wilson and Johnny Kilbane, would be dealt with more leniently, provided of course that they exhibit their wares in New York on a regular basis. Seizing upon this and hoping to ingratiate himself to the commission Johnny Wilson announced that he would no longer call Boston home and would instead relocate to New York City. It was a clumsy gesture but one Wilson hoped would pay dividends.[62]

Much to their disappointment Greb and Mason arrived in Hot Springs only one day before the Pirates finished training. Nevertheless Greb was received by locals and ball players alike as a conquering hero. After checking in to the luxurious Eastman he and Mason were loaned Pittsburgh uniforms by Pirates manager and future baseball hall of famer Bill McKechnie. The two fight bugs were as giddy as school children to train with the team while wearing their colors. At the end of the day Harry was exhausted. It had been nearly a month since he had boxed his exhibition with Tom Higgins and he had a lot of work ahead of him before he could round into the kind of shape needed to challenge for two championships.

"I am going to go through with a systematic course of training," he said, "and started the program today with my first bath. My ticket calls for 20 more dips in the hot water and I am drinking regularly from the mineral spring. Mason closed arrangements shortly after we arrived for a workout each day at the Fordyce gymnasium. Beginning tomorrow I will play 18 holes of golf every morning and also take daily hikes over the hills and do some horseback riding."

I have refused all offers to fight but I intend to get into the greatest condition of my career and go after Gene Tunney, for of course he is the one I am eager to meet. I'm not worried about that 160 pounds that must be made to fight Johnny Wilson for I can make this weight and will post the forfeit in due time. It had been my plan to make a trip to Europe, but right now it looks as if this will have to be postponed as I probably will accept several offers later in the season."[63]

On April 6th Greb was ringside for the Red Herring-Bobby Green fight. Announcer Johnny White hailed Greb as the "popular champion of the light-heavyweight division" to great applause. When Greb was asked to say a few words he stated that he was in Hot Springs to get into the kind of condition necessary to restore the title that had been "stolen" from him.[64]

Greb quickly began rounding into shape and as the life returned to his limbs he became more and more eager to get a rematch with Tunney. "I would much prefer not to go to London now," he said "and prefer to stay here and force Tunney into another match. I have never felt so good. This is a wonderful place to train, and I expect to be in better condition than ever before in a short while, and then I am going to force the issue in the east and recover my title. Of course if I have to fulfill the London engagement I will do so, but I would rather stay here now." Off the record Greb intimated that the blow caused by his wife's death had made him hesitant to travel abroad at the moment.[65]

Greb and Mason returned home on April 20 after first stopping off in Chicago to watch the Pirates-Cubs series. Greb pronounced himself in perfect condition and was eager to fight before his local fans the following month.

Five days after arriving Greb appeared in an exhibition bout at an event thrown by the Knights of Columbus for the entertainment of veterans. His opponent was Frank Munroe and when Harry entered the ring he was given a rousing ovation.

Top: Harry Greb fielding balls with his beloved Pittsburgh Pirates on their last day of spring training in 1923. Above: left to right Pirates outfielder Reb Russell, Greb, and Red Mason pose together.

A few days after the exhibition with Munroe it was announced that Greb would meet Jimmy Darcy at Motor Square Garden on May 7. Darcy had been scheduled to meet Greb six months previous. When Greb cancelled bouts that Engel had signed on his behalf Darcy was left without a payday. This, combined with the two previous losses he had suffered at the hands of Greb, left him eager to even the score.

Since the last time he and Greb had fought, Darcy had left Jack Kearns management in favor of Leo P. Flynn. The change had done little to bolster his career. Indeed, it had been nearly a year since Darcy had won a fight despite middling competition. In fact his recent record had been uninspiring enough that combined with the fact that he had already lost to Greb on two occasions one member of the local commission was prompted to vote against sanctioning Darcy as an opponent. He was overruled by the other five members.[66]

Despite Darcy's faded reputation Greb was taking the bout seriously and training as if it were a championship. The fans came in droves to watch Greb spar daily at Motor Square Garden against the likes of Harry Fay and Ditty Woods. It had been months since they had seen their hero in a real bout and, despite the talk that he was now slowing down and showing wear from the long years and many engagements, they marveled at the speed and endurance he displayed.

On the day of the fight Greb's recent bad luck flared up again. Harry had developed a boil on his right arm during preparation for the Darcy fight. During training the boil had been scratched. Initially it was a minor annoyance but the small wound became infected and the day before the fight he was unable to train. He was taken to see Dr. Grover Well who was immediately alarmed at the advanced stage of the infection. The doctor tried to convince Greb to admit himself to Mercy Hospital but Harry refused thinking he might still go on with the fight and admit himself after.

At noon on Monday the seventh Greb arrived for the weigh in at Motor Square Garden, his arm wrapped in bandages and smelling of the opiate anesthesia Laudanum. Dr. Briney, the commission's doctor, immediately declared that Greb would not be allowed to go on. When Greb was presented to Darcy the west coast fighter stated: "Gee, that's more than I could do to you in a week, I guess it's all off."[67] Harry stated his intention to go on with the show if the doctors thought he could but he added that not only his arm hurt but his chest as well. The fight was called off and Greb was rushed to the hospital where his badly swollen arm was lanced.

Greb's condition was serious enough that four doctors conferred and determined that surgery would be necessary to relieve the infection otherwise Harry might lose his right arm. The following day surgery was performed successfully and just in the nick of time. The tissue around the wound had become wasted by the poison. Had surgery not been performed immediately his condition would have deteriorated rapidly. When Greb awoke from the anesthesia he stated that his arm felt somewhat better but was told he would need plenty of rest before he was able to be up and about again.

Harry would spend most of the following week at the hospital under close observation. The infection and resulting surgery had forced Greb to call off matches in both Chicago and Peoria the following week. While Greb lay confined in bed his thoughts were troubled by the dark cloud that seemed to hang over him with the loss of his title, death of his wife, and near amputation of his arm all coming one right after another.

Upon being discharged from the hospital Harry and Red Mason immediately boarded a train bound for the east coast where Mason would negotiate fights for Greb against Johnny Wilson for the Middleweight title and Mike McTigue for the light heavyweight title. While Mason took care of business Greb planned to relax further at Atlantic City.

When Greb and Mason returned from the east they notified the press that a fight with McTigue would take place in the near future. Joe Jacobs, McTigue's manager, also announced that Greb and McTigue would likely fight in Chicago on June 20. Days later when Tex Rickard could not secure Georges Carpentier to face McTigue at Boyles Thirty Acres in July he offered to promote a Greb-McTigue bout there, to which the parties quickly agreed.

The match meant a great deal to Greb as it would be staged before a large audience and would provide Greb with the opportunity to win a world championship if he could win inside the distance. On June 3 Harry and his retinue left for Conneaut Lake, where Greb would set up a formal training camp to prepare for the match. McTigue had set up camp at Babylon, Long Island.

As a tune-up for the McTigue bout Greb hoped to shake off the ring rust by fighting Len Rowlands in Uniontown on June 15. In preparation for these two bouts Greb hired Cuddy DeMarco, Harry Fay, Johnny Francis, Johnny Byers, and Walter Maloy to serve as sparring partners and set about working himself into shape.

Unfortunately ten days into Greb's camp word was received that the McTigue fight was off. As the price for McTigue's services crept higher and higher Tex Rickard refused to meet the Irishman's increasingly exorbitant demands. Believing McTigue had priced himself out of the fight Rickard called off the match. Having the rug pulled out from under him so close to a championship fight with a man he had already defeated twice must have seemed like one more bit of bad luck in a seemingly unending stream of misfortune.

With the McTigue match now a thing of the past Mason began looking over the flood of offers for Greb's services. Harry was still booked to face Jeff Smith in Atlanta, a match that had been discussed for weeks but was having difficulty gaining approval due to local opposition to prize-fighting. He was also scheduled to face Len Rowlands in Uniontown. It would be his first fight in four months, one of the longest layoffs of his career, and he would have to put on a dominating performance over a man he had already defeated twice before to show that he had not lost a step.

After a two day delay due to rain Greb did not disappoint. For two rounds he toyed with Rowlands showing his speed, strength, and aggression, before finally ending matters with a

Above: Harry Greb (left) trains with Harry Fay at Conneaut Lake for his June 22 fight with Mike McTigue. Facing page, top: Greb in various phases of training. Facing page bottom: Greb (left) and Harry Fay sparring.

well-placed right to the chin in the third. Rowlands crumpled to the canvas unconscious. As his handlers worked over him feverishly Greb moved in with his hands still gloved and began administering to Rowlands as well, splashing cool water on his face to help revive him. When Rowlands finally came too he was dazed and confused but eventually shook Greb's hand, and congratulated him.[68]

After the fight Greb was interviewed by local newspapermen. He told them that after all of the trouble he had experienced in recent months he considered retiring from the sport. He was only convinced otherwise by the urgings of Red Mason and his sisters. He also hoped to fight in Uniontown again soon and suggested Luis Firpo as an opponent, adding that promoters should sign the toughest opponent possible for him.[69]

Finally on June 23 it seemed that Greb's fortunes had changed for the better. It was announced that Greb and Johnny Wilson had been matched for August 31 at the Polo Grounds in a bout scheduled for 15 rounds to a decision with the middleweight championship of the world at stake. In order to gain the match Greb was forced to post a $10,000 weight forfeit. Wilson believed, or hoped, that Greb would fail to make weight resulting in Wilson claiming the sizeable forfeit and rendering the match a non-title affair.[70]

It was the chance Greb had spent six years waiting for. Ever since 1917 when he faced middleweight champion Al McCoy and light-heavyweight champion Battling Levinsky in no-decisions matches which he won handily Greb had yearned for a match with a champion, any champion, to a decision. Johnny Wilson had avoided Greb for two years to the point where he was willing to drive his career nearly to ruin and fight only four times during that period against poor competition for less than a fraction of what he could have made against Greb. But Wilson knew what Greb knew, what most knew, which was that as soon as the ink was set down on the contract Wilson's title was as good as Greb's, provided Greb could make weight and provided making weight didn't severely weaken him. It was on this hope that Wilson finally found the courage to fight Greb.

On July 3rd Greb's right arm became infected again from another boil, this time on his elbow. He made an appointment for the following day to have his arm operated on. That day Greb had motored to Gorley's Lake, near Uniontown, in order to scout his training camp for the Wilson fight. Along for the ride were his sister Ida, brother-in-law Elmer, Helen Austin, and his three year old daughter Dorothy. On the way back the group passed through Connellsville. While trying to bypass a traffic jam Greb was stopped by traffic officer V. Bert Ritchie. From here the story changes depending on who was recounting it. What seems clear is that Greb and the officer got into an argument at which point the officer asked Greb to follow him to the police station.

Upon arriving at the police station Greb was thrown in a jail cell and, according to him, beaten by a huge officer named Andy Thomas and two others. Greb was made to pay $25 in bail until the mayor, C. C. Mitchell, was phoned. The mayor immediately had Greb's bail returned

and released him. By his own admission Harry had already made up his mind to get even with Thomas and upon leaving his cell he wheeled around and landed a terrific blow on the officer, and then promptly left. Once again Greb was arrested and held, this time being made to pay $100 in bail.

The mayor arrived on the scene clearly unhappy with the turn of events, and sensing a situation was developing, immediately demanded that Greb be released and his bail returned. Greb admitted he was wrong to strike the officer but added that he had lost his temper after hearing his daughter and sister crying in the next room. He was asked only to return if called for a hearing to which he agreed.[71]

Mitchell was so flustered by what could have rapidly developed into a public relations nightmare that he immediately fired his brother, city detective J. W. Mitchell, for mishandling the fiasco. Detective Mitchell had apparently been on duty and in charge on the night of the fourth. It was alleged that detective Mitchell had been intoxicated while on duty

Scenes of Greb sparring at his Conneaut Lake train- which contributed to the situation *ing camp in 1923. In the top photo Greb is sparring* getting out of control.[72] *an unknown opponent, likely Leo Caghil. Below we* *see Greb squaring off with his lightweight stable-* For Greb's part the incident was *mate Cuddy DeMarco. DeMarco, known as the Sheik* quickly forgotten but former detec- *of Charleroi, was a frequent member of Greb's train-* tive Mitchell spent the next several *ing staff.*

weeks fighting to get his job back. Mayor Mitchell, to his credit, held his ground and eventually abolished the position of city detective altogether. The mayor's actions on the night of the fourth and thereafter were upheld by the city council.[73]

20

TRIUMPH

The same day that Greb was speeding back to Mercy Hospital two thousand miles away under the hot July sun a different drama was playing out. Jack Dempsey was defending his championship against Greb's old foe Tommy Gibbons in Shelby, Montana. Drama is likely too extreme a term to apply to what would ever after be called the "Sack of Shelby."

In order to obtain Dempsey's services the promoters and their backers were forced to give in to Doc Kearns' exorbitant demands. These included that Dempsey receive $300,000 for his services, plus $10,000 in training expenses. In addition to this Kearns demanded that the money be paid in three equal installments, the last of which was to be made two days before Dempsey and Gibbons exchanged a single blow. Furthermore, Kearns reserved the right to call off the fight, and keep any payments he had collected up to that point if any succeeding payments were not met.

Despite being held in a seemingly remote venue the promotion initially looked like it would be successful. Advance ticket sales were brisk. Despite this promoters were nervous. Doc Kearns had refused to put his or Dempsey's full backing on the match in public. When promoters temporarily had difficulty making the second installment of $100,000 Kearns threatened to pull out of the fight completely. The promoters, particularly those backing the match with their own finances, realized too late that Kearns had them where he wanted them and if they were to recoup any of their investment they would have to give in to his demands. The second $100,000 was cobbled together and paid. It was too late though, what should have been a minor and private speed bump was made all too public. Ticket sales slowed, as did train bookings. Then, shortly before the third installment of $100,000 was due, it was announced that it would be impossible to pay such a sum before the gate receipts had been collected. Without batting an eyelash Kearns called the fight off, more than happy to walk away with a $200,000 payday for nothing. Suddenly ticket sales didn't simply cool, they ground to a halt and the box offices were flooded with cancellations. The promotion was effectively dead.

In order to salvage the fight Kearns was persuaded to take the first $100,000 from the gate receipts. With this agreement in place Kearns finally announced, on the day of the fight, that Dempsey would indeed defend his championship against Tommy Gibbons who had gotten his shot at the heavyweight title by losing to a man who was now in training to challenge for the 160 pound championship.

The fight itself lacked the drama of the promotion. Dempsey characteristically charged out in the opening round, intent on finishing Gibbons quickly. Tommy smothered Dempsey's rushes, seemingly finding solace, if not success, in the clinches. In the second round Dempsey seemed to slow slightly; he was still keeping ahead of Gibbons on points but Tommy was now finding it easier to create the distance he needed to pot shot Dempsey, even landing several jarring blows against the champion that brought the crowd to its feet.

By the fourth round Dempsey's punch output had slowed down. The champion seemingly realized that the fight might go longer than expected. The slower pace allowed Gibbon's to get back into the fight by utilizing his long range skills. As Dempsey grew frustrated he fought dirty, throwing a litany of rabbit punches, kidney punches, and even hitting on the break while Gibbons was tied up in the ropes. Never the less Gibbons continued to peck and poke and smother Dempsey or make him miss.

As the fight wore on Gibbons' pace slowed as well, which now allowed Dempsey more success. Apparently the heat, or Dempsey's heavy blows, or both, were telling on Gibbons. As the rounds wore on, witnessing clinch after clinch, Gibbons fell further and further behind due to his lack of aggression.

When Dempsey's hand-picked referee, Jimmy Daugherty, raised his hand there was no great surprise as to the winner. Indeed, Dempsey had been expected to win, and win far more emphatically than he did. Dempsey had by now been built up as such a giant killer that even a seasoned professional like Tommy Gibbons, who had never been stopped and who possessed excellent defensive skills, was expected to be bowled over by the champion with little effort.

Gibbons emerged from the bout as a hero for staying the full fifteen rounds and doing so knowing full well that he would likely not receive a dime for his trouble. He would go on to make up the loss by leveraging his new found notoriety into stage appearances and more lucrative bouts.

After the fight Kearns quickly collected the entire gate receipts (which totaled only about $55,000) and left town that night. Dempsey's reputation had taken a major hit due to the fiasco. Kearns' handling of the promotion reminded many of a stickup man, which did not sit well with jaded fans already tired of the

Despite defeating Tommy Gibbons in Tex Rickard's elimination bout it was Gibbons who got the heavyweight title shot. Here Gibbons is seen in the dark trunks fending off one of Jack Dempsey's attacks in their 15 round championship bout at Shelby, Montana.

increasing commercialization of the sport. As the public face of their partnership Dempsey bore the brunt of Kearns' business decisions. It didn't help that Dempsey had been idle for two years, seemingly resting on his laurels and had now been taken the distance by a man who had lost his most important fight to a middleweight and who himself was only a few years removed from being a middleweight. It was said that the champion no longer retained his edge and that he would have to fight more often. Plans had already been in place for months to match Dempsey against Luis Firpo and with Firpo's victory over former champion Jess Willard eight days later the match was now a certainty for late summer or early fall.

As Kearns counted his money and plotted his escape from Montana, Uniontown promoter Fred Kelley was desperately seeking an audience with him. Kelley had traveled to Montana with the hope of signing Dempsey to face Harry Greb on August 15 near Uniontown. Harry had already agreed to Kelley's terms while in Uniontown to face Len Rowlands. Kelley had financial backers willing to pay Dempsey $100,000 to fight the middleweight.[1] To this end Kelley chased Doc Kearns half way across the country trying to get Kearns to sign. The closest he got was a conference with Tom O'Rourke acting on behalf of Kearns.[2] It was a long shot, made more so by Kearns, Dempsey, and Tex Rickard hungrily eyeing the Luis Firpo.

The futility of his quest escaped Kelley even when in mid-July Dempsey was signed to fight Firpo on Labor Day. Even then Kelley continued his quixotic quest to stage a Dempsey-Greb bout for over a month. Kelley's ambitions were finally curbed when the outdoor season drew to a close as no indoor venue in the area could accommodate the amount of people needed to make such a venture profitable.

Greb looked upon the Dempsey-Firpo bout with disdain. He reasoned that Dempsey had just been extended the distance by a man that he (Greb) had dominated and Firpo had been extended the distance by a man that Greb had knocked out in five rounds (Homer Smith).[3] Harry intended to wager heavily that Dempsey would stop Firpo within five rounds, reasoning that Firpo was too slow, crude, and inexperienced to give the champion a proper challenge.

Peeved as he may have been by losing yet another opportunity, as remote as the possibility was, at Dempsey, Greb was focused on his own upcoming championship match. By late July his arm had healed sufficiently to begin training. He spent time in both Pittsburgh and Conneaut Lake working with Jack Barry, Leo Caghil, and Cuddy DeMarco.

DeMarco himself was training for an upcoming bout in Johnstown against Tony Ross and a hoped for position on the undercard of the Greb-Wilson bout. Greb accompanied DeMarco to Johnstown to help Mason work the corner. When Tony Ross refused to face DeMarco during a dispute at the weigh in Harry stepped in and boxed a three round exhibition with Cuddy and another three rounds with Leo Caghil thereby saving the show and placating the grumbling fans. Fred Kelley had promoted the DeMarco-Ross bout and his handling of the controversy put the final nail in the coffin of his hopes to promote a Dempsey-Greb bout.[4] Soon after, Tom O'Rourke forsook working with Kelley on the match and instead opened negotiations with

Barney Dreyfuss to stage the Dempsey-Greb bout at Forbes Field.[5]

Two days after the DeMarco-Ross debacle Greb fought a six round exhibition with Leo Caghil for the Conneaut Lake Fireman's Association. Two days after the exhibition Greb broke camp in Conneaut Lake and relocated to Gorley's Lake near Uniontown for a week. Along with Greb came his daughter Dorothy, sister Ida, brother-in-law J. Elmer Edwards, Red Mason, Caghil, DeMarco, as well as his own personal cook Mrs. Braun and her daughter Mary. More sparring partners would follow when Greb transferred operations to his Manhasset, Long Island camp where he would put the finishing touches on his training.

The fresh air and hills around Uniontown agreed with Greb. His condition was already excellent, his spirits were up, and he felt supremely confident that he would soon be the middleweight champion. He even found time to give a couple of exhibition bouts for the locals who showed up to watch the contender's training routine which included rowing, swimming, and rock climbing in addition to his boxing workouts.

Wilson had setup his training camp at Johnny Collins' health farm at Summit, New Jersey under the watchful eye of trainer Harry Kelley. Wilson sparred daily with Jack Taylor, Wild Bill Houlihan, and Jack Delaney and would later add Georgie Ward, Jimmy Amato, and Frankie Quill. The champion was rounding into arguably the best shape of his career and seemed to be taking no notion of the press' assertion that it was a foregone conclusion that a new champion would be crowned on the 31st. Regardless, when the odds makers began taking bets Greb was installed as a 2 to 1 favorite.[6]

As both fighters trained feverishly, troubling reports began to filter out that Greb would once again face a handicap of biased officiating as he had in his bout with Tunney. Other disturbing rumors began to spread that Greb would throw the fight.[7] Those that did not totally accept the rumors that the fight was fixed outright for Wilson to win one way or another, wondered allowed if Greb would weaken himself making weight. Such gossip served only to slow ticket sales.

Tom O'Rourke began frantically contacting every media outlet in hopes of curbing the rumors. Greb himself was livid when told

Johnny Wilson, right, is seen sparring with Jack Taylor in preparation for his middleweight title defense against Harry Greb.

Scenes from Harry Greb's Manhasset, Long Island training camp as he prepares for his title shot against Johnny Wilson. Top, left to right, Leo Caghil, Greb, Ida Greb Edwards, Dorothy, J. Elmer Edwards, and unknown, do roadwork for the cameras. Bottom left, Greb (right) prepares to spar as Red Mason looks on. Bottom right, Harry recieves Red Mason's famous Chinese laundry spray between sparring sessions. Facing page, Top left, Harry Greb in characteristic pose. Top middle, Greb jumping rope. Top right and bottom left, Greb poses with Dorothy. Bottom right, Greb shares a quiet moment with Dorothy and his sister Ida. The press who visited Greb's camp were taken with Greb's dedication to his family and stated goal of fighting to build a nest egg for his little girl. They reported at length on the subject and published numerous photos of the family together.

Greb's training retinue. Red Mason, top row center white shirt, stands among Greb's sparring partners. Bottom row, left to right, Jack White, camp cook Mrs. Braun's daughter Mary Braun, Mrs. Braun, Greb, Dorothy, Ida, and J. Elmer Edwards.

of the stories. "My friends here and all over the world know that I have never quit and never will," he said. "I'll make the weight and they can weigh me every day as suggested to keep an eye on me. I'll beat Wilson and beat him so badly that there will be no chance of cheating me. This is my big chance, and although there are some who think my day as a big league fighter is over, I hope to prove otherwise. Wilson is tough and can punch, but I'll beat him in front of his friends and show that I can come back. Then for Tunney, Gibbons, and even Dempsey. I'm getting a late start, but will 'go some' when I do get started."[8]

On August 17 Greb arrived in New York City to give the press a good look at him. He immediately went to Philadelphia Jack O'Brien's gym for a public workout before heading out to his Manhasset training camp. While at O'Brien's gym Harry gave a fascinating interview which gives us a candid snapshot of his mental outlook in the months leading up to the Wilson fight:

> "Yes, there were days when I was through with everything and didn't care if I never entered the ring again, or what became of me. Inside of a period of three weeks it seemed that I had lost everything. My title of light heavyweight champion, they got that away from me. A few days later my wife died. About two weeks after that came the trouble with my arm which had developed an infection, and when they put me under ether for the operation I was warned that I might wake up with only one arm.

By then I was in a state of mind that I didn't care what happened. For nearly three years I had been worried by the illness of my wife. When they discharged me from the hospital it was worse than ever. I had to tear myself away and find life and lights and wild parties. Anything to try and forget. Yes, I guess all those stories you heard about my dissipation were only too true.

I went away to Conneaut Lake for a spell and now everywhere I go my sister and little girl go with me. I started resuming training and it felt so good to feel right again physically. To an athlete there is nothing like the feeling of being in shape. I am cured of dissipation and now I have something to work for. I want to be a champion again and make a lot of money and save it for my little girl. I know I can beat Wilson. I am not underestimating him, and they tell me he is in wonderful shape. But after Gibbons, Gene Tunney, Bill Brennan and a lot of other men many pounds heavier than myself I look forward to the Wilson match with every confidence."[9]

On August 21 Greb amazed the assembled press at his training camp with a marathon sparring session with six sparring partners, going two rounds apiece. Greb fought faster in the eleventh and twelfth rounds than he had in the first and left his partners bruised and bloody. Greb then cooled down by skipping rope for a round and was hardly breathing heavy.[10] Two days later Harry again amazed observers when in addition to his regular routine of shadow boxing, rope skipping, and bag punching he sparred three rounds with Harry Fay, three rounds with Ed Keeley, three rounds with Kid Carter, two rounds with Eddie Bitzel, and another three rounds with Young Frankie taking only thirty second breaks between rounds. He then jumped on the scales and weighed 159 pounds.[11]

Greb was working so hard in camp that Philadelphia Jack O'Brien warned him to ease up or risk going stale. Greb would have none of it and continued at his frantic pace to the delight of the hordes that showed up to watch him train for free. Throughout his training Greb had been wildly popular with Long Islanders.

Two days before fight night Greb and company breezed into Manhattan to finish their final day of training at Philadelphia Jack O'Brien's gym. Greb's skin was bronzed and underneath it every muscle rippled. He was below weight and so confident of victory that he had bet heavily on himself to win by knockout.[12] "I have more at stake in this fight than in any fight I have ever had and I must win," he said. "I think I have demonstrated that I am in great shape. I have had no trouble making the weight. I will be too fast and strong for Wilson and I will surprise the public by showing that I can hit. I must beat Wilson in order to get Tunney back and then Dempsey. I want to end my career as a boxer with three championships."[13]

At 2pm on the day of the fight Greb and Wilson weighed in at the offices of the Athletic

Commission. Both men weighed in at 158 pounds, two pounds under the limit now stipulated by the commission, likely at Wilson's insistence as he had loudly proclaimed that he had won the championship at 158 and anyone expecting to make a claim to the title would have to make that poundage as well. Greb likely wanted to be on the side of tradition as well as the commission when he made such a low weight. The select few reporters chosen by the commission to be present at the weigh in noted that while Wilson appeared to have made the weight easily; Greb seemed weakened by the experience.

According legend passed down in the family of Cuddy DeMarco, who fought on the undercard, as Greb, Red Mason, and DeMarco sat in the dressing room waiting for the main event they were approached by underworld figures hoping to bribe Greb to throw the fight. The men were told in no uncertain terms that Harry was out to win the championship after which they were shown the door. For the rest of his life Cuddy would blame Greb and Mason's unwillingness to play ball with the mob for his inability to gain a title shot when he was at the height of his abilities.[14]

Between the persistent rumors that dogged the fight and the combination of Wilson's unpopularity, the belief that the fight was something of a mismatch, and the fact that it was scheduled just two weeks before Jack Dempsey's heavyweight championship defense against Luis Firpo at the same venue, resulted in a disappointing attendance of just over 10,000 persons.

Harry entered the ring first at 9:53pm in a green robe, Wilson followed. Greb received the larger ovation of the two. Among those present to cheer the fighters were the entire team of the New York Yankees who had been given tickets as a prize for defeating the Washington Senators.

Frank Marlowe, whose real name was Gandolfo Curto, was a gambler and bootlegger with deep and dangerous connections to organized crime. In 1923 he took over Johnny Wilson's contract. According to some sources he eventually became a mob boss before being murdered gangland style in 1929. Both Johnny Wilson, and Wilson's early manager, mob underboss Ciro Terranova were questioned about the murder.

Wilson showed early on that he intended to follow his pre-fight game plan as advertised, going for the body almost exclusively. Greb surprised onlookers by fighting flat footed. Despite this change in tactics he set a pace immediately that was too quick for Wilson. From the outset the gulf in class was apparent. As expected, Wilson quickly fell behind on points and even his attempts to work Greb's body were met with only mixed success as Harry proved too fast, even fighting flat footed, to allow Wilson many opportunities to land.

Greb's willingness to box flat footed puzzled many. It was felt in some quarters that the effort to make weight had indeed robbed him of a portion of his vitality. Others felt he was boxing flat footed in an effort to put more power into his punches and thereby collect on the heavy wagers he had made to stop Wilson. And still others felt that Greb was boxing in this more conservative style out of fear of the same type of officiating that had robbed him of his victory over Gene Tunney. Likely it was a combination of these factors which prompted Greb to make such a puzzling change in his style in such an important fight.

Wilson won his first round in the sixth by finally breaking through with several powerful blows to the body which momentarily slowed Harry and echoed around the ball field.

By the midway point of the fight Wilson was so tired his corner was forced to use "restoratives" in order to bring him out for each new round. In the final two rounds Greb's lead was so insurmountable that he let out slightly, coasting, this as well led some to opine that Greb was weak from making weight. As they shook hands for the final round Wilson said "Good luck to you, Harry." Greb answered back "Good luck to you, too, Johnny. They'll say the best man won." They did.[16]

Johnny Wilson (left) and Harry Greb pose for photographers prior to their 15 round middleweight championship fight at the Polo Grounds on August 31, 1923. Referee Jack O'Sullivan and announcer Joe Humphries look on as does Red Mason (far right).

Facing page top: Harry Greb (center) cocks his right in preparation for an assault on Johnny Wilson. Facing page middle: The intensity on Harry's (left) face is apparent as the cameraman catches the instant Greb leaps to the attack. Facing page bottom: Wilson (facing the camera) is about to absorb one of Greb's sweeping left hands. Top left: Fourth round action as Greb (lighter trunks) tries to work in close with Wilson holding on. Top right: Wilson (right) covers up as Greb pounds away to the head and body with his right in a clinch. Bottom: Greb (right) has just bounced out of range of Wilson's left hand swing in an unspecified round.

Various action photos of the August 31, 1923 middleweight championship between Harry Greb and Johnny Wilson. Top: Fifth round action as Wilson (left) tries to find an opening to Greb's body. Bottom: Greb (center) prepares to launch an assault as Wilson stands off during the second round. Facing page top left: Wilson (back to the camera) covers up as Greb gives him some of his own medicine by going to the body in the eighth. Top right: Greb peers over Wilson's shoulder in a clinch during the thirteenth round giving a knowing smile to the cameraman. At this point Greb knew he had the fight in hand. Facing page bottom: Referee Jack O'Sullivan watches the action closely as Greb (center) launches one of his trademark two fisted attacks, forcing Wilson to give ground in an unspecified round.

Few if any were surprised when Joe Humphries announced Greb as the winner. Only long time Greb detractors Fred Keats and Bob Edgren had anything truly negative to say about Greb. Edgren, comically, intimated that at the close of the fight it was anyone's guess who the victor would be. Nobody, not even Keats, agreed with this assessment. It illustrates the lengths to which some of Greb's enemies were willing to reach in order to defame him, his character, or his ability. The majority of newspapermen ringside gave Wilson only two rounds, a few others with more generous inclinations gave Wilson four rounds.

Joe Humphries (left) has just announced that Harry Greb has won the middleweight championship. Greb's second, Tom Dolan, looks on as Red Mason climbs through the ropes. Greb's other cornerman, Tom Holleran, lifts Greb into the air in jubilation as Greb waves to the audience.

Greb was elated. After over ten years as a professional, six years spent as a legitimate contender, he was a world champion. A few days later it was revealed the lengths to which Greb was willing to go in order to become a world champion. Johnny Wilson, it was said, refused to face Greb for the championship for anything less than fifty percent of the gate. To that end Greb was forced to sign a contract stating that if Wilson won the bout he would receive $37^1/_2$ percent while Greb would receive $12^1/_2$ percent of the gate receipts. If Greb won the championship Wilson would receive the full 50 percent of the gate receipts.[17] Essentially it was a win-win situation for Wilson. Had Wilson won he would keep his title and the future earnings that would entail as well as a purse three times the size of Greb's (who was the actual drawing card) in losing his title he kept the entire purse. As a result Wilson took nearly $30,000 home to keep him company as he nursed a closed eye, and various cuts and bruises. Greb took home no purse, but he had cemented his place in history.

21

...AND STILL CHAMPION

After the Wilson fight, Harry was treated to a lavish celebratory banquet which lasted long into the night. As Harry sat in the Hotel Pennsylvania the following day, basking in the glow only a newly crowned champion can know, word was received that Piero Provano, the man who had attempted to promote a bout between Jeff Smith and Greb in Atlanta back in July, was suing Greb for $2,500 for Greb's failure to appear in the bout. Greb ducked the matter and Provano would continue to chase Harry for the next several months without much success. The match itself had been fraught with disaster even before Greb pulled out due to the fact that a committee of Atlanta Evangelical Ministers appeared before an Atlanta Grand Jury in an effort to prevent the bout. The Grand Jury agreed and instructed the local Sheriff and Chief of Police to use all measures to stop the bout. When Greb notified the promoter that he was unwell and would not be able to appear Captain Bob Roper was substituted in Greb's place and, in an effort to appease those opposed to the match, Provano was compelled to move its location. Finally, on fight night the crowd that turned out to see the event was so small that both Roper and Smith refused to fight as their percentage would not be worth the effort. It would seem in hindsight that Provano was trying to salve his wounds on Greb's future earnings.

Within days of winning the title Greb motored down to Atlantic City for a much deserved period of rest and relaxation. Initially plans had been made for Greb to tour the vaudeville circuit as he had when he defeated Tommy Gibbons the previous year but those plans were quickly scrapped in favor of actual fighting. Harry had made it known that he would be an active champion, defend against all comers, and attempt to secure both the light heavyweight and heavyweight championships as well. It was an ambitious goal and vaudeville would do little to further the cause.

To this end promoters were hard at work trying to match Greb. Tex Rickard was trying to arrange a bout between Greb and Mike McTigue for Madison Square Garden. If successful this bout would feature both the middleweight and light heavyweight championships on the line and crown a dual champion. Greb had readily agreed to the match but Rickard was having difficulty acquiring the services of McTigue.[1]

Nick Kline of Newark had offered Jack Dempsey $100,000 to face Greb in a no-decision bout to be staged at his newly erected arena. When Greb was approached with the offer, while in training for Wilson, he replied "Can you get Dempsey? Well if you get him, I'll be willing to fight three days after I beat this Wilson and win the middleweight title."[2] With Greb's approval the club approached Doc Kearns. Dempsey's manager replied: "We're perfectly willing to fight Greb," answered Kearns, "and the $100,000 offer looks good. But we don't want the fight now. Next year it will be O.K."[3] Kearns cited tax reasons for not wanting the fight, but whenever Dempsey and Greb were mentioned in the same sentence Kearns was never at a loss for excuses.

When Luis Firpo was told of the big money being offered in Newark, while in training for his upcoming challenge of Dempsey, he stated "I'll gladly fight anybody. I'd like to go back again to Newark where I started my career in America. My price? Well, name the man I'm to meet and I'll name my price!" Someone threw out Greb's name, "Harry Greb?" Firpo asked, "No. He's too small."[4] Then he suggested Cliff Kramer instead, noting that when he fought Willard Kramer fought on his undercard to admittedly mixed reviews. Again, when Greb's name was thrown around in Firpo's presence he was never at a loss for excuses or sub-par alternatives. Greb had attended Firpo's training camp while vacationing in Atlantic City, even authoring his opinion on Firpo's chances for the Universal News Service. What Greb saw in camp now being called a title challenger for the sports richest prize disgusted him. Firpo was slow of movement and slow of thought, lumbering, clumsy, and crude. Greb's official verdict: Dempsey by KO in no more than four rounds.[5]

When Harry arrived in Pittsburgh on September 10 he was again hailed as a conquering hero, just as he had been after his defeat of Tommy Gibbons nearly a year and a half earlier. When he got off the train that afternoon he was greeted once again by the strains of Danny Nirella's brass band and a massive throng of well-wishers. Harry was escorted through the city by a contingent of mounted policemen until the parade reached the City-County building were councilman Daniel Winters spoke in his honor, this time outside in order to avoid the chaos that ensued during the last such event, and presented Greb with a key to the city. Then Harry was led to the Elks Club where a luncheon was given in his honor.

Offers for fights flooded in from all over the country, as well as endorsement deals, offers to guest referee, and requests to appear in benefits. Harry and Red were so busy fielding such offers and working out a fight schedule that they both missed out on one of the most legendary fights in boxing history. On September 14, 1923 Jack Dempsey met Luis Angel Firpo at the Polo Grounds in New York before 80,000 enthusiastic fans. The Polo Grounds had witnessed 4 championship bouts that year and in all four the championship had changed hands. Despite the fact that both Greb and Red Mason felt the fight would be a fairly easy set up for the champion, Dempsey came within a hair of being the fifth champion to lose his title at the Polo Grounds in 1923.

In the first round Dempsey, intending to wade into the lumbering Firpo and end matters early, was caught with a wild right hand and sent to the canvas for a flash knockdown.

Top left: Heavyweight Champion Jack Dempsey topples through the ropes after the onslaught of Argentina's Luis Angel Firpo. The fight would be one of the most legendary events of the roaring twenties. Moments later Dempsey would scramble back into the ring to resume the action. Top right: After a total of twelve knockdowns between the two fighters in less than two rounds Firpo was finally pummeled to the canvas by the raging champion for the fateful ten count.

Dempsey sprang up, fighting like a wild man. Firpo was knocked down five times in the brawl that followed before he landed a wild punch causing Dempsey to touch both gloves to the canvas. Incredibly Firpo was then knocked down twice more with Dempsey standing over him waiting to pounce as the referee tolled off the count. Firpo sprang up and made his escape. Then, after a long range exchange, Firpo pressed Dempsey to the ropes with a wild attack. As Firpo rained blows down on Dempsey the champion tumbled backwards out of the ring and onto the newsmen seated ringside.

As Dempsey scrambled back into the ring, still groggy, Firpo pressed the attack, sensing that victory and the championship were within his grasp. But Firpo quickly became arm weary and by the time the bell rang ending one of the wildest first rounds in history Dempsey had seemingly recovered and was again on the attack. As the bell sent the fighters out for the second round it was plain to see that Firpo was slower, weaker, and still arm weary from his efforts in the first. Dempsey attacked, dropping Firpo again and then once more for the final ten count.

Former heavyweight champion Jess Willard had been ringside for the fight and left for California immediately afterwards. On a stopover in Arizona Willard was interviewed, giving his opinions on the affair as a man who had lost to both Firpo and Dempsey. During the course of the conversation he was asked who he thought had the best chance of beating Dempsey "There is one man who has a chance of beating Dempsey," said the giant former champion, "and that man is Harry Greb. You remember how Greb beat Gibbons and then he beat Tunney. He has a peculiar style that baffles the best of them. He is not the kind of fighter that the fans like to watch. But he has a perfect defense and can pile up a lot of points. He might beat Dempsey on points. He also has a chance of defeating Gene Tunney and winning the light-heavyweight championship. This would present a situation unique in boxing history -one man holding three world titles. Of course I am not saying Greb will beat Dempsey, but as I said before, he is the one good man in the world today who has a good chance to beat Jack Dempsey. Harry Greb's style of fighting is marvelous in itself, despite the criticisms directed at him."[6]

To this day the Dempsey-Firpo contest remains one of the wildest fights in the history of the sport. If one counts Dempsey touching his gloves to the canvas there had been a total of twelve knockdowns in less than four minutes of fighting. Dempsey had broken the curse of the Polo Grounds, retained his title, and added to his legend.

Three days after the Dempsey-Firpo fight it was formally announced that Harry Greb would make his first appearance as champion in Pittsburgh against Bryan Downey on September 27 at Forbes Field. The following day it was announced that McTigue was close to signing articles for the double championship bout Tex Rickard had been trying to arrange and that his manager Joe Jacobs would be meeting with Rickard in the coming days to finalize details. Rickard was hoping to schedule the bout for mid-October or early November but, curiously, on a stopover in Atlanta while on his way to sign articles to face eighteen year old Georgian prodigy Young Stribling McTigue was quoted as saying that the fight would likely be held in January.[7]

There was obviously more going on behind the scenes than the Greb party was aware of because when they left Pittsburgh on September 20, bound for New York they were under the impression that it was to be a quick trip for the purpose of signing the articles of agreement for the McTigue fight. When they returned home on the 22nd they did so empty handed. McTigue had not signed articles and gave no explanation. Greb had been told that New York power brokers had blocked his efforts to fight McTigue in favor of Gene Tunney getting the match.[8] At least outwardly Greb gave little sign of being annoyed by the situation. He had the utmost confidence that if Tunney got to McTigue first he would simply end up defeating Tunney for the championship, it mattered little to him who he won the championship from as long as he got his shot in due time.

In addition to failing to sign the McTigue fight Mason was notified when he stepped off the train that Bryan Downey had called off his match with Greb. Downey's infant daughter had tragically died leaving Downey too distraught to think about fighting.

With Downey out of the picture indefinitely, Jimmy Darcy was quickly acquired to face Greb on October 4. Greb had gotten larger offers to make his first appearance elsewhere but he was adamant about making his debut as champion in front of his hometown fans, even if it meant taking less money.

Harry had also agreed to face Tommy Loughran at Boston on October 11 and rising Bridgeport contender Lou Bogash at Newark on October 22. Harry then received word that Gene Tunney had decided he would be unable to face McTigue for at least two months, leaving Harry once again the front runner for Rickard's planned show.[9]

On September 29 Greb made his first unofficial appearance as champion when he faced Pittsburgh police officer George Hook in a three round exhibition bout at the Annual Police Meet. 20,000 people were on hand and they showered their champion with adulation. In return for

Above: Greb (left) lands a right hand to the head of George Hook during Pittsburgh's Annual Police Meet on September 29, 1923. The exhibition marked Greb's first boxing appearance in his hometown as champion.

such a warm welcome Greb gave them a dose of real fighting; Only the large gloves and Greb's willingness to ease up when he had Hook in trouble allowed the policeman to complete the three rounds. It was also announced that Greb had accepted the honor of training the police force in self-defense. Given Greb's busy schedule this was likely a largely ceremonial gesture.[10]

Greb assured anyone who would listen that he was not taking Darcy lightly in light of the fact that Darcy had scored a flash knock down over him two years earlier in Buffalo. Yet Darcy had lost far more fights than he had won since Greb had battered him in Buffalo and it was plain to see when Greb entered the ring that he had not trained diligently. Despite weighing only 163 pounds he looked soft and fleshy.

A sudden cold snap had forced many to stay away and hurt the gate resulting in an audience of only 6,000 to 7,000. Starting at 10pm both KDKA and WCAE broadcast the bout live from ringside blow by blow and what the fans heard huddled by their radios was Greb win as he pleased over Darcy. In the sixth Greb attacked relentlessly bringing blood from both Darcy's mouth and ears. Even as Harry rendered his opponent a bloody mess Darcy continued to try to land a game changing blow, even teasing Greb for his lack of a knockout punch at times. Harry was awarded the decision and after the fight Darcy's seconds worked over him for several minutes before he was fit to leave the ring. Despite the lopsided victory it was once again noted that Greb was not the same fighter he had been in previous years. He seemed slower, his timing was off, and at times he seemed to tire where once his energy seemed inexhaustible.[11]

On the same day that Harry defeated Darcy in Pittsburgh light-heavyweight champion Mike

McTigue was defending his championship in Columbus, Georgia against 18 year old boxing schoolboy Young Stribling. Boxing fans in the Deep South were enamored with their young fighter and felt that in him they had a coming champion. When McTigue signed to face Stribling southern fans went wild and the gate was expected to be a record breaker in the area. McTigue and his manager Joe Jacobs likely felt they would breeze into this southern hick town and take these hayseeds for all they were worth. When they arrived in Georgia and realized they had a real fight on their hands they balked, realizing a loss would ruin any opportunity for the big money fights McTigue hoped for against Greb, Tunney, Siki, and Carpentier.

Early on October 3 a rumor began spreading through the local community that the fight was off, with McTigue claiming an injured hand. A large crowd began gathering at McTigue's hotel looking for confirmation or denial of the story. When McTigue made an appearance on the balcony with his left hand swaddled in bandages the rumor seemed confirmed. As the largely peaceful crowd grew and some voiced their disapproval, police and American Legion officials were stationed outside of the hotel and in the lobby, barring entrance to all except the local press and those associated with the promotion. Captain Bob Roper, and a contingent of doctors, lawyers, and city councilmen met with McTigue in order to convince him to go on with the match. X-Ray's had been taking which showed McTigue suffered nothing more than an old, improperly healed fracture of his left thumb. To many it appeared as if McTigue was trying to avoid the match. When it became apparent that the locals were not buying McTigue's excuse his personal referee, imported to Georgia to protect McTigue, appealed to the local officials to make the fight a no-decision match. If anyone had previously doubted McTigue's integrity those doubts were now confirmed.

McTigue finally acquiesced and the resulting fight was a dull one. McTigue fell back on his tried and true tactic of covering up and clinching to see out the final bell. When the fight ended those newspapers in attendance were fairly unanimous: Stribling had won the fight by a wide margin. When the fight was over Ertle pointed to both fighters signaling a draw. The crowd quickly began to sense that once again the wool was being pulled over their eyes and for a time it looked as if they would riot. Major John Paul Jones, promoter of

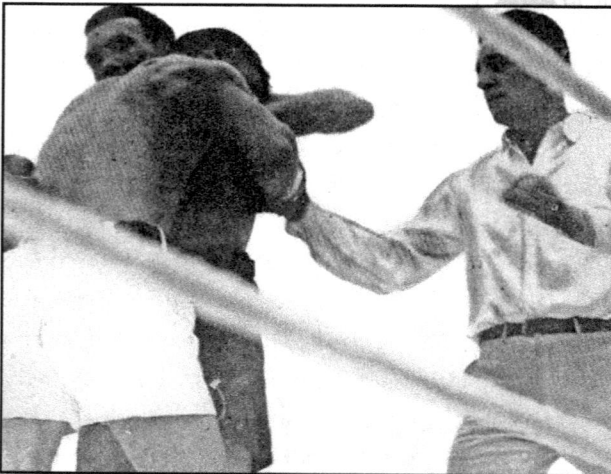

Above: Referee Harry Ertle (right) tries to break Young Stribling from one of Mike McTigue's incessant clinches. Stribling would go on to defeat McTigue only to have the victory and the light heavyweight championship snatched from his grasp by Ertle's biased ruling.

the bout, told Ertle to render a decision. Ertle then announced that Stribling had won the fight and was quickly whisked away by McTigue, Jacobs, and a contingent of policemen, and apparently did not look back until they reached Atlanta. When they felt safe Ertle then changed his decision, once again rendering a draw verdict.[12]

Stribling, the fans, and reporters who had traveled far and wide to see the fight were enraged. Their anger was made worse when Jacobs, McTigue, and Ertle returned north with wild tales feeding off the public's fascination with the newly resurgent Ku Klux Klan, that they were threatened at gunpoint with lynching if McTigue did not go through with the contest and intimated the entire ordeal had been a Ku Klux Klan conspiracy. McTigue himself had the gall, after his behavior and pitiful showing, to say he handled Stribling easily and called the young fighter a joke. The fight was compared by those who actually saw it to the Johnny Wilson-Bryan Downey robbery two years earlier.

McTigue continued to show his true colors the following month when after being signed to fight Gene Tunney, a fight which virtually guaranteed the loss of his title, he promptly fired his manager Joe Jacobs and walked out on the bout.

As all of this was playing out behind the scenes Greb awaited his coming bout with Loughran. After having defeated Loughran in all three of their previous bouts Harry appears to have been somewhat overconfident. Loughran, for his part, was highly focused on defeating Greb. Loughran spent the entire buildup to the fight telling anyone who would listen that he had defeated Greb in every one of their previous bouts, despite overwhelming evidence to the contrary and intended to show Boston fans upon his first appearance in the city that he was Greb's master. In fact Loughran would spend the rest of his life swearing that he always had Greb's number and beat him every time they met. Loughran was the type of fighter whose supreme confidence left him convinced he had never lost a fight.

Initially there was talk of Loughran coming in under 160 pounds in an effort to win the championship but Loughran could no longer comfortably make the middleweight limit and retain his strength so this idea was quickly scrapped in favor of Loughran coming in strong and trying to make a name for himself by beating the champion. In the intervening months since his last bout with Greb he had already added light heavyweight champion Mike McTigue's scalp to his collection and now hoped to add a middleweight champion as well.

Signs that Greb was not taking the contest seriously emerged when he missed a 3pm deadline to appear before the club the day before the fight. Instead Greb and Red Mason were indulging another of their great loves: Baseball. At the moment they should have been in Boston they were in fact sitting in the grandstands of Yankee Stadium taking in the first game of the World's Series. As time went by the club officials began to worry that the star of the show would not arrive at all. It was not until late that night that the champion finally arrived in Boston.

Greb's cavalier attitude would come back to haunt him when the 10 round decision was awarded to Loughran. Both the Boston Post and Boston Globe felt the decision was justified with the Globe editorializing that Greb's loss could be attributed to his holding and hitting tactics. Both fighters in fact fought outside of the rules but it was universally agreed that Greb was the worst offender.

The Boston Advertiser and Boston Traveler also agreed that the decision was justified and felt that through his showing Greb had lost a lot of prestige in the city. The Boston Herald gave the best account of the fight, illustrating that while Greb seemed slower, and more apt to load up on his punches, his cleverness prevented the quick fisted Loughran from being able to land anywhere but to the body.

The only dissenting opinion was that of Jack Conway writing for the Boston American whose article was accompanied by the headline "Greb Robbed of Decision..." Conway felt that the fans, with which Loughran was the favorite, had influenced the judges' decision through loud rooting.[13]

Harry was surprised by the verdict but took it in stride, likely realizing that he had only himself to blame. He would explain his loss by saying "I know I did not make the greatest hit in my bout with Loughran in Boston, but what is a fellow going to do when these World's Series has a guy almost crazy?"[14] Red Mason added to that when asked for an explanation of Greb's half-hearted performance "Harry had a little too much of the World Series before coming to Boston."[15] was his answer.

Eleven days later Greb was in Newark to face Lou Bogash. Bogash was an Italian fighter from Bridgeport who had turned professional as a fifteen year old lightweight. Over the years as he added weight he had developed into a talented contender. In one of his earliest bouts he fought on the undercard of Harry Greb's 1918 bout with Zulu Kid in Bridgeport, now he would be facing Greb himself. In recent years Bogash had worked himself to the forefront of middleweight contention by defeating such men as welterweight champion Mickey Walker, Tommy Loughran, Jackie Clark, Panama Joe Gans, and drawing with Mike O'Dowd and Mike McTigue. His most recent victory was one that brought him to the top of the list of viable contenders for Greb's throne, a ten round decision victory over highly rated Jock Malone, who had twice defeated Bogash in previous bouts.

Greb had seemingly learned his lesson from the Loughran fight and after returning to Pittsburgh had gotten down to hard training. When Harry stepped in to the ring to face Bogash a contract for the winner to face former light heavyweight champion Battling Siki was on the line. Siki had recently arrived in the United States seeking larger purses and the championship he had lost to McTigue.

There was a great deal of anticipation and anxiety about the match. Two weeks earlier welterweight champion Mickey Walker had faced Jimmy Jones in a highly unsatisfactory bout in which both fighters were accused of not trying. The pressure would be on Greb and Bogash to perform.

The fight itself was a good one and served to restore the fans faith in the sport locally. With Johnny Wilson and Harry Wills looking on, Greb was adjudged the winner by the local press and several reporters who attended from Pittsburgh. Yet, Harry was once again hounded from across the river by the New York press, many of whom voted against him in the match. It was clear however that local opinion was with Greb and negotiations were started for the Siki match based upon on his performance against Bogash.[16]

After the fight Harry and Red Mason were approached by Frank Flournoy hoping to sign Greb for a title defense in New York. Still stinging from the Tunney decision and from his treatment by the New York sportswriters Harry and Mason gave Flournoy the brush off. "They won't get me in there and tell me what to do. They did that once with Tunney and he got beat. Our plans are to stay away from New York as long as possible, meet anyone in the world anywhere else and make the title mean something. When the time comes, I'll go into New York, but not before, for it seems they want me to learn something new and I'm getting a little too old for that. The Newark club is dickering for Battling Siki, and the chances are that the match will be made. That's the kind of stuff I'm after. I can beat him, even though he looks like a good fighter, and then maybe the winner of the Tunney-McTigue match will give me a shot. New York owes me plenty and I'm going to make them come to me."[17]

Lou Bogash, born Luigi Bogassio on February 24, 1901 in the province of Foggia, Italy turned pro at the tender age of 15 and in 1918 fought on a couple of Harry Greb's undercards. By 1923 he had established himself as a leading contender for the middleweight championship with wins over Jock Malone, Bryan Downey, Panama Joe Gans, and Tommy Loughran.

Things quickly began to unravel with the proposed Greb-Siki bout in Newark. It turned out that Siki was obligated to a match with Kid Norfolk in New York by a previous manager, Gene Sennet. After tiring of Siki's erratic behavior and fights over money Sennet sold Siki's contract to Bob Levy for $6,000. Initially Siki had hoped to avoid both the match with Greb in Newark and the match with Kid Norfolk before the powerful New York commission stepped in and

Above: Battling Siki (left) faces off against Kid Norfolk in his first bout in the United States. Greb had been hoping for a lucrative match with Siki when New York flexed its muscles and enforced a contract for Siki to face Norfolk.

ruled that Siki must fight Norfolk on November 20 which all but killed any possibility of Siki facing Greb in the near future.

All of this played out as Harry trained for his upcoming bout with Soldier Jones in Pittsburgh on November 5. Harry had a healthy respect for Jones' punching power after being dropped by Jones in one of their previous matches and wobbled in another, but he had also given Jones frightful beatings in those fights and felt that once again his speed would make the difference.

With the Siki match dead, and Greb's options for a large purse limited, he finally agreed to face Johnny Wilson in a rematch in New York at Madison Square Garden. The Jones bout and a fight Greb picked up against old adversary Chuck Wiggins in Grand Rapids on November 15, would serve to keep him shape going into the holiday season.

Most reports recapping the sensational bout agreed that Greb had once again come in to the ring out of shape and over confident. This gave Soldier Jones the opportunity to present Pittsburgh fans and Greb with the thrill of their lives. Jones attacked at the opening bell throwing hard punches which Greb was able to avoid. Greb was making Jones miss with his wild, powerful swings and countering on the inside when Jones suddenly got home a left which backed Greb up and then followed up with a dynamite right that sent Greb to the floor.

The entire arena erupted and then just as quickly fell into a hushed silence as the referee tolled the count. With each passing second it became clear that this was no flash knockdown, Greb was hurt. Murmurs of "he's out" could be heard around the ring. Greb began to struggle up but his mind was a fog and he went back down to one knee to clear his head. He jumped up at the count of eight and ran right in to another right hand which sent him to his knees. Harry was up without a count but he reeled and staggered around the ring. Jones chased him down, pinned him to the ropes and began to strafe him with long, clubbing rights and lefts. Greb's legs trembled as he lay on the ropes, wobbling to and fro. For a time it looked as if he would go down again but he was saved by the bell.

Greb staggered drunkenly to a neutral corner, not knowing where he was. Red Mason leapt into the ring and dragged Harry back to his stool. He quickly went to work, bringing color back to the champion's pallid complexion.

Greb was still groggy in the second and trying to find himself when Jones again rocked him and sent him wobbling. As Jones tried to press his advantage Greb lashed out wildly, stopping Jones in his tracks which brought Harry a much needed respite. In between rounds Harry began to perk up. He began talking to Mason and his color had returned.

Greb came out for the third renewed. Jones had been within an inch of defeating the champion, he did not yet realize it but the moment had passed. Now it was Greb's turn. As Jones waded in Harry's head bobbed and weaved, deftly avoiding Jones' punches, then Harry opened with a quick combination that ripped a jagged cut over Jones' left eye.

From that point on Greb pounded Jones mercilessly. He opened another cut under Jones' left eye, swelled both eyes shut, and had blood boiling from the Canadian's nose and mouth. In the eighth Greb dropped Jones for an eight count. Jones rose unsteady, crying, and looking a pitiful, forlorn sight. Referee Ed Keally asked if he wished to continue. Jones lurched forward, grimly accepting his task like the warrior he was. He was helpless for the final two rounds and Greb continued to pour in punches to every part of Jones' anatomy. Harry was so intent on punishing Jones that the effort he exerted in the final round left him utterly exhausted and speechless when the final bell had rung.[18]

Ten days after nearly being separated from his senses by Jones Greb was set to fight Chuck Wiggins and it was hoped by Wiggins that Greb would once again enter the ring under prepared allowing him the opportunity to defeat a world champion.

Prior to leaving for Grand Rapids to face Wiggins Greb agreed to fight Bryan Downey on December 3 in Pittsburgh and to take Mike McTigue's place against Gene Tunney one week later in New York at Madison Square Garden, McTigue having once again wormed out of a dangerous bout. Despite his misgivings about ever getting a fair shake against Tunney in New York Greb hoped that a victory over the former marine would lead to a big money bout with the winner of the proposed Siki-Norfolk fight and a shot at world champion Mike McTigue.

The Wiggins fight was greatly anticipated in Michigan with reserve seats coming from all over. A Chicago motion picture company even approached Promoter W.T. Morrissey about filming the bout. Wiggins started the contest fast with the intention of catching Greb by surprise and scoring a quick knockout. After his experience with Soldier Jones Greb was not going to be taken unawares. He fought Wiggins off and what ensued was one of the fastest, most scientific, and often roughest contests ever witnessed in Grand Rapids.

The two fighters set such a hellacious pace that the Grand Rapids Press and Grand Rapids Herald were unable to provide a round by round description. The club's physician Dr. R. H. DeCoux stated the contest was "as much faster and more scientific than the average ring contest as a horse is faster than a cow in a race."[19]

Early in the fight Greb cut Wiggins' eye. In between rounds Wiggins' manager Jack Druley accidentally spilled coagulant into Wiggins' eye and from that moment on Wiggins was a one-eyed fighter. This combined with Greb's advantage in speed nullified Wiggins' eleven pound weight advantage. When the contest had completed Greb was once again judged the winner.[20]

Within the week Greb was doing light training in New York where he had gone to see Kid Norfolk face Battling Siki, who Greb still hoped to meet in a big money bout in the near future. Greb felt that Siki, despite his status as a former champion, was something of an unknown quantity but felt he would defeat Norfolk, arguing that Norfolk was now on the downside of his career and no longer the fighter he once was.[21] It would be one of the few recorded times that Greb's prediction proved wrong as Norfolk pounded Siki mercilessly to take a 15 round decision.

Greb opened hard training for the Downey and Tunney bouts on November 27 at the Pittsburgh Lyceum sparring Leo Caghil, Frank Senk, and Cuddy DeMarco.

The bout with Downey would be the first fight in Pittsburgh held under the newly enacted McBride Act which legalized ten round decisions in Pennsylvania. An added sidelight to the match was that regardless of Greb's weight if Downey came in under the 160 pound limit Greb's title would be on the line.

In hindsight Harry's bout with Downey must have seemed like little more than a tune-up with the news announced the day before that Greb had agreed to terms to defend his championship against Johnny Wilson in New York on January 18 and with the Tunney fight just a week away. Greb helped to cement this notion when he utterly dominated Downey. For the first two rounds Greb was wary of Downey's reputation as a right hand puncher but after sampling Downey's power Harry opened up with both barrels and sent Downey careening out of the ring. Greb then reached over the top rope, hauled Downey back into the ring, and despite criticisms that Greb was once again not at his best, proceeded to batter Downey around the ring leaving him a bloody, swollen mess after the tenth and final round. Downey had weighed 158^1/$_2$ pounds to Greb's 161.[22]

Downey was so disheartened by the loss and the death of his daughter that he promptly retired from boxing only to return to the sport six months later with a victory over future light-heavyweight champion Jack Delaney, one of the several champions Downey was credited with defeating during his career.

Three days after his victory over Downey Harry left for New York with his manager and sparring partners in tow as well as his three sisters and young daughter. The fight had all the makings of a classic grudge match. Greb was eager to get Tunney back into the ring and beat him so bad in the process that nobody could deny him the victory. If by chance, like their previous meeting, victory was denied Tunney would know for weeks to come he had been in the ring with Harry Greb. Harry carried a load of resentment towards Tunney. He resented Tunney's accusations of foul tactics leveled against Greb. He resented Tunney's litany of excuses for his failure to subdue Greb, the most recent being that in their previous match he had been bedridden for three days prior to the bout, a story which is not supported by the multitudes of press and friends who witnessed Tunney's daily training in Red Bank. Finally, Greb resented that Gene Tunney had a "win" next to his name in a fight that Greb felt to the core of his soul he had won.

Tunney himself would admit years later in his autobiography that "realizing there was some justice in Greb's claim of a bad decision, I offered him a return engagement."[23] To Tunney's credit he wanted the match as much as Greb in order to prove that he could indeed defeat the little man from Pittsburgh.

Both fighters trained hard for the bout. Gene went to work once again at his Red Bank training camp, employing Charlie Nashert, Billy Shine, and Jock Malone as sparring partners. Greb worked out daily at Philadelphia Jack O'Brien's gym and did roadwork in Central Park. During one of these training sessions cub reporter Paul Gallico walked into the gym and noticed a dark haired fighter in red training togs working tirelessly and was immediately smitten with the fighter's ability. Gallico approached one of the gym instructors and stated his intention to take his new discovery around to New York Daily News boxing expert Harry Newman in order to get him some publicity. When the instructor pointed out that Gallico's "discovery" was indeed

Left to right: Red Mason, Harry Greb, Tom Dolan, Bryan Downey, Eddie Kennedy, and Jimmy Dunn pose before the December 3, 1923 match between Greb and Downey. Despite coming in over the middleweight limit Greb's title was on the line if Downey won. Downey was at the tail end of a respectable career which saw him defeat several world champions across several weight divisions including his controversial first fight with Johnny Wilson in Cleveland in 1921 which should have won him the championship.

middleweight champion Harry Greb, currently in training for the Tunney fight Gallico slunk off sheepishly.[24]

Once again as the two fighters prepared for the fight a publicity campaign was set in motion to hamper Greb, albeit not as aggressive as was found prior to their previous bout. As Greb trained for the bout a rumor began to make the rounds that he was soon to be remarried.[25] Harry was immediately bombarded with questions from curious associates, fans, and reporters looking for a good story. Harry felt the rumor had been spread by parties close to Tunney to distract him from his training. "These fellows around here are trying every way to get my mind off the thing I've got to do tomorrow, but you can say for me that there is nothing to that marriage story. I'm not even thinking about it."[26] In addition to this Harry intimated his ongoing concern that New York officials would look for any excuse to disqualify him or hamper his style. Even Red Mason was notified that he would not be able to use his famous Chinese laundry shower to cool down Greb as it was against the rules, what rules specifically frowned on this act were not explained.[27]

A capacity crowd of just over 11,000 people came to view the grudge match between Greb and Tunney, paying just over $43,000. Once again Tunney proved to be the fan favorite. Among the celebrities announced from the ring prior to the fight was Battling Siki, who despite his loss to Norfolk, still hoped for a big money bout with the winner. The weights were announced as 175 pounds for Tunney (Ray Coll of the Pittsburgh Gazette-Times alleged that Tunney actually weighed a quarter pound over the limit but it was agreed to forget about the extra weight) and an unusually high $171^1/_2$ pounds for Greb, who had added ten pounds in a week in hopes of dealing with Tunney's greater size. Just before the start of the bout Harry was presented with a loving cup from the volunteer fire department of Manhasset, Long Island.

With the preliminaries completed, and introductions finished all that was left was to decide the supremacy of these two bitter rivals. The bout itself was hard fought. Greb would dance around the ring, before leaping in, throwing himself bodily at Tunney while landing eye catching flurries to the head. Tunney continually and almost exclusively met these rushes with body punches.

In the second round Greb brought blood from Tunney's nose. In the third Tunney began to butt Greb and by the fifth round the pro Tunney crowd was beginning to boo their man's use of tactics he had once criticized Greb for. In the sixth Tunney nearly doubled Greb over with a left hook to the body but was warned for rabbit punching. Greb opened a cut under Tunney's right eye with a combination. By the end of the round Tunney was bleeding from his nose, mouth, and his damaged eye.

Greb landed the hardest punch of the fight to this point in the seventh and attacked Tunney relentlessly who stood calmly in the face of these rushes hammering home body punches. Greb seemed to slow in the eighth under a terrific body beating by Tunney, who was once again being booed for using his head.

In the tenth Tunney was again booed for using his head and despite that continued through much of the round with his rough tactics. Both men were momentarily stunned by hard punches. In the eleventh Greb once again seemed to be weakening under Tunney's hard body punching. Tunney continued to butt Greb but it was Greb who drew a warning for excessive holding.

Greb was back on his toes bouncing around the ring in the twelfth. At the end of the round Greb leapt at Tunney, the fighters wrestled and Tunney fell through the ropes. Greb and referee Lou Magnolia had just gotten Tunney back in the ring as the bell ended the round.

The thirteenth started badly for Greb with Tunney pouring in withering body punches. But Greb, showing his incredible fortitude and durability, continued to launch himself at Tunney. Instead of peppering Tunney with volume punches he was now trying to land a powerful blow that might end the fight. At the end of the round one of these blows opened a cut under Tunney's left eye.

The fifteenth round was likely Greb's best. He fought at a frantic pace in hopes of putting an exclamation point on his performance.[28]

According to Ray Coll of the Pittsburgh Gazette-Times Tunney walked over to Greb and congratulated him on his victory then began to leave the ring before it was announced that once again Tunney had defeated Greb. According to Coll Tunney exhibited a stunned look at the announcement and both Tunney's manager Billy Gibson, and Greb's former manager George Engel, who worked Tunney's corner, admitted that Greb deserved no worse than a draw.[29]

The audience, which began as a pro-Tunney crowd, was in an uproar. For twenty minutes they stood around the ring hissing and booing. One irate fan began screaming at announcer Joe Humphries and the judges. This fan was making his way into the ring when several police officers intercepted him and escorted him out of the Garden where he stood on the sidewalk voicing his irritation with like-minded fans.

Greb stood silently and surveyed the scene as the crowd booed Tunney all the way back to his dressing room. "I knew it was against me from the start, but I went in and gave my best. I'm sorry over the outcome, but can expect nothing else," said a bemused Greb after the fight.[30] Referee Lou Magnolia had to be escorted from the ring by a contingent of police officers. When Harry finally left the ring, his sides red and raw from the body punishment he had sustained, the audience raised the roof with their cheers for him.

The following day newspapermen were once again divided as to the winner. Among those feeling Tunney won the bout by varying degrees were Fred Keats of the Sun and Globe, Harry Newman of the Daily News, James Dawson of the Times, Bert Igoe of the World, Jack Lawrence of the Tribune, George Underwood of the Evening Telegram, Seabury Lawrence of the Evening Post, W. O. McGeehan of the Herald, Dan Lyons of the Evening Mail, Ed Van Every of the Evening World, Jim Jab of the Pittsburgh Press, and Bert Dodge of the Newark Star-Eagle. Among those feeling Greb deserved the victory were Ray Coll of the Pittsburgh Gazette-Times,

Regis Welsh of the Pittsburgh Post, Westbrook Pegler of the UPI, James P. Sinnot of the Morning Telegraph, The Newark Evening News official opinion was that Greb was robbed. Ferd Frick of the Evening Journal felt the fight was a draw.

The difference of opinion was as wide as the ocean. Most of those voting for Tunney felt that the Marine was dominant, while those voting for Greb felt he was equally as dominant. There was very little middle ground. While the difference of opinion is notable, it is equally notable that many of those papers who had felt Greb was robbed against Tunney in their previous engagement now agreed with the decision which illustrates that Tunney was likely the deserved victor this time around in a bout far more close and competitive than history now remembers.

The newspapermen agreed almost

Top: Harry Greb and Gene Tunney square off prior to their December 1923 rubber match. Bottom: Greb (back to the camera) looks for an opening. Facing page top: Greb (left) eyes Tunney before launching into one of his trademark attacks. Facing page middle: In this photo, commonly and incorrectly attributed to the first bout between Tunney and Greb, Tunney (left) slips Greb's right and prepares to fire off a right to the ribs. Facing page bottom: Greb (facing camera) extends a range finding left as Tunney waits to counter the attack during the eighth round.

The third bout between Greb and Tunney was marred by occasional clinches and wrestling by both fighters. Top left: Greb (facing the camera) wrenches Tunney's head. Bottom left: Tunney and Greb (back to the camera) work in close. Top right: Tunney (back to the camera) and Greb battle furiously on the inside. Facing page top right: Greb (left) evades one of Tunney's attacks. Facing page bottom right: Greb and Tunney fall through the ropes during a clinch in the twelfth round.

unanimously that Greb had fought a clean and sportsmanlike fight. They noted that Greb never once complained or tried to curry favor when Tunney resorted to foul tactics. Much was made by those who felt Greb had won that the judges, Frankie Madden and Charles Mathison, had also handed down the decision on the undercard bout between Tommy Loughran and British champion Roland Todd. Todd had seemingly made a successful American debut by defeating Loughran when the officials ruled that Loughran had won. Their decisions caused many to wonder if they knew their business. In fairness to the judges it should be noted that they officiated over Greb's title bout against Johnny Wilson in August without complaint.

Those who supported Tunney tried to deflect criticism by stating that the outrage voiced ringside was by those who had bet large sums of money on Greb. James Sinnot gave the best rebuttal of this argument:

Echoes of the Gene Tunney-Harry

Greb fight are still heard about town. It seems that most of the New York writers agree with the decision of the referee and judges and declare that Tunney earned the victory.

I filed a dissenting opinion on Tuesday morning. It is a minority report so far as local fistic experts are concerned, but I believe a majority one if the crowd that witnessed the contest could be polled.

Certainly there has been no more violent demonstration of protest over a decision in a long time than that which the fight fans made after Tunney had been declared the winner.

Everyone is entitled to his own opinion as to the relative merits of fighters. Mine, in regard to the Tunney-Greb contest, is that Greb won easily.

Some of the boys have been rather unfair in attributing the demonstration made against the official decision in the Garden on Thursday night to disgruntled gamblers who had bet on Greb...

The boys know, or should know, that there was little Greb money. If there had been, how could Tunney jump from 8-5 to 2 ½ to 1 favorite?

If there was Greb money around, the price would have been shortened, and not lengthened, the smart money was supposed to be on Tunney.

I defy anyone to say that the result of the first two bouts between Harry Greb and Gene Tunney warranted Tunney being made 8-5 choice over the middleweight champion. How did the price go to 2 ½ to 1 if there was Greb money about?

Those who booed and hooted the decision in Tunney's favor on Monday night were not disgruntled bettors. It was a Tunney crowd when the battle began. Why

wasn't it a Tunney crowd after the verdict?

Tunney is a local boy, and is unusually intelligent, pleasant, and has a lot of personality. Greb is from Pittsburgh, has often been branded here as a roughhouse fighter and is hardly a popular idol.

Is it too much to assume that, under the circumstances, this crowd that came hoping to see Tunney beat Greb and then hooted the decision in the Greenwich Village lad's favor, really thought that Greb had the better of the fight? I don't think it is.[31]

In fairness to Tunney he had shown better against Greb this time around than in their previous two meetings. His punches to the body clearly bothered Greb on several occasions and it is possible that those voting for Greb were influenced by his flashier punching and neglected to score Tunney's body punching. Greb himself paid Tunney respect. "I never knew a fighter to improve as much and as fast as Gene Tunney," said Harry, "He certainly handed me a surprise. I think he would knock out Georges Carpentier, the Frenchman, in five rounds, and I am sure that he will beat Tom Gibbons if they ever meet."[32] Tunney in turn remarked that Greb's greater weight allowed him to punch harder than in their previous engagements.[33]

The New York papers made much of Greb alleging a fix was in but Harry quickly backed down on these claims. He had been bitterly disappointed with his treatment in the city but within days he was expected to finalize his rematch with Johnny Wilson at the Garden and he desperately hoped for a big money match with Georges Carpentier in the summer which Tex Rickard had been dangling before the winner of the Greb-Tunney fight. That possibility seemed distant now but if Greb hoped to receive favorable treatment in these endeavors he realized that he would need to back off on some of the more harsh criticisms directed at the New York establishment.

One week after the third Greb-Tunney bout, with the merits of the decision still being discussed, Jack Bernstein lost his junior lightweight championship to Johnny Dundee on a highly controversial decision. The uproar prompted the New York State Athletic Commission to meet and alter the way it oversaw boxing matches so as to address, and curb recent criticisms of decisions handed down by its officials. It banned known or suspected gamblers; judges were now to be situated on opposite sides of the ring, with the time keeper no closer than six feet away. No persons would be allowed ringside on either of the sides occupied by the officials. The judges were not to speak, or listen to conversation, instead focusing all of their attention on the boxing match they were to officiate. Finally, no person would be allowed in a fighter's dressing room either before or after the fight excepting the fighter's manager and handlers.[34]

Whether the new changes by the commission would have changed the outcome of the third fight between Greb and Tunney will never be known but Harry was certainly still smarting from the decision when he was called to the offices of Tex Rickard to finalize the details of his upcoming title defense against Johnny Wilson. Greb had already agreed in principle to

Rickard's offer but now Harry was holding out for more money. Ostensibly the reason Greb gave for holding out for more money was the fact that despite being acknowledged as Wilson's top contender for years he was paid nothing when he finally received the opportunity to fight for the title. It was now Greb's title, and he intended to dictate terms, particularly in New York where they were now going to have to pay for the privilege of Greb's services after the past treatment he received there.

After two days of intense negotiations the match was signed, details were not released but it was believed that Tex Rickard and Frank Flournoy acquiesced and that Greb would receive a guarantee in excess of $30,000.[35]

In the meantime Greb had been matched with Tommy Loughran on Christmas afternoon at Motor Square Garden. It would be the fifth time Greb had faced Loughran, and an opportunity for Greb to avenge the loss he suffered to Loughran in Boston two months earlier. The bout was promoted as a middleweight championship but Loughran was now no longer able to make the middleweight limit and there was a great deal of speculation about Greb's own ability to make 160 pounds given his unusually high weight for the Tunney bout, despite weighing only 161 for Downey the week before. KDKA would broadcast the match live from ringside.

As Greb and Loughran moved to the center of the ring to hear referee Eddie Kennedy's instructions they did so with only honor on the line. Loughran had weighed $168^1/_2$ pounds to Greb's 168 leaving the championship off the table. Kennedy told the fighters to "go in and fight. You are both the same size and capable of taking care of yourselves. Fight and protect yourselves at all times." He then sent the fighters to their corners and the match began.

Despite suffering from boils Loughran was competitive early on. He utilized his deadly accurate left jab and, theorizing that Greb would still be feeling the effects of Gene Tunney's body punishment two weeks previous, directed his heavier blows to the body in an effort to slow the champion down. Very quickly the fight turned ugly. Greb was using his favorite tactic of holding and hitting while Loughran wrestled, heeled, and elbowed.

In the second round Greb opened an old cut under Loughran's left eye and had the beginnings of other cuts around the same eye. In the fifth round Harry ran into a wild right hand swing by Loughran. Greb reeled back a few steps and Loughran jumped on him trying to seize on the opportunity. Instead it was Loughran who ran into a hornet's nest and was forced to give ground. The fight was fairly close after five rounds with Greb holding a slight lead when after being booed for his holding and hitting tactics in the sixth Greb suddenly stood off, quit the questionable tactics being mindful of his own fans' criticism and promptly put on a display that rendered Loughran impotent. It left those unaware of the condition of Greb's eyesight wondering why he so often held and hit when he could seemingly fight so well without such tactics.

By the eighth Greb had matters well in control and Loughran was tiring. In the ninth Greb took advantage of Loughran's exhaustion and launched a powerful left which immediately closed Tommy's right eye with a grotesque swelling. For the remainder of the fight Loughran reeled around the ring blindly and at times unwilling or unable to fight. In the final round Greb dominated Loughran so thoroughly some felt he could end the fight at any time. When the final bell ended the bout Loughran was relieved and had to be assisted to his corner by Greb.[36]

With Loughran behind him Harry had three weeks to focus on his title defense against Johnny Wilson. There was a great deal of speculation surrounding the match. In many corners it was believed that Wilson had an improved chance of beating Greb. This theory was based on the belief that when they first met Wilson had only four fights in the previous two years. This time around Wilson had fought three times in the previous three months and each time he had won convincingly and came in right around the middleweight limit. There would be no rust this time around.

Another factor in those thinking Wilson's chances were improved were the concerns of Greb's ability to comfortably make the middleweight limit. This anxiety was increased when Greb made it known that he would remain in Pittsburgh to train, away from the prying eyes of New York reporters. Wilson, for his part, trained enthusiastically at Freddie Welsh's Summit, New Jersey health farm.

The concerns about Greb's weight and Wilson's improved chances caused the betting odds to open closer than the results of their previous bout would have foretold. Greb was installed as an 8 to 5 favorite but so much Wilson money trickled in that by fight time the odds were almost even with Greb a slight favorite.

On the morning of the fight Wilson weighed in at $159^1/_2$. When it was Greb's turn to step on the scales Wilson's eyes nearly bugged out of his head. Greb tipped the beam at one pound less than Wilson despite the raging debate surrounding his status as a middleweight. Greb gingerly stepped off the scale, took a sip of beef broth from a thermos and then retired to the Tavern Restaurant, a favorite haunt of his when in the city, to eat a large steak. By afternoon Greb's weight was about 169 pounds in his street clothes. Whether making weight had weakened him remained to be seen.

The bout would be broadcast live from ringside with Major J. Andrew White giving the round by round commentary.

In the first five rounds Wilson made a good showing. In the fifth his body punching seemed to bother Greb and many believed Wilson was beginning to take over. After the fifth Mason worked feverishly over Greb. Harry sat focused on Wilson across the ring. Watching the drama play out from ringside foxy trainer Jimmy DeForrest, who had taken Dempsey to the championship against Willard, commented "Greb is studying his man, he will shift his style if he has anything left."[37]

Greb smiled as he rose for the sixth and quickly showed that rather than fading he had simply been waiting, letting Wilson show his hand. Harry came out and began to step around Wilson's southpaw left to the body, then quick as a cat he would leap in with hard right hand leads to Wilson's head and body. Greb would then tie up Wilson's left, preventing counters. Once Greb brought this tactic into play it quickly became obvious that Wilson had no plan B.

From the seventh round on Wilson slowed up measurably and Greb began piling up points. Before long Harry had built an insurmountable lead. Those who had questioned Harry's ability to make weight comfortably were shocked that it was Wilson who was rapidly fading and Greb who seemed to be getting stronger.

As Wilson became frustrated he started looking for alternate ways to either win or get out of the fight. He complained incessantly to referee Eddie Purdy that Harry kept blocking his vision by waving an open glove in Wilson's face (not strictly against the rules but Greb was warned for it). In one round Wilson came out with his trunks hitched up nearly to his arm pits, obviously in hopes that one of Greb's body punches would be called low garnering a disqualification win for Wilson. Purdy was having none of it and ordered Wilson's trunks lowered. Finally, late in the fight Wilson struck Harry low several times in what many felt was an attempt to take an easy way out of the fight by fouling out. Greb never complained he simply went about his business, smiling happily all the while.

When Greb was announced the winner the decision was popular with both the newspaper men and the audience. Compared with some of the recent decisions handed down in New York

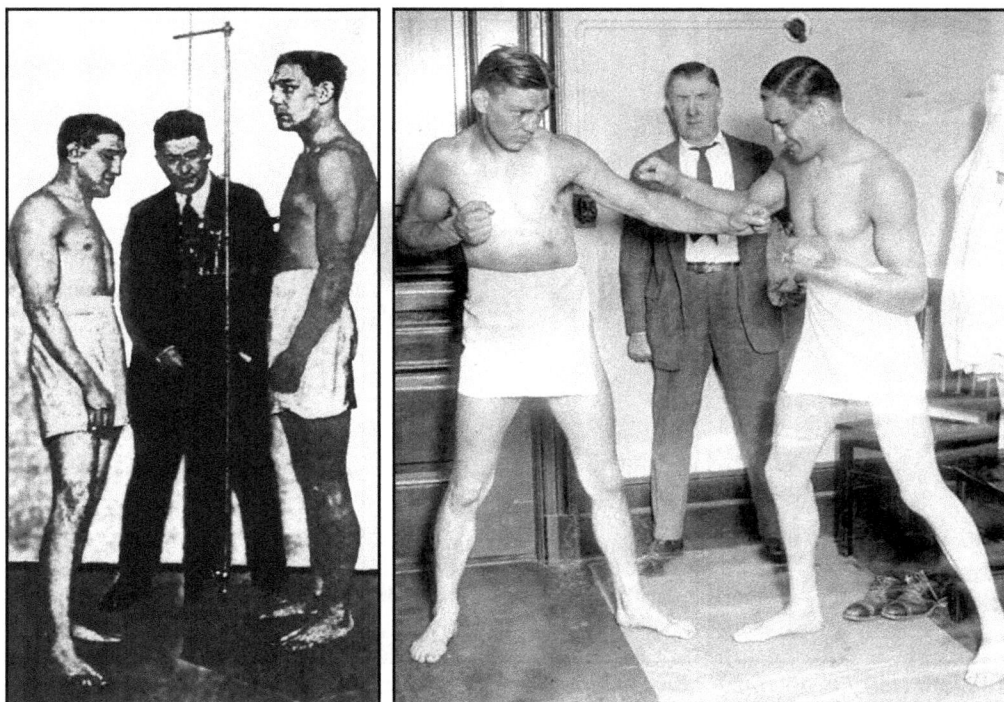

Above left: Johnny Wilson and William McCormack watch as Greb weighs in for their championship rematch. As the beam settled Wilson was shocked that Greb had made the weight. Above right: Greb and Wilson pose for the cameras during the weigh in. Red Mason referee's the pretend sparring match.

Top left: Harry Greb and Johnny Wilson pose for cameramen just before the start of their 1924 championship rematch. Top right: Greb (right) and Wilson work in close. Bottom row left: Wilson with his back to the camera tries a left while in a clinch. Center: Another clinch in the fifth round. Bottom row right: Greb (right) launches an attack on Wilson as the southpaw tries to work his right hook to the body.

Above left: Greb (right) is backed into the ropes in the second round as referee Eddie Purdy rushes to seperate them. Above right: Wilson (center) tries to mount an offense as Harry ducks away from a long left. Right: Harry (right) the instant before launching into one of his characteristic windmill attacks. Throughout the contest Harry would work around Wilson from the outside, always concious of staying outside of Wilson's southpaw right jab and hook. Then he would leap in and pepper Wilson before tying his man up. Wilson had no answer.

it was a rare moment of unanimity. Harry showed little if any effects from the fight while Wilson left the ring with a cut below his left eye, and a bleeding ear, nose, and mouth.[38]

After the match $2,602 of Greb's purse was withheld due to an attachment awarded to Piero Provano as damages for the failed bout Greb was supposed to have against Jeff Smith the previous summer. Rather than defend himself against the claims of Provano Greb and Mason had simply tried to duck the matter, hoping it would go away. Several times they had managed to stay one step ahead of sheriff's deputies trying to serve Greb with a summons. Finally after much frustration Provano was awarded a default judgment against Greb, resulting in the $2,602 being withheld.

Harry had originally hoped to quickly be signed for important and lucrative bouts with Carpentier, and McTigue. But he slowly came to the realization that Rickard would not be able to induce Carpentier to fight him, and that McTigue, who was now embroiled in a messy contract dispute with his former manager, was chronically unable (or more likely unwilling) to

These photos were taken as Greb arrived in California for what he hoped would be a relaxing vacation and several bouts for easy money.

defend his championship against qualified fighters. As a result Harry began making plans for a tour of the West Coast and Hawaii.

At the eleventh hour Rickard sent Greb a telegram pleading for him to remain in the East long enough for Rickard to finalize a McTigue match. Not willing to postpone his plans to wait for the unreliable McTigue Greb ignored Rickard's pleas and headed for the West Coast on February 5.

Harry viewed the trip as little more than a vacation for rest and relaxation. He arrived in California after a cross country journey of four days only to be met with a telegram from Tex Rickard offering him a match with Rickard's new favorite Paul Berlenbach within ten weeks. Sensing an opportunity, Greb and Mason cancelled all plans for an extensive tour of the West in favor of taking a short vacation in California and then returning to the East to face Berlenbach.

The proposed match with Berlenbach must have seemed like easy money to Greb for him to cancel his plans. Berlenbach was a twenty-three year old middleweight fresh out of the amateurs with only eight professional fights to his credit. Despite his incredible lack of experience Rickard had thrown his full support behind Berlenbach due to the fighter's punching power which had been electrifying fan's with exciting knockouts. Rickard viewed Berlenbach as a pocket version of Jack Dempsey and planned to have Berlenbach annex the middleweight championship, light heavyweight championship, and then challenge Dempsey. Harry likely reasoned that if Rickard was willing to throw good money away matching a prospect with less than ten fights against a battle hardened champion who was he to turn down free money?

When Greb chanced to pick up a match with Jack Reeves over four rounds (the maximum length of boxing matches allowed by California law) in Oakland, California he hardly took it seriously. He demanded that the match be a non-title affair with both fighters obligated to weigh in above the middleweight limit. In a letter home he admitted that he had not trained since his defeat of Wilson the previous month and ultimately trained little for Reeves. Despite this Harry dominated Reeves through his speed and skill but it was a lackadaisical performance. Harry smiled throughout and often laughed over the shoulder of his opponent while in clinches. Despite his easy supremacy Greb made few friends with the performance which he obviously looked on as little more than an exhibition.[39]

With Tex Rickard eager to secure Greb's services Harry and Red planned to head back East in mid-March. The team toured Los Angeles and Tijuana before returning to San Francisco in hopes of getting one more four round fight in before heading home. When a bout with either Jimmy Delaney or George Manley failed to materialize Harry and his team headed south to Paso Robles where they spent a couple of days with the Pittsburgh Pirates who were now in spring training.

As Harry was speeding his way back to Pittsburgh in hopes of closing the match with Berlenbach the rug was pulled out from under him. The fans had tired of hearing the ballyhoo surrounding Berlenbach after each successive knockout over the retreads he was being

Above is a photo of Harry Greb squaring off against Jack Reeves in his first bout on the coast. Left to right: Reeves' manager Bill Reeves, Jack Reeves, announcer Eddie Ryan, referee Bob Shand, Greb, Red Mason, and Greb's sparring partner Leo Caghil.

matched with and demanded that he be matched with a young gun like himself. In answer to these cries Tex Rickard matched Berlenbach with young Bridgeport boxer/puncher Jack Delaney. Delaney had shown promise in his best performances but he was likely chosen as an opponent for Berlenbach due to knockout losses he had suffered at the hands of Augie Ratner and Young Fisher. Yet, Delaney was far more experienced than Berlenbach and could boast of wins over the highly touted Lou Bogash and Tommy Loughran.

Berlenbach and Delaney met the day before Harry and company returned home. Delaney stood up to Berlenbach's early assault and by the third round was returning his own heavy fire and even dropped Berlenbach near the end of the round. In the fourth round, after scoring another knockdown, Delaney finally sent Berlenbach to the canvas unconscious. The crowd stormed the ring and a new sensation was born. Tex Rickard immediately began working on matching Greb and Delaney for a big outdoor bout in the summer.

Harry took the loss of the opportunity in stride. "So they finally stopped this fellow Paul Berlenbach before I could get to him," he said on his return. "It just saved the job, for I feel certain I could have polished him off in a manner which would have left no doubt in the minds of those who thought the so-called punchin' fool would dethrone me. Berlenbach's gloves would have been as useless to him as a shoe horn to a goldfish."[40]

While still in California Red Mason had agreed to terms for Harry to defend his championship against Fay Keiser. The bout would be held in Baltimore at the Fourth Regiment Armory on March 24. It would be almost exactly ten years to the day since Harry and Fay had first met in the ring as young prospects.

Since Keiser and Greb had last met more than two years previous Keiser's career had begun to slow. He continued to fight some of the best men of the middleweight and light heavyweight divisions but was now losing, although not disgraced, more often than not. He had gotten married and his wife was now pregnant with the couple's first child. Keiser had done little in recent years to earn a shot at Greb's middleweight championship but he remained popular in Baltimore as a result of his victory over Bob Martin. Promoter Benny Franklin reasoned that Keiser would be a marketable name locally for Greb to defend his title against.

Despite being a relatively inconsequential bout the match was plagued by Controversy nearly from the start. A few days prior to the fight Red Mason notified the Maryland State Athletic Commission that he would only accept a referee of his choosing. He intended to bring either Eddie Kennedy or Al Foss from Pittsburgh to the scene of the battle as the official arbiter. The commission, to their credit, flatly refused this demand. Mason ignored the commission and brought Al Foss to Baltimore. When the commission steadfastly refused to bend to Mason's demands he threatened to pull Greb out of the match. Noting that the largest indoor gate in Baltimore's history was waiting for the fighters to face off promoter Benny Franklin offered his services as referee as a means of compromise. Greb agreed and the show continued.

As this drama was playing out Keiser's manager John Snyder was registering his own com-

Harry Greb (left) squares off against long time rival Fay Kaiser before their 1924 middleweight championship bout. The fight would be a source of much controversy both before and after its conclusion. Promoter Benny Franklin stands between the two fighters. He took on the role of referee as a last minute replacement when Greb refused to fight before the original referee.

plaint with the commission. Keiser had weighed in the afternoon of the fight, making the stipulated limit of 160 pounds. Greb however failed to weigh in. When Snyder tried to collect his weight forfeit he was notified that Greb had not been contracted to make the middleweight limit and that his forfeit was for appearance only. Snyder felt he had been duped and vowed not to drop the matter.

It turned out that there was far more excitement outside of the ring than inside. Greb outclassed Keiser at every facet of the game, as should have been expected. For most of the fight Keiser looked silly as he flailed about in an attempt to land punches on his elusive rival. As the fight wore on it became more one sided until Harry floored Fay hard with a left hook in the twelfth round.

The knockdown was preceded by two or three rounds in which Keiser had taken a pummeling and was near defenseless. Keiser was so dazed that he failed to keep a knee in order to take a count and a much needed respite. Instead he arose at the count of three and immediately wobbled backwards into a neutral corner where Greb leapt at him like a panther. Harry landed a fusillade of unanswered blows prompting Franklin to jump in shouting "enough!"[41]

The fight was over. Greb had defended his championship via a twelve round technical knockout but there was more controversy to come. Snyder made it known that he would remain in Baltimore for a week until the next meeting of the Athletic Commission in order to plead his case and try to acquire Greb's $500 forfeit. When the Commission finally did meet Snyder was nowhere to be found and a great deal was revealed in his absence.

According to testimony and evidence given at the hearing Greb had been notified that a plot was underway to have his title stolen in Baltimore. A plan had been hatched to buy the services of the referee who would then render a decision against Greb awarding Greb's championship to Keiser. Benny Franklin testified that on the day of the fight he was offered three thousand dollars and the future services of Keiser (as champion) by Snyder to "fix" the referee. Franklin refused this offer. A letter warning Greb of the plot was also submitted as evidence. In answer to the complaint against Greb for failing to make weight Greb's contract and forfeit check were displayed showing plainly that Greb was contracted at catch weights and that his forfeit only bound his appearance at the fight, not his weight.[42]

Another week went by before the commission was ready to make a decision and this time Snyder was present. He labeled Franklin's story "damnable lies" and alleged that Franklin had concocted the entire story to prevent him from claiming Greb's weight forfeit. The commission ruled against Snyder in the matter of the weight forfeit. The terms of Greb's contract made it clear Snyder had no claim. However, they refused to act on the charges leveled against him by Franklin due to lack of evidence. For his part in the episode Al Foss was suspended by the Pennsylvania Athletic Commission.[43]

In late March it was announced that Harry had agreed to fight Kid Norfolk in Boston on April 14. Within days of the announcement newspapers carried the story that Greb had been injured in an automobile accident and would need to postpone the fight. In reality Harry was buying more time to get into shape after neglecting hard training for over four months.

The Norfolk bout was put back until April 19 and in the week leading up to the fight Boston newspapers were filled with stories of Greb's first encounter with Norfolk, no doubt originating from the fertile mind of Norfolk's manager Leo P. Flynn. The flash knockdown Greb suffered in the third round was twisted into four knockdowns in the first round. Greb's dominance in the final round was turned so that Greb was the fighter being battered. The various newspaper decisions being split down the middle for each fighter became a complete whitewash in favor of Norfolk. According to these accounts it was Greb, who went on to fight a week later, who cancelled all of his future fight dates to convalesce, not Norfolk, who in reality had been sent to the hospital and would not fight again for four months.

Harry left Pittsburgh on April 16 for New York where he would begin negotiations for a proposed summer bout against Jack Delaney. From New York Harry, with Red Mason, Happy Albacker, and Al Foss in tow, arrived in Boston on the 17th on the same train as Norfolk.

Norfolk had trained very hard for the bout and while Red Mason admitted that Greb had been lax in his training over the previous months he assured promoters that Greb had trained faithfully for Norfolk. The weigh in was conducted behind closed doors and no members of the press were allowed to witness. One paper deduced that this was because Boston had a rule in place stating that there could not be a difference of more than seven pounds between fighters facing one another below heavyweight. [44] The weights were announced for both fighters as being exactly 172³/₄ pounds despite more than one report stating that Norfolk appeared at least ten pounds heavier than Harry.

Odds opened at even money but by fight night Harry ruled as favorite by margins of 7 to 5 or 10 to 8 in some quarters. [45]

As Greb and Norfolk posed for photographs there was a palpable tension that could be felt throughout the hall. With Johnny Wilson, Jock Malone, and Augie Ratner all in attendance and hoping to challenge Greb the fighters left their corners for the first round.

The various accounts of the bout itself differed wildly and featured many interesting side-lights and details. All accounts agree that the match was one of the roughest and most bitterly contested of the era.

From the opening round both fighters fought using increasingly foul tactics. The two Pittsburgh newspapermen in attendance lay blame for this squarely with Kid Norfolk. The Boston Herald writer blamed Greb. The other Boston writers avoided laying blame and took a much more neutral stance. Those newspapermen from Pittsburgh, who issued by far the two most detailed accounts of the fight, claimed that early in the first round Norfolk began hitting low and throwing kidney punches. This angered Greb who asked the referee to watch Norfolk's tactics. When it was plain that the referee could not or would not reign in the situation Harry took matters into his own hands.

Things went from bad to worse in the third round when Norfolk (depending on which account the reader prefers) either butted, pushed, or threw Greb out of the ring and into press row. Greb was furious and from that point on the fight was less a boxing match and more a street fight in which both fighters fought along the foulest lines possible. The bout featured a dazzling array of low blows, kidney punches, head-butts, wrestling, thumbing, heeling, and every other dirty trick known to the sport.

As the fight degenerated the rowdy audience was in an uproar yelling for a knockout and admonishing the referee, who had long since lost control, to let the men fight any way they wanted. Both fighters were warned several times without paying the least bit of attention.

The sixth round opened with a low blow from Norfolk and the free for all continued. When the bell rang ending the round Greb dropped his hands, turned, and began walking to his cor-

Harry Greb (right) faced Kid Norfolk for a second time on April 19, 1924. The bout would go down in history as one of the roughest fights in Massachusetts history. Greb would lay blame with Norfolk and referee Jack Sheehan (center) who he, and others, deemed too feeble and timid to control the fight.

ner. Norfolk turned and struck Greb. Harry became enraged and leapt at Norfolk landing several blows to his body. The two fighters continued fighting for nearly a minute as their handlers entered the ring and began fighting amongst themselves. The audience, which had been whipped to a fever pitch, surged forward prepared to get in on the fighting. A soda bottle was tossed from the audience and the ring filled with police. It was nearly twenty minutes before order was restored.

In the middle of this maelstrom the befuddled referee, Jack Sheehan, wildly gesticulated in Norfolk's direction, signaling that he had awarded the bout to Norfolk on a foul and then quickly exited the ring and beat a hasty retreat. The audience and fighters were stunned and confused by Sheehan's actions and milled around waiting for an official announcement. As the waiting dragged on the already irate audience demanded that the two fighters fight.

Greb was being restrained in his corner by several men as he cursed Norfolk and continued trying to get at him. Norfolk stood in his corner, had his gloves removed, and taunted Greb. As he left the ring he made one final attempt to get at Greb and another small melee was nearly set off.[46]

Commissioner Gene Buckley, interviewed at ringside, gave the unofficial statement that it was his opinion that Norfolk had fouled first and that he expected the decision to be reversed but first needed to consult with the referee who was now nowhere to be found.[47]

Interviewed in his dressing room after the fight Greb stated: "Norfolk refused to fight cleanly from the early part of the first round. The referee, who, to start with, has no business in the ring, was helpless and I quickly saw, that unless I protected myself at all times I would be a victim of rough play. I tore into Norfolk with everything I had and had him crazy, I guess, when the sixth round closed. I started to my corner and he swung and hit me four times. I thought he hadn't heard the bell and told him it had rung. He called me a foul name and swung again. Then I started swinging to protect myself. You know the rest."[48]

Leo P. Flynn had a similar story to tell when he issued a press release on the matter. "Greb many times tried to deliberately foul Norfolk, but the Kid was too smart and gave him no openings. In desperation, Greb waited till after the bell had sounded ending the round, and on pretext of going to his corner, would turn around and hit Norfolk. He did this on several occasions till the referee, tiring of his unsportsmanlike tactics, called a halt to the proceedings and handed the bout to Norfolk—thereby cheating Norfolk of a sure knockout."[49] Flynn's version of the ending of the fight is not supported by ringside accounts which were unanimous, with one exception, stating that Norfolk did indeed strike Greb first after the bell ending the sixth round. All told Norfolk would be disqualified three more times in his two remaining years as a prizefighter after facing Greb. It was the first and only disqualification of Greb's career.

There was plenty of blame to go around for the debacle. Both fighters clearly fought foul. The audience encouraged the men and when it began to get out of hand the referee was too timid to bring matters under control. Interviewed again the day after the fight Harry stated that he felt referee Sheehan had become alarmed by the rowdy crowd and the thrown soda bottle, prompting a split second judgment call and a hasty retreat.[50]

Two days after the fight with Norfolk, while still awaiting an official ruling from the Boston commission, Greb signed to defend his championship against Jack Delaney at Yankee Stadium in what was hoped to be a blockbuster promotion. Initially Harry and Red had held out for $40,000 but settled on $37,500. The bout would be the headliner of a card staged for the benefit of the Milk and Ice Fund.

Greb was still eager to conclude matters with Norfolk and quickly agreed to meet Norfolk in Boston once again during the second week of May. However, the Boston commission had seen enough of Greb and Norfolk and quickly banned both fighters from fighting in the state for six months, while upholding Jack Sheehan's decision as final, in order to prevent a reoccurence of their last bout.[51]

Initially the edict handed down in Boston was not expected to affect Greb's schedule outside of his proposed rubber match with Norfolk. It was unlikely that the New York State Athletic Commission would follow suit with Massachusetts due to the importance of Harry's defense against Delaney and the amount of money it would bring to the state and its promoters. This reasoning was upended when Delaney took a seemingly easy warm up fight with Bryan Downey in Columbus, Ohio. Downey had not fought since his lop sided defeat at the hands of Greb but had rethought his decision to retire from the ring sixth months earlier. Downey easily defeated the highly touted Delaney and seemingly had the younger fighter ready for a knockout at conclusion of the contest.

Such a massive upset greatly devalued not only Delaney's stock but his challenge against Greb. The promoters of the contest could no longer expect to pay Greb the $37,500 they promised and still hope to profit. The fight now looked to be a financial loser for but they had one option. The New York Commission promptly did an about face and acknowledged that it too would enforce the Massachusetts ban on Greb and Norfolk thereby eliminating the need for the promoters to live up to their contract.

The motivations of the New York State Athletic Commission became all the more obvious when it allowed Norfolk to fight Bob Lawson in Buffalo just three days after acknowledging the ban, only to have Norfolk lose to Lawson on disqualification for use of the same tactics Greb complained of in Boston. Publicly the commission stated that it had allowed Norfolk to honor his obligation to face Lawson because his contract pre-dated the commission's decision to ban him. However, Greb's contract with Delaney also predated the commission's ban and even pre-dated Norfolk's contract to face Lawson.

On the same day that Jack Delaney was losing to Bryan Downey Harry easily stopped Jackie Clark in two rounds just outside of Washington, D.C.[52] He followed this performance up a week later with a crowd pleasing victory over Pal Reed at Pittsburgh in which Greb was once again far over his best weight. In the Reed fight Harry injured his right hand forcing a layoff of nearly a month.[53]

Between the injury and his ban Harry found himself unable to earn the kind of money a champion deserved. He lobbied aggressively for New York to lift the ban on him. He was desperate for the payday that the Delaney fight would bring but in the end he was forced to agree to cut his purse from $37,500 to $20,000 in return for the ban to be lifted. Despite this concession the commission would only consent to lift the ban if he could gain the consent of Massachusetts. Harry had already been advised that the Massachusetts commission had no intention of lifting his ban so for the time being the Delaney fight seemed like a lost cause.

As soon as Harry's hand was healed Mason began booking a busy summer schedule. Ever since his title defense against Johnny Wilson in January Harry's conditioning had left much to be desired. It was Mason's hope that a busy schedule would keep Harry in shape and focused. First up would be an exhibition at Olean, New York's St. Bonaventure College against his sparring partner Frank Senk, on his thirtieth birthday. Greb made a hit with the audience by sparring two rounds with George Kenneally of the college and finishing off with four rounds against Senk. Afterwards he was awarded an honorary letter from the college.[54]

Six days later Greb faced light heavyweight Martin Burke at Brooklyn, Ohio, just outside of

Cleveland. Burke had been an amateur stand out from New Orleans for years before turning pro in 1919. He was a solid, if unspectacular fighter who had recently temporarily relocated to Cleveland in order to give his career a jump start. At six feet three inches he would tower over Greb yet was still an underdog. Greb easily dominated Burke. In the fourth Greb opened a bad cut over Burke's right eye and from that point on Burke was a badly beaten man. He held on gamely to the finish but failed to win a single round. Seaburn Brown writing for the Cleveland Press estimated that Burke managed to land only two punches per round on Greb.[55]

It had been 8 years since Greb first faced Jackie Clark. Clark was now in the twilight of his career as Greb faced him in a non-title bout to stay busy.

Greb's next opponent looked, on paper, to be one of his more difficult recent propositions. Welshman Frank Moody was on his second trip to the United States, having arrived in early May. He had visited the States six months earlier winning ten of his twelve bouts, losing only to Lou Bogash and Allentown Joe Gans by decision. Moody returned to the United States desperately seeking a title shot against Greb. In just over two weeks after entering the country he won his first bout, a surprise stoppage of Lou Bogash. Moody's victory made headlines due to the fact that no other fighter had ever been able to stop Bogash. Nine days later he would go on to defeat fring contender George Robinson. His surprise victory over Bogash had propelled him into a match with Greb at Waterbury, Connecticut. Just three days prior to the Greb bout Moody once again pulled off an upset by defeating Jock Malone in Boston and once again removing one of Greb's most persistent challengers.

The bout was thrown into jeopardy initially when it was discovered that Moody had a prior agreement to face Pal Reed in Bridgeport on June 23. According to the laws governing boxing in Connecticut a fighter could not fight twice in the state within seven days. Given the circumstances the commission had no other choice but to void Moody's agreement with promoter George Mulligan to face Greb. Mulligan was frantic to save his promotion. Initially he offered Bridgeport promoters $1,500 to postpone their show, which was refused. Then Mulligan approached another British import, Ted Moore, who held several wins over Moody in the old

Top: Martin Burke of New Orleans had been a highly touted amateur and had faced some of the best fighters in the country. He had temporarily relocated to Ohio where he faced Greb in 1924. Bottom: Frank Moody was a very experienced fighter from England who had traveled to the United States looking for a shot at Greb's championship. He earned a non-title fight with Greb in 1924 by winning two major upsets over Jock Malone, and Lou Bogash.

country and who had also defeated Bogash. Finally Bridgeport promoters consented to allow Moody to first face Greb in exchange for the right to co-promote the bout with Mulligan.[56]

While preparing for Moody Greb received word that the Massachusetts commission had agreed to lift his ban for one day to allow him to face Jack Delaney in New York, in light of the fact that the bout was to be held for charity. Only days later it was announced that Delaney had been stricken with appendicitis and would be unable to accommodate Greb. Seizing on George Mulligan's idea the promoters for the Delaney bout secured Ted Moore as a substitute. The way was now paved, Greb need only defeat Moody.

Both Greb and Moody weighed in at 167 lbs. for their match and both looked to be in excellent condition. The bout itself started out slowly with Greb getting in close and feeling Moody out. In each successive round Greb increased his pace and work rate and by the third he had Moody's right eye reddened and his mouth bleeding. In the fourth round Harry landed a left hook which sliced open Moody's already damaged eye. The flow of blood bothered Moody and shortly after, while in a clinch, Greb landed a heavy left to the heart which traveled mere inches and dropped Moody for a nine count.

Moody rose, clearly hurt, and Greb pounced. Moody clinched but Harry dropped him again for a count of three. Once again Moody rose unsteadily but showed enough presence of mind to clinch until the round ended.

In the fifth Moody tried to box at long range with Greb and, despite landing a solid right hand, could not cope with his rival's speed. Greb came out for the sixth in full control, picking his spots. As he worked his way inside he saw his opening and shot a short powerful uppercut to the point of Moody's jaw, dropping the Welshman to the canvas. As referee Jim Galvin's count reached nine Moody got to his feet but his unsteady legs betrayed him and he tumbled back down. Galvin immediately called the fight off despite protests from Moody and his corner men. He had lost every round of the fight. As Greb administered the knockout Rudolph Freidler, a real estate agent from New Haven who had complained of pains in his arm on the way to the bout dropped dead of heart failure. When Greb's hand was raised in victory Red Mason jumped into the ring and turned a cartwheel to the delight of the audience.[57]

Harry arrived in New York to complete training for his defense against Ted Moore only to once again be met by attacks from the New York press. Several New York papers printed the story that Greb had defeated Moody by using exceedingly foul tactics, stories which are not supported by any of the ringside accounts of the Moody bout. In addition to this several outlets ran reports that Greb had weighed 172 pounds for Moody, ignoring the official weigh in figures. Such hostility reminded Greb of the attacks on him prior to his bouts with Tunney and served to make him apprehensive over the officiating of the fight.

Harry immediately set about training at Philadelphia Jack O'Brien's gym, while Moore impressed reporters with his conditioning at his Pompton Lakes training camp. "They tell me Harry will make a rushing fight of it," said Moore. "I hope he does. That's just the kind of fighter I can whip. I'll win sure." Greb was no less confident despite speculation that he was having difficulty making weight. "Don't be surprised if I knock the skids from under Moore's legs. I can whip those kind of fighters every day of the week."[58]

The card itself was a hot ticket and expected to sell extremely well. In only nine days after ticket sales opened there had been $100,000 worth sold. Promoter James J. Johnston expected Yankee Stadium to be

Harry Greb poses for photographers while training at Philadelphia Jack O'Brien's gym in preparation for his upcoming title defense against Ted Moore.

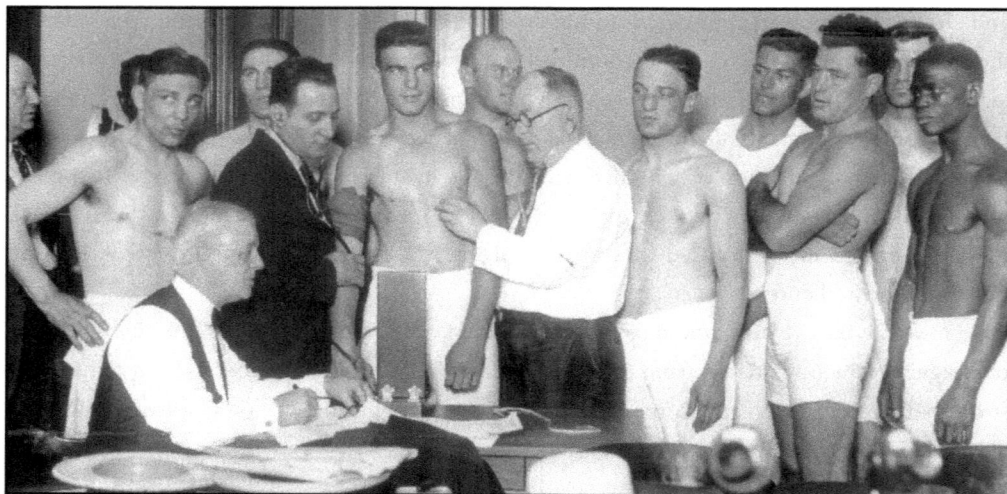

The fighters on the Greb-Moore Milk Fund fight card are examined by commission doctors at the weigh in. Fighters are left to right: Larry Estridge (barely visible behind Greb), Harry Greb, Tommy Loughran, Young Stribling, Sandy Seifert, Ted Moore, Gene Tunney, Erminio Spalla, Dan Leiber (barely visible), and Panama Joe Gans.

sold out before the first bout commenced.

In addition to Greb headlining the event against Moore, fans were excited over the prospect of an international bout between Gene Tunney and Erminio Spalla of Italy as the semi-final. While they could also expect to see Tommy Loughran (a last minute replacement of Paul Berlenbach) facing Young Stribling, Panama Joe Gans against Larry Estridge, and Dan Leiber against Sandy Seifert in the curtain raiser. Motion pictures would be taken of the stellar event and shown in theaters all over New York State.

Harry was installed as a 2 to 1 favorite and even as high as 3 to 1 in some areas. Despite the disparity in the odds Moore was considered a live underdog.[59] This was due in part to Moore's pedigree as a fighter: He had defeated Frank Moody three times in England, and had traveled to Greb's hometown to defeat Lou Bogash in order to gain recognition as a challenger. In addition to this Moore was considered to be a brave and durable fighter with a respectable punch. However, the fact that he was conceded a chance against the champion was due in part to the belief that Greb was slipping, and the rumors about his struggles to make weight.

Two days before the fight representatives of the athletic commission went to both fighters camps to ascertain their condition. It was found that Greb weighed 165$^{1}/_{2}$ lbs. The following day Greb was expected to weigh just over 161 lbs. and intended to dry out that night in order to make weight.[60]

The fighters weighed in at 2pm on the afternoon of the fight. Moore weighed 160 pounds on the dot, while Greb weighed a half pound under, looking weak, drawn, and nervous. After posing for photographers Harry rehydrated, ate a steak dinner, and brought his weight back up to 168$^{1}/_{2}$ pounds. He then took a nap and after a rub down estimated that he entered the ring weighing 166 pounds.[61]

After the preliminaries fans warmed up for the Greb-Moore showdown by watching Panama Joe Gans lose his colored middleweight championship to Larry Estridge. Young Stribling, who Harry had signed to fight the following week at Michigan City, defeated Tommy Loughran in a close, competitive bout, and Gene Tunney had a few rocky moments with Italy's Erminio Spalla before finally gaining a technical knockout after damaging the Italian's left eye.

By the time Greb and Moore had entered the ring roughly 50,000 people had filled the stands paying over $200,000 to see the fighters. The audience was studded with luminaries who arrived less out of interest in the sport than to be seen at the event.

For the first seven rounds Greb fought at a measured pace which led some to the conclusion that making the middleweight limit had indeed weakened him or that he was boxing under wraps for fear of being disqualified by hostile New York officials.

Top: Greb and Ted Moore pose for cameramen at the weigh in prior to their championship match. Below: Greb (right) attacks a bewildered Ted Moore.

Both of these may have been factors in Greb's performance but the fact of the matter is that as Greb had aged he had begun to fight more conservatively in the early rounds of his bouts, increasing his pace as the fight wore on. Against Moore that is exactly what happened.

In the third round Greb brought blood from Moore's nose and kept it bleeding round after round.

Moore continually played for Greb's body. He would work in close and bang away at the ribs. Greb fought best at long range where Moore could not cope with the champions speed. Time and time again Harry would bound around, bobbing and weaving, confounding Moore by popping up behind him, befuddling the challenger with blows from all angles. Whenever Moore threatened to assert himself Greb would rock him to show him who was boss.

After the mid point of the fight Harry increased his pace and took total control. He constantly kept Moore on the defensive, spinning him and popping up behind him at indefensible angles, as the two photos above illustrate.

Moore tried to rally in the sixth and seventh, hoping to regain command of the fight. Instead Harry increased his pace and when Moore could not keep up Harry outclassed his opponent the rest of the way.

In the eleventh round Moore's right eye was cut and from that point on the Englishman grew increasingly weaker and more reticent to engage. By the end of the fight Moore clung to Greb at every opportunity and when the unanimous decision was announced Moore seemed more than happy to have simply finished the fight on his feet.

After the fight members of the press were unanimous that Greb had won, and by a large margin. They also made note that Greb fought an exceedingly clean fight and never resorted to tactics that Moore himself did not use. However, the reviews were not all good. More than one paper felt the fight was a poor one. This was due in part to Greb's dominance over Moore but also due to the fact that Greb was apparently aging. He was clearly not the fighter he had once been and some of the more critical elements felt that he was ripe for the taking. Still others noted that Moore had been a good and highly touted opponent who Greb handled with relative ease. Those members felt that if Moore was handled so easily by a Greb that was not at his best it would be a long time before anyone upset the champion.[62]

After the fight Harry stayed in New York for a few days where he would rebuild his strength after the ordeal of making weight and relax a bit before heading west to Michigan City for his bout with Young Stribling. Yet even as he relaxed plans were beginning to take shape for an ambitious campaign that would pit him against some of the most formidable names in the sport over the coming months.

22

FIGHTING FATHER TIME

After his victory over Ted Moore Harry had intended to head straight for Chicago where he would train for a day or two before moving on to the scene of his bout with Young Stribling at Benton Harbor, Indiana but a bout of homesickness prompted him to stop off in Pittsburgh for a short visit with friends and family.

The Stribling bout was a 10 round catch weights bout with no decision being given, promoted by the Arena Boxing and Athletic Club, which was controlled by Joe Coffey, Frank Parker, and Floyd Fitzsimmons. The same club had promoted the successful Tommy Gibbons-Georges Carpentier bout just over one month previous which witnessed Gibbons dominate the former champion. As an added attraction the semi-final to the Greb-Stribling bout would feature bantamweight champion Abe Goldstein.

When Harry arrived in Chicago he immediately set about training at the Arcade gym, playing handball with Red Mason for forty minutes and sparring several rounds with Frank Senk, to the delight of onlookers. Greb was made a solid favorite over Stribling once his condition had been assessed.

You're lucky if you are an exhibitor in N.Y. State
for then you can show 2nd Annual
MILK FUND FIGHT PICTURE
PRODUCED EXCLUSIVELY BY INTERNATIONAL — RELEASED THRU UNIVERSAL — FEATURING THE GREATEST FIGHTS OF THE YEAR STAGED AT YANKEE STADIUM, JUNE 26

THE greatest boxing card of the year—title contenders in a group of bouts that will make ring history. Four or five rounds on length of bouts) of close-up action. Held under the supervision of the Mayor's Committee of Women, Mrs. William Randolph Hearst, Chairman. All proceeds from the picture rights go to provide funds to buy free milk for babies. Released the day these fights in New York State only.

Invaluable publicity will be given the bout films (including mention of the theatres showing films) in the Evening Telegram, Times-Union, Albany; Evening Journal, Rochester; the New York American and Journal in New York City in addition to headline articles on sporting pages of papers everywhere.

Special posters, scene stills and slides at Exchanges! The biggest sporting event of the season—an opportunity to cash in on thousands of dollars worth of publicity!

Phone or Wire Your Universal Exchange Immediately.
GET YOUR PLAY DATES NOW!

NOW BOOKING AT UNIVERSAL'S NEWYORK, BUFFALO AND ALBANY EXCHANGES
Starts off with a Bang at New York City
MOSS' BIG BROADWAY THEATRE JUNE 27TH

TED MOORE
HARRY GREB

YOUNG STRIBLING
PAUL BERLENBACH

GENE TUNNEY
ERMINIO SPALLA

PANAMA JOE GANS
LARRY ESTRIDGE

The day after Greb and co. arrived in Chicago the Stribling bout was cancelled under mysterious circumstances, mere days before it was scheduled to take place. Initially it was announced by the mayor of Michigan City that the bout had been called off due to concerns over a virulent smallpox outbreak in neighboring Michigan.[1] However, Michigan health officials quickly shot back stating there was no smallpox epidemic in their state.[2] Shortly thereafter it was revealed that promoters had postponed the bout after becoming spooked by slow ticket sales prompted by the siphoning off of sports fans in the area to other nearby events.[3] Both fighters left the scene. Greb intended to stay in Chicago while promoters tried to salvage the event, Stribling left for Macon.

Hoping to salvage the match, and their profits, promoters asked both fighters to accept a percentage of the gate, as opposed to the guarantees which had originally been agreed upon. Harry accepted, Stribling refused and the match was permanently cancelled, and with that one of the more intriguing matchups of the mid-1920s was lost.[4]

Even as the Stribling bout was falling apart Red Mason was negotiating with former lightweight championship claimant turned promoter Ray Bronson for a bout between Harry and a little known African American fighter out of Georgia who was now making rapid strides to the forefront of the middleweight and light-heavyweight divisions.

Theodore "Tiger" Flowers had found his way into the boxing fraternity under the tutelage of prizefighter Rufus Cameron. During the war Flowers migrated from Georgia to Philadelphia, eventually finding work as a riveter in the shipyards supplying vessels for the war effort. There he continued to train and caught the eye of Philadelphia Jack O'Brien who further encouraged Flowers. Flowers turned professional in 1918 and labored for years on what would eventually be known as the "chitlin circuit," clubs in the southern United States that catered primarily to black patrons where black fighters faced one another to little or no publicity, and with little financial reward.

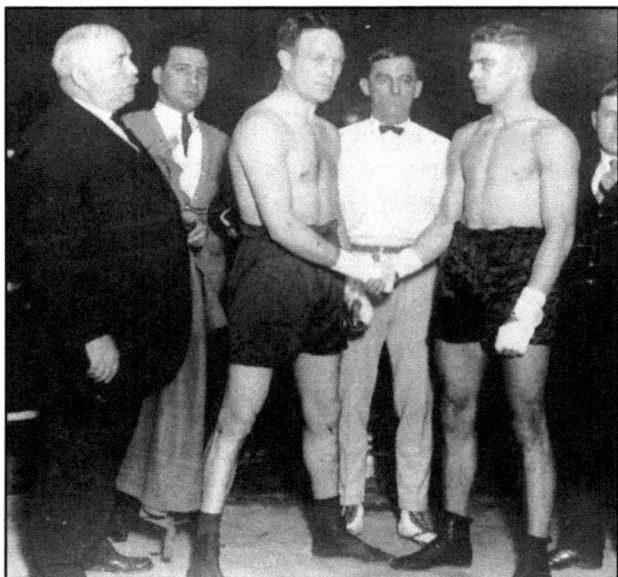

Mike McTigue (center left) and Young Stribling pose for camera men prior to their March 31, 1924 no-decision rematch held in Newark, New Jersey. Once again the nineteen year old Stribling easily defeated McTigue, managing to knock him down in the process. McTigue's performance, or lack thereof, cemented him in the minds of the public as a cheese champion. The fighters are flanked by Paddy Mullins (far left) McTigue's manager, Referee Henry Lewis (center), and Pa Stribling (far right).

During these early years Flowers fought many recognizable names in the sport, particularly among African American fighters, and was often billed as having never lost a decision. This was true but it was often left unsaid that Flowers had been knocked out in all of his losses. However in the previous year he had been making rapid advances since the defeat of his old nemesis Panama Joe Gans. Flowers had developed into a supremely conditioned fighter who relied on blinding speed and an aggressive two fisted attack much along the same style as Greb. Flowers was an awkward, slapping fighter made more difficult to figure out due to his left handed style. He had two weaknesses, he was not a heavy puncher, and he had been dropped and stopped fairly frequently.

Flowers had only recently gained any kind of recognition outside of the south through a series of fights in the upper Midwest and New York City arranged by his ever present manager Walk Miller. Along with his greater professional publicity Flowers personal character also became a matter of great interest to the public in light of the controversy that had followed Jack Johnson around the globe. In Flowers the press found a colorful figure who met with a great deal of acceptance in the still racially charged times. In Flowers they found a soft spoken, unassuming man, deeply religious, devoted to his family, and reputed to be a vegetarian. In addition to this Flowers had a strong work ethic and a happy disposition. In short Flowers was the type of man who could break racial barriers without threatening the white establishment.

Flowers was so eager to show what he could do against a champion that he agreed to face Greb for nothing if the gate did not exceed $15,000 and even then he only got a percentage if the gate exceededthat figure.[5] Harry agreed to the contest but set several conditions to protect his championship, being unfamiliar with Flowers, Miller, and having never boxed under a promotion by the Fremont A.C.. Greb stipulated that the bout must be held at catch weights, it would be a 10 round no decision match, and Greb would be allowed to dictate the referee. With these protections in place the bout was signed for August 14 to be staged at an arena specially constructed for the event outside of Fremont, Ohio.

Fremont, Ohio was situated on the Sandusky River and most of the town's income came from river trade or farm-

Tiger Flowers' remarkable conditioning is evident in this photo of him jumping rope. His stamina was such that he was the only fighter who could compare with Greb in terms of speed and punch output. By the summer of 1924 he was rapidly making a name for himself in the division.

ing. With a population of about thirteen thousand it seemed an unlikely location to host what promised to be an intriguing matchup. Yet, Fremont was centrally located, allowing fairly easy access from larger population centers like Cleveland, Toledo, Detroit, Columbus, and Sandusky, as well as many surrounding smaller communities. The Greb-Flowers match would be the biggest thing to come to little Fremont in years, with press passes being requested and large blocks of tickets being purchased from all over the Midwest.

Instead of setting down to hard training Harry headed back to Atlantic City for more rest and relaxation. On July 17 he would watch approvingly as his former opponent Kid Norfolk stopped Mexican Joe Lawson in eight rounds.

Two weeks later Harry traveled to New York City to get a glimpse of Tiger Flowers for the first time as Flowers fought Jack Townsend at the Commonwealth Sporting Club. What Greb saw convinced him he had greatly underestimated Flowers. Harry left in the middle of the fight[6] and two days later reportedly asked for a delay of ten days to face Flowers.[7] Instead, the fight was postponed one week. Greb himself denied that he was to blame for the delay stating that it was Bronson who had approached him for a delay citing an inability to complete the arena by fight time.[8] It was likely a mutual decision that benefited both men equally. Bronson was indeed having difficulty getting the arena erected and in fact it would not be completed until August 20, six days after the original fight date and the day before the fight was eventually held. Regardless, Greb definitely saw something in Tiger Flowers that convinced him to get down to hard training. He immediately left the relative comfort of Atlantic City for a train-

Harry Greb loved cars, the faster and flashier the better. This Jordan roadster was a favorite of his. He drove it to Fremont, Ohio to prepare for his bout with Tiger Flowers. As he toured the streets with the top down locals looked on in awe.

ing camp at Conneaut Lake.

When Harry finally arrived in Fremont the week of the fight in his blue Jordan Roadster he was tanned and confident despite still carrying slightly more weight than usual. Harry stayed at the Jackson Hotel with Red Mason, Jack Barry, and Jim Tennor. He trained at the American Legion A.C. sparring with Cleve Hawkins, Johnny Lewis, and Barry among others. In the evenings Harry and friends would stroll the streets of Fremont, accompanied by great fanfare and crowds of people. On August 17 they took in a minstrel show where Greb was asked to the stage and gave a short speech. On the 18th they were treated to a luncheon by the Women's Relief Corps, to which Greb donated, and on the 19th the Pittsburgh contingent attended a screening of the film of the famous boxing match between Ad Wolgast and Battling Nelson.

In the days leading up to the fight Greb had made such a popular impression on the locals that the Fremont Daily Messenger commented: "Greb is a popular fellow down town and he is followed to and from his walks between the Hotel Jackson and the restaurant where he dines. The trim built and neatly dressed boxer is a hit and that's that. They are selling Greb hats, Greb suits, Greb shoes, while the barbershops are giving Greb haircuts and shaves and shampoos. In the refreshment parlors they have Greb sundaes, Greb milkshakes, Greb colas, and a lot of folks are thinking of buying cars just like the big blue roadster that the champion pilots about. It's great to be boss of the walk."[9]

On August 18 Harry gave the hundreds of fans who attended his training a glimpse at his conditioning. He sparred nine rounds with four different sparring partners, added two rounds of shadow boxing, two rounds of rope skipping, and one round of tossing around the medicine ball and barely broke a sweat. In the audience was Flowers' manager Walk Miller who rarely missed a chance to watch Greb train in the days leading up to the fight.[10]

Flowers had arrived in Ohio on August 17

GREB vs. FLOWERS
Thursday, Aug. 21st, 1924
8:00 O'clock P. M. Eastern Time

BLEACHER SEAT

Price $3.00 War Tax 30cts Total $3.30

The FREA

A.C. MOORE
PRES.

206 South F.

HUNGRY? TRY HODE'S LUNCH

Official Program

The

Harry "Tiger"

GREB-FLOWERS

World's Championship
BOXING CONTEST

::

FREMONT, OHIO

Thursday, August 21, 1924

PRICE 25c

READ THE SANDUSKY REGISTER

The Two Fastest Boxers in the World	World's Middleweight Championship Boxing Match!

HARRY GREB
WORLD'S CHAMPION, VS.
TIGER FLOWERS
LEADING TITLE CONTENDER

Everything Set—Harry Greb and Tiger Flowers both in Fremont and training hard. Big Mammoth Open Air Arena Seating 11,000 People now up and ready for big match.

BRONSON AND MILLER'S OPEN AIR ARENA **Fremont, Ohio, Thursday, August 21** 8:15 P.M.

4 GREAT PRELIMINARIES THAT ARE CLASSED AS MAIN EVENT MATCHES ON ANY CARD

K. O. Williams vs. Kid Ryle	Let Philbin vs. Jack Hallet	Charley Scherer vs. Norm Genet	Red Herring vs. Eddie Briney
4 Rounds at 122 Pounds	Toledo — Detroit 6 Rounds at 147 Pounds	Sandusky — Barberton 6 Rounds at 158 Pounds	Gulf Port, Miss. — Louisville, Ky. 6 Rounds at 140 Pounds

Better get your tickets right away. Advance sale already beyond expectations. Prices $3.30, $5.50, $8.25, $11.00, including war tax

from Texas where he had defeated Oscar Mortimar five days earlier. Flowers set up training camp at Toledo, sparring daily with Joe Packo, "Let" Philbin, Johnny Andrews, Toledo Knockout Brown, and Pinkey Mitchell. Flowers exhibited a cool confidence that only a fighter in peak physical condition knows. George Pulford of the Toledo Blade was greatly impressed by Flowers, having seen him fight several times before and made note of the fact that Greb did not seem in the best condition despite his training.

By the 20th everything was set. The Arena had finally been completed. The fighters concluded their training. Ticket sales had been a success. Flowers wife and young daughter had arrived in Fremont to witness what they hoped would be a triumph. The Light Guard and M.W.A. bands had been enlisted to provide entertainment before the first match and between contests. Pathé films had been enlisted to film the contest. Eddie Kennedy of Pittsburgh had been selected by Greb as referee with the approval of the Pennsylvania Commission. On that day Flowers and Greb met for the first time as they arrived at Dr. Schultz's office to take a preliminary physical. The two men shook hands "Mr. Flowers, I'm glad to meet you," said Greb.[11] Both fighters checked out in excellent physical condition with Flowers weighing 161^1/$_2$ pounds and Greb reportedly weighing between 165 and 170 pounds. All that was left now was to return to their quarters and rest up for tomorrow's bout.

The following day, prior to the fight, Walk Miller and Flowers had tried to persuade the commission to allow Flowers to weigh in secretly in order to prove that Flowers was under the middleweight limit in the event of a knockout or disqualification in Tiger's favor, allowing them to claim Greb's championship. This was refused by the commission under the terms of the contract that Flowers and Miller had signed to face Greb, which stipulated the fight be fought at catch weights despite publicity calling the match a championship.[12]

Flowers entered the ring at 9:55pm followed by Miller and two seconds. Greb, trying to gain a psychological advantage kept Flowers waiting several minutes before entering the ring himself, followed by Red Mason, Cleve Hawkins, Jack Barry, and Jim Tennor. The two managers inspected their opponents hand wraps as Izzy Weinstein, who had been the announcer for the Dempsey-Willard championship contest, made the necessary introductions.

The fighters came out for the first round feeling each other out. Greb allowed Flowers to do the leading as he studied his opponent. The champion wore the demeanor of a man who had been here before. Flowers seemed slightly nervous and anxious. About thirty seconds before the end of the round Flowers landed a body shot that woke up the champion and the fight began in earnest.

Over the course of the fight both fighters took turns displaying dazzling speed, a blistering offense, and defensive wizardry rarely seen in the ring. If Harry had been fighting down to the level of his competition in recent months Flowers was bringing out the best in him. There was no laying back and saving a reserve for a late round burst. Flowers was forcing Harry to use every trick he had learned in his career, all of his speed, and dig deep into that seemingly bottomless well of stamina. And yet Greb smiled throughout the contest, always confident that he had matters in hand.

It was no different for Flowers. He had never faced a champion and this was the opportunity all fighters yearn for. This was Flowers chance to test himself against the best and see if he had what it takes to be a champion. This fight could elevate Flowers from humble beginnings to a different professional and economic stratosphere and he was proving he was equal to the task. Flowers was giving the performance of his life.

It was considered by almost all who saw the fight as being one of the fastest and greatest exhibitions of boxing ever staged. The majority of newspapers felt Greb had won the bout but the difference of opinion as to Greb's margin of victory or the overall outcome of the fight itself illustrates just how competitive the bout was.[13] Flowers was adjudged the winner by the Fremont Daily News, Toledo Blade, Toledo News-Bee, the Akron Press, and the Columbus Citizen. Greb was given the decision by the Columbus Evening Dispatch, Fremont Daily Messenger, Toledo Times, Detroit News, Sandusky Star Journal, Pittsburgh Gazette Times, Lorain Times Herald, Tiffin Advertiser, Mansfield News, Pittsburgh Post, Fostoria Daily Review, Cleveland News, and Findlay Morning Republican. The Sandusky Register had the bout a draw as did the Grand Rapids Herald, Lima News, and both referee Eddie Kennedy and promoter Ray Bronson. Even those papers voting for Greb gave Flowers a world of credit for his showing.

Greb, who took home $7,012 for his work, was magnanimous towards Flowers, giving the Atlanta fighter high praise. For once Greb, in describing Flowers, sounded like one of his own opponents trying to describe the style that for years had befuddled contenders across several divisions. "He is an awkward target, a weaving, moving fellow who throws his punches from any angle," said Greb after the fight. "While I believe I'm safe in saying I beat him I want to say that he will give any first-class man a tough session and will lick a lot of the best ones. That goes especially for Loughran, Stribling, Berlenbach, and Slattery. Furthermore I think he is one man who can give Jack Dempsey a merry time for six or eight rounds. When I say that I know what I am talking about. Dempsey would probably eventually get to him because Flowers doesn't carry a knockout punch, but he'd mark the champ up before the latter would get to him. I think so well of Flowers that I am going to draw the color line from here on in. That goes."[14]

The comment, which was meant as a compliment to Flowers and not to be taken literally, was immediately taken out of context, picked up by various media outlets, and widely report-

Buffalo, New York's Jimmy Slattery (top) was a boy phenom much like Young Stribling. He had a flashy style, combined with speed and a respectable punch. Despite being too young to fight in anything but six round matches in his home state he was already considered a likely future champion. Above he can be seen sparring with Young Fisher in preparation for his bout with Harry Greb.

ed as an admission of Flowers' superiority.

After the fight Walk Miller gathered up his collection of press clippings stating Flowers had won and, completely ignoring the fact that more than twice as many papers voted for Greb, began assailing press outlets all over the country calling his man the uncrowned champion. The tactic worked and Flowers began to find himself in the national press and flooded with offers. Flowers was so pleased with Miller's managerial acumen that one month later he signed himself to a lifetime contract with Miller, something unheard of in the modern era. Flowers took home $2,743.65 and regardless of whether or not Miller's claim of victory for Flowers was believed or not the Tiger from Georgia was now in great demand.

While still preparing for Flowers Greb was signed to face Jimmy Slattery in Buffalo on September 3 and Gene Tunney in Cleveland five days later. Promoters from all over the East and Midwest had been after a fourth bout between Greb and Tunney for months. Even millionaire steel magnate Charles Schwab had tried to entice Tunney to face Greb in central Pennsylvania with a huge purse.[15] Tunney spurned all offers to meet Greb in Pennsylvania fearing that Greb would benefit from a home court advantage, despite having benefited from some of the most biased officiating in recent memory in his last two fights against Harry. Instead, the neutral offer from promoters Matt Hinkle and Tommy McGinty was

accepted by both parties.

Before Harry faced Tunney, he first had to get by Buffalo's Jimmy Slattery. Only 20 years old, Slattery had been making a name for himself as a phenom. He had been moved along carefully, as one might expect for such a young fighter, but of late he had increased his level of competition significantly and continued to excel. In less than three years as a professional he had fought nearly fifty times and only lost once, that being a decision loss to Joe Eagan who had turned professional when Slattery was only five years old. To date his greatest win had been over fellow prodigy Young Stribling in a six round decision match. In fact Slattery had only fought more than six rounds once owing to the fact that the law in his home state of New York prohibited a fighter of his age fighting longer.

The fight with Greb was scheduled to take place at Bison Stadium which could potentially seat between fifteen and twenty thousand spectators. It would be fought over six rounds at a stipulated weight of 165 lbs.

To prepare for the fight Slattery enlisted Young Fisher as a sparring partner. In addition to this Greb's old opponent from nearly a decade past, Willie "KO" Brennan, had expressed his willingness to help Slattery prepare. Brennan still harbored a grudge for Greb all these years later and if he could not defeat the man himself he wished to at least assist the fighter who could.

A smaller than expected crowd of paid customers sat in anticipation as the two fighters readied themselves across the ring from one another. Slattery weighed 163 lbs. to Greb's 163^1/$_2$. Greb admitted that he was now in the best condition he had been in since he won the championship.

In the first Slattery showed a great deal of speed and cleverness as he danced around the ring with his hands down, dodging punches. He landed some heavy punches which caught Greb's attention and when Harry worked in close Slattery showed that he was strong enough to tie up the champion.

For three rounds Slattery held his own and stood up well despite a frantic pace. In the third Greb, realizing the fight might be slipping away from him, switched his attack to the body and this immediately started to pay dividends. At the end of the round Slattery suffered a relatively small cut yet his corner seemed unable to stem the flow of blood.

In the fourth Slattery slowed perceptibly. From that point on Harry became increasingly more dominant. He seemed to grow stronger even as Slattery weakened. When the sixth round was over the decision in Greb's favor was well received. Every paper covering the fight conceded that Slattery had given Greb a handful for three rounds but his lack of experience had told and had the fight been scheduled for ten or fifteen rounds Greb likely would have stopped his man.[16]

Harry gave Slattery all the credit that was due to him for being such a young, developing fighter. "This is a great boy," he said after the fight. "I will not be surprised if he becomes a light heavy or heavy champion, not a middleweight, for he is young and growing. He can hit. One

Harry poses here with his new Lincoln Sedanette purchased in the late summer/fall of 1924. This is one of a series of photos that came from Greb's personal collection.

punch in the opening round was all I care for of the kind. And he's very fast and hits well. I thought Tiger Flowers was about the fastest thing I have yet confronted, but this kid beats him."[17]

In 1927 Harry's prediction came true, Slattery gained recognition as the light-heavyweight champion by defeating Maxie Rosenbloom. Slattery went on to be inducted into the Hall of Fame in 2006.

The day after the fight Harry and friends went to Niagara Falls, then down to Erie, and finally stopped off to pick up his training gear before heading to Ohio to prepare for the Tunney fight. The fight was set for September 8 but rain storms forced the promoters to postpone the bout to the following evening. When rain storms again forced a postponement the match was set back to the 17th in order to accommodate a contract Greb had signed to face Billy Hirsch in Mingo Junction on the 15th.

The Mingo Junction bout promised to be a fairly easy paycheck for Harry. Billy Hirsch was an experienced but limited club fighter who despite being game did not have the skill set to challenge a fighter of Greb's caliber. Harry drove to Canton in his new Lincoln Sedanette and entered the ring weighing seventeen pounds heavier than Hirsch at 172 lbs.

The most interesting thing that happened at the contest took place not in the ring but outside of it when a section of the bleachers erected for the contest collapsed under the weight of the audience. Harry outclassed Hirsch easily, forcing the referee to stop the contest in the eighth round to save Hirsch from further punishment.[18]

In facing Tunney next Greb was fighting a man who was now being groomed as an opponent for heavyweight champion Jack Dempsey. After defeating Erminio Spalla on the undercard of Greb's title defense against Ted Moore Tunney fought Georges Carpentier who was only just coming off of his disastrous loss to Tommy Gibbons two months earlier. Carpentier was dominated for nine rounds of cautious, tactical boxing before Gene finally broke through in the tenth to floor Carpentier three times en route to giving the faded Frenchman a brutal beating. Somehow Carpentier found the strength and courage to continue and Tunney went back to patiently breaking his man down when'in the fourteenth round Carpentier was hit with a punch that many felt was low. With Carpentier unable or unwilling to continue Tunney was awarded the victory.

Billy Hirsch was a twenty-two year old middleweight from Canton, Ohio with several years experience in Ohio clubs when he was signed as a "stay busy" opponent for Greb. He had never faced anyone remotely of the caliber of the champion when they met and it showed.

The victory left a sour taste in the mouths of many onlookers. Tunney was clearly winning the fight and winning it handily as was expected but winning such an important battle, which was designed to establish a challenger for Dempsey, in this fashion prompted some in the press to once again point to a bias in favor of Tunney in his home city. Ray Coll of the Pittsburgh Gazette-Times who was seated ringside for the match was prompted to remark:

> **Fight fans have become disgusted with Tunney. Nobody is being fooled about him. They all know he can't lose unless knocked cold. He never fights outside of New York unless he has a set-up. He is the most pampered and protected fighter in the game.**[19]

Coll was probably being somewhat harsh in his criticism (particularly in light of the fact that Tunney had indeed agreed to face Greb outside of New York). Carpentier had a long history of trying to win fights by claiming foul when he could win in no other way. However there was a growing feeling that Tunney was being manufactured as an eventual opponent for Jack Dempsey rather than having to fight his way up the way ladder.

When Greb and Tunney finally met on neutral territory Tunney had once again tried to stack the deck in his favor. He and Billy Gibson had again filled the press with stories of Greb's unfair tactics and hoped the referee would handcuff him. To this end they lobbied hard with promoter Matt Hinkle who was announced as referee to keep a discerning eye on the middleweight champion. On fight night Tunney had not only Billy Gibson working his corner but

Greb's old manager George Engel as well, in hopes of gaining a psychological edge. Greb and Mason for their part tried to have Hinkle replaced unsuccessfully. They defended themselves as best they could in the press and waved off Engel's presence as nothing more than a publicity stunt.

It was a great crowd that witnessed the show. Among those present were former middleweight champion Frank Klaus, and Eddie Kane, manager of Tommy Gibbons who was now negotiating with Tunney for a bout. Greb was accompanied into the ring by Mason and Tom Dolan. The crowd grew restless as both fighters had their gloves put on. Tunney was met with laughter and razzberries when he was announced as the "light heavyweight champion of New York." It looked to most that Tunney outweighed Greb anywhere from twenty to twenty-five pounds although no weights were announced. A long conference was held in ring center as Matt Hinkle went over the final instructions and Greb questioned what would and would not be allowed.

As the fight opened Greb took the offensive and built a strong lead over Tunney, who was criticized for being overly cautious. Greb would continually launch his flying attacks at Tunney who worked primarily to Harry's body. Greb would then tie Tunney up on the inside and work with his right hand free. It was a perplexing strategy to Greb's fans because when he boxed from the outside Greb was far faster than Tunney, who was unable to land. Only when Greb worked his way in close was Tunney able to have any success. Little did those fans know that Greb's accuracy from long range had been greatly reduced with the loss of sight in his eye.

As the rounds wore on, particularly after the seventh, Tunney seemed to put more effort in to his showing and had his best round in the tenth and final round. The few papers that voted for Tunney did so largely based on this last round rally.

When the smoke had cleared three of the four Cleveland newspapers gave the decision to Greb, as did the Pittsburgh Press. Barney McGuire of the Associated Press called the bout a draw while the Pittsburgh Gazette-Times announced the bout a draw but actually had Greb winning more rounds (five rounds to Tunney's three with two even). The Pittsburgh Post and Cleveland News awarded the bout to Tunney by a slim margin, while referee Matt Hinkle stated that had he been allowed to render a decision it would have been a draw or a win for Greb.[20] It is notable that the Cleveland News decision was handed down by Ray Campbell who would go on to work part time as Tunney's press agent.

Both the Cleveland Press and Pittsburgh Press were highly critical of Tunney who they felt had been far too timid for someone who styled himself a champion.

"If Gene Tunney will fight me I'll let him bring his own referee and judges with him and will guarantee as much money as he got in Cleveland Wednesday night," said Harry the day after the fight.

"Of more than twenty writers at ringside only two gave the bout to Tunney, and one of them from his own home town. Three Cleveland papers gave me the fight without question while the Associated Press and The Gazette-Times called it a draw. I think that is conclusive proof that Tunney did not beat me. Gene is one man I can beat and I want to show my friends here that I can beat him. That's why I want to get Tunney in to a local ring with me. He can have the official decision if that means anything to him. All I want is to prove to the fans that I can beat him and will leave it to their judgment. If the light-heavy champ wants a soft piece of change let him fight me in Pittsburgh. I'll grant him the official decision before the start, but I'll prove to everybody that I can beat him."

"If Tunney ever fights me in New York and defends his title by making 175 I'll whip him by a city block. He'll never make that weight and have a show with me. I may not get the decision because of Tunney's position in New York, but I'll satisfy everybody in the house that I can lick the light-heavy champ."[21]

Three days after facing Tunney Greb appeared in an exhibition bout against Harry Meyers as part of the annual Police Athletic Field Day. After this Greb intended to take three weeks off before he was scheduled to meet Tommy Loughran in Philadelphia. It had been rumored that Loughran, who by now had outgrown the middleweight division, had nearly $100,000 in boxing matches lined up over the coming months and Harry hoped that by defeating Loughran he might be able to steal away some of those matches for himself.

Loughran had been inactive for several months owing to an injured hand acquired in training for an aborted match with Tunney earlier in the summer. The hand was now healed and Loughran was focused on gaining a measure of revenge for the previous losses he had sustained at Greb's hands.

Harry, apparently not learning from his loss in Boston to Loughran, intended to train in New York so that he could follow the World Series. While there he was approached by Tex Rickard who wanted to match Greb with Jack Delaney that winter for a middleweight title fight provided Delaney win his upcoming bout against Jimmy Slattery in Madison Square Garden. Harry gave his consent, hoping that Delaney could rehabilitate his reputation enough to garner a large purse. Delaney had already made a step in the right direction by knocking out Frank Moody in August and a win over the rapidly rising Slattery would only help to further his climb back into contention. Unfortunately the match fell through when Delaney was outpointed by Slattery and Harry was once again left wondering when he would be able to break into the big purses.

Greb's stated intention in fighting Flowers, Tunney, and now Loughran was to force a fight with either the light-heavyweight or heavyweight champion, preferably Dempsey. "Give me a ten-round bout with the man-killer, and nothing would suit me more. Jack likes the moving picture game, he has just had that beak re-modeled. I know that if I plastered a few punches on that $10,000 nose, he would lose his head and I could swat it often. Fighting is my business and I could get a lot of money if I could pry my way into that circle."[22]

"I know just what a defeat means," said Greb upon arriving in Philadelphia. "I am ready and will carry Loughran faster than he ever traveled in his life. I am after the light heavy-weights and the heavyweights and a defeat by Loughran would certainly ruin my chances. I am going to fight as Philadelphians have never seen me fight. I cannot be satisfied with just edging this fellow out of the decision at the end of ten rounds. I must knock him out if I can. Yes, I am going to work today, and then I am ready for the fastest fight of my life. I cannot get any middleweight matches and here is where I start to prove I have a punch and compel the big fellows to meet me."[23]

Loughran was more reserved in his prediction yet no less confident. "I met him before. I don't say I can knock him out. I don't believe Jack Dempsey could do that. So he plans a speedy fight, eh. Well, right into my hands if he does, for that is exactly what I am going to make him do, battle every second. I am the faster man, the better boxer. Him knock me out, never. I hope he opens up as he always does, I might nail him."[24]

The crowd of six or seven thousand were fully behind their local hero and it didn't help that Greb drew the ire of referee Frank McCracken before the fight even started. When the men were called to ring center for their final instructions Greb remarked "You don't have to tell us the Pennsylvania boxing rules. We know them."

The bout itself was a fast one that found Greb warned for rough tactics, primarily holding and hitting, a back hand punch, and using his head. All which counted against Harry when the scores were tabulated. Judge Jack Kelly, who would one day be the father of Grace Kelly, gave the fight to Loughran. The other judge, Harry McGrath, awarded the bout to Greb while refer-ee Frank McCracken called the bout a draw. The Philadelphia Evening Bulletin felt that Greb had deserved the decision and even Frank McCracken, writing for the Public Ledger hinted that Greb had fought better than Loughran but only awarded the draw due to Greb's rough fighting.

When the decision was announced Harry just smiled and shook his head in disbelief. Red Mason literally doubled over in laughter at what he considered one of the poorest decisions he had ever seen rendered. One fan who had been loudly rooting for Loughran throughout the bout walked away from the ring admitting his man had lost.[25]

"Rotten!" said Tommy, when asked his thoughts on the decision. "I think I outpointed him enough to earn the decision and besides Greb's foul fighting counted against him."[26]

Harry was incredulous. "It was a worse decision than the one they handed me when I lost my American light-heavyweight title to Tunney in New York. I licked Loughran worse tonight than I did last time in Pittsburgh and he knows it. I think the decision was a joke."[27]

In less than two months Harry had faced four young men who would soon be recognized as champions and would one day be inducted into boxing's Hall of Fame. Greb had at least held each of the four opponents even and could easily argue victory in all four bouts. It was a great accomplishment for a faded, aging fighter. It seemed as if Greb was attempting to defeat father time himself.

Once again Harry took several weeks off to recuperate. He had suffered from a rib injury acquired in the fight with Tiger Flowers which had been aggravated by both the Tunney and Loughran fights. Harry took nearly a month to heal before he was scheduled to face Otto Hughes in Phillipsburgh as part of the Armistice Day celebration there on November 11.

When Hughes refused to fight, claiming sickness, Lou Comasana of the Philippines, sparring partner of Pedro Campo, who appeared on the undercard was substituted. Comasana was a total unknown and to make matters worse he was described as a "a grinning old yellow man, introduced as the middleweight champion of the Philippine Islands but who, some of the boys who swam the river with Funston back in 1898, said looked like Emilio Aguinaldo's grand-pap."[28] Harry toyed with Comasana, giving the audience their money's worth before stopping him in the second.[29]

Six days later Harry would face Jimmy Delaney of Saint Paul at Motor Square Garden in Pittsburgh, turning in one of the most dramatic performances of his career. The local fans had not seen Harry perform in his hometown since his May bout with Pal Reed and they were anxious to see their hero. Harry was anxious to give the his fans a good show.

Delaney was a twenty-three year old protégé of Mike Gibbons. He was a natural light heavyweight, standing over six feet tall and weighing 175 lbs. He boxed in the classic Saint Paul style, working in and out, setting everything up with the jab, and trying to draw leads over which he could counter. Against Greb he planned to utilize a body attack in hopes of slowing Harry up. He had only lost four times since turning pro in 1919, two of those losses coming at the hands of Gene Tunney. Delaney was just returning from a tour of the west coast which saw him participate in six fights in just under one month. Harry had originally been scheduled to face Delaney two years earlier but a combination of his impending split with George Engel, his eye troubles, and Mildred's health had forced him to cancel the match. Ever since then Delaney had been telling anyone who would listen that Greb had ducked the match. Greb intended to pay him back in kind for his slight.

There was much riding on the match. For the two previous weeks Motor Square Garden had promoted two unsatisfactory shows. On November 3 Cuddy Demarco had turned in a listless performance against Pep O'Brien which left the fans unsatisfied. A week later it seemed that the Garden had scored a hit when Jack Zivic and Nate Goldman put on a vicious battle. Yet, in the third round, as the crowd was reaching a boiling point, Zivic claimed a foul. Many in the audience left the arena muttering that Zivic had quit just as Goldman was beginning to make things too hot for him. A third successive unsatisfactory show could put future boxing promotions at the Garden in jeopardy.

It had been planned to have both Delaney and Greb hold public training sessions every day for a week leading up to the fight in order to build interest but Greb was called away to New York to negotiate with promoters eager to feature him in a big bout. While out east he took in the boxing match between Luis Firpo and Charlie Weinert in Newark, New Jersey, cheering

Jimmy Delaney was a talented protege of Mike Gibbons. Delaney had been after Greb since late 1922 when he accused Greb of ducking out of a match with him. When they finally met in November 1924 it provided Greb with one of his most dramatic victories.

Weinert and shouting tactical advice from ringside. Back in New York Paul Berlenbach had been scheduled to face Tony Marullo but backed out when he suffered an injury. Battling Siki was substituted for Berlenbach. Greb was eager to make a quick purse and offered promoters to face either Siki or Marullo on short notice. The promoters were eager but both Siki and Marullo declined leaving Greb to focus on Jimmy Delaney.

Greb opened his public sparring sessions by working with Cuddy DeMarco, Johnny King, and Jack Barry. He showed excellent conditioning and it was thought by many that he had regained some of the form he seemed to have lost when he let his conditioning slide the previous winter. Delaney as well made several supporters with his showings in the gym and everything looked set for a terrific show.

Harry entered the ring weighing four pounds less than Delaney who weighed in at 173. As the first round began both men met in ring center and began exchanging punches. Neither fighter had yet warmed up when Delaney landed a foul blow directly on Greb's protective cup which sent Harry to his knees with a cry of agony. The audience shot upright and began to grumble that another bloomer had been pulled off at Motor Square Garden. Harry was dragged back to his corner by Red Mason and Tom Dolan while Eddie Kennedy, and Commissioner Havey Boyle oversaw club physician Doc Briney administer to Greb. Delaney stood in his corner explaining that the blow was an accident.

After five minutes a loud cheer rang out when it was announced that Greb wished to continue. As the round resumed Greb looked weak and shaken from the blow but still managed to take that round and the next on heart and determination.

In the third Harry had regained some of his strength and was tearing into Delaney when another low blow landed on Greb's cup with an audible clunk. Harry collapsed in a heap moaning. The audience was in an uproar with cries of "Throw Delaney out!" Greb was dragged to his corner where he lost consciousness and vomited over the side of the ring.

Members of the audience began milling around and heading for the doors. After more than five minutes Greb was brought around and seeing the commotion in the audience announced that he would finish the fight "if it killed him."

A murmur began to wash over the crowd which carried to the ears of those outside of the arena who had left in disgust. People were saying that Greb would continue. In utter disbelief those who had left filed back into the arena dumfounded and saw that their hero would resume the contest. As they took their seats announcer Al Foss took to the ring and confirmed the rumor that Harry would indeed continue. The crowd went wild, standing on their chairs and cheering Harry to the rafters.

When the fight continued Harry went on the offensive. He continually bulled his way inside, refusing to give Delaney a chance to breath or get set. On top of his man all the time Greb punched incessantly refusing to permit Delaney to counter, or to create distance with which to use his height and reach advantages. When it was all over Greb had remarkably won every round despite the damaging fouls and in refusing to claim victory on a foul had saved the show and the reputation of Motor Square Garden.[30]

After the fight Delaney gave Greb the credit he was due. "Both blows were unavoidable," he said sheepishly, "and I know they hurt because I had everything behind them. Greb is the greatest fighter I have ever seen or ever hope to see."[31]

Within days of defeating Delaney Harry agreed to face Jeff Smith in Pittsburgh on December 1. Smith had been complaining for over a year that Greb was ducking him and so Harry was eager to prove this accusation false. While he waited for the match to be finalized he picked up some easy money by knocking out twenty-four year old West Virginia club fighter Frankie Ritz at Wheeling.[32]

The Smith fight fell through when it was discovered that Smith was obligated to face Gene Tunney in New Orleans the following week and did not want to face two such daunting opponents so close together. Instead Kansas contender Billy Britton was substituted for Smith. Britton had been making a name for himself in the division as a young and developing fighter of whom great things were expected. However, as negotiations opened for the match Britton was defeated handily in Detroit by a twenty five year old law school graduate named Bob Sage. Promoters instead attempted to sign Sage to face Greb but when Sage injured his wrist in training the card was postponed and ultimately scrapped when Harry decided that he could get a bigger purse in Detroit where Sage was better known on January 9.

Smith drew Harry's ire when Harry offered to box Smith New Year's Eve to accommodate his schedule. When Smith backed out of the fight owing to an injured hand acquired in the Tunney fight Greb went to the press and gave Smith some of his own medicine. "That guy has been popping off for two years about fighting me," said Harry, "and now he crawls out of it when I offer him a chance. This is the last time. I'll never give him another chance as long as I'm in the game. S'final!"[33]

Harry took most of December off, only appearing as a guest referee or in exhibitions and doing light training. On December 9 he was ringside at Madison Square Garden to watch Tommy Gibbons knock out Kid Norfolk in the sixth round and Tiger Flowers stop Johnny Wilson in the third. If the two performances worried Harry he didn't show it. Rather, he saw dollar signs, hoping to challenge the two winners in the near future. "I've fought and beaten the four of them," said Harry the following day, "I whipped Gibbons in the same ring two years ago, trounced Norfolk in Pittsburgh in 10 hard rounds, made a mess of Flowers in his own bailiwick and repeated over Wilson in Madison Square Garden... I'd have liked to have been in there last night with any of the four and I'd have won under wraps."[34]

Two days after Flowers stopped Wilson Harry was approached by Jimmy Johnston with an offer to defend his title against Flowers the following summer at one of the major league ball parks for $50,000. It was a tremendous opportunity and one which Greb was eager for but he was also leery of the far off date. "Fifty grand, eh? Sounds good, and coming from Johnston, too. Well, maybe, but June is a long ways off and a lot of things can happen between now and seven or eight months hence."[35] His words could not have been more prophetic.

One week after Greb had received the offer to face Flowers news of a most sensational variety broke. It was announced that Harry was soon to be wed. The story emanated from Chicago where Harry had been on "business." While in the Windy City Greb had reacquainted himself with a pretty blonde chorus girl named Louise Walton, whom he had met the previous month in Pittsburgh. Walton had been performing in the musical comedy Plain Jane, which had won rave reviews in New York and was now traveling the circuit. The show featured a mock boxing match. At every opportunity the producers had acquired popular local boxers to act as the referee in the match in order to increase interest. In November, while the show was being performed at the Nixon in Pittsburgh, Harry had appeared in the production to positive reviews.

While in Chicago under the pretense of working out details with Frank Mulkern for a bout in Milwaukee, Harry and Louise had reconnected. During a night of revelry Louise, Kid Howard, and Harry blundered in to the night court and, according to Harry, what had been intended as a practical joke was quickly embellished by the press.[36] "The report of a marriage, or of an intended one," said Harry, "was the result of a practical joke."

"The Judge asked me if I would like to marry Louise. I said I'd marry her in a minute, but that was only in jest. The judge asked Louise if she would marry me. She said she would have to keep on with her part in the 'Plain Jane' company. Still joking, we began to argue. I said I wouldn't allow my wife to work. Louise said she wouldn't quit. 'Kid' Howard dashed out, borrowed a wedding ring, came back and handed it to the Judge."

"Then a flock of reporters and photographers rushed in. I hid my face, but Louise got her picture taken. When we denied we were married no one would believe us. We went to dinner, and they played the wedding march for us, and turned the spotlights on us. At her performance that night, Louise was introduced as 'Mrs. Harry Greb.'"

"She's a nice girl, and we are the best of friends. But there was no wedding."[37]

Harry explained away their being at the night court simply enough by stating that Louise, Kid Howard, and he had gone there to meet Judge Jacobs for a dinner date when the joking began.

Walton seemed to enjoy the publicity and ran with the story. She granted interviews and talked at length of her engagement to Harry even as Greb continued to deny those reports. For three weeks the press continued to print stories on the affair and every time they began to die down Walton was quick to grant another interview to keep her name in the papers. Harry seemingly ended the matter in a statement made in Detroit as he prepared for his upcoming bout with Bob Sage. "It is difficult for me to believe that Miss Walton gave out such a ridiculous and untrue statement."

"However I desire to make this much plain, I am not engaged to be married to Miss Walton. I do not care to comment further on the subject as I regard marriage as sacred and therefore prefer not to speak lightly concerning it."[38]

The matter had caused Greb a great deal of embarrassment. He had been romantically involved for several months with a young Beaver County girl named Naomi Braden who was decidedly unhappy when she discovered in the newspapers that Harry was being seen around Chicago with another woman, much less one he supposedly intended to marry.[39]

Coming off an easy New Year's Day victory over Augie Ratner,[40] Harry went into the Sage fight with controversy once again surrounding the articles of agreement. The bout had been advertised as a title fight but when Harry signed the contract he had written into the articles that the match would be above 160 pounds relegating the fight to non-title status. The articles Sage signed had no such stipulation. When Harry arrived in Detroit and learned that some parties and the press were pushing for a championship match Greb became wary. He demanded that the articles he signed stand and added that he would not fight unless he

Harry had a brief relationship with chorus girl Louise Walton in late 1924 and early 1925 which provided much fodder for tabloid journalists. Walton apparently reveled in the publicity and seemed more than willing to feed the reporters copy at every opportunity.

got to pick the referee and incredibly one of the judges. The promoters of the match saw no other way to salvage the situation and relented. Harry chose Al Foss as his referee and close friend Bernard "Happy" Albacker as a judge.[41]

As it turned out Harry did not need the extra protection. He defeated Sage easily, winning every round. The press was critical of the job Al Foss had done as referee but even Sage's most ardent supporters admitted that he could have had his closest family members as officials and still would have lost by a wide margin.[42]

Despite having a busy winter campaign planned out with matches lined up against Jimmy Delaney, Johnny Klesch, Billy Britton, Johnny Papke, and Young Fisher, interspersed with exhibition appearances, Harry was distracted by the upcoming bout between Tiger Flowers and Jack Delaney in Madison Square Garden which would determine his next logical contender. Much was made of Delaney's inconsistent performances and of Flowers' great showing against Greb in Fremont to the point where many felt it was a forgone conclusion that the Tiger from Atlanta would be Harry's next opponent. Promoters were already lining up in hopes of securing the lucrative match and Harry himself had bet $500 on Flowers.

Prior to the match Harry and Paul Berlenbach were introduced from ringside and it was announced that Berlenbach would face the winner and Harry would face the winner of that match.

Flowers came out with his usual rush, weaving like a snake as he forced Delaney around the ring. Delaney seemed puzzled by Flowers' speed and aggression and spent most of the round laying back defensively with his left hand extended trying to gauge Tiger's speed and time his rushes.

In the second round Flowers again came out aggressively but now Delaney began to prod and poke with his left, finding the range and just trying to touch Flowers, while hiding his right behind his left shoulder. Less than a minute into the round Flowers weaved to his left and Delaney finally unleashed his right, straight from the shoulder snapping Flowers head back. Delaney then followed up with a right uppercut that dropped Tiger in a heap on the canvas and sent the crowd to their feet. Flowers rolled over and tried to rise at the count of seven but failed. When the referee reached ten Flowers crawled on all fours toward his corner with blood bubbling from his nose and mouth. With that image dancing before him Harry's hoped for $50,000 bout with Flowers in the summer evaporated.[43]

Immediately Flowers' diminutive manager Walk Miller began a campaign whereby he tried to convince anyone who would listen that Delaney had cheated his way to victory and that he had in fact used loaded gloves during the fight. He became so insistent, and so exasperating to the press that he was ever after labeled "Squawk" Miller. The tactic may not have halted the media scrutiny into Flowers' susceptibility to the knockout but it did get him a rematch with Delaney the following month.

While waiting for the outcome Red Mason kept Harry busy, fearing that he would again let

HARRY GREB

The Middleweight Champion of the World

And the Champion of Champions

Greb fights them all. All sizes all Colors and all Weights. Will even tackle a Klu-Kluxer in a Klu Klux City. The One and only fighting Champion.

JACK DEMPSEY who seldom fights is now a Picture Actor and don't want his new nose hurt. MIKE McTIGUE who won it in Ireland and won't fight anywhere else. BENNY LEONARD who fights Lew Tendler every three years and wants to take Edwin Booth's place as a legitimate Actor and is suffering from a bad case of to much thumb. JOHNNY DUNDEE who is to old to fight, but was a good one in his day. ABE GOLDSTEIN who will fight anyone the Undertaker selects. PANCHO VILLA who fights when things are fixed just right!

Greb has fought and defended his title five times inside a year, at 158½ pounds. Greb only whipped Tom Gibbons four times, while Jack Dempsey the greatest heavyweight of all time, also won a 15 round decision over the same Gibbons. Greb will fight Dempsey any time, any place although Kearns and Dempsey states Greb is to small. Greb only murdered Jack Renault three times and now the latter is said to be ready for Dempsey. Greb will fight all the Foreign Greasers like Firpo Carpentier, Romero Rojas, Spalla and the like, every week.

The Cry set up by Dempsey and the other big Hulks now adays is that Greb is to small. In the Old Days it was the other way, a fellow was too big.

Greb is the one and only present day Champion that always gives the fans what they pay for a Fight. The present day Commissions and Club matchmakers say that Greb is the one fighter that gives them no trouble and fights for a reasonable amount of what he draws.

All the above is sworn to and can be verified by writing to JAMES MASON. Manager of HARRY GREB, The World's Middleweight Champion. 5527 Claybourne Street, Pittsburgh, Pa. Bell Phone, Montrose 1421.

This promotional flyer was likely issued by Red Mason in late 1924 or early 1925. The reference to the Ku Klux Klan is a thinly veiled jab at Young Stribling who was accused by Mike McTigue of having been supported by the Klan.

his conditioning slide as it had the previous spring. He easily defeated Cleveland's Johnny Papke on a seven round TKO when Papke's manager Jimmy Dunn threw in the towel to save Papke from Greb's onslaught.[44]

Harry then faced Jimmy Delaney in a rematch of their controversial November bout. Several locations had bid on the bout but Harry elected to accept the offer from Delaney's hometown of St. Paul. Mike Gibbons drilled Delaney tirelessly on how to beat Greb and offered a unique first-hand account of Greb's puzzling style:

> Mike explained that Harry has a habit of going through a number of busy but wholly useless motions calculated to upset an opponent and prepare him for the damaging punches. Like a sleight of hand performer, he throws in a lot of gestures to conceal the sudden movement that turns the trick.
>
> The problem is to be able to ignore the flashing feints and meaningless steps and to pick out the sign that advertises the real attack. If that can be done there is a fair chance to landing solidly upon this dancing target and Mike believes it can be done.[45]

Detroit's law student boxer Bob Sage who fought Greb in January 1925. Sage would go on to have a successful law career before murdering an associate and taking his own life in the 1940s.

Gibbons and Delaney sold the fight to the public on the idea that Greb had not been fouled by Delaney in Pittsburgh but had been legitimately knocked down, despite their earlier admission. This irritated Harry who was intent on not only avoiding any similar mishaps but punishing Delaney for the stories he was putting out.

For two rounds Harry started at an even pace, easily outpointing Delaney but never really pouring on the speed that he was known for. In the third and fourth Delaney slowed Greb up with body punches and for a time it looked as if Delaney had solved Greb's style. In the fifth Greb halted Delaney's momentum and from the sixth round on steadily increased the pace and so exhausted Delaney that no one doubted the champion had won. Harry scored a flash knockdown in the seventh and by the final rounds Delaney had suffered cuts under both eyes and on his nose, as well as a pair of swollen, bloody lips. Despite being fined $250 for arriving in town three days later than contracted Harry had made a hit with local fans and plans were already under way to bring him back against Jock Malone or Gene Tunney on St. Patrick's Day.[46]

Harry followed up the win with a surprisingly competitive victory over a young Kansas fighter named Billy Britton at Allentown, Pennsylvania. During the fight Harry seemed to be protecting his left hand and rarely threw it, he also suffered a cut left eye in the fourth round.[47] Six days later Harry defeated Young Fisher by a sixth round disqualification in Scranton. The fight was an unsatisfactory one with Greb never showing to his full arsenal and Fisher totally outclassed and unwilling, or unable to mount any kind of offense against Greb. Finally Fisher was disqualified for failing to give an effort and his entire purse was confiscated, less $47 for hotel and traveling expenses.[48]

Three days after the poorly received fight with Young Fisher Harry was once again ringside to watch Tiger Flowers and Jack Delaney square off to decide whether the first fight was held on its merits or if Flowers could reverse the stunning defeat. The fight itself began almost exactly as the first fight. Flowers rushed from his corner and jumped

Cleveland's Johnny Papke, who faced Greb at Zanesville in early 1925 was a respected if somewhat limited fighter. However, as a trainer Papke became an Ohio legend. Developing fighters for decades from the amateurs all the way through to some of the most celebrated professionals of the sport.

out to an early lead. Once again Delaney laid back, content to allow Flowers to force the fight. Then suddenly, near the end of the fourth round, Delaney saw his opening and uncorked a right hand that caused Flowers to crumple along the ropes and onto the canvas.

Referee Patsy Haley quickly stepped in and waved Delaney to a neutral corner. Flowers got up quickly but was clearly dazed and when Haley waved the fight on Delaney rushed at Flowers intent on finishing his man. Flowers, seeing Delaney charging at him, dropped to the canvas without being hit. In the heat of the moment Delaney threw a right hand that by some accounts either landed on the shoulder, or full on the face of Flowers. Haley once again jumped between the fighters and sent Delaney to a neutral corner. This time though Haley signaled his intention to disqualify Delaney for hitting Flowers while he was down. Immediately the crowd erupted. Many in the audience shouted reminders that Flowers had gone down without being

hit, a foul in New York State punishable by disqualification. Those parties argued that it was Flowers who should have been disqualified. Haley seemed unsure of what to do and after several minutes decided to allow the fight to continue and the fourth round fought over as if nothing had ever happened. Just over a minute into the second fourth round Delaney caught Flowers with a terrific right hand on the jaw that sent Flowers sprawling in the center of the ring and out.[49]

Immediately after the fight Tex Rickard and Frank Flournoy sent word to Red Mason, who had remained in Pittsburgh, to come to New York in order to discuss terms for the proposed Greb-Delaney match. Mason left that night for New York and before he had arrived in the city Jack Delaney inexplicably announced that he was done with the middleweight division and would henceforth set his sights on the light-heavyweight division.[50] Completely ignoring the fact that he had now blown two proposed title fights with Greb, he blamed Harry, stating he felt like he was being avoided. In reality Tex Rickard was already planning on matching Mike McTigue with Paul Berlenbach for the title in the near future, a match that most felt Berlenbach would win handily. Delaney and his manager Pete Reilly likely felt that the easiest way to a championship was through either McTigue, one of the weakest champions of that or any other era, or Berlenbach, whom Delaney had already knocked out once.

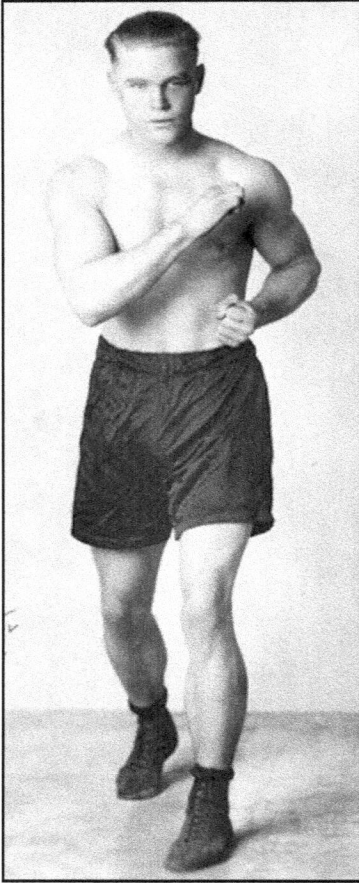

Billy Britton of Cherokee County, Kansas was born a coal miner but blessed with the skills of a fighter. He fought his way out of the mining camps often beating men much older and larger then he. By the time he faced Greb three times in 1925 he was being called the Kansas Cyclone and drawing comparisons to Stanley Ketchel.

With Delaney forsaking the middleweights Harry was left once again without a dance partner for the big open air match he had been waiting over a year to take part in. His greatest opponent was time. He was an aging fighter, battle scarred and ring worn. His dedication to the sport was waning and it was more difficult to attain the kind of conditioning that once came easily. Harry was nearly thirty-one years old and in the twilight of his career. He had never made the kind of bonanza purses that some of the other popular fighters of the era benefited from and if he did not start finding the big paydays soon it was a very real possibility that he would retire without his financial future secure, half blind, and without any skills. It was a daunting thought.

Harry had committed himself to face Gene Tunney in St. Paul on St. Patrick's Day but while in New York he was taken aside by Frank Flournoy and asked why he had done such a foolish thing when he could have received far more money facing Tunney in New York. Greb replied that he would rather risk a possible loss to Tunney in a fair fight for less money in St. Paul, than face a certain loss to Tunney in a fixed fight in New York for greater financial gain.[51]

Harry returned to Pittsburgh and intended to leave within a few days for Hot Springs, Arkansas where he would condition himself for the Tunney bout. The trip was delayed several days when in the early morning hours of March 1 Harry, accompanied by his girlfriend Naomi Braden and acquaintance Patricia Jones, was returning to his apartment where the party were to meet Mrs. Jones' husband after spending the evening at an event at Motor Square Garden. The party decided to take a detour through Highland Park when Naomi noticed a vehicle following them. The vehicle sped past them and a few minutes later the party came across a man waving them down. Harry stepped out to help the man and was told that he had been beaten and robbed by four friends he had been riding with. The men had thrown him from the vehicle and left him.

The man appeared to be bleeding but as he got closer Harry noticed the blood looked more like paint and began to feel uneasy about the situation. Just then several men approached from the bushes and were identified by the first man as his assailants. Sensing a setup Greb warned the men "Listen fellows, you know me, I'm Harry Greb." "The dickens you are," one replied before taking a swing at Greb. As Harry fought with the attackers the first man hopped into Greb's car in an effort to rob the two young women. Mrs. Jones fainted, while Naomi kicked the man in the face with her heal, bit, and scratched him before he was able to make off with her purse and a diamond ring. Naomi then swung into action. She jumped into the driver's seat, wheeled the car around and shouted for Harry, who had knocked one man out and was fighting off the others, to jump in.

They sped off and dropped Patricia off at Harry's apartment where they picked up a revolver and a baseball bat before returning to the scene of the crime. The men were still there, apparently in the midst of fighting amongst themselves. Greb exchanged words with them, intent on continuing the fight before Naomi convinced him to leave and report the incident to the police.[52] Early the next day George A. Seibert was arrested when his wife called the local police station to see if anyone had reported their vehicle found in the vicinity of Highland Park. Seibert claimed to have been drinking the night before and had little memory of the events despite wearing the tell-tale marks Naomi had left him, chiefly a severely scratched face and the bruised imprint of her heel on his forehead.[53]

Within days five more men had been arrested in connection with the nights events, Edward Brendle, William Saunders, Earl Conway, George Dietz, William Grant, and Robert Killen, who was tracked to a hospital bed after his blood was found all over the crime scene. Remarkably, and hinting that there was much more to the story than has been revealed to history, after several of the suspects had been positively identified by Greb and Naomi, Harry refused to press charges and even changed his story to exonerate the men and offered to pay Brendle's bond if police would free him.[54] Despite this there was enough evidence to hold the men on suspicion but the case fell apart when it went before a judge who had no choice but to rule that Harry and his companions had happened upon and became entangled in a drunken brawl.[55] The Pittsburgh Gazette-Times noted immediately after the event that there were persistent rumors that the attack had not been a robbery at all, as was first surmised, but had been devised as an act of revenge against Greb for a "personal grudge."[56]

As the apparent holdup was being investigated Harry once again found himself in the newspapers. A few days after the incident in Highland Park a complaint was made by Harry Meyers to the police that he and Greb had been cheated in a game of craps by two women at Greb's apartment. According to Meyers he and Greb had met the two women at the State House, a speakeasy on Wylie Avenue. An interesting description of the nightclub can be found in a 1925 pamphlet titled "A Study Of Dance Halls In Pittsburgh" published by the Pittsburgh Girls Conference.

The hall is not very large and the dance floor is very small. While not particularly unattractive, it is very plainly furnished and little effort has been made to make it aesthetically pleasing. During the singing colored spot lights are used and tend to create an impression of "art" in excess of actuality.

As we entered we were greeted in the most familiar manner by the waiters. The things they said and the way they said them gave me the impression that, perhaps, regular habitués were acquainted with some "pass-word" that would identify them as reliable frequenters and friends of the establishment. At any rate, quite a bit of whiskey was sold, yet I was unable to buy any.

This cabaret caters to a sort of sporting class and has been identified by some people as Harry Greb's "hangout". Some two months ago it received free advertisement as a result of this champion boxer's being duped by two young girls he had met here. Some of the patrons present on the occasion of my visit were vaudeville actors.

The patrons seem to be "good spenders" and from all appearances were having a good time. The vocal selections were greeted with much enthusiasm. In fact, I felt as if unusual interest was manifested in all that was taking place. A great many of the people danced, few of them using freakish or objectionable steps.[57]

According to Meyers the two women had accompanied Harry and he back to Greb's apartment where a crap game was started. Several hours later one of the women allegedly switched the dice for a loaded pair and "cleaned out" Harry and Meyers. The two women matched the description of two women who had recently been accused in a similar incident which began at another nightclub.[58]

Harry went on damage control and gave his own version of events which seemed somewhat flimsy at best. "A story like that is humiliating," he said, "because it puts a fellow in the light of being a squawker, besides making it appear that he's pretty careless about what goes on in his apartment. Here's what really happened."

"I dropped in at a cabaret in Wylie avenue early this morning with a friend, and when we were about to call a cab and go to my apartment Harry Meyers, who was sitting nearby with two young women and who overheard our conversation, volunteered to take us home in his car. He did so, my friend and I and the two young women entering the machine."

"When we arrived at my house I said to our companions, because it seemed only courteous to do so, 'Will you come up for a while?'"

"Meyers and his two friends accepted the invitation. I supposed they would stay only a few minutes. I was very tired and after a little time I excused myself and went to bed, leaving my friend to entertain our three guests, whom I supposed would go very soon."

"I quickly fell asleep. Later I was aroused by the sound of quarreling. Only half awake, I called out, asking what was the matter. Meyers answered, 'She stole my money.'"

"I responded that if they had a dispute to settle they would have to go outside to settle it. I heard them leave in the car."

"I not only did not shoot craps with those folks, but I did not know till I was awakened that there had been any crap shooting. As a matter of fact that's a form of diversion that I don't indulge in and never has been practiced in my apartment with my knowledge. But let me say this, if I had been in the game and I had been trimmed, I wouldn't have gone to the detective bureau about it."[59]

The following day Harry left for Hot Springs where he intended to train for the Tunney fight and no doubt to get away from the prying questions of the press. While he was away the two women involved in the rigged crap game were arrested and fined $25 each on a charge being suspicious persons. Apparently the two did not learn their lesson as five years later they appeared before the same judge for the same offense.

Harry had a lot of ground to cover in a little time. The rib injury suffered against Tiger Flowers had plagued him off and on and had been re-aggravated in the fight with the alleged bandits in Highland Park. Harry would need extra time to heal if he was to give his best effort against a damaging body puncher like Tunney. He asked for a postponement of ten days from St. Paul promoters. Initially the promoters, eager to have a St. Patrick's Day promotion tried to get Jack Delaney or Young Stribling to face Tunney in Greb's stead. Delaney flat out refused and Stribling's demands were so excessive that promoters were forced to abandon the March 17 date and grant Greb his delay.

While Greb had been the subject of what today would be tabloid headlines for his early morning activities Tunney had been down in Florida training like a Spartan. The young former marine had continued to improve steadily. He sacrificed his personal life in order to continually perfect his style, technique, and physical conditioning. He had one goal in mind: To win the heavyweight championship and his dedication was rapidly paying dividends. Tunney had now essentially forsaken the light heavyweight division and announced his intention to work toward a fight with Jack Dempsey. To that end, even as he prepared to face Greb, he was in deep negotiations for a major bout with Tommy Gibbons in New York which would determine Dempsey's top white challenger.

In Pittsburgh Greb's fans worried that he was taking a chance fighting Tunney in St. Paul, Gibbons' hometown. They feared that with negotiations already under way it would be difficult for Greb to win a decision over Tunney that would upset the proposed Gibbons-Tunney match. Tunney himself intended to use a victory over Greb as leverage in the negotiations. The idea of Tunney beating him, much less looking ahead to using him as leverage irritated Greb. As confident as always and still convinced that he had beaten Tunney four times out of four Harry looked on the fight as a golden opportunity. He declared that when he beat Tunney he should be given the shot at Gibbons. He felt he had Tunney's number and by beating Tunney he would then place himself squarely in line to face Gibbons and once again establish himself as Dempsey's leading white contender.

The fight was greatly anticipated in the Twin Cities. Not since hometown heroes Mike Gibbons and Mike O'Dowd faced each other before the motion picture cameras in 1919 had a fight been so eagerly awaited. Speculation on the outcome was a topic of discussion in all corners of the sporting community locally. Jimmy Delaney who had faced both men publicly stated that he favored Greb, who opened as a 6 to 5 favorite in the betting odds.[60]

The press took a poll of local personalities opinions on who would win. Tommy Gibbons, and amateur golf champion Jimmy Johnston picked Tunney. Mike Gibbons and Jimmy Potts picked Greb. Fred Fulton said it was too close to call but called both men the best in the business. Jimmy Delaney who visited the camps of both men when they arrived in St. Paul marveled at Tunney's improvement since he last faced him a year ago and switched his vote from Greb to Tunney. Jock Malone, who had been in Hot Springs while Greb was there sent back reports to the commission, which had been concerned about Greb's conditioning in light of his recent after hours activities, that Greb was rounding in to

Gene Tunney (right) jogs with sparring partner Kid Muskie across the Wabasha Street Bridge in preparation for his match with Greb.

excellent shape and picked Greb to win, despite being squarely in Tunney's camp when Greb fought Gene in December of 1923.

Prior to the fight Red Mason discovered that the contracts he had signed made no mention of weight. How he missed such an important factor is a mystery but quickly Mason scrambled to try unsuccessfully to have Tunney forced to make the light heavyweight limit. It was a major oversight on Mason's part and one which gave Tunney an advantage that Greb had been eager to erase when he challenged Tunney after their last bout. When the men weighed in Greb weighed $167^1/_2$ to Tunney's $181^1/_2$. It was the largest announced weight disparity of any of their contests.

Harry got off to an early lead against Tunney. Nearly all reports credit him with win-

Top: Harry and Red Mason arrive in St. Paul March 24, 1925 for Harry's fight with Gene Tunney. Below: Greb hops a fence while jogging six miles along Lake Harriet in training for his match with Tunney.

ning the second and third rounds handily while getting at least a draw in the first round (some credit that round to Greb as well). Harry had come out characteristically fast and aggressive, showering Tunney with punches then tying him up on the inside. In the second he landed a perfect combination that sent Tunney flailing back onto his heels. The tide began to change in the fourth round when it seemed that the body punching of Tunney was beginning to tell on Greb. The round was close but it was Tunney's. From the fifth round on Greb became unusually passive. His rapid fire attacks ceased and instead he continually clinched and held, trying to minimize the action, and only showing spurts of token offense.

During the fight Red Mason kept up a constant chatter from ringside, at times coaching Greb and at others directed at Tunney to rattle the fighter. In the seventh Tunney landed a perfect

Harry (left) shakes hands with Tunney prior to their fifth bout held in St. Paul on March 27, 1925. Referee George Barton is seen between the two men.

punch to Greb's nose causing it to bleed. Greb paid him back in kind in the eighth opening an old cut over Tunney's left eye, yet still lost the round. The pace of the fight had slowed increasingly from the fifth round on until the tenth when the disgusted audience began to file out, weary of the uninteresting contest. The fault lay squarely with Greb who seemed to be fighting only to survive and seemed glad when the contest was finished. Every paper present awarded the victory to Tunney by varying margins. Some awarded Greb as many as three rounds to Tunney's five with two even. Most gave Greb two rounds, Tunney six, and two even. A small minority gave Tunney as many as eight rounds to Greb's two.[61]

While Greb was guilty of rendering the fight a disappointment several supported him and sympathized with his tactics citing the weight disparity. Tommy Gibbons himself defended Greb stating that he found the fight interesting.[62] Mike Gibbons, seated ringside, called Tunney one of the craftiest ring generals he had seen in years, a compliment that Tunney no doubt appreciated as he had worked hard to learn and emulate the St. Paul style which Mike originated.[63] George Barton noted that the weight difference, combined with Tunney's improvement and Greb's decline, were all too much for Harry to overcome.[64] What nobody realized was that the rib injury suffered against Tiger Flowers, which had seemingly never healed, was re-aggravated by Tunney's body blows in the fourth round of the fight causing Greb's sudden change in tactics. Rather than use the injury as an excuse Harry went to Gene's dressing room after the fight and congratulated his bitter rival. "You are getting too big and too strong for me," he told Gene. "You are hitting better and harder than ever. If you fight Tommy Gibbons my money will go down on you."[65]

23

THE TOY BULLDOG

After his bout with Tunney Harry ignored his injured ribs and committed himself to a busy spring schedule which he hoped would keep him in shape and out of trouble, with the ultimate goal being a successful title defense in one of the large New York venues during the summer for a fat purse. His two most likely options for such a fight were Jack Delaney and welterweight champion Mickey Walker. Greb was more eager for the Delaney fight feeling that Delaney's reputation and greater size would add interest and make for a better gate. Walker had been interested in a fight with Greb for nearly two years and talk of matching the two had intensified over recent months.

Walker, like Greb, had found difficulty in getting the big money bouts. Most recently he had signed to meet lightweight champion Benny Leonard in a very attractive match up. The bout was a natural but at the eleventh hour Leonard pulled out claiming an injured thumb and then promptly retired, leaving Walker without a dance partner.

Promoter Humbert J. Fugazy was eager to make the match between Walker and Greb for his Italian Hospital Fund charity card. The likelihood of this initially seemed remote as Jack Delaney had announced that he had changed his mind about facing Greb and would soon be posting a forfeit to bind the match. In addition to this Walker was under suspension in New York for his refusal to face his top challenger Dave Shade. It remained for all of these obstacles to be ironed out while Greb continued to fight and stay in shape.

As Greb waited for the big fight to materialize he signed to face Johnny Wilson in Boston on April 17. Wary of Wilson, and Boston's reputation for dodgy decisions, he made steps to protect his championship by forcing Wilson to post a $1,000 forfeit to weigh in over the middleweight limit.

Wilson had been, and would continue for the rest of his life, telling anyone who would listen that he was robbed against Greb in their first two matches. The Boston papers remarkably printed stories suggesting that Greb's victories over Wilson had been unjust. Whether Boston sportswriters actually believed these stories or were simply trying to add interest to the match and increase the gate is debateable considering that those Boston papers which covered the first two Greb-Wilson fights voted for Greb. Regardless, Harry was eager to defeat Wilson in front of his hometown fans to silence his critics there.

Since last facing Greb Wilson had fought five times yet only won two of those, losing three times, most recently by stoppage to Tiger Flowers, in a bout he claimed to have taken on short notice without adequate time to prepare. Wilson was so intent on victory that he went into training at Johnny Collins' Health Farm in New Jersey immediately after the fight was announced.

On April 2nd Harry and Red Mason traveled to New York to discuss terms for his title defense that summer. Greb first approached Tex Rickard about the likelihood of a Delaney fight. Rickard informed him that he had tried repeatedly to get Delaney to commit to a fight with Greb without success.[1] With Delaney not interested in fighting Harry for the title and seemingly waiting on the outcome of the proposed Berlenbach-McTigue fight there was only one option left. Humbert Fugazy was intent on promoting the Walker fight and Greb stated that he was willing provided Walker's ban was lifted. The match was tentatively scheduled for June 19 at the Polo Grounds. It would be a much needed shot in the arm for Harry who was guaranteed the largest purse of his career.[2]

The bout itself was nearly torpedoed when the New York State Athletic Commission would only agree to lift the ban on Walker if he agreed to defend against Dave Shade. Shade saved the day when he agreed to step aside on the condition that Walker sign to fight him next. Shade eventually replaced Tiger Flowers who was scheduled to go on against Jimmy Slattery on the undercard.

After a tentative agreement had

Top: Greb watches as Wilson weighs in for their third match in Boston. Below: Wilson (left) and Greb pose for photographs just prior to the start of their third bout in Boston. The referee is Johnny Brassil.

been reached for the Walker fight Greb and Mason left for Boston to face Wilson. With Greb's injured ribs still healing it was a dangerous fight to take given Wilson's propensity for body punching. Yet any fear that Greb might be in danger was quickly shown to be unfounded. Harry had Wilson figured from their earlier engagements. Employing a right uppercut, which would pop Wilson's head into place for repeated quick left hooks, Greb was always in command. In the second it seemed like Wilson might slow Greb up but the moment was fleeting and by the third Wilson's nose bled to such an extent that his seconds could not stop the flow. The steady stream hampered Wilson throughout and after the decision was given in Greb's favor even those local papers which perpetuated the myth that Wilson had deserved victory against Greb in their previous two meetings were forced to admit their error.[3]

Five days later Harry and Red Mason were in New York for the formal contract signing of the Mickey Walker fight. The signing was staged at the Hotel Brevoort before an impressive array of newspapermen, photographers, and motion picture cameras. During last minute negotiations Greb was angered to find that Harry Wills, scheduled to face Charlie Weinert on the card, was demanding that he go on last as the star attraction. "Where do they get off with that stuff ballyhooing a bout between Harry Wills and Charlie Weinert as the main event?" declared Greb. "Both Walker and I are world's champions, and neither Wills nor Charley Weinert ever so much as saw a title at close range."

"So far as I am concerned, either Walker and I will fight the main bout or the works are off. I'll tell you gentlemen what I'll do if you don't think my argument is sound. Toss Weinert off the bill and I'll fight Wills myself. I'll fight him in the gym, if you want me to, to prove that he

On April 22, 1925, on the roof of the Hotel Brevoort, Harry (right) signed to face Mickey Walker for the largest purse of his career. Presiding over the formalities is matchmaker Jimmy DeForrest, chomping on his ever present stogie.

doesn't belong ahead of a couple of champions. The idea? Asking two world's champions to play runners-up to a couple of second-rate heavyweights! I never heard of such a thing."[4]

When Fugazy admitted that Greb had a point and relented the contracts were signed as the henpecked promoter breathed a sigh of relief. The two fighters joked with each other, signed contracts, and then posed for pictures. Afterwards they were treated to a luncheon to celebrate the occasion.

When the festivities had completed Greb and Mason departed for Toronto where Harry was scheduled to face Jack Reddick. In keeping with the plan to keep Harry in fighting trim he was matched with Reddick, Quintin Romero Rojas in Detroit, and Billy Britton in Columbus, Ohio, all within a span of two weeks. Walker departed the following day for California where he planned to take his only tune-up against Lefty Cooper.

Reddick was the son of a farmer who had immigrated to Canada from the United States in 1911. He had built up a solid if unspectacular record and managed to win the Canadian light heavyweight championship by stopping Soldier Jones. Whenever Reddick had stepped up his competition he had given a good account of himself but ultimately lost each time. He had garnered a reputation as a tough fighter by nearly upending Paul Berlenbach in Madison Square Garden the year before. Reddick was popular in Canada but his fans were growing weary of his bouts against what they considered carefully selected opposition and demanded he up the level of his competition. As a result Greb was imported.

When Harry arrived with Red Mason and Red Carr, manager of Jimmy Slattery, in tow the Toronto Daily Star noticed that he was no longer the handsome young man he had been nearly three years earlier. His nose was now flat, his face lined with scars, and his eyes were hidden beneath thick, calloused brows. Harry, who was sensitive about his looks and took great pride in his appearance,[5] was keenly aware of the toll that his career had taken on his body and took offense to the Star's characterization.

Carr had come along to help Mason work Greb's corner during the fight and was shortly joined by Jimmy Slattery who intended to challenge Greb soon. Greb had become a great admirer of Slattery and sang his praises to the press whenever the subject came up.

With between seven and eight-thousand present it was a record gate for an indoor boxing match in Toronto. True to form Reddick gave an exhibition of gameness and courage but was easily defeated by Harry. Reddick was so groggy after

John Runner, who fought professionally as Jack Reddick was a strong, determined, yet limited fighter. He had garnered a decent reputation off of his gutsy albeit losing performance against the streaking Paul Berlenbach.

only the first round that on several different occasions after a round he started for the wrong corner. Local reports felt Greb could have ended the fight any time he chose. Reddick failed to win a round but had satisfied his fans that he was not afraid to face any man in the ring.[6]

One week later Harry was in Detroit to face Chilean heavyweight import Quintin Romero Rojas. Rojas had been brought to the United States by Tex Rickard who hoped to build Rojas into an exotic attraction much like he had done with Luis Firpo, the ultimate goal being another million dollar gate with Jack Dempsey. Unfortunately for Rickard Rojas failed to live up to expectations and scored only a handful of wins while suffering far more telling losses. However, those losses where against heavyweights and against Greb Rojas would sport a five inch height advantage and whopping $26^1/2$ pound weight advantage.

Several special telegraph lines had been installed ringside to send returns of the fight from Detroit to New York and then on to South America. The South Americans who waited at their local newspaper and telegraph offices got to share in the same experience as so many fans of Greb's opponents. Round after round Greb outpointed his much larger opponent and made it look easy. He was far too fast for Rojas and even matched the heavyweight's strength on the inside where he was the Chilean's master at every turn.

Greb won every round of the contest and at the close of the match referee Dickerson raised Greb's hand without waiting for the judges' decision. Dickerson was taken with Greb's performance and for the next two days devoted space in his column to Greb's greatness.[7]

Harry was now rapidly rounding himself in to the kind of condition he had not seen in months, if not years. While in New York to sign for Walker Greb had stopped off at Philadelphia Jack O'Brien's gym to work out. "I tell you, I can't for the life me understand where he gets all his stamina," commented O'Brien. "I've been in the fight racket 30 odd years, but over that stretch of time I've never met a boxer so strong and one who has so much vitality as Harry. I don't care what anybody else says, I will go on record as saying the middleweight king is the greatest specimen of physical manhood in modern history. He is the enigma of the prize ring."

"All your Johnny Dundees, Jack Dempseys, and Harry Wills don't compare with this champion. Marvelous, marvelous boy is Harry."

Quintin Romero Rojas, the Lion of the Andes, had been imported to the United States by Tex Rickard as a second Luis Firpo in hopes that he could build him into an attraction for an eventual showdown with Jack Dempsey for another million dollar gate. Unfortunately Rojas would not live up to Rickard's hopes.

"He came in to my gym yesterday a half hour after he signed articles to box Mickey Walker and right off he plunged into hard work. He boxed four rounds with Eddie Bitzell and two more with me. He punched the bag four rounds and played two games of handball with his manager, Red Mason. He was sore because there weren't any more boys around to give him a hand with the gloves. He jumped on the scales and tipped the beam at the 165-pound notch. He has seven more fights before tackling Walker. He thrives on fighting and his only recreation is knocking around town when his manager can't find any work for him."[8]

Mason's plan to work Greb into shape and keep him there was baring fruit. He easily defeated Billy Britton in Columbus. The fight had been postponed two days due to poor weather conditions. The weather was cold when the fighters finally met and it seemed to hamper the action to a degree. Yet, Greb still managed to cut Britton's face to ribbons and win much more comfortably than their first meeting.[9]

A scheduled fight with Pat McCarthy on May 22 in Boston fell through when McCarthy injured his back two days before the match. That left a gap of more than two weeks without a fight. When Greb resumed his schedule he fought three times inside of a week. First defeating Detroit's Tommy Burns in Indianapolis on the eve of the Indianapolis 500, much like he had Billy Britton, slicing him up but never really showing everything he had.[10]

Then it was on to Louisville where he defeated Soldier Buck, winning every round and breaking Buck's nose in the first round with a loud crack. In the tenth round Greb was warned by referee Marvin Hart for pushing Buck through the ropes. Greb hurled an insult at Hart and for fully one minute the fight was halted while champion and referee engaged in a war of words. After the fight Hart made clear his intention to fine Greb $500 for his behavior. This was then reduced to $50 and finally the fine was lifted altogether when Greb explained himself.[11]

In these three previous fights Greb showed a slight alteration to his style which is illustrative. For the fights in question, and other previous assorted bouts, Greb had waited for several rounds before opening up with the speed and ferocity which he had become renowned for. In days past he would open the fight with a rush that often swept away his opponents and then remarkably would increase his speed throughout. Now Greb seemed to wait, fighting just enough to stay one step ahead of his opponents on points. Then between the third and fifth rounds depending on the opponent and the length of the fight, the real Greb would begin to emerge. He would dance, leap about the ring, and begin throwing the multitude of blows that garnered him the nickname "the Pittsburgh Windmill." In hindsight it seems that Greb may no longer have had the bottomless well spring of stamina he was well known for.

This tactic also illustrates the ring intelligence Harry possessed. He understood that he could let his opponents break themselves on him while he had another gear to slip into just as they began to tire. Most importantly it illustrates that Harry was exercising a level of self-preservation in order to extend his career. Fighters that cannot make adjustments lose, sometimes brutally, and with that comes an end to the big paydays, and maybe even a career. That would come soon enough, too soon for Harry's liking; he had no intention of hastening it.

Two days after the fight with Buck, in the early morning hours of June 3, Harry was involved in another incident which added fodder to the newspaper stories about his night time antics. Details of the incident and what precipitated it are murky but what is known is that about 3 a.m. Patrolman Edward Donahue was alerted by screams coming from an automobile at the corner of Pittsburgh's Federal Ave and East Ohio St.

When Donahue approached the vehicle he stated that the occupants began to shout insults at him. The officer ordered the occupants of the vehicle to follow him to local police station at which time Harry Greb leapt from the vehicle, chased down a passing taxi, and sped off. The patrolman quickly hailed another cab and gave chase. Donahue was only able to bring Greb's cab to a halt after firing several shots from his revolver.

While Greb was being arrested by Donahue his companions were taken into custody by other officers who had arrived on the scene. When the gun smoke had cleared it was determined that those in custody were Mack Moore, Alan Jones, Harry Newman, Naomi Braden, Patricia Jacobson (who turned out to be Patricia Jones, Alan's wife, who had been with Naomi and Greb on the night of the Highland Park incident), and Greb.[12]

Later the cab driver who had sped Greb from the scene of the arrest was brought in and told his version of events. He stated that Greb, returning from a nightclub, had found Naomi in a vehicle with several men and attacked her. He stated that when police arrived Greb grabbed Braden, pushed her into the cab, and ordered the driver to ignore the police officer and speed away. The cab driver added that he had failed to heed the first several shots from the officer's gun because he feared Greb's fists more than bullets.[13]

Harry and his five friends posted $30 each and then forfeited the money when they failed to show up at Morals Court, at which time the police considered the matter closed.

The left jabs of Soldier Buck had given Greb a nasty cut lip requiring two stitches. He had intended to call off his last bout before facing Walker, a match with Jimmy Nuss, in Marquette, Michigan but this latest episode had convinced him that he needed to get out of town while the story died down. Cut lip or no he would be facing Jimmy Nuss on June 5.

Nuss' story was a sad one. He had been born July 16, 1899 in DuPere, Wisconsin. The family was poor and what meager income they had was brought in by Nuss' father Charles who worked in the local lumber camps. When Nuss was just 13 years old his mother died and his father sent him to live with his elderly grandparents. He picked up boxing when he was 13 or 14 years old and about the same time he left school for good. During the war he fought in France with the 121st Field Artillery. After the war Nuss returned home and resumed boxing. He turned pro in 1920 and quickly ran up a respectable record. By the time he faced Greb he had a solid reputation as a willing, if somewhat limited, brawler who always gave his best.

As expected Nuss fought a good, determined fight but was outclassed by the champion. Nuss was aggressive throughout the contest which allowed Greb to hammer home the blows that finally stopped Nuss in the fourth round. Despite his early exit Nuss left the fans satisfied with his performance.[14] Sadly Nuss was paid nothing for what should have been the biggest purse of his career. He promptly fired his manager and witnessed his career take a downward spiral before he finally retired in 1929. In the mid 1930's while working in a lumber camp he was severely injured leaving him crippled for life. He lived the remainder of his life on a $66 a month pension from the army before passing away in 1973.[15]

The same night Greb defeated Nuss Gene Tunney and Tommy Gibbons finally faced off in a match three years in the making. Harry and Red Mason had argued over who would win, Red being adamant that Gibbons would be victorious and Harry betting $500 that Tunney would win.

Once again Greb's ability to analyze a fight won out the day. Tunney easily dominated Gibbons before stopping him in the twelfth round. To most it looked as though Gibbons had gotten old overnight. He seemed clueless as to how to handle Tunney who was fighting in much the same style that Gibbons himself was accustomed to employing. Finally it appeared equal parts frustration and exhaustion which finished Gibbons. As soon as the match was over the hype for a Dempsey-Tunney championship fight began.

"A man has to fight Tunney to appreciate what he really is," said Harry. "He wastes no energy, hits hard and clean, is exceptionally strong in the arms and his mightiest blows travel only a few inches. I have never considered Dempsey a great champion. He has been the best of a bad crop. Before crediting him with being one of the greatest fighters of all time do not forget that he has yet for the first time to face any opponent the equal of Tom Sharkey, Gus Ruhlin, Peter Jackson, Kid McCoy, or Stanley Ketchel. In other words he has been a 2:10 horse in a 2:20 class race."

"Since I have fought Tunney a half dozen times I feel that I am better qualified to judge than anyone who has ever faced him. I have boxed Dempsey and found the task anything but a hard one."[16]

With Greb's schedule now clear he could focus on getting down to hard training for his defense against Mickey Walker. The 23 year old Walker was a sensational fighter in his own right. Labeled the "Toy Bulldog" for his diminutive stature and pugnacious fighting style, he loved nothing better than to get in close and bang away with short, powerful left hooks. But Walker was versatile as well. He could box going backward, he had excellent judgment of distance, was extremely durable, and remarkably strong for his size. In short, Walker was a complete fighter. He had won the welterweight championship in November of 1922 at the tender age of 21. Not content Walker dreamed of fighting for the middleweight championship, light-heavyweight championship, and remarkably even hoped someday to fight Jack Dempsey. The irony of his penchant for tilting at windmills was not lost on the press when he signed to fight Greb.

Shortly after Walker agreed to face Greb he acquired Jack Kearns as his manager. Kearns had been in the midst of a very public row with Jack Dempsey which threatened their relationship. The two were barely on speaking terms and Kearns was desperate to find another meal ticket.

Kearns was publicly optimistic about Walker's chances against Greb but the wily manager was not unwilling to use any trick in the book to secure victory for his charge. So it was that when Kearns announced on June 8 that Walker would have to postpone the bout due to an infected ingrown toenail many felt that it was a ruse designed to allow more time for Walker to train or to throw off Greb's training, knowing that aging fighters have a more difficult time maintaining peak form.

When the promoters and the New York State Athletic Commission met to decide a new date for the match Kearns appeared and announced that he would like to renew his second's license to work Walker's corner, his license having lapsed in the two years since Dempsey had last fought. The commission flatly denied his request, citing his continued reluctance to answer Harry Wills' persistent challenge of Dempsey. Kearns was told that he would not be officially recognized in any capacity until he appeared before the commission with Dempsey to explain their avoidance of Wills. This put Kearns in a tight spot. As his relationship with Dempsey deteriorated the champion had fled to Europe with his new wife Estelle Taylor, ostensibly to celebrate a belated honeymoon but ultimately to be rid of reporters who had continually questioned him about what would ultimately be his permanent split from Kearns. With Kearns unceremoniously ushered from the chambers the new date was set down as July 2.[17]

Greb opened as a narrow favorite over Walker.[18] This was due in large part to the questions surrounding Greb's age, ring wear, and the continued rumors about his lack of dedication and training. Most admitted that the Greb of years past would be too much for Walker but they reasoned that someday soon Greb would grow old overnight and a fighter of Walker's caliber was just the man to make him feel his age.

"I'll admit that if Greb was the man he was two or three years ago I wouldn't go so strong on Walker's chances," stated Kearns. "But Harry isn't the man he was by a long shot, and couldn't be after all his years of fighting. The fact that Greb is making the middleweight limit without trouble is a tipoff to the fact that the years are beginning to tell."[19]

"So they've dubbed Mickey Walker a miniature Dempsey?" answered Greb when told that Walker was modeling his style and training habits after the heavyweight champion. "Great! I only hope Mickey fights along the same style that Jack does. I've tried to get Jack into the ring but he won't give me a tumble. As I said before I sincerely hope that Walker fights, as they say, 'just like Dempsey,' for then I'm certain my crown will be safe."[20]

Harry trained at Bacharach Park, Atlantic City for the contest before arriving in New York a few days before the bout to taper off training at Philadelphia Jack O'Brien's. He mystified the press and onlookers by supplementing the usual boxer's training with what many older boxing devotees considered unusual additions to his regimen: rowing along the coast, swimming, baseball, and his favorite: handball. Walker trained at Johnny Collins' Health Farm working daily with a small army of sparring partners.

On June 30 Kearns made a formal application to the commission for a second's license. Kearns was nearly struck dumb when this was not only denied but he was informed that he would be barred from the Polo Grounds in any capacity. Desperate to gain admittance to the fight Kearns relented and stated that he would agree to allow Dempsey to face to Wills in 1926 but only after his request for a license was granted.[21] The members of the commission were as aware of the reputed split between he and Dempsey as anyone else who read the daily newspaper stories and once again denied his request. Kearns then stated that he would attend the fight in the capacity of a newspaper reporter to which he was told that any attempt to gain admittance would be denied, by physical force if necessary.

The following day, the final day of training, Harry trained before motion picture cameras for the benefit of the newsreels. He appeared in excellent condition, light hearted but focused on the task at hand. In truth both fighters were supremely confident of victory. Walker was quoted as saying he intended to try for the knockout but if it did not come early the fight would go the distance and be determined by the fighter with the most endurance.[22] "I'll win in a walk," answered Harry. "I look for it to be a one-sided fight after the early rounds. I don't think Mickey can keep up with me in speed. I am sure he cannot knock me out and I am not going to try to knock him out. I will be satisfied to win an undisputable margin on points."[23]

Early on the morning of the fight rain threatened a postponement of the match but eventual-

Top: Mickey Walker jumps rope in preparation for his upcoming match with Harry Greb. Below: Greb poses for photographs in Pittsburgh just prior to leaving for his Atlantic City training camp for the bout with Mickey Walker.

ly passed. That afternoon a large crowd had gathered outside of the weigh in. Excitement was at a fever pitch as the fighters each where given a healthy cheer; with Walker arriving last and being cheered the loudest. Once again Harry Wills, who had continually harried the promoters for the top spot on the card, appealed for the main event but was denied once and for all when the commissioners agreed that the championship should get top billing.

Harry claimed to have made weight easily but some present felt that he displayed the telltale signs of nervous tension which accompany a fighter who has struggled to cut weight. Walker weighed in at 152 lbs. while Greb hopped on the scale and weighed 159 lbs. He was then called in to an inner office to renew his license after which he quickly rushed from the building without even taking his coat and hat, leaving many including Red Mason wondering and causing further speculation as to the strain of making weight.[24]

That evening the Polo Grounds was packed with everyone in attendance anxiously awaiting what was being hailed as one of the greatest cards in years. The bouts were being broadcast live by WBGS in New York with Paul Gallico and Sigmund Spaeth doing the live commentary. KDKA in Pittsburgh would broadcast fight returns telegraphed in from Regis Welsh. A novelty had been enacted whereby a live radio microphone had been placed on a ring post to better catch all of the action. Many of the fighters before and after their fights approached the microphone and spoke directly to the fans at home, a first in radio history. Immediately seeing the potential of this WHN announcers climbed into the ring after each fight to interview the fighters, managers, referee, and anyone else, which would be the first time in history fighters would be interviewed live from ringside after the fight, a tradition that continues to this day.

Top: The week before Greb left for Atlantic City to train for Walker he was photographed in a variety of training stunts including a new found love: Golf. Below: Greb (left) and Leo Caghil spar as Greb prepares for Mickey Walker.

Top: The day before Harry Greb fought Mickey Walker he posed for motion picture cameras while training. The outtakes of that film are the only motion pictures in existance of Greb in action. It was lost for nearly seventy years before turning up in the archives of the University South of Carolina. Bottom left and right: Stills from the motion picture of Greb training. Facing page top left: Still showing Greb working the speedbag. Facing page top right: Still showing Greb sparring with Philadelphia Jack O'Brien. Facing page bottom left: Greb and O'Brien playing handball. Facing page bottom right: Naomi Braden toweling Harry off after a strenuous workout.

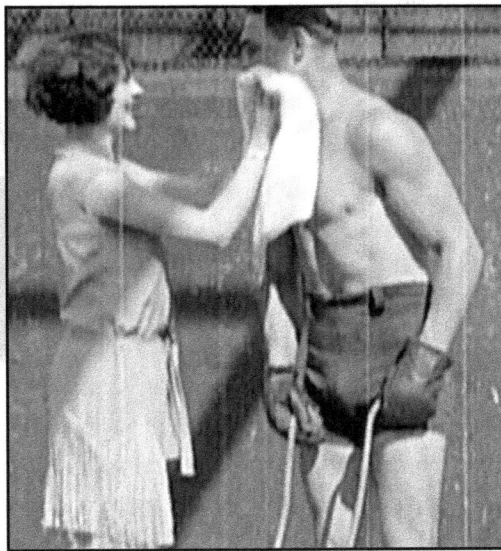

Motion pictures would be made of the event and distributed throughout New York. Special busses had been arranged in various nearby cities to shuttle fans to and from the Polo Grounds.

The undercard featured a four round curtain raiser between former Bantamweight champion Joe Lynch and Jack Sharkey. This was followed by the most stunning upset of the year when Mickey Walker's top contender Dave Shade blitzed Jimmy Slattery, repeatedly catching him with punches to the amazement of everyone. In the third Shade dropped Slattery twice before a towel came flying into the ring to save the helpless fighter. The victory left most sure they knew the reason why Walker had been so hesitant to fight Shade. In the semi-final Harry Wills unceremoniously ended yet another of Charlie Weinert's comebacks. Weinert, nearly thirty pounds lighter than Wills, seemed intimidated before getting stopped in the second round.

Mickey Walker arrived late to the arena, not expecting the preliminaries to be over so quickly. This caused a delay of nearly thirty minutes before the championship could start. As the audience waited with anticipation they passed around the rumors that had been spreading throughout the stadium that Doc Kearns had tried to enter the arena in various disguises, each with greater hilarity than the last. First he attempted to enter disguised as a woman, he then plucked out his eye hoping to be mistaken for the famous gate crasher One-Eyed Connelly only to be discovered when it was noticed he had removed the wrong eye, finally it was said he attempted to enter the arena concealed in a hot dog cart. In truth Kearns listened to the reports of the fight via radio at Billy La Hiff's tavern. However, it was not expected that Kearns' absence would be a detriment to Walker as Kearns had only worked Walker's corner on one occasion; that being the one round knockout of Left Cooper in which Kearns likely had little or nothing to do in the corner on that occasion.

Finally a cheer went up from the audience as Mickey made his approach to the ring wearing an old sweater after the fashion of his idol Jack Dempsey. He was followed a minute later by Greb, wearing his customary green trunks. Walker was seconded by Teddy Hayes, Greb by Red Mason and Tom Dolan.

The audience was dotted with such luminaries as Babe Ruth, Gentleman Jim Corbett, Jacob Rupert, George M. Cohen, Bernard Gimbel, James J. Walker, John McGraw, Carl Laemle, and William Fox. By fight time odds in some areas had been bet down to even money but in others Greb still remained a slight a favorite.

After the introductions and instructions the fighters returned to their corner and the entire arena seemed to hold its breath as it awaited the opening bell.

Walker opened with a rush, throwing almost exclusively to Greb's body hoping to reduce Greb's advantage in speed. Only occasionally did he throw to the head. Greb, for his part, mixed his punches evenly to the head and body. He would continually work around Walker, often popping up behind him and befuddling the welterweight champion. It was noted that Walker's punches seemed to carry more power. Near the end of the round the two fighters brought the crowd to its feet it with a blistering toe to toe exchange.

Harry opened the second round with a torrent of punches that forced Walker to break ground. Greb followed, rocking the smaller man. Walker lashed out with two powerful drives to the body that forced Greb back. For a moment Walker took the initiative, following Greb before Harry stopped in his tracks, stood flat footed and fought Walker to a standstill. Suddenly it was Walker in full retreat. The welterweight was forced into a corner where Greb continued his onslaught. Again, Walker clawed his way back by forcing Greb back only to be met with terrific drives to the head by Harry. A combination forced Walker to his knees but he was up without a count. Embarrassed and intent on showing he had not been hurt Walker stood toe to toe with Greb and the two traded punches furiously. Greb was staggered at the end of the round but it was noted that Walker returned to his corner bleeding from the nose.

The audience was by now whipped into a frenzy by the viciousness of the fighting. Only two rounds had passed and there had already been more action than is seen in most ten round fights.

Greb came out for the third, once again flat footed, left arm extended from the shoulder as a range finder. Walker crouched looking for an opening. The two clinched and Greb, looking for any opportunity to impose his size, pushed Walker into the ropes and leaned his weight him. The two broke and Walker fired several hard punches to the body. Greb wrapped his left arm around Walker, fired several right hands to the head and body and once again draped his weight over Walker.

Walker opened the fourth with a left to the body but was immediately countered with three rapid rights to the face which sent him reeling. The pace slowed in this round with much of the round spent wrestling with Greb once again using his weight in the clinches to tire Walker.

Greb came out for the fifth with a rush, forcing Walker to the ropes and pouring in punches. Walker fought Greb off with a powerful left hook that landed with a smack on Greb's mouth. Greb stepped back, spat, and then felt the hole in his mouth where two teeth had been. The two then went in close and there was much more infighting and wrestling which continued to tire Walker as his pace slowed considerably.

By the sixth round Walker had fought admirably, even winning to this point by a narrow but convincing margin on several scorecards. Yet, Greb's plan was now becoming clear. He had forced Walker to expend an incredible amount of energy for the first three rounds, while taking a great deal of punishment, only to have the thinnest of margins. And now, even before Greb had begun to fight at full speed Mickey was tiring badly, made worse by the gore which now poured constantly from his nose, with ten rounds to go.

The sixth was hailed universally as the turning point of the fight, where Greb began to take over and assert his dominance. Walker was continually backed to the ropes and tattooed at close quarters. True, Mickey continued to strafe Harry with left hooks to the body but the middleweight champion seemed none the worse for wear as he jogged back to his corner sprightly at the end of the round.

In the seventh Walker attempted to stem the tide but every time he landed one of his powerful blows Greb would counter with an equally damaging punch, followed by an additional torrent of blows to put an exclamation point on the exchange. At the end of the round referee Eddie Purdy was attempting to separate the fighters from a clinch along the ropes when he slipped, fell, and painfully wrenched his knee. Walker and Greb stepped over the stricken referee and as Greb attempted to help Purdy to his feet the audience joined in a chorus to count Purdy out. It was a rare moment of hilarity in an otherwise dramatic contest.

Greb continued outpunching Walker several blows to one in the eighth and splitting Walkers lip with a left uppercut. Walker continued to fight valiantly, equating himself well.

Indeed, a less formidable opponent than Greb would have likely wilted in the face of Walker's dogged determination. But, Greb, even an aging, half blind, battle scarred Greb was a far different proposition than most fighters and at the end of the round a dazed and confused Walker started for the wrong corner.

The ninth was fought primarily at close quarters with Greb forcing Walker to the ropes, pinioning him there, and belaboring him with short, choppy punches, particularly the uppercut. Walker continued to try to drive forward but his punch output had steadily decreased and Harry had sapped him of much of his stamina.

Greb opened the tenth with an assault that clearly bothered Walker. The middleweight champion had now found an effective defense for most of Walker's best blows but Walker, ever dangerous, lashed out with a desperate right that reached Greb and spun him around. Greb rushed back at Walker and remarkably began fighting at a much faster pace than he had at the start of the fight.

The two went to close quarters again in the eleventh where Greb pounded Walker along the ropes. When they were separated Walker attacked, dazing Greb with a bevy of powerful punches. Greb blunted the assault by smothering Walker, clinching until his head cleared. In trying to separate the fighters Eddie Purdy once again fell. The two fighters ignored the prostrate arbiter and continued to fight toe to toe like wild animals in a corner at the bell.

Top: Walker and Greb square off prior to their fight as referee Eddie Purdy and announcer Joe Humphries look on. Bottom: First round action as Walker (left) launches a left hook. Note Greb's right hand already in position to protect against the blow as he jabs at Walker with his left.

The previous two rounds illustrated that Walker, despite fading round by round, was still a dangerous tiger when cornered. Still, his rallies broke upon Greb like the surf upon a stony shore and the effort left Walker ever weaker.

Walker made a magnificent rally in the twelfth. Sensing the fight had slipped away, rushed across the ring at the bell and attacked. The two fighters once again stood toe to toe for most of the round with Greb landing more punches and Walker landing harder. The thirteenth picked up where the previous round left off. The two stood together throwing everything they had but now Walker's stamina, and with it his rally, had run its course. The little Irishman was taking severe punishment and as the round ended his left eye was beginning to close and his face showed bumps and other signs of swelling where Greb had battered him relentlessly. The cut on Walker's lip had reopened and he once again seemed dazed and confused as he returned to his corner.

Again, the fourteenth opened with both fighters going toe to toe. Then Greb began to dance and Walker simply could not find him or deal with his speed. As Walker chased Greb around the ring Harry suddenly planted his feet and Mickey walked into a dynamite right hand that exploded on the side of his head and sent him reeling across the ring and into the ropes. Greb immediately saw that Walker was helpless and jumped on him. He rained blows down upon the welterweight champion. Walker tottered side to side, his hands down at sides defenseless as blow after blow landed on his unprotected chin. For at least a full minute Walker was battered into a drunken, bloody haze, completely out on his feet. As Greb landed each blow Walker's knees sagged a little more and the crowd

Top: Greb (right) has Walker on the run in the second round. Bottom: Walker (right) launches a body attack in the third round as Greb covers up. This is an early example of a photo transmitted via telegraph or telephone.

Top: Walker (left) works Greb's body in an unknown round. Bottom: Walker (right) works out of a crouch, trying to penetrate Greb's defense in an unknown round. Facing page top: In the seventh round referee Eddie Purdy fell to the canvas while attempting to separate the fighters from a clinch. Greb (back to the camera) and Walker are seen here stepping over Purdy. Facing page center: Greb (right) sinks a left hook to Walker's liver in the eighth round. By this point in the fight the pace had begun to tell on Walker and Greb was rapidly gaining momentum. Facing page bottom: Eddie Purdy once again fell in the eleventh round. He had painfully injured his knee in the two falls and from this point on could do little but hobble after the fighters. Walker can be seen over Greb's shoulder wiping the blood from his nose.

Top left: Greb (right) lands a right hand high on Walker's head in the twelfth round. Top right: Greb (back to the camera) pounds away at Walker in close during the fourteenth round. Bottom: Greb (left) lands the dynamite right hand on Mickey Walker's jaw that nearly knocked the welterweight champion out. It was the beginning of a brutal, minute-long beating for Walker.

screamed, some for the knockout, some for mercy. People listening to the fight at home on the radio reported hearing Walker beg Greb not to knock him out.[25] Then suddenly, showing the courage that had defined Walker this night, Mickey lashed out desperately. Greb was momentarily forced back, buying Walker a brief respite. Greb was quickly on Walker again but this time the bell rang saving the little fighter from a possible knockout.

Dazed and bloody, Walker again started for the wrong corner. Smiling, Greb caught him by the shoulders, turned him, and gave him a gentle shove in the direction of his corner. Harry then turned, laughing, and trotted off to his own corner. Clearly Harry was enjoying himself.

They shook hands to start the fifteenth and final round. Greb spun Walker around with a left hook that had opened a bad cut below Walker's right eye. Streaming blood, Walker, with a rage that surprised even Greb, attacked. One of Walker's powerful left hooks staggered Harry. The two traded blows with Greb being driven backwards. Walker stumbled forward, ever forward, spraying crimson clouds from his battered nose as he snorted like a wounded bull. The audience urged Mickey on but Greb smiled and took the assault in stride, riding out the round, confident that the fight was his and that Mickey's final rally was too little too late.[26]

The two fighters embraced and returned to their respective corners. Harry showed little sign of having been in such a trying contest. Walker was a mess. He bled from the cut below his eye, his nose, split lips, and a cut inside his mouth. His right eye was now almost completely closed, his left was puffed, and knots had been raised all over his swollen face and head. He was clearly exhausted and sat down heavily on his stool where Teddy Hayes administered to him.

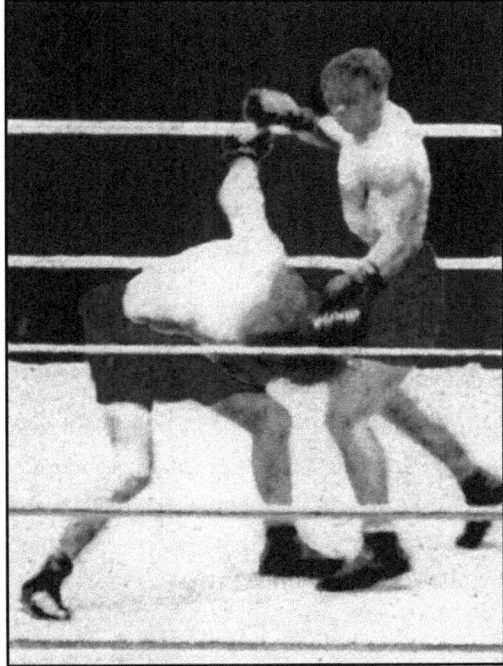

Walker (facing the camera) made a remarkable comeback in the fifteenth round. Fighting on heart and instinct alone he forced Greb backwards and traded blows with the champion bringing the crowd to its feet. The rally typified the courage he displayed throughout the contest

Joe Humphries gathered up the slips and after a quick calculation walked over and raised Harry's right hand in token of his victory. There wasn't a dissenting voice in the house. Walker had turned in a great performance. He had given everything he had, had come out battered, bloodied, bruised, and completely exhausted and it still had not been enough to topple Greb. When this became official he buried his head in a towel and wept. His tears were all he had left to give.

24

WAY OUT WEST

"I gave Mickey everything I had in the fourteenth round and I couldn't put him away," said Harry after the match. "I knew I had the decision safely sewed up and I thought it best to play safe in the fifteenth. I'm glad I didn't knock Mickey out as I am mighty fond of that kid. He is one of the greatest little fighters in the world and I think there are only two middleweights in the world that can beat him. Of course, I'm not mentioning any names.

"I do think, though, that Mickey is making a mistake in going out of his class. I guess I gave them a real scrap at that."[1]

Walker was too badly damaged to give an interview, leaving the arena quickly and refusing any comment.[2] It would be several days before he emerged from his hotel, as pugnacious as ever, demanding a rematch and promising to knockout Greb the next time they met.

The contest proved something of a renaissance for Greb. It had been an artistic and financial success. The bout had drawn nearly $400,000, the largest gate by far of the season and was being talked about as one of the greatest fights ever witnessed. Within days motion pictures of the fight and its undercard were playing to packed movie houses all over the state. New York promoters were falling over themselves to quickly match Harry for another big contest before the end of the summer, and once again offers flooded in from all over the United States for his services.

Harry stayed in New York just long enough to pick up a check for $50,856 and then planned to return to Atlantic City where he intended to spend two weeks of rest and relaxation at the shore before beginning a new campaign. However this trip was

HIPPODROME

TODAY AND TOMORROW

VICTOR HUGO HALPERIN'S

"SCHOOL FOR WIVES

WITH
CONWAY TEARLE
SIGRID HOLMQUIST
PEGGY KELLY

EXTRA ADDED ATTRACTION

EXCLUSIVE PICTURES OF ITALIAN HOSPITAL BENEFIT FIGHT FILMS.

GREB vs. WALKER
WILLS vs. WEINERT
SHADE vs. SLATTERY

TAKEN FROM A RINGSIDE SEAT.

Pictured left to right are: Dave Shade, Harry Greb, Leo P. Flynn, A. A. Bertini, and Humbert Fugazy on July 6, 1925 on the event of Greb and Shade picking up their checks for the Italian Hospital Fund fights. Greb took home a career high purse of $50,856.

cut short when Red Mason was severely injured while staging a fireworks display for his daughter to celebrate the fourth of July. For a time it was feared Mason would lose the sight of one or both of his eyes. Harry picked up his check, posed for photos with Dave Shade, and asked Humbert Fugazy to match him with Paul Berlenbach. He then rushed to Pittsburgh to visit Mason in the Hospital.

Harry found the tough old fight manager, his face swaddled in bandages, working feverishly on booking Greb for a busy fight schedule throughout the Midwest, seemingly in defiance of the possibility that he may lose his vision.

Harry returned to the seashore to begin training for the first of the bouts, a match in Cleveland on July 16 against young New York middleweight Maxie Rosenbloom. Rosenbloom was being hailed as a considerable talent who had only suffered three defeats in more than forty contests but in fighting Greb he was taking a monumental leap in class from the fighters he had previously faced. When they met that leap in class showed immediately.

At the start Greb toyed with Rosenbloom, coasting and allowing the younger fighter to force the fight while doing just enough to stay out in front. As early as the third round the Cleveland Plain Dealer felt that Greb could end the fight any time he pleased. Greb began to open up by the fifth round and in the sixth he dropped Rosenbloom hard, flat on his back, for a count of seven. When Rosenbloom clambered to his feet the one sided contest continued. Rosenbloom managed to finish the fight but lost every round.[3] Joe Williams, writing for the Cleveland Press, felt that Greb could have stopped Rosenbloom any time he wished but allowed him to finish on his feet:

> Further Proof of the glittering genius of Harry Greb was displayed when he went ten full rounds with young Maxie Rosenbloom of New York, Thursday night at the Taylor arena, without knocking him out. It required artistry of a high caliber to keep Young Maxie in a vertical position for that length of time, but the middleweight champion was, as the phrase goes, equal to the occasion.[4]

Slapsie Maxie Rosenbloom was an 18 year old, developing prospect from New York when he faced Greb in the summer of 1925. He would go on to win the light-heavyweight championship five years later and eventually be inducted into the Hall of Fame. He would call Greb the greatest fighter he ever fought and admit that "I guess Greb could have murdered me if he wanted. He was great."

Harry's busy schedule continued with bouts slated against Billy Britton in Columbus, Kansas on July 23, Ralph Brooks at Wichita on July 27, and Jack Matlock at Colorado Springs on August 3 (which later fell through). After a short rest he headed west for Kansas with Red Mason and Leo Caghil in tow and while on the road picked up two more fights; one against Otis Bryant on July 31 at Tulsa, Oklahoma, and another with Knockout Ed Smith on August 4 at Kansas City.

The ten round bout with Britton, the third fight between the two this year, was being promoted by William F. Kurtz and the Anti-Horse Thief Association to be held in conjunction with a rodeo and stock show and was fairly indicative of the pattern Greb's fights would take during this tour both in tone and purpose. It would prove a fairly easy bout for a relatively small purse. With a half dozen low risk bouts Greb could make nearly $20,000, have a relaxing trip out west, stay out of trouble, and stay in shape while waiting for the bigger matches. At 172 pounds Britton outweighed Greb by $4^{1}/_{2}$ pounds but once again class was the story of the fight. Despite taking things fairly easy Greb left Britton with two black eyes and a loss.[5]

Greb and company then made the 165 mile

trek to Wichita to face Ralph Brooks of Hunnewell, Kansas. Brooks was a 26 year old former soldier who was now promoting himself as the "heavyweight champion of the occupation forces." Brooks had lived a hard life. His father had died before he was a year old and by the time he was ten he and his brother had been separated and shipped off to live with relatives. He was a rugged farm boy who was known for his willingness to assimilate punishment but occasionally showed up in less than stellar condition. Kansas fans had expected great things from him but five months earlier he had been stopped in eight rounds by Bob Roper, slowing his rise, and in May he had been arrested for drunkenness. Knowing that this would be the most difficult proposition of his career and realizing that he would have to contend with Greb's speed Brooks set up training camp at Excelsior Springs, Missouri with a goal of reducing his weight and increasing his speed.

Brooks had an added incentive for defeating Greb. As Harry was fighting his way through Kansas Floyd Fitzsimmons had floated him an offer to face Jack Dempsey. When Dempsey had returned from Europe he was still under notice from the New York Status Athletic Commission that he needed to appear in person and explain his continued reluctance to meet Harry Wills' challenge. Enormous pressure was being brought to bear on Dempsey to force him into the match. Senator James J. Walker, architect of the current law legalizing boxing in the state, demanded that Dempsey defend his title against Wills or retire. He added that if Dempsey continued to hide behind the color line then Walker's bill may as well be abolished. Dempsey informed the commission that he was willing to accept Wills' challenge but would first need several tune-up fights. The commission was briefly appeased when Dempsey promised to appear in person on July 21 and sign articles to face Wills.

Floyd Fitzsimmons, Seizing upon Dempsey's professed intent to begin a campaign of tune-up bouts, began working on arranging a bout between Dempsey and Greb. Upon being approached by Fitzsimmons to assess their willingness for the match Greb and Mason were eager but cautious. They had been down this road before with the champion. They were also wary of the financial arrangements, remembering that Tommy Gibbons had received almost nothing to face Dempsey in 1923. "If Fitz makes the price right, there is nothing else to worry about," said Greb. "I'll take the match with Dempsey in a minute. There was never a time that I did not think I could out speed the champion and even though the chance is coming a few years later than it should, I'll take it, Dempsey has not been doing much for the last few years. I have been active and proved in the Walker fight that I still have something."[6]

Greb and Mason met with Fitzsimmons in Chicago on their way to Kansas to discuss terms for the match, then headed to Wichita while they waited for Fitzsimmons to get the details in order.[7] Brooks hoped that by defeating Greb he would be able to usurp his place against Dempsey.

The Dempsey-Greb bout seemed doomed almost as soon as it was announced. When Dempsey failed to appear before the commission in New York to sign articles for Wills, New

York officials were furious. Tex Rickard tried to smooth things over stating that he would act as Dempsey's proxy. The commission had enough of this nonsense and promptly declared Dempsey ineligible to fight in New York until he personally explained himself. Rickard promised to produce Dempsey within two weeks. On the same day that Greb faced Billy Britton Floyd Fitzsimmons hosted a dinner for Chicago sportswriters to determine the best opponent for Dempsey's return. The sportswriters were notified that Dempsey had refused to face either Wills or Tunney so five names were floated: George Godfrey, Jack Renault, Tommy Gibbons, Bartley Madden, and Harry Greb. Tommy Gibbons had informally retired; Godfrey, Renault, and Madden were all deemed unworthy leaving only Greb.[8] A date of either September 19 or 25 was selected. Red Mason gave his consent to either date for Greb's services and promised to come to Chicago. Dempsey as well verbally agreed "That's O.K. with me," said the champion at home in Los Angeles, "I'll be in training before another week's gone by."[9]

While in Tulsa Greb was hopeful but expressed some doubts as to whether Dempsey would agree to the match, citing the fact that Dempsey had too much to lose by taking him on.[10] Several sportswriters echoed this line of thought. Walter Trumball felt Dempsey would never agree to Greb as an opponent because "the Pittsburgh Wildcat might make Dempsey look foolish in a limited-round bout."[11] Ed Wray of the St. Louis Post-Dispatch agreed advising Dempsey to take a tune-up before facing Greb. "Its risky business fooling with a tarantula of Greb's type when not equipped against him," finished Wray.[12] Harry Newman of the New York Daily News was another who felt it was a dangerous match for Dempsey stating "I think Greb would smack Dempsey's ears off in a limited round bout. Dempsey knows that about Greb and I don't think Dempsey would dare go with Greb with the decision at the end of it."[13] Bob Dunbar of the Boston Herald weighed in stating that Greb would give Dempsey at least as good an argument as Tommy Gibbons had.[14] Some in the press ridiculed Dempsey for the match but Davis J. Walsh of the International News Service shot them down as jealous that a Midwestern promoter had stolen what would have been a great promotion in New York.[15]

Greb was treated to several lavish dinners while in Wichita as a guest of the Elks, the Rotary club, and the Kiwanis. He impressed the gatherings as a well-spoken man of intelligence and humility when asked to speak before them. Against Brooks he showed that he had brawn to go along with his brains. Brooks had trained himself down to his lowest weight and finest condition. He stood four and a half inches taller than Greb and despite this, and a reach advantage, rarely landed a solid punch. Greb won every round of the contest opening a dozen cuts on Brooks' battered face and closing both of his eyes. At one point Greb lay on the ropes, swaying back and forth with his hands down, as Brooks unloaded punch after punch without landing a single a blow.[16]

Wichita was thoroughly impressed with the performance. C. Lee McPherson, writing for the Wichita Beacon, stated that neither Young Stribling, who had recently appeared in Wichita, nor Jack Dempsey could compare to Greb. He added that Greb made lightweights Charlie White

Top: Fred Bell (left), county treasurer and head of the Eagles Boxing Committee which promoted the Greb-Brooks bout proudly poses with the champion (center) and Red Mason. Center, left to right: Greb's sparring partner Leo Caghil, Manager Red Mason, Harry Greb, Referee Johnny Husong, Ralph Brooks, Brook's manager Mike Curran, and an unknown pose before their July 27, 1925 bout in Wichita, Kansas. Right: In this rare action photo referee Johnny Husong, left, steps back after seperating Harry (back to the camera) and Ralph Brooks during their fight.

and Ever Hammer look slow by comparison.[17] Greb praised Brooks, stating that he had tried hard for a knockout but couldn't bring him down, although many felt Greb had allowed Brooks to stay the distance and could have stopped him at any time in the last three rounds, which were described as a "merciless slaughter."[18]

Harry, Mason, and Caghil lingered in Wichita for a day or two before heading south to Tulsa where they had picked up a fight against Otis Bryant. Bryant was a veteran of Midwestern rings hailing from Southeast Missouri. During the war he had been stationed at Great Lakes Naval Training Center with the Hospital Corps. He had first become acquainted with Greb when together they were on the Navy team competing in the Tournament for the King's Trophy in London back in 1918, Bryant serving as an alternate in the welterweight class. Bryant had continued to fight occasionally out of Chicago, St. Louis, and generally anywhere he could find work. He had a wealth of experience and had been fighting for at least eleven years but he was not a very durable fighter and Greb represented a massive step up in competition. He was not expected to defeat Greb, but it was hoped by Tulsa fans that he could at least force Greb to show some of his ability.

William Otis Bryant of Sikeston, Missouri was a 29 year old middleweight who had been in the fight game since at least 1914. He had first become associated with Greb in late 1918 when he served as an alternate for the Inter-Allied boxing tournament in London, England.

From the opening bell Bryant seemed overwhelmed by the sight of a champion in the opposite corner. He tried to force the fight but Greb easily avoided his clumsy attacks and at the end of the first round he dropped Bryant with a left to the chin. The bell saved Bryant at the count of five. Things only got worse for Bryant in the second when he was dropped twice, the bell again saving him on the second knockdown. Referee Johnny Husong halted the mismatch in the third to save Bryant any further embarrassment.[19]

While in Tulsa, Greb and Mason received word that Dempsey had reconsidered the offer to face Greb. He had finalized his split from Kearns and under the terms Dempsey would handle his own business affairs while Kearns would get a 50% split of Dempsey's ring earnings until September 1926. Meanwhile Dempsey had once again missed his date to appear before the New York State Athletic Commission. He had been negotiating with Tex Rickard to face Gene Tunney and was trying to get Kearns to accept a 35% stake in his earnings as opposed to the agreed upon 50%.

Dempsey's options were now rapidly shrinking. Even while simultaneously negotiating with Rickard and Fitzsimmons he was trying to get an easy, no-decision match in New Jersey. Immediately the bars went up on the match. Frustrated, as almost everyone in boxing was with Dempsey's continued excuses for not facing Wills, New Jersey stated that the only match Dempsey would be allowed to fight there was against his top challenger. With Dempsey's credibility now at it's lowest point he publicly stated that if he decided to fight in 1925 it would definitely not be against Harry Greb.[20]

Undaunted by the somewhat anticipated news Harry rushed to Kansas City where he hoped to meet Floyd Fitzsimmons and sign articles for the fight. When he arrived Fitzsimmons was a no-show. The same day Greb was scheduled to face Knockout Ed Smith on the last leg of his tour Jack Dempsey was officially placed on the ineligible list in New York for ignoring yet another request to appear. In retaliation Dempsey refused to ever face Wills in New York if the match ever came off at all. The Commission made it known that if they had the power they would declare his title vacant. As it stood any fighter who faced Dempsey before Dempsey formally signed to fight Wills and bound the match with a bond would be banned by New York and all of the states that it held a reciprocal relationship with. It was the final nail in the coffin of Greb's hopes for a match with Dempsey.

Without mussing his hair Greb knocked out Ed Smith one minute and twenty-five seconds into the fourth round with a short right hand on the inside. Oddly, Smith was said to have weighed only 160 lbs. after weighing in at 180 lbs. only the day before. After the count Smith hopped to his feet so gingerly that many in the audience felt he had been looking for a soft place to lay down after being cut and battered in the first three rounds.[21]

Harry and Red then headed back east. After a brief stop in Pittsburgh they went to Atlantic City where Harry had agreed to meet

Edward "Knockout" Smith was a big, 29 year old heavyweight from Carterville, Missouri, just outside of Joplin. He reportedly began boxing at the age of 17 along the Kansas-Missouri border and, by the time he fought Greb, claimed over 80 bouts, half of which he had won by KO.

Cincinnati's Pat Walsh for charity on August 12. While on the coast Harry and Mason intended to meet with promoters in hopes of arranging a bout with Dave Shade. When they arrived they found that Shade was already in talks for a title fight with Walker to be held in September. Harry's options for another big fight before the end of the outdoor season were drying up quickly. With Walker, Shade, Berlenbach, and Delaney all either scheduled for other matches or out of action the only opponent New York was interested in for Greb was the still popular Jimmy Slattery. Preliminary arrangements were made for Greb to defend his championship against Slattery at the Polo Grounds in September.

After stopping Walsh in 2 rounds Harry returned to Pittsburgh where less than a week later he amazed boxing fans by pulling a feat which was unheard of for a champion. Jack Delaney had been scheduled to face middleweight Tommy Burns in Detroit on August 17 as part of a charity card arranged for the benefit of veterans but was forced to cancel on short notice when doctors ordered surgery on a tonsular abscess he was suffering from. The frantic organizers contacted Greb, who was reticent to substitute for Delaney. "That fellow won't even give me a fight, why should I substitute for him?"[22] was Greb's reply. The organizers pleaded with Greb telling him that without his services the show would fail. Greb agreed to help out for charity's sake and immediately hopped a train for Detroit. The middleweight champion of the world had taken the fight on twelve hours' notice.

The match itself was remarkably one sided. Greb toyed with Burns for the full ten rounds without taking a single solid punch.[23]

After returning to Pittsburgh Harry had a couple of days to prepare for his upcoming fight with Jimmy Darrah at Erie. The day before the bout, on August 20, Harry set out in his new Studebaker for Erie with Leo Caghil and Allan Jones. About fifteen miles north of Pittsburgh, while attempting to pass a car on a steep downgrade made slick by a light rain, Greb's car skidded and left the road. The large vehicle rolled over three times before landing in a ditch. Harry was pinned behind the wheel of the demolished automobile as Caghil and Jones went to flag down help. Greb was unconscious and when he awoke he found that he and his companions had been taken to West Penn Hospital. Caghil and Jones suffered only minor cuts and bruises but Greb's condition was more serious. He had suffered a broken rib, internal

Harry poses inside his new Studebaker Big Six in front of the Robert Burns statue out-side of Phipps Conservatory. It is believed that this was the car Greb was driving when he skidded off the road on the way to fight Jimmy Darrah and was nearly killed. The car was demolished.

injuries, as well as various cuts and bruises. He was ordered to stay hospitalized for three weeks and would be unable to box for six weeks. Harry remembered nothing of the accident.[24]

Almost as depressing as being confined to his hospital bed was the thought that the accident threatened postponement or cancellation of his planned defense against Slattery and the $50,000 it promised. Showing the iron will and constitution that had seen him through nearly 300 fights Harry made a remarkably quick recovery. After a minor operation to remove some glass he had picked up in the accident he was released into his mother's care after just over a week in the hospital, and much earlier than the predicted stay of two weeks.

Harry lingered at his parents' house for a few days before traveling to New York with Red Mason to try to salvage the Slattery fight. They begged to postpone the match until October 5 which they hoped would give Greb enough time to recover sufficiently to train for the match. Promoter James J. Johnston agreed and petitioned the Athletic Commission to allow the delay. From there Greb headed south to Atlantic City to continue his recovery before resuming light training.

While in Atlantic City, Greb followed the National League intently. The Pittsburgh Pirates were close to winning the National League Pennant and Greb felt sure they would participate in the World Series. His only concern was making sure his fight schedule did not conflict with his fans ability to see the Pirates. "You see," he said while in New York, "I must cater to some extent to my customers in Pittsburgh. If I fight within airplane distance of Pittsburgh, I will have certain Pittsburgh rooters at ringside, which is always comforting. If I should happen to box in some important bout while the Pittsburgh team is handing a lacing to the combination that happens to win the American League flag, it would be quite impossible for these cus-

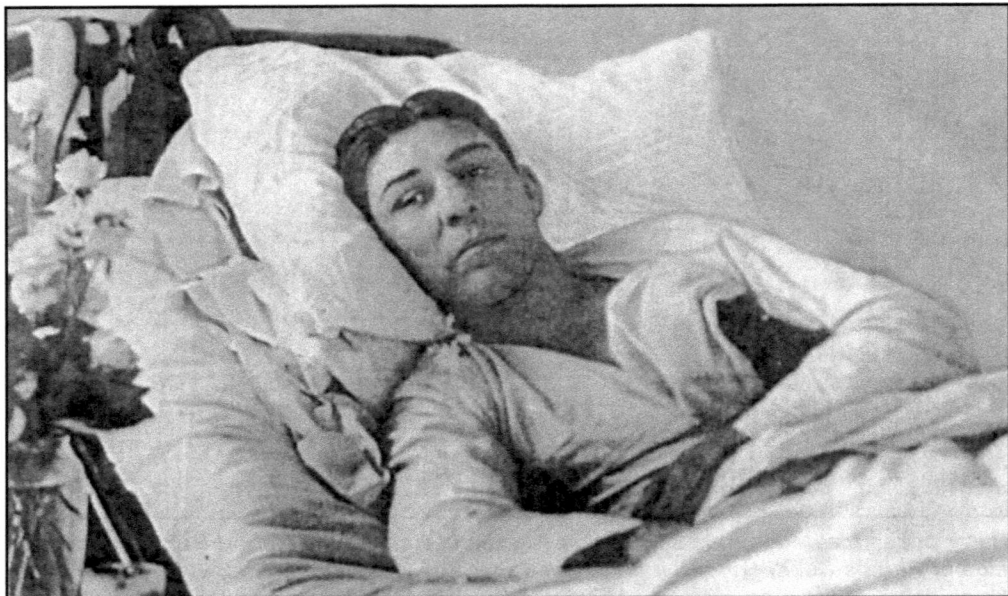

Never one for sitting in one place too long Harry looks dejected as he is confined to bed rest and observation at West Penn Hospital following his harrowing accident. Initial reports called it the end of Greb's career, doctors stated he would be laid up for at least two months. In less than two weeks he was in New York hunting up another big fight.

tomers to be present, as they will all be intent on watching their home club win a world's series, which is something they haven't seen for many years. They have seen me win many fights, and, while they never lacked interest in this particular diversion, they can't be blamed for giving their undivided attention, to the rather rare spectacle of the Pirates taking the world's championship. I do not intend to interfere with their pleasure. Neither do I intend to curtail it by mixing in some important match while they are anchored to their seats in the Pittsburgh ball park or, perhaps, in Washington or Philadelphia."

"If I boxed in some show for the purpose of making a show of a boy like Jimmy Slattery, for instance, and the date of the contest happened to conflict with the world's series in which Pittsburgh is to participate, it might work to the detriment of the so-called national pastime. The real national pastime, of course, is boxing, but the baseball fans have their pet obsessions and far be it from me to interfere with them. Let them have their world's series and get the business over with. I will wait until the baseball uproar has subsided. Baseball needs the business and we boxers should do everything to help the poor diamond magnates out. I for one, shall not offer myself as a counter-attraction to a world's series in which Pittsburgh is involved."[25]

Greb's match with Slattery had fascinating potential. In just over a week's time Slattery, who had recently turned 21 and could now box 15 rounds in New York, would challenge Paul Berlenbach for the light-heavyweight championship. Slattery had replaced the ailing Jack Delaney, who after the surgery on his throat had contracted blood poisoning forcing him to bow out of the match with Berlenbach. If Slattery could win he would drop down to 160 pounds placing both the middleweight and light heavyweight championships on the line when he and Greb met. It would be no easy task dealing with the power punching Berlenbach as questions still remained about Slattery's durability in the wake of his loss to Dave Shade.

Harry and Red Mason were present at ringside for the fight. Prior to the match Harry climbed into the ring and was introduced. Slattery started out in his customary style, dancing on his toes with his hands down at his waist. Fleet of foot and incredibly accurate Slattery made Berlenbach look slow by comparison, perforating his defense whenever the light-heavyweight champ left an opening. In the second round Berlenbach broke through and twice pinned Slattery on the ropes, hammering him with powerful hooks. After the round was over Red Mason, fearing Greb's payday could be in jeopardy, rushed to Slattery's corner and coached him throughout the bout.

Slattery had another shaky round in the third before regaining his momentum. In the fifth Slattery electrified the crowd by turning the tables on Berlenbach, pinning him to the ropes, and strafing him with several punches which brought the crowd to its feet. In the next several rounds he either outpointed Berlenbach or held him even. He often made Berlenbach look slow and foolish but as the rounds progressed Slattery began to slow.

Slattery had only been ten rounds twice in his career and had never traveled the scheduled fifteen round route. The duration told and as Slattery slowed Berlenbach got closer and closer. In the tenth Berlenbach broke through and dropped Slattery three times. The bell ending the round found Slattery on his knees and as he rose and trotted off to his corner he stumbled and fell again. When he came out for the eleventh he was still on shaky legs and for the next minute

Jimmy Slattery (facing the camera) slips one of Paul Berlenbach's dangerous blows as he challenges for Berlenbach's light-heavyweight title. Slattery survived a few scary moments to do well against the champion before finally succumbing in the eleventh round, ruining a $50,000 payday for Greb.

and a half Berlenbach battered him, dropping the young challenger three times before Patsy Haley stepped in and saved Slattery from further punishment.[26]

Jimmy Johnston had made it clear that Slattery would still be given a shot at Greb regardless of whether he won or lost but in the face of this second devastating loss in three months Slattery demurred. He stated that he would temporarily retire from the sport and go into seclusion for a number of months in order evaluate his career and to regain his confidence. With that Harry's last hope for a big money title defense by the end of the outdoor season went up in smoke.

The only possible alternative for a big fight was the winner of the upcoming Mickey Walker-Dave Shade fight. It was a long shot. Shade and Walker were scheduled to face one another at the end of the month, leaving little time to promote a major title defense with the winner. Harry was ringside to watch Walker take a disputed and somewhat controversial decision over Shade who immediately expressed his disgust with the welterweight division and intent to move up to middleweight and challenge Greb. Tex Rickard was willing to arrange the match with either Greb or Shade but he had no intention of staging the bout until early December when the new Madison Square Garden, which was currently under construction, would be open.

Anthony "Young" Marullo was a 24 year old Brooklyn born New Orleans fighter who had recently risen to contender status with several creditable showings against Paul Berlenbach, Jack Delaney, and Battling Siki, culminating in becoming the first man to stop Jeff Smith inside the distance.

Harry continued to take things easy in New York and Atlantic City for the next few weeks before returning to Pittsburgh on October 7, just in time to sit with Gene Tunney ringside at the Jack Zivic-Sailor Friedman fight and compare notes.

Harry had returned to face Tony "Young" Marullo at Motor Square Garden on October 12. The bout was to be held in conjunction with game six of the World Series. The Pirates had made it to the Series as Greb predicted. A massive influx of sports fans was expected to the city and promoters hoped to take advantage of the carnival-like atmosphere. When the game was postponed due to bad weather Greb's bout was set back a day.

Marullo would be a good opponent to challenge Greb. He had recently risen to the top of the light-heavyweight division by giving creditable performances against Tommy Loughran and Jack Delaney, as well as outpointing Paul Berlenbach before their contest was controversially declared a no-contest in a move some thought designed to preserve Berlenbach's championship. Most importantly Marullo had become the first man to stop Jeff Smith only two months previous, sending the aging veteran into temporary retirement. Despite these performances Marullo carried the reputation of being a fighter who pushed the elite fighters but ultimately came up short.

With many fans more focused on the now tied World Series heading into its final game there was a smaller than hoped for turnout for the Marullo bout. As the majority of fans sat home listening to the fight being broadcast live by KDKA Greb turned in what was probably one of his worst performances. Whether still hampered by his injuries, or the resulting inability to train properly, or as in the past, a preoccupation with baseball, Greb seemed out of shape and unusually short of breath. He dropped Marullo in the second round and hurt him again in the third but his efforts to put Marullo away left him winded and for the remainder of the bout he fought only in spurts as the contest began to look more and more like a wrestling match as opposed to a fight.

Greb was given the decision, and every round of the fight, but it had been a dismal affair. Blame for the poor showing rested squarely with Harry and he was booed by even his own fans as he left the ring. Sadly, in an odd twist of fate, this unsatisfying fight would be the last bout Greb ever fought in Pittsburgh before the fans he cherished.[27]

For the next several weeks Harry laid low while waiting for promoters in New York to arrange the big match he had been desperate for. The frontrunner was Tex Rickard who was trying to arrange a fight featuring Greb against Dave Shade, Mickey Walker, or Paul Berlenbach. Harry wanted a guarantee of $50,000 reasoning that he had made more than that against Walker and that Walker had been paid $100,000 to defend his championship against Shade. Rickard refused stating he was no longer going to play Santa Claus to fighters, once again delaying any possibility of Greb making a sizeable purse.

In the meantime Greb accepted terms for a rematch with Marullo in New Orleans for fifteen rounds on November 13. Angry over the rough fight Greb had put up in their first bout Marullo talked long and loud about his plan to pay Greb back in kind with his pet kidney punch, which despite being outlawed in most states was still legal in New Orleans. Greb was scheduled to arrive in New Orleans to help with the promotion on November 9 but true to form was three days late. When he finally arrived he sparred with Big Boy Peterson and Young Scotty to shake out the cobwebs of the long train ride.

After a fairly even first round Greb took over and outclassed Marullo until the tenth round when he noticeably began to tire. Once again it seemed Harry had not fully recovered the level of conditioning he had attained prior to the accident. Marullo took the tenth and the twelfth; the rest of the rounds went to Greb or were even. Any time Marullo threatened to use his greater size to advantage Greb would tie him up and toss him around the ring to show that he was stronger. Several times when frustrated by his lack of success Marullo attempted to use his much publicized kidney punch but Greb would expose his flanks to the blows and laugh when they had no effect. Despite his lack of condition Greb won the fight easily.[28]

Harry spent the next two weeks between Pittsburgh and New York hunting up fights but finally became frustrated when nothing could be arranged and decided to head for Hot Springs, where he hoped to get himself back into condition for a barnstorming tour across the country and into California. Harry had been in Hot Springs for less than a week when he got the call from Rickard to return to New York to discuss a proposed bout with the winner of the Berlenbach-Delaney fight being staged by Rickard on December 11. Greb caught the first train from Hot Springs on December 4 and made New York on December 10.

Harry was disappointed when he arrived to discover that Rickard had called Greb to the city under false pretenses. Rather than attempting to arrange a bout for Greb he had hoped to have Greb on hand to substitute for Delaney in case Delaney could not pass the physical. After the throat surgery which resulted in Greb substituting for Delaney against Tommy Burns Delaney had experienced a long and difficult recovery. Some felt Delaney was not sufficiently recovered to fight, prompting Rickard to con Greb into being present as an alternate.[29]

Delaney proved healthy enough to face Berlenbach and gave the champion a scare by dropping him in the fourth. Greb was in the audience watching and had been introduced from the ring prior to the match. Berlenbach ultimately won a close decision after Delaney faded over the second half of the fight. The fight was the first of its kind in New York to be judged on the basis of the number of rounds won.

On the day of the fight, whether he had any intention of honoring the agreement or not, Rickard came to terms with Greb for a two fight deal totaling $100,000 for Greb. The first fight of the agreement was supposed to be the winner of the Berlenbach-Delaney fight but when offered the chance Berlenbach demurred, stating he intended to take a rest and then face the winner of the upcoming bout between Tiger Flowers and Mike McTigue. Once again Greb was left out in the cold.

Harry left New York to travel directly to Nashville where he had a scheduled rematch with Soldier Buck. Harry approached the bout as little more than a workout. He smiled throughout the contest and never really opened up on Buck despite staying far out in front on points. There were no knockdowns and this, combined with the impression that Greb was fighting under wraps, left some in the audience unsatisfied with the champion's performance.[30]

The Flowers-McTigue fight scheduled for December 23 was promoted as being a ten round elimination bout to decide an opponent for Berlenbach. In getting the bout Walk Miller had once again been suspended by the athletic commission for continuing to spread the rumor that Jack Delaney had defeated Flowers by using leaden gloves. The suspension was finally lifted when Miller appeared in person to apologize and promise for the second time that it would not happen again.

Fought for the New York American Christmas Fund, the Flowers-McTigue bout would go down in history as one of the worst decisions ever rendered in New York. For ten rounds Flowers attacked McTigue, who fought largely on the defensive with only occasional bursts of offense. Two inexperienced guest judges were being used as part of the charity promotion, Bernard Gimbel of department store fame, and Peter J. Brady of the Federation Bank. When the decision was announced it was discovered that Brady and Gimbel had voted for McTigue while referee Eddie Purdy, the only experienced official, had voted for Flowers. For ten minutes after Joe Humphries read the decision the audience of twelve thousand hurled a cascade of boos and catcalls down on the ring.[31]

Walter F. Buckrop, known professionally as Soldier Buck, was a club fighter from Louisville, Kentucky who faced Greb twice in 1925. At only 24 years old he gave a good account of himself despite losing both fights.

Walk Miller was understandably livid and protested the decision to the commission but the result stood. Instead, Miller posted a $2,500 forfeit to bind Flowers' challenge of Greb. The commission immediately ordered that Greb must sign to defend his title against Flowers within thirty days. The Pittsburgh newspapers laughed over the thought of anyone having to order Greb to fight. "Will I fight Flowers," laughed Greb as he left for New York, "Will I? Say don't you remember a few months back when I offered to fight that bird in Duquesne Gardens here? That show didn't go through, but it wasn't any fault of mine. I wanted the Tiger to get even with him for some dirty cracks he and his manager have been making about our fought down in Fremont, Ohio last summer a year ago. I won the popular decision but he has been claiming he gave me a whipping. I wasn't in any sort of shape that night, but I will be when I fight him again and I'll show 'em what a fine challenger he is. The commission is doing me a favor ordering me to fight him. It is creating a demand in New York for a match that wasn't well enough thought of in Pittsburgh to serve as opening show of a new club, and I'll get myself around $40,000 smackers for smacking the Tiger into a tabby cat. Pardon me while I laugh up the other sleeve a while. This one has had all the chuckles it can stand."[32] Indeed, Greb was so eager for the match that the day the commissions announcement was made public he boarded a train for New York and finalized the match within the week for a purse of $60,000. Combined with the fact that Harry gleefully announced that he was in negotiations with a club in Miami to face Gene Tunney a sixth time in a ten round no-decision bout for $35,000, Harry was finally back in the big money.[33]

Before heading west to California Greb first traveled to Toronto to face Britain's Roland Todd. Todd had turned professional at seventeen and quickly racked up an impressive string of wins which included wins over previous Greb opponents Frank Moody and Ted Moore. In early 1923 Todd defeated Britain's legendary Ted "Kid" Lewis for the British, Commonwealth, and European middleweight titles. Late that same year he traveled to the United States in hopes of getting a fight with Greb but met with mixed success and left for home. He had arrived back in the States in December and quickly acquired a fight with Dave Shade on New Year's Day which he lost. Undaunted he traveled to Toronto to face Greb in hopes that a victory or a good showing would force Greb to enter into a championship fight with him.

Todd proved no match for Greb. Slower of hand and foot Todd was made to order for Harry with his stand up European style. As had been increasingly his custom Greb laid back in the early rounds, doing just enough to stay out in front on points. He countered and preserved his energy for his usual late round push. He began to speed up in the fourth round and in the sixth opened a cut over Todd's left eye which slowed the challenger. After gaining a wide lead Greb went all out in the eleventh and twelfth hitting Todd with everything in his arsenal and leaving no doubt as to the victor.[34]

Harry returned to Pittsburgh for a brief stay before he left in the early morning hours of January 17 for Omaha, Nebraska accompanied by Red Mason, Jack White, and Eddie Deasy. In Omaha he would face Toledo's Joe Lohman on January 19. The plan was for Greb to fight his way out west, and fight his way back in order to be in shape by the time he arrived in New York to defend against Tiger Flowers but Greb had other ideas. In light of Flowers' two knockout losses to Jack Delaney, a recent newspaper loss to Chuck Wiggins, and the unjust loss he suf-

Roland Todd was the British and Commonwealth middleweight champion in 1926 and had held the European championship. He had come to the United States with the express intention of challenging for the world's title. He had defeated such battlers as Ted "Kid" Lewis, Jock Malone, and also held wins over previous Greb opponents from Britain Ted Moore, and Frank Moody.

fered at the hands of McTigue, Greb seemed to be over confident and taking Flowers lightly. According to an exasperated Red Mason Greb was up until four in the morning the night before his fight with Lohman.[35] Harry took the fight itself as nothing more than a workout despite Lohman's advantage in size and wealth of experience. Harry held back and never showed his full range of ability.[36]

During the fight a fourteen year old newsboy, anxious to see the world champion, had climbed to a second story window of the auditorium, lost his footing, and plummeted head first to the pavement below, knocking out all of his teeth and leaving him unconscious. The boy was taken immediately to the hospital where he remained in a coma. He passed away the following day. Harry left Omaha unaware of the tragedy. When he finally heard of the young boy's fate he was grief stricken. He immediately sent $50 (equivalent to nearly $700 in today's currency) to the boy's father to help with the funeral expenses.[37]

Joe Lohman, seen here (left) posing with Jack Barry in 1931, was a big light-heavyweight from Toledo, Ohio who had been fighting for over 10 years when he met Greb in early 1926. He had met some of the greatest names in the sport and would go on to fight for nearly another ten years. His match with Greb would result in a tragedy.

Harry and his entourage arrived in Los Angeles on January 22. The party was greeted by an enthusiastic crowd which included former middleweight champion Billy Papke, young power punching bantamweight Bud Taylor, and promoter Jack Doyle, who would promote Greb's first bout in California against Ted Moore at his Vernon Arena. Harry quickly made it plain that this trip was as much or more about pleasure than it was about preparing for Flowers. He intended to do a minimum of training and a lot of sight-seeing. "I don't want to get too fine while on this trip as I have to make 160 pounds on February 26 for Tiger Flowers in New York in a championship fight," he said. "I will only box about ten days in the gym for that fight."[38] Instead Harry inquired where he could rent a car to see as much of California as possible.

Harry's rematch with Ted Moore was heavily promoted on the myth that their first bout had been a controversial decision. Since facing Greb Moore had continued to get fights in the United States but had run into Tiger Flowers in a pair of fights, losing a decision in one and being stopped in the other. His most recent fight had been against rising West Coast contender

Leo Lomski, in which he lost a closely contested decision. Moore was being trained for Greb by Jack Dempsey's trainer Jerry "The Greek" Luvadis and hoped some of the champions skills would rub off on him.

Much as he had in their first fight Moore worked almost exclusively to Greb's body as Greb beat a tattoo wherever Moore left an opening. Claude Newman of the Hollywood Daily Citizen perfectly captured Greb's style and the flow of the fight:

> "Perpetual Motion Harry" rollicked through the ten rounds and seemed to enjoy himself fully while plastering Moore with punches that came from nowhere and many times ended up in the same place.
>
> Like any freak, Greb is a sideshow attraction, He does nothing according to Hoyle but does everything efficiently.
>
> Sometimes he leads with his right -- Something the critics say should never be done. But then, Harry never does anything he should, only win fights as middleweight champion of the universe. Harry leads with his right but doesn't get his jaw broken.
>
> Leaping forward with the agility of a gymnastic, the "Pittsburgh windmill" surprises everyone and his opponent by starting a lead with his left and before the

Left to right front row: Red Mason, Billy Papke, Bud Taylor, Jack Doyle, Harry Greb, unknown, as Greb is met at the train station in Los Angeles by well wishers.

motion is completed landing with his right. At times he gets his hands all wrapped around in front of himself but punches materialize out of thin air and the man opposite is the sufferer.

Built loosely, strong and fast, "Hopping Harry" is indeed a showman. After seeing his relaxation it is easy to understand why Greb fights and fights but never wears out. He does things without apparent effort. He was as fresh as a daisy in the tenth round and seemed capable of five more rounds of agile effort.

It is uncanny the way Greb can windmill around without getting hurt and at the same time belabor an opponent with wallops that the devotees didn't know existed. When Harry isn't punching he is bobbing up and down like a buoy on a rough sea.

Greb is the type you have to see fight to know how he does it. His flailing arms hook, jab, and uppercut with equal alacrity from all points of the compass. Part of the time he comes crouching off the floor. Again he is standing straight up, flapping his arms lashing out accurately.

Moore was no worry whatever to Greb, who won about as he pleased and without putting the punch windmill into high gear. This Moore person is tough, aggressive, smart, and game but he can never match the brains and experience of Greb's thirteen years in the ring.[39]

Newman gave Moore only one round to Greb's seven with two even. The Los Angeles Evening Herald agreed with Newman's assessment but gave Greb six rounds to Moore's three with one even. The Los Angeles Times neglected to give their score but stated the fight was close.

Continuing his barnstorming, Harry got special permission from the local commission to box Buck Holley three days after his bout with Moore. Typically a fighter could not have more than one bout a week but the commission recognized the fact that Greb had a limited amount of time in which to squeeze in fights and offered the rare opportunity for fans to see a champion. Holley had been a favorite club fighter of the four round era in California. By the time he faced Greb Holley was semi-retired from the ring and training fighters. His lack of experience and class told against Greb who easily dominated the fight's action. Holley missed often, and badly. At times the momentum of his wild swings sent him reeling to the floor. He was wide open for Greb's counters and by the fifth he was reeling. After the round Greb helped him to his corner where Holley's seconds threw in the towel to save him further punishment.[40]

Harry left Los Angeles and set up camp across the bay in San Francisco, which irritated some fans, who felt he should stay in city where he would be earning his paycheck against Jimmy Delaney. Delaney had spent much of his time on the West Coast since last facing Greb the previous year and had gone undefeated in all of his fights save a ten round loss to Young Stribling

29 year old Ardent Hollingsworth aka Buck Holley had been a favorite in California during the four round era. Never more than a trial horse, he was called out of a semi-retirement which found him training fighters to face Greb on his second West Coast tour.

in September. Harry was expected to win the bout but much was made of his refusal to adhere to a strict training regimen. He took only a light workout the day before the fight upon arriving in Oakland and according to Bob Shand, who was no fan of Greb's, Harry spent the day of the fight sightseeing with a carload of women and only stopped long enough to face Delaney before resuming the party.[41]

Weighing in at 172 Delaney was eight pounds heavier than Greb who once again took things easy. Delaney seemed to lack confidence either in his ability or conditioning against Greb and this combined with Greb's obvious careless approach to the fight soured some fans. Yet, despite Greb's less than Spartan training he was clearly in better condition than Delaney who noticeably tired after the third round allowing Greb to waltz to an easy decision.[42]

Harry continued to enjoy the weather in California for several more days before boarding a train east. Despite the New York State Athletic Commission's attempt to prevent him from signing any fights between February 1 and the date of his defense against Flowers Harry picked up another easy money bout against a young local pug in Phoenix, Arizona named Owen Phelps.

Phelps had begun boxing in late 1923 and according to local press had fought thirty-five bouts, losing only one. Phelps was a rugged middleweight with a lot of promise but he was young and inexperienced. Greb had sent a scout ahead to watch Phelps' bout with Tiger Johnny Cline the week before he was scheduled to face Greb. The scout brought back a report that Phelps was a willing, awkward battler who Greb should be able to defeat without much concern but against whom Greb should not take any chances. Phelps understood full well the opportunity he had been presented and planned to fight every second of every round.

When Greb arrived in Phoenix he brought news that he had agreed to terms for a sixth bout with Gene Tunney in Miami. Phoenix sportswriters found Greb to be a fun loving fighter, more than willing to dispense his seven rules for success in the ring:

1. Live naturally - you'll last longer.

2. Fight yourself into condition and keep fighting.

3. Don't pay sparring partners to fight you - let promoters pay you to fight sparring partners.

4. A fight a week makes the bankroll speak.

5. Keep the other fellow so busy stopping 'em that he hasn't time to backfire.

6. A boxing glove is harmless unless you keep it hitting.

7. If there is no fun being champion, why be champion?[43]

"I just gotta catch the 11 o'clock train Friday night in order to be in Pittsburgh Wednesday morning and not disappoint Dorothy and my home-town folks," said Harry. "I'm gonna catch the midnight choo choo if I have to board the train on a stretcher. Don't get the idea that Dorothy is my sweetie back in Pittsburgh for she's my little seven year-old daughter who was left motherless three years ago when lung trouble claimed Mrs. Greb before we could get to Arizona, where we had planned to come."

"Dorothy is Owen Phelps' hardest foe tomorrow night for it will be largely for her sake that I'll try to turn the lights out for the Arizona boy and catch the train that'll carry me back to the old smoky home town where I started my career. Dorothy is my strongest rooter and never loses a chance to tell her school chums that her Daddy licked Tom Gibbons and it is for Dorothy's sake that I've reached the position in the fight which I hold today."[44]

Harry added that he intended to retire in 1927, an assertion he had been making for several months now, but first hoped to clean out the light-heavyweight division, win a title there and then challenge Jack Dempsey. He also addressed the stories of his hard partying. "The fight fans have me all wrong. They think I hit the booze pretty hard. As a matter of fact, I never drink any of it."[45] But Harry said nothing of spurning late nights.

The same day Harry arrived in Phoenix, the day before his bout with Phelps, with barely enough time to shake the trail dust, he was treated to a luncheon by the Lions Club, trained for eight rounds in the

Left to right: Red Mason, Harry Greb, referee Al Wainright, Jimmy Delaney, announcer Eddie Ryan, and Mike Collins pose prior to Greb's 1926 bout with Delaney in Oakland, California.

Owen Phelps was a 21 year old fighter from Mesa, Arizona who had previously fought under the name "Roughhouse Nelson." He gave Greb the best fight of Greb's western barnstorming tour, prompting Red Mason to attempt to purchase his contract for $5,000.

gym (claiming it was only his third gymnasium workout in five weeks), took in a comedy, and then attended the local Elk's ball that evening.

The following day Greb met Owen Phelps. Surprisingly the betting odds were even, illustrating Phelps popularity in the region. Phelps had agreed to come in over the middleweight limit and at 163 was outweighed by six pounds. He gave Greb the best workout of anyone on his western tour, drawing blood from the champion's mouth early in the fight which Greb paid back in kind. Yet, despite his willingness Phelps was outclassed by Greb in every aspect of the sport. When the referee's decision was announced many in the audience were unhappy, hoping for a draw for their home-town boy, but both the referee and the Arizona Gazette agreed that Greb had won six rounds, Phelps three, and one round was even. The Arizona Republic gave Greb nine rounds and called one even.[46] Red Mason was so impressed with Phelps that he unsuccessfully tried to buy the young fighter's contract for $5,000 before leaving for home.[47]

Harry and his entourage hopped on a train headed east and meandered their way toward Pittsburgh. When they passed Omaha Harry learned of the circumstances surrounding young Morris Osterman's death the previous month. Harry was grief stricken and arranged for money to be sent to his father to helo defer funeral expenses. When they arrived in Chicago he notified curious reporters that the planned fight with Tunney in Miami was likely off as he had not received word from the promoters since agreeing to their terms. The day after Greb had agreed to terms for the bout Young Stribling was announced as Tunney's opponent. Tunney had now been placed on the fast track to challenge for Dempsey's championship by Tex Rickard and likely viewed Stribling as the lesser threat, and thereby unlikely to upset his plans. In any case Tunney eventually abandoned the fight altogether, preferring to stay inactive and protect his status as Rickard's favorite for Dempsey's next challenger.

As Harry continued eastward, he headed toward a historic title defense against Tiger Flowers, and an outcome that was utterly inconceivable to him. As Harry had lived life to the fullest during the previous weeks out west, enjoying the fruits of his long years of labor, there was no hint that over the next several months Harry's life would spiral out of control leaving the usually happy-go-lucky fighter despondent and questioning his future.

25

THE GEORGIA DEACON

When Harry pulled into Pittsburgh on the morning of February 18 he was met with a summons from Garden matchmaker Jess McMahon requesting his immediate presence in New York. Harry left that evening for New York and arrived the following day, exhausted from his cross country journey. That same day he began formal training at Philadelphia Jack O'Brien's gym for his title defense against Tiger Flowers. Feeling that his western tour had left him sharp, Harry focused his training primarily on cutting weight.

The match would be a history making event. Tiger Flowers was the first African-American to challenge for the middleweight championship, and as a result would be the first African-American middleweight champion in history if he succeeded in defeating Greb. In addition to this the match was the first mixed race championship bout held in New York since the implementation of the Walker Law, and indeed it would be the first mixed race championship in the United States in over a decade. As a result ticket sales were brisk and the match was expected to do very well at the box office.

Harry was installed by the bookmakers as a slight favorite over Flowers at odds of 8 to 5, and in some quarters as much as 2 to 1.[1] He continued to pay lip service to Flowers' ability publicly but he was taking the challenger lightly, failing even to have a single southpaw in his training camp to prepare him for the Flowers' stance. On the relatively few occasions that he actually sparred, chief sparring partner George Courtney was ordered to box left handed, but invariably as soon as Harry opened up on him Courtney would switch back to an orthodox stance in order to better defend himself. After less than six days of formal training, spent mostly playing handball, Harry wound up his training camp the day before the fight.[2]

Harry's unusually relaxed preparation for a fight of this magnitude and an opponent of this caliber was due in part to the prevailing opinion among sportswriters and fans that Flowers had been exposed in his bouts with Delaney. This belief was echoed, even magnified to some extent, by the black press who felt their faith in Flowers had been misguided after his shocking losses. W. Rollo Wilson, dean of black sportswriters, working at the Pittsburgh Courier, was one such writer:

The majority of my readers hope Tiger Flowers will lick Harry Greb and some

of them may be foolish enough to wager their guilders and kronen and kopecks and guineas thereon. So this comes as a word of caution. DON'T BET AGAINST GARFIELD HARRY IN A CHAMPIONSHIP FIGHT!

...Flowers has a YELLOW STREAK which may, or may not, crop out in this bout. The Georgia Jungaleer quit cold to Jack Delaney in their second bout and I am not the only one who says so! If Delaney kayoed Flowers then Cum Posey and Romeo Daugherty are blood brothers. This throwback of Flowers' -fear complex, if you please -has never exhibited itself against any other boxer. Certainly he did not trot it out when he mixed with Greb in Fremont...

...That's the story to date. If both men go at top speed and each gives his best from bell to bell it will be a helluva fight when they meet on the 26th.

But don't bet on it.[3]

The New York Amsterdam News echoed Wilson's opinion of Flowers:

...His quick retreat on two occasions, to the canvas, hastened by the blows of Monsieur Chapedelaine, has left colored Harlem in doubt of the ability of Theodore Flowers to win from Harry Greb, and that in spite of his victory over Mike McTigue.

The colored sport when stung twice in the same place becomes wary, and while he will turn out in large numbers to Mr. Rickard's Garden on Friday night, it will not be with the same spirit of confidence that marked his first trip to the big amphitheater when he hearkened unto the call of Walk Miller and Jess McMahon to see Tiger cut loose against Mr. Delaney.[4]

Harry agreed with this assessment of Flowers, and felt that since the Delaney fights Flowers had been somewhat off form. This outlook and resulting lack of adequate preparation completely ignored the fact that Flowers had only lost one official decision in his entire career, that being his loss to McTigue which was universally considered a terrible decision. In short Harry would have to be at his best to win a points victory over Flowers, particularly in light of the fact that the fight was expected to go the full route, given that neither fighter was known as a particularly hard puncher.

"I expect Flowers to give me one of the hardest fights I have ever had, but I expect to win," said the champion the day before the fight. "I am in great shape and ready for the rest. The Tiger gave me what I consider the toughest fight of my career when we met at Fremont, Ohio nearly two years ago, and I have not forgotten it. I will go right after Flowers from the start, and I believe the winner will be the man who can stand up best under the hot pace."

"I cannot look for a knockout either way and will not start the battle with the idea of 'taking' Flowers. However, if he weakens I may make a big try for a decisive finish in the later rounds. Also, if my opponent should get off to a big lead and be out in front at the end of the tenth round, I will throw everything I have into every punch thereafter, even swinging from the floor if necessary and either will knock him out or be knocked out in the attempt."

"If I lose I will go down fighting, as a real champion should."[5]

Finishing his training at Sprague's gym in Harlem Flowers, who had been bothered by the fact that he was being taken so lightly by the press and fans, exuded a quiet confidence. He had spent several weeks in training camp in the south hunting, chopping wood, and doing road-work. He polished this off with a week of heavy training in the gym and was now in magnificent condition. It was clear that he understood the magnitude of the opportunity he had been given and planned to make the most of what he believed was divine providence. "All I can say is I am confident," said Flowers in his final interview before the fight. "The better man will win and I believe I am the better man. I learned a lot about Greb in our first bout and just as sure as Jack Delaney is my admitted master, I am sure I have the edge on Greb. I know I am going to face one of the fastest and greatest fighters of modern times, but I do not fear the issue. I am asking my friends to back me to win."[6]

The afternoon of the fight Harry arrived at the weigh in looking drawn and pale, the sure sign of a man who has struggled to make weight, while Flowers had been below weight for several days. Greb weighed 159^1/$_2$, just half a pound under the limit and a pound heavier than Flowers. The two men posed for photographers and Greb assured Chairman Muldoon that he was in the best of condition before leaving.

That night, after the preliminaries, Flowers entered the ring first followed a few minutes later by Greb, wearing a dark satin robe trimmed in purple, still looking pale and worried. He crossed the ring and shook hands with Tiger before returning to his corner to listen to Joe Humphries give the announcement. By fight time odds had lengthened in Greb's favor to as much as 5 to 1 in some areas, though few bets were being made.[7] As predicted the fight was excellently attended. 16,311 people paid $105,134.70 to see the event, making it an overwhelming financial success. Greb's purse of 37^1/$_2$ percent would generate one of his largest paydays.

Flowers was so eager to get the fight underway that he leapt from his corner before the gong had even had a chance to ring and was turned back. When the bell finally started the round he was still facing his corner and turned to meet Greb, catching the champion in a clinch. It quickly became apparent that both fighters had a great deal of respect for the other, and that their unusual styles would not make for a pretty fight. After being parted Flowers lashed out at Greb with rights and lefts to the head and body. Harry seemed surprised by Flowers' attack and was momentarily staggered when caught off balance. Flowers pinned Greb in a neutral corner pouring in punches before Greb seemed to wake up. He threw his weight behind a right hand which sent Flowers reeling. Greb gave chase with a volley of punches and landed a short right uppercut before the bell which gave Flowers a slight cut above the left eye.

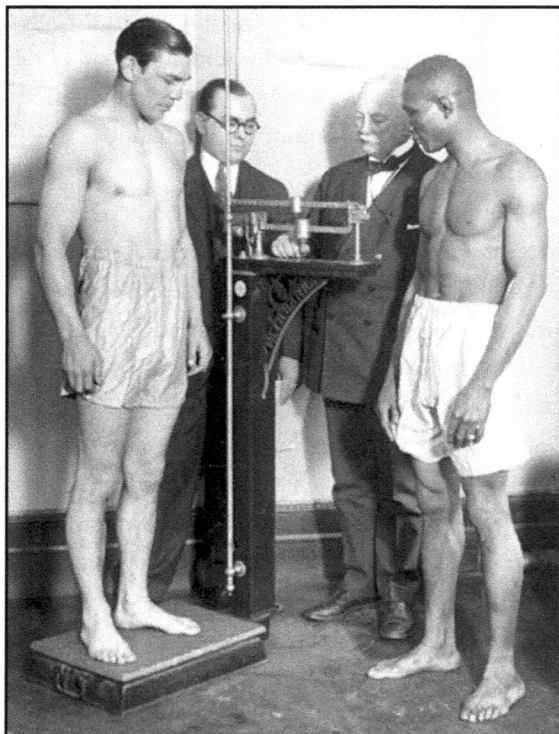

Top: Tiger Flowers (right) watches intently as Greb weighs in for the championship bout. Boxing Commission members Bert Stand (center left) and William Muldoon (center right) officiate. Above: Greb and Flowers pose for photographers at the weigh in ceremonies.

Harry improved upon his tepid performance in the second to a degree. He was missing a lot of punches though those that landed seemed to bother Flowers. During an accidental clash of heads (a common occurrence when an orthodox fighter meets a southpaw) Harry suffered a bad cut over the left eye which extended partially down the side of his nose.

Flowers immediately reopened the cut above Harry's left eye at the start of the third and very quickly blood streamed into the eye and cascaded down Harry's face. Blind in one eye for nearly five years, and now with blood rendering his good eye all but useless Harry was in serious trouble. The only success Harry could find was when he was able to work in close, grip Flowers with his left, and hammer away with his right to the body and head. During these exchanges inside Flowers complained that Greb was thumbing him, while Flowers was accused of heeling and slapping with open glove. At long range Harry was nearly helpless and fought almost the exclusively on the defensive. The two were locked in an embrace and fighting so furiously at the close of the round that neither heard the bell and had to be pried apart by referee Gunboat Smith.

When Greb emerged from his corner for the fourth round with his eye cleaned, and the flow of blood halted, the newspapermen ringside (who had no idea of the condition of his right eye) noted that Greb was now more accurate and more aggressive. It was easily his best round of the fight so far as he forced Tiger Flowers to break ground in numerous exchanges.

The fifth was a slightly better round for Flowers but with the flow of blood seemingly staunched Greb was still able to hold his own. The round was fought at a slower pace than the previous four. Despite the lack of action Greb was able to reopen Flower's left eye before the close of the round.

The sixth was another slow round and the fight now seemed to be settling into a more measured pace in anticipation of a long fight. Harry was able to rock Flowers once and got a laugh from the audience by disdainfully mocking Flowers' body punching.

The fight was shaping up to be a sloppy affair by the seventh with both fighters missing more than they landed. Flowers once again complained that Harry was using his thumbs in close even as he himself had been accused of kidney punches and repeatedly slapping with the open glove. There was a great deal of clinching and wrestling to be seen and the audience booed or admonished both fighters in turn, Greb for his dirty tactics and Flowers for his inability to take command of a fighter who was apparently badly faded.

In the eighth Flowers again complained that he was being thumbed and Greb drew a warning from the referee for his tactics. Both fighters had their moments in this round and fought furiously after the bell.

By the ninth several reporters had begun to

Top: Greb (left) and Flowers exchange lefts during the first round of their second fight. Above: Greb parries a left and lands his own left hand during the second round.

notice that Greb had been fighting much of the fight one handed. He relied almost solely on his right hand and used his left only sparingly or to block or throw light punches to the body. Several reporters noted that this seemed to confirm a pre-fight rumor that Harry had injured his left hand in training.

The tenth and eleventh were uninteresting rounds, featuring more clinching, missed punches, and sloppy fighting. Flowers, looking to take command, was now beating Greb to the punch. He was faster, more accurate, and his judgment of distance was better. Whenever Harry

Top: Greb launches a left as Flowers backs out of range during the third round. Above: The fight was marred by a series of mauling clinches as seen above in this photograph taken during the fourth round.
Facing Page top: Flowers ducks under a right hand thrown by Greb.
Facing page center: The two fighters square off during a lull in the action.
Facing page bottom: An excellent example of the tactic which Greb became most associated with during the latter portion of his career. He is seen here holding Flowers around the neck with his left while buffeting him about the head and body with his right.

attempted to mount an offense Flowers either avoided the issue or tied Greb up.

Between rounds Red Mason was heard to exclaim "You'll have to step on it, Harry. Go out and give it to him next round. Let him have both barrels." And for the first time in the fight Greb came out for the twelfth round and looked like the Greb of old, instead of just an old Greb. He immediately sailed into Flowers with both fists churning in his famous windmill style and rocked the challenger. An uppercut snapped Flowers head back and a right hand spun him completely around. In his fury Greb bulled Flowers through the ropes and nearly pushed him completely out of the ring. He was booed by the crowd for this overzealous act and warned by the referee but he had clearly won the round.

Flowers rushed out intent on regaining lost ground in the thirteenth but his attack was smothered in a clinch. Coming out of the clinch Flowers complained of being butted and once again the fight devolved into a series of mauling clinches.

The fighters sparred conservatively in the fourteenth, seemingly saving up for a big finish. Each took turns taking control of the momentum, first one, and then the other chasing his opponent across the ring.

They shook hands for the fifteenth and final round in ring center as the crowd waited in anticipation of what could be the deciding round. Harry tried desperately but he was weak and once again there was much clinching and mauling. Flowers landed a hard punch which wobbled Greb and, as he had in the past when stung, Harry tried to counter-attack but the old fire was gone. The fighters were mixing at the bell with Greb landing the

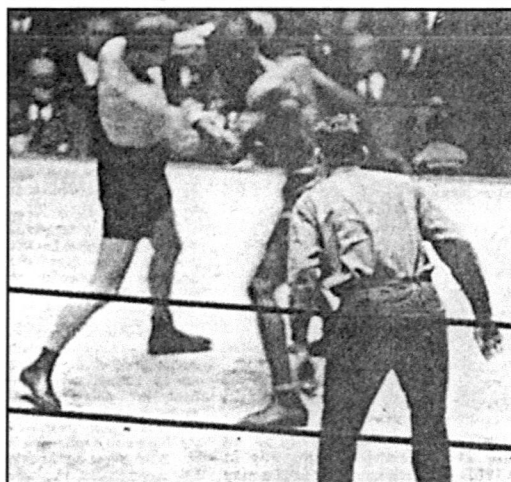

Top: Flowers sidesteps one of Harry's attacks.

Center: Harry is on guard as Flowers starts a punch.

Left: The two fighters work furiously inside.

Facing page top: Flowers holds on as Greb attempts to break a clinch in the sixth round.

Facing page center: Flowers leaps away from an attack started by Greb during the eighth round.

Facing page bottom: Flowers lands a two fisted attack during the ninth round.

final blow to punctuate the fight.[8]

The bout had been close, remarkably close. Nobody could deny that. Even Greb had sensed the urgency of the situation as the rounds ticked by and tried everything to take Flowers off his game from rough tactics to cursing his man in the clinches. His handlers as well sensed the fight was close and repeatedly admonished Harry to "Go Into him. Carry him along fast. Give him all that you have, Harry!"[9]

Flowers himself understood the match to be close as evidenced by his behavior when Joe Humphries stepped to the center of the ring to announce the winner. The announcer held his arms aloft in a sign universally recognized throughout the arena as symbolizing a draw. Greb stood puzzled as Flowers leapt from his stool and approached with a broad smile and a congratulatory handshake, clearly pleased with the outcome. He was halted mid-ring by Joe Humphries and ushered back to his corner. Humphries then returned to the center of the ring and announced "The winner and new champion, Tiger Flowers!"

Flowers exploded in a show of emotion, kicking his heels together, running around the ring, and hugging his handlers before nearly toppling over in the arms Walk Miller as the two embraced. Harry stood in his corner as if stricken. Nearly in tears he buried his head in the ring ropes before Flowers came to shake hands. Harry managed a weak smile but could not find any words. His sister sat a few rows away with tears streaking down her cheeks.

The vast majority of critics ringside scored

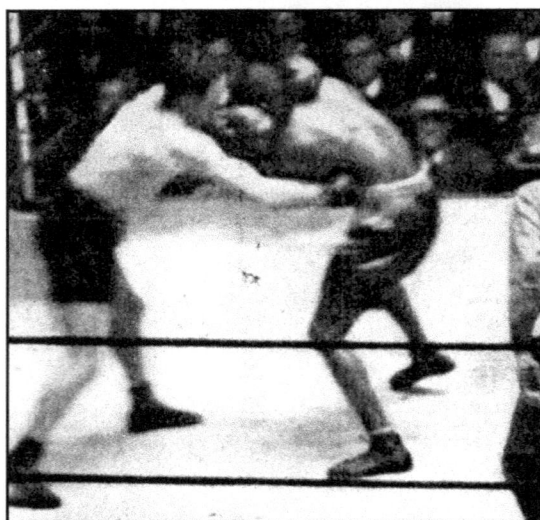

Top: Greb launched a furious attack in the twelfth and nearly pushed Flowers out of the ring.
Above: Once again Greb is seen holding Flowers by the neck and pounding away at any opening the challenger leaves.

the fight for Flowers but had it no more than a two round swing, meaning that had just two rounds been scored differently Greb would have retained his championship. Many felt that Harry had either won the fight, or that Flowers' margin of victory was too small for the championship to change hands. The decision itself had been split with the two judges awarding victory to Flowers while the referee, Gunboat Smith, voted for Greb. Everyone admitted that Harry had fought his worst fight and that he was very likely through as a great fighter. He had fought at times as though he was sleepwalking through the bout. Even those who felt Flowers had legitimately defeated Greb predicted that his reign as champion would be a short one if he could not prove a more conclusive victory over a fighter who had fought as poorly as Greb.

The following day the match was written up by the press as a morality play. It became a struggle of the god-fearing, quiet, reserved, family man against the rambling Good Time Charlie who preferred the life of wine, women, and song to one of hard work and who paid the price for burning the candle at both ends. Some of this was at least partially true, particularly in the past couple of years, but for the most part it was, and has continued to be greatly exaggerated. In reality Greb was now an aging fighter with an incredible amount of ring wear. How much longer he could continue fighting at such a high level had been in question for years and even now he was talking about retirement. Greb's days as champion were numbered long before he ever stepped into the ring with Flowers. Injuries suffered in training and in the ring as well as his maddeningly relaxed method of preparation for what was admittedly one of his more difficult opponents combined to render him a blunted weapon in the squared circle. Even then Flowers had only beaten the champion, a shadow of the Greb who had cut a swath through three divisions back in 1919, by a whisker. And, while Harry may not have recited the 144th Psalm between rounds as Flowers did, he was equally devoted to his church, having donated thousands of dollars and hours of his time to it's benefit. He may not have worn his religion on his sleeve but he was not the denizen of the streets that he had been portrayed as, even if he had strayed somewhat from the path of late.

Harry slowly returned to his dressing room, making his way through the crowd to a mingled chorus of boos and cheers. In his dressing room he sat with his head in his hands for nearly a half an hour before finally granting interviews. "I just could not get started," he said. "I thought I was as good as ever but I was not up to snuff. If anyone had told me I would do no better than I did I would not have believed it. But, at that, I thought I deserved at least a draw. I never was hurt. I want to fight him again and I don't care how soon it is either. Let me get him again and I will win back the title."[10]

Focusing on the fact that the fight contract stipulated that Flowers would give Greb a shot to regain the title within ninety days, in the event he won the championship, Greb was eager for a rematch. "Give me another crack at Flowers, and I'll reverse the decision. I thought I won and I am disappointed over my defeat. However, if the judges thought I lost that settles that. Get him again for me. He's a clean fighter, and I congratulate him. But get him in there again."[11]

After the fight Flowers continued to express his confidence and joy at winning the title. "When I was free Mr. Greb could not hurt me, but he slapped me around when he had me in close and held me. I feel proud to be champion of the world. It has always been my ambition and through the years I have been trying I have always dreamed of the day that I would wear the title. Mr. Greb fought a good battle. He is a fast fighter and a man who is hard to meet. But I was confident all the way through. I met him out in the Middle West and defeated him, according to the newspapers. I am open to defend my title and will fight Greb again in ninety days."[12]

"I always have been confident that I could beat Greb in a championship since the day, in the summer of 1924, that I outpointed him in Fremont, Ohio. I trained for speed particularly and I had no complaint to make on the score of condition when I went into the ring. The long rest I had after my bout with Mike McTigue did me a lot of good. Greb never hurt me badly. I did slow down in one round when Mr. Miller told me to rest up a little for a fast finish. I could have gone along without that rest but I always do what Mr. Miller says. Greb fought a pretty clean fight. He stuck his thumb in my eye a couple of times and almost pushed me out through the ropes a couple of times and he used some profane language. But outside of that I had no complaint. He is all right."[13]

Red Mason echoed what many in the press had expressed. "I'll grant that the fight was close, but there were no knockdowns in it nor any other decisive features, and, in such a case it is the tradition of the ring that the champion is entitled to the doubt, if any exists, as to the winner."[14]

Another of Greb's seconds was more pointed in his assessment of the bout. "You can't enjoy yourself and do what you like and expect to hold a championship."[15]

For the most part Flowers victory was a popular one. Flowers was an eminently likeable man who presented the less progressive elements of American society with a "safe" alternative to the controversy that plagued Jack Johnson's reign. Among the black press Flowers was placed on a pedestal as a man who might break barriers and would go a long way toward shattering the color line that had held back so many worthy black fighters. Indeed it was not lost on them that even as Tex Rickard was doing everything in his power to prevent Harry Wills from getting a shot at Jack Dempsey's championship he was promoting Tiger Flowers' challenge of Harry Greb.

Dempsey himself had reportedly stated that he could not understand why Greb had given a title shot to a Negro[16] which caused an outcry among the black press. In answer the Pittsburgh Courier printed a scathing rebuttal and at the same time praised Greb:

> **Is it a question of race or color? Or an attempt on the part of Dempsey to cast a dark shadow over the fighting record of Greb? The colored fighting fans regret the passing of Harry Greb as much as does anybody else. Harry Greb was a champion and he acted like one.**
>
> **He was always willing to meet any challenger, regardless of whether they were black or white. He was champion by record, and not merely in name, as Dempsey is. He never ran out of a fight in fear of getting whipped. It's a pity Dempsey cannot say that. Our Mr. Greb has shown that he was a man among men, and not a 'race horse,' like the famous Mr. Dempsey.**[17]

Within days Harry had signed articles for a return bout with Flowers to be held on May 21 and then left for a short stay in Pittsburgh before traveling with Red Mason, Eddie Deasy, and Jack White to Hot Springs, Arkansas where he intended to clear his head and work his body back into physical condition. While in Hot Springs Harry finally admitted to himself and the public that he had not adequately prepared for Flowers, adding "I know the followers of the game feel that I haven't led the right kind of life and it may be hard for me to them I am going to be different, but I am. Why I've even cut out ice cream sodas and I am doing everything that will tend to make me stronger."[18] Harry set about a program of long hikes, taking recuperative mineral baths, and training with the Milwaukee Brewers and Little Rock Travelers.

While Greb worked at Hot Springs Walk Miller attempted to have Flowers' defense against Greb switched from Madison Square Garden to an outdoor venue where more money could be made. Mason and Greb had no objection to this idea but feared that Miller was trying to get Flowers out of the agreement to face Greb and demanded that whether the venue was changed or not that Flowers be obligated to defend against Greb on the scheduled date of May 21.

Greb and Mason's fears were borne out when Walk Miller attempted to side step Greb completely by signing Flowers to defend his title against Mickey Walker and stating that Greb would need to prove himself as Flowers' top challenger before he got a title shot.[19]

Back in Hot Springs Harry and Red Mason got into a heated argument, reportedly over Harry's belief that Mason had withheld $1,000 from his purse for the Flowers fight. Harry reportedly threw Mason's clothes from the locker they shared at the bathhouse. When Mason was warned by a friend that the argument could threaten his relationship with Greb Mason boasted that he had a two year contract on Greb signed the day of the Flowers fight. Greb denied any knowledge of the contract and left Hot Springs immediately for New York to ascertain the existence and legitimacy of the document.[20]

When Harry arrived in New York he found that Mason had indeed filed the contract in question with the Athletic Commission. Greb immediately went before the commission stating that on the day of the Flowers fight Mason had approached him in the outer offices of the commission during the weigh in with a boxing license renewal application and two other pieces of paperwork he understood to be duplicates which needed to be signed. In reality the extra paperwork was the contract and Greb alleged that he had been duped. Harry asked the commission to annul the contract and allow his immediate professional separation from Mason.

Mason denied all of Greb's allegations stating instead that Greb was attempting to leave him because he was jealous of the time Mason was spending with Cuddy DeMarco and that Greb knew all along exactly what he was signing the afternoon of the Flowers fight. "There is nothing wrong with the contract," he said. "Harry was well aware of what he was doing when he signed it. He is a bit erratic at times and does things he regrets afterward and I am sure he will see his mistake this

Above: Harry and Red Mason are seen here in Atlantic City in 1926. Shortly after losing the championship to Flowers Harry and Red would get into a heated argument at Hot Springs that resulted in Harry leaving the resort and firing Mason. The resulting legal battle would drag on for months.

time."[21]

Before the Athletic Commission would render a decision on the subject they wanted to hear Mason's side of the story. Yet, Mason denied ever being summoned by the commission and when he finally admitted his presence had been requested he begged off stating that he was still in Hot Springs and too ill to travel. The Hot Springs newspapers make it clear that Mason was not ill but instead was enjoying his extended vacation.

While in New York Harry succeeded in getting the New York State Athletic Commission to back him and prevent Flowers from sidestepping him though the date of the match was pushed back to May 27. The day after the commission handed down their ruling Flowers fought Allentown Joe Gans at Wilkes-Barre. Soon after the fight Walk Miller issued a statement that Flowers had been cut in the fight, and injured his hand, forcing a postponement of the bout until at least mid-June. Many in the press were skeptical of Flowers' excuse as he had nearly six weeks in which to heal, far more time than most fighters of this era utilized when injured.

Harry's difficulties increased when on May 4 he was sued by a young struggling chorus girl using the stage name Sally Bronis. Bronis was suing Greb for breach of promise, alleging that she and Harry had carried on a two year affair during which Harry made promises of marriage. According to Bronis she had met Harry two years previous in Chicago. The two began a romance that cooled when Bronis began soliciting funds from Greb to take a European vacation. Harry, it was alleged, refused, calling Bronis a gold digger. Later Bronis was stranded in Havana when a show she was performing in failed and once again reached out to Harry for financial support only to be rebuked. It was then that Bronis decided to sue; alleging she wanted nothing more than Harry's love but in absence of that $100,000 would salve her wounded heart.[22]

The depth of their relationship remains somewhat of a mystery but it is clear there was some truth in both stories. Yet, there were problems with Sally's case from the start. Harry denied most of Bronis' story and was supported in his denials by mutual acquaintances of both he and Bronis. Instead Harry stated that he had met Bronis less than a year previous while her show was performing in Pittsburgh. Apparently she became immediately infatuated with him and began writing him frequently. Some of these letters were answered but Greb denied ever making any promises of marriage.[23]

In addition to this Bronis alleged that at one of Harry's bouts she attended at the new Madison Square Garden Greb had introduced her to Tex Rickard as his future wife. The new Garden had only been completed in December and the only bout Harry had fought there was against Tiger Flowers which took place nearly two months after Bronis alleged that Greb ended their relationship. Evidence more damning to Bronis' case was yet to emerge.

The day after Bronis publicly announced her suit the entire case fell apart. Sally's husband, from whom she was separated, saw the opportunity for a payday and surfaced to throw his hat into the ring. Her attorney, citing the fact that she signed a sworn affidavit stating that she was not married, dropped her. The press chided her, stating that she needed to drop one husband before she could sue for another. For his part in the sordid affair Alfred John Bronis (or Bronstein) announced that he intended to sue Harry for $250,000 for alienation of affection, alleging that he was happily married until his wife became infatuated with the fighter. Alfred Bronis stated that he had gotten wind of the matter when Sally approached him and offered him a cut of the money if he kept quiet about their marriage. Alfred refused, sent her away, and immediately approached his attorney, who he claimed had been looking for the evidence he needed for months to bring suit against Greb.[24] The case had all of the ear marks of a good old fashioned shakedown but it would be months before any more light would be shed on the matter or movement in the case.

The same day that the press reported on the implosion of Sally's suit against Greb both Harry and Red Mason finally appeared before the New York State Athletic Commission to resolve their contract dispute. Harry was represented by attorney Jeremiah O'Leary. Mason was accompanied only by his brother William, prompting the commission to refuse O'Leary's participation in the proceedings. After listening to the testimony of Mason, Greb, and notary Dan Donegan the commission announced "The commission, after listening to the evidence from both sides, decided that Greb signed the contract without having a complete knowledge of the document." Mason vowed to take the matter to the state supreme court answering "This has put me in the light of having induced Greb to sign this contract by trickery, and I cannot too strongly deny that. That is why I intend to institute court proceedings. I don't care if I never have anything more to do with Greb, but I resent the charge even by imputation."[25]

Above: Marcella Dolphin, better known by her stage name Sally Bronis, sued Greb for $100,000 for allegedly backing out of a promise to marry her in mid 1926. The suit would generate a lot of tabloid ink but barely lasted twenty-four hours before it was discovered Bronis was already married.

The appearance of O'Leary as legal counsel to Greb lent credence to the rumor that Harry intended to employ Jimmy Johnston as his new manager, as O'Leary had been associated with Johnston in the past. Johnston was a well-connected and influential figure in the sport who had first become associated with Greb back in 1917 when he gave Harry his first opportunity to appear in New York. When Mike McTigue won his controversial decision over Flowers many

believed it was due to Johnston's influence. It was reasoned that Harry looked to Johnston hoping that his influence would sway a close decision against Flowers in his favor. For now though Harry refused to confirm the rumor and publicly acted as his own manager.

His first order of business as a free agent was to sign himself for a fight in Buffalo on June 1st. He signed a blank contract stipulating he was willing to fight any man, black or white, provided he weigh less than 175 pounds. In short order popular Buffalo southpaw Art Weigand was signed to face Greb. Weigand was a big, strong middleweight who had only recently grown into the light heavyweight division. He boasted wins over Battling Siki and Maxie Rosenbloom as well as draws with Jock Malone and Mike McTigue but he was relatively inexperienced, having only recently turned 21, particularly over the ten round distance which he had only traveled twice. In short he could be expected to give Greb an excellent workout to prepare for Flowers but a victory in his favor was a remote possibility.

It had been nearly ten years since Harry had become an instant sensation in Buffalo, electrifying fans with his breakout performance against Willie "KO" Brennan. His bout with Weigand was now being promoted as possibly the last time Buffalo fans would be able to see Harry in action, acknowledging that his career was now rapidly winding down. Brennan, who still harbored a grudge against Greb after all of these years dusted off his training gear after four years of retirement and once again, as he had done in the past when Greb fought a local boy, offered his services to prepare Weigand for the Pittsburgh Windmill in hopes that he might aid in Greb's defeat and share in the glory.[26] Weigand was also sparring daily with middleweight contender Frankie Schoell. Schoell had defeated Weigand the previous year but now told of the vast improvements Weigand had made in both his skill and strength.

Harry was taking the match seriously as well. He could not afford a setback with a shot at Flowers just around the corner. "I have come along slowly for this bout," wrote Harry in a telegram to the Buffalo Courier, "for I have builded on a solid foundation. I expect to get to about sixty-five and stay there, and will not try to come below it, for Weigand is young and strong and I do not think it

Above: Art Weigand was a young up and comer from Buffalo when he faced Greb. Left handed, big for a middleweight, and strong as a bull he was the perfect opponent to prepare Greb for a third bout with Tiger Flowers.

would be well for me to make lower weight with a Tiger Flowers bout in prospect."

"I have worked for six weeks, four weeks of slow preparation, and doing harder work the past two weeks. By Saturday I will be at the point I aim to be, and will do enough work in Buffalo Sunday and Monday to keep there. I expect to win as quickly as eight rounds. You may say that for me."[27]

Since the loss of his title and recent legal troubles Harry had surrounded himself with his family. He arrived in Buffalo the night before the fight with his three sisters and brother-in-law in tow and checked into the Statler. The party settled in and relaxed, waiting for Harry to break one of the longest layoffs of his career.

Against Weigand Harry started with his characteristic rush but quickly realized that he was facing a young, strong, and aggressive battler. He soon fell back on his tactic of allowing Weigand to force the fight early while conserving his strength. Despite this Weigand finished the first round with a cut eye.

For the first three or four rounds Weigand gave Harry as good as he got but by the midway point of the fight he started to weaken and Greb took over, never looking back. In the fifth round Greb cut Weigand's mouth and the blood clearly hampered the tiring young fighter. By the ninth round Greb was in complete control. In that round Harry got a laugh from the audience when Weigand missed a blow, landing on Greb's arm, and Harry dismissively dusted off the spot where the blow landed.

When the fight had finished Greb was awarded the unanimous decision but many were surprised by the difficult fight Weigand had given him.[28] The Buffalo Courier noted that Greb appeared pale and clumsy, no longer the same fighter who had terrorized three divisions. The

Above: Harry having fun in Atlantic City with his sweetheart Naomi Braden (center) and sister Catherine. For the past year Harry had been spending an increasing amount of time at the seashore and maintained an apartment there.

Buffalo Morning Express had Greb ahead by only one round, much to Harry's consternation. If Harry intended to reclaim his title he was going to have to improve upon his performance against Weigand.

Just prior to his fight with Weigand Greb was served with a summons to appear in a Manhattan court on June 4 in regards to his contract dispute with Mason. Mason was seeking to prevent Greb from fighting until the case could be heard in October. Justice Charles Guy heard both sides of the argument but reserved his decision for a later date. In the meantime Greb signed himself to face Allentown Joe Gans at Wilkes-Barre on June 15 for ten rounds to a decision. It would be Harry's last fight before challenging Tiger Flowers for the championship, a proposed match with King Solomon having fallen through when Solomon declined to face Greb.

Gans was a talented fighter who could hold his own with anyone, as evidenced by his bouts with Jock Malone, Tiger Flowers, and Jack Delaney. In the past year he had greatly improved and was now considered a top ten contender for the middleweight title. After giving Flowers all he could handle in April Gans hoped that a victory over Greb would propel him to a championship bout with the Tiger. With this in mind Gans worked at a secluded training camp at Harvey's Lake, situated roughly fifteen miles from Wilkes-Barre.

Greb arrived on the scene the day before the bout and was met with the news that Mason's

injunction had been granted. It was feared this would prevent Greb from fighting but after lawyers were consulted it was decided that the injunction was only good in New York, Mason would have to pursue further legal action in Pennsylvania before he could prevent Greb from facing Gans. Yet the action served Mason's desired purpose by threatening to prevent Greb's return match with Flowers. Before he could salvage that fight he first had to get past Gans.

Gans showed up for the fight trained to the minute. He had trained to deal with Greb's speed and cut his weight to a svelte $157^1/_2$ pounds. Despite newspapermen noting that Harry seemed fat around the midsection, weighing nearly eight pounds more than Gans, he was quoted as saying "I just wish I had been in as good shape as I am now the night I took on Flowers and the

Above: Three young women pose with newly purchased tickets to the bout between Harry Greb and Allentown Joe Gans at Wilkes-Barre. For better or worse Harry was always popular with the ladies.

title never would have changed hands."[29]

Excess weight or not Harry turned in a wonderful performance. He entered the ring to a hostile crowd. The fans had heard much of his high living and wicked ways and were prepared to cheer Gans to victory. Early on Greb virtually hypnotized Gans with a lead right that he would hold out in front of him and just when Gans thought there was no harm in the extended hand Greb would snap out at him with the punch like a cobra. Several times Greb landed the blow through sheer speed, a blow that no trained professional should ever be hit with.

Harry began to win over the audience in the fourth when Gans missed a punch and tripped to the canvas. Greb stood over him for half a heartbeat as the crowd thought he was going to take advantage of Gans position. Instead Greb put to rest the stories they had heard of his unsportsmanlike behavior by reaching down and helping Gans to his feet before backing off and letting his opponent get his bearings. Greb cemented his popularity in the ninth round when Gans struck Greb after the bell accidentally. Greb made a halfhearted show of the blow and pretended there would be trouble then smiled and stuck out his glove to shake Gans' hand in acceptance of his apology.

When the fight had ended Greb had made a hit with the fans and was awarded the decision. He was credited with six rounds, three were even. Gans was awarded only one round, the sixth.[30]

Immediately after the fight Greb headed to New York in order to fight Justice Guy's ruling favoring Red Mason. The ruling itself had a ripple effect through the state. By upholding the contract the court had trampled on the authority of the New York State Athletic Commission. It was a serious blow to the Commission and a rare moment of weakness after years of dictatorial behavior. The move served to embolden Tex Rickard who had been locked in a titanic struggle with the commission over his plan to stage the Dempsey-Tunney bout while ignoring Harry Wills' years old challenge of the champion. The

Above: Arphelius Hicks fighting as Allentown Joe Gans, was a talented middleweight of the 1920s. He possessed a good right hand and was always in shape. By 1925 he had made a list compiled by Tex Rickard of the top ten middleweights in the country. He had fought Jock Malone, Tiger Flowers, Roland Todd, and Jack Delaney among others, always holding his own.

controversy led some politicians in the city and state government to voice the opinion that if the commission could exert no greater control or influence over the sport than was seen in the Greb-Mason case and in the Dempsey-Wills affair then it might to be time to return to the days when boxing was outlawed in the state.

Against this backdrop Harry arrived in New York to battle Red Mason's injunction. He was able to move forward with the Flowers fight when attorneys for both parties came to an agreement. In exchange for allowing the fight forty percent of Greb's purse would be held up pending the outcome of the contract dispute in October. The agreement served both parties, Mason's percentage was protected and Greb would still be allowed to earn an income by fighting Flowers. Never-the-less Harry was defiant, vowing that Mason would never see the forty percent.[31]

With the agreement in place the Greb-Flowers bout was formally announced for August 12 but pushed back one week later to August 19 when Flowers requested more time to train. Harry left for Atlantic City where he would train for several weeks before moving on to Dr. Bier's health farm at Pompton Lakes, New Jersey. Once again Harry surrounded himself with family in Atlantic City, taking his mother, sisters, and daughter.

While in Atlantic City Greb once again found his name sensationalized in the papers. In early August, forty miles outside of Atlantic City a man was cornered by police after a chase of several miles for speeding. When approached by the officers the man gave his name as Harry Greb and a struggle nearly ensued before the man was hauled before the local justice of the peace. It was discovered that the man was actually L. J. Dickey of Chicago, Illinois. He was fined $60 and barred from driving in New Jersey, yet it was Greb's name splashed across the headlines.[32] Greb was quick to deny any participation in the event. "Will you please rectify the story in reference to me being blacklisted and barred from driving an automobile in New Jersey," he wrote the Pittsburgh Post. "On the date of the supposed arrest I was in Atlantic City and on that day I got up at 9 o'clock and ran five miles, had breakfast and rested until the afternoon, when I went to the Elks' Club gymnasium and worked for an hour. I then had dinner and about 8 o'clock that evening mother, my daughter and myself took a ride on a rolling chair on the Boardwalk and at 10:30 I was in bed. I have been doing this same routine for the past three weeks, have never so much as been out of Atlantic City. I know nothing at all about the arrest. I have Pennsylvania licenses, not Illinois."[33]

After several weeks of light conditioning at Atlantic City, Harry traveled up to Pompton Lakes where he would begin hard training. With him were Jackie Kerrigan, Jack Favor, George Courtney, and Leo Caghil acting as sparring partners. His sister Ida was along as well to oversee the housekeeping and acting as Harry's cook. Greb's friends Jack Albacker and Jack White also came along to help Harry round into shape for the bout.

By all accounts Harry trained hard and felt confident enough of winning that he placed a $5,000 bet on himself.[34] "Am doing everything in my power at my training camp here to get back in tip-top shape to enhance my chances of winning back the middleweight championship of the world," said Harry in a letter to the Pittsburgh Gazette-Times. "I surely have been working hard. I have five sparring partners, all husky fellows, and we tangle into each other every day. Most of them box with their right hand extended in Flowers' fashion. I feel stronger and am boxing harder than any time in the last three years, and after my workout yesterday I scaled $163^1/_2$ pounds, which means that I am making the weight gradually and should be strong in the ring."[35]

Leo Caghil backed this up in a follow-up letter to the Gazette-Times stating: "Greb is going to be in the same excellent condition he was in for his bout with Mickey Walker back in July of last year. We are out here at Dr. Bier's health farm at Pompton Lake and are going through a routine calculated to send Harry into the ring at his best. We get up promptly at 7 o'clock each morning and run three or four miles on the road as fast as we can travel and then we have breakfast at 9 o'clock. We indulge in fishing before noon and at 2 o'clock we go to the gym, where the champ that was and will be again takes on his whole flock of sparring partners. One of these is Johnny Wilson, southpaw former middleweight champion, from whom Greb won the title. Others include George Courtenay, the Oklahoma cowboy, Mike Carrin, a southpaw who boxes exactly like Flowers and myself, a lightweight. Harry weighed $163^3/_4$ pounds this morning and will not have any trouble making the weight, 160 pounds."

Above left: Left to right, Jack Albacker, Harry Greb, Leo Caghil, and Jack White relax at Harry's training camp at Doc Bier's health farm at Pompton Lakes, New Jersey as the former champion prepares to attempt to regain his championship from Tiger Flowers. Above right: Greb poses with Leo Caghil during training for his third bout with Tiger Flowers.

"Harry is punching much harder then ever before and it would not surprise me to see him knock out Flowers this trip. We all know that Flowers can't take a solid smack on the jaw, and he is in for plenty of them from Greb in this fight, as Harry has been concentrating on his wallop, as he realizes the success Jack Delaney and others have had in belting Flowers squarely on the button."

"Harry boxes three rounds each day with each of his sparring partners and then shadow-boxes two rounds, punches the bag two rounds, hits the sandbag two more and works on the weights and pulleys. Everybody hits the hay at 9:30 o'clock at night, for that is the time the lights go out at this place, and Dr. Bier will stand for no infractions of his strict rules. The late Pancho Villa trained for all of his important bouts here and it's a great spot."

"We trained for three weeks at Atlantic City before coming here last Tuesday and will remain here until the morning of the fight. I have worked with Harry for a lot of his bouts and never felt his punches as I am feeling them now. Two meals a day, regular daylight hours and plenty of hard work and boxing have made a new fighter of him, and you can broadcast the fact to the world that after Thursday night Harry and his little old title will be heading back to Pittsburgh together."[36]

As Greb trained at Pompton Lakes rumors continued to fly that he intended to employ Jimmy Johnston as his manager. It was said that in so doing the decision in the Flowers bout would be "in the bag" for Harry. When Greb formally announced that Johnston would indeed be acting as his manager Walk Miller was livid. Johnston had been manager for Mike McTigue when McTigue had won his infamous decision over Flowers. Johnston had also been managing Yale Okun when Okun won a controversial decision over George Cook who was being handled by Miller at the time. Upon hearing that Johnston would be in Greb's corner Miller approached Rickard and tried to have the fight cancelled. When this failed he went before the commission pleading with them to protect his fighter to which the commission agreed.[37]

The odds for the fight opened at 7 to 5 in favor of Flowers but betting was light and by the day before the fight had settled at only 8 to 5 in Tiger's favor. When Harry arrived in New York he mapped out his strategy for the press. "I may be a little slow getting started," he said "but that will be because I intend to let Flowers be the aggressor in the first few rounds. I will not step in and slug unless I get him in trouble, and I know that I will be there with the speed at the finish while he will be tiring fast after the first half of the fight."[38]

As Greb was being interviewed in his hotel across town Red Mason had gone to Flowers' gym to watch him train and, according to rumor, give him pointers on how to more easily defeat Greb. Mason denied these accusations but he was invited to the weigh in as a guest of Flowers and Miller in hopes that his presence with the champion would unnerve Greb.[39]

At the weigh in the afternoon of the fight Greb was tanned and ready for battle. He had clearly trained more faithfully than for their previous fight and showed none of the tell-tale signs of having difficulty making weight. Greb weighed in at 159 pounds while Flowers weighed in a quarter pound more. During the weigh in ceremony Harry was served with papers giving him twenty days to respond to the alienation of affection suit which had finally been filed by Sally Bronis' husband. Under this mental handicap Greb entered the ring against Flowers that evening in hopes of winning back his championship.

After the preliminaries ended Flowers entered the ring at 9:35pm wearing a dark robe emblazoned with the head of a tiger on the back. Afterwards Greb entered the ring wearing a purple silk robe. He was treated to a much greater ovation than that received by the champion, punctuated by calls of "we want Greb!" Harry crossed the ring and gave Flowers a warm greeting before returning to his corner where Jimmy Johnston and his brother Charlie prepared to handle Greb between rounds.

Prior to the start of the bout there was a ceremony whereby Joe Humphries, on

Above: Harry weighs in for his third bout with Tiger Flowers, others in the photo are left to right Tiger Flowers, commissioner Edward Curry, secretary Bert Stand, chairman Jim Farley.

behalf of the New York Boxing Writers Association, awarded Flowers a gold belt, emblematic of his championship. As Greb eyed the proceedings some in the audience shouted to him "It will be yours tonight!"

Harry stayed true to his promise in the early rounds by letting Flowers take the initiative. He came out dancing and the fighters went into a clinch. After a bit of sparring Tiger stumbled and nearly fell through the ropes in a clinch. The fight was once again shaping up to be a sloppy, clumsy affair. Flowers sent a wicked left to the body after a series of mauling clinches. Greb landed a hard uppercut near the close and the fighters ended the round in an embrace.

During the second round Flowers began to play for the body but was warned for punching low. In an odd role reversal Harry countered from the outside and seemed to control the action from a distance while Flowers looked to outfight Greb in the clinches. Both fighters missed frequently but at the end of the round Flowers once again opened a cut over Greb's left eye with a solid right hook.

Flowers won his first clear round in the third as Greb missed several wild swings only to be countered with hard body shots. Yet, despite his success in the third, Flowers fought more con-

servatively in the fourth frame, continuing to aim for the body. It was once again noted that he was landing low blows even as he was complaining of having his eyes gouged by Greb. Greb managed to bring blood from Flowers' mouth but likely lost the round by a close margin.

Greb opened the fifth complaining that Flowers was holding incessantly and refusing to fight. Flowers answered to "come and fight!" As Harry rushed in to meet him Flowers caught him with a hard right to the chin and a bevy of body blows before, once again, complaining of being thumbed. The fighters exchanged punches for the duration of the round with Flowers forcing the fight.

Flowers nearly fell again during a clinch in the sixth, sensing weakness Greb pounced and launched an attack that had Flowers on the defensive. Flowers once again tried to clinch to save

Facing page top left: Greb and Flowers in an exchange during the second round. Facing page top right: Flowers and Greb flail away at each other during an unspecified round. Facing page bottom: Greb chases Flowers after the bell ending the eighth round. Top left and top right: Flowers trips, going to the floor during the eighth round. Above: Greb is wrestled to the floor during the twelfth round.

himself but Greb got the champion in a choke hold and was warned by the referee. The fight was shaping up as more of an alley fight than a boxing match. As the round ended Flowers was bleeding from the mouth and cut over his left eye.

Greb came out for the seventh and picked up right where he left off, landing several hard right hands to the head. A furious exchange followed with Greb continuing to land hard shots to the head as Flowers punched to the body. Just as it seemed as if Greb might be taking control Flowers rallied, battling back, refusing to relinquish his title so easily. Near the end of the round Greb slipped and Flowers stepped back to allow him to gain his feet. As the round ended Greb once again complained of Flowers' excessive holding.

The eighth started with a series of clinches. After landing a left Flowers tripped going backwards and upon arising danced around the ring to the crowd's amusement. The round featured several exchanges. A split second before the bell ending the round Flowers landed a punch. Greb attempted to chase Flowers back to his corner to pay him in kind but the referee caught him and directed him back to his own corner.

The ninth and tenth rounds featured several sloppy exchanges with more punches missed than landed. The fight broke open again in the eleventh as champion and challenger traded punches. Greb landed several hard blows but Tiger continued to take them, wade in, and land a series of body punches which forced Greb to break ground.

Harry opened the twelfth with a hard right to the body. In a clinch he was wrestled to the floor. After Flowers landed a series of body blows Greb clinched repeatedly. He was tiring and saving himself for a fast finish. Just before the end of the round Flowers opened deep, jagged cut over Greb's right eye with a left.

A sloppy exchange opened the thirteenth and Flowers was wrestled to the floor but on rising caught Greb coming in. Both of Harry's eyes were now bleeding and his face was a mask of blood. As a result his accuracy suffered and Flowers was able to counter him effectively, staggering him before the close.

Greb roared back in the fourteenth, forcing Flowers around the ring. For a full three minutes Greb was on the attack constantly, never ceasing. For a brief, shining moment Greb was the Greb of old. The two fighters were trading so furiously that they failed to hear the bell closing the round and had to be separated.

The fighters came out for the fifteenth and final round cautiously shaking hands. Greb renewed his assault. Flowers tried to stem the tide by clinching and Greb, desperate to get free, nearly pushed Flowers from the ring. Referee Crowley was so exhausted from prying the fighters from clinch after clinch that he was having difficulty getting the fighters apart and once again Greb nearly threw Flowers through the ropes. As the round ended Flowers did a handspring to show that he still retained his strength.[40]

The fight had once again been close, a near repeat of their first bout with both fighters slightly improved since February. Despite this improvement the fight was considered an aesthetic disaster. Due to the awkward nature of the fighters, and indeed the fight itself, it was anyone's guess which way the decision would go. As the fighters stood in their corners waiting for the scores to be tabulated fans on each side of the ring began to shout their favorite to victory.

When Joe Humphries stepped to the center of the ring and bellowed "The winner and still champion, Tiger Flowers!" Greb looked stunned. A chorus of boos followed as did a shower of torn paper. Naomi Braden and one of Greb's sisters rushed press row, mistaking some of the reporters for the judges. Greb's sister screeched "YOU ROBBERS!" and the two women attacked. One slapped Dick Murphy of Western Union and attacked Harry Cross of the New York Herald-Tribune. The other just missed a blow aimed at W. O. McGeehan, also of the Herald-Tribune; she then picked up a chair with which to further continue her mayhem before police officers intervened. Another group of fans rushed the ringside and asked Humphries if the decision had been unanimous. It had not. As in the previous bout the referee, Jimmy Crowley, had voted for Greb. The judges, Harold Barnes and Charles Mathison had voted for Flowers.

According to Westbrook Pegler "It was a hard fight to score, for they were both so bad that it became a case of assigning the blame at the end of each round instead of awarding credit. Greb just happened to be consistently wilder and generally worse than Flowers, a fellow who happens to fight better than Harry does in Harry's own carefree way."[41] Despite his improvement it was still a consensus of onlookers that Greb was finished as a great fighter. "The Windmill who faced the Deacon last night was a sorry wreck of the former Windmill that beat Tommy Gibbons and that held his own with Gene Tunney," wrote McGeehan. "It was evident from the start of the bout last night that this was so. The Tiger armed with righteousness and perhaps with the strength of more careful living, was too strong for him."[42]

With a relative few dissenting opinions it is clear that Flowers won a close but deserved victory. Flowers left the ring first followed a short time later by Greb, who was cheered all the way back to his dressing room.

"I thought I defeated Tiger Flowers tonight by a margin that left no room for doubt in the minds of the judges," said Greb as he sat dejected in his dressing room. "I cannot conceal my disappointment over the unfavorable verdict. Right now after having had my title taken away from me by a questionable margin in my second bout with Flowers and having been denied the return of it after, in my own mind and the minds of many of my friends and the spectators and the referee, having beaten Flowers tonight, I am just about disgusted enough to hang up the gloves and quit boxing. I don't know what I shall do. I'll have to take some time to think things over."[43]

Harry's depression over the result carried him through a sleepless night. He rose for breakfast early the following morning and then spent the morning at a bath house soothing his aches and pains. He had two black eyes, a small cut over the left eye and a long jagged cut over the right. Yet he was still defiant. "I am confident that if I ever won a fight I beat Flowers last night and it breaks me up to think of how hard I trained for this bout and the money I spent preparing for it only to have the judges pick Flowers after I led him in a majority of the rounds. I can't understand how they could have arrived at such a finding."[44]

The financial aspect of the fight was foremost on Greb's mind. His purse totaled only $9,343 and forty percent of that was being withheld pending the resolution of his contract dispute with Mason. His training expenses, including the time he had spent in Hot Springs, totaled nearly the entire amount of his purse and he still owed Jimmy Johnston his fee for handling Greb for the bout in addition to the $5,000 he lost betting on himself to win. In short Greb didn't just fight Flowers for nothing; he was operating at a loss. In addition to this Harry would very shortly discover that his livelihood was in danger.

Within days Harry traveled to Atlantic City to recuperate. The cut over his blind right eye was in bad shape and forced him to visit the specialist who had recently been treating it. He was warned that the eye's condition could cause a sympathetic reaction in his good eye leaving him completely blind.[45] He was advised to retire from the sport that had been his life for over thirteen years and have the eye completely removed and replaced with a glass eye.

Harry had a difficult decision to make. He was in desperate need of money. With legal expenses mounting rapidly, the threat of two large lawsuits, and the fact that his savings were almost entirely tied up in stocks and bonds, Greb would need to do something quick to resolve his myriad of financial issues or face retirement with nothing to show for his long years of service but scars.

While Harry considered his options he spent a great deal of time at the Atlantic City training camp of Jack Dempsey. Rickard, emboldened by the perceived weakness in the New York State Athletic Commission, set about an ambitious plan to circumvent its authority. He moved the entire massive promotion of the proposed Dempsey-Tunney championship to Philadelphia, completely ignoring Harry Wills' challenge. The move met with controversy in Pennsylvania as well but Rickard found a commission much more willing to look the other way as Rickard, Dempsey, and Tunney trampled on the principles of fair play and equality. When the only African-American member of the Pennsylvania commission, Charles Fred White, spoke out against circumventing Wills' rights he was removed from the board and the last obstacle to the Dempsey-Tunney fight went with him.

Initially Greb thought Tunney would need to show more aggressiveness than he had in the past to defeat Dempsey. He had always reasoned that you needed to stay on top of Dempsey, not give him any room to punch, and keep forcing him back so that he could not get any leverage on his blows. As the days wore on Harry's opinion changed. He was disappointed with what he saw in Dempsey's camp. The champion had initially surrounded himself with a poor stable of sparring partners. Those that showed any ability seemed to be holding back when facing Dempsey to make him look better than he actually was. Harry spent some time with the champion, giving him tips on what to expect from Tunney, but after a week of watching

Dempsey spar Greb decided that Tunney had an excellent chance to win. He felt that Dempsey's three years of easy living without a fight had left him unable to capture the old fire that once typified his performances.

Greb had come to a decision about his future. He would retire from the sport, open a gymnasium which catered to white collar clientele, and submit to have his useless right eye substituted with a glass replacement. Publicly he would state that he intended to continue fighting but would abandon the middleweight division and make a run at the light-heavyweights. The subterfuge would keep him in the public eye, reasoning that it would be good publicity and advertising for his gym while also duping Red Mason into believing that he would get a percentage of Greb's earnings.

To that end Greb met with Red Mason in order to patch up their differences. Without telling Red of his plans the two worked out a deal whereby Greb would accept Red Mason as his manager for twenty-five percent of his future ring earnings, Red Mason would drop his suit, and the forty percent of Greb's purse from the Flowers fight would be released. New contracts would be drawn up and submitted to the New York State Athletic Commission, effectively killing any future possibility of retribution from Mason when Red found out he had been duped into dropping his claim on Greb's previous earnings. It was a stroke of tactical brilliance on Greb's part.

The public and Mason (who had never known the full extent of the injury to Greb's right eye) were told that Greb would be operated on for the removal of cataract. This would explain his convalescence and eye patch that he would be forced to wear while the eye healed. Harry submitted to the surgery on September 16 and spent nearly a week healing before he attended the Dempsey-Tunney battle in Philadelphia with a black patch over his eye. What Greb witnessed must have filled him with regret.

After nearly ten years of trying to get a match with Dempsey without success, and with the loss of his title fresh on his mind, he sat ringside and witnessed his bitter rival utterly dominate Dempsey to win the heavyweight championship of the world. Round after round Tunney stabbed at Dempsey with long left jabs, and raked him with left hooks and right crosses on the rare occasions when Dempsey was able to get in close. Dempsey was such a battered swollen mess after the fight that he had to be led to Tunney by his handlers in order to congratulate him on his victory.

Greb witnessed as Tunney became an overnight sensation and had to believe that had he gotten the shot at Dempsey and won it would be he who would have reaped fame and fortune. Newspapers featured serialized stories of Tunney's life, he appeared in countless newsreels, his every move was written about with great anticipation, and he was even currently starring in a motion picture which had been filmed prior to winning the championship. Even the newspapers in Pittsburgh were not immune to Tunneymania. Harry Keck, in writing Tunney's life story recounted the Greb-Tunney bouts. How his story had changed in years since those bouts took place. Where Keck originally reported that Greb had broken Tunney's nose in the first round of their first fight with a punch, he now wrote that it was an accidental head butt which broke Tunney's nose. Where once he had been indignant over the decision awarded to Tunney in their second bout now he wrote that it was justified. He wrote that the consensus favored Tunney in their fourth bout. And on it went.

Harry was furious that his legacy was being rewritten to suit the story of the conquering Hero. He confronted Keck stating "I would like to meet this Mr. Tunney whom you praise so highly right here in Pittsburgh for his title. He won his title in a 10-round bout, so let him fight the only man who holds a decision over him, and I assure you that I will bring the world's heavyweight championship to dear old Pittsburgh. I wish you would give a little credit where it is due to me, a man who will fight Tunney for charity right here in Pittsburgh."[46]

Only Greb knew that his threats were empty. It was all for naught. He would never fight again with only one eye and the thought sent him into a deep depression. He began to speak with an increasingly morbid outlook, often punctuating discussions of his plans for the future with "if I live." He spoke often of his death, what arrangements should be made in such an eventuality, and the care of Dorothy.[47]

On October 10 Harry traveled to Steubenville to watch a semi-pro football team he was sponsoring, the Fort Pitt Bulldogs, play the Steubenville Hope Harveys. The Hope Harveys were actually a Pittsburgh team featuring Art and Dan Rooney. They had been forced to take on the Steubenville banner in order to play Sunday games in Steubenville when Pittsburgh refused to allow semi-pro football on Sundays. Greb watched as his team was defeated 38-0 and then returned to Pittsburgh. On the way home the car Harry was driving was involved in an accident. Mysteriously Greb was whisked away from the accident without treatment and Jack White, who had been with him, was left at the scene with a broken arm.[48] Immediately the report that Greb had been involved in the accident was denied and when reporters attempted to reach Greb at his apartment they were unsuccessful. It would be two weeks before the mysterious circumstances of this accident were revealed.

It became clear that something was wrong when Harry missed his appointment in New York to sign the new contracts with Mason that would formally end their dispute. Harry was finally confronted at his apartment, ostensibly about a loud party the night before. The years of frustration with the press, always eager to sensationalize or invent the salacious details of his life, boiled over. Appearing in a silk robe and slippers with a bandage over his re-injured right eye, he went after the reporter with both barrels "Let's get this right. You fellows come here to ask me about some scandal, some scandalous party. I have been in bed four days and not once outside of my apartment. I have been ill. There wasn't any party held here last night. I tell you that and it is the absolute truth. But that won't satisfy newspapers. There's no news in that -the fact that Harry Greb is sick in bed because of a bad eye. But if he was sick in bed because of a black eye received in a cabaret brawl -well that would get on the front page."

Harry spent an increasing amount of time with family after his first loss to Flowers in February, often bringing them with him to Atlantic City. Above left: Harry is seen in his Atlantic City apartment with his sisters Ida (left) and Catherine. Above right: Harry poses on the same day (likely Easter 1926) with his mother.

"Why, do you fellows know that Harry Greb never walked out of a cabaret in his life? No sir, not once. He always staggered out. Look back at the files and you'll see."

"But what's the truth? I haven't had but two drinks of whisky in the last four years. Just two drinks. And I'll repeat that and make it stronger. I have had only two drinks of liquor in the last four years, and I say that with God as my judge."

"But what do the papers do? It's Harry Greb in this scandal with this woman and Harry Greb in that liquor drinking cabaret party. Can I help because some woman may take a notion to sue me for breach of promise? One did sue for $100,000. What happened? It didn't take long to show that she was married."

"Then? She couldn't get the money that way so her husband sued for alienation of affections. All he wanted was $225,000. That suit is still pending."

"Publicity and plenty of it. Scandal, scandal, and scandal," He continued, taking a dig at Tunney while he was at it. "But don't get me wrong in this. I don't claim to be a member of all of the literary societies, the art clubs and the reading circles. I have my fun just like others. But I'm not the Harry Greb that I have been painted."

"Ever see anything in the papers about Harry Greb giving thousands of dollars to charity? Not a line. I didn't want it published but no one ever tried to find it out."

"Ever see anything in the papers about the $15,000 I gave in one year to the Catholic Church?

I never wanted it published, but no one ever tried to dig that up on me."

"Never a line in the papers if they see me in church every Sunday morning, but Harry Greb coming out of a cafe or cabaret at midnight is good for plenty."

"What did they say about me being in church last Tuesday night making a novena? See any headlines about that?"

"I'm not asking you to print this, I just had to get it out of my system."[49]

Shortly thereafter Harry visited the office of Dr. Frank Goehring complaining of pain in his side, shoulder, and exhibited a large cut above his eye. Dr. Goehring treated his shoulder and told him to look after the eye. He asked Harry to return to his office in a day or so for a follow up. Greb answered that he was going to Atlantic City to see the surgeon who had treated his eye and would seek care there. Goehring noted that Greb "did not appear any too chipper."[50]

The following day Harry called his mother before leaving for Atlantic City. "Good-bye mother," he said, "I won't be long."[51]

26

AFTERWARDS

Larry Murray remembered the day well, nearly eighty years later. He was six going on seven and lived around the corner from Pius and Annie Greb. He idolized their famous son and laughed as he recalled Greb tossing pennies to he and his friends whenever he came back to the old Garfield neighborhood. He remembered seeing women running across the street that day to discuss the dark news with their neighbors and heard talk he did not understand that "she" was inconsolable, near collapse. "She" turned out to be Harry's mother Annie. The news was spreading through Pittsburgh's streets like wildfire. Harry Greb, former middleweight champion, and idol of Pittsburgh was dead.[1]

Harry visited the private hospital of Dr. Charles Berenda Weinberg on October 21 accompanied by his sweetheart Naomi Braden. He was seen by Dr. Charles McGivern and complained of severe headaches and dizziness. An examination found that during his recent automobile accident Greb had suffered a fracture above the bridge of his nose, just below his brow which was causing difficulty breathing. It was decided to undergo a minor operation to remove the bone fragment blocking the nasal passage.

The surgery was started under local anesthetic. As the surgery progressed Harry was given nitrous oxide and oxygen. Greb left the operating table at 8:30 that evening in good condition. At 10am the following morning he began to grow weaker and his heart began to fail despite the use of stimulants. Harry asked for his sister Ida to be brought from Pittsburgh to be by his side. Shortly after Ida received the call and rushed to Atlantic City Harry's parents were notified that his condition was serious and that they too should travel with all haste to Atlantic City. But a short while later, before they could board a train for Atlantic City, word was received that Harry had died.[2]

Harry's father and brother-in-law J. Elmer Edwards left for Atlantic City that night to escort Ida, Naomi, and Harry's body back to Pittsburgh. While in Atlantic City Harry's body lay in state at the J. Bunker Plum funeral home where several members of the boxing fraternity and local friends paid their last respects.

Dr. Weinberg and Dr. McGivern disagreed on the cause of death. According to Weinberg a post mortem examination, made through the wound caused by the surgery, discovered that a bone fragment had broken off at the bridge of the nose and caused a blood clot on the brain.

When the bone was removed relieving the blockage it permitted the clot to flow to the brain causing a hemorrhage which resulted in Greb's death. Weinberg, likely trying to allay any stigma that might be attached to his clinic after such a high profile death, stated that Harry's nose and skull had been weakened by previous cosmetic surgeries which contributed to the injuries and added that Greb would not have survived another six months without the surgery.[3]

McGivern felt that death was caused by cardiac arrest from shock caused by the surgery and accident which resulted in his injuries. He further stated that he was unable to determine the cause of death with any certainty adding that Weinberg's theory could not be proven by means of the limited examination made through the surgical incision.[4] Greb's death certificate lists the cause of death as traumatic thrombosis of the cerebral artery (the purported clot caused by the accident) and aortic fibrillation of the heart (an irregular heartbeat which can lead to heart failure or stroke). Contributing factors are listed as operative shock and, interestingly, cardiac hypertrophy which in laymen's terms is an enlarged heart.[5]

In hindsight there is no way to parse out the true cause of death, particularly given so many mitigating factors. Harry's ring career, the automobile accident, the dangerous use of nitrous oxide at the time, and the surgery itself could all have been contributing factors or each one individually could have been the cause.[6] The relative lack of knowledge by experienced, well-meaning physicians of the era would have made it very difficult during that era even had a thorough autopsy been performed.

That night at Madison Square Garden a ceremony was held where the New York Boxing Writers Association awarded Gene Tunney his championship belt. During the ceremony a minute of silence was observed in memory of Greb.

Eddie Dugan (center) and Jack Albacker pay their last respects as Harry lies in state at the J. Bunker Plum funeral home in Atlantic City on October 23, 1926.

The solemn party quietly arrived at the East Liberty station on the morning of October 24 amid a slow, steady rain. Harry's body was taken to Ida's home where the funeral would be held three days later. The house had already begun to look awash in a sea of flowers as floral arrangements arrived from all parts of the country, including one from Tiger Flowers. At 4pm Harry's mother, who had been under constant care since receiving the news of Harry's death and accompanied by members of the family, viewed Harry's remains. Thereafter the public was allowed admittance to the home and a steady stream of well-wishers shuffled through to say their final good-byes to the fallen warrior.[7]

The flowers and telegrams poured in. Johnny Wilson, Jack Dempsey, Johnny Dundee, Jimmy Delaney, the wife of Greb's murdered opponent Bill Brennan, Pete Latzo, and Joe Dundee were just a few of the boxing notables who sent their sympathies to the Greb family.[8] At noon on the 25th Reverend James Cox of Old St. Patrick's Church gave a tribute to Greb during his sermon on the subject of diligence over the air on WJAS. Cox had been the director of the Pittsburgh Lyceum when Greb was just a young boy begging to be become a member so he could train with the boxers there. He chastised those who perpetuated the myth that Greb never trained and spoke of how he drew inspiration in his own life from watching Harry train for hours in the gym.[9]

John Blackwell, speaking on behalf of African-American boxing fans wrote the Press: "The colored sport lovers of Pittsburgh sadly miss Harry Greb. We wonder if we will ever have another fighter of his type. He was just what he represented himself to be -and that was a real sport and a real fighter. He never barred anybody of quality. He had the heart of a fighter."

"Color of skin made no difference to him. He gave everybody a chance. If the fighting ring had more men like Greb, the game would be better off. He left a good record for other ringsters to follow. He was a fighter, and not a would-be."[10]

Ira F. Lewis, writing in the Pittsburgh Courier would reaffirm this position only days later. "The record of Harry Greb," he wrote, "goes down in history as a credit to the game of boxing and to the honor of America. He deserves to take his place along with Ketchel, Frank Erne, Terry McGovern, Rube

This floral arrangement honoring Greb greeted boxing fans as they entered Motor Square Garden two days before Harry's funeral. Tribute was paid to the fallen fighter that evening as fans all over the city mourned his loss.

Ferns, "Philadelphia" Jack O'Brien and hundreds of other illustrious gladiators of the past, who were fighters in every sense the word implies."

"Contrasting Greb's career and his interpretation of what constitutes a world's champion with the pussyfooting of most white fighters and sport writers, colored America may well stand at ATTENTION at the tomb of Harry Greb and truthfully say: "THERE LIES AN AMER-ICAN."[11]

The evening before Harry's funeral, during the boxing matches being staged at Motor Square Garden, tribute was paid to Greb. Four large colored photographs of Harry were placed in the ring facing out over each direction. The lights were extinguished except for those illuminating the ring and the audience was asked to rise, bare their heads, and observe a moment of silence. The timekeeper tolled the bell for the fatal ten count and then Taps was played followed by a drum roll to end the ceremony.[12]

Gene Tunney, while stopping off in Pittsburgh on his way to an engagement in Ohio, personally visited the Greb family to give his condolences. He was asked by organizers of the funeral to be a pallbearer and sent a wire from Ohio in answer:

If Greb family wishes me to act as pallbearer, will do so, as I believe that is a tribute I owe Harry, who was one of the greatest men of his weight, and inches I ever saw. Wire me in regard to such arrangements as may be necessary.

Gene Tunney[13]

That same day friends of Harry finally broke their silence and revealed that Greb had been blind in one eye since his first fight with Kid Norfolk five years earlier.[14] Even those who were aware Greb had bad eyesight were shocked to discover that he had won two titles and defeated some of the greatest fighters in the sport with only one eye but Dr. McGivern confirmed the rumor. "Harry Greb was made blind by a blow on his right eye during a fight with Kid Norfolk, negro heavyweight, in New York City (sic) in 1921," said McGivern when confronted with the story. "He told no one about it. Several years ago he was advised by physicians and friends to have the eye removed, but refused to do so in fear that it would be discovered that he was half blind and he would be barred by boxing commissions and promoters from the ring."[15]

Ida was angry that Greb's confidants had revealed his secret. "Harry was sensitive about the affliction," she said, "that made it necessary for him to have his right eye removed and a glass eye substituted, and even in death I am sure he would not have wanted the world to know about it."[16]

Harry may have been prompted to finally have the eye removed by the fact that his vision was rapidly becoming public knowledge. Jack Kofoed, discussing the news, admitted that "everyone in the ring game knew that, but the fact was never broadcast out of respect for a real gamester."[17] Months before Harry underwent the surgery to remove his bad eye, and long before his condition was publicly revealed Tiger Flowers was deemed ineligible by the California boxing commission when a conversation was overheard between Walk Miller and Jimmy DeForrest as they discussed Greb's bad eye. It was believed at the time that they were discussing Flowers and not Greb resulting in their action against Flowers.[18] At the time the conversation was publicly reported and it is reasonable to assume that the more publicized Greb's condition became the less likely it would be for him to continue to fight.

At 9:25am on October 27 Gene Tunney arrived at the Edwards home amid a dense fog. Thousands had already begun lining the streets to catch a glimpse as Harry was taken to his final resting place. A Grey hearse pulled to the curb which was lined with a police detachment headed by Greb's old sparring partner George Hook. The pallbearers, Red Mason, Tom Dolan, Happy Albacker, Leo Caghil, Eddie Deasy, Jack White, Jack Barry, Sam Pender, Daniel Winters, and Tunney, carried the copper and bronze casket down the walkway lined with members of the American Legion and gently slid it into the waiting vehicle.

A contingent of motorcycle policemen escorted the funeral procession on a slow meandering course through the streets of Pittsburgh. The procession took an hour and ten minutes to make its way through the massive crowds that lined Pittsburgh's streets before finally arriving at St. Philomena's Church. They were met there by a massive throng that stretched as far as the eye could see. Some onlookers had climbed trees to gain a better vantage point. A motion picture crew was present to film the spectacle and cameramen snapped photos, some even climbing to the upper stories of the church to better capture the enormity of the event.

Harry's mother collapsed while following the casket into the church. She had to be supported by Pius, a doctor, and a nurse who had been in constant attendance at her side for days as a result of the physical and emotional shock brought on by Harry's death.

After the solemn high mass the procession wound its way slowly to Calvary Cemetery where Harry was laid to rest next to Mildred as Taps was played.[19]

A few days after the funeral Sally Bronis resurfaced. A report had spread the week of Harry's death that she had attempted suicide because of Greb's continued rejection.[20] The reality of the situation at once shed light on Greb's final accident and further clouded the extent of his relationship with Bronis. The reason Harry had been whisked away from the scene of the accident and his condition kept a guarded secret was that Sally Bronis had been with him at the time. The cuts on her wrists had not been the result of a suicide attempt but rather had been received when she shielded herself from the shattered windshield.[21]

Her presence in Greb's company, at a time when he was being sued by her husband for alienation of affection and when he was publicly acknowledging Naomi Braden as his sweetheart, would explain the subterfuge. What is unclear is whether Harry was actively involved in a relationship with Bronis at the time, or if he was simply using the star struck chorus girl in hopes that she would help him sink her husband's case.

Facing page, top: Gene Tunney leaves the Edwards home at the head of Greb's ornate casket. Funeral director William N. Winter is to the right of Tunney. Bernard "Happy" Albacker is just behind Tunney to the left. Facing page bottom: Tunney and Winter lead the casket down the steps of St. Philomena's Church after the funeral Mass. Harry's sparring partner Jack Barry can be seen just above and to the left of Winter. Top: Harry's casket is navigated through the vast crowd that awaited outside of St. Philomena's church to pay their final respects to Pittsburgh's greatest boxing icon. This photo was shot from one of the upper floors of the church. The white arrow indicates Tunney. Above: Another photo showing the casket leaving the church the crowd pushes in to get a final glimpse.

Top: Two large trucks carrying floral arrangements make their way through the multitude of people. So many floral arrangements were received at the Edwards home that they filled both floors of the house. Above: Harry's mother (center) nearly collapsed on her way into the church and had to be assisted by Pius (left) and a physician. Anna Greb had suffered an emotional breakdown at the news of her son's death and had been under constant care ever since.

Early estimates of Harry's estate were that he had left behind $200,000. When the actual estate was appraised it valued only $77,114.55, still a great deal of money in 1926 (nearly one million dollars at current values) but far below the estimated $200,000. It would be over two years before Harry's estate was finally settled due to a complex web of legal entanglements. Chief among these was Harry's unresolved contract dispute with Red Mason. When Harry's injuries prevented him from being in New York to sign the new contract with Mason the door was left wide open for Mason to continue legal proceedings against Greb's estate, particularly in light of the fact that it was now public knowledge that Harry never intended to fight for Mason, or anyone else again. A handwriting expert was even hired by the Greb family to ascertain if Harry had actually signed the contract in question. The case dragged on through the middle of March the following year when Mason was paid the sum of $15,000 to settle the matter. There were other debts as well and much of Harry's investments in stocks and bonds were sold at a loss. In the end, when the estate was paid out in January of 1929 there was only $37,057.51 left. It all went to Dorothy, who had been adopted by Harry's sister Ida and her husband J. Elmer Edwards.

Time marched on. The years passed. Newspapers grew dusty and unread. Films were lost. Those who had seen Greb in his prime were spread far and wide, grew old and passed away. A large gap in understanding regarding Greb opened and grew. In place of an educated historical perspective on Harry and his accomplishments the lies and legends that had been created or embellished by a largely hostile New York press and self-serving opponents grew and became accepted as fact. The perpetuation of these myths was only aided by the fact that a significant portion of those writers who had slandered Greb mercilessly during his life retired from their newspapers in old age and took up work as regular columnists in the burgeoning boxing magazine market.

Prior to losing the sight in his right eye in 1921, which really signaled the beginning of Greb's decline, Harry had been seen in New York City only a handful of times. Some of these appearances were only exhibition bouts. The writers in New York who helped to formulate Greb's legacy for the next sixty-plus years had in reality rarely, if ever, seen him at his best. Once Harry lost the use of his right eye, hampering his depth perception, his style changed. He was often forced to hold an opponent with his left hand in order to be able to land punches with his right. This is a foul but a relatively minor one. Yet, from the pens of New York boxing writers Harry went from being a rough fighter to one of the dirtiest fighters in history, an assertion which simply is not supported by the writers of any other town outside of New York, and particularly not prior to the summer of 1921. In short Harry's legacy has been colored by opinions which were only being formed as his career was slowly winding down.

Those same writers who contributed to Greb's reputation as a dirty fighter wrote endlessly of Harry's womanizing, nightlife, lack of training, and drinking. By all accounts, except those emanating from New York, Harry was a devoted family man. Only after the death of Mildred was he known to chase women. Again, this period only encompassed the last few years, at most, of a thirteen year career, yet to many it became representative of his entire career. As for his drinking, and love of the nightlife Harry's close friends were all in agreement. "Harry drank, I'll say that," said Jack Barry years later, "but he didn't drink that much, and when he trained he drank hardly at all. Those stories about how much he'd drink got started because he did like to stay out late."

"I can remember we were in New York once, while Harry was training for a fight, and there was a nightclub across the street from the old Theresa Hotel in the Bronx. Harry'd be in there every night, but he wasn't doing any drinking. He just liked people, and they were always asking him out, and he never turned anybody down."[22]

Leo Caghil agreed. "There never was a more conscientious trainer in the business, and he didn't drink. He would sip a little ginger ale and would set them up for his friends, but he himself stayed away from the stuff."[23]

"I never saw him take more than two drinks," stated Cuddy DeMarco, "yet he always tried to act tight. He'd go out the night before a fight, play around, and next night give his opponent the licking of his life. He liked people to point out that fact. But he was always in shape."[24]

These defenders of Greb rarely saw their stories published outside of their local papers while those responsible for embellishing Greb's story were nationally syndicated writers, or published in magazines with an international readership. As a result, this fiction became the Greb story.[25]

Former opponents piled on as well. If every opponent that claimed to have defeated Greb actually did gain a victory over him we would not be discussing his legacy today. Tommy Loughran would claim that he never lost a fight to Greb. Maxie Rosenbloom, likewise, would claim to have beaten Greb in Cleveland in 1925. In rare moments of candor he would admit that Harry had been not only defeated him easily but had indeed been the greatest fighter he ever faced.

Mickey Walker would claim that their fight had been close and to salve his wounds would eventually invent a story whereby he and Greb got into a street fight following their championship battle and Walker won. "That never happened," said Leo Caghil, "We went to the Silver Slipper after the bout and stayed together until Greb went to bed. We didn't see Walker again that night. We met up at the club with Jimmy Slattery, who was knocked out by Dave Shade in a preliminary but we didn't run across Mickey."[26] Walker simply couldn't accept that he had lost to Greb so he invented a story where he defeated him.

Gene Tunney spent years taking liberties with the story of his five fights with Greb, to the point that Greb's family went from having a mutually respectful relationship with the former champion to scorning him. Jack Dempsey would tell several different versions of why he never saw fit to fight Greb and none of them reflected the truth.[27] Even Johnny Wilson, arguably the most mob influenced fighter of the early twentieth century, ludicrously claimed that he lost his championship to Greb when the fight was fixed in Greb's favor.[28] Harry never got to tell his side of the story.

Matters were only made worse in 1946 when James R. Fair published a biography of Greb which bordered on pulp fiction. Claiming to be one of Harry's closest friends, he wrote a salacious tale of Harry's supposed sexual escapades, run-ins with gangsters, and ridiculous array of fight stories, including a completely fictional account of Harry biting off the tip of Chuck Wiggins' nose during a bout at Grand Rapids.

Fair had gotten the help of Harry Keck and Happy Albacker, and even wormed his way into an interview with the Greb family by promising to write a truthful account of Harry's career. Harry's friends immediately jumped to his defense. Happy Albacker's willingness to go along with the project caused a permanent rift between he and his brother Jack, who felt Happy had sold out Greb's memory.[29]

Johnny Houck, brother of Greb's opponent Leo Houck, was similarly outraged. Writing for The Veteran Boxer, Houck blasted the book. "The author of this book always pretended to be a friend of the late Greb. Since Greb is dead, this would be the one, the friend thought. Who could be a better subject than the great Harry Greb?"

"Any person who ever participated in any athletic contest knows it would have been impossible to carry out these fantastic fairy tales which he wrote about Greb. When the writer read the book, it made him laugh out loud, and at the same time, hurling the book of lies into a corner. I became violently angry to think that any person who thought himself so brilliant as to write such untruths about one of our greatest champions. He would have you believe that Greb was one of the most immoral pugilists that ever stepped into a ring. Also one of the foulest."

Houck went on to refute the claims that Greb was a foul fighter by quoting his brother Leo, George Barton, and recounting the fights he had personally seen Greb in and went on to detail Greb's more admirable qualities, left out of the book. "For the benefit of the readers of The Veteran Boxer Magazine, I have given you the true side of Harry Greb. I am not trying to make a fortune by writing this article, like the fellow who tried to make Harry Greb a male Amber, and the foulest fighter that ever stepped into a ring. You may ask why I do not expose his name or mention the title of his story. I will gladly give you the reason clearly. This fellow pretended to be such a good friend of Greb's. What he did not know of the late champion's life he thought he would go to Pittsburgh and investigate. He visited the most famous sports writer of the Smoky City and when the said writer learned of the fellow's mission he tried to tell him to write a clean book on Harry's career, but he insisted a sexy story is what the public would go for. Then he visited Greb's sister, who was very hospitable to him and gave him all the information he desired about her famous brother. He promised he would write a fine book about the late champion, but when it came off the stand, and she read what type of book it was, she and the rest of the family became frantic. She threatened a law suit against this man and had him brought to Pittsburgh, but at the advice of her attorney she dropped the charges, the reason being that it would bring more publicity for the book. Now, dear readers I do hope you understand why I have not mentioned the title of this book or the name of the author, as I do not want to give it publicity or advertisement for the author to derive benefits from its publicity. It is often stated, the meanest thief in the world is the one who steals pennies from a dead man's eye."[30]

Jimmy Kilty backed up Houck's assertions. "Wine, women and song might be the author's sales-talk in selling the book, but it is far from the truth when he associates the former champion with them."

"That Harry's sister was disillusioned when she read the book would be putting it mildly and, the annoyances that came after were more than her family could bear."

"Parts of her letter is as follows: 'The book brought no end of embarrassment to my family and particularly myself...'

'In Houck's story, he explained of how the author came to us and when the book was published we apparently took it lying down. I want to assure it wasn't an easy thing to do. I received letters from all over the nation, asking why I did not declare the book to be an untruth.'

'I am praying for the day when a true book will be written about my brother, for as you know, his training was not on women and song, but on real hard work, for I was with him all the time helping him to attain his goal. Words fail me in trying to express my appreciation to

Mr. Houck and you for defending my brother the way you have, for you have let the world know it, as it should be.'

"It is too bad the author couldn't have written the story in a decent, kindly and tolerant manner. He should have never engaged in a crusade of such a celebrity as the late Harry Greb. Whatever effectiveness he might otherwise had if it was the true story of Harry Greb's life, it was lost right at the beginning through the title. The dollar and cents sign was plastered on the front cover."

"There are too many stories written like the Greb book that are not based on facts and, those of us who knew Greb will never tolerate the untruths said about him."[31]

As the next generation of boxing writers took over during the latter half of the twentieth century they primarily rehashed the same tired stories that had plagued Greb during the latter portion of his career and became inflated after his death. Beginning in the early 1990's Harry's legacy witnessed something of a revival. A new breed of dedicated researchers began to track and document all of Greb's fights. The vast array of newspaper decisions were documented which further shed light on Greb's dominance and greatness.

Around 1990 boxing enthusiast Bill Herr discovered the only known film footage of Harry Greb to have survived to the present day. The footage consisted of two short outtakes of the newsreel clips of Harry signing contracts with Mickey Walker at the Hotel Brevoort and Harry training for the Walker fight the day before the bout. Finally historians saw Harry Greb come to life before their eyes. On display was a living, breathing man who previously had only been seen as a two dimensional figure and whose story seemed almost too unreal to be true.

As the facts of Harry's life came to light there was a renewed interest in the Pittsburgh Windmill. With his achievements placed in their proper perspective Harry has now attained a place suitably high in the pantheon of boxing greats. He regularly makes the top three of lists compiling the greatest fighters in the history of the sport often taking the top position. Memorabilia related to Greb is highly sought after and very expensive. His standing in the sport, impact, and record are all hotly debated among boxing enthusiasts.

In the 21st century during an era that has seen the popularity of boxing wane, the proliferation of boxing championships, lack of competition at the highest level of the sport, and scandals prompted by the use of performance enhancing drugs, Harry is often held up as an example of what all boxing fans appreciate in the sport. His was the quintessential American story; the son of an immigrant father, and first generation mother, who was raised in the very hub of the industrial revolution. He was a product of the burgeoning class of sports superstars that would come to influence generations of young boys, prompting him to try his hand at boxing. He came up through the ranks the hard way, forging his ability, like the steel of his hometown's namesake, over hundreds of fights in dozens of towns before ever getting a shot at the title. He fought anyone who would sign to face him regardless of size or weight, and always fought to win. He gave no quarter and asked none in return. Finally forcing the champions to take notice

he attained the goal he dreamed of since childhood, a world championship. Even during the last years of his career, when he was slowly slipping into physical decline, he actively sought the most challenging fights and, remarkably, rarely ever held up negotiations over the price of his purse.

Throughout his career Harry was often on the road for weeks at a time, leaving behind a sick wife and a small child. One should not judge him too harshly for this. This was simply the reality of his occupation and the only way he knew to give them a standard of living that far exceeded the average laborer in the mills of Pittsburgh. He left the sight of one eye in the ring and the greater part of his youth and vitality. In short, Harry gave everything to sport he loved and when he was no longer able to fight his life seemed to lose purpose. Boxing could do with a great many Harry Greb's in this day and age. If it had them the sport might once again reclaim its position rivaling baseball as the national past time. While reflecting on Harry's life and early demise we truly are reminded of the words of Ira F. Lewis, "THERE LIES AN AMERICAN."

APPENDIX A

HARRY GREB'S FIGHTING RECORD

Harry Greb

Alias	Pittsburgh Windmill
Birth Name	Edward Henry Greb
Country	United States of America
Hometown	Pittsburgh, PA, USA
Birthplace	Pittsburgh, PA, USA
Division	Middleweight/Light-Heavyweight
Born	June 6, 1894
Died	October 22, 1926
Managers	James "Red". Mason, Billy Kelly, Billy Reynolds, George Engel, Jimmy Johnston

	Date	Opponent	Location	Result
	1913-03-10	William Miller	Pittsburgh, PA, USA	W3 (Am)
	1913-03-11	Arthur Story	Pittsburgh, PA, USA	W3 (Am)
	1913-03-12	Red Cumpston	Pittsburgh, PA, USA	W4 (Am)
	1913-04-04	George Koch	Pittsburgh, PA, USA	W4 (Am)
1.	1913-04-05	Red Cumpston	Pittsburgh, PA, USA	NWS 6
2.	1913-05-08	Red Cumpston	Pittsburgh, PA, USA	W KO 3
3.	1913-05-29	Knockout Kirkwood	Pittsburgh, PA, USA	W NWS 6
4.	1913-07-19	Battling Murphy	Pittsburgh, PA, USA	W TKO 2
5.	1913-08-13	Lloyd Crutcher	Punxsutawney, PA, USA	W KO 1
6.	1913-10-11	Hooks Evans	Pittsburgh, PA, USA	L NWS 6

7.	1913-10-22 Mike Milko	Pittsburgh, PA, USA	L NWS 6
8.	1913-11-17 Mike Milko	Pittsburgh, PA, USA	W NWS 6
9.	1913-11-29 Joe Chip	Pittsburgh, PA, USA	L KO 2
10.	1913-12-06 Battling Sherbine	Pittsburgh, PA, USA	W NWS 6
11.	1913-12-12 Bud "Young Bat" Nelson	Altoona, PA, USA	W KO 3
12.	1914-01-01 Whitey Wenzel	Pittsburgh, PA, USA	W NWS 6
13.	1914-01-09 Whitey Wenzel	Pittsburgh, PA, USA	W NWS 6
14.	1914-03-02 Mickey Rodgers	Steubenville, OH, USA	W DQ 5
15.	1914-04-14 Fay Keiser	Pittsburgh, PA, USA	W NWS 6
16.	1914-05-13 Fay Keiser	Pittsburgh, PA, USA	W NWS 6
17.	1914-05-25 George Lewis	Pittsburgh, PA, USA	D NWS 6
18.	1914-05-29 Whitey Wenzel	Pittsburgh, PA, USA	W NWS 6
19.	1914-06-15 Walter Monaghan	Pittsburgh, PA, USA	W NWS 6
20.	1914-06-29 Irish Gorgas	Pittsburgh, PA, USA	W NWS 6
21.	1914-07-20 John Foley	Pittsburgh, PA, USA	W NWS 6
22.	1914-07-27 George Lewis	Steubenville, OH, USA	L NWS 10
23.	1914-08-10 Irish Gorgas	Pittsburgh, PA, USA	W NWS 6
24.	1914-08-24 Whitey Wenzel	Pittsburgh, PA, USA	D NWS 6
25.	1914-08-31 John Foley	Pittsburgh, PA, USA	W NWS 6
26.	1914-09-26 Jack Fink	Philadelphia, PA, USA	W NWS 6
27.	1914-11-14 Terry Martin	Philadelphia, PA, USA	D NWS 6
28.	1914-12-07 Joe Borrell	Philadelphia, PA, USA	L NWS 6
29.	1915-01-01 Billy Donovan	Philadelphia, PA, USA	L NWS 6
30.	1915-01-08 Howard Truesdale	Philadelphia, PA, USA	W NWS 6
31.	1915-01-12 Billy Miske	Philadelphia, PA, USA	D NWS 6
32.	1915-01-25 Jack Blackburn	Pittsburgh, PA, USA	W NWS 6
33.	1915-02-10 Harry "KO" Baker	Pittsburgh, PA, USA	W NWS 6
34.	1915-03-04 Whitey Wenzel	Pittsburgh, PA, USA	W NWS 6
35.	1915-03-06 Tommy Mack	Washington, PA, USA	W NWS 6
36.	1915-03-13 Jack Lavin	McKeesport, PA, USA	W NWS 6
37.	1915-03-25 Harry "KO" Baker	Pittsburgh, PA, USA	W NWS 6
38.	1915-04-15 Whitey Wenzel	Pittsburgh, PA, USA	W NWS 6
39.	1915-04-22 Joe Borrell	Pittsburgh, PA, USA	L NWS 6
40.	1915-05-24 Whitey Wenzel	Pittsburgh, PA, USA	W NWS 6
41.	1915-05-31 Fay Keiser	Connellsville, PA, USA	L NWS 6
42.	1915-06-25 Fay Keiser	Cumberland, MD, USA	D NWS 10
	1915-07-08 Red Robinson	Keystone Park, PA, USA	EXH 6
43.	1915-07-12 Tommy Gavigan	Pittsburgh, PA, USA	W NWS 6

44. 1915-07-21 George Hauser   Elwyn Grove, PA, USA   W KO 6
45. 1915-07-22 Fay Keiser   Cumberland, MD, USA   D NWS 10
46. 1915-08-23 Al Rogers   Pittsburgh, PA, USA   W NWS 6
47. 1915-09-13 Al Rogers   Pittsburgh, PA, USA   W NWS 6
48. 1915-10-18 George Chip   Pittsburgh, PA, USA   D NWS 6
49. 1915-11-16 Tommy Gibbons   St. Paul, MN, USA   L NWS 10
50. 1915-12-16 Kid Graves   Pittsburgh, PA, USA   L TKO 2
51. 1916-02-26 Walter Monaghan   Pittsburgh, PA, USA   W NWS 6
52. 1916-04-01 Kid Manuel   Pittsburgh, PA, USA   W NWS 6
53. 1916-04-27 Grant "Kid" Clark   Johnstown, PA, USA   NC 5
54. 1916-05-06 Whitey Wenzel   Charleroi, PA, USA   W NWS 6
55. 1916-06-03 Kid Manuel   Pittsburgh, PA, USA   W KO 1
56. 1916-06-17 Whitey Wenzel   New Kensington, PA, USA   W NWS 10
57. 1916-06-26 George Chip   New Castle, PA, USA   L NWS 10
58. 1916-08-07 Al Grayber   Pittsburgh, PA, USA   W NWS 6
59. 1916-08-28 Jerry Cole   Pittsburgh, PA, USA   W NWS 6
60. 1916-09-04 Fay Keiser   Cumberland, MD, USA   W PTS 10
61. 1916-10-16 Jackie Clark   Lonaconing, MD, USA   D PTS 10
62. 1916-10-21 Harry "KO" Baker   Pittsburgh, PA, USA   W NWS 6
63. 1916-11-04 KO Sweeney   Pittsburgh, PA, USA   W NWS 6
64. 1916-11-08 Willie "KO" Brennan   Erie, PA, USA   W NWS 10
65. 1916-11-14 Jackie Clark   Lonaconing, MD, USA   W KO 3
66. 1916-11-17 Willie "KO" Brennan   Buffalo, NY, USA   W NWS 10
67. 1916-11-24 Tommy Burke   Buffalo, NY, USA   W NWS 10
68. 1916-11-27 George "KO" Brown   Pittsburgh, PA, USA   W NWS 6
69. 1916-12-26 Bob Moha   Buffalo, NY, USA   W NWS 10
70. 1917-01-01 Joe Borrell   Pittsburgh, PA, USA   W NWS 6
71. 1917-01-13 Eddie Coleman   Charleroi, PA, USA   W KO 2
72. 1917-01-20 Jules Ritchie   Philadelphia, PA, USA   W TKO 4
73. 1917-01-29 Fay Keiser   Lonaconing, MD, USA   W PTS 20
74. 1917-02-10 Mike Gibbons   Philadelphia, PA, USA   L NWS 6
75. 1917-02-12 Willie "KO" Brennan   Buffalo, NY, USA   W NWS 10
76. 1917-03-05 Frankie Brennan   Pittsburgh, PA, USA   W NWS 6
77. 1917-03-20 Tommy Gavigan   McKeesport, PA, USA   W TKO 5
78. 1917-03-23 Herman Miller   Johnstown, PA, USA   W TKO 5
79. 1917-04-02 Young Ahearn   Pittsburgh, PA, USA   W KO 1
80. 1917-04-14 Al Rogers   Charleroi, PA, USA   W NWS 10
81. 1917-04-16 Zulu Kid   Pittsburgh, PA, USA   W NWS 6

82. 1917-04-30 Al McCoy	Pittsburgh, PA, USA	W NWS 10
83. 1917-05-03 Jackie Clark	Cumberland, MD, USA	D PTS 20
84. 1917-05-09 Harry "KO" Baker	Uniontown, PA, USA	W KO 5
85. 1917-05-19 Jeff Smith	Buffalo, NY, USA	W NWS 10
86. 1917-05-22 George Chip	Pittsburgh, PA, USA	W NWS 10
87. 1917-06-14 Frank Mantell	Uniontown, PA, USA	W KO 1
88. 1917-07-02 Buck Crouse	Pittsburgh, PA, USA	W TKO 6
89. 1917-07-30 Jack Dillon	Pittsburgh, PA, USA	W NWS 10
90. 1917-09-06 Battling Levinsky	Pittsburgh, PA, USA	W NWS 10
91. 1917-09-11 Jeff Smith	Milwaukee, WI, USA	W NWS 10
92. 1917-09-14 Jack London	New York, NY, USA	W TKO 9
93. 1917-09-17 George "KO" Brown	Dayton, OH, USA	W TKO 9
94. 1917-09-22 Battling Kopin	Charleroi, PA, USA	W TKO 3
95. 1917-09-25 Johnny Howard	Brooklyn, NY, USA	W TKO 9
96. 1917-10-06 Billy Kramer	Philadelphia, PA, USA	W NWS 6
97. 1917-10-11 Gus Christie	Buffalo, NY, USA	W NWS 10
98. 1917-10-19 Len Rowlands	Milwaukee, WI, USA	W NWS 10
99. 1917-10-23 Gus Christie	Chattanooga, TN, USA	W PTS 8
100. 1917-11-02 Soldier Bartfield	Buffalo, NY, USA	L NWS 10
101. 1917-11-19 George Chip	Cincinnati, OH, USA	W NWS 10
102. 1917-12-03 Willie Meehan	Philadelphia, PA, USA	W NWS 6
103. 1917-12-05 George Ashe	Johnstown, PA, USA	W NWS 10
104. 1917-12-08 Terry Martin	Charleroi, PA, USA	W KO 3
105. 1917-12-17 Gus Christie	Cincinnati, OH, USA	W NWS 12
106. 1917-12-25 Whitey Wenzel	Homestead, PA, USA	W NWS 10
107. 1918-01-04 Terry Kellar	McKeesport, PA, USA	W NWS 10
108. 1918-01-14 Battling Kopin	Charleroi, PA, USA	W KO 1
109. 1918-01-21 Augie Ratner	New Orleans, LA, USA	W PTS 20
110. 1918-01-29 Zulu Kid	Bridgeport, CT, USA	W PTS 14
111. 1918-02-04 Jack Hubbard	Lonaconing, MD, USA	W KO 3
1918-02-07 Frank Klaus	Pittsburgh, PA, USA	EXH 3
112. 1918-02-18 Bob Moha	Cincinnati, OH, USA	W PTS 10
113. 1918-02-25 Mike O'Dowd	St. Paul, MN, USA	L NWS 10
114. 1918-03-04 Jack Dillon	Toledo, OH, USA	W NWS 12
115. 1918-03-11 Mike McTigue	Cleveland, OH, USA	W NWS 10
116. 1918-03-18 Willie Langford	Buffalo, NY, USA	W NWS 6
1918-05-04 Jim Coffey	New York, NY, USA	EXH 3
1918-05-04 Joe Bonds	New York, NY, USA	EXH 3

	1918-05-04 Al McCoy	New York, NY, USA	EXH 3
117.	1918-05-13 Al McCoy	Cincinnati, OH, USA	W NWS 10
118.	1918-05-15 Clay Turner	Bridgeport, CT, USA	W PTS 15
119.	1918-05-20 Soldier Bartfield	Pittsburgh, PA, USA	W NWS 10
	1918-05-24 Gunboat Smith	New York, NY, USA	EXH 6
120.	1918-05-29 Soldier Bartfield	Toledo, OH, USA	W NWS 15
121.	1918-06-20 Zulu Kid	New York, NY, USA	W NWS 6
122.	1918-06-24 Frank Carbone	Bridgeport, CT, USA	W PTS 15
123.	1918-07-04 Bob Moha	Rock Island, IL, USA	W NWS 10
	1918-07-06 Oscar Anderson	Cleveland, OH, USA	EXH 4
124.	1918-07-16 Soldier Bartfield	Philadelphia, PA, USA	W NWS 6
125.	1918-07-27 Eddie McGoorty	Ft. Sheridan, IL, USA	W PTS 10
126.	1918-08-06 Battling Levinsky	Philadelphia, PA, USA	W NWS 6
127.	1918-08-09 Clay Turner	Jersey City, NJ, USA	W NWS 8
128.	1918-09-21 Billy Miske	Pittsburgh, PA, USA	L NWS 10
	1918-12-11 L. Cpl. E. C. Baker	London, England	W KO 1
	1918-12-12 Sgt. Ring	London, England	L PTS 3
129.	1919-01-14 Leo Houck	Boston, MA, USA	W PTS 12
130.	1919-01-20 Young Fisher	Syracuse, NY, USA	W NWS 10
131.	1919-01-23 Paul Sampson Korner	Pittsburgh, PA, USA	W NWS 10
132.	1919-01-27 Soldier Bartfield	Columbus, OH, USA	W NWS 12
133.	1919-01-31 Tommy Robson	Cleveland, OH, USA	W NWS 10
134.	1919-02-03 Len Rowlands	Pittsburgh, PA, USA	W TKO 4
135.	1919-02-10 Bill Brennan	Syracuse, NY, USA	W NWS 10
136.	1919-02-17 Battling Levinsky	Buffalo, NY, USA	W NWS 10
137.	1919-02-28 Chuck Wiggins	Toledo, OH, USA	W NWS 12
138.	1919-03-03 Chuck Wiggins	Detroit, MI, USA	W NWS 8
139.	1919-03-06 Leo Houck	Lancaster, PA, USA	W NWS 6
140.	1919-03-17 Bill Brennan	Pittsburgh, PA, USA	W NWS 10
141.	1919-03-25 Happy Howard	Johnstown, PA, USA	W NWS 10
142.	1919-03-31 Billy Miske	Pittsburgh, PA, USA	W NWS 10
143.	1919-04-02 Tommy Madden	Butler, PA, USA	W KO 2
144.	1919-04-07 Young Fisher	Syracuse, NY, USA	W NWS 10
145.	1919-04-08 One Round Davis	Buffalo, NY, USA	W NWS 10
146.	1919-04-25 Leo Houck	Erie, PA, USA	W NWS 10
147.	1919-04-28 Battling Levinsky	Canton, OH, USA	W NWS 12
148.	1919-05-06 Clay Turner	Boston, MA, USA	W PTS 12
149.	1919-05-08 Willie Meehan	Pittsburgh, PA, USA	W NWS 10

150. 1919-05-13 Bartley Madden	Buffalo, NY, USA	W NWS 10
151. 1919-05-26 Tommy Robson	Syracuse, NY, USA	W NWS 10
152. 1919-06-16 Joe Borrell	Philadelphia, PA, USA	W TKO 5
153. 1919-06-18 Happy Howard	Erie, PA, USA	W NWS 10
154. 1919-06-20 Yankee Gilbert	Wheeling, WV, USA	W TKO 4
155. 1919-06-23 Mike Gibbons	Pittsburgh, PA, USA	W NWS 10
156. 1919-07-04 Bill Brennan	Tulsa, OK, USA	W PTS 15
157. 1919-07-14 Battling Levinsky	Philadelphia, PA, USA	W NWS 6
158. 1919-07-16 George "KO" Brown	Wheeling, WV, USA	W NWS 10
159. 1919-07-24 Joe Chip	Youngstown, OH, USA	W NWS 12
160. 1919-08-11 Terry Kellar	Dayton, OH, USA	W PTS 15
161. 1919-08-23 Bill Brennan	Pittsburgh, PA, USA	W NWS 10
162. 1919-09-01 Jeff Smith	Youngstown, OH, USA	W NWS 12
163. 1919-09-03 Battling Levinsky	Wheeling, WV, USA	W NWS 10
164. 1919-09-18 Silent Martin	St. Louis, MO, USA	W NWS 8
165. 1919-10-13 Sailor Ed Petroskey	Philadelphia, PA, USA	W NWS 6
166. 1919-11-17 George "KO" Brown	Canton, OH, USA	W NWS 12
167. 1919-11-24 Larry Williams	Pittsburgh, PA, USA	W NWS 10
168. 1919-11-27 Zulu Kid	Beaver Falls, PA, USA	W NWS 10
169. 1919-11-28 Soldier Jones	Buffalo, NY, USA	W KO 5
170. 1919-12-10 Clay Turner	Buffalo, NY, USA	W NWS 10
171. 1919-12-12 Mike McTigue	Endicott, NY, USA	W NWS 10
172. 1919-12-15 Billy Kramer	Pittsburgh, PA, USA	W NWS 10
173. 1919-12-22 Clay Turner	Philadelphia, PA, USA	W NWS 6
174. 1920-02-06 Zulu Kid	Kalamazoo, MI, USA	W NWS 10
175. 1920-02-21 Bob Roper	Pittsburgh, PA, USA	W NWS 10
176. 1920-03-09 Clay Turner	Akron, OH, USA	W NWS 12
177. 1920-03-17 Tommy Robson	Dayton, OH, USA	W PTS 12
178. 1920-03-22 Larry Williams	Pittsburgh, PA, USA	W NWS 10
179. 1920-03-25 George "KO" Brown	Denver, CO, USA	W PTS 12
180. 1920-04-05 Bob Roper	Denver, CO, USA	W PTS 12
181. 1920-05-15 Tommy Gibbons	Pittsburgh, PA, USA	L NWS 10
182. 1920-06-02 Clay Turner	Philadelphia, PA, USA	W NWS 8
183. 1920-06-28 Frank Carbone	Rochester, NY, USA	W NWS 10
184. 1920-07-05 Bob Moha	Canton, OH, USA	W NWS 12
185. 1920-07-08 Larry Williams	Buffalo, NY, USA	W NWS 10
186. 1920-07-31 Tommy Gibbons	Pittsburgh, PA, USA	W NWS 10
187. 1920-08-14 Bob Moha	Cedar Point, MI, USA	W NWS 10

188. 1920-08-20 Chuck Wiggins	Kalamazoo, MI, USA	W NWS 10
189. 1920-08-28 Ted Jamieson	Grand Rapids, MI, USA	W NWS 10
190. 1920-09-06 Chuck Wiggins	Benton Harbor, MI, USA	W NWS 6
191. 1920-09-22 Ted Jamieson	Milwaukee, WI, USA	W TKO 6
192. 1920-10-21 Gunboat Smith	South Bend, IN, USA	W KO 1
193. 1920-10-28 Mickey Shannon	Pittsburgh, PA, USA	W NWS 10
194. 1920-11-10 Bartley Madden	Kalamazoo, MI, USA	W NWS 10
195. 1920-11-22 Bob Moha	Milwaukee, WI, USA	W NWS 10
1920-11-28 Jack Burke	Pittsburgh, PA, USA	EXH 3
196. 1920-12-11 Jack Duffy	Pittsburgh, PA, USA	W TKO 6
197. 1920-12-21 Bob Roper	Boston, MA, USA	W PTS 10
198. 1920-12-25 Jeff Smith	Pittsburgh, PA, USA	W NWS 10
199. 1921-01-20 Johnny Celmars	Dallas, TX, USA	W PTS 10
200. 1921-01-29 Pal Reed	Boston, MA, USA	W PTS 10
201. 1921-02-25 Jeff Smith	Boston, MA, USA	W PTS 10
202. 1921-03-16 Jack Renault	Pittsburgh, PA, USA	W NWS 10
203. 1921-04-01 Happy Littleton	New Orleans, LA, USA	W NWS 15
204. 1921-04-06 Jack Renault	Montreal, QC, Canada	W NWS 10
205. 1921-04-11 Soldier Jones	Toronto, ON, Canada	W KO 4
206. 1921-05-04 Bartley Madden	Pittsburgh, PA, USA	W NWS 10
207. 1921-05-13 Jimmy Darcy	Boston, MA, USA	W PTS 10
208. 1921-05-20 Jeff Smith	New Orleans, LA, USA	D PTS 15
209. 1921-05-28 Chuck Wiggins	South Bend, IN, USA	D NWS 10
210. 1921-06-24 Chuck Wiggins	Terre Haute, IN, USA	W NWS 10
1921-08-15 Mike Burke	New York, NY, USA	EXH 3
1921-08-24 Jack Burke	Millvale, PA, USA	EXH ??
1921-08-27 Johnny Howard	Pittsburgh, PA, USA	EXH 4
211. 1921-08-29 Kid Norfolk	Pittsburgh, PA, USA	D NWS 10
212. 1921-09-05 Chuck Wiggins	Ashland, KY, USA	W NWS 10
213. 1921-09-20 Joe Cox	Brooklyn, NY, USA	W PTS 12
214. 1921-10-24 Jimmy Darcy	Buffalo, NY, USA	W PTS 10
215. 1921-11-04 Charley Weinert	New York, NY, USA	W PTS 15
216. 1921-11-11 Billy Shade	Pittsburgh, PA, USA	W NWS 10
217. 1921-11-25 Homer Smith	Newark, NJ, USA	W TKO 5
218. 1921-12-06 Fay Keiser	Philadelphia, PA, USA	W NWS 8
219. 1921-12-23 Whitey Allen	Syracuse, NY, USA	W TKO 6
220. 1922-01-02 Chuck Wiggins	Cincinnati, OH, USA	W NWS 10
221. 1922-02-01 Hugh Walker	Grand Rapids, MI, USA	W NWS 10

222. 1922-02-20 Jeff Smith	Cincinnati, OH, USA	W NWS 10	
1922-02-25 George Hook	Pittsburgh, PA, USA	EXH 3	
1922-02-26 George Hook	Pittsburgh, PA, USA	EXH 4	
223. 1922-03-13 Tommy Gibbons	New York, NY, USA	W PTS 15	

Harry boxed three rounds twice daily at the Gayety Theatre in Pittsburgh
against Young Frank Gotch from Mar. 20 thru the 23th and the 25th as part of a theatrical tour.
On the 24th Gotch sparred 2 rounds with Greb and Patsy Scanlon boxed another two
Rounds with Harry.

1922-03-26 Jack Barry	Pittsburgh, PA, USA	EXH 4	

Harry boxed three rounds twice daily against Pittsburgh Heavyweight Red Flaherty
in Toronto as part of his theatrical tour from March 27 to March 31.

1922-03-28 Tiny Guthrie	Toronto, ON, Canada	EXH 2	
1922-03-28 Les Blackie	Toronto, ON, Canada	EXH 2	

Harry boxed three rounds twice daily against Pittsburgh Heavyweight Red Flaherty
in Montreal as part of his theatrical tour from April 3 to April 7.

Harry boxed three rounds twice daily against Pittsburgh Heavyweight Red Flaherty
in Buffalo as part of his theatrical tour from April 10 to April 14.

Harry boxed three rounds twice daily against Pittsburgh Heavyweight Red Flaherty
in New York City as part of his theatrical tour from April 17 to April 21.

224. 1922-05-12 Al Roberts	Boston, MA, USA	W KO 6	
225. 1922-05-23 Gene Tunney	New York, NY, USA	W PTS 15	
226. 1922-06-26 Hugh Walker	Pittsburgh, PA, USA	W NWS 10	
227. 1922-07-10 Tommy Loughran	Philadelphia, PA, USA	W NWS 8	
1922-09-02 Jimmy Darcy	Saranac Lake, NY, USA	EXH 3	
228. 1922-09-26 Al Benedict	Toronto, ON, Canada	W TKO 2	
229. 1922-09-29 Bob Roper	Grand Rapids, MI, USA	W NWS 10	
230. 1922-10-27 Larry Williams	Mariesville, RI, USA	W TKO 4	
231. 1922-11-10 Bob Roper	Buffalo, NY, USA	W PTS 12	
232. 1923-01-01 Bob Roper	Pittsburgh, PA, USA	W NWS 10	
1923-01-14 Frank Munroe	Pittsburgh, PA, USA	EXH 3	

233. 1923-01-15 Tommy Loughran	Pittsburgh, PA, USA	W NWS 10
234. 1923-01-22 Billy Shade	Jersey City, NJ, USA	W NWS 12
235. 1923-01-30 Tommy Loughran	New York, NY, USA	W PTS 15
236. 1923-02-05 Pal Reed	Newark, NJ, USA	W NWS 12
237. 1923-02-16 Young Fisher	Syracuse, NY, USA	W PTS 12
238. 1923-02-23 Gene Tunney	New York, NY, USA	L PTS 15
1923-03-11 Tom Higgins	Pittsburgh, PA, USA	EXH 3
1923-04-25 Frank Munroe	Pittsburgh, PA, USA	EXH 3
239. 1923-06-16 Len Rowlands	Uniontown, PA, USA	W KO 3
1923-08-07 Cuddy DeMarco	Johnstown, PA, USA	EXH 3
1923-08-07 Leo Caghil	Johnstown, PA, USA	EXH 3
1923-08-09 Leo Caghil	Conneaut Lake, PA, USA	EXH 6
1923-08-12 (Likely Leo Caghil)	Uniontown, PA, USA	EXH ?
1923-08-12 (Likely Cuddy DeMarco)	Uniontown, PA, USA	EXH ?
240. 1923-08-31 Johnny Wilson	New York, NY, USA	W PTS 15
1923-09-29 George Hook	Pittsburgh, PA, USA	EXH 3
241. 1923-10-04 Jimmy Darcy	Pittsburgh, PA, USA	W NWS 10
242. 1923-10-11 Tommy Loughran	Boston, MA, USA	L PTS 10
243. 1923-10-22 Lou Bogash	Jersey City, NJ, USA	W NWS 12
244. 1923-11-05 Soldier Jones	Pittsburgh, PA, USA	W NWS 10
1923-11-06 Harry Fink	Pittsburgh, PA, USA	EXH 3
245. 1923-11-15 Chuck Wiggins	Grand Rapids, MI, USA	W NWS 10
1923-12-02 Frank Senk	Pittsburgh, PA, USA	EXH 3
246. 1923-12-03 Bryan Downey	Pittsburgh, PA, USA	W UD 10
247. 1923-12-10 Gene Tunney	New York, NY, USA	L PTS 15
248. 1923-12-25 Tommy Loughran	Pittsburgh, PA, USA	W PTS 10
249. 1924-01-18 Johnny Wilson	New York, NY, USA	W PTS 15
250. 1924-02-22 Jack Reeves	Oakland, CA, USA	W PTS 4
251. 1924-03-24 Fay Keiser	Baltimore, MD, USA	W KO 12
252. 1924-04-19 Kid Norfolk	Boston, MA, USA	L DQ 6
253. 1924-05-05 Jackie Clark	Kenilworth, MD, USA	W KO 2
254. 1924-05-12 Pal Reed	Pittsburgh, PA, USA	W PTS 10
1924-06-06 George Kenneally	Olean, NY, USA	EXH 2
1924-06-06 Frank Senk	Olean, NY, USA	EXH 4
255. 1924-06-12 Martin Burke	Brooklyn, OH, USA	W NWS 10
256. 1924-06-16 Frank Moody	Waterbury, CT, USA	W KO 6
257. 1924-06-26 Ted Moore	Bronx, NY, USA	W PTS 15
258. 1924-08-21 Tiger Flowers	Fremont, OH, USA	W NWS 10

259.	1924-09-03 Jimmy Slattery	Buffalo, NY, USA	W PTS 6
260.	1924-09-15 Billy Hirsch	Steubenville, OH, USA	W TKO 8
261.	1924-09-17 Gene Tunney	Cleveland, OH, USA	W NWS 10
	1924-09-20 Harry Meyers	Pittsburgh, PA, USA	EXH KO 2
262.	1924-10-13 Tommy Loughran	Philadelphia, PA, USA	D PTS 10
263.	1924-11-11 Lew Comasana	Phillipsburg, PA, USA	W KO 2
264.	1924-11-17 Jimmy Delaney	Pittsburgh, PA, USA	W PTS 10
265.	1924-11-25 Frankie Ritz	Wheeling, WV, USA	W TKO 3
	1924-12-28 Tony Ross	Pittsburgh, PA, USA	EXH 2
	1924-12-28 Jack Barry	Pittsburgh, PA, USA	EXH 2
266.	1925-01-01 Augie Ratner	Pittsburgh, PA, USA	W PTS 10
267.	1925-01-09 Bob Sage	Detroit, MI, USA	W NWS 10
268.	1925-01-19 Johnny Papke	Zanesville, OH, USA	W TKO 7
	1925-01-22 Kid Lewis	Pittsburgh, PA, USA	EXH KO 1
269.	1925-01-30 Jimmy Delaney	St. Paul, MN, USA	W NWS 10
	1925-02-12 Frank Munro	Pittsburgh, PA, USA	EXH 3
270.	1925-02-17 Billy Britton	Allentown, PA, USA	W PTS 10
271.	1925-02-23 Young Fisher	Scranton, PA, USA	W DQ 6
272.	1925-03-27 Gene Tunney	St. Paul, MN, USA	L NWS 10
273.	1925-04-17 Johnny Wilson	Boston, MA, USA	W PTS 10
274.	1925-04-24 Jack Reddick	Toronto, ON, Canada	W PTS 10
275.	1925-05-01 Quintin Romero Rojas	Detroit, MI, USA	W NWS 10
276.	1925-05-06 Billy Britton	Columbus, OH, USA	W PTS 12
277.	1925-05-29 Tommy Burns	Indianapolis, IN, USA	W NWS 10
278.	1925-06-01 Soldier Buck	Louisville, KY, USA	W NWS 10
279.	1925-06-05 Jimmy Nuss	Marquette, MI, USA	W KO 4
280.	1925-07-02 Mickey Walker	New York, NY, USA	W PTS 15
281.	1925-07-16 Maxie Rosenbloom	Cleveland, OH, USA	W NWS 10
282.	1925-07-23 Billy Britton	Columbus, KS, USA	W PTS 10
283.	1925-07-27 Ralph Brooks	Wichita, KS, USA	W NWS 10
284.	1925-07-31 Otis Bryant	Tulsa, OK, USA	W KO 3
285.	1925-08-04 Ed Smith	Kansas City, MO, USA	W KO 4
286.	1925-08-12 Pat Walsh	Atlantic City, NJ, USA	W TKO 2
287.	1925-08-17 Tommy Burns	Detroit, MI, USA	W NWS 10
288.	1925-10-12 Tony Marullo	Pittsburgh, PA, USA	W PTS 10
	1925-10-27 Charles Dixie Allen	Pittsburgh, PA, USA	EXH 4
289.	1925-11-13 Tony Marullo	New Orleans, LA, USA	W PTS 15
290.	1925-12-14 Soldier Buck	Nashville, TN, USA	W PTS 8

291.	1926-01-11 Roland Todd	Toronto, ON, Canada	W PTS 12
292.	1926-01-19 Joe Lohman	Omaha, NE, USA	W PTS 10
293.	1926-01-26 Ted Moore	Vernon, CA, USA	W PTS 10
294.	1926-01-29 Buck Holley	Hollywood, CA, USA	W TKO 4
295.	1926-02-03 Jimmy Delaney	Oakland, CA, USA	W PTS 10
296.	1926-02-12 Owen Phelps	Prescott, AZ, USA	W PTS 10
297.	1926-02-26 Tiger Flowers	New York, NY, USA	L PTS 15
	1926-04-01 Fred Switzer	Little Rock, AK, USA	EXH 3
	1926-05-25 Jack Barry	Pittsburgh, PA, USA	EXH 3
298.	1926-06-01 Art Weigand	Buffalo, NY, USA	W PTS 10
299.	1926-06-15 Allentown Joe Gans	Wilkes-Barre, PA, USA	W PTS 10
300.	1926-08-19 Tiger Flowers	New York, NY, USA	L PTS 15

APPENDIX B

FILM SOURCES

Augie Ratner Vs. Paul Berlenbach (Tunney-Carpentier film)

Bartley Madden Vs. George Christian

Battling Levinsky Vs. Jim Savage

Battling Siki Vs. Georges Carpentier

Battling Siki Vs. Marcelle Niles II

Billy Miske Vs. Jack Renault I (Dempsey Vs. Carpentier undercard)

Billy Papke sparring Jeff Smith (Papke-Carpentier film)

Billy Papke Vs. Georges Carpentier

Primo Carnera Vs. Tommy Loughran

Frank Klaus Vs. Georges Carpentier

Frank Moody Vs. Tommy Milligan

Gene Tunney Sparring Jim Corbett

Gene Tunney Sparring Jimmy Delaney (Tunney-Dempsey I film)

Gene Tunney Vs Soldier Jones (Dempsey Vs. Carpentier undercard)

Gene Tunney Vs. Georges Carpentier

Gene Tunney Vs. Jack Dempsey I

Gene Tunney Vs. Jack Dempsey II

Gene Tunney Vs. Ted Jamieson

Gene Tunney Vs. Tom Heeney

Gene Tunney Vs. Tommy Gibbons

Georges Carpentier Vs. Arthur Townley

Georges Carpentier Vs. Dick Smith

Georges Carpentier Vs. George Cook

Georges Carpentier Vs. Georges Grundhoven

Georges Carpentier Vs. Jeff Smith

Georges Carpentier Vs. Joe Beckett I

Georges Carpentier Vs. Joe Beckett II

Georges Carpentier Vs. Marcel Nilles

Georges Carpentier Vs. Ted Kid Lewis

Georges Carpentier Vs. Tommy Gibbons newsreel

Georges Carpentier Vs. Willie Lewis

Gunboat Smith Sparring Bob Armstrong

Harry Greb and Mickey Walker Sign Contracts.

Harry Greb Trains For Mickey Walker

Harry Wills Vs. Bartley Madden

Jack Delaney Training

Jack Delaney Vs. Paulino Uzcudan

Jack Delaney Vs. Tom Heeney

Jack Dempsey Sparring Jock Malone (Dempsey-Willard film)

Jack Dempsey Sparring Larry Williams (Dempsey-Carpentier film)

Jack Dempsey Sparring Martin Burke (Dempsey-Sharkey film)

Jack Dempsey Sparring Terry Keller (Dempsey-Willard film)

Jack Dempsey Sparring Tommy Loughran (Tunney-Dempsey I film)

Jack Dempsey Training Aboard The U.S.S. Granite State 1920

Jack Dempsey Training at Van Kelton Stadium 1920

Jack Dempsey Trains With Terry Keller in early 1919

Jack Dempsey Vs. Bill Brennan II

Jack Dempsey Vs. Billy Miske III

Jack Dempsey Vs. Georges Carpentier

Jack Dempsey Vs. Jess Willard

Jack Dempsey Vs. Luis Firpo

Jack Dempsey Vs. Tommy Gibbons

Jack Johnson Vs. Frank Moran

Jack Renault Sparring Dave Shade

Jack Sharkey Vs. Mike McTigue

Jack Sharkey Vs. Tommy Loughran I

Jack Sharkey Vs. Young Stribling

Jess Willard Vs. Frank Moran

Jess Willard Vs. Jack Johnson

Jock Malone Vs. Navy Rostan (Dempsey-Willard film)

Kid From Kokomo, The (Maxie Rosenbloom)

Kid Norfolk Vs. Bill Tate III (Dempsey-Brennan II film)

Les Darcy Vs. Eddie McGoorty I

Les Darcy Vs. George Chip

Les Darcy Vs. George K.O. Brown II

Les Darcy Vs. Jimmy Clabby II

Les Darcy Vs. Dave Smith I

Luis Firpo Vs. Bill Brennan

Max Schmeling Vs. Mickey Walker

Max Schmeling Vs. Young Stribling

Mickey Walker In Hollywood 1925

Mickey Walker Training

Mickey Walker Training for Ace Hudkins

Mickey Walker Trains for Harry Greb

Mickey Walker Vs. Ace Hudkins II

Mickey Walker Vs. Jack Sharkey

Mickey Walker Vs. Mike McTigue I

Mickey Walker Vs. Tommy Milligan

Mike Gibbons Training With Tommy Gibbons

Mike Gibbons Training Troops in World War I

Mike Gibbons Vs. Packey McFarland

Mike McTigue Training

Mike McTigue Vs. Battling Siki

Mike O'Dowd Sparring Bob Armstrong (O'Dowd-Gibbons film)

Mike O'Dowd Sparring Jimmy Delaney (O'Dowd-Gibbons film)

Mike O'Dowd Vs. Al McCoy I

Mike O'Dowd Vs. Mike Gibbons I

Paul Berlenbach Vs. Jack Delaney III

Paul Berlenbach Vs. Jimmy Slattery

Roland Todd Vs. Ted Kid Lewis II

Roland Todd, Our New Champion

Single Standard, The (Captain Bob Roper)

Ted Kid Lewis Vs. Augie Ratner II

Tom Heeney Vs. Bartley Madden

Tommy Gibbons Vs. Jack Bloomfield

Tommy Loughran Vs. Jim Braddock

Tommy Loughran Vs. Jimmy Delaney II (Tunney-Dempsey I film)

Tommy Loughran Vs. Leo Lomski

Tommy Loughran Vs. Maurice Strickland

Tommy Loughran Vs. Mickey Walker

Young Stribling Training

Young Stribling Vs. Ambrose Palmer

Young Stribling Vs. Don McCorkindale

Young Stribling Vs. Phil Scott

NOTES

PROLOGUE

1 Lorant, Stefan, **Pittsburgh: The Story of an American City**. New York: Doubleday & Company, Inc., 1964.

2 Ibid.

3 Foner, Philip S., **History of the Labor Movement in the United States: From Colonial Times to the Founding of the American Federation of Labor**. New York: International Publishers, 1947.

4 Krause, Paul, **The Battle for Homestead, 1880-1892: Politics, Culture, and Steel**. Pittsburgh: University of Pittsburgh Press, 1992.

5 Harvey, George, **Henry Clay Frick, The Man**. Beard Books, 2002.

6 Yellen, Samuel, **American Labor Struggles**. New York: Harcourt, Brace and Company, 1936.

7 Hoffmann, Charles, **The Depression of the Nineties: An Economic History**. Westport, CT: Greenwood Publishing, 1970.

8 Stefan Lorant, **Pittsburgh: The Story of an American City**. New York: Doubleday & Company, Inc., 1964.

9 Schwantes, Carlos A., **Coxey's Army: An American Odyssey**. Lincoln: University of Nebraska Press, 1985.

NOTES

CHAPTER 1

1 The story of Pius' clandestine journey to the United States is recounted in the Rossdorf Church records. The 1900 United States Census lists Edward Greb as having arrived in 1878 while Edward's Application for citizenship, filed in 1885 states that he had been in the country for at least five years. However there is a ship passenger record from 1881 on file at the National Archives which lists an Eduard Greb (the original spelling of his name) this date corresponds almost exactly with the date listed by Edward as his arrival on a later passport application.

2 Richard Greb's application for citizenship filed in 1886 lists him as having been in the country for no less than five years.

3 Ship Passenger records on file at the National Archives list Elizabeth Greb and Peter Riehl as arriving together in 1882.

4 The 1900 U.S. Census lists Pius as arriving in 1880 and states that he was naturalized in Pennsylvania (he wouldn't be naturalized until 1902). The 1910 Census lists 1880 as the year of arrival as well. However, the 1920 census lists Pius as having arrived in 1885. The 1930 census also states that Pius arrived in 1885.

5 It is believed that Pius helped out in the Riehl family butcher shop because some later accounts list Pius as being a butcher as opposed to a private contractor. This is supported by Pius' will which left behind many items commonly found in a commercial butcher shop.

6 One of the many myths that has grown up about Harry Greb is that he was born in a car on the way to the hospital. This myth originated in the 1950s when a certified copy of Greb's birth certificate surfaced. It was noted that the location of his birth was given as the corner of Fitch and Dauphin. In reality the corner of Fitch and Dauphin was where the home of Pius and Annie Greb was located. The confusion comes from the fact that shortly after Greb's birth the street names changed. Fitch became Millvale Ave and Dauphin became Broad. As stated in the text Harry Greb was born at home under the care of Mary Werle, acting as midwife. This is all aside from the simple fact that in 1894 there were only

a handfull of automobiles (at most) in the United States for Harry to have been born in.

7 Pius and Edward's participation in the Woolslair School and St. Joseph church construction is part of an oral tradition passed down through the family of Edward Greb.

8 Ibid.

9 Clement, Priscilla Ferguson. ***Growing Pains: Children in the Industrial Age, 1850-1890***. Twayne's History of American Childhood Series. NY: Twayne Publishers, 1997.

10 The 1910 census lists Edward (Harry) Greb working as an Electrician's Apprentice. Later accounts of James Mason, George Engel, and various Pittsburgh sportswriters place Greb in the Westinghouse plant and it is a logical leap to the assumption that this is where he was employed as an Electrician's Apprentice considering this was one of the lowest level jobs an applicant could find at the plant. Harry may have moonlighted as a tinsmith's apprentice while working at the Westinghouse plant as he later stated that he worked as a tinsmith's apprentice from the ages of 14 to 18.

11 Weber, Max. ***The Protestant Ethic and the Spirit of Capitalism***, London, Routledge, 1992.

12 This is certainly up to debate since Klaus had moved his base of operations to New York and had not yet won a championship. Klaus was Pittsburgh's only fighter who at the time was making daily news on the world scene with major bouts from California to New York and as far away as Paris.

NOTES

CHAPTER 2

1 This story has almost become tradition in the Greb legend. Both James Mason and George Engel (Greb's most prominent managers) retold this story in later accounts of Greb's life. Its likely the story has some basis in fact but the details remain shrouded.

2 Stoney Ritz was described in the August 17, 1912 edition of the Wheeling Register as coming close on the heels of Walter "Goo" Stewart for the honors of Wheeling's best boxer.

3 This story probably originated with George Engel. Engel's accounts of Greb's early career are full of factual inaccuracies but it is likely that Greb acted as a towel waver in his early days since this was the type of duty relegated to young hangers-on and up and coming fighters.

4 Skipper Manning is first associated with Greb in print in the March 11, 1913 edition of the Pittsburgh Press: "One Feature of the evening was the fact that Skipper Manning esquired a winner. James has been picking dead ones, but the cards shifted on him last night. He groomed a starter who trimmed W. J. Miller, a medal sporter from the famous O'Toole club."

5 Pittsburgh Gazette-Times: ***Harry Greb's Life Story***, November 9, 1926.

6 William J. Miller had been fighting in local amateur competitions since at least 1911. Both Art Story and Red Cumpston had been fighting in the amateur ranks since at least late 1912. There has been some confusion as to W. J. Miller's identity in various published records of Greb. Later records for Greb list Miller's name as "Buck" Miller yet Buck Miller and W. J. Miller were two different people boxing in roughly the same weight division at the same time in the amateurs which may have led to some confusion. Buck Miller continued his career into the professional ranks but no mention has been found of William J. Miller turning professional. Indeed William J. Miller would be indicted for murder a few years later. Adding to the confusion is the fact that a Buck "Twin" Miller gained some prominence in Philadelphia not long before William and Buck Miller gained some recognition for their amateur careers and one "Bull" Miller of Monesson was active in the Pittsburgh area at the same time that William and Buck were fighting.

7 Pittsburgh Chronicle-Telegraph: ***AM. BOXING BOUTS THRILL THE FANS***, March 11, 1913.

8 Pittsburgh Press: ***AMATEUR TOURNEY AT LAWRENCEVILLE CLOSES TONIGHT***, March 12, 1913.

9 McVicker, W. B., Pittsburgh Press: *What the Local Amateur Athletic Stars Are Doing,* March 16, 1913.

10 Cleveland Press: *Victory Friday Night May Cause G. Koch to Turn Professional,* March 11, 1913.

11 There is a story associated with Greb's presence in the Cleveland tournament. It has been alleged that Greb was only a participant in the tournament because a more experienced fighter was unable to attend and Greb took his place by default. This story is obviously faulty in that Greb clearly won his place on the squad. However, Cumpston was sent along as 135 lb entry due to the fact that no bouts in that division had been held during the Pittsburgh elimination tournament and also as a 145 alternate. Indeed the story may have some basis in fact, while being unrelated to Greb, as up until the time of the tournament Cumpston's name was being listed as the entry for the 135 pound class. At the last minute Victor Wright, who hadn't even competed in the Pittsburgh tournament, was sent in against Dick Stosh and lost. Its possible that Wright and not Greb was the late sub and the only thing tying the two stories together is Cumpston.

12 Cleveland Plain Dealer: *CLEVELAND BOXERS WIN MEET BY SLIGHT MARGIN,* April 5, 1913.

13 The two early professional bouts with Cumpston are listed on early records for Greb, and even one published in the Pittsburgh papers after his death. However, there are several seemingly factual mistakes in Mason's narrative found in the following footnote. For instance, the six rounder which Mason is presumably referring to as the first time he saw Greb fight was not held at Waldemier Hall according to the advertisements (unless the venue was changed on short notice). Another factual error on Mason's part is that the rematch was not held two weeks later but an entire month later. This may simply be nitpicking of an older man's recollection of events 13 years previous but it also gives the naysayer ammunition to level at Greb's record.

Further evidence of these bouts having taken place is that in a newspaper advertisement for Greb's rematch with Cumpston (their third bout) dated May 9, 1913 both Greb and Cumpston are listed as ex-amateurs. Still later, on May 31, 1913 in a short editorial in the Pittsburgh Press we find the story of how Greb came into boxing: "Harry Greb, latest debutant into pro ranks is the son of a Millvale Ave. contractor. Harry was stung by the fight bug less than six months ago. His rise has been rapid. Pewter prizes satisfied him until the night Battery B boys held a smoker. Then Greb heard the jingle of coin and promptly proceeded to look for a manager." Finally, Greb himself discussed the bout, as detailed in footnote 15, several years later although himself mixing up the decision and the knockout. All strong evidence that these bouts did indeed take place and were in fact professional bouts.

14 Pittsburgh Gazette-Times: *Harry Greb's Life Story,* November 11, 1926.

15 Corbett, James J., Binghamton Press: *"Jim" Corbet's Daily Column,* September 9, 1920.

16 Pittsburgh Press: *Fistic Foibles,* May 12, 1913.

17 Taken from Red Mason's numerous obituaries, most notably those published in the Pittsburgh Post-Gazette by Jack Sell and the Pittsburgh Press on August 16, 1935.

18 This specific date was gathered from the above listed obituaries but it was commonly mentioned throughout Mason's later career that he had at one time been professionally associated in some capacity with the Pittsburgh Pirates, variously as a trainer and groundskeeper.

19 Dr. Laurence McNamee, when interviewed, remembered Mason's antics well and commented that the fans were generally entertained by his quick witted remarks and zany behavior. The above mentioned obituaries were also helpful in adding more detail to this aspect of Mason's life, particularly his harassment of Cuban baseball player Adolpho Luque and the fact that Mason continued his habit of carrying a megaphone to games and razzing players when he moved to Chicago at the end of his life.

20 Pittsburgh Gazette-Times: *Harry Greb's Life Story,* November 11, 1926.

21 Pittsburgh Press: *Fistic Foibles,* May 31, 1913.

22 Ibid.

23 Pittsburgh Press: *ROBINSON AND RODGERS READY FOR THEIR BOUT,* July 18, 1913.

24 Pittsburgh Press: *BOXING SHOW WILL BE HELD HERE AUGUST 9,* July 21, 1913.

25 Punxatanwey Spirit: *GETZ BESTS ROBINSON IN CLEAN BOXING SHOW AT JEFFERSON THEATRE,* August 14, 1913. This account is interesting because if the quote attributed to Greb's friends is accurate then that would account for his bout with Cumpston which is lacking corroboration, his bout with Stoney Ritz which lacks corroboration and a bout of which no mention has ever been made.

26 The Frank Klaus - George Chip bout was not a decision bout and was not even promoted as a championship match. However, given the context of the day, if Chip succeeded in weighing in below the middleweight limit, and managed to

knockout Klaus, he would be considered the new Middleweight Champion.

27 Youngstown Vindicator: *GRIFFITHS IS WINNER OVER BRESNAHAN,* October 21, 1913.

28 Pittsburgh Post: *DEATH NOTICES,* October 20, 1913.

29 Burial Records of Northside Catholic Cemetery.

30 Pittsburgh Post: *AMATEUR HEAVYWEIGHT CLEANS UP IN BRADDOCK,* June 4, 1913.

31 Pittsburgh Gazette-Times: *Kid Milko Against Owen Moran,* December 30, 1910.

32 Pittsburgh Gazette-Times: *Finals in Amateur Boxing Tournament,* February 26, 1911. "There was a protest entered against Mike Melco (sic), the winner of the 135 pound event. It is claimed that he fought against professionals at the Gayety Theatre in exhibition bouts."

33 Pittsburgh Leader: *Three Bouts on Card For Tariff Club,* October 22, 1913.
Pittsburgh Press: *GREBB AND MILKO TO MEET TONIGHT,* October 22, 1913.

34 Youngstown Telegram: *GREBBS FEARS CHIP BUT MEETS PITTSBURG BOXER,* October 23, 1913.

35 Pittsburgh Leader: *Will Finish Brawl In Roped Arena,* October 30 1913.

36 Pittsburgh Post: *AMoNG the BoXERS,* November 10, 1913.

37 Pittsburgh Press: *MASON MAKES BOLD DEFI TO PUGILISTS,* November 23, 1913.

38 Pittsburgh Post: *AMoNG the BoXERS,* November 5, 1913.

39 Pittsburgh Leader: *Moha and McMahon Will Battle Tonight,* November 29, 1913.

40 Accounts of Joe Chip's knockout win over Harry Greb are derived primarily from the Pittsburgh Daily Dispatch, which had the most detailed coverage of their fight, and was supplemented by the Pittsburgh Press, Pittsburgh Leader, and Pittsburgh Gazette-Times. The Coverage of the Pittsburgh Post was minimal at best. It has become a part of the Greb legend that Greb was to have fought Hughie Madole but that at the last minute Joe Chip was substituted in Madole's place and thus Greb was forced to a fight a bigger, more difficult opponent at a moments notice. This story is erroneous and is disputed by the simple fact that Joe Chip had been announced as a part of the card as, early if not earlier than, Greb. The story of the late substitution was probably a distortion of Greb's bout against Hooks Evans in which Greb substituted for Madole against Evans. It has also been stated by more recent writers that Greb was on his feet when the bout was stopped and actually thanked the referee for stopping the fight. Nothing could be further from the truth as illustrated in this books description of the fight taken from eye-witness sources. One final myth in relation to this fight which needs addressing is that Buck Crouse, as Greb's stablemate, had made an attempt to reach the bell and ring it before the final 10 count, giving Greb a minutes rest. Again, this account is completely false as Crouse had not only split with Mason but had recently relocated to Buffalo, New York when this fight took place.

NOTES

CHAPTER 3

1 Pittsburgh Post: *AMoNG the BoXERS,* December 1, 1913.

2 Pittsburgh Leader: *Deal to Crimp Boxing By Underhand Method,* November 30, 1913.

3 Based on reports gathered from the Pittsburgh Daily Dispatch, Leader, Post, Gazette-Times, and Press all of which voted the bout a victory for Greb.

4 Altoona Mirror: *THREE BOUTS HALTED BEFORE REACHING LIMIT,* December 13, 1913.

5 Descriptions of the bout were taken from the Altoona Mirror and Altoona Times. Later records credit this bout as hav-

ing been against a certain "Terry" Nelson. This however is incorrect as the two most prominent boxers named Terry Nelson, active during Greb's lifetime, were from Ohio and Georgia respectively. This fighter, one "Young Bat" or "Bud" Nelson was called a "local" boy by the Altoona newspapers and indeed upon further research one finds that "Young Bat" Nelson was a preliminary fighter from Altoona who at the time had been making a name for himself locally by running up a string of knockouts.

6 Reports of the Greb-Wenzel bout are gathered from the Pittsburgh Sun, Post, Gazette-Times, and Daily Dispatch. The quote is taken from the January 2, 1914 edition of the Pittsburgh Post.

7 McCarty, S. E., Pittsburgh Leader: *ONLY BY STALLING OF VISITING PUG DID LOCAL BOXER LAST FIVE SESSIONS*, January 11, 1914.

8 Pittsburgh Daily Dispatch: *Monoghan a Chopping Block For Clever Gus Christie*, January 11, 1914.

9 McCarty, S. E., Pittsburgh Leader: *A Brief Summing Up Of Local Mitt Maulers And Their Prospects*, January 11, 1914.

10 Pittsburgh Post: *AMoNG the BoXERS*, January 12, 1914.

11 Pittsburgh Gazette-Times: *Mickey Rodgers Takes the Count*, July 26, 1913.

12 Pittsburgh Daily Dispatch: *RODGERS HELD FOR COURT*, February 9, 1918.

13 Pittsburgh Post: *AMoNG the BoXERS*, February 17, 1914.

14 Pittsburgh Daily Dispatch: *Rodgers-Greb Bout Postponed*, February 22, 1914.

15 Pittsburgh Post: *Rodgers Bars None In Lightweight Ranks*, February 26, 1914.

16 Davis, Ralph, Pittsburgh Leader: *Ralph Davis' Column*, March 4, 1914.

17 Accounts of the Harry Greb - Mickey Rodgers bout are gathered from the various Pittsburgh newspapers. Most if not all of these accounts appear to be wire reports which generally do not give the most accurate picture of events. These reports differ as to whether Greb was hit low or received a "well placed knee to the abdomen." Questions arise in regard to exactly how Rodgers fouled Greb in Steubenville when on March 9, 1914 a letter is written to the Sporting Editor of the Pittsburgh Press asking: In their recent fight, Rodgers fouled Greb. Did he hit him or kick him? The Editor responded by stating: Rodgers hit Greb several times below the belt. He did not kick him.

18 Pittsburgh Post: *Going After Scalp Of Big John Foley*, April 5, 1914.

19 It has been stated that Chip took the McCoy bout on a moments notice, stepping in for his brother Joe. This is a more romanticized version of the facts. In truth, George had known that he would be fighting McCoy several days (possibly as much as a week or more) in advance.

20 New York Tribune: *CHIP KNOCKED OUT IN FIRST ROUND*, April 8, 1914.

21 The Pittsburgh Sun, Gazette-Times, and Post all agreed that Greb deserved the verdict. The Pittsburgh Press declined to award victory.

22 Pittsburgh Gazette-Times: *Red Robinson Is Beaten at The Finish*, May 14, 1914.

23 Pittsburgh Press: *ROBINSON BEATEN BY MICKEY RODGERS IN FURIOUS BATTLE*, May 14, 1914.

24 Pittsburgh Press: *JACK DILLON IS IN EXCELLENT TRIM FOR BATTLE WITH CROUSE*, April 9, 1913.

25 Pittsburgh Press: *A PUNCHER AMONG THE PASTRY COOKS*, January 25, 1914.

26 Pittsburgh Post: *AMONG THE BOXERS*, May 26, 1914.

27 Pittsburgh Press: *GREB AND LEWIS PRINCIPALS IN SLOVENLY BOUT*, May 26, 1914.

28 Pittsburgh Gazette-Times: *Lewis Has Better of Greb*, May 26, 1914.

29 Pittsburgh Press: *Fistic Foibles*, May 28, 1914.

30 The account of Greb's bout with Whitey Wenzel is derived from reports found in the Pittsburgh Post, Gazette-Times, and Daily Dispatch.

31 Walter Monaghan should not be confused with the heavyweight Walter Monoghan who served as sparring partner for Jess Willard. The reader will note different spellings used when discussing Monaghan. The author has chosen to use the "gh" as Monaghan did himself on official documents. However, most contemporary sources leave off the "g." The point may be only academic as "Walter Monaghan" was in fact a pseudonym. Monaghan's real name was Earl C. Monnin.

32 Pittsburgh Press: **BIG CROWD LIKELY TO WITNESS BOUTS**, June 12, 1914.

33 Pittsburgh Press: **GREB AND MONOGHAN READY FOR BATTLE**, June 13, 1914.

34 Reports of the Greb-Monoghan bout are taken from the Pittsburgh Post, Pittsburgh Press, Pittsburgh Gazette-Times, and Pittsburgh Sun.

35 Pittsburgh Post: **Harry Greb Hands Monoghan Bad Beating in Six Round Bout**, June 16, 1914.

36 Pittsburgh Press: **MONOGHAN CUT TO RIBBONS BY GREB'S BLOWS**, June 16, 1914.

37 Pittsburgh Press: **LEWIS CLAIMS GREB IS AFRAID TO TACKLE HIM**, June 23, 1914.

38 Pittsburgh Post: **GREB DOWN TO WEIGHT**, June 27, 1914.

39 The account of the Greb-Gorgas bout is derived from reports printed in the Pittsburgh Sun, Post, Press, Daily Dispatch, and Gazette-Times.

40 Pittsburgh Sun: **Kyser Takes Place of Parks Against Greb**, July 20, 1914.

41 Pittsburgh Sun: **Kyser Hits Foley and Dislocates His Nose**, July 14, 1914.

42 Pittsburgh Press: **FOLEY IS MARK FOR HIS FOE**, July 21, 1914.

43 The Pittsburgh Daily Dispatch and the Pittsburgh Chronicle-Telegraph voted the Greb -Foley bout a draw. The Pittsburgh Press, Gazette-Times, and Post voted for Greb.

44 Pittsburgh Press: **LEWIS AND GREB WILL BOX AT STEUBENVILLE**, July 22, 1914.

45 Steubenville Herald-Star: **Good Bouts**, July 28, 1914.

46 Ibid.; Steubenville Daily Gazette: **LITTLE THINGS BRIEFLY TOLD**, July 28, 1914.

47 Below is the wire report found in the July 28, 1914 edition of the Pittsburgh Press:

Steubenville, O., July 28. - In one of the best 10-round contests ever pulled off here, Harry Greb, of Pittsburgh, bested George Lewis last night before the Steubenville Athletic Club. From the first round until the tenth Greb carried the fighting to Lewis, and had him weary from the punishment handed out. In the second round he broke Lewis' nose with a right hand punch. After this round Greb did not use his right hand to speak of, and after the fight it was found to be fractured.

Only one round could be said to be even, and that was the tenth, when Lewis tried to make a rally for a few seconds, but Greb came back and finished it with an even break.

This release or versions of it appeared in every Pittsburgh newspaper with the exception of Daily Dispatch which presented its own wire report that found the bout a draw.

48 Pittsburgh Sun: **DENIES THAT GREB BEAT LEWIS**, July 30, 1914.

49 Pittsburgh Sun: **GREB WILLING TO FIGHT AT CATCHWEIGHTS**, August 3, 1914.

50 Pittsburgh Sun: **To Settle With Lewis If He Defeats Gorgas**, August 4, 1914.

51 Accounts of the Greb-Gorgas bout are drawn from the Pittsburgh Chronicle-Telegraph, Post, Gazette-Times, Press, and Daily Dispatch.

52 Pittsburgh Sun: **Wenzel and Greb Go Six Rounds to a Draw**, August 25, 1914.

53 Pittsburgh Sun: **Foley takes Place of Lewis in Greb Match**, August 29, 1914.

54 Reports of the Greb-Foley bout are taken from the Pittsburgh Gazette-Times, Press, Daily Dispatch, and Chronicle-

Telegraph.

55 Apparently Greb had two managers during his stay in Philadelphia, Billy Reynolds being the most prominent. Interestingly Reynolds, with George Engel, seems to have been co-managing Buck Crouse who was also in Philadelphia at the time. Several weeks after Greb abandoned his Philadelphia invasion a letter appeared in the Philadelphia Public Ledger signed by one "Billy Kelly" naming himself manager of Harry Greb and asking for a rematch with Joe Borrell.

56 Philadelphia Public Ledger: **Reynolds Has Two Champions**, September 13, 1914.

57 Philadelphia North American: **JACK M'CARRON HANDS K.O. BAKER A BEATING**, September 27, 1914.

58 Philadelphia Public Ledger: **HOUCK OUTBOXED BY YOUNG AHEARN**, November 15, 1914.

59 The Description of the Joe Borrell-Harry Greb fight is comprised from accounts found in the Philadelphia Inquirer, North American, Press, Public Ledger, Philadelphia Evening Bulletin, and Philadelphia Evening Public Ledger.

NOTES

CHAPTER 4

1 Taken from interviews with Harry Wohlfarth. Knockout Harry Baker should not be confused with the Jewish fighter of the same name from the West Coast who fought Ad Wolgast and Abe Attell. The two fighters can be difficult to differentiate between because both fought in the lightweight division at the same time (early in the career of the Harry Baker from Wilmington, Delaware and late in the career of Harry Baker from San Francisco) and both fought in Philadelphia, Pennsylvania in roughly the same time frame.

2 Accounts of Greb's bout with Billy Donovan were taken from the Philadelphia Inquirer, Philadelphia Press, Philadelphia North American, Philadelphia Evening Public Ledger, Philadelphia Record, and Philadelphia Public Ledger.

3 Accounts of Greb's bout with Howard Truesdale are drawn from the Philadelphia Public Ledger, Philadelphia Record, and Philadelphia North American.

4 Accounts of Greb's bout with Billy Miske are drawn from the Philadelphia Public Ledger, Philadelphia Record, Philadelphia North American, Philadelphia Evening Public Ledger, and Philadelphia Evening Bulletin.

5 Pittsburgh Press: **HARRY GREB IS HERE TO TRAIN FOR BOUT**, January 17, 1915.

6 Pittsburgh Gazette-Times: **Preacher's Son Is Blackburn, The Pugilist**, May 10, 1914.

7 Pittsburgh Sun: **BLACKBURN TO RE-ENTER RING AS A WELTER**, December 22, 1913.

8 Pittsburgh Press: **JACK BLACKBURN HERE FOR BATTLE WITH HARRY GREB**, January 24, 1915.

9 Davies, David J., Pittsburgh Dispatch: **Director Morin Bars Whites From Meeting Negro Boxers**, January 14, 1913.

10 Davies, David J., Pittsburgh Dispatch: **Crouse-Chip Fight Causing Row Among Rival Promoters**, January 27, 1915.

11 Jerpe, James, Pittsburgh Gazette-Times: **"AFFY-DAVITS"**, January 20, 1915.

12 Accounts of the Greb-Blackburn fight are drawn from the Pittsburgh Post, Gazette-Times, Daily Dispatch, Press, Sun, and Leader.

13 Jerpe, James, Pittsburgh Gazette-Times: **"AFFY-DAVITS"**, January 27, 1915.

14 This is reflected in published reports of his address found later in the narrative.

15 The account Harry Baker's January 19, 1915 bout with Jack Blackburn is derived from reports found in the Philadelphia Press, Philadelphia North American, Philadelphia Record, and Philadelphia Evening Public Ledger.

16 Pittsburgh Press: *CROUSE AND GREB MIX IT?*, February 8, 1915.
  Davies, David J., Pittsburgh Dispatch: *LIVE WIRES ON SPORTS*, February 9, 1915.

17 Keck, Harry, Pittsburgh Post: *Harry Greb Scores Victory Over Baker in Vicious Bout*, February 11, 1915.

18 Guy, Richard, Pittsburgh Gazette-Times: *BAKER LOSES HOT BATTLE TO GREB*, February 11, 1915.

19 Keck, Harry, Pittsburgh Post: *Boxing Public Proves Loyalty By Patronizing Shows of Merit*, March 7, 1915.

20 Pittsburgh Press: *BOUT BY HOME LADS PLEASES FISTIC FANS*, March 5, 1915.

21 Washington Observer: *CLEVER HARRY GREB DELIGHTS BIG CROWD*, March 8, 1915.

22 There would have been several fighters in Cleveland who would have disputed Reddy Mason's claim that Jack Lavin was the best Cleveland had to offer. Lavin was a fairly poor fighter, the high point of his career was likely when he briefly served as a sparring partner to both Jack Dempsey and Jess Willard during their training to face one another. Lavin was sent away from Dempsey's training camp after a day or two sparring because he wasn't able to furnish the challenger any competition. He eventually wound up in Jess Willard's camp where he fared slightly better.

23 Flynn had been spending the week in Pittsburgh after having fought Gunboat Smith the previous month in Cincinnati.

24 Accounts of the Greb's second bout with Harry Baker are derived from the Pittsburgh Post, Press, Sun, Dispatch, Chronicle-Telegraph, and Gazette-Times.

25 Pittsburgh Sun: *Wenzel Is Confident Of Victory Over Greb*, April 13, 1915.

26 Pittsburgh Sun: *Wenzel and Greb to Clash at Best Weight*, May 22, 1915.

27 Macpherson, Jr., Leslie C., Pittsburgh Post: *Wenzel Has Slight Shade On Garfield Middleweight In Terrific Encounter*, April 16, 1915.

28 Reports of the April 15, 1915 clash between Harry Greb and Whitey Wenzel were compiled from the Pittsburgh Post, Dispatch, Chronicle-Telegraph, Gazette-Times, Press, and Sun.

29 Descriptions of Joe Borrell's fight with Al McCoy in Philadelphia on January 25, 1915 are taken from the Philadelphia Record, and Philadelphia North American. In the buildup to Greb's rematch with Borrell the Pittsburgh newspapers intimated that Borrell deserved the victory against McCoy. This is refuted by eyewitness reports.

30 Pittsburgh Post: *Among the Boxers*, April 20, 1915.

31 The account of the Greb-Borrell bout was compiled from reports found in the Pittsburgh Daily Dispatch, Gazette-Times, Post, Chronicle-Telegraph, Press, and Sun.

32 Pittsburgh Post: *Among the Boxers*, May 14, 1915.

33 The Greb-Wenzel fight description was compiled from accounts printed in the Pittsburgh Sun, Press, Post, Daily Dispatch, Gazette-Times, and Chronicle-Telegraph.

34 Initially reports surfaced after the Grayber-Keiser bout in Frostburg, MD. That Keiser had won the decision. Grayber returned to Pittsburgh denying this and claiming that Jack Stevens (Kaiser's manager) had sent his own version of the fight out over the wire.

35 The description of Greb's bout with Keiser and the eventual promotional fallout was found in the ringside report of the June 1, 1915 edition of the Connellsville Daily Courier. The Pittsburgh papers all published wire accounts of the bout which deviate dramatically from the ringside report (and all have Greb winning a fast and exciting bout) giving the impression that these reports originate with Red Mason.

36 Cumberland Times: *Greb And Keiser Engage In Fast Ten Round Contest*, June 26, 1915.

NOTES

CHAPTER 5

1 Pittsburgh Post: **AMONG THE BOXERS**, July 9, 1915.

2 The account of the Greb-Gavigan bout in Duquesne Gardens was drawn together from reports found in the Pittsburgh Post, Gazette-Times, Daily Dispatch, Press, Sun, and Chronicle-Telegraph. The amount of Tommy Gavigan's purse was discussed in the Fistic Foibles section of the July 27, 1915 edition of the Pittsburgh Press.

3 The account of the Greb-Hauser bout at Elwyn Station is drawn together from reports found in the Pittsburgh Post, and Pittsburgh Chronicle-Telegraph. Most of the Pittsburgh papers did not cover the bout. The Press gave an anecdotal account of the bout two days later. George Hauser's account of the bout was found in the Fistic Foibles section of the July 27, 1915 edition of the Pittsburgh Press.

4 Long, James J., Pittsburgh Sun: **HARRY GREB AFTER MATCH WITH GEORGE CHIP.**, July 19, 1915.

5 Long, James J., Pittsburgh Sun: **AL ROGERS WANTS TO FIGHT HARRY GREB.**, July 15, 1915.

6 The account of the Greb-Keiser bout is derived from the ringside report found in the July 23, 1915 edition of the Cumberland Times.

7 The account of the bout between Crouse and Rogers is taken from the January 14, 1913 Pittsburgh Gazette-Times. Dillon's comments on Rogers are taken from the January 19, 1913 Pittsburgh Gazette-Times.

8 The description of the first Greb-Rogers bout is derived from accounts found in the Pittsburgh Post, Press, Sun, Daily Dispatch, Gazette-Times, and Chronicle-Telegraph.

9 Long, James J., Pittsburgh Sun: **SPORTING Gossip & Comment**, August 26, 1915.

10 Long, James J., Pittsburgh Sun: **SPORTING Gossip & Comment**, August 27, 1915.

11 Pittsburgh Press: **ROGERS ASSERTS HE WILL TACKLE CHIP**, September 11, 1915.

12 The description of the second Greb-Rogers bout is derived from accounts found in the Pittsburgh Post, Press, Sun, Daily Dispatch, Chronicle-Telegraph, and Gazette-Times.

13 Pittsburgh Sun: **Fighter Fells Negro After Man Is Wounded**, September 27, 1915.
  Pittsburgh Daily Dispatch: **NEGRO SHOOTS WHITE MAN**, September 27, 1915.
  Pittsburgh Gazette-Times: **Negro Shoots White Man When Reproved for Actions**, September 27, 1915.
  Pittsburgh Post: **Pugilist Fells Man With Gun; One Is Shot**, September 27, 1915.
14 Pittsburgh Post: **After Facing Revolver Harry Greb Is Signed To Oppose George Chip**, September 27, 1915.

15 Pittsburgh Post: **Greb and George Chip Nearly Come to Blows, October 6**, 1915.

16 The description of the Greb-Chip bout is derived from accounts found in the Pittsburgh Post, Sun, Press, Daily Dispatch, Chronicle-Telegraph, and Gazette-Times.

17 St. Paul Dispatch: **More About Harry Greb.**, November 4, 1915.

18 St. Paul Dispatch: **GREB DECLARES HE DOES NOT FEAR ANY MIDDLEWEIGHT FOE**, November 9, 1915.
  St. Paul Daily News: **SOLDIER BARTFIELD DUE HERE TODAY**, November 10, 1915.

19 St. Paul Dispatch: **GREB'S PLAN IS TO DEFEAT TOMMY AND THEN MEET PHANTOM**, November 10, 1915.

20 St. Paul Daily News: **SOLDIER BARTFIELD ARRIVES FOR BOUT**, November 11, 1915.

21 Minneapolis Journal: **GIBBONS AND GREB MAKE THE WEIGHT FOR TUESDAY'S BOUT**, November 15, 1915.

22 St. Paul Dispatch: ***How Greb Views It***, November 15, 1915.

23 The account of the Greb-Gibbons bout is compiled from reports found in the St. Paul Daily News, Minneapolis Journal, Minneapolis Tribune, St. Paul Pioneer Press, and St. Paul Dispatch.

24 Pittsburgh Post: ***Jimmy Mason Defended By St. Paul Matchmaker; Fears We Mistreat Him***, November 27, 1915.

25 Pittsburgh Daily Dispatch: ***COURT NOTES***, November 24, 1915.
   Pittsburgh Gazette-Times: ***HARRY GREB ACCUSED OF PUNCHING NEGRO***, November 24, 1915.

26 Clarence Jackson criminal record is on file at the Allegheny County Courthouse and lists no less than twenty arrests or convictions from 1915 to 1961.

27 The account of the Graves-Greb bout is compiled from reports found in the Pittsburgh Daily Dispatch, Gazette-Times, Press, Leader, Sun, Chronicle-Telegraph, and Post.

28 M'Carty, S. E., Pittsburgh Leader: ***M'Carty's Comment,*** December 17, 1915.

NOTES

CHAPTER 6

1 Pittsburgh Sun: ***GREB NOT A QUITTER; X-RAY PROVES INJURY***, December 21, 1915.

2 Keck, Harry, Pittsburgh Post: Al McCoy no Piker; Will Fight for $1,000, February 14, 1916.

Brooklyn, N. Y., Feb. 9, 1916.

    Mr. James Mason,
       Dear Sir- Will take $1,000 and three (3) round trip tickets for
the champion to box Greb six rounds in Pittsburgh, if I don't sign
the champion up to far ahead before we come to terms, as I have
a lot of propositions for him.
      Hoping that my terms will be satisfactory to you, I remain,
Yours very truly,
A. J. RUDOLF

3 The report of the Greb-Monaghan bout is derived from accounts found in the Pittsburgh Leader, Press, Gazette-Times, and Daily-Dispatch.

4 The report of Harry Greb's bout with Kid Manuel is derived from accounts found in the Pittsburgh Post, Pittsburgh Press, Pittsburgh Leader, Pittsburgh Daily Dispatch, and Pittsburgh Gazette-Times.

5 Pittsburgh Post: ***Best Local Amateur Boxers To Fight in P.A.A. Tourney; Dispute Over Manuel Bout***, April 26, 1916.

6 Johnstown Tribune: ***BOUT IS STOPPED BY REFEREE BUSER***, April 28, 1916.

7 Charleroi Mail: ***GREB PROVES HIMSELF TOO FAST FOR WENZEL***, May 12, 1916.

8 Pittsburgh Gazette-Times: ***GUS CHRISTIE PASSES UP BOUT HERE***, May 14, 1916.

9 The account of Greb's rematch with Kid Manuel is derived from reports found in the Pittsburgh Daily Dispatch, Pittsburgh Gazette-Times, Pittsburgh Post, and Pittsburgh Press.

10 Gibson, Florent, Pittsburgh Post: ***Greb Knocks Out Manuel In First Round; Battle Is Over in 52 Seconds***, June 4, 1916.

11 Gibson, Florent, Pittsburgh Post: *Whitey Wenzel Through; A Musical Moulder*, June 6, 1916.

12 Pittsburgh Post: *Moran and Dillon Begin Training for Their Bout*, June 8, 1916.

13 The account of the June 17, 1916 bout between Harry Greb and Whitey Wenzel is derived from wire reports found in the Pittsburgh Daily Dispatch, Pittsburgh Post, and Pittsburgh Gazette-Times.

14 Pittsburgh Post: *AMONG THE BOXERS*, June 19, 1916.

15 Much of the animosity toward Greb and Red Mason was played out in the "Jabs and Stabs" section of the New Castle Herald.

16 New Castle Herald: *JABS AND STABS*, June 14, 1916.

17 New Castle Herald: *JABS AND STABS*, June 15, 1916.

18 Pittsburgh Post: *AMONG THE BOXERS*, June 19, 1916.

19 Youngstown Telegram: *DELMONT LOSES TO INDIAN KID*, June 20, 1916.

20 New Castle News: *GEORGE CHIP WOULD FIGHT AT LEAST ONCE EVERY WEEK IN SUMMER*, June 22, 1916.

21 Pittsburgh Post: *Among the Boxers*, June 22, 1916.

22 Pittsburgh Post: *AMONG THE BOXERS*, June 24, 1916.

23 New Castle Herald: *GEORGE CHIP WILL FIGHT HARRY GREB TONIGHT IN 'COLLIE'*, June 26, 1916.

24 Youngstown Telegram: *GREB STAYS LIMIT WITH CHIP BUT IS BADLY OUTPOINTED*, June 27, 1916. As poor as they may sound Mason likely had an ulterior motive. A man who could boast of going the distance with the power-punching Chip, especially if Chip were to defeat Darcy, would find himself in demand.

25 Ibid.

26 Ward, Frank B., Youngstown Vindicator: *GREB STALLS THROUGH BOUT WITH GEO. CHIP*, June 27, 1916.

27 Fritz, E. H., New Castle Herald: *HARRY GREB LOST TO GEORGE CHIP IN TEN ROUNDS*, June 27, 1916.

28 Glenn, A. B., New Castle News: *Greb Proves Master of Hanging On And Shows Little More*, June 27, 1916.

29 Keck, Harry, Pittsburgh Post: *"Most Loyal in World," Says Greb of Followers*, July 4, 1916.

30 New Castle Herald: *WELL, HERE'S A JOKE*, June 28, 1916.

31 Pittsburgh Press: *GREB HOPEFUL OF LANDING K.O. BLOW*, August 3, 1916.

32 Pittsburgh Press: *GREB AND GRAYBER WILL BOX*, August 7, 1916.

33 The account of the Greb-Grayber bout is derived from reports found in the Pittsburgh Press, Pittsburgh Chronicle-Telegraph, Pittsburgh Sun, Pittsburgh Leader, Pittsburgh Post, Pittsburgh Gazette-Times, and Pittsburgh Daily Dispatch.

34 Pittsburgh Press: *"Fighting Al" Rogers Meets Canal Zone Champ Tonight*, April 1, 1915.

35 Pittsburgh Press: *COLE HERE TOMORROW FOR BOUT WITH GREB*, August 25, 1916.

36 The report of Greb's bout with Jerry Cole is derived from reports found in the Pittsburgh Press, Pittsburgh Leader, Pittsburgh Daily Dispatch, Pittsburgh Gazette-Times, and Pittsburgh Post.

37 Cumberland Evening Times: *Greb Wins Over Fay Keiser In Fast Ten Round Bout*, September 5, 1916.

38 Keck, Harry, Pittsburgh Post: *Australia Beckons Greb and Ray; To Make Trip in April*, September 29, 1916.

39 Cumberland Evening Times: *FANS VOTE CLARKE AND GREB FIGHT GREATEST EVER STAGED*, October 17, 1916.

40 The account of the Greb-Baker bout held in Pittsburgh on October 21, 1916 is derived from reports found in the

Pittsburgh Leader, Pittsburgh Daily Dispatch, Pittsburgh Post, Pittsburgh Gazette-Times, and Pittsburgh Press.

41 Gibson, Florent, Pittsburgh Post: **Knockout Sweeney Tosses Scare Into Greb Camp**, November 5, 1916.

42 Ibid.

43 The account of Greb's bout with Knockout Sweeney is derived from reports found in the Pittsburgh Leader, Pittsburgh Daily Dispatch, Pittsburgh Gazette-Times, Pittsburgh Post, and Pittsburgh Press.

44 Pittsburgh Post: **George Chip Tips His Hat To Les Darcy, 'Better Man'**, November 6, 1916.

45 Erie Dispatch: **Greb Arrives in City For Bout With Brennan Tonight**, November 8, 1916.

46 Ibid.

47 The account of Greb's bout with Willie "KO" Brennan at Erie, Pennsylvania is derived from reports found in the Erie Dispatch, and Erie Herald, the Herald report being reprinted in the Pittsburgh Post.

NOTES

CHAPTER 7

1 Buffalo Morning Express: **HARRY GREB PLASTERED KAYO**, November 10, 1916.

2 Buffalo Morning Express: **RIGHT INTO KAYO'S LAIR THEY COME**, November 13, 1916.

3 Cumberland Times: **RECORD CROWD WILL SEE GREB FIGHT CLARKE**, November 13, 1916.

4 Cumberland Times: **GREB WINS OVER CLARKE WITH KAYO**, November 15, 1916.

5 Buffalo Courier: **K.O. BRENNAN, BURKE, WAGNER, GREB AND MEYERS READY FOR MIDDLEWEIGHT CARNI-VAL**, November 17, 1916.

6 Buffalo Morning Express: **KAYO FACES GREB IN TONIGHTS RING**, November 17, 1916.

7 Buffalo Courier: **K.O. BRENNAN, BURKE, WAGNER, GREB AND MEYERS READY FOR MIDDLEWEIGHT CARNI-VAL**, November 17, 1916.

8 Buffalo Courier: **GREB BEATS BRENNAN IN SEASON'S GREATEST BATTLE; TOM BURKE STOPS WAGNER**, November 18, 1916.
   The description of the Greb's bout with Brennan fight was compiled from reports found in the Buffalo Courier, Buffalo Morning Express, Buffalo Enquirer, and Buffalo Evening News.

9 Buffalo Morning Express: **BURKE MATCHED WITH HARRY GREB**, November 18, 1916.

10 Ibid.

11 Parker, Marion F., Saint Louis Globe-Democrat: **Tommy Burke's Showing Against Rowlands Poor**, December 2, 1915.

12 Buffalo Courier: **NELSON AND FINCH FIGURE ON K.O. OVER JOHNNY O'LEARY; BRENNAN COACHING BURKE**, November 22, 1916.

13 Buffalo Morning Express: **GREB AND O'LEARY THE VICTORS**, November 25, 1916.

14 The account of the Greb-Burke bout is derived from reports found in the Buffalo Courier, Buffalo Morning Express,

Buffalo Enquirer, and Buffalo Evening News.

15 The account of Greb's bout with Knockout Brown is derived from reports found in the Pittsburgh Leader, Pittsburgh Daily Dispatch, Pittsburgh Post, Pittsburgh Gazette-Times, and Pittsburgh Press.

16 Buffalo Courier: *Greb and Moha Great Pair*, December 20, 1916.

17 Buffalo Evening News: *KAYO BRENNAN THINKS WELL OF GREB AND MOHA*, December 20, 1916.

18 Buffalo Courier: *MISKE, DILLON, MOHA, NOW LEAD LIGHT HEAVY BRIGADE; GREB HAS CHANCE TO CLIMB*, December 21, 1916.

19 Buffalo Courier: *HUSTLING LOGS IN LITTLE LUMBER CAMP, BOB MOHA PREPARES FOR HARRY GREB*, December 22, 1916.

20 Buffalo Morning Express: *HARRY GREB WINS OVER BOB MOHA*, December 27, 1916.

21 Ibid.

22 The Description of the Greb-Moha bout was derived from reports found in the Buffalo Courier, Morning Express, Buffalo Enquirer, and Buffalo Evening News.

23 Buffalo Morning Express: *HARRY GREB WINS OVER BOB MOHA*, December 27, 1916.

24 Buffalo Courier: *GREB'S SPEED AND YOUTH BEAT BOB MOHA IN BOUT FULL OF REAL SENSATIONS*, December 27, 1916.

25 Buffalo Courier: *Moha and Greb Depart*, December 28, 1916.

26 Ibid.

27 Pittsburgh Post: *Darcy Not Alone in Demanding Big Coin*, December 29, 1916.

28 The account of Greb's bout with Joe Borrell in Pittsburgh on January 1, 1917 is derived from reports found in the Pittsburgh Post, Pittsburgh Gazette-Times, and Pittsburgh Press.

29 Pittsburgh Post: *Darcy Challenged For Harry Greb*, January 5, 1917.

30 Buffalo Courier: *Darcy Gets a Frost*, January 19, 1917.

31 Charleroi Mail: *GREB WINS OVER ED. COLEMAN OF OHIO BY THE KNOCKOUT ROUTE*, January 19, 1917.

32 The Account of the Greb-Ritchie bout was derived from reports found in the Philadelphia Press, and Philadelphia Public Ledger.

33 Buffalo Courier: *Jeff Smith to Darcy*, January 23, 1917.
    Buffalo Courier: *About Smith and Greb*, January 30, 1917.
    Buffalo Courier: *Jeff Smith to Darcy*, February 1, 1917.

34 Buffalo Courier: *About Smith and Greb*, January 30, 1917

35 Buffalo Morning Express: *A LAST STAND!*, February 4, 1917.

36 Buffalo Courier: *GREB AND KAISER BOUT A REMINDER OF THE OLD DAYS; WANTS TO MEET DARCY HERE*, January 28, 1917.
    Some reports list the $1,500 purse as being "winner take all."

37 The Account of the Greb-Keiser bout is taken primarily from the Cumberland Times and Pittsburgh Post, which sent a special correspondent to the fight.

38 Keck, Harry, Pittsburgh Post: *Greb Loses 10 Pounds In 20-Round Battle*, January 31, 1917.

39 Buffalo Evening News: *DARCY INTERESTED IN GREB-BRENNAN BOUT*, January 31, 1917.

40 Buffalo Courier: *GREB HERE ON SATURDAY TO TRAIN FOR BRENNAN GO; DANGER FOR BOXING GAME*, February, 1, 1917.

41 Buffalo Morning Express: *Greb sorry that he could not get here to meet Darcy.*, February 2, 1917.

42 Milwaukee Sentinel: *$50,000 OFFERED FOR DARCY-GIBBONS BOUT*, September 5, 1916.

43 Pittsburgh Post: *GREB MATCHED TO BOX WITH MIKE GIBBONS*, February 7, 1917.

44 Buffalo Morning Express: *OLD KAYO WILL BE IN PRIME FORM*, February 3, 1917.

45 Buffalo Courier: *BRENNAN WAIVES WEIGHT LIMIT FOR GREB; TELLS HIM TO COME IF HE WEIGHS A TON*, February 9, 1917.

46 Buffalo Courier: *GREB HELD TO PHILLY MATCH WITH MIKE GIBBONS, WILL TACKLE PHANTOM TONIGHT*, February 10, 1917.

47 The account of Greb's bout with Mike Gibbons is derived from reports found in the Philadelphia Evening Public Ledger, Philadelphia Public Ledger, and Philadelphia Press.

48 The description of the Greb's bout with Brennan fight was compiled from reports found in the Buffalo Courier, Buffalo Morning Express, Buffalo Enquirer, and Buffalo Evening News.

49 Gibson, Florent, **Pittsburgh Post: Is G. Chip Evading Scrap With H. Greb?**, February 19, 1917.

50 Gibson, Florent, Pittsburgh Post: *Greb Stops Ahearn In Opening Minute; Johnny's Lesson Off!*, April 3, 1917.

51 The description of Greb's knockout over Young Ahearn is derived from reports found in the Pittsburgh Post, Pittsburgh Gazette-Times, and Pittsburgh Press.

52 Gibson, Florent, Pittsburgh Post: *Greb Stops Ahearn In Opening Minute; Johnny's Lesson Off!*, April 3, 1917.

53 Miller, Nathan, **Theodore Roosevelt: A Life**. New York: William Worrow and Co., 1992.

54 Guy, Richard, Pittsburgh Gazette-Times: *PITTSBURGH TO SEE LONGER BOUTS, REPORT*, April 19, 1917.

55 Keck, Harry, Pittsburgh Post: *SPORTING CHIT-CHAT*, April 23, 1917.

56 Keck, Harry, Pittsburgh Post: *SPORTING CHIT-CHAT*, April 25, 1917.

57 Gibson, Florent, Pittsburgh Post: *With Darcy Bout Off, Chip Would Box Here*, April 26, 1917.

58 New Castle News: *Outlook For Chip-Darcy Match Dull*, April 26, 1917.

59 Pittsburgh Daily Dispatch: *McCoy Coming in Style; Just Like Real Champion*, April 27, 1917.

60 Pittsburgh Daily Dispatch: *McCoy Confident He'll Win In Battle With Harry Greb*, April 28, 1917.

61 Pittsburgh Daily Dispatch: *McCoy Confident He'll Win Over Harry Greb Tonight*, April 30, 1917.

62 The account of the match between Harry Greb and Al McCoy was derived from reports found in the Pittsburgh Daily Dispatch, Gazette-Times, Post, Sun, Chronicle-Telegraph, Leader, and Press.

63 Davies, David J., Pittsburgh Daily Dispatch: *Harry Greb Is an Easy Winner In His Fight With Al McCoy*, May 1, 1917.

64 Pittsburgh Sun: *GREB TAKES PLACE WITH TOPNOTCHERS*, May 1, 1917.

65 Guy, Richard, Pittsburgh Gazette-Times: *Middleweight Title Holder Is Beaten at All Stages Before Big Fight Crowd*, May 1, 1917.

NOTES

CHAPTER 8

1 Cumberland Evening Times: *Harry Greb Meets His Match In Jackie Clark*, May 4, 1917.

2 Pittsburgh Post: *Hinkle Calls Greb-Clark Fight Draw*, May 4, 1917.

3 The description of the Greb-Baker fight is derived from reports found in the Uniontown Morning Herald and Pittsburgh Daily Dispatch.

4 Keck, Harry, Pittsburgh Post: *SPORTING CHIT-CHAT*, June 3, 1917.

5 Buffalo Morning Express: *HOT SHOT FROM JEFF SMITH*, May 17, 1917.

6 Buffalo Evening News: *JEFF SMITH NO JOKE FOR HARRY GREB*, May 19, 1917.

7 Buffalo Morning Express: *JEFF SMITH PUZZLES GREB*, May 20, 1917.

8 Buffalo Courier: *GREB'S PERSISTENT ATTACK EARNS SHADE OVER SMITH, DESPITE CLEVER DEFENSE*, May 20, 1917.

9 The account of Harry Greb's bout with Jeff Smith in Buffalo is derived from reports found in the Buffalo Courier, Evening News, Buffalo Enquirer, and Morning Express.

10 Gibson, Florent, Pittsburgh Post: *"Madison Miner" Working Like a Beaver For His Fight Here Tuesday Against Local Middle in Music Hall.*, May 20, 1917.

11 Gibson, Florent, Pittsburgh Post: *What F. Klaus Thinks of Greb-Chip Battle*, May 21, 1917.

12 The account of the Greb-Chip bout is derived from reports found in the Pittsburgh Daily Dispatch, Post, Gazette-Times, Leader, Chronicle-Telegraph, Sun, and Press.

13 Guy, Richard, Pittsburgh Gazette-Times: *HARRY GREB WINNER OVER GEORGE CHIP IN TEN HARD ROUNDS*, May 23, 1917.

14 Gibson, Florent, Pittsburgh Post: *YOUNGSTER BEATS EX-CHAMP, BUT HAS MITTS ALWAYS FULL*, May 23, 1917.

15 Davies, David J., Pittsburgh Daily Dispatch: *GREB DEFEATS CHIP; LOCAL BOY SUPREME*, May 23, 1917.

16 Keck, Harry, Pittsburgh Post: *SPORTING CHIT-CHAT*, June 6, 1917.

17 The Description of the Harry Greb-Frank Mantell fight is derived from the report found in the Uniontown Morning Herald.

18 Husted, Bob, Dayton Journal: *SPORT COMMENT*, March 16, 1920.

19 Guy, Richard, Pittsburgh Gazette-Times: *PERMIT IS NOT GRANTED BY LOCAL CLUB*, January 27, 1917.

20 Pittsburgh Daily Dispatch: *Greb and Crouse Matched at Last*, June 17, 1917.

21 Keck, Harry, Pittsburgh Post: *SPORTING CHIT-CHAT*, June 14, 1917.

22 Gibson, Florent, Pittsburgh Post: *Crouse Must Put Up Weight Coin, or Bout Is Off, Opines Mason*, June 19, 1917.

23 Pittsburgh Daily Dispatch: *Buck Crouse Is Angry Over Mason's Statement*, June 20, 1917.

24 Pittsburgh Leader: *Crouse-Greb Battle to Be Bitter One*, June 22, 1917.

25 Pittsburgh Leader: *Crouse Resumes Hard Training For Big Fight*, June 25, 1917.

26 Keck, Harry, Pittsburgh Post: *SPORTING CHIT-CHAT*, June 24, 1917.

27 Pittsburgh Leader: *GREB AND CROUSE AGAIN TRAINING FOR BIG MATCH*, June 26, 1917.

28 The account of the bout between Harry Greb and Buck Crouse is derived from reports found in the Pittsburgh Leader, Post, Press, and Gazette-Times.

29 Keck, Harry, Pittsburgh Post: *SPORTING CHIT-CHAT*, July 4, 1917.

30 Pittsburgh Post: *Greb's Title Claim Popular With Fans*, July 16, 1917.

31 Pittsburgh Post: *Greb Relieves Training With Canoeing Trip*, July 20, 1917.

32 Pittsburgh Press: *GREB'S ABILITY TO HOLD JACK DILLON EVEN QUESTIONED*, July 24, 1917.

33 Pittsburgh Press: *GREB INJURED IN BOUT WITH HOOK*, July 29, 1917.

34 The account of the Greb-Dillon bout is derived from reports found in the Pittsburgh Press, Post, Leader, Gazette-Times, Daily Dispatch, and Sun.

35 Gibson, Florent, Pittsburgh Post: *"ICKY" TAKES NINE ROUNDS OF FIGHT; OTHER ONE IS EVEN*, July 31, 1917.

36 Ibid.

37 Guy, Richard, Pittsburgh Gazette-Times: *GREB OUTFIGHTS DILLON IN TEN ROUNDS*, July 31, 1917.

38 Pittsburgh Press: *DILLON BEATEN BY GREB*, July 31, 1917.

39 Interview with former Pittsburgh Press sports writer Roy McHugh.

40 Keck, Harry, Pittsburgh Post: *SPORTING CHIT-CHAT*, August 3, 1917.

41 Andrews, Tom S., Milwaukee Leader: *JEFF SMITH WILL HAVE REAL BATTLE ON HIS HANDS WHEN HE MEETS HARRY GREB IN MILWAUKEE; RING GOSSIP*, August 25, 1917.

42 Pittsburgh Post: *Murray Wants To Know About Wimler Battle*, August 17, 1917.

43 Pittsburgh Post: *Greb in Fine Condition for Coming Fight*, August 29, 1917.

44 Gibson, Florent, Pittsburgh Post: *Greb-Levinsky Bout Is Set for Thursday*, September 2, 1917.

45 Gibson, Florent, Pittsburgh Post, September 4, 1917.

46 Gibson, Florent, Pittsburgh Post: *Greb and Levinsky Resume Training for Thursday Night's Bout*, September 5, 1917.

47 Gibson, Florent, Pittsburgh Post: *Greb-Levinsky Set For Fight Tonight*, September 6, 1917.

48 The account of Greb's bout with Levinsky is derived from reports found in the Pittsburgh Sun, Pittsburgh Press, Pittsburgh Chronicle-Telegraph, Pittsburgh Gazette-Times, Pittsburgh Post, Pittsburgh Daily Dispatch, and Pittsburgh Leader.

49 Gibson, Florent, Pittsburgh Post: *GREB WORRIES BAT LEVINSKY ALMOST DOWN TO HIS SIZE*, September 7, 1917.

50 Ibid.

NOTES

CHAPTER 9

1 Andrews, Tom S., Milwaukee Leader: *JEFF SMITH WILL HAVE REAL BATTLE ON HIS HANDS WHEN HE MEETS HARRY GREB IN MILWAUKEE; RING GOSSIP*, August 25, 1917.

2 Milwaukee Leader: *JEFF SMITH DUE HERE FRIDAY FOR MATCH WITH GREB*, September 6, 1917.

3 Milwaukee Leader: *Boxing*, September 8, 1917.

4 Milwaukee Free Press: *CREAM CITY CLUB OFFERS OPENING BOUTS TONIGHT*, September 11, 1917.

5 The account of the Harry Greb's bout with Jeff Smith in Milwaukee are derived from reports found in the Milwaukee Free Press, Milwaukee Sentinel, Milwaukee Journal, and Milwaukee Leader.

6 Milwaukee Sentinel: *JEFF SMITH SUSPENDED; FAILS TO POST FORFEIT*, September 13, 1917.

7 New York Tribune: *Greb Knocks Out London in Ninth*, September 15, 1917.

8 Knox, P. T., New York Evening Telegram: *MUSIC HELPS BOXER TRAIN FOR HIS BOUT*, September 12, 1917. Pittsburgh papers scoffed at this story as fiction.

9 Dayton Journal: *BRAND-NEW CARD FOR THE MIAMI CLUB SHOW*, September 17, 1917.

10 The description of Harry Greb's bout with George "KO" Brown in Dayton is derived from reports found in the Dayton Journal, Dayton Daily News, and Dayton Herald.

11 First hand accounts of Harry Greb's bout against Battling Kopin in Charleroi are lacking as there was no local newspaper published on Sundays (the bout being held on a Saturday). The account published here is drawn from the various news wire reports that were published in Pennsylvania the following day.

12 Hawthorne, Fred, New York Tribune: *Boxing News and Notes*, September 25, 1917.

13 The account of Harry Greb's bout against Johnny Howard was drawn from reports found in the New York Times, New York Tribune, New York Morning Telegraph, New York Herald, New York Sun, and New York Evening World.

14 Pittsburgh Post: *FOUR BOUTS FOR GREB*, October 2, 1917.

15 The account of Greb's bout with Billy Kramer is derived from reports found in the Philadelphia Public Ledger, Philadelphia North American, and Philadelphia Evening Public Ledger.

16 The description of Harry Greb's bout with Gus Christie in Buffalo is taken from reports found in the Buffalo Morning Express, Buffalo Evening News, Buffalo Enquirer, and Buffalo Courier.

17 Keck, Harry, Pittsburgh Post: *Al McCoy Runs Out Of Match With Greb; Latter Claims Title*, October 15, 1917.

18 Ibid.

19 Harry had registered for the draft on June 5, 1917, Christie had signed May 28.

20 Chattanooga Daily Times: *WILLARD IN GOOD SHAPE*, October 17, 1917.

21 Milwaukee Sentinel: *"GREB IS TERROR," SAYS GUS CHRISTIE*, October 18, 1917.

22 Chattanooga Daily Times: *MIDDLES IN SLOW FIGHT*, October 24, 1917.

23 Buffalo Morning Express: *SOLDIER BARTFIELD NOW WANTS GREB*, October 22, 1917.

24 Ibid.

25 Buffalo Courier: *BARTFIELD AND GREB HAGGLE OVER ONE POUND LIKE KIDS IN QUARREL OVER RED APPLE*, October 27, 1917.

26 Buffalo Morning Express: *GREB CLEAR TO THE BARTFIELD BOUT*, October 30, 1917.

27 The description of Harry Greb's bout with "Soldier" Jacob Bartfield was derived from reports published in the Buffalo Courier, Buffalo Morning Express, Buffalo Enquirer, and Buffalo Evening News.

28 Buffalo Courier: *GREB DECAMPS, INCENSED AT DECISION GIVEN AGAINST HIM; SAYS HE CAN STOP BARTFIELD*, November 4, 1917.

29 Buffalo Morning Express: *HARRY GREB AGGRIEVED*, November 4, 1917.

30 Buffalo Courier: *GREB DECAMPS, INCENSED AT DECISION GIVEN AGAINST HIM; SAYS HE CAN STOP BARTFIELD*, November 4, 1917.

31 Ibid.

32 Gibson, Florent, Pittsburgh Post: *Ten-Round Boxing Here After Election---Rumor*, November 4, 1917.

33 The account of Mike O'Dowd's title winning victory over Al McCoy is derived from reports found in the New York Times and New York Tribune.

34 Cincinnati Enquirer: *BOXERS DUE TO-DAY*, November 17, 1917.

35 The account of Greb's bout with George Chip at Cincinnati is derived from reports found in the Cincinnati Commercial-Tribune, and Cincinnati Enquirer.

36 Philadelphia Public Ledger: *GREB VICTOR OVER 'MOUNTAIN' MEEHAN*, December 4, 1917.

37 Johnstown Tribune: *GREB EASY WINNER OVER GOTHAM MIDDLEWEIGHT*, December 6, 1917.

38 First hand accounts of Harry Greb's bout against Terry Martin in Charleroi are lacking as there was no local newspaper published on Sundays (the bout being held on a Saturday). The account published here is drawn from the various news wire reports that were published the following day. Sadly, less than one year later Terry Martin would be dead. He passed away on October 14, 1918 of what was thought to be pneumonia at the time but was likely Spanish Influenza.

39 Cincinnati Enquirer: *NO STOP To Pittsburgh Wild Man.*, December 18, 1917.

40 Keck, Harry, Pittsburgh Post: *Sporting Chit-Chat*, August 29, 1917.

41 Pittsburgh Post, December 21, 1917.

42 Keck, Harry, Pittsburgh Post: *Greb and Wenzel Bout Features Xmas Card*, December 25, 1917.

43 The account of Greb's bout with Wenzel is derived from reports found in the Pittsburgh Post, Pittsburgh Gazette-Times, and Pittsburgh Press.

44 Pittsburgh Post: *Wenzel Not Through*, December 30, 1917.

NOTES

CHAPTER 10

1 Pittsburgh Post: *Harry Greb Was Busiest Boxer in Country Last Year; Earned $28,753*, January 3, 1918.

2 The account of Harry Greb's bout with Terry Keller at McKeesport was derived from reports found in the Pittsburgh Post, Pittsburgh Gazette-Times, Pittsburgh Daily Dispatch, and McKeesport Daily News.

3 Pittsburgh Daily Dispatch: *AMONG THE BOXERS*, January 11, 1918.

4 Gibson, Florent, Pittsburgh Post: *Greb Kayos Kopin In The First Round*, January 15, 1918.

5 Saint Paul Pioneer Press: *Capital City Club Closes for Contest*, January 20, 1918.

6 New Orleans States: *Ratner Expects To Surprise Harry Greb; Middleweights Ready For Tulane A.C. Bout*, January 20, 1918.

7 The description of Harry Greb's bout with Augie Ratner in New Orleans is derived from reports found in the New Orleans Times-Picayune, and New Orleans States.

8 Keck, Harry, Pittsburgh Post: *Greb Comes Right in, Turns Around, Goes Right Out Again Tonight*, January 26, 1918.

9 Bridgeport Telegram: *HARRY GREB ON WAY TO THIS CITY FOR BIG BOUT*, January 24, 1918.

10 Ferri, Roger, Bridgeport Telegram: *Live Comments on All Sports*, January 29, 1918.

11 Ferri, Roger, Bridgeport Telegram: *HARRY GREB MAKES HUMAN TARGET OF GAME ZULU KID*, January 30, 1918.

12 The account of Harry Greb's bout with Zulu Kid in Bridgeport is derived from accounts found in the Bridgeport Telegram, and Bridgeport Post.

13 Bridgeport Post: *SHOOTING 'EM OVER BY PAS*, January 30, 1918.

14 Cincinnati Enquirer, February 3, 1918.

15 Cumberland Evening Times: *HUBBARD EASY MEET FOR BEARCAT GREB*, February 5, 1918.

16 Pittsburgh Post: *Frank Klaus Fights Greb in Headliner; 10 All=Star Bouts*, February 3, 1918.

17 Pittsburgh Daily Dispatch: *Gibbons Dares Greb; Wants to Bet $1,000*, February 4, 1918.

18 The account of Harry Greb's exhibition bout with Frank Klaus is derived from reports found in the Pittsburgh Post, Pittsburgh Gazette-Times, Pittsburgh Press, and Pittsburgh Daily Dispatch.

19 Keck, Harry, Pittsburgh Post: *Sporting Chit-Chat*, February 15, 1918.

20 Hosking, E. R., Saint Paul Dispatch: *TOMMY GIBBONS IS AFTER MIKE O'DOWD*, February 13, 1918.

21 Hosking, E. R., Saint Paul Dispatch: *CHAMPION O'DOWD IMPROVES AS BOXER*, February 11, 1918.

22 The account of the bout between Harry Greb and Bob Moha at Cincinnati on February 18, 1918 was drawn from reports found in the Cincinnati Post, Times-Star, and Enquirer

23 Cincinnati Enquirer: *LOOK OUT For Wild Man of Ring!*, February 19, 1918.

24 Tompkins, Tinear, Minneapolis Journal: **REDDY TAKES OVER THE GREB FORFEIT**, February 18, 1918.

25 Cobrun, Fred R., Minneapolis Tribune: **Harry Greb Has a Shade Over O'Dowd**, February 26, 1918.

26 Minneapolis Tribune: **WHAT THEY SAY.**, February 25, 1918.

27 Ibid.

28 Flagg, Harriet T., Minneapolis Journal: **ART AT THE RINGSIDE**, February 26, 1918.

29 The account of the championship bout between Harry Greb and Mike O'Dowd held on February 25, 1918 was derived from reports found in the Minneapolis Journal, Minneapolis Tribune, Minneapolis News, Saint Paul Dispatch, Saint Paul Pioneer Press, and Saint Paul Daily News. It should be noted that no copy of the Minneapolis News dated February 26, 1918 could be found However George Barton's description of the fight for that paper was republished in the March 3, 1918 edition of the Pittsburgh Post.

30 Shave, Ed L., St. Paul Daily News: **O'Dowd Retains His Title; Greb Gets But a Draw**, February 26, 1918.

31 Barton, George A., Minneapolis News (republished in the Pittsburgh Post March 3, 1918): **Greb Outpoints O'Dowd in Ten-Round Struggle**, February 26, 1918.

NOTES

CHAPTER 11

1 Pulford, George R., Toledo Blade, March 2, 1918.

2 Toledo Blade: **DILLON WOULD MEET DEMPSEY**, March 4, 1918.

3 The account of the bout between Jack Dillon and Harry Greb, held on March 4, 1918 at Toledo, Ohio, is derived from reports found in the Toledo Blade, Toledo Times, and Toledo News-Bee.

4 Pulford, George R., Toledo Blade: **Dillon Makes Sorry Showing With Harry Greb, Stem=Winder Phenom**, March 5, 1918.

5 Pulford, George R., Toledo Blade, March 7, 1918.

6 Dillon, Jack, Toledo Times: **Dillon Believes Harry Greb Will Be Boss of Middleweight Fighters**, March 13, 1918.

7 Edwards, Henry P., Cleveland Plain Dealer: **Pittsburger Hammers Opponent Around Ring**, March 12, 1918.

8 The description of the bout between Mike McTigue and Harry Greb held at Cleveland on March 11, 1918 is taken from the Cleveland Plain Dealer, and Cleveland Press.

9 Pulford, George R., Toledo Blade, March 14, 1918.

10 Cleveland Plain Dealer: **HARRY GREB FAILS TO WEIGH IN FOR MOOSE CLUB BOUT**, March 12, 1918.

11 Cleveland Plain Dealer: **COMPLETE PLANS FOR C.A.C. SHOW**, March 27, 1918.

12 Buffalo Courier: **YOUNG MENDO WILL TACKLE ELMER DOANE ON Q.A.C. CARD; LANGFORD EAGER FOR GREB**, March 16, 1918.

13 Buffalo Morning Express: **GREB WILL TAKE HIS TURN TONIGHT**, March 18, 1918.

14 The account of Greb's bout against Willie Langford in Buffalo was derived from reports found in the Buffalo Courier,

Buffalo Morning Express, and Buffalo Evening News.

15 Buffalo Morning Express: *TALK OF KAYO-GREB AWAKES EAST SIDE*, March 20, 1918.

16 The list of fights Greb had scheduled for April was taken from various wire reports of the time. Some of them appear to either be erroneous or tentative. Following up on some of the dates proved to be a wild goose chase with little or no corroboration.

17 Toledo Blade: *HARRY GREB HAS NOTHING TO DO UNTIL TOMORROW*, March 30, 1918.

18 Muncie Evening Press: *FRANK MANTELL WILL TAKE ON H. GREB MONDAY*, April 5, 1918.
Toledo Times: *GREB-CHRISTIE FIGHT CALLED OFF BY AN OFFICIAL*, April 6, 1918.

19 The report of Greb's cancelled bout with Bill Scott/Jack Reed/Frank Mantell/Terry Keller was derived from the Muncie Star and Muncie Evening Press.

20 Toledo Blade: *GREB IN BAD SHAPE*, April 15, 1918.

21 The account of Greb's three exhibition bouts aboard the land battleship U.S.S. Recruit was derived from accounts found in the New York Tribune, New York Times, New York Morning-Telegraph, New York Herald, New York Sun, Stars and Stripes, and the National Police Gazette.

22 Hawthorne, Fred, New York Tribune: *Boxing News and Notes*, May 8, 1918.

23 Ibid.

24 Ed W. Smith, Chicago Evening American: *"I'LL KNOCK HIM OUT, SURE," IS WORD GREB SENDS*, July 27, 1918.

25 The account of the bout between Harry Greb and Al McCoy held at Cincinnati was derived from reports found in the Cincinnati Enquirer, Post, and Commercial Tribune.

26 The account of the bout between Harry Greb and Clay Turner held at Bridgeport was derived from reports found in the New Haven Evening Register, Bridgeport Telegram, and Bridgeport Post.

27 The account of the bout between Harry Greb and Soldier Bartfield held at Pittsburgh was derived from reports found in the Pittsburgh Post, Pittsburgh Leader, Pittsburgh Gazette-Times, Pittsburgh Dispatch, Pittsburgh Sun, Pittsburgh Chronicle-Telegraph, and Pittsburgh Press.

28 Gibson, Florent, Pittsburgh Post: *Greb Not Signed With Bartfield in Toledo*, May 18, 1918.
Toledo Times: *Harry Greb's Manager Is Going to Give Local Fistic Board Something to Work On When the Members Meet Today*, May 22, 1918.

29 The account of the Red Cross benefit is derived from reports found in the New York Times, New York Evening-Telegram, New York Morning-Telegraph, New York Sun, and New York Evening-World.
This bout should be considered an exhibition bout on Greb's official record. The rounds were two minutes long as opposed to three minutes and the contestants wore larger gloves than standard professional boxing gloves.

30 Pittsburgh Leader: *HARRY GREB TO AID RED CROSS*, May 26, 1918.

31 Meade, Dick, Toledo News-Bee: *BARTFIELD SAYS HE WILL PUT AWAY GREB HERE ON WEDNESDAY*, May 27, 1918.

32 The description of the bout between Harry Greb and Soldier Bartfield at Toledo was compiled from reports found in the Toledo Blade, Toledo News-Bee, and Toledo Times.

33 The description of the bout between Harry Greb and Zulu Kid at Madison Square Garden was derived from reports found in the New York Herald, New York Evening Telegram, New York Evening World, New York Morning Telegraph, New York Tribune, New York Sun, and New York Times.

34 The description of the bout between Harry Greb and Frank Carbone is derived from reports found in the Stamford Daily Advocate, Bridgeport Telegram, and Bridgeport Post.

35 Johnson, L. C., Rock Island Argus: *GREB ARRIVES; IN FINE SHAPE FOR MOHA BOUT*, July 4, 1918.

36 The account of Harry Greb's bout in Rock Island against Bob Moha is derived from reports found in the Moline Daily Dispatch, and Rock Island Argus.

37 The account of Greb's exhibition bout against Oscar Anderson was derived from reports found in the Cleveland Plain Dealer, Chicago Tribune, Philadelphia Public Ledger, Buffalo Courier, and Cleveland Press. Those papers listed which did not originate in Cleveland were quoted because the sports editor or writer of that paper was present at the event.

38 Rocap, William H., Philadelphia Public Ledger: **FULTON NO MATCH FOR DEMPSEY**, July 29, 1918.

39 Rocap, William H., Philadelphia Public Ledger: **WHY BOXING IS POPULAR IN PHILA.**, July 20, 1918.

40 The account of Greb's bout against Soldier Bartfield in Philadelphia was taken from reports found in the Philadelphia Inquirer (voted for Bartfield), Philadelphia Press (voted for Bartfield), Philadelphia Public Ledger (voted for Greb), Philadelphia Evening Bulletin (voted for Greb), Philadelphia Record (voted for Greb) and Philadelphia Evening Public Ledger (voted a Draw).

41 National Police Gazette: **GOOD BOXING AT OSHKOSH.**, April 14, 1900.

42 Ed W. Smith, Chicago Evening American: **"I'LL KNOCK HIM OUT, SURE," IS WORD GREB SENDS**, July 27, 1918.

43 Chicago Herald-Examiner: **TITLE AT STAKE IN M'GOORTY-GREB GO**, July 25, 1918.

44 Chicago Herald-Examiner: **FURLOUGH FOR GREB IF HE IS VICTORIOUS**, July 26, 1918.

45 The account of Greb's bout against Eddie McGoorty at Ft. Sheridan is derived from reports found in the Chicago Tribune, Chicago Daily News, Chicago Evening Post, and Chicago American.

46 Philadelphia Inquirer: **HARRY GREB WANTS FIGHT WITH DEMPSEY**, August 6, 1918.

47 The result of Greb's fight against Battling Levinsky in Philadelphia in August of 1918 was derived from reports found in the Philadelphia Inquirer, Philadelphia Public Ledger, Philadelphia Evening Public Ledger, Philadelphia Evening Bulletin, Philadelphia Press, and Philadelphia Record.

48 The account of Greb's fight against Clay Turner was derived from reports found in the Hudson Dispatch, New York Sun, and Jersey Journal.

49 Pittsburgh Sun: **ENLISTED FIGHTERS MUST GET PERMISSION TO BOX AT CLUBS.**, September 3, 1918.

50 Pittsburgh Leader: **Greb and Miske Ready For Hard Battle Today**, September 21, 1918.

51 Gibson, Florent, Pittsburgh Post: **Greb and Miske Meet In Local Ring Today**, September 21, 1918.

52 The account of the bout between Harry Greb and Billy Miske held on September 21, 1918 was derived from reports found in the Pittsburgh Post, Pittsburgh Press, Pittsburgh Leader, Pittsburgh Sun, Pittsburgh Dispatch, and Pittsburgh Gazette-Times.

53 Gibson, Florent, Pittsburgh Post: **MISKE OPENS CUT OVER HARRY'S EYE TURNING THE TIDE**, September 22, 1918.

54 Pittsburgh Post: **The Morning Hatchet**, September 23, 1918.

55 Pittsburgh Leader: **Greb-Robson Fight at Boston Is Called Off**, October 6, 1918.

56 Keck, Harry, Pittsburgh Post: **Greb Drives New Car Like He Fights; Help!**, October 12, 1918.

57 Keck, Harry, Pittsburgh Post: **GREB TO FIGHT CARPENTIER IN LONDON**, November 11, 1918.

58 Keck, Harry, Pittsburgh Post: **SEEKING XMAS TOYS, SON OF JAMES MASON BADLY BURNED**, November 26, 1918.

59 Keck, Harry, Pittsburgh Post: **Burns Prove Fatal To Wee Jimmy Mason; Gritty to the Last**, November 28, 1918.

60 Buffalo Courier: **GREB HAS AN ALIBI FOR LOSING ABROAD BUT IT'S FISHY**, December 25, 1918.

61 New York Times: **ENGLISH FOG SLOWS UP YANKEE BOXERS**, December 24, 1918.

62 Milwaukee Journal: **CUPID MAY ROUT JINX THAT HAS PURSUED HARRY GREB FOR WEEKS**, January 30, 1919.

63 London Daily Telegraph: **KING'S BOXING PRIZE WON BY BRITISH ARMY.**, December 13, 1918.

64 The account of Greb's participation in the tournament for the King's Trophy was derived from reports found in the London Times, Pall Mall Gazette, London Morning Post, London Daily Telegraph, The Sporting Life, Boxing magazine, and the various account of the fighters present at the tournament.

65 Keck, Harry, Pittsburgh Post: **HARRY GREB, BACK FROM LONDON, TELLS OF BOUTS**, December 26, 1918.

66 Ibid.

67 The Sporting Life: **ALBERT HALL AFTERMATH.**, December 14, 1918.

68 Keck, Harry, Pittsburgh Post: **HARRY GREB, BACK FROM LONDON, TELLS OF BOUTS**, December 26, 1918.

NOTES

CHAPTER 12

1 Coverage of Greb's aborted bout with Jack Heinen was taken from reports found in the Pittsburgh Dispatch, Chicago Tribune, Pittsburgh Gazette-Times, and Pittsburgh Sun.

2 The description of Harry Greb's victory over Leo Houck at Boston was derived from reports found in the Boston Post, Boston Globe, Boston Herald, and Lancaster Examiner.

3 Syracuse Post-Standard: **FISHER READY TO MEET GREB IN FINAL BOUT**, January 20, 1919.

4 The account of Greb's bout against Young Fisher at Syracuse in January of 1919 is derived from reports found in the Syracuse Post-Standard, Syracuse Journal, and Syracuse Herald.

5 Syracuse Herald: **GREB WINS FROM FISHER IN 10 FAST ROUNDS**, January 21, 1919.

6 The account of Greb's bout against Paul Sampson was derived from reports found in the Pittsburgh Dispatch, Pittsburgh Press, Pittsburgh Sun, Pittsburgh Chronicle-Telegraph, and Pittsburgh Gazette-Times.

7 Columbus Evening Dispatch: **WEIGHT DISPARITY HELPED GREB TO DEFEAT BARTFIELD**, January 28, 1919.

8 The account of Greb's wedding was derived from reports found in the Pittsburgh Post, Pittsburgh Chronicle-Telegraph, Pittsburgh Gazette-Times, as well as interviews with members of the Greb family and that of best man Leo "Puff" Kelly.

9 Cleveland Plain Dealer: **HARRY GREB FINALLY SHOWS HE WEIGHS ABOUT 168 POUNDS**, February 1, 1919.

10 The account of Greb's bout in Cleveland against Tommy Robson was derived from reports found in the Cleveland Press and Cleveland Plain Dealer.

11 Pittsburgh Sun: **ROBSON SAYS DEMPSEY IS ONLY MAN WHO CAN STOP GREB.**, February 3, 1919.

12 The account of Greb's victory over Len Rowlands at Pittsburgh is derived from reports found in the Pittsburgh Sun, Pittsburgh Press, and Pittsburgh Gazette-Times.

13 The report of Greb's bout against Bill Brennan at Syracuse is derived from accounts found in the Syracuse Herald, Syracuse Post-Standard, Syracuse Journal.

14 Syracuse Journal: **GREB REGISTERS VICTORY BILL BRENNAN**, February 11, 1919.

15 Syracuse Post-Standard: **GREB WINNER OVER BRENNAN IN MAIN GO OF GOOD BOXING CARD**, February 11, 1919.

16 Buffalo Morning Express: *HARRY THE PLUNGER HITS THE TOWN*, February 12, 1919.

17 Pittsburgh Press: *"GREB WINS," "GREB LOSES;" HELP, HELP!*, February 11, 1919.

18 Pittsburgh Chronicle-Telegraph: *Brennan to Meet Greb Here Next Monday Night*, March 10, 1919.

19 Buffalo Courier: *GREB DROPS OFF 'TWEEN TRAINS LONG ENOUGH TO PROMISE BAT LEVINSKY BEATING HERE*, February 12, 1919.

20 Buffalo Courier: *Harry Greb Would Pattern Career After Dempsey, Sees Levinsky as Stepping Stone*, February 13, 1919.

21 Boyle, Havey J., Pittsburgh Chronicle-Telegraph: *THROUGH THE SPORT LENS*, February 13, 1919.

22 The description of Harry Greb's bout against Battling Levinsky held in Buffalo was derived from reports found in the Buffalo Enquirer, Buffalo Courier, Buffalo Morning Express, Buffalo Enquirer, and Buffalo Evening News.

23 Buffalo Courier: *Christie Pops Surprise of Season, Stopping Doane; Greb Beats Bat Levinsky*, February 18, 1919.

24 Pulford, George R., Toledo Blade, February 24, 1919.

25 Pulford, George R., Toledo Blade, February 28, 1919.
   Pittsburgh Sun: *TOLEDO IS LATEST TO BID FOR BATTLE*, February 28, 1919.

26 The description of Greb's bout with Wiggins in Toledo is derived from reports found in the Toledo News-Bee, Toledo Blade, and Toledo Times.

27 Meade, Dick, Toledo News-Bee: *HARRY GREB HAS TOO MUCH CLASS AND SPEED FOR CHUCK WIGGINS*, March 1, 1919.

28 Toledo Blade: *DETROIT'S ELKS EAGER FOR BOUT*, March 2, 1919.

29 Meade, Dick, Toledo News-Bee: *THEY SAY GREB CAN'T HIT, BUT DONT BELIEVE 'EM*, March 4, 1919.

30 The description of the bout between Harry Greb and Chuck Wiggins at Detroit was derived from reports found in the Detroit Free Press, Detroit News, Detroit Times, and Toledo News-Bee.

31 The bout description of the bout between Harry Greb and Leo Houck at Lancaster is derived from reports found in the Lancaster Examiner, Lancaster Intelligencier, and Lancaster New Era.

32 Boyle, Havey J., Pittsburgh Chronicle-Telegraph: *THROUGH THE SPORT LENS*, March 17, 1919.

33 Pittsburgh Chronicle-Telegraph: *Greb Going Up Against Hard Foe, Dempsey Says*, March 15, 1919.

34 The description of Greb's bout against Bill Brennan was derived from reports found in the Pittsburgh Gazette-Times, Pittsburgh Press, Pittsburgh Chronicle-Telegraph, Pittsburgh Dispatch, Pittsburgh Leader, Pittsburgh Sun, and Pittsburgh Post.

35 Pittsburgh Chronicle -Telegraph: *James Mason's Wife Is Dead*, March 20, 1919.

36 Johnstown Tribune: *LOCAL FIGHT FANS ONCE MORE GIVEN THE "GRAND RAZZ"*, March 26, 1919.

37 The description of Harry Greb's third and final bout with Billy Miske held in Pittsburgh in 1919 was derived from reports found in the Pittsburgh Press, Pittsburgh Dispatch, Pittsburgh Leader, Pittsburgh Gazette-Times, Pittsburgh Sun, Pittsburgh Post, and Pittsburgh Chronicle-Telegraph.

38 Guy, Richard, Pittsburgh Gazette-Times: *REFEREE DECLARES MISKE FAKED HERE*, April 3, 1919.

39 Pittsburgh Chronicle-Telegraph: *OFFICIALS SAY BOXERS MUST GUARANTEE THEY WILL FIGHT*, April 3, 1919.

40 Pittsburgh Chronicle-Telegraph: *MISKE'S MANAGER SAYS DILLON DID NOT KNOW HIS DUTIES*, April 4, 1919.

41 Butler Citizen: *GREB PUT MADDEN TO SLEEP IN THE SECOND ROUND*, April 3, 1919.

42 Syracuse Post-Standard: *JACK DEMPSEY MAKES HIT BEFORE BIG AUDIENCE AT THE ARENA SHOW*, April 6, 1919.

43 The description of Harry Greb's bout with Young Fisher at Syracuse in April 1919 is derived from reports found in the Syracuse Post-Standard, Syracuse Journal, and Syracuse Herald.

44 Buffalo Courier: *Greb Will Not Be Content With Point Victory, Says He Will Knock Davis Out*, April 4, 1919.

45 The account of Greb's bout with George "One Round" Davis is derived from reports found in the Buffalo Courier, Buffalo Evening News, Buffalo Morning Express, and Buffalo Enquirer.

46 Buffalo Courier: *DAVIS NOT DISCOURAGED AT DEFEAT BY THE FASTER GREB; MICHAELS MAKES REAL HIT*, April 10, 1919.

47 Gannon, William C., Erie Dispatch: *IS THE BOXING COMMISSION TO QUEER THE GAME?*, April 17, 1919.
    The feud between Oppenheimer and Finneran had played out before the press for several weeks however the above article gives a basic summation of the events thus far.

48 Canton Daily News: *The Gift Of Gab*, April 29, 1919.

49 The account of Greb's bout against Battling Levinsky was derived from reports found in the Canton Daily News, and Canton Repository.

50 The account of Harry Greb's bout against Clay Turner at Boston was derived from reports found in the Boston Herald, Boston Post, and Boston Globe.

51 The account of Harry Greb's rematch with Willie Meehan held in Pittsburgh was derived from reports found in the Pittsburgh Gazette-Times, Pittsburgh Leader, and Pittsburgh Post.

52 Keck, Harry, Pittsburgh Post, May 19, 1919.

53 Pittsburgh Post: *JESS WILLARD WANTS GREB TO HELP HIM TRAIN FOR JACK DEMPSEY*, June 7, 1919.

54 Pittsburgh Press: *GREB NOT TO HELP WILLARD*, June 8, 1919.

55 The description of Greb's bout against Joe Borrell held in 1919 is derived from reports found in the Philadelphia Public Ledger, Philadelphia Inquirer, Philadelphia Evening Public Ledger, and Philadelphia Evening Bulletin.

56 The brief description of Greb's bout against Happy Howard at Erie was derived from the reports found in the Erie Tribune and Erie Dispatch. The description of Greb's bout against Yankee Gilbert at Wheeling, West Virginia was derived from accounts found in the Wheeling Register and Wheeling Intelligencier.

57 Pittsburgh Press: *H. GREB BECOMES ANGRY*, June 21, 1919.

58 The account of Greb's bout with Mike Gibbons held in Pittsburgh in 1919 is derived from reports found in the Pittsburgh Post (both editions), Pittsburgh Gazette-Times, Pittsburgh Press, Chicago Evening American, and Pittsburgh Leader, Pittsburgh Chronicle-Telegraph, Pittsburgh Sun, and Pittsburgh Dispatch.

59 Guy, Richard R., Pittsburgh Leader: *The Sporting Editor's Musings*, June 24, 1919.

60 Davis, Ralph, Pittsburgh Press: *RALPH DAVIS' COLUMN*, June 25, 1919.

61 Pittsburgh Post: *The Morning Hatchet*, June 25, 1919.

62 Randy Roberts, *Jack Dempsey The MANASSA MAULER*. Baton Rouge: Louisiana State University Press, 1979.

63 Pittsburgh Leader: *New Champion Now Wishes To Meet Georges Carpentier*, July 6, 1919.

64 Duffy, Lou, Tulsa Democrat: *Brennan and Greb Finish Preparatory Work This Afternoon*, July 3, 1919.

65 Tulsa Daily World: *CHICAGOAN MUST HIT HARD TO WIN*, July 3, 1919.
    Duffy, Lou, Tulsa Democrat: *Greb as Light on His Feet as Three Dollars' Worth of Feathers*, July 3, 1919.

66 The description of Greb's bout against Bill Brennan is derived from reports found in the Tulsa Democrat, and Tulsa Daily World.

67 Philadelphia Press: *Will Dempsey Last Long.*, July 13, 1919.

68 The description of the bout between Harry Greb and Battling Levinsky was derived from reports found in the

Philadelphia Inquirer, Philadelphia Public Ledger, Philadelphia Evening Bulletin, Philadelphia Press, Philadelphia Evening Public Ledger, and Philadelphia Record.

69 Philadelphia Press: ***Dempsey Stands Alone.***, July 16, 1919.

70 The account of Greb's bout against George "KO" Brown at Wheeling is derived from reports found in the Wheeling Register and Wheeling Intelligencier.

71 Edgren, Robert, Pittsburgh Press: ***WILLARD WEIGHS 248 NOW***, June 20, 1919.

72 Youngstown Telegram: ***Would Match Greb With Champ Jack***, July 18, 1919.

73 Cincinnati Enquirer, July 20, 1919.

74 Youngstown Telegram: ***CAPACITY CROWD IS ASSURED FOR THURSDAY'S BOUT***, July 22, 1919.

75 New Castle News: ***Joe Will Have To Flash Kayo To Win***, July 24, 1919.

76 Erie Daily Tribune: ***CHIP MAY GET CRACK AT DEMPSEY***, July 18, 1919.

77 New Castle News: ***"Tough And Fast," Says Joe's Brother***, July 24, 1919.

78 McHale, M. J., Youngstown Telegram: ***New Castle Boy Never Has a Chance With Rugged Pittsburgh Lad; Fails To Go Down Only Because of Fine Condition and Stamina***, July 25, 1919.

79 The account of Greb's rematch with Joe Chip was derived from reports found in the Pittsburgh Gazette-Times, Youngstown Telegram, Youngstown Vindicator, New Castle News, and New Castle Herald.

80 New Orleans Times-Picayune: ***Joe Chip Looks Lot Like George***, July 20, 1921.

NOTES

CHAPTER 13

1 Dayton Journal: ***HARRY GREB MAY MEET CHAMP JACK DEMPSEY***, August 4,1919.

2 Pittsburgh Leader: ***Mike O'Dowd Has High Ideas as to Worth***, August 27,1919.

3 The account of Greb's bout with Terry Keller at Dayton, Ohio is derived from reports found in the Dayton Evening Herald, Dayton Journal, and Dayton Daily News.

4 The account of Harry's bout with Bill Brennan at Forbes Field is derived from reports found in the Pittsburgh Gazette-Times, Pittsburgh Press, Pittsburgh Leader, Pittsburgh Dispatch, and Pittsburgh Post.

5 Youngstown Telegram: ***PREMIER BOXING BOUT OF SEASON BOOKED SEPT. 1***, August 18, 1919.

6 Youngstown Vindicator: ***STAMBAUGH IS SEEKING BEST BOUT IN MARKET***, August 17, 1919.

7 Youngstown Vindicator: ***MONDAY EVENING'S MITT SHOW AT IDORA SHOULD BE PREMIER FISTIC EXHIBITION OF SEASON***, August 31, 1919.

8 The account of Harry Greb's bout with Jeff Smith at Youngstown is derived from reports found in the Youngstown Telegram, New Castle Herald, and Youngstown Vindicator.

9 Wheeling Register: ***Greb-Levinsky Bout Wednesday***, September 1, 1919.

10 Wheeling Intelligencier: *FIRST CHAMPIONSHIP BOUT EVER IN STATE OF WEST VIRGINIA*, September 3, 1919.

11 The account of Greb's bout with Battling Levinsky is derived from reports found in the Wheeling Register and Wheeling Intelligencier.

12 The account of Greb's bout with Silent Martin at Saint Louis is derived from reports found in the St. Louis Globe-Democrat, Saint Louis Post-Dispatch, and St. Louis Star.

13 Wray, John E., St. Louis Post-Dispatch: *Greb's Prancing And Fast Hitting Bewilder Martin,* September 19, 1919.

14 The account of Greb's bout with Sailor Petroskey is derived from reports found in the Philadelphia Press, Philadelphia Evening Bulletin, Philadelphia Inquirer, Philadelphia Public Ledger, Philadelphia Record, and Boxing Blade.

15 Moran's bout with Jack Geyer in Pittsburgh was heavily criticized. Geyer was announced as being 24 years old. When he appeared it was clearly evident that he was closer to 40 and posed little threat to Moran. When Moran was again matched against a hapless opponent at Cumberland a few days later, and won without difficulty in two rounds, it became clear that he would need to step up his competition before he could hope to get a big a fight with either Greb or Dempsey.

16 The account of Greb's bout with George "KO" Brown at Canton is derived from reports found in the Canton Daily News, Pittsburgh Gazette-Times, and Canton Repository.

17 The account of Greb's bout with Larry Williams at Pittsburgh is derived from reports found in the Pittsburgh Gazette-Times, Pittsburgh Press, and Pittsburgh Post.

18 Beaver Falls Evening Tribune: *GREB DEFEATS "ZULU KID" IN CLEVER FIGHT,* November 28, 1919.

19 Buffalo Courier: *SOLDIER JONES, SMILING YOUNG GIANT, SAYS HE AIN'T AFRAID OF REPUTATIONS,* November 27, 1919.

20 Ibid.

21 The account of Greb's bout with Soldier Jones at Buffalo is derived from reports found in the Buffalo Courier, Buffalo Morning Express, Buffalo Evening News, and Buffalo Enquirer.

22 Buffalo Morning Express: *HARRY GREB KAYOS SOLDIER JONES,* November 29, 1919.

23 Buffalo Morning Express: *GREB ADVISES JONES,* November 30, 1919.

24 The account of Greb's cancelled bout with Clay Turner and the eventual fallout involving Panama Joe Gans is derived from various reports found in the Syracuse Post-Standard, Syracuse Journal, and Syracuse Herald.

25 Buffalo Morning Express: *Harry Greb and Jimmy Mason pay a brief visit.,* December 4, 1919.

26 The account of Greb's bout with Clay Turner at Buffalo is derived from reports found in the Buffalo Evening News, Buffalo Morning Express, Buffalo Courier, and Buffalo Enquirer.

27 Buffalo Courier: *TURNER WOULD RATHER FIGHT TEN LEVINSKYS THAN GREB; SAYS HE'S NEXT TO DEMPSEY,* December 12, 1919.

28 The account of Greb's second bout with Mike McTigue is derived from reports found in the Binghamton Morning Sun, Union News-Dispatch, Endicott Record, and the Binghamton Press and Leader.

29 Williams, Gordon, Binghamton Press and Leader: *THE REALM OF SPORTS,* December 12, 1919.

30 The account of Greb's bout with Billy Kramer at Pittsburgh is derived from reports found in the Pittsburgh Gazette-Times, Pittsburgh Post, and Pittsburgh Press

31 Britt, Willus, Philadelphia Public Ledger: *Where Was the Referee?,* December 21, 1919.

32 The account of Greb's bout with Clay Turner is derived from reports found in the Philadelphia Evening Bulletin, Philadelphia Record, Philadelphia Public Ledger, Philadelphia Inquirer, Philadelphia Press, and Philadelphia Evening Public Ledger.

33 Philadelphia Evening Bulletin: *GREB SEEKS CLASH WITH JACK DEMPSEY,* December 23, 1919.

NOTES

CHAPTER 14

1 Keck, Harry, Pittsburgh Gazette-Times: *GREB, ILL, CALLS OFF BOUT WITH AUGIE RATNER,* December 27, 1919.

2 Gibson, Florent, Pittsburgh Post: *MICKEY RODGERS IS PRIMING M'GUIRE TO LICK ZIP KIRK; GREB HIDES FRACTURED ARM,* January 18, 1920.

3 Welsh, Regis M., Pittsburgh Post: *GREB MEETS DEMPSEY DECORATION DAY IN BUFFALO, RUMORED,* January 30, 1920.

4 Ibid.

5 Battle Creek Enquirer And Evening News: *GREB WINNER WITH ONE HAND,* February 8, 1920.

6 Hall, Howard P., Kalamazoo Gazette: *All Kinds of Happenings Uncorked Hurt Class of Friday Evening's Boxing,* February 7, 1920.
   The account of Greb's bout with Zulu Kid at Kalamazoo was derived from reports found in the Kalamazoo Gazette, Grand Rapids Herald, and Battle Creek Enquirer And Evening News.

7 Welsh, Regis M., Pittsburgh Post: *ANOTHER DOC COOK BREAKS INTO PRINT; FIGHT FANS WAITING,* February 8, 1920.

8 Welsh, Regis M., Pittsburgh Post: *KLAUS COMES BACK,* February 9, 1920.

9 Pittsburgh Post: *BOB ROPER'S BIOGRAPHY SHOWS HE'S NO NOVICE; HAS FOUGHT FOR YEARS,* February 19, 1920.
   Roper's first recorded bout was held in Manila June 13, 1914. He lost a six round decision to Bob Harris while fighting as Ernest Hammond, Roper's real name being William Ernest Hammond.

10 The account of Greb's bout with Roper is derived from reports found in the Pittsburgh Gazette-Times, Pittsburgh Leader, Pittsburgh Daily Dispatch, Pittsburgh Press, and Pittsburgh Post.

11 Akron Evening Times: *STAR BOXERS TO SHOW ON CARD MAR. 9,* February 28, 1920.

12 Akron Evening Times: *AKRON FANS STRONG FOR STAR BOXERS,* March 5, 1920.

13 The account of the match featuring Johnny Ray against Johnny Kirk and the resulting riot is derived from reports found in the Pittsburgh Post, Pittsburgh Gazette-Times, and Pittsburgh Press.

14 Pittsburgh Press: *KIRK DISCHARGED AFTER HEARING,* March 9, 1920.
   Pittsburgh Gazette-Times: *"WHO TACKLED JOE THOMPSON?",* March 9, 1920.
   Accounts differed as to whether Greb was involved or not and no sanctions were ever levied against him.

15 Akron Evening Times: *PITTSBURGER TAKES FIGHT ALL THE WAY,* March 11, 1920.
   The account of the bout between Greb and Clay Turner at Akron is derived from reports found in the Akron Beacon-Journal and Akron Evening Times.

16 Gibson, Florent, Pittsburgh Post: *GREB WILL FIGHT DEMPSEY ON MAY 31 IN BUFFALO ARENA,* March 13, 1920.

17 Kelly, Billy, Buffalo Courier: *BEFORE AND AFTER,* March 16, 1920.

18 Pittsburgh Post, March 14, 1920.

19 The account of Greb's bout with Tommy Robson is derived from reports found in the Dayton Journal, Dayton Daily News, and Dayton Evening Herald.

20 Skid, Syracuse Herald: *THE HERALD LISTENING POST OF SPORTDOM,* November 13, 1920.

21 The account of Greb's bout with Larry Williams is derived from reports found in the Pittsburgh Gazette-Times, Pittsburgh Press, Pittsburgh Leader, Pittsburgh Daily Dispatch, Pittsburgh Sun, Pittsburgh Chronicle-Telegraph, and Pittsburgh Post.

22 Pittsburgh Gazette-Times: *NEGOTIATIONS FOR DEMPSEY BOUT ARE ON, SAYS GREB,* March 23, 1920.

23 The account of Greb's bout with George "KO" Brown at Denver is derived from reports found in the Rocky Mountain News, and Denver Post.

24 Ricketson, Rick, Denver Post: *WINNER OF ROPER-GREB TILT WILL MEET GIBBONS IN DENVER MEMORIAL DAY,* March 30, 1920.

25 Denver Post: *Greb Admits He's Not Champ But Fighting for Pair of 'Em,* April 1, 1920.

26 The account of Greb's bout with Captain Bob Roper at Denver is derived from reports found in the Denver Post, and Rocky Mountain News.

27 Pollack, Abe, Rocky Mountain News: *GREB OUTPOINTS BOB ROPER IN BOUT AT STOCKYARDS,* April 6, 1920.

28 Ricketson, Rick, Denver Post: *Greb Shades Bob Roper In Dandy Feature Event,* April 6, 1920.

29 Pittsburgh Post: *WITH THE BOXERS,* April 19, 1920.

30 Long, James J., Pittsburgh Sun: *SPORTING GOSSIP & COMMENT,* April 28, 1920.

31 Ibid.

32 Ricketson, Rick, Denver Post: *TOM GIBBONS ISN'T OVERLY ANXIOUS TO MEET EITHER GREB OR ROPER,* April 3, 1920.

33 Ibid.

34 Pittsburgh Gazette-Times: *Kirk Injures Ribs; Cancels Dunn Bout,* April 26, 1920.

35 Keck, Harry, Pittsburgh Gazette-Times: *SPORT CHAT,* May 30, 1920.

36 Gibson, Florent, Pittsburgh Post: *CARPENTIER IMPRESSES FANS WITH SPEED AND VERSATILITY OF ATTACK; BOGASH IS WINNER,* May 4, 1920.

37 Pittsburgh Post: *Greb Wants Him,* May 6, 1920.

38 Farrell, Henry L., Pittsburgh Chronicle-Telegraph: *WILSON SOUTHPAWS WAY TO VICTORY OVER TITLE-HOLDER,* May 7, 1920.

39 Long, James J., Pittsburgh Sun: *SPORTING GOSSIP & COMMENT,* May 13, 1920.

40 Keck, Harry, Pittsburgh Gazette-Times: *Defeat Makes O'Dowd Fight Here Uncertain,* May 7, 1920.

41 Ibid.

42 Keck, Harry, Pittsburgh Gazette-Times: *Greb Issues Challenge to New Champ,* May 8, 1920.

43 Keck, Harry, Pittsburgh Gazette-Times: *Greb Out to Wipe Slate Clean Against Gibbons,* May 9, 1920.

44 Keck, Harry, Pittsburgh Gazette-Times: *Kirk-Ward Box Tonight; Gibbons Arrives Today,* May 11, 1920.

45 Pittsburgh Sun: *Kirk-Ray Postponed; Gibbons Must Weigh,* May 14, 1920.

46 The account of Greb's first match with Tommy Gibbons at Pittsburgh is derived from reports found in the Pittsburgh Gazette-Times, Pittsburgh Daily Dispatch, Pittsburgh Press, Pittsburgh Leader, Pittsburgh Post, Pittsburgh Chronicle-Telegraph, and Pittsburgh Sun.

47 Guy, Richard, Pittsburgh Leader: *THE SPORTING EDITOR'S MUSINGS,* May 17, 1920.

48 Keck, Harry, Pittsburgh Gazette-Times: *Greb Wants to Fight Gibbons Again May 29,* May 17, 1920.

49 Pittsburgh Post: *The Morning Hatchet,* May 17, 1920.

50 Keck, Harry, Pittsburgh Gazette-Times: *SPORT CHAT,* May 30, 1920.

51 Keck, Harry, Pittsburgh Gazette-Times: *Greb Wants to Fight Gibbons Again May 29,* May 17, 1920.

52 Davis, Ralph, Pittsburgh Press: *RALPH DAVIS' COLUMN,* May 18, 1920.

53 Long, James J., Pittsburgh Sun: *SPORTING GOSSIP & COMMENT,* May 18, 1920.

54 The account of Greb's bout with Clay Turner at Philadelphia is derived from reports found in the Philadelphia Public Ledger, Philadelphia Inquirer, and Philadelphia Evening Public Ledger.

55 Pittsburgh Chronicle-Telegraph: *Greb Training for Carbonne Battle,* June 22, 1920.

56 Pittsburgh Chronicle-Telegraph: *Greb Anxious for Bout With Gibbons,* June 25, 1920.

57 The account of Greb's bout with Frank Carbone at Rochester is derived from reports found in the Rochester Herald, Rochester Democrat and Chronicle, Rochester Post-Express, and Rochester Times-Union.

58 Canton Daily News: *DEMPSEY BOUT FOR GREB HERE NOW ON TAPIS,* July 3, 1920.

59 Davis, Ralph, Pittsburgh Press: *RALPH DAVIS' COLUMN,* July 2, 1920.

60 Peet, William, Pittsburgh Daily Dispatch: *FIGHT STUFF,* July 4, 1920.

61 The description of Greb's bout with Bob Moha at Canton is derived from reports found in the Canton Daily News, and Canton Repository.

62 The description of Greb's bout with Larry Williams at Buffalo is derived from reports found in the Buffalo Morning Express, Buffalo Evening News, Buffalo Courier, and Buffalo Enquirer.

63 Buffalo Morning Express: *HARRY GREB BATS AS WELL AS EVER,* July 9, 1920.

64 Pittsburgh Press: *GREB CONFIDENT HE CAN BEAT GIBBONS,* July 19, 1920.

65 Pittsburgh Chronicle-Telegraph: *GREB PLANS FOR REVENGE IN RETURN SCRAP WITH GIBBONS,* July 23, 1920.

66 Pittsburgh Post: *FANS WARMING UP TO GIBBONS AND GREB BOUT,* July 24, 1920.

67 Pittsburgh Daily Dispatch: *Not News But Views,* July 28, 1920.

68 Pittsburgh Daily Dispatch: *Greb and Dempsey Workout,* July 29, 1920.

69 New York Morning-Telegraph: *DOUG BOXES WITH DEMPSEY,* July 30, 1920.

70 Underwood, George B., New York Evening-Telegram: *Lynch Will Try to Do What Carpentier Couldn't,* July 31, 1920.

71 Pittsburgh Press: *GREB TO OPPOSE GIBBONS,* July 31, 1920.
   Pittsburgh Chronicle-Telegraph: *ST. PAUL BATTLER IS SURE OF WINNING AS HE AWAITS BELL,* July 31, 1920.

72 Keck, Harry, Pittsburgh Gazette-Times: *LOCAL BATTLER ATONES FOR DEFEAT AT TOMMY'S FISTS TWO MONTHS AGO,* August 1, 1920.

73 The account of Greb's second bout with Tommy Gibbons at Pittsburgh is derived from reports found in the Pittsburgh Post, Pittsburgh Press, Pittsburgh Leader, Pittsburgh Gazette-Times, Pittsburgh Daily Dispatch, and Pittsburgh Chronicle-Telegraph.

74 Peet, William, Pittsburgh Daily Dispatch: *Gibbons Defeated By Greb,* August 1, 1920.

75 Pittsburgh Gazette-Times: *GREB-GIBBONS FIGHT DRAWS $17,365, LARGEST "GATE" IN LOCAL HISTORY,* August 2, 1920.

76 Scrapbook compiled by Tommy Gibbons detailing his career.

NOTES

CHAPTER 15

1 Pittsburgh Gazette-Times: **GREB MAKES HIT BOXING WITH DEMPSEY,** July 29, 1920.

2 New York Morning-Telegraph: **GREB WANTS TO BOX LEVINSKY FOR TITLE,** August 5, 1920.

3 The account of Greb's bout with Bob Moha at Cedar Point is derived from reports found in the Sandusky Register, and Sandusky Star-Journal.

4 Kalamazoo Gazette: **Bumper Crowd Will Gather for All-Star Boxing Show This Evening at Armory,** August 20, 1920.

5 Ibid.

6 Hall, Howard P., Kalamazoo Gazette: **Greb Winner in Brilliant Battle With Chuck Wiggins; Johnny Lewis Stops Dalton,** August 21, 1920.

7 The account of Greb's bout with Chuck Wiggins at Kalamazoo is derived from the report found in the Kalamazoo Gazette.

8 Grand Rapids Herald: **GREB WILL BATTLE JAMIESON AT RAMONA SATURDAY NIGHT,** August 27, 1920.

9 Ibid.

10 Grand Rapids Press: **HARRY GREB TO MEET JAMIESON,** August 27, 1920.

11 Grand Rapids Herald: **FANS CERTAIN TO SEE GRAND FIGHT BETWEEN LIGHT HEAVIES,** August 28, 1920.

12 The account of Greb's bout with Ted Jamieson at Grand Rapids is derived from reports found in the Grand Rapids News, and Grand Rapids Herald.

13 Grand Rapids Herald: **PITTSBURGH BOXER IS FLOORED BY OPPONENT IN THE FIRST ROUND,** August 29, 1920.

14 Grand Rapids News: **WHAT HAPPENED IN THE SPORT WORLD OVER THE WEEK END,** August 30, 1920.

15 The Capital Times: **DOCTORS ORDER MISKE TO REST FOR A MONTH,** July 10, 1919.

16 Dempsey, Jack with Barbara Piattelli Dempsey, **DEMPSEY.** New York: Harper & Row, Publishers, Inc., 1977.

17 Hall, Sam, Saint Louis Post-Dispatch: **Dempey-Miske Fight Will Be a No-Decision Affair, Hall Predicts,** September 1, 1920.

18 The account of Greb's first sparring session with Dempsey at Benton Harbor is derived from reports found in the Chicago Herald and Examiner, Chicago Evening American, Chicago Tribune, and Pittsburgh Gazette-Times.

19 Knox, P. T., Pittsburgh Gazette-Times: **Dempsey and Greb Stage Lively Training Battle,** September 2, 1920.

20 The account of Greb's second sparring session with Dempsey at Benton Harbor is derived from reports found in the Pittsburgh Gazette-Times, Chicago Tribune, Pittsburgh Post, Chicago Herald and Examiner, and Chicago Evening American.

21 The account of Greb's third and final sparring session with Dempsey at Benton Harbor is derived from reports found in the Chicago Evening American, Pittsburgh Gazette-Times, Chicago Herald and Examiner.

22 Dickerson, E. W., Grand Rapids Herald: **DICK SAYS DEMPSEY IS A REAL CHAMPION, MISKE EASY PICKING,**

September 7, 1920.

23 Hall, Sam, Saint Louis Post-Dispatch: **Dempsey Coin at 10 to 4 Fails to Lure Miske Bets,** September 5, 1920.

24 The account of Greb's bout with Chuck Wiggins on the undercard of the Dempsey-Miske title fight is derived from reports found in the Benton Harbor News-Palladium, South Bend Tribune, South Bend News-Times, Detroit News, Pittsburgh Press, Chicago Tribune, Grand Rapids Herald, and the Chicago Herald and Examiner.

25 Dickerson, E. W., Grand Rapids Herald: **DICK SAYS DEMPSEY IS A REAL CHAMPION, MISKE EASY PICKING,** September 7, 1920.

26 The account of Greb's bout with Chuck Wiggins on the undercard of the Dempsey-Miske title fight is derived from reports found in the Benton Harbor News-Palladium, South Bend Tribune, South Bend News-Times, Detroit News, Pittsburgh Press, Philadelphia Public Ledger, Grand Rapids Herald, and the Chicago Herald and Examiner.

27 Keck, Harry, Pittsburgh Gazette-Times: **Greb Still Anxious To Battle Dempsey,** September 11, 1920.

28 Milwaukee Sentinel: **CARPENTIER MAY BOX VICTOR HERE,** September 20, 1920.

29 The account of Greb's bout with Ted Jamieson in Milwaukee is derived from reports found in the Milwaukee Sentinel, Milwaukee Journal, Madison Capital Times, and Milwaukee Leader.

30 Pittsburgh Gazette-Times: **GREB SIGNS FOR 10-ROUND FIGHT WITH JACK DEMPSEY,** September 23, 1920.

31 Koeppel, Chet, Milwaukee Sentinel: **DEMPSEY-GREB SCRAP UNLIKELY,** September 24, 1920.

32 Levy, Sam, Milwaukee Journal: **Journal Readers Oppose a Dempsey-Greb Go Here,** September 25, 1920.

33 South Bend Tribune: **MAY MATCH DEMPSEY.,** September 27, 1920.

34 South Bend Tribune: **ARRANGE FOR PRELIMS TO SMITH-GREB MATCH,** September 30, 1920.

35 South Bend Tribune: **STARRING IN SPORTS,** October 12, 1920.

36 Trenton Evening Times: **COMMISSIONER CRAIN MAY BE ASKED TO TELL WHY HE CALLS CARPENTIER-LEVINSKY GO FAKE,** October 18, 1920.

37 Milwaukee Sentinel: **MANNING VAUGHN'S COLUMN,** October 15, 1920.
    Milwaukee Sentinel: **ANDREWS FAILS TO LAND MATCH,** OCtober 14, 1920.

38 Scully, M. F., South Bend News-Times: **PITTSBURGER'S FIRST BLOW BLINDS GUNNER,** October 22, 1920.

39 The account of Greb's bout with Gunboat Smith at South Bend is derived from reports found in the South Bend News-Times, South Bend Tribune, Chicago Evening American, and Chicago Post.

40 South Bend News-Times: **MATCH GREB TO FIGHT DEMPSEY AND IRISH CHAMP,** October 23, 1920.

41 The account of Greb's bout with Mickey Shannon is derived from reports found in the Pittsburgh Sun, Pittsburgh Daily Dispatch, Pittsburgh Gazette-Times, Pittsburgh Post, and Pittsburgh Press.

42 Gibson, Florent, Pittsburgh Post: **GREB HANDS MICKEY TERRIBLE CLUBBING BUT SHANNON STAYS,** October 29, 1920.

43 Gibson, Florent, Pittsburgh Post: **ONE-SIDED BOXING BOUTS HURT SPORT; GAMBLING ELEMENT,** October 31, 1920.

44 Ibid.

45 Pittsburgh Gazette-Times: **Greb Ordered to Fight Madden or Be Barred,** November 2, 1920.

46 Kalamazoo Gazette: **BOXERS CLAIM VICTORY NOW!,** November 10, 1920.

47 The description of Greb's bout with Bartley Madden at Kalamazoo is derived from reports found in the Kalamazoo Gazette.

48 New Orleans Times-Picayune: **GREB ARRIVES FOR MONDAY SCRAP HERE,** November 13, 1920.

49 Ibid.

50 Koeppel, Chet, Milwaukee Sentinel: *"GREB CAN WHIP DEMPSEY" -KANE*, November 19, 1920.

51 The account of Greb's bout with Bob Moha at Milwaukee is derived from reports found in the Milwaukee Journal, Milwaukee Sentinel, and Milwaukee Leader.

52 Andrews, T. S., Milwaukee Journal: *How Harry Greb Bluffed V. Moha*, November 24, 1920.

53 The account of Mickey Shannon's death is derived from reports found in the Cumberland Evening Times, Pittsburgh Gazette-Times, Pittsburgh Sun, Pittsburgh Daily Dispatch, and Pittsburgh Post.

54 The account of Greb's bout with Jack Duffy at Pittsburgh is derived from reports found in the Pittsburgh Post, Pittsburgh Gazette-Times, Pittsburgh Daily Dispatch, and Pittsburgh Press.

55 The account of Jack Dempsey's title defense against Bill Brennan is derived from reports found in the New York Times, New York Tribune, New York Evening Telegram, Brooklyn Standard Union, and Brooklyn Daily Eagle.

56 Pittsburgh Daily Dispatch: *Motor Square Club Offers $50,000 For Jack Dempsey to Meet Greb*, December 15, 1920.

57 The account of Greb's bout with Captain Bob Roper at Boston is derived from reports found in the Boston Post, Boston Herald, Boston Globe, and Boston Evening Transcript.

58 Peet, William, Pittsburgh Daily Dispatch: *Greb and Mason Split; Engle Is to Manage The Garfield Battler*, December 31, 1920.

59 Peet, William, Pittsburgh Daily Dispatch: *Pride of Garfield Gives Bayonne Man Neat Boxing Lesson*, December 26, 1920.

60 The account of Greb's bout with Jeff Smith at Pittsburgh is derived from reports found in the Pittsburgh Daily Dispatch, Pittsburgh Post, Pittsburgh Gazette-Times, Pittsburgh Press, and Pittsburgh Sun.

NOTES

CHAPTER 16

1 Welsh, Regis, Pittsburgh Post: *LOCAL BOXER DROPS VETERAN PILOT AS RESULT OF MATCHES*, December 31, 1920.

2 Correspondence between Harry Greb and George Engel, Author's collection.

3 Ibid.

4 Pittsburgh Post: *FORMER LOCAL FIGHT FAN WANTS TO STAGE GREB-GIBBONS MATCH*, January 12, 1921.

5 Pittsburgh Post: *The Morning Hatchet*, January 12, 1921.

6 Pittsburgh Post: *The Morning Hatchet*, January 14, 1921.

7 Dallas Morning News: *Celmers Must Pay For Greb's Teeth*, January 19, 1921.

8 Dallas Daily Times Herald: *"Bigger They Are The Harder They Fall," Says Greb; Hot After Dempsey; Believes Wills or Frenchman Could Whip Champion*, January 19, 1921.

9 Dallas Morning News: *Celmers Must Pay For Greb's Teeth*, January 19, 1921.

10 The account of Greb's bout with Johnny Celmars at Dallas is derived from reports found in the Dallas Daily Times Herald, Fort Worth Star-Telegram, and Dallas Morning News.

11 The account of Greb's bout with Pal Reed at Boston is derived from reports found in the Boston Herald, Boston Globe, Boston Post, and Boston Daily Advertiser.

12 Saunders, Daniel J., Boston Globe: *JEFF SMITH HERE, READY FOR HIS BATTLE WITH HARRY GREB IN MECHANIC'S TOMORROW NIGHT,* February 24, 1921.

13 The account of Greb's bout with Jeff Smith at Boston is derived from reports found in the Boston Post, Boston Herald, and Boston Globe.

14 Almy, Doc, Boston Post: *Boxing Gossip,* February 28, 1921.

15 Guy, Richard, Pittsburgh Leader: *The Sporting Editor's Musings,* March 18, 1921.

16 Pittsburgh Post, March 1, 1921.

17 The account of Greb's bout with Jack Renault in Pittsburgh is derived from reports found in the Pittsburgh Post, Pittsburgh Leader, Pittsburgh Press, Pittsburgh Sun, and Pittsburgh Gazette-Times.

18 The account of the rematch between Johnny Wilson and Mike O'Dowd is derived from reports found in the Pittsburgh Press, New York Times, New York Morning Telegraph, New York Tribune, New York Evening Telegram, New York Sun, Brooklyn Daily Eagle, Brooklyn Standard Union, and Boston Globe.

19 New Orleans Item: *Madden Shows Littleton How Greb Battles,* March 26, 1921.

20 New Orleans Times-Picayune: *HARRY GREB COMES FOR FRIDAY'S BOUT; WORKS AT MANDOT'S,* March 31, 1921.

21 New Orleans Times-Picayune: *"Friday Is April Fool Day," Says "Happy"; Greb Smiles,* April 1, 1921.

22 The account of Greb's bout with Happy Littleton is derived from reports found in the New Orleans States, New Orleans Times-Picayune, and New Orleans Item.

23 Keefe, Wm. McG., New Orleans Times-Picayune: *PITTSBURGH WARRIOR IS TOO EXPERIENCED; HAP TRIES GALLANTLY,* April 2, 1921.

24 The account of Greb's bout with Jack Renault at Montreal is derived from reports found in the Montreal Gazette, Montreal Star, Le Devoir, and La Presse.

25 The account of Greb's bout with Soldier Jones at Toronto is derived from reports found in the Toronto Star, Toronto Globe, and Toronto Evening Telegram.

26 Rothman, Sheila M., *Living in the Shadow of Death: Tuberculosis and the Social Experience of Illness in American History*. Baltimore: The Johns Hopkins University Press, 1995.
    Interview with Dr. Lee B. Reichman, 2012.

27 Utica Morning Telegram: *GREB WILL FIGHT AT SARANAC LAKE,* April 22, 1921.

28 Pittsburgh Daily Dispatch: *BENEFIT CARD MADE PUBLIC; GREB NOT ON,* April 25, 1921.

29 Utica Morning Telegram: *GREB WILL FIGHT AT SARANAC LAKE,* April 22, 1921.

30 Pittsburgh Daily Dispatch: *Harry Greb And Madden Are Matched,* April 28, 1921.

31 The account of Greb's benefit bout with Bartley Madden is derived from reports found in the Pittsburgh Leader, Pittsburgh Daily Dispatch, Pittsburgh Post, Pittsburgh Gazette-Times, and Pittsburgh Press.

32 The account of Greb's bout with Jimmy Darcy at Boston is derived from reports found in the Boston Herald, Boston Post, and Boston Globe. the Boston Globe stated that the knockdown occured in the fourth round.

33 New Orleans States: *20 Rounds? Yes, If Paid For It -- Greb. Ring Sharps Make Harry 7-5 Shot,* May 20, 1921.

34 The account of Greb's bout with Jeff Smith at New Orleans is derived from reports found in the New Orleans States, New Orleans Times-Picayune, and New Orleans Item.

35 South Bend Tribune: *WIGGINS CONFIDENT HE CAN WHIP HARRY GREB,* May 27, 1921.

36 South Bend Tribune: *GREB HERE TO TRAIN FOR WIGGINS CONTEST,* May 24, 1921.

37 South Bend News-Times: *GEORGES UNABLE TO REFEREE HERE,* May 26, 1921.

38 South Bend Tribune: *WIGGINS CONFIDENT HE CAN WHIP HARRY GREB,* May 27, 1921.

39 South Bend News-Times: *HOOSIER IN FAST FINISH TO EQUAL GREB'S BIG LEAD,* May 29, 1921.

40 Fitzgerald, C. F., New York Tribune: *Joe Jeanette Knocked Flat By Carpentier,* June 7, 1921.

41 Farrell, Henry L., South Bend News-Times: *CARPENTIER MADE 'BOOT' IN PASSING UP AMERICAN PUGS,* June 22, 1921.

42 Keck, Harry, Pittsburgh Gazette-Times: *BATTLE OF KEEN RIVALS ASSURED FOR NEW YORK,* June 15, 1921.

43 Fitzgerald, C. F., New York Tribune: *Georges Invited To Watch Rival Train for Bout,* June 10, 1921.

44 White, Ralph H., Terre Haute Tribune: *WIGGINS OUT TO HAND HARRY GREB LACING,* June 21, 1921.

45 White, Ralph H., Terre Haute Tribune: *GREB ARRIVES HERE FOR GO WITH WIGGINS,* June 22, 1921.

46 M'Afee, Olin E., Terre Haute Star: *OPEN AIR BOUTS LIKED BY FANS,* June 24, 1921.

47 Pittsburgh Chronicle-Telegraph: *DEMPSEY CELEBRATES HIS 26TH BIRTHDAY BY 24-HOUR LAYOFF; GREB NOT TO JOIN JACK'S STAFF,* June 24, 1921.

48 Boyle, Havey J., Pittsburgh Chronicle-Telegraph: *THROUGH THE SPORT LENS,* June 29, 1921.

49 Ibid.

50 Pittsburgh Daily Dispatch: *GREB PROMISED MATCH IF CHAMPION WINS,* July 1, 1921.

51 Pittsburgh Daily Dispatch: *Dempsey Confident As Big Mille Nears,* July 1, 1921.

52 The account of Dempsey's title defense against Georges Carpentier is derived from reports found in the Pittsburgh Press, Pittsburgh Gazette-Times, Pittsburgh Daily Dispatch, New York Times, New York Tribune, Brooklyn Standard Union, New York Evening Call, and Brooklyn Daily Eagle.

53 Peet, William, Pittsburgh Daily Dispatch: *Struggle Ends in 4th Round With Champion Standing Over Victim,* July 3, 1921.

54 Boyle, Havey J., Pittsburgh Chronicle-Telegraph: *THROUGH THE SPORT LENS,* July 13, 1921.

55 Peet, William, Pittsburgh Daily Dispatch: *Not News but Views,* July 14, 1921.

56 Peet, William, Pittsburgh Daily Dispatch: *FIGHT STUFF,* August 14, 1921.

57 Smith, Frank, Chicago Tribune: *Johnny Wilson to Take on Greb at E. Chicago Aug. 16,* July 24, 1921.

58 The account of Johnny Wilson's controversial bout with Bryan Downey at Cleveland is derived from reports found in the Cleveland Press and Cleveland Plain Dealer.

59 Peet, William, Pittsburgh Daily Dispatch: *Not News but Views,* August 21, 1921.

60 Keck, Harry, Pittsburgh Gazette-Times: *Greb-Norfolk Bout Given Official O. K.,* August 27, 1921.

61 Keck, Harry, Pittsburgh Gazette-Times: *Club Invites Probe Of Greb-Norfolk Bout,* August 23, 1921.

62 The account of Greb's exhibition bout with Johnny Howard at the third annual Victory Field Day in Pittsburgh is derived from reports found in the Pittsburgh Gazette-Times, Pittsburgh Daily Dispatch, and Pittsburgh Press.

63 The account of Harry Greb's bout with Kid Norfolk at Pittsburgh is derived from reports found in the Pittsburgh Post, Pittsburgh Press, Pittsburgh Sun, Pittsburgh Chronicle-Telegraph, Pittsburgh Leader, Pittsburgh Gazette-Times, and Pittsburgh Daily Dispatch.

64 While the Sun voted for Norfolk its report is so similar in structure and wording to that of the Chronicle-Telegraph and Gazette-Times that it seems possible if not likely that this report was also a rewritten version of Keck's article.

65 Welsh, Regis, Pittsburgh Post: **VERDICT WOULD HAVE GONE TO GREB, STATES BOUT REFEREE**, August 31, 1921.

66 Keck, Harry, Pittsburgh Gazette-Times: **WILSON-DOWNEY BATTLE FEATURES LABOR DAY CARD**, September 6, 1921.

67 Pittsburgh Leader: **BOXING**, September 3, 1921.

68 It has since become vogue for recent historians to second guess exactly when Harry Greb lost the sight in his right eye. The author prefers to take the word of Greb's physicians and close friends who knew better than anyone today and stated categorically that he lost his vision during the fight with Kid Norfolk in 1921.
   This trend likely came about due to the misinformation which originally surrounded the event during and immediately after Greb's life. Several sources close to Greb, but likely unaware of the extent to which his eye was damaged until the condition was made public after his death, told different stories in later years as to the extent of his blindness and it's origin. Red Mason who was never told and never fully aware of its extent stated that Greb only suffered a cataract. This however was the story Greb had released publicly and was refuted by the physicians who looked after Greb's eyes. As Mason was not acting as Greb's manager when the injury occurred he would not have been privy to the information.
   When Greb and Mason finally reconciled Greb would have kept it from Mason knowing that he would use it against Greb if they ever split again. Indeed, it is unlikely that George Engel was ever told the extent of the injury as well, as his stories often varied wildly from the official version of events, though it must be noted that Engel was a most unreliable source.
   Another source of confusion is the fact that Harry left the ring after the Norfolk fight without any outward sign of trauma. However, interviews conducted with Dr. Margaret Goodman, formerly of the Nevada State Athletic Commission and Dr. Howard Schatz, a prominent retinal specialist and boxing enthusiast, note that it is not uncommon to suffer an injury of this sort (likely a retinal detachment) without visible signs of injury. In fact a retinal tear, which can lead to detachment is often experienced with little or no symptoms discerned by the victim. Unreliable anecdotal sources record Red Mason stating that Greb often complained of a "ball of fire" before his eye, which, if those sources are accurate, would indicate a retinal tear. However, Greb researchers should be wary about giving this statement too much credence as the original source for the story is Mason, who was kept in the dark about Greb's condition.

69 The account of Greb's bout with Wiggins at Ashland, Kentucky is derived from reports found in the Huntington Advertiser, and Huntington Herald Dispatch.

70 The account of Johnny Wilson's bout with Bryan Downey at Boyle's Thirty Acres is derived from reports found in the New York Times, New York Morning Telegraph, New York Tribune, New York Evening World, New York Evening Telegram, Boston Globe, Jersey Journal, and Brooklyn Daily Eagle.

71 New York Morning Telegraph: **WILSON SCORED BY BOXING CHIEFS**, September 9, 1921.

72 The account of Greb's bout with Joe Cox is derived from reports found in the New York Evening Telegram, New York Tribune, New York Times, New York Evening World, New York Herald, and Brooklyn Daily Eagle.

73 Underwood, George B., New York Evening Telegram: **GREB NOW READY FOR BEST OF 'EM**, September 21, 1921.

74 Buffalo Morning Express: **SPORT DAY by DAY**, October 21, 1921.

75 The account of Greb's bout with Jimmy Darcy at Buffalo is derived from reports found in the Buffalo Courier, Buffalo Morning Express, Buffalo Evening News, and Buffalo Enquirer

76 New York Herald, November 3, 1921.

77 The account of Greb's bout with Charlie Weinert is derived from reports found in the New York Evening Telegram, New York Herald, Newark Star-Eagle, New York Daily News, New York Tribune, New York Times, Newark Evening News, New York Evening World, and Brooklyn Standard Union.

NOTES

CHAPTER 17

1 This assertion by Shade's representatives is not supported by Australian sources. Shade did defeat Australian middleweight champion Tommy Uren but if that title did indeed change hands there is no indication that any of the other titles did. In fact it is unlikely that Shade could have physically made the weight necessary to win a welterweight championship of Australia.

2 The account of Greb's bout with Billy Shade in Pittsburgh is derived from reports found in the Pittsburgh Post, Pittsburgh Daily Dispatch, Pittsburgh Press, and Pittsburgh Gazette-Times.

3 Welsh, Regis, Pittsburgh Post: **GREB RENEWS CONTRACT WITH ENGEL; SPIKES RUMOR OF RETURN TO MASON,** November 28, 1921.

4 The account of Greb's bout with Homer Smith at Newark is derived from reports found in the Newark Star-Eagle and Newark Evening News.

5 New York Tribune: **Johnny Wilson Cancels Bout With Harry Greb in Garden,** January 3, 1922.

6 The account of Greb's bout with Fay Keiser at Philadelphia is derived from reports found in the Philadelphia Public Ledger, Philadelphia Inquirer, Philadelphia Evening Bulletin, and Philadelphia Evening Public Ledger.

7 Treanor, Vincent, New York Evening World: **V. Treanor's COLUMN,** December 13, 1921.

8 Hawthorne, Fred, New York Tribune: **Leonard Offered 50 Per Cent Of Gate for Bout at Garden,** December 14, 1921.

9 The account of Greb's bout with Whitey Allen at Syracuse is derived from reports found in the Syracuse Journal, Syracuse Post Standard, and Syracuse Herald.

10 Vila, Joe, New York Sun: **Setting the Pace,** December 30, 1921.

11 The account of Greb's bout with Chuck Wiggins at Cincinnati is derived from reports found in the Cincinnati Enquirer, Cincinnati Post, Cincinnati Commercial-Tribune, and Cincinnati Times-Star.

12 Cincinnati Enquirer: **SHADE FOR GREB,** January 3, 1922.

13 Cincinnati Enquirer: **WILSON TURNS DOWN MATCH,** January 3, 1922.

14 New York Times: **WILSON IS BARRED BY N. Y. COMMISSION,** January 4, 1922.

15 New York Tribune: **Boxing Body Would Bar Johnny Wilson One Year,** January 17, 1922.

16 Lawrence, Jack, New York Tribune:**Wilson Must Go Through With Greb Bout, Commission Rules,** January 18, 1922.

17 Grand Rapids Herald: **HARRY GREB BOXES HUGH WALKER HERE INSTEAD OF BOB ROPER,** January 25, 1922.

18 Grand Rapids Herald: **GREB IS NOTIFIED BY BIGGER THAT RULES MUST BE ENFORCED,** January 27, 1922.

19 Grand Rapids Herald: **GREB READILY AGREES TO POSTPONEMENT OF HIS CONTEST HERE,** January 27, 1922.

20 Ibid.

21 Dickerson, E. W., Grand Rapids Herald: **Dick's Dope,** January 25, 1922.

22 Grand Rapids Herald: **Greg To Meet Gibbons,** January 31, 1922.

23 The account of Greb's bout with Hugh Walker at Grand Rapids Herald is derived from reports found in the Grand Rapids Herald and Grand Rapids Press.

24 Grand Rapids Herald: *HARRY GREB CLEARLY OUTPOINTS HUGH WALKER IN ARMORY BOUT,* February 2, 1922.

25 The account of Greb's bout against Jeff Smith at Cincinnati is derived from reports found in the Cincinnati Post, Cincinnati Enquirer, and Cincinnati Commercial-Tribune.

26 Greb, Harry, The Ring: *My Hardest Fight,* February, 1925.

27 Ibid.

28 Doyle, Charles J., Pittsburgh Gazette-Times: *GREB AND OTHERS PLEASE IN CASEYS' BOXING SHOW,* February 26, 1922.

29 Uppercut, Pittsburgh Daily Dispatch: *LYCEUM HOLDS SMOKER; HARRY GREB, HERB WADDELL AND OTHERS FEATURE EVENTS,* February 27, 1922.

30 Pittsburgh Chronicle-Telegraph: *KEARNS'S COLOR LINE EXCUSE SAID TO BE MERE SUBTERFUGE TO ESCAPE LIKELY CHALLENGER,* February 17, 1922.

31 Pittsburgh Daily Dispatch: *Georges Carpentier Will Fight Winner Of Elimination Series in United States,* February 4, 1922.

32 Lawrence, Jack, New York Tribune: *Brilliant Crowd at Garden Will See Greb-Gibbons Bout,* March 12, 1922.

33 Pittsburgh Chronicle-Telegraph: *CHAMPION BEMOANS INABILITY TO FIND SUITABLE OPPONENT; TIRED OF THEATRICAL DUTIES,* February 16, 1922.

34 New York Sun: *14,000 Seats Requested For Greb-Gibbons bout,* February 25, 1922.

35 Runyon, Damon, Cincinnati Enquirer: *KEARNS MEETS MULLINS,* February 21, 1922.

36 Pittsburgh Daily Dispatch: *Harry Greb Blows Into Big Town, Looking Fit and Apparently Sure He Can Stow Away Brother Gibbons,* March 3, 1922.

37 Rickard was being sued by a former business associate, Frank C. Armstrong, the suit threatened to place Rickard's business dealings in receivership. In addition to this Rickard was indicted on charges of sexual assault against three young girls, aged 11, 12, and 15.

38 The account of Harry Wills' elimination bout against Kid Norfolk is derived from reports found in the New York Times, New York Tribune, New York Daily News, New York Evening World, New York Evening Telegram, Queensborough Daily Star, New York Evening Post, Brooklyn Standard Union, New York Age, New York Call, and Yonkers Statesman and News.

39 Pittsburgh Daily Dispatch: *TOM GIBBONS AND HARRY GREB COMPLETE PREPARATIONS FOR FIGHT ON MONDAY -PITTSBURGER OUTWEIGHED,* March 10, 1922.

40 Keats, Fred, New York Sun: *Boxing Needs Larger Arenas,* March 10, 1922.

41 Rice, Grantland, New York Tribune: *The SPORTLIGHT,* March 11, 1922.

42 Boyle, Havey J., Pittsburgh Chronicle-Telegraph: *THROUGH THE SPORT LENS,* March 7, 1922.

43 The account of Greb's bout with Tommy Gibbons at Madison Square Garden is derived from reports found in the New York Times, New York Tribune, New York Daily News, Pittsburgh Leader, New York Sun, New York Evening World, Pittsburgh Gazette-Times, New York Morning Telegraph, Pittsburgh Chronicle-Telegraph, Philadelphia Inquirer, Brooklyn Daily Eagle, Queensborough Daily Star, Brooklyn Standard Union, Philadelphia Evening Public Ledger, New York Evening Telegram, New York Post, Pittsburgh Press, New York Evening Mail, Grand Rapids Herald, and New York Call.

44 McGeehan, W. O., Pittsburgh Daily Dispatch: *Pittsburg Lad Gains Big Lead On Famed Rival,* March 14, 1922.

45 Guy, Richard, Pittsburgh Leader: *The Sporting Editor's Musings,* March 14, 1922.

46 Tunney, Gene, **ARMS FOR LIVING**. New York, N.Y.: Wilfred Funk, Inc, 1941.

47 Greb, Harry, Illinois State Journal: **Refusal To Let Gibbons Get Set Won Battle For Me, Harry Greb Declares,** March 17, 1922.

48 Greb, Harry, Illinois State Journal: **Need Not Be Giant To Win Fight Championship, Says Greb; Speed Is Big Asset,** March 18, 1922.

49 Greb, Harry, Illinois State Journal: **Gibbons Struck Only 3 Hard Blows, Greb Claims; Each Carried Knockout,** March 19, 1922.

50 Greb, Harry, Illinois State Journal: **Gibbons Outgamed, Fight Should Silence Critics Is Claim Of Harry Greb,** March 20, 1922.

51 Greb, Harry, Illinois State Journal: **Could Outbox Dempsey, Is Harry Greb's View; Hopes For Fight With Champion,** March 21, 1922.

52 Greb, Harry, Illinois State Journal: **"Wilson and Tunney With Titles Are Made For Me" Says Gibbon's Conqueror,** March 22, 1922.

NOTES

CHAPTER 18

1 Pittsburgh Leader: **Harry Greb And Engel Reach Here,** March 20, 1922.

2 Keck, Harry, Pittsburgh Gazette-Times: **Welcome Home Keeps Greb Hopping; Forced to Show Best Footwork,** March 21, 1922.

3 Pittsburgh Daily Dispatch: **HARRY GREB IS HONORED BY FRIENDS AT BANQUET,** March 24, 1922.

4 Pittsburgh Gazette-Times: **GREB IS FETED AGAIN; LEAVES FOR TORONTO,** March 27, 1922.

5 New York Morning Telegraph: **DEMPSEY TELLS PLANS FOR ENGLISH TRIP,** March 21, 1922.

6 Toronto Globe-Mail: **Harry Greb Entertains Convalescent Soldiers,** March 29, 1922.

7 Keck, Harry, Pittsburgh Gazette-Times: **Local Boy Is Beaten Badly by Gene Tunney at Motor Square,** April 11, 1922.

8 Graham, Frank, New York Sun: **GREB SURE OF BEATING JACK,** April 19, 1922.

9 Dawson, James, Pittsburgh Gazette-Times: **GREB-TUNNEY BOUT AWAITS AGREEMENT ON TERMS; CARP SOUGHT FOR PITTSBURGHER,** April 27, 1922.

10 Newman, Harry, Buffalo Morning Express: **CARPENTIER IS CABLED OFFER FOR A MATCH,** April 27, 1922.

11 The account of Tunney's bout with Levinsky is derived from reports found in the New York Times, New York Tribune, Brooklyn Daily Eagle, Philadelphia Evening Public Ledger, New York Evening World, New York Evening Telegram, Queensborough Daily Star, and Yonkers Statesman.

12 Sullivan, Timothy, Pittsburgh Daily Dispatch: **Greb Is Favorite By 6 to 5,** May 21, 1922.

13 The account of Greb's bout with Al Roberts at Boston is derived from reports found in the Boston Post, Boston Herald, Boston Globe, Boston American, and Boston Traveler.

14 Pittsburgh Gazette-Times: *Boston Scribes Pan Greb After Victory Against Al Roberts,* May 14, 1922.

15 Sullivan, Timothy, Pittsburgh Daily Dispatch: *Greb Hitting Better; Is All Set for Gene,* May 19, 1922.

16 Edgren, Bob, New York Evening World: *Edgren Sees It,* May 15, 1922.

17 New York Morning Telegraph: *GREB IS CONFIDENT OF BEATING TUNNEY,* May 20, 1922.

18 Walsh, Davis J., Saint Louis Post-Dispatch: *Bagley Expects Tunney to Beat Greb by Knockout,* May 22, 1922.

19 Jack Lawrence of the New York Tribune quoted odds of 7 to 5 in favor of Greb while Harry Keck quoted odds of 2 to 1 in favor in Greb the day before the fight. Hype Igoe quoted odds of 3 to 1 in favor of Greb.

20 Interestingly Jim Jab, in his report the following day, claimed that it was Tunney who demanded Greb's hands be rewrapped. This is refuted by Tunney himself in his book "A Man Must Fight" as he recounts George Engel demanding the bandages be removed, although he leaves out the part about the hard tape being wound on his hands. Regis Welsh also alluded to the fact that it was Tunney who had "loaded" wraps when he fought Greb in his column of the November 26, 1922 found in the Pittsburgh Post, as well as his column found in the February 18, 1923 edition of the Pittsburgh Post.

21 The account of Greb's bout with Gene Tunney is derived from reports found in the New York Tribune, New York Times, New York Daily News, Pittsburgh Gazette-Times, New York Evening World, New York Sun, Pittsburgh Daily Dispatch, Brooklyn Daily Eagle, Philadelphia Evening Public Ledger, Pittsburgh Press, New York Evening Telegram, Brooklyn Standard Union, New York Evening Call, New York Post, and Yonkers Statesman and News.

22 Lawrence, Jack, New York Tribune: *Pittsburgh Boxer Outpoints Gene Tunney by Wide Margin,* May 24, 1922.

23 Van Every, Ed, *The Life of Gene Tunney: The Fighting Marine*. New York: Dell Publishing Co., 1926.

24 Jack Lawrence of the Tribune claimed it was the first blow, a long left, of the fight that broke Tunney's nose. James Dawson writing for the Times agreed that it had been a looping left hook at the start of the fight which started the blood from Tunney's nose. The Daily News also stated that it was a left in the first round. William Peet of the Pittsburgh Daily Dispatch stated it was a right "jab" in the first that brought the blood from Tunney's nose. George Underwood of the Evening Telegram also stated it was the first punch of the fight which broke Tunney's nose, despite being squarely in Tunney's camp and going so far as to call the bout a draw. Westbrook Pegler in the Call also stated it was a left, the fourth punch thrown, that drew blood from Tunney's nose. Tunney himself indicated that the clash of heads which produced the cut in the sixth round was accidental when interviewed immediately after the fight: "I guess I got a pretty tough break. When our heads came together it was my eye that opened. It could have happened to Greb Instead of to me, but the luck was the other way."

25 Pittsburgh Daily Dispatch: *Tunney to Receive Return Match With Greb, Engel States,* June 4, 1922.

26 Pittsburgh Chronicle-Telegraph: *Dempsey Says Greb Is Too Light to Get Title Fight,* May 25, 1922.

27 New York Times: *Rickard to Offer $150,000 For Greb-Carpentier Bout,* May 24, 1922.

28 Walsh, Davis J., Illinois State Register: *RICKARD ASKS CARPENTIER TO BOX HARRY GREB,* May 24, 1922.

29 New York Times: *CARPENTIER READY TO DEFEND TITLE,* May 26, 1922.

30 Pittsburgh Daily Dispatch: *Tunney to Receive Return Match With Greb, Engel States,* June 4, 1922.

31 Mathison, Charles F., Pittsburgh Daily Dispatch: *Georges Avoids Greb,* June 12, 1922.

32 Pittsburgh Gazette-Times: *ENGEL TO CLAIM CARP'S WORLD'S TITLE FOR GREB,* June 19, 1922.

33 Pittsburgh Daily Dispatch: *Wilson Must Fight Harry Greb,* June 7, 1922.

34 Boyle, Havey, Pittsburgh Chronicle-Telegraph: *THROUGH THE SPORT LENSE,* June 16, 1922.

35 Pittsburgh Gazette-Times: *COMMISSION RULES OUT WILSON FOR NOT SIGNING TO BOX GREB,* June 24, 1922.

36 Pittsburgh Chronicle-Telegraph: *HUGHEY WALKER DUE HERE TODAY,* June 23, 1922.

37 The account of Greb's bout with Hugh Walker at Pittsburgh is derived from reports found in the Pittsburgh Gazette-Times, Pittsburgh Chronicle-Telegraph, Pittsburgh Daily Dispatch, Pittsburgh Press, and Pittsburgh Post.

38 Peet, William, Pittsburgh Daily Dispatch: *Greb-Dempsey Matched Here On Labor Day,* June 28, 1922.

39 Dawson, James, New York Times: *DEMPSEY-GREB BOUT IS NOW SUGGESTED,* June 29, 1922.

40 Chicago Tribune: *JACK IN FLYING VISIT,* July 7, 1922.

41 Chicago Tribune: *DEMPSEY-WILLS FAIL TO AGREE ON TERMS FOR GO,* July 9, 1922.

42 New York Times: *KEARNS WAITS FOR $100,000 PROMOTER,* July 10, 1922.

43 New York Times: *WILL NOT PROMOTE BOUT ON LABOR DAY,* July 10, 1922.

44 Jaffe, Louis H., Pittsburgh Gazette-Times: *Tommy Loughran Ring Sensation; Looms as Opponent for Dempsey,* February 19, 1922.

45 The account of Greb's first bout with Tommy Loughran is derived from reports found in the Philadelphia Evening Bulletin, Philadelphia Public Ledger, Philadelphia Inquirer, Philadelphia Record, and Philadelphia Evening Public Ledger.

46 Philadelphia Evening Bulletin: *"I Can Beat Harry Greb Any Time," Asserts Tommy Loughran, and He Did,* July 11, 1922.

47 New York Times: *GREB AND MANAGER DRAW SUSPENSIONS,* July 19, 1922.

48 The account of the Rosenberg-Krug "championship fight" is derived from reports found in the New York Times, New York Tribune, New York Evening World, New York Evening Telegram, New York Evening Post, Yonkers Statesman and News, Brooklyn Daily Eagle, Brooklyn Standard Union, and New York Call.

49 Benson, Peter, *BATTLING SIKI.* Fayettville: The University of Arkansas Press, 2006.

50 Chicago Tribune: *GREB READY TO ACCEPT,* July 27, 1922.

51 The account of Greb's bout in Toronto against Al Benedict is derived from reports found in the Toronto Evening Telegram, Toronto Globe-Mail, and Toronto Star.

52 Grand Rapids Press: *GREB, GIANT KILLER, IS SURE HE CAN WHIP DEMPSEY,* September 29, 1922.

53 The account of Greb's bout with Bob Roper at Grand Rapids is derived from reports found in the Grand Rapids Herald, and Grand Rapids Press.

54 New York Times: *HARRY GREB ASKS FOR REINSTATEMENT,* October 3, 1922.

55 New York Times: *COMMISSION READY TO REINSTATE GREB,* October 4, 1922.

56 New York Times: *BOXING COMMISSION REINSTATES GREB,* October 7, 1922.

57 The account of Greb's bout with Larry Williams is derived from reports found in the Providence Evening Bulletin, and Providence Journal.

58 Buffalo Morning Express: *GREB COVETS THE DECISION OVER ROPER,* November 1, 1922.

59 Pittsburgh Post: *ENGEL OFFERS TO SEND GREB AGAINST JOHNSON, BRENNAN SAME NIGHT,* November 4, 1922.

60 The account of Greb's bout with Bob Roper at Buffalo is derived from reports found in the Buffalo Evening News, Buffalo Courier, Buffalo Morning Express, and Buffalo Enquirer.

61 Welsh, Regis M., Pittsburgh Post: *BREAK COMES AFTER REPEATED RUMORS; MAY GO TO MASON,* November 19, 1922.

62 Keck, Harry, Pittsburgh Sun-Telegraph: *SPORTS,* August 29, 1947.

63 Davis, Ralph, Pittsburgh Press: *Ralph Davis' Column,* November 23, 1922.

64 Pittsburgh Post: *TUNNEY MATCH IS SCHEDULED DEC. 29, DAY CONTRACT ENDS,* November 21, 1922.

65 New York Evening Telegram: *Greb Training Here,* January 10, 1923.

66 Davis, Ralph, Pittsburgh Press: **Ralph Davis' Column,** December 9, 1922.

67 Welsh, Regis M., Pittsburgh Post: **Greb Admits Strained Relations With Engel,** November 18, 1922.

68 Lawrence, Jack, New York Tribune: **Harry Greb Severs Relations With Manager George Engel,** November 21, 1922.

69 Lawrence, Jack, New York Tribune: **Boxing Commission Insists on Greb-Tunney Bout in Garden,** November 23, 1922.

70 Pegler, Westbrook, Pittsburgh Post: **"OUGHT TO RUN OUT OF MATCH" OPINION OF EASTERN EXPERT,** November 24, 1922.

71 Pittsburgh Post: **Greb in New York,** November 24, 1922.

72 Davis, Ralph, Pittsburgh Press: **Ralph Davis' Column,** December 9, 1922.

73 Pittsburgh Press: **BIG CROWD TO SEE GREB AND ROPER BATTLE,** December 27, 1922.

74 The account of Greb's bout with Bob Roper at Pittsburgh is derived from reports found in the Pittsburgh Leader, Pittsburgh Press, Pittsburgh Post, Pittsburgh Daily Dispatch, and Pittsburgh Gazette-Times.

NOTES

CHAPTER 19

1 Welsh, Regis, Pittsburgh Post: **MOVE MAY PAVE WAY TO REUNION; CHAMP STILL UNDECIDED,** January 15, 1923.

2 The account of Greb's exhibition bout with Frank Munroe in which Red Mason was his second is derived from reports found in the Pittsburgh Daily Dispatch, Pittsburgh Post, Pittsburgh Gazette-Times, and Pittsburgh Press.

3 The account of Greb's bout with Tommy Loughran in Pittsburgh is derived from reports found in the Pittsburgh Gazette-Times, Pittsburgh Leader, Pittsburgh Daily Dispatch, Pittsburgh Post, and Pittsburgh Press.

4 Pittsburgh Post: **FRENCH AUTHORITIES TRYING TO FIND WAY TO DETHRONE CHAMP,** January 17, 1923.

5 Ibid.

6 Pittsburgh Daily Dispatch: **Signs Articles With Former Manager For One Year of Fights,** January 24, 1923.

7 The account of Greb's bout with Billy Shade at Jersey City is derived from reports found in the Newark Star Eagle, New York Daily News, New York Sun, New York Evening Telegram, New York Evening World, New York Tribune, New York Times, Brooklyn Daily Eagle, and New York Evening Call.

8 Welsh, Regis, Pittsburgh Post: **MATING OF OLD PAIR TO MEAN INTENSIVE DRIVE FOR MATCHES,** January 24, 1923.

9 Ibid.

10 Pittsburgh Daily Dispatch: **Will Fight Anyone; Greb Is Ordered To Complete Tunney Go,** January 24, 1923.

11 New York Sun: **Billy Gibson Is Now Gene Tunney's Manager,** January 23, 1923.

12 Newark Star-Eagle: **GREB OFFERS BROAD A.C. PROMOTERS $800 TO CALL OFF FIGHT WITH PAL REED,** January 24, 1923.

Pittsburgh Post: **GREB-MASON HOME FOR DAY, LEAVE TONIGHT,** January 26, 1923.

13 McGuinness, James K., New York Evening Telegram: **SPORTING SPOTLIGHT,** January 29, 1923.

14 Pittsburgh Daily Dispatch: **GIBBONS SAYS LOUGHRAN HAS CHANCE TO BEAT GREB,** January 29, 1923.

15 The account of Greb's bout with Tommy Loughran at Madison Square Garden is derived from reports found in the New York Tribune, New York Times, New York Sun, New York Evening World, New York Evening Telegram, New York Daily News, New York Call, Brooklyn Daily Eagle, New York Evening Post, Boxing Blade, Brooklyn Standard Union, and Yonkers Statesman and News.

16 Pittsburgh Post: **JOHNNY WILSON WILL BE REINSTATED SOON TO MEET TOMMY ROBSON,** February 3, 1923.

17 The account of Greb's bout with Pal Reed at Newark is derived from reports found in the New York Evening Telegram, New York Sun, New York Tribune, Newark Evening News, Newark Star-Eagle, and New York Daily News.

18 The account of Greb's bout with Young Fisher is derived from reports found in the Syracuse Post Standard, Syracuse Telegram, Syracuse Journal, and Syracuse Herald.

19 Time: **Sport: Championship Business** November 17, 1930.

20 Treanor, Vincent, New York Evening World: **V. Treanor's COLUMN,** June 13, 1922.

21 Articles of Agreement between Gene Tunney, Billy Gibson, and Max "Boo Boo" Hoff dated September 22, 1926. Authors Collection.

22 Mara eventually settled out of court with Tunney for $30,000 after a sensational trial which detailed the backroom deals and influence peddling which circumvented Harry Wills' title challenge, and placed Tunney in a position to win the championship. Much of Mara's damning testimony was supported by Tunney himself who was more interested in fending off the monetary damages than protecting his reputation.

23 Cavanaugh, Jack, **TUNNEY: BOXING'S BRAINIEST CHAMP AND HIS UPSET OF THE GREAT JACK DEMPSEY.** New York: Random House, Inc, 2006.
    Cavanaugh suggests that Tunney was an unwilling participant in such activities but the evidence throughout the latter half of Tunney's career clearly indicates that he not only condoned such methods but was an eager participant.

24 Welsh, Regis, Pittsburgh Post: **GREB-TUNNEY TITLE BOUT OFFICIALLY ANNOUNCED IN NEW YORK FOR FEB. 23,** February 15, 1923.

25 Haley's record as a referee shows him to have an unusually high amount of disqualifications rendered. Some of these were in very high profile fights showing Haley's willingness to take matters into his own hands. Such fights include O'Dowd-Rosenberg, Wills-Sharkey, and Britton-Leonard.

26 Lawrence, Jack, New York Tribune: **Greb Not Likely to Get By With Foul Tactics in Tunney Bout,** February 20, 1923.

27 New York Sun: **"Enforce Boxing Rules!" Says Tunney's Manager,** February 22, 1923.

28 New York Sun: **GREB HINTS RING PLOT AGAINST HIM,** February 22, 1923.

29 Pittsburgh Post: **MULDOON REASSURES TITLE HOLDER'S WIFE,** February 23, 1923.

30 Welsh, Regis M., Pittsburgh Post: **LOCAL FAN TELLS OF SITUATION IN PRE-FIGHT FEELING,** February 21, 1923.

31 New York Evening Telegram: **TUNNEY WEIGHS 174; GREB 165 1-2,** February 23, 1923.

32 The account of Greb's second bout with Gene Tunney is derived from reports found in the New York Morning Telegraph, New York Evening Mail, Newark Star-Eagle, Newark Evening News, New York Sun, New York Evening Telegram, New York Evening World, New York Times, New York Tribune, Syndicated columnists Davis J. Walsh, Henry L. Farrell, New York Daily News, Pittsburgh Post, Pittsburgh Gazette-Times, Brooklyn Daily Eagle, New York Herald, New York Globe, New York Evening Journal, New York Morning World, New York Evening Post, Philadelphia Public Ledger, Brooklyn Standard Union, Brooklyn Daily Times, New York Call, Pittsburgh Press, New York American, Staten Island Advance, Boxing Blade, and Ring Magazine.

How they voted:

Greb:

New York Morning Telegraph (Sam Taub) Greb won 10 of 15 rounds.
New York Morning Telegraph (James Sinnott) Greb won 8 rounds, Tunney 5, 2 even.
New York Evening Mail (Ed Hughes) The worst Greb should have gotten was a draw.
New York Evening Mail (Warren Brown) The worst Greb should have gotten was a draw.
Newark Star-Eagle (Bert Dodge) "Aside from the fourteenth round I fail to see how the officials could pick Tunney over Greb."
Brooklyn Daily Eagle (W. C. Vreeland) Greb won 8 rounds, Tunney 5, 2 even.
New York Tribune (Grantland Rice) Greb deserved the decision, at worst it could have been called a draw.
International News Service (Davis J. Walsh) Greb won 6, Tunney 5, and 4 even.
New York Herald (Charles Mathison)
New York Evening Journal (Sid Mercer)
Philadelphia Public Ledger (Louis Jaffe)
Newark Evening News
Pittsburgh Post (Regis Welsh) Tunney won only two rounds.
Pittsburgh Gazette-Times (Harry Keck) Greb won 7 rounds, Tunney 4, 4 even.
Pittsburgh Press (Jim Jab) Greb deserved the shade, no worse than a draw but even that would have been unjust.
Brooklyn Standard Union Greb won 9 rounds, Tunney 5, 1 even.
Boxing Blade (Clarence Gillespie)
Staten Island Advance (Jim Halliday) Greb won 13 rounds, Tunney 1, 1 even.
Brooklyn Daily Times Tunney won only 1 round.

Other experts who felt Greb won were:

Joe Lynch (bantamweight champion)
Frank Flournoy (Promoter/matchmaker)
Tom O'Rourke (Manager/matchmaker)
"Dumb" Dan Morgan (Manager)

Tunney:

New York Sun (Fred Keats) Tunney won more because Greb put up a poor fight than because of anything remarkable that he accomplished.
New York Evening Telegram (George Underwood)
New York Times (James Dawson) Tunney won 9 rounds, Greb 6.
New York Morning World (Bert "Hype" Igoe)
New York American (Ed Curley)
New York Globe (Dan Lyons) Tunney won 8 rounds, Greb 5, 2 even.
New York Call (Westbrook Pegler)
New York Post

Draw:

New York Evening World (Ed Van Every) Greb won 6, Tunney won 6, 3 even.
New York Tribune (Jack Lawrence) Greb won 5, Tunney won 5, 5 even.
New York Herald (Walter Trumball)
New York Daily News (Harry Newman)

33 Welsh, Regis M., Pittsburgh Post: ***Hoots, Jeers, Catcalls Greet Greenwich Villager, Departing From Ring With "Gift" Victory***, February 24, 1923.

34 Van Every, Ed, New York Evening World: ***'I WAS ROBBED,' SAYS GREB, AS TUNNEY GETS DECISION***, February 24, 1923.

35 O'Neil, Frank, New York Sun: ***GREB HOWLS AS TUNNEY WINS***, February 24, 1923.

36 New York Evening Telegram: ***AWARD INFLUENCED BY FOUL TACTICS***, February 24, 1923.

37 New York Evening World: ***REFEREE HALEY SAYS GREB FOULED FROM SECOND ROUND ON***, February 24, 1923.

38 Welsh, Regis M., Pittsburgh Post: ***GREB IS HERALDED AS ACTUAL WINNER IN MANY QUARTERS***, February 25, 1923.

39 Keats, Fred, New York Sun: ***Gene Tunney Regains Title***, February 24, 1923.

40 Underwood, George B., New York Evening Telegram: ***TUNNEY REGAINS TITLE FROM GREB***, February 24, 1923.

41 Dawson, James, New York Times: *TUNNEY REGAINS HIS RING HONORS,* February 24, 1923.

42 Igoe, Bert, New York Morning World (as printed in the St. Louis Post-Dispatch): *Tunney Regains Lightheavy Title, Defeating Greb in Rough 15-Round Contest,* February 24, 1923.

43 Lyons, Dan, New York Globe (as printed in the Pittsburgh Gazette-Times): *DETHRONED CHAMPION TO ISSUE FORMAL DEFI FOR RETURN CONTEST,* February 25, 1923.

44 Taub, Sam, New York Morning Telegraph: *NEWS OF THE SQUARED CIRCLE,* February 25, 1923.

45 Sinnott, James P., New York Morning Telegraph: *IN MID-CHANNEL,* February 25, 1923.

46 Hughes, Ed, New York Evening Mail: *Decision Depriving Greb of Light Heavyweight Crown Calls for Sweeping Inquiry,* February 24, 1923.

47 Dodge, Bert, Newark Star-Eagle: *BILLY GIBSON'S PROPAGANDA ABOUT GREB'S ALLEGED FOUL WORK FACTOR IN GENE'S WIN,* February 24, 1923.

48 Newark Evening News: *Tunney Is Again King of Division,* February 24, 1923.

49 Gillespie, Clarence S., Boxing Blade: *Gene Tunney Regains U. S. Light Heavyweight Title By Getting a Decision over Harry Greb,* March 10, 1923.

50 Vreeland, W. C., Brooklyn Daily Eagle: *Boxing Judges at Garden Decide Against Greb, Who Had Lead on Points,* February 24, 1923.

51 Van Every, Ed, New York Evening World: *'I WAS ROBBED,' SAYS GREB, AS TUNNEY GETS DECISION,* February 24, 1923.

52 Rice, Grantland, New York Tribune: *Poor Fight, and a Poor Decision, Says Rice,* February 24, 1923.

53 Newman, Harry, New York Daily News: *VILLAGE BOY BEATS ROUGH-GOING HARRY GREB,* February 24, 1923.

54 Welsh, Regis M., Pittsburgh Post: *Hoots, Jeers, Catcalls Greet Greenwich Villager, Departing From Ring With "Gift" Victory,* February 24, 1923.

55 Keck, Harry., Pittsburgh Gazette-Times: *GREB LOSES HIS TITLE IN BOUT WITH TUNNEY IN NEW YORK,* February 24, 1923.

56 Lawrence, Jack, New York Tribune: *Greb, Insisting He Was Robbed, Asks Return Bout With Tunney,* February 25, 1923.
   Mathison, Charles, New York Herald (as printed in the Pittsburgh Post): *Haley's Decision Wrong in Opinion Of Billy Muldoon,* February 25, 1923.

57 Dawson, James: *MULDOON SAYS GREB OUTPOINTED TUNNEY,* February 25, 1923.

58 Welsh, Regis M., Pittsburgh Post: *GREB IS HERALDED AS ACTUAL WINNER IN MANY QUARTERS,* February 25, 1923.

59 Doyle, Chilly, Pittsburgh Gazette-Times: *Chilly Sauce,* February 26, 1923.

60 Pittsburgh Post: *Lost title But- Won Fight, on Cup Presented Greb By Lyceum Pals,* March 12, 1923.

61 Lawrence, Jack, New York Tribune: *Muldoon's Power as Boxing Head To Be Curbed by License Board,* April 1, 1923.

62 Pittsburgh Post: *JOHNNY WILSON AND KILLILEA QUIT BUSINESS,* March 28, 1923.

63 Balinger, Edward F., Pittsburgh Post: *GREB ARRIVES FOR TRAINING AS CORSAIRS LEAVE OZARKS,* April 3, 1923.

64 Hot Springs Sentinel-Record: *HERRING-GREEN BOUT WAS A DRAW,* April 6, 1923.

65 Hot Springs Sentinel-Record: *GREB'S LONDON BOUT MAY BE CANCELLED,* April 8, 1923.

66 Keck, Harry, Pittsburgh Gazette-Times: *COMMISSION TO STAND PAT,* May 5, 1923.

67 Welsh, Regis M., Pittsburgh Post: **GREB, THREATENED WITH POISONING UNDERGOES KNIFE,** May 8, 1923.

68 The account of Greb's bout with Len Rowlands at Uniontown is derived from reports found in the Uniontown Herald, and Uniontown Daily News Standard.

69 Uniontown Herald: **OPPONENT TO BE SELECTED VERY SHORTLY,** June 18, 1923.

70 Smith, Chester L., Pittsburgh Gazette-Times: **Greb Signs to Meet Wilson,** June 24, 1923.

71 Connellsville Daily Courier: **HARRY GREB, IN POLICE MIX-UP HERE, USES FIST,** July 5, 1923.
  Pittsburgh Press: **CONNELLSVILLE OFFICERS GIVE THEIR SIDE OF CLASH IN WHICH GREB STRUCK COP,** July 6, 1923.
  Thomas, outside of the Greb case and a few other minor complaints, seems to have been a respected member of the police force in Connellsville and would eventually rise to chief of police. As reported he was a large man who weighed over 220 pounds and at least once won a fattest man competition at a local fair. Despite his size Thomas was a respected athlete who years earlier had been a crack baseball player.

72 Uniontown News Standard: **Mayor Mitchell Fires Brother Who Threatens Action,** August 14, 1923.
  Mayor Mitchell's action in firing his own brother seems to add weight to some of Greb's complaints of misconduct on the part of the Connellsville police. However, Mitchell was also being hounded by political rivals who viewed his appointment of his brother to the position as an example of nepotism despite J. W. Mitchell's twenty years of service in local law enforcement. Mayor Mitchell may have taken the opportunity to remove what he likely viewed as a political albatross from around his neck.

73 Connellsville Weekly Courier: **CITY DETECTIVE JOB ABOLISHED BY COUNCIL'S ACT,** August 30, 1923.
  Mitchell had been forced to resign as Fire Chief fifteen years earlier for a similar incident in which he had drunkenly attempted to extort money from several people.

NOTES

CHAPTER 20

1 Indiana Evening Gazette: **JACK DEMPSEY MAY MEET GREB AT JOHNSTOWN,** July 6, 1923.

2 Johnstown Tribune: **TOM O'ROURKE HERE TO CONFER WITH PROMOTERS,** August 4, 1923.

3 Johnstown Tribune: **NEWS, VIEWS & COMMENT By The SPORTS EDITOR,** August 8, 1923.

4 Johnstown Tribune: **Two Boxers Fail to Appear for Open Air Fistic Event at Ideal; Conlon Is Winner,** August 8, 1923.

5 Peet, William, Pittsburgh Post: **Treat Em Rough!,** August 8, 1923.

6 New York Sun and Globe: **GREB FAVORITE TO BEAT WILSON,** August 16, 1923.

7 Pittsburgh Gazette-Times: **New York Gamblers Charge Greb Will "Quit" in Bout For Wilson's Fight Crown,** August 8, 1923.

8 Pittsburgh Post: **GREB LEAVES TOMORROW FOR WILSON BOUT,** August 10, 1923.

9 Van Every, Ed, New York Evening World: **Greb's Little Daughter Makes Him Ambitious to Win Three Titles,** August 18, 1923.

10 New York Sun and Globe: **GREB READY FOR WILSON MATCH,** August 22, 1923.

11 New York Sun and Globe: *GREB ALREADY IS DOWN TO WEIGHT*, August 24, 1923.

12 Pittsburgh Press: *Greb in Trim for Battle*, August 26, 1923.

13 Pittsburgh Post: *STATEMENTS BY FIGHTERS*, August 31, 1923.

14 Interview with Charles DeMarco August 28, 2003.

15 Igoe, Bert, New York Morning World (as printed in the Boston Globe): *GREB WINS TITLE, BEATING WILSON*, September 1, 1923. (Quote).
   The account of Greb's world championship bout with Johnny Wilson is derived from reports found in the Pittsburgh Gazette-Times, New York Evening Telegram, New York Sun and Globe, New York Evening World, New York Morning World (via the Boston Globe), Newark Star-Eagle, New York Tribune, St. Louis Post-Dispatch, New York Times, Boston Post, New York Daily News, Pittsburgh Post, Brooklyn Daily Eagle, Boston Herald, Pittsburgh Press, Brooklyn Standard Union.

16 Pollack, John, New York Evening World: *$29,733 TO WILSON FOR LOSING TITLE; NOTHING FOR GREB*, September 4, 1923.

NOTES

CHAPTER 21

1 Coll, Ray, Pittsburgh Gazette-Times: *Mason For Go Between Greb And M'Tigue*, September 8, 1923.

2 Newark Star-Eagle: *"I NEVER FAILED TO GIVE 'EM A GOOD FIGHT AND I WON'T FOOL NEWARKERS NOW," IS PROMISE HARRY GREB MAKES*, October 18, 1923.

3 Dodge, Bert, Newark Star-Eagle: *THAT BLOODY SET-TO IS SURE PROVES MAGNET*, September 11, 1923.

4 Dodge, Bert, Newark Star-Eagle: *LUIS FIRPO WOULD LIKE TO HERE*, September 7, 1923.

5 Pittsburgh Gazette-Times: *GREB PICKS DEMPSEY TO DEFEAT FIRPO IN FOUR ROUNDS AT MOST*, September 5, 1923.

6 Arizona Republic: *Willard Says Greb Has Chance to Defeat Dempsey*, September 20, 1923.

7 Allen, Henry, Atlanta Constitution: *Mike McTigue Arrives Here On Way to Columbus to Sign Articles for Big Title Bout*, September 3, 1923.

8 Welsh, Regis, Pittsburgh Post: *BATTLE WITH WALKER MAY BRING CROWN TO YOUNGSTOWN BOY*, September 24, 1923.

9 Pittsburgh Post: *YOUNGSTOWNER GETS CHANCE OF LIFETIME IN JERSEY, MONDAY*, September 26, 1923.

10 The account of Greb's exhibition bout with George Hook is derived from reports found in the Pittsburgh Gazette-Times, Pittsburgh Post, and Pittsburgh Press.

11 The account of Greb's bout with Jimmy Darcy is derived from reports found in the Pittsburgh Post, Pittsburgh Press, and Pittsburgh Gazette-Times.

12 The account of the first bout between Young Stribling and Mike McTigue is derived from reports found in the Columbus Ledger, Atlanta Georgian, Macon Telegraph, Jacksonville Journal, Montgomery Advertiser, and Atlanta Journal.

13 The account of Greb's bout with Tommy Loughran at Boston is derived from reports found in the Boston Post,

Boston Globe, Boston Daily Advertiser, Boston Herald, Boston Traveler, Pittsburgh Gazette-Times, and Boston American.

14 Duffey, Athur, Boston Post: **Arthur Duffey's SPORT COMMENT,** October 16, 1923.

15 Duffey, Athur, Boston Post: **Arthur Duffey's SPORT COMMENT,** October 13, 1923.

16 The account of Greb's bout with Lou Bogash at Newark is derived from reports found in the Newark Star-Eagle, Newark Evening News, New York Tribune, New York Evening World, Pittsburgh Post, New York Sun and Globe, New York Evening Telegram, and the syndicated column written by Fairplay.

17 Welsh, Regis, Pittsburgh Post: **GREB STARTS HOME TO BEGIN TRAINING FOR JONES BATTLE,** October 24, 1923.

18 The account of Greb's bout with Soldier Jones is derived from reports found in the Pittsburgh Post, Pittsburgh Gazette-Times, Pittsburgh Chronicle-Telegraph, Pittsburgh Sun, and Pittsburgh Press.

19 Grand Rapids Herald: **5,000 Fans Treated to a Scientific Boxing Lesson,** November 16, 1923.

20 The account of Greb's bout with Chuck Wiggins at Grand Rapids is derived from reports found in the Grand Rapids Herald, and Grand Rapids Press.

21 Pittsburgh Post: **MEETS KID NORFOLK IN 15 ROUND BOUT AT MADISON GARDEN,** November 20, 1923.

22 The account of Greb's bout with Bryan Downey is derived from reports found in the Pittsburgh Post, Pittsburgh Sun, and Pittsburgh Gazette-Times.

23 Tunney, Gene, **A MAN MUST FIGHT**. Boston/New York: Houghton Mifflin Company, 1932.

24 Gallico, Paul, New York Daily News: **Tunney Will Be Glad to Hear of This!,** December 8, 1923.

25 Welsh, Regis, Pittsburgh Post: **BOUT LOOKS TO BE ON LEVEL; LITTLE BETTING ON OUTCOME; HARRY WILL WEIGH 167 POUNDS,** December 10, 1923.

26 Ibid.

27 Welsh, Regis, Pittsburgh Post: **HARRY VICTIM OF ANOTHER RAW DECISION OF JUDGES AFTER GENE TAKES SEVERE LACING,** December 11, 1923.

28 The account of Greb's third bout with Gene Tunney is derived from reports found in the Pittsburgh Post, Pittsburgh Gazette-Times, New York Sun and Globe, New York Daily News, New York Times, New York Morning World, New York Tribune, New York Evening Telegram, New York Morning Telegraph, United Press, New York Herald, Pittsburgh Press, Brooklyn Standard Union, Brooklyn Daily Eagle, Newark Star-Eagle, Newark Evening News, New York Evening Journal, New York Evening Mail, New York Evening World, and New York Evening Post.

How they voted:

Tunney:

New York Sun and Globe (Fred Keats) Tunney won 11 rounds, "but his margin was not as great as that sounds because he had only a shade in most of the rounds."
New York Daily News (Harry Newman) Tunney was clearly entitled to the decision.
New York Times (James Dawson) Tunney won 10 rounds, Greb 4, 1 even.
New York Morning World (Bert "Hype" Igoe) Tunney clearly outpointed Greb.
New York Tribune (Jack Lawrence) Tunney won 9 rounds, Greb won 3, with 3 even.
New York Evening Telegram (George B. Underwood) "There was absolutely no question of Tunney being entitled to the decision."
United Press (Henry L. Farrell) Tunney won 10 rounds, Greb 4, 1 even.
Pittsburgh Press (Jim Jab) The decision was fair. It was a close fight with possibly some slight favoritism shown to Tunney but Greb had not done enough to take the title.
Brooklyn Standard Union Tunney won 10 rounds, Greb 4, 1 even. (This article might be a wire report and thus a reprint of an earlier cited source.)
Brooklyn Daily Eagle (W. C. Vreeland) Tunney won 8 rounds, Greb won 5, 2 even.
Newark Star-Eagle (Bert Dodge) There could be no question to the fairness of the decision.
New York Evening Post (Seabury Lawrence) Tunney won fairly.
New York Evening Mail (Dan Lyons) "It wasn't even close."
New York Evening Mail (Ed Hughes) "He'll (Tunney) beat him any time they meet."

New York Evening World (Ed Van Every) "There was no other decision to be given."

Greb:

Pittsburgh Post (Regis Welsh) Tunney won 6 rounds, Greb won 6 rounds, 3 even. Welsh stated that Greb's margin in his six rounds was greater than Tunney's and that, combined with Tunney's foul fighting, should have earned Greb the decision.
New York Morning Telegraph (James P. Sinnot) Greb won 10 rounds, Tunney won 4, 1 even. By the tenth round Tunney was so far behind on points he needed a knockout to win.
Pittsburgh Gazette-Times (Ray Coll) Greb won 10 rounds, Tunney 2, 3 even.
Newark Evening News "Thousands of boxing followers will proclaim, perhaps, that Greb's only hope of victory over Tunney in New York is apparently via the knockout route."
United News (Westbrook Pegler) "By what obscure processes the judges of the bout arrived at their decision it was not possible to see."
Consolidated Press (Fairplay) "Perhaps next year whether Greb loses or retains his middleweight crown we shall be treated to that annual comedy entitled "Handing the Decision to Tunney.""

Draw:

New York Evening Journal (Ford Frick)

29 Coll, Ray, Pittsburgh Gazette-Times: *CROWD HISSES VERDICT WHICH ROBS LOCAL MAN OF BOUT WHICH IS HIS,* December 11, 1923.

30 Ibid.

31 Sinnott, James R., New York Morning Telegraph: *IN MID-CHANNEL,* December 13, 1923.

32 Lawrence, Jack, New York Tribune: *Champion Holds Out for Larger Offer to Sign*, December 14, 1923.

33 Dayton, Alfred, New York Sun: *TUNNEY READY FOR M'TIGUE,* December 12, 1923.

34 Welsh, Regis, Pittsburgh Post: *IMMEDIATE REMEDY IMPERATIVE TO SAVE FUTURE ARGUMENTS,* December 21, 1923.

35 Pittsburgh Gazette-Times: *MIDDLEWEIGHT CHAMP AGREES TO TOSS CROWN INTO NEW YORK RING,* December 13, 1923.
   Guarantees were forbidden in New York State at the time but were often paid under the table by promoters eager to secure fighters and stay competitive with states where promoters were legally allowed to offer guarantees.

36 The account of Greb's bout with Tommy Loughran is derived from reports found in the Pittsburgh Press, Pittsburgh Gazette-Times, and Pittsburgh Post.

37 Van Every, Ed, New York Evening World: *SHOWS BEST IN NINE OF FIFTEEN ROUNDS,* January 19, 1924.

38 The account of Greb's second fight with Johnny Wilson is derived from reports found in the Pittsburgh Press, United Press, New York Daily News, New York Times, New York Tribune, New York Morning Telegraph, International News, New York Evening World, Brooklyn Daily Eagle, Pittsburgh Gazette-Times, Brooklyn Standard Union, New York Evening Telegram, New York Evening Post, Queensborough Daily Star, and Newark Star-Eagle.

39 The account of Greb's bout with Jack Reeves at Oakland is derived from reports found in the Oakland Post-Enquirer, and Oakland Tribune.

40 Camins, Harry, Pittsburgh Gazette-Times: *Harry Greb, Back From Coast, Must Turn to Match With Jack Delaney,* March 16, 1924.

41 The account of Greb's title defense against Fay Keiser is derived from reports found in the Baltimore American, Baltimore Sun, and Pittsburgh Gazette-Times.

42 Polo, Marco, Baltimore Morning Sun: *FRANKLIN SPURNED GREB "FRAME-UP"*, April 1, 1924.

43 Davis, Ralph, Pittsburgh Press: *SPORT CHAT,* March 31, 1924.

44 Coll, Ray, Pittsburgh Gazette-Times: *REFEREE RULES CHAMP HIT KID AFTER BELL AT CLOSE OF SIXTH ROUND,* April 20, 1924.

45 The Boston Post reported odds of even money on April 17. The following day odds were reported in the Boston Daily Advertiser as 7 to 5 in favor of Greb. The same day the Boston American reported that odds had shifted from even money to 10 to 8 in favor of Greb. April 19 the Advertiser reported odds of 10 to 7 in favor in Greb.

46 The account of Greb's bout with Kid Norfolk at Boston is derived from reports found in the Boston Post, Boston Herald, Boston Globe, Boston American, Pittsburgh Post, Chicago Defender, and Pittsburgh Gazette-Times.

47 Coll, Ray, Pittsburgh Gazette-Times: *REFEREE RULES CHAMP HIT KID AFTER BELL AT CLOSE OF SIXTH ROUND,* April 20, 1924.

48 Ibid.

49 Almy, Doc, Boston Post: *BOXING GOSSIP,* April 29, 1924.

50 Coll, Ray, Pittsburgh Gazette-Times: *THROWN POP BOTTLE RESPONSIBLE FOR LOSING BOUT, GREB SAYS,* June 17, 1924.

51 The account of Greb's bout with Jackie Clark is derived from reports found in the Washington Post, and Washington Herald.

52 The account of Greb's bout with Pal Reed is derived from reports found in the Pittsburgh Gazette-Times, Pittsburgh Press, Pittsburgh Chronicle-Telegraph, Pittsburgh Sun, and Pittsburgh Post.

53 Olean Evening Times: *Harry Greb Makes Instant Hit With Local Fight Fans in Exhibition at College,* June 7, 1924.

54 The account of Greb's bout with Martin Burke at Cleveland is derived from reports found in the Cleveland Plain Dealer, Massillon Evening Independant, and Cleveland Press.

55 Bridgeport Post: *BRIDGEPORT A. & A. TO WORK WITH MULLIGAN IN PROMOTING CHAMPIONSHIP SCRAP JUNE 16,* June 8, 1924.

56 The account of Greb's bout with Frank Moody at Waterbury is derived from reports found in the New Haven Evening Register, Bridgeport Post, Bridgeport Telegram, and Waterbury Republican.

57 New York Telegram and Evening Mail: *Wills Finally Lands Bout,* June 24, 1924.

58 New York Telegram and Evening Mail: *HARRY GREB EXPECTS TO KNOCK OUT MOORE,* June 18, 1924.

59 New York Times: *60,000 TO SEE GREB BOX MOORE TONIGHT,* June 26, 1924.

60 New York Times: *BOXING BODY DEFERS DECISION ON ZIVIC,* June 25, 1924.

61 Coll, Ray, Pittsburgh Gazette-Times: *MIDDLEWEIGHT CHAMP NEVER EXTENDS SELF IN 15-ROUND STRUGGLE WITH ENGLISHMAN,* June 17, 1924.

62 The account of Greb's bout with Ted Moore is derived from reports found in the New York Evening Post, Brooklyn Daily Eagle, Pittsburgh Gazette-Times, New York Herald Tribune, New York Evening World, New York Telegram and Evening Mail, New York Daily News, New York Times, Brooklyn Standard Union, and New York Sun.

NOTES

CHAPTER 22

1 Michigan City News: *Mayor Orders Stribling Greb Fight For July 4th Off Because of Epidemic,* July 2, 1924.

2 Chicago Tribune: *SMALLPOX TALK BUNK, MICHIGAN OFFICIAL SAYS,* July 4, 1924.

3 Chicago Herald-Examiner: *NEW DEAL ON FOR FIGHT AT MICHIGAN CITY,* July 4, 1924.

4 Michigan City News: *BOXING FALLS ON EVIL DAYS IN OUR SKY BLUE ARENA,* July 15, 1924.

5 Fremont Daily Messenger: *GREB-FLOWERS TITLE GO ALL SET FOR FREMONT,* July 9, 1924.

6 New York Age: *TIGER FLOWERS WINS BY TECHNICAL KAYO OVER JACK TOWNSEND,* August 9, 1924.

7 Fremont Daily Messenger: *GREB ASKS FOR POSTPONEMENT IN BIG BOUT DATE,* August 6, 1924.

8 Coll, Ray, Pittsburgh Gazette-Times: *THROUGH THE ROPES,* August 8, 1924.

9 Fremont Daily Messenger: *FINISHING TOUCH BEING PLACED ON BIG ARENA,* August 19, 1924.

10 Fremont Daily Messenger: *HARRY GREB TO COMPLETE HIS TRAINING HERE,* August 19, 1924.

11 Fremont Daily News: *FIRST MEETING,* August 21, 1924.

12 Fremont Daily News: *FINAL DETAILS,* August 21, 1924.

13 The account of Greb's bout with Tiger Flowers at Fremont is derived from reports found in the Fremont Daily News, Fremont Daily Messenger, Lorain Times Herald, Akron Press, Pittsburgh Post, Pittsburgh Gazette-Times, The Lima News, Sandusky Star-Journal, Findlay Morning Republican, Columbus Evening Dispatch, Columbus Citizen, Toledo Blade, Grand Rapids Herald, Toledo News-Bee, Toledo Times, Sandusky Register, Detroit News, Tiffin Daily Advertiser, and Fostoria Daily Review.

14 Coll, Ray, Pittsburgh Gazette-Times: *MIDDLEWEIGHT CHAMP MAKES ANNOUNCEMENT AFTER FLOWERS BOUT,* August 24, 1924.

15 Schwab was eventually able to acquire Tunney's services to disastrous results. Tunney faced Ray Neuman at Schwab's newly constructed venue at Ebensburg only to be fined and suspended for three months by the Pennsylvania Athletic Commission for his poor performance, despite being warned in advance to give his best effort.

16 The account of Greb's bout with Jimmy Slattery is derived from reports found in the Buffalo Enquirer, Buffalo Evening News, Buffalo Morning Express, Buffalo Courier, and Pittsburgh Gazette-Times.

17 Lerch, Horace, Buffalo Morning Express: *YOUNG BISON BRILLIANT IN OPENING ROUNDS; SLOWS IN GREAT BOUT,* September 4, 1924.

18 Steubenville Herald-Star: *Middleweight Champ Shows To 3000 Fans; Takes Away $2,000,* September 16, 1924.

19 Coll, Ray, Pittsburgh Gazette-Times: *DISCUSSION WAXES WARM OVER CLIMAX OF BOUT THURSDAY,* July 26, 1924.

20 The account of Greb's bout with Gene Tunney at Cleveland is derived from reports found in the Cleveland Press, Pittsburgh Post, Cleveland News, Cleveland Plain Dealer, Pittsburgh Gazette-Times, and Pittsburgh Press.

How they voted:

Greb:

Cleveland Press (Russell Needham) Greb won 8 rounds, Tunney won 1, 1 even.
Cleveland Plain Dealer (Stuart Bell) Greb won 5 rounds, Tunney won 4, 1 even. Bell actually claimed in his headline that Greb won 6 rounds, with Tunney winning 3, and 1 even. The round by round report credits Tunney with 4 rounds and Greb with 5. This discrepancy occasionally occurs when a separate, unnamed reporter issues the round by round report. Therefore the above discrepancy may be the result of two separate ringside opinions in favor of Greb. Without corroboration the author has chosen to err on the side of caution giving Greb only credit for the more conservative victory.
Pittsburgh Press (Jim Jab) Greb won 7 rounds, Tunney scarcely won 3.

Tunney:

Pittsburgh Post (Regis Welsh) Tunney won 5 rounds, Greb won 3, 2 even. Welsh added that Tunney won by "one of the slightest shades possible."
Cleveland News (Ray Campbell) Tunney won 5, Greb won 3, 2 were even. Campbell stated that Greb vomited from Tunney's body punches after the seventh and eighth rounds. It should be noted that Campbell, who issued the most

favorable report to Tunney would later work as Tunney's press agent and secretary.

Draw:

Pittsburgh Gazette-Times (Ray Coll) Coll had the fight dead even at the end but interestingly once again we have a discrepancy in his report and the round by round account reported by his newspaper. The round by round account credits Greb with 5 rounds, Tunney 3, and 2 even. Again, this could be the result of two separate authors: Coll writing the main account of the fight for the newspaper, and an unnamed reporter keeping tabs of the round by round description for later print as was often the case during the era.
Associated Press (Barney McGuire) McGuire did not give a tabulation of the rounds awarded to each fighter but stated that the fight was fought on "fairly even terms."

21 Coll, Ray, Pittsburgh Gazette-Times: ***Greb Makes Tunney Tempting Offer For Bout in Pittsburgh,*** September 19, 1924.

22 Philadelphia Evening Bulletin: ***GREB AFTER HEAVIES,*** October 7, 1924.

23 Philadelphia Inquirer: ***HARRY GREB HERE FOR LOUGHRAN BOUT,*** October 12, 1924.

24 Ibid.

25 The account of Greb's bout with Tommy Loughran is derived from reports found in the Philadelphia Inquirer, Philadelphia Evening Bulletin, and Philadelphia Public Ledger.

26 Philadelphia Evening Bulletin: ***Loughran Gets Draw in Renewal of "Roughhouse Act" With Greb,*** October 14, 1924.

27 Ibid.

28 Clearfield Progress: ***Philipsburg Legion Men Put On Big Celebration Of Armistice Signing,*** November 12, 1924.

29 The account of Greb's bout with Lou Comasana is derived from reports found in the Altoona Mirror, Altoona Tribune, and Clearfield Progress

30 The account of Greb's bout with Jimmy Delaney at Pittsburgh is derived from reports found in the Pittsburgh Post, Pittsburgh Press, and Pittsburgh Gazette-Times.

31 Pittsburgh Gazette-Times: ***MIDDLEWEIGHT KING IS TWICE FOULED IN TERRIFIC BOUT,*** November 18, 1924.

32 The account of Greb's bout with Frankie Ritz is derived from reports found in the Wheeling Register and Wheeling Intelligencer.

33 Coll, Ray, Pittsburgh Gazette-Times: ***THROUGH THE ROPES,*** December 22, 1924.

34 Pittsburgh Gazette-Times: ***Greb, After Watching Gibbons, Norfolk, Flowers, and Wilson in Action, Says He Beat 'Em All Once and Can Do It Again,*** December 11, 1924.

35 Coll, Ray, Pittsburgh Gazette-Times: ***Harry Greb Receives Offer of $50,000 to Box Tiger Flowers,*** December 13, 1924.

36 Pittsburgh Gazette-Times: ***REPORT OF MARRIAGE A JOKE, SAYS GREB, RETURNING HERE,*** December 20, 1924.

37 Ibid.

38 Pittsburgh Gazette-Times: ***Not Engaged, Says Greb; It's Up Harry -Louise,*** January 9, 1925.

39 Pittsburgh Gazette-Times: ***REPORT OF MARRIAGE A JOKE, SAYS GREB, RETURNING HERE,*** December 20, 1924.

40 The account of Greb's bout with Augie Ratner is derived from reports found in the Pittsburgh Post, Pittsburgh Gazette-Times, and Pittsburgh Press.

41 Greene, Sam, Detroit News: ***DETROIT READY FOR TITLE BOUT,*** January 9, 1925.

42 The account of Greb's bout with Bob Sage is derived from reports found in the Detroit Free Press, and Detroit News.

43 The account of Jack Delaney's bout with Tiger Flowers is derived from reports found in the New York Times, New York Amsterdam News, Pittsburgh Courier, Brooklyn Daily Eagle, and New York Sun.

44 Zanesville Signal: *Middleweight Champ Was Master of the Situation Throughout Every Round*, January 20, 1925.

45 St. Paul Pioneer Press: *Jimmy Delaney Well Versed In Greb's Ring Maneuvers*, January 29, 1925.

46 The account of Greb's bout with Jimmy Delaney at St. Paul is derived from reports found in the St. Paul Dispatch, St. Paul Pioneer Press, Minneapolis Tribune, and Minneapolis Journal.

47 Allentown Morning Call: *HARRY GREB WINS THE DECISION OVER BRITTON; BIG CROWD THERE*, February 18, 1925.

48 The account of Greb's bout with Young Fisher at Scranton is derived from reports found in the Scranton Times and Scranton Republican.

49 The account of Jack Delaney's second bout with Tiger Flowers is derived from reports found in the New York Times, Pittsburgh Courier, Chicago Defender, New York Age, Brooklyn Standard Union, Brooklyn Daily Eagle, and New York Sun.

50 Hartford Courant: *Delaney Gives Up Hope Of Winning Middleweight Crown, Starts After Light Heavies*, February 28, 1925.

51 St. Paul Pioneer Press: *DAWSON ACTS TO PREVENT CHANGE IN FIGHT PLANS*, March 9, 1925.

52 Pittsburgh Post: *Harry Greb, With Two Girls, Beats Up Bandit Gang in Highland Park*, March 2, 1925.

53 Pittsburgh Press: *Greb Attack Suspect Held*, March 3, 1925.

54 Pittsburgh Chronicle-Telegraph: *GREB OFFERS SUSPECTS BOND*, March 4, 1925.

55 Ibid.

56 Pittsburgh Gazette-Times: *HARRY GREB, 2 GIRLS BATTLE FOOTPADS IN HIGHLAND PARK*, March 2, 1925.

57 Stocking, Collis A., *A STUDY OF DANCE HALLS IN PITTSBURGH: MADE UNDER THE AUSPICES OF THE PITTSBURGH GIRLS' CONFERENCE*. Pittsburgh: Pittsburgh Council of the Churches of Christ, 1925.

58 Pittsburgh Chronicle-Telegraph: *2 Girls Swindle Greb And Pal in Crap Game*, March 5, 1925.

59 Pittsburgh Sun: *GREB DENIES BEING SWINDLED AT CRAPS*, March 6, 1925.

60 Walker, Edward G., Minneapolis Journal: *Middleweight Champion Makes Impressive Showing in Workout*, March 25, 1925.

61 The account of Greb's fifth and final bout with Gene Tunney is derived from reports found in the Minneapolis Journal, St. Paul Pioneer Press, Minneapolis Tribune, and St. Paul Dispatch.

62 Minneapolis Journal: *GREB'S STYLE HAS GENE HANDICAPPED*, March 28, 1925.

63 St. Paul Dispatch: *JIMMY DE FOREST REMAINS HERE FOR FINAL CONFERENCE*, March 28, 1925.

64 Barton, George A., Minneapolis Tribune: *WATCHING the SPORT SHOW THROUGH the REFEREE'S EYES*, March 29, 1925.

65 St. Paul Dispatch: *SPORT COMMENT*, March 28, 1925.

NOTES

CHAPTER 23

1 Keck, Harry, Pittsburgh Gazette-Times: **Between Rounds,** April 7, 1925.

2 Strictly speaking Guarantees for prizefighters were not allowed in the state of New York but most promoters made promises to fighters "under the table" in order to secure their services, thus there was often a discrepancy between the publicized purse size and what was actually paid to the fighter.

3 The account of Greb's third and final bout with Johnny Wilson is derived from reports found in the Boston Daily Advertiser, Boston Globe, Boston Evening Transcript, and Boston Post.

4 Keck, Harry, Pittsburgh Gazette-Times: **Between Rounds,** April 24, 1925.

5 Toronto Daily Star: **JAGUAR OF THE RING HERE FOR REDDICK,** April 23, 1925.

6 The account of Greb's bout with Jack Reddick is derived from reports found in the Toronto Evening Telegram, Toronto Daily Star, and Toronto Globe Mail.

7 The account of Greb's bout with Quintin Romero Rojas is derived from reports found in the Detroit Times, Detroit Free Press, Grand Rapids Herald, and Detroit News.

8 Pittsburgh Gazette-Times: **CHAMPION ANSWERS GONG 277 TIMES IN 12 YEARS' FIGHTING,** April 26, 1925.

9 The account of Greb's bout with Billy Britton at Columbus, Ohio is derived from reports found in the Columbus Citizen, and Columbus Dispatch.

10 The account of Greb's bout with Tommy Burns at Indianapolis is derived from reports found in the Indianapolis Star, and Indianapolis News.

11 The account of Greb's bout with Soldier Buck at Louisville is derived from reports found in the Louisville Courier-Journal, and Louisville Times.

12 Pittsburgh Sun: **Cop Shoots at Greb In Northside Chase,** June 3, 1925.

13 Pittsburgh Gazette-Times: **Feared Greb's Fists More Than Bullets Is Driver's Story in Court,** June 7, 1925.

14 The account of Greb's bout with Jimmy Nuss is derived from reports found in the Marquette Mining Journal, and Grand Rapids Herald.

15 Brumm, Bob, Marquette Mining Journal: **Jimmy Nuss, Who Once Fought For Title Here, Living In Kiva Area,** April 16, 1957.

16 Dickerson, E. W., Grand Rapids Herald: **DICK'S DOPE,** June 7, 1925.

17 Newman, Harry, New York Daily News: **JACK HEARS IT'S COLD TURKEY IN GOTHAM FOR HIM,** June 13, 1925.

18 Greb opened as a favorite at odds of 6 to 5. A persistent myth has been handed down in regards to Greb that on the night before the fight he appeared with two women at a popular New York nightclub drunk. The story goes that Greb's appearance was an act devised to lengthen the odds in Walker's favor so that Greb could make more money on any bets he placed on himself. This story is a myth. The odds for the bout stayed relatively close and never dipped further in Walker's favor than even money. This is beside the obvious fact that the two fighters were heavily featured in the press and their condition was well noted, including the example of Greb exhibiting his condition before motion picture cameras the day before the fight. Occasionally this story has also been stated to have happened prior to the first bout between Greb and Johnny Wilson. Again, this supposed occurrence never happened at that time either. The commission was keeping a close eye on Greb's conditioning due to the rumor that he would throw the fight and the stories of his difficulty making weight. Greb opened against Wilson as a heavy favorite at 3 to 1 odds. The odds shortened in the days

leading up to the fight (which is common) but even despite the odds shortening Greb still remained a 2 to 1 favorite on the day of the fight and betting was very light.

19 Van Every, Ed, New York Evening World: *KEARNS SAYS WALKER WILL KNOCK OUT GREB,* July 1, 1925.

20 Farrell, Jack, New York Daily News: *SMITH MEETS GOODMAN FOR CHARITY AT DEXTER PARK,* June 25, 1925.

21 New York Morning Telegraph: *KEARNS FAILS TO MOVE BOARD,* July 3, 1925.

22 Jenkins Jr., Burris, New York Evening World: *Walker, Bigger, Heavier in Shoulders, Looks Stronger, as Training Nears End,* June 30, 1925.

23 Keck, Harry, Pittsburgh Gazette-Times: *HARRY SCALES 158½ POUNDS; IS CONFIDENT,* July 2, 1925.

24 Van Every, Ed, New York Evening World: *MIDDLEWEIGHT CHAMPION WEIGHS IN AT 159 POUNDS,* July 2, 1925.

25 Farrell, Henry L., Oswego Palladium-Times: *RADIO AT RINGSIDE MAY BRING CHANGE IN BOXERS' LANGUAGE,* July 25, 1925.

26 The account of Greb's bout with Mickey Walker is derived from reports found in the Newark Evening News, Philadelphia Inquirer, New York Morning Telegraph, New York Herald Tribune, New York Evening World, Pittsburgh Gazette-Times, Pittsburgh Post, New York Morning World, New York Times, International News, United Press, New York Daily News, Pittsburgh Press, Pittsburgh Chronicle-Telegraph, Brooklyn Daily Eagle, Queensborough Daily Star, Elizabeth Journal, New York Evening Post, and Brooklyn Standard Union.

NOTES

CHAPTER 24

1 New York Evening World: *GREB SAYS HE GAVE WALKER EVERYTHING HE HAD IN FOURTEENTH,* July 3, 1925.

2 Ibid.

3 The account of Greb's bout with Maxie Rosenbloom is derived from reports found in the Cleveland Press, Pittsburgh Post, and Cleveland Plain Dealer.

4 Cleveland Press: *IT TOOK REAL ART, BUT GREB LET MAXIE "STAY",* July 17, 1925.

5 The account of Greb's third and final bout with Billy Britton is derived from reports found in the Columbus Daily Advocate, and Iola Daily Register.

6 Pittsburgh Post: *"Money Is Only Thing Uncertain," Says Greb On Way To Meet Promoter,* July 21, 1925.

7 Eckersall, Walter, Chicago Tribune: *'TIGER' FLOWERS HERE FOR BOGASH BATTLE,* July 22, 1925.

8 Smith, Frank, Chicago Tribune: *DEMPSEY-GREB GO GETS O. K. OF BOXING WRITERS,* July 24, 1925.

9 Chicago Tribune: *Greb Gets Jack's O. K.,* July 24, 1925.

10 Duffy, Lou, Tulsa Tribune: *WORLD'S CHAMP IN TULSA FOR BOUT FRIDAY,* July 30, 1925.

11 Trumbull, Walter, New York Evening Post: *The Listening Post,* July 26, 1925.

12 Wray, John, St. Louis Post Dispatch: *WRAY'S COLUMN,* July 26, 1925.

13 Newman, Harry, New York Daily News: *O'CONNEL MAY HAVE SURPRISE FOR TERRIS,* July 26, 1925.

14 Dunbar, Bob, Boston Herald: **Bob Dunbar,** July 28, 1925.

15 Walsh, Davis J., Tulsa Daily World: **STAGE BELIEVED RIPE FOR MATCH,** July 28, 1925.

16 The account of Greb's bout with Ralph Brooks is derived from reports found in the Wichita Beacon, and Wichita Eagle.

17 McPherson, C. Lee, Wichita Beacon: **BROOKS OF KANSAS TOOK ALL CHAMPION HAD AND FINISHED,** July 28, 1925.

18 Wichita EAGLE: **CHAMP DISPLAYS DAZZLING SPEED DURING FIGHT,** July 28, 1925.

19 The account of Greb's bout with Otis Bryant is derived from reports found in the Tulsa Daily World, and Tulsa Tribune.

20 Chicago Tribune: **Dempsey Rules Greb Fight Out; Jacks Split Property,** July 31, 1925.

21 Kansas City Times: **SMITH IS KNOCKED OUT,** August 5, 1925.

22 Green, Sam, Detroit News: **GREB REPLACES JACK DELANEY,** August 17, 1925.

23 The account of Greb's bout with Tommy Burns at Detroit is derived from reports found in the Detroit News and Detroit Free Press.

24 Pittsburgh Post: **Harry Greb Injured When Auto Plunges Down Embankment,** August 21, 1925.
   Pittsburgh Gazette-Times: **RING CHAMPION UNDERGOES SECOND X-RAY EXAMINATION,** August 22, 1925.

25 Pittsburgh Post: **CHAMPION ISSUES OPEN DEFI TO ANY FIGHTER IN WORLD,** September 3, 1925.

26 The account of Jimmy Slattery's loss to Paul Berlenbach is derived from reports found in the New York Times, New York Herald Tribune, Brooklyn Daily Eagle, Brooklyn Standard Union, New York Evening Post, Buffalo Morning Express, and New York Sun.

27 The account of Greb's bout with Tony Marullo at Pittsburgh is derived from reports found in the Pittsburgh Post, Pittsburgh Gazette-Times, and Pittsburgh Press.

28 The account of Greb's bout with Tony Marullo at New Orleans is derived from reports found in the New Orleans Times-Picayune, New Orleans Tribune, and New Orleans States.

29 Keck, Harry, Pittsburgh Gazette-Times: **Between Rounds,** December 31, 1925.

30 The account of Greb's bout with Soldier Buck at Nashville is derived from reports found in the Nashville Tennessean, and Nashville Banner.

31 The account of Tiger Flowers controversial loss to Mike McTigue is derived from reports found in the New York Times, New York Herald-Tribune, Brooklyn Standard Union, New York Sun, and Brooklyn Daily Eagle.

32 Keck, Harry, Pittsburgh Gazette-Times: **Between Rounds,** December 31, 1925.

33 Pittsburgh Gazette-Times: **Greb to Box Flowers In Garden, February 26,** January 2, 1926.

34 The account of Greb's bout with Roland Todd at Toronto is derived from reports found in the Toronto Globe, and Toronto Star.

35 Los Angeles Times: **GREB SEEKING FIGHT RECORD,** January 25, 1926.

36 Omaha World Herald: **CHAMP A PUZZLE TO HERR LOHMAN,** January 20, 1926.

37 Pittsburgh Gazette-Times: **Greb Sends Check To Father of Lad Who Fell to Death As Greb Fought,** February 20, 1926.

38 Los Angeles Times: **GREB ARRIVES FOR BOUT,** January 23, 1926.

39 Newman, Claude, Hollywood Daily Citizen: **GREB OUT-MAULS ENGLISH FIGHTER,** January 27, 1926.

40 The account of Greb's bout with Buck Holley is derived from reports found in the Los Angeles Times, Los Angeles

Evening Herald, and Hollywood Daily Citizen.

41 Shand, Bob, Oakland Tribune: *BOOING OF FANS FAILS TO PERTURB GREB OR MANAGER*, February 7, 1926.

42 The account of Greb's bout with Jimmy Delaney at Oakland is derived from reports found in the Oakland Tribune, and Oakland Post-Enquirer.

43 Arizona Republic: *Ring King Denies Adopting Young Griffo's Method of Training On Beer And Beef*, February 8, 1926.

44 Brady, Tim, Arizona Gazette: *MIDDLEWEIGHT CHAMPION SCOFFS AT PHELPS RECORD; ANNOUNCES HE'LL STOP MESAN IN 3 ROUNDS*, February 11, 1926.

45 Arizona Republic: *Ring King Denies Adopting Young Griffo's Method of Training On Beer And Beef*, February 8, 1926.

46 The account of Greb's bout with Owen Phelps is derived from reports found in the Arizona Republic, and Arizona Gazette.

47 Arizona Gazette: *Phelps Turns Down $5,000 to Become Protege of Mason*, February 13, 1926.

NOTES

CHAPTER 25

1 Taub, Sam, New York Morning Telegraph: *Harry Greb Defends Title Against Flowers To-Night*, February 26, 1926.

2 Keck, Harry, Pittsburgh Gazette-Times: *Middleweight Champ Rules Big Favorite Over Flowers*, February 26, 1926.

3 Wilson, W. Rollo, Pittsburgh Courier: *EASTERN SNAPSHOTS*, February 6, 1926.

4 New York Amsterdam News: *Tiger Flowers Trial at Madison Square Garden on Friday Night*, February 24, 1926.

5 Keck, Harry, Pittsburgh Gazette-Times: *GREB Predicts Close Fight, But Says He'll Win; Place Your Money on Me, Tiger Tells Friends*, February 26, 1926.

6 Ibid.

7 Keck, Harry, Pittsburgh Gazette-Times: *RING TRADITION SAYS CHALLENGER MUST BEAT CHAMP TO WIN TITLE*, February 28, 1926.

8 The account of Greb's second bout with Tiger Flowers is derived from reports found in the New York Herald Tribune, New York Times, Pittsburgh Post, Pittsburgh Gazette-Times, New York Morning World, New York Daily News, New York Evening Post, New York Evening Journal, New York Sun, New York Morning Telegraph, New York Amsterdam News, Brooklyn Standard Union, Pittsburgh Courier, New York Age, and Brooklyn Daily Eagle.

9 Vreeland, W. C., Brooklyn Daily Eagle: *In a Poor Title Bout of 15 Rounds, the "Tiger" Finds Harry out of Form*, February 27, 1926.

10 New York Sun: *FLOWERS WILL BOX IN 90 DAYS*, February 27, 1926.

11 New York Evening Journal: *GREB SEEKS ANOTHER CHANCE*, February 27, 1926.

12 New York Evening Journal: *FLOWERS PROUD TO BE CHAMPION*, February 27, 1926.

13 New York Sun: **FLOWERS WILL BOX IN 90 DAYS,** February 27, 1926.

14 Pittsburgh Gazette-Times: **"I THOUGH I DESERVED THE DECISION" -GREB,** February 27, 1926.

15 Vreeland, W. C., Brooklyn Daily Eagle: **In a Poor Title Bout of 15 Rounds, the "Tiger" Finds Harry out of Form,** February 27, 1926.

16 Welsh, Regis, Pittsburgh Post: **FALLEN CHAMPION FOLLOWS ZIVIC IN UNEXPECTED DEFEAT,** March 2, 1926.

17 Pittsburgh Courier: **GREB AND DEMPSEY,** March 13, 1926.

18 Hot Springs New Era: **Greb Indicates He Means Business in Starting New Life,** March 17, 1926.

19 Pittsburgh Gazette-Times: **"Get a Reputation," Hint Given Greb as He Demands Flowers Meet Him Again,** April 6, 1926.

20 Keck, Harry, Pittsburgh Gazette-Times: **Feud at Hot Springs Precipitates Break Between Greb, Mason,** April 7, 1926.

21 Hot Springs New Era: **GREB'S ACTION DOES NOT ALARM MANAGER,** April 7, 1926.

22 Albell, Alfred, New York Daily News: **Pugilist Now Cool After Asked Her to Wed, Chorine's Plaint,** May 5, 1926.

23 Pittsburgh Post: **Greb Facing $250,000 Alienation Suit as Sally's Husband Appears,** May 6, 1926.

24 Albell, Alfred, New York Daily News: **CHORINE'S HUBBY PUTS $250,000 BOUT ON GREB,** May 6, 1926.

25 New York Times: **GREB-MASON DEAL VOIDED BY BOARD,** May 8, 1926.

26 Buffalo Evening News: **WILLIE BRENNAN TO HELP ART WEIGAND,** May 29, 1926.

27 Buffalo Courier: **Greb Seriously Training, to Weigh 165 For Weigand,** May 28, 1926.

28 The account of Greb's bout with Art Weigand is derived from reports found in the Buffalo Courier, Buffalo Morning Express, and Buffalo Times.

29 Pittsburgh Post: **REVERSES OPINION OF BOXING BOARD IN CONTRACT FUSS,** June 15, 1926.

30 Wilkes-Barre Record: **HARRY GREB MAKES HIT IN VICTORY OVER GANS,** June 16, 1926.

31 Pegler, Westbrook, Pittsburgh Post: **JIMMIE JOHNSTON BECOMES BIG FACTOR IN FIGHT TONIGHT,** August 19, 1926.

32 Pittsburgh Post: **"GREB" IS MY NAME, SPEEDER TELLS MOTOR COP; IS BARRED FROM DRIVING CAR IN NEW JERSEY,** August 5, 1926.

33 Pittsburgh Post: **"I Don't Do Such Things," Says Greb, Denying Wild Jersey Auto Ride,** August 6, 1926.

34 Keck, Harry, Pittsburgh Gazette-Times: **PITTSBURGHER REACHES NEW YORK PRIMED FOR BATTLE WITH FLOWERS,** August 19, 1926.

35 Pittsburgh Gazette-Times: **Greb and Sparring Partner Write He's Primed for Battle,** August 15, 1926.

36 Ibid.

37 New York Morning Telegraph: **FLOWERS WILL BE PROTECTED IN BATTLE WITH HARRY GREB,** August 18, 1926.

38 Keck, Harry, Pittsburgh Gazette-Times: **PITTSBURGHER REACHES NEW YORK PRIMED FOR BATTLE WITH FLOWERS,** August 19, 1926.

39 Keck, Harry, Pittsburgh Gazette-Times: **TIGER FLOWERS AWARDED DECISION BY 2-TO-1 VOTE; MANY BELIEVE FORMER CHAMP WON BOUT,** August 20, 1926.

40 The account of Greb's third and final bout with Tiger Flowers is derived from reports found in the Pittsburgh Post, Pittsburgh Gazette-Times, New York Evening Post, New York Evening World, Brooklyn Daily Eagle, New York Sun, New York Times, New York Daily News, New York Herald Tribune, New York Morning Telegraph, New York

Amsterdam News, Cleveland Dispatch, New York Age, Pittsburgh Courier, Pittsburgh Press, United News (Frank Getty), Brooklyn Standard Union, International News (Davis J. Walsh), and Chicago Tribune (Westbrook Pegler).

41 Pegler, Westbrook, Chicago Tribune: *DEACON TIGER OUTHUGS GREB IN SLOW BOUT,* August 20, 1926.

42 McGeehan, W. O., New York Herald Tribune: *Windmill Seems On Down Grade In Garden Bout,* August 20, 1926.

43 Greb, Harry, Pittsburgh Gazette-Times: *I Was Robbed; Am Disgusted Enough Greb Says Of Flowers Bout,* August 20, 1926.

44 Keck, Harry, Pittsburgh Gazette-Times: *"HARRY TO START DRIVE ON LIGHT-HEAVYWEIGHT DIVISION, HE DECIDES,* August 21, 1926.

45 The condition referred to is Sympathetic Ophthalmia which is an inflammation of both eyes following damage to one eye. This condition can occur immediately or years after the initial injury and given the nature of Greb's injured eye he would have been at a great deal of risk for this condition.
   Interview with Howard Schatz January 4, 2009.

46 Keck, Harry, Pittsburgh Gazette-Times: *HARRY GREB An Appreciation,* October 24, 1926.

47 Pittsburgh Gazette-Times: *GREB HAD PREMONITION OF DEATH ACTIONS SHOWED, HIS BROTHER IN LAW DECLARES,* October 27, 1926.

48 Pittsburgh Press: *REPORT HARRY GREB ACCIDENT VICTIM,* October 12, 1926.

49 Pittsburgh Post: *Greb, Indignant, in Last Interview Here, Told Of Unjust Notoriety Given Him,* October 23, 1926.

50 Pittsburgh Gazette-Times: *Doctor He Visited Before Leaving For Atlantic City Sheds Light On Physical Condition of Greb,* October 23, 1926.

51 Pittsburgh Gazette-Times: *Mother Inconsolable Over Greb's Death,* October 23, 1926.

NOTES

CHAPTER 26

1 Interview with Larry L. Murray, Jr. August 2003.

2 Pittsburgh Gazette-Times: *Mother Inconsolable Over Greb's Death,* October 23, 1926.

3 Pittsburgh Chronicle-Telegraph: *PLASTIC SURGERY CAUSE OF GREB'S DEATH, CLAIM,* October 23, 1926.

4 Pittsburgh Gazette-Times: *Doctors at Odds on Cause Of Greb's Death; Brain Hemmorhage, One Says,* October 24, 1926.

5 Greb, Edward Henry, Death Certificate on file at Atlantic County, Atlantic City, New Jersey.
   An enlarged heart can be cause for concern but is often found in endurance athletes as a result of their regular aerobic exercise and has been anecdotally found to be a common trait among several of the great boxers known for unusually high stamina, Henry Armstrong for example. In these cases the condition is quite normal and natural, posing no threat to the athlete's health.

6 Interview with Dr. Bradley E. Smith October 2012.

7 Pittsburgh Chronicle-Telegraph: *Large Crowds View Body of Harry Greb,* October 25, 1926.

8 Pittsburgh Chronicle-Telegraph: *Tunney to Be Pallbearer At Greb Funeral Tomorrow,* October 26, 1926.

9 Pittsburgh Gazette-Times: *Father Cox Lauds Diligence of Greb In Radio Sermon,* October 26, 1926.

10 Davis, Ralph, Pittsburgh Press: *RALPH DAVIS SAYS,* October 28, 1926.

11 Lewis, Ira F., Pittsburgh Courrier: *THE SPORTIVE REALM,* October 30, 1926.

12 Pittsburgh Chronicle-Telegraph: *Large Crowds View Body of Harry Greb,* October 25, 1926.

13 Pittsburgh Post: *WORLD CHAMP COMES BACK TO SERVE AS PALLBEARER,* October 26, 1926.

14 Pittsburgh Chronicle-Telegraph: *Greb Blind in One Eye For Past Five Years, Boxer's Friends Say,* October 26, 1926.

15 New York Times: *GREB HAD A GLASS EYE FOR PAST TWO MONTHS,* October 27, 1926.

16 Pittsburgh Gazette-Times: *Greb Relatives Regret Secret Of Glass Eye Became Known,* October 27, 1926.

17 New York Evening Post: *GREB SCALED PEAK UNDER HANDICAP OF IMPAIRED EYESIGHT,* October 27, 1926.

18 New York Morning Telegraph: *CALIFORNIA BOARD IN A PICKLE OVER RULING ON TIGER FLOWERS,* June 20, 1926.

19 The account of Harry Greb's funeral is derived from reports found in the Pittsburgh Press, Pittsburgh Sun, Pittsburgh Post, Pittsburgh Gazette-Times, and Pittsburgh Chronicle-Telegraph.

20 Pittsburgh Gazette-Times: *'I Loved Him So!',* October 23, 1926.

21 New York Morning Telegraph: *DENIES TRYING SUICIDE FOR GREB,* October 30, 1926.

22 Christine, Bill, Pittsburgh Post-Gazette: *Playing Games,* May 14, 1973.

23 Keck, Harry, Pittsburgh Sun-Telegraph: *Sparring Mate Explodes Greb Myths,* Undated, 1942-1943.

24 Biederman, Les, Pittsburgh Press: *DeMarco Earned Half-Millions And He Spent and Enjoyed It,* January 24, 1946.

25 Abrams, Al, Pittsburgh Post-Gazette: *Sidelights on Sports,* March 28, 1941.

26 Keck, Harry, Pittsburgh Sun-Telegraph: *Sparring Mate Explodes Greb Myths,* Undated, 1942-1943.

27 Dempsey was often questioned about a proposed fight with Greb over the years. In an interview with Harry Keck in 1951 Dempsey curiously denied ever sparring Greb in New York City adding that no promoter could be found to promote a bout between he and Greb and no commission would sanction such a bout. Dempsey knew better in regards to both assertions. In another interview, this time with Ned Brown, Dempsey stated that he had taken it easy on Greb in their sparring session and never considered a fight with the middleweight.
  In 1931 Doc Kearns stated "You could not have dragged him (Dempsey) into a ring with Harry Greb, who whipped him every time they boxed in a training camp." In 1941 in an interview with Jack Miley Kearns admitted that Greb would have defeated Dempsey and stated that they weren't willing to risk the championship on such a fight. When speaking of Greb and Dempsey in 1943 Kearns intimated that he felt Greb would have always beaten Dempsey based on his style. However, it should be noted that by the time of these interviews the feud between Kearns and Dempsey was in full swing and Kearns may have been using the opportunities to take a jab at his former fighter.

28 Heller, Peter, *"In This Corner...!".* New York: Da Capo Press, 1994.
  Wilson makes several incorrect statements when telling his tale of the first Greb fight, not the least of which is that the officials had been orchestrated to take his title away, and that one of those officials was Bat Masterson. Masterson had been dead for two years when Wilson lost his title to Greb. This of course is above and beyond the ludicrous picture Wilson paints of a New York born fighter, managed by a powerful New York mobster, losing a crooked decision in New York to a fighter from out of town. Wilson may have been unpopular but he completely ignores the fact that his standing with the public was due in large part to his avoidance of Greb for two years.

29 Interview with Phyllis Albacker Roseberry August 2003.

30 Hauck, Johnny, Veteran Boxer: *HAUCK'S CORNER,* Winter 1946.

31 Kilty, Jimmy, Huntington Park Daily Signal: *JIMMY KILTY,* March 17, 1947.

www.ingramcontent.com/pod-product-compliance
Lightning Source LLC
Chambersburg PA
CBHW050401110426
42812CB00006BA/1765